Praise for Kay Showker's
Caribbean Ports of Call series

"Written by travel expert Kay Showker is a first-of-its-kind guide that shows anyone how to plan a carefree vacation at sea and make the most of the limited time in each port of call."

—Modern Bride

"Adds to cruise clients' enjoyment by tipping them off to fun things to do while ashore."

—Travel Life

"There are shelffuls of guidebooks on the Caribbean, and there are books that deal with cruising in general (and with ships in particular), but there has been no comprehensive work that effectively combines the two. Kay Showker's admirably fills that void."

—Oceans

"Very, very comprehensive, a complete and invaluable book."

—Joel Rapp, WABC Radio, New York

"Check out *Caribbean Ports of Call* to get an inside line not only on the cruise 'personalities' and itineraries, but also where to go, what to do, and what to skip when the ship pulls into shore."

—Self magazine

"Her book will become a standard in its field that fills a need people have referred to but no one has taken the time to prepare. For both the first-time cruiser as well as the aficionado, this book is perfect. It is absolutely indispensable to any person taking a cruise and can lend a totally added dimension to the cruise experience."

—Arthur Frommer, "Arthur Frommer's Almanac of Travel,"
The Travel Channel

"Has much to offer both the most experienced old salt and the first-time passenger . . . Pulls together various aspects of Caribbean cruising that often are covered in separate books . . . More than lives up to its title."

—The Washington Times

Help Us Keep This Guide Up to Date

Every effort has been made by the author and editors to make this guide as accurate and useful as possible. However, many things can change after a guide is published—establishments close, phone numbers change, facilities come under new management, etc.

We would love to hear from you concerning your experiences with this guide and how you feel it could be improved and kept up to date. While we may not be able to respond to all comments and suggestions, we'll take them to heart, and we'll also make certain to share them with the author. Please send your comments and suggestions to the following address:

The Globe Pequot Press
Reader Response/Editorial Department
P.O. Box 480
Guilford, CT 06437

Or you may e-mail us at:

editorial@GlobePequot.com

Thanks for your input, and happy travels!

Caribbean
Ports of Call

EASTERN AND SOUTHERN REGIONS

KAY SHOWKER WITH MARY BRENNAN

SEVENTH EDITION

travel

Guilford, Connecticut

In memory of Audrey Palmer Hawks,
a credit to her homeland of Grenada
and a beloved friend who radiated the
warmth and charm of the Caribbean
and the strength of its women.

Text design by Nancy Freeborn
Photo research by Sue Preneta
Cartography by Multi-Mapping, Ltd. © Morris Book Publishing, LLC.

ISSN 1537-0100
ISBN 978-0-7627-4538-8

Printed in the United States of America

10 9 8 7 6 5 4 3 2 1

The 2007 hurricane season brought a string of destructive hurricanes to the Caribbean. As a result, we recommend that readers check with the cruise lines, establishments, and attractions listed in this guide before making firm travel plans. Also, please bear in mind that prices, exchange rates, schedules, etc., change constantly. Readers should always check with a cruise line regarding its ships and itineraries before making final plans.

Caribbean
Ports of Call

EASTERN AND SOUTHERN REGIONS

a photo essay

Aruba

British Virgin Islands

British Virgin Islands

British Virgin Islands

British Virgin Islands

Puerto Rico

Puerto Rico

St. Thomas/ U.S. Virgin Islands

St. Thomas/ U.S. Virgin Islands

Martinique

St. Maarten

Dominica

Tobago

Trinidad

Trinidad

St. Vincent and the Grenadines

Bonaire

Barbados

St. Lucia

Curaçao

Aruba

Aruba

Grenada

Contents

Part Six

South America's Caribbean and the Panama Canal

List of Maps

Eastern and Southern Caribbean Islands

Anguilla
Antigua/Barbuda
Aruba
Barbados
Bonaire
British Virgin Islands
Curaçao
Dominica
Grenada/Carriacou
Guadeloupe/Iles des Saintes (Les Saintes)
Martinique
Montserrat

Puerto Rico
Saba
St. Barts
St. Eustatius
St. Kitts/Nevis
St. Lucia
St. Maarten/St. Martin
St. Vincent and the Grenadines
   (Bequia, Mustique, Mayreau, Palm, Union,
   Tobago Cays)
Trinidad and Tobago
U.S. Virgin Islands

MAP LEGEND

Boundary:

▦ ♠	National Park / Forest	
—·—·—·—	International	
—··—··—··	Provincial	

Transportation:

═══════	Major
───────	Other
----------	Trail

Hydrology:

～～～	Rivers/Creeks
▬	Lake
⫽	Waterfall

Symbols:

♠	Accommodation
∴	Archaeological Site / Ruin
⑧	Bank
🚌	Bus Station
†	Cemetery
⚰	Church
⚔	Customs / Immigration

⚑	Embassy
🚢	Ferry / Cruise
⛿	Fort
⚓	Golf Course
✚	Hospital
■	Important Building
❶	Information
✈ ✈	International / Domestic
📖	Library
🗼	Lighthouse
🏛	Museum
🗽	Observatory
★	Point of Interest
✉	Post Office
🕊	Sanctuary
🏫	School
🚕	Taxi
👁	View Point
🌋	Volcano

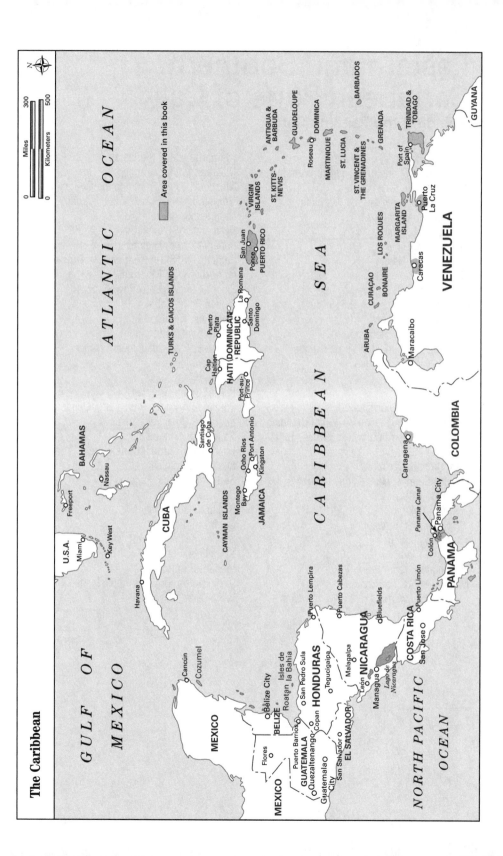

The Caribbean

Eastern and Southern Caribbean Ports of Call
Including the Panama Canal

Anegada, British Virgin Islands
Basse-Terre, Guadeloupe, French West Indies
Basseterre, St. Kitts
Bequia, St. Vincent and the Grenadines
Bridgetown, Barbados
Cartagena, Colombia
Castries, St. Lucia
Charlestown, Nevis
Charlotte Amalie, St. Thomas, U.S. Virgin Islands
Christiansted, St. Croix, U.S. Virgin Islands
Codrington, Barbuda
Cristobal (Colon), Panama
Cruz Bay, St. John, U.S. Virgin Islands
English Harbour, Antigua
Falmouth, Antigua
Fort Bay, Saba
Fort-de-France, Martinique
Frederiksted, St. Croix, U.S. Virgin Islands
Gustavia, St. Barthélemy (St. Barts), French West Indies
Hillsborough, Carriacou
Iles des Saintes, Guadeloupe, French West Indies
Jost Van Dyke, British Virgin Islands
Kingstown, St. Vincent
Kralendijk, Bonaire
La Guaira (Caracas), Venezuela
Los Roques, Venezuela
Marie Galante, French West Indies
Marigot, St. Martin, French West Indies

Margarita Island (Porlamar), Venezuela
Mayreau, St. Vincent and the Grenadines
Mustique, St. Vincent and the Grenadines
Norman Island, British Virgin Islands
Oranjestad, Aruba
Oranjestad, St. Eustatius
Panama Canal, Panama
Palm Island, St. Vincent and the Grenadines
Philipsburg, St. Maarten
Pigeon Point/Rodney Bay, St. Lucia
Pigeon Point, Tobago
Plymouth, Montserrat
Pointe Bout, Martinique
Pointe-à-Pitre, Guadeloupe, French West Indies
Ponce, Puerto Rico
Port of Spain, Trinidad
Portsmouth/Prince Rupert Bay, Dominica
Puerta La Cruz, Venezuela
Road Town, Anguilla
Road Town, Tortola, British Virgin Islands
Roseau, Dominica
San Blas Islands, Panama
San Juan, Puerto Rico
Scarsborough, Tobago
Soufrière, St. Lucia
St. George's, Grenada
St. John's, Antigua
Vieques, Puerto Rico
Virgin Gorda, British Virgin Islands
Willemstad, Curaçao

Cruising and the Caribbean

The Winning Combination

Every year, more than thirteen million people take cruises, and almost half of them cruise in the waters of the Bahamas and the Caribbean. Superb year-round weather, proximity, prices, and the region's great variety—of cultures, activity, scenery, sports, and attractions—all are reasons that make the combination of cruising and the Caribbean a vacation choice that's hard to beat.

Caribbean Ports of Call: Eastern and Southern Regions is one of three books in the Caribbean Ports of Call series. From its first publication in 1987, the series has been intended to fill the gap between two kinds of books: books about cruising and books about the Caribbean.

Typically, books about cruising describe the ships in great detail and are useful in selecting a cruise; however, these books give little or no attention to ports of call. Generally, once you are on board your ship heading to the Bahamas or the Caribbean, their value is marginal.

Guidebooks on the Bahamas and the Caribbean invariably assume that their readers will arrive at a destination by plane and remain several days or longer and have plenty of time to explore the attractions. They are not written for cruise passengers who spend only a few hours in port and need a special kind of guidance.

Indeed, neither the standard cruise guide nor the typical Caribbean guidebook has the kind of information cruise passengers need to help them plan and set priorities for their time in port. And that has been the aim of my series from the outset.

Caribbean Ports of Call: A Guide for Today's Cruise Passenger was the first of its kind when it was first published, and although other cruise guides and Caribbean books have appeared with "Ports of Call" added to their titles, a comparison of their content would show that the books in my series are still the only ones designed specifically with the goal of helping readers plan their time in each port of call as well as serving as a guide to be taken along in port.

Caribbean Ports of Call: A Guide for Today's Cruise Passenger has been divided into three volumes for the most practical reasons. We want each of the three books to be portable and their inclusion of ports to reflect the pattern of Caribbean cruises.

This volume, *Caribbean Ports of Call: Eastern and Southern Regions,* includes the islands of the Eastern and Southern Caribbean plus the northern coast of South America and the Panama Canal. It describes the ports in the Eastern Caribbean visited by ships departing from San Juan and elsewhere in the region; longer cruises departing from Florida and other U.S. ports; and cruises that include ports in the Southern Caribbean and Panama Canal.

How to Use This Guide

Part One is an introduction to the Caribbean and particularly to the Eastern and Southern Caribbean, with an overview of their attractions and contrasts with the northern and western regions. It is also a guide for selecting and buying your cruise, with information on ways to save money on your cabin, no matter which ship you select, and it provides tips to help you get ready for your trip.

Part Two is a guide to the cruise lines that sail in the Eastern and Southern Caribbean. It is designed to help you find the line and ship most likely to match your tastes and pocketbook. A chart at the end of the book capsulizes the ships and their ports, listing cruise ships/lines with their various ports of call and the price range of their cruises. This information is intended for general planning only.

Parts Three through Six cover the ports of call in the Eastern and Southern Caribbean and the Panama Canal. For easy reference an alphabetical list of the ports follows the Contents. Every effort has been made to be consistent in the presentation of information for each port of call, but some slight variations are inevitable because of the differences in the islands.

All major port chapters open with At a Glance, a generic list of attractions with one ★ star to five ★★★★★ stars. The stars are not used in the sense of a restaurant critique; they are intended as an objective guide to what the island has to offer, that is, which of its attractions are comparatively the best. The purpose is to give an instant picture of the port to help you judge how best to use your time.

Major port chapters include an introduction to the country with a general map, Fast Facts, and Budget Planning. Brief descriptions of popular tours—or shore excursions, as cruise lines call them—are provided for those who like to tour with a group.

The Port Profile has information on embarkation, port location and facilities, and local transportation. The Author's Favorite Attractions are then listed; these can be used as a guide to tailor your own priority list. Sections on the capital or main city, historic, and other attractions are followed by those on shopping, sports, dining, entertainment, cultural events, holidays, and festivals.

For those who want to be on their own, each chapter has a walking tour with map, where appropriate, and descriptions of island attractions to see when you rent a car or hire a taxi.

Prices are not uniform in the Caribbean; they tend to be highest in the most popular places. You might sometimes have the feeling that there's a "soak the tourist" attitude, but try to remember that a place like St. Maarten, which has no industry and only minimal agriculture, must import almost all of its food and other supplies. Since the islands cater mainly to Americans, costs are high because American tastes often cost a great deal to satisfy.

Mapping the Caribbean

The Caribbean roughly has the shape of a rectangle. The sides of the rectangle—north, east, south, and west—represent four regions that are quite different from one another, each with its particular qualities and special appeal.

The northern leg—Cuba, Jamaica, Haiti, Dominican Republic, and Puerto Rico—is known as the Greater Antilles. These are the largest, most developed islands, with the largest populations and closest to the United States, with direct air service (except for Cuba). Historically they have had the closest ties with the United States and from a visitor's standpoint, cater mainly to American tourists. Indeed, for most Americans, they are the Caribbean.

But far more numerous and more "Caribbean" in the tropical sense are the islands of the "other" Caribbean—the string of tiny jewels that starts east of Puerto Rico and arches south to South America. Sometimes called the Bali Hai of the Western Hemisphere, the islands of the Eastern Caribbean are serene, seductive hideaways with grand landscapes of savage beauty. Most are intensely green and very mountainous, often rising almost directly from turquoise seas to jagged, cloud-covered peaks.

Known in history as the Lesser Antilles, they fall into two groups: the Leewards on the north (composed of U.S. and British Virgin Islands that bridge the northern and eastern Caribbean, Anguilla, St. Maarten/St. Martin, St. Barts, Saba, St. Eustatius, St. Kitts/Nevis, Antigua/Barbuda, Montserrat, and Guadeloupe); and the Windwards on the south (Dominica, Martinique, St. Lucia, St. Vincent and the Grenadines, and Grenada). Barbados, technically neither a Leeward nor a Windward island, is 100 miles to the east of St. Vincent. The islands on the south side of the Caribbean rectangle—Trinidad and Tobago, Aruba, Curaçao, and Bonaire—form what is known as the Southern Caribbean.

What's in a Name?

After battling with the French and Dutch for 200 years in the seventeenth and eighteenth centuries, the British gained control over most of the Antilles in the late eighteenth century and divided them into two administrative groups, calling them by the nautical terms—the Leeward Islands and the Windward Islands. Following World War II, when some of the former British colonies obtained a measure of independence, they formed a loose alliance, called the Eastern Caribbean Associated States, with a common currency and protection in trade agreements under the British Commonwealth, of which they are members.

Lesser Antilles and *Leewards* and *Windwards* are terms still used by mapmakers, but *Eastern Caribbean* has gradually replaced the nautical and colonial administrative terms as the popular name to define the small islands of the east, to differentiate them from the big islands of the north. Along with the former British colonies, the Eastern Caribbean now also includes the Dutch West Indies, the French West Indies, and the U.S. territories.

Until recently the islands of the Eastern Caribbean were visited only by yachts and small cruise ships and an occasional large ship en route to the Panama Canal or South America, but in the past decade, there have been significant changes for two reasons. First, since 1987, the number of cruise ships sailing to the Caribbean has more than doubled. As the competition for Caribbean cruises departing from Florida intensified with the arrival of new ships, more ships, and larger ships, cruise lines felt the pressure to find new destinations.

Most lines have moved some of their fleet to San Juan, from which they sail through the Eastern Caribbean on a wide variety of itineraries. The development of San Juan as the major air hub of the Caribbean also was an important consideration in its selection as an alternative home port. During the winter season, there are almost as many ships based in San Juan as there are in either Miami or Fort Lauderdale. St. Maarten and Barbados are used as home ports as well.

Meanwhile, most islands of the Eastern Caribbean have improved and expanded their port facilities, roads, and transportation, as well as shopping, sports, and other tourist facilities, specifically to attract more and larger ships. Small islands that were minor players in the past have developed into major ports.

Planning Your Time

All cruise lines would like you to believe that their ships are the main reason to take a cruise, but they are the first to admit that most passengers select a cruise for its destinations. In the Eastern Caribbean the destinations are as different as the U.S. or British Virgin Islands, the French West Indies, and the Netherlands Antilles. Some, like Grenada and St. Lucia, are mountainous and lush with tropical greenery; others, like Aruba, are flat and dry, resembling the American Southwest. Some, like Barbados and St. Croix, are steeped in history; others, like Bequia and Carriacou, are the hideaways time has left behind.

Together the ports on an Eastern Caribbean cruise provide a kaleidoscope of the region's history and cultures, scenery and sights, language and music. It is a window onto the islands with an ever-changing panorama. The Eastern Caribbean offers every warm-weather sport, along with magnificent weather in which to enjoy them, and a year-round calendar of feasts, festivals, and special events.

A cruise is the best and sometimes the only way to visit several Eastern Caribbean islands in one vacation—that's one of cruising's main attractions. But if you don't plan, you might come back thinking the islands are all alike. Each island has its own special features, personality, and appeal. This book explains their differences and will enable you to plan your activity in each port in order to have an interesting cruise full of variety.

Since cruise passengers are a diverse group with changing interests, this book is intended to address a variety of needs. Some readers may want to pursue sports; others may be more interested in history, art, and culture. Others may want to stroll around and shop. Any of these activities are available in Eastern Caribbean ports, but you will need to decide which activity you prefer to do at a particular destination. You also need to decide if you want to take an organized tour or see the sights on your own. Some Eastern Caribbean ports lend themselves to organized touring; others are best seen by walking or touring on your own.

San Juan, Barbados, and some Caribbean ports are both a home base and a port of call for cruise ships. Passengers arrive by plane to board their ships and often come early or plan to stay a few days after their cruises, when time is less of a constraint. They might want to plan both organized tours and independent travel.

To ensure that this book has the broadest possible application and can be used by many different kinds of cruise passengers, a great deal of specific information is provided on sports, sightseeing, shopping, culture, and how to see the port of call whether you take a tour or travel on your own. In any case the primary objective has been to help you organize and maximize your time in port to ensure that you get the most out of your visit.

The Caribbean with a Difference

Often called the Undiscovered Caribbean, most of the Eastern Caribbean islands are idyllic hideaways, still natural and unspoiled. It is of course difficult to generalize, since the islands are at various stages of development and sophistication, but with a few exceptions the Eastern Caribbean islands are less developed and hence less commercial than those of the Northern Caribbean.

For the most part these off-the-beaten-track destinations are little known to most Americans. They have retained a more local ambience, not one geared to American tourists. Their economies, generally, are based on agriculture. The people live closer to the land and are more self-reliant. There is a warm, easy, natural quality about them.

The islands also differ from those of the north in origin, size, and history—elements that give them their character and ambience. Most islands are mountainous and volcanic in origin; some still have smoking craters and other evidence of continuing volcanic activity. St. Lucia even boasts a "drive-in volcano." From their jagged, smoldering peaks, often shrouded in mist and white clouds brought by the trade winds, the terrain falls through exotic rain forests and lush green valleys crisscrossed by cascading rivers to coastlines scalloped with pearly beaches fringed by coral reefs floating in turquoise seas. On approach from a cruise ship, the panorama is breathtaking and fits the popular image of the tropics.

The island chain acts as a barrier between the Atlantic and Caribbean. On the east, or windward side, the rolling Atlantic Ocean pounds against rocky shores often covered with wind-sheared vegetation. On the west, or leeward side, the crystal waters of the calm Caribbean lap gently at the white—or black—sand beaches of reef-trimmed coves. These protected leeward waters have long been among the world's most popular yachting waters. Indeed, although the Eastern Caribbean is newly discovered for many cruise ships, it has been the favorite of yachtsmen for decades.

Most of the islands are less than 20 or 30 miles in length, yet often they have scenery so grand, it belies their small size. Sharp contrasts make up one of their most outstanding attractions. Martinique, for example, in a distance of only 50 miles, drops from an active volcano at almost 5,000 feet and razorback peaks thick with rain forests to flowing meadows and pastureland—complete with grazing cows—to bone-dry desert. On its east coast, white-capped Atlantic waves crash against weather-beaten shores. On the western Caribbean side, quiet, dreamy beaches hide in little coves—and all within a day's drive.

Sprinkled throughout this volcanic region are low-lying islands and coral atolls rung by pristine white sand beaches and coral reefs. These are often the popular destinations of day-sailing trips from the main ports of call.

The islands of the Eastern Caribbean are close together, like stepping-stones. Cruise ships sailing on these routes are seldom out of sight of land and sometimes visit two islands in one day. These itineraries, unfortunately, make for a hurried trip in a part of the world where the tranquil, relaxing pace is one of the most delightful attractions.

Added to the visual diversity of the land and the coral gardens of the sea, the Eastern Caribbean is a cultural kaleidoscope. It changes from the Spanish heritage in San Juan—from which most of the ships depart—to the Danish legacy in the U.S. Virgin Islands, to the Dutch in the Dutch Windwards, the French in the French West Indies, and the British in a dozen or so stops from Anguilla to Barbados. Throughout the region monuments, old forts, plantation homes, sugar mills, churches, and synagogues—often beautifully restored and used as art galleries, boutiques, restaurants, and museums—reflect that region's rich cultural heritage.

Out of this melting pot, the islands of the Eastern Caribbean have evolved a culture of their own—more Creole or West Indian than the islands of the north—which is reflected in their festivals, dances, music, and cuisine. The islands have a year-round calendar of events that showcase the Eastern Caribbean's cultural diversity. Carnival, held at various times of the year in different islands, is a wonderful opportunity to see the region's creative talents at their best.

The Southern Caribbean

The southernmost islands—Trinidad and Tobago, Aruba, and the Netherlands Antilles islands of Curaçao and Bonaire—are on the south side of the Caribbean rectangle and lie along the north coast of South America. Sometimes called the Deep Caribbean, they form separate units and are quite different in appearance, culture, and history from the islands of the Eastern Caribbean. The contrasts offered by these islands are delightful.

Due to their location they are normally ports of call on itineraries of longer than one week from Florida and San Juan and on cruises en route to South America or the Panama Canal.

They, too, are coming into their own now as ports of call on itineraries starting from Barbados or Curaçao. Also, some ships based in Jamaica, and others that visit it from Florida ports, drop south to Aruba or Curaçao. Adventure and nature-type cruises frequently combine the islands of the Deep Caribbean with journeys up the Orinoco or Amazon Rivers.

The Spice of Life

Each island is different, and discovering this difference is part of the fun and fascination of a Caribbean cruise. You can maximize the enjoyment of your cruise by taking advantage of the unique or unusual features of each port of call rather than repeating the same activity in each port. Plan activities that take in the cultural as well as the scenic variety the ports offer. Enjoy a sport or learn a new one in at least one port, and select an activity in each port that you cannot do elsewhere.

In other words, if you were to spend all your time on a walking tour in Old San Juan, you might want to have a gourmet lunch in Guadeloupe, take a snorkeling or diving lesson in St. Maarten, and go hiking in a rain forest in St. Lucia. If you plan to shop for perfume and other French products in Martinique, you should plan another activity as well, because most people finish their shopping in an hour or two and then don't know what to do with themselves.

Facts to Remember

Climate While the sun keeps the islands warm, the trade winds that blow from the northeast and east throughout the year keep the temperatures comfortable and consistent, averaging about 78 to 82 degrees Fahrenheit year-round. The difference between summer and winter temperatures seldom varies more than five to ten degrees. December through March are normally the driest, coolest months, when temperatures on some islands might drop to 65 degrees Fahrenheit on mountain peaks. July, August, and September are the hottest, wettest months, when temperatures reach 86 to 90 degrees Fahrenheit and the humidity can be 100 percent. Fortunately, during this period, frequent tropical showers quickly cool the air.

The lay of the land has a direct impact on weather on every island. Some islands, such as Antigua, Barbados, and St. Barts, which do not have the high mountains and thick foliage characteristic of most Eastern Caribbean islands, tend to be dry, with rainfall averaging only 46 inches annually. Even on the islands with high mountains, such as St. Kitts, the climate can vary, from 148 inches of annual rain on forested mountain peaks to less than 40 inches per year in dry lowlands.

Trinidad and Tobago, Aruba, Bonaire, and Curaçao fall south of the Caribbean hurricane belt. Aruba, Bonaire, and Curaçao are similar in climate, which, typically, is much drier than in other parts of the Eastern Caribbean. On these islands where the terrain is low, the winds are strong and constant, reaching their greatest intensity in June and July.

Clothing Cotton and lightweight fabrics are recommended year-round. Informal, casual but conservative dress is appropriate throughout the islands. Bathing suits, tank tops, and revealing attire are not acceptable anywhere except on the beach. West Indians generally are conservative and are offended by tourists wearing such attire in public places. Some casinos require jackets.

In the French West Indies, on an island like St. Barts the dress code is informal, with slacks, shorts, or jeans by day and only a slightly more fashionable look at night. As in France, topless is not only allowed, it's expected. Guadeloupe and

St. Martin have topless and nudist beaches, but Martinique does not.

Remember that the sun is very strong. Wear a sun hat or visor for protection, and always use sunscreen lotion. For hiking at high altitudes, take a sweater and good hiking shoes.

Departure tax All the islands covered in this book, with the exception of Puerto Rico, U.S. Virgin Islands, Guadeloupe, and Martinique, have departure taxes. Cruise passengers do not pay these taxes, unless they leave their ship during the cruise to return home by air. The amount is noted in Fast Facts for each island.

Electricity Aruba, St. Maarten, and U.S. Virgin Islands have 120 volts AC, 60 cycles; Barbados, Bonaire, Curaçao, and Puerto Rico have 110–120 volts AC, 50 cycles.

The French West Indies and all other islands (Anguilla, Antigua/Barbuda, British Virgin Islands, Dominica, Grenada, Montserrat, St. Kitts/Nevis, St. Lucia, St. Vincent, Trinidad and Tobago) have 220 volts AC, 60 or 50 cycles. Appliances made in the United States need transformers or models with converters built into them. Hotels on most islands, however, have 110 volts AC, 60 cycles or both currents. If in doubt, inquire at the hotel front desk.

Entry formalities U.S. and Canadian citizens do not need visas, but if you leave your ship, you will need proof of citizenship with photo (passport in most cases). Most islands also require visitors to have a valid onward or return ticket. Beginning January 1, 2009, all U.S. citizens will be required to show a passport to enter or leave the United States.

In the French West Indies (Guadeloupe, Martinique, St. Barts, St. Martin), if proof of citizenship is a document other than a passport (such as a notarized birth certificate), it must have a raised seal and photo identification.

Port security No special identity or security measures are required on any island covered in this book. Passengers are allowed to come and go from their ships freely; every cruise ship has its own system for identifying its passengers. Large ships usually issue identity cards like a credit card, whereas small ships may simply use cabin keys or tabs.

Time All the islands covered here fall into the Atlantic standard time zone, which is one hour ahead of eastern standard time. When daylight savings time is in effect in the United States, only a few of the islands change their time. In those months Atlantic standard time is the same as eastern daylight time.

Vaccination requirements There are no inoculation requirements for U.S. and Canadian citizens to visit any island in the Caribbean.

Selecting a Cruise: Tips and Advice

With so many cruises going to so many different places, selecting one can be difficult. My suggestion is to start your planning at a travel agency. About 85 percent of all cruises are purchased through travel agents. It will not cost more than buying a cruise directly from a cruise line, and it will save you time. Alternatively, if you are a wiz on the Internet, there is a wealth of information on cruises. All cruise lines have their own sites with descriptions of their ships and itineraries—none of them objective, of course, any more than the cruise line brochures are objective. Many travel agencies also have sites, which usually service sales via e-mail. For ship reviews and the latest deals, check out AOL's Cruise Critic (keyword: Cruise Critic), www.cruisemates.com, or subscribe to some of the e-mail newsletters published by cruise lines or large travel agencies that feature weekly cruise specials. In all cases, however, be guided by your interests and needs—and not by price alone. If it's your first cruise, you should seek the expertise of a travel agent.

Using a Travel Agent

A good travel agency stocks the brochures of the leading cruise lines; these show prices and details on the ship's itineraries and facilities. An experienced agent will help you understand the language of a cruise brochure, read a deck plan, and make reservations. The knowledgeable agent can help you make comparisons and guide you in the selection of a ship and an itinerary to match your interests. Your agent can book your dining room table and handle a particular request such as for an anniversary party or a special diet. Agents also know about packages and discounts that can help you save money.

The Built-In Value of a Cruise Vacation

Of all the attractions of cruising, none is more important than value. For one price you get accommodations, meals, entertainment, use of all facilities, and a host of recreational activity. Air transportation may or may not be included, depending on the cruise line and the destination (see Cruise-Only Fares). The only items not included are tips, drinks, photographs, shore excursions, personal services such as spa services and hairdressers, and, in some cases, port tax. There are no hidden costs.

Dollar for dollar, it's hard to beat a cruise for value. To make an accurate assessment of how the cost of a cruise compares with other types of holidays, be sure to compare similar elements. A holiday at sea should be compared with a holiday at a luxury resort, because the quality of service, food, and entertainment on most cruises is available only at posh resorts or top-level all-inclusive resorts.

The average brochure price of a 1-week Caribbean cruise can range from $150 to $400 per person per day including the ingredients previously described, but with current discounts and advance purchase plans, these prices can be cut in half. Shorter 3- and 4-day Bahamas cruises range from $130 to $250 per day, and there are plenty of low promotion fares available for them, too. No luxury resorts give you a hotel room, four full meals plus two or three snacks each day, nightly entertainment plus a myriad of activity—all for the one price of $150 to $300.

Stretching Your Budget

Air/sea combinations are available in two forms: an all-in-one package combining a cruise and air transportation in one price; or a second type, in which the cruise is priced separately and an air supplement is added on to the cruise price or a credit for air transportation from one's hometown

to the ship's nearest departure port is offered. The amount of the supplement or credit varies from one cruise line to another. But, usually, the supplement is slightly more the farther away from the departure port you live. Still, the total cost is far less to you than if the cruise and air transportation were purchased separately. The details are spelled out in the cruise line's brochure. Ask your travel agent to explain how the package works as it can be confusing.

Is Free Air Free?

If you are skeptical—you don't get something for nothing—every cruise company publishes pamphlets that show the rates for every cabin on its ships, regardless of how passengers elect to get to the ship. If the cruise offers "free" air transportation and quotes one price for the package without a breakdown for each component, you can still know the value by reading the section intended for those prospective passengers who live in or near the departure port of the ship.

Although air/sea packages save you money, it goes without saying that some definitely represent larger savings than others, depending on the cruise line, the cruise, and the time of year. Every line's policy is different, and policies vary not only from line to line, but even from cruise to cruise on any specific ship. The introduction of new cruise ships or new itineraries creates a buyer's market with real bargains. It pays to shop around.

Cruise-Only Fares

Most cruise line brochures quote "cruise-only" fares rather than air/sea packages. The reasons: Crowded airplanes and crowded skies have often made it difficult for cruise lines to negotiate the low airfares of the past. Even when they can, the airlines—not cruise lines—control the routing, which often has deviations that lead to passenger complaints. Also, many cruise passengers have acquired frequent-flyer miles they want to use for vacation travel.

Selecting a Ship

The ship and the cruise line's reputation are other considerations in making your selection. Not only do ships differ, so do their passengers. You are more likely to enjoy a cruise with people who are seeking a similar type of holiday and with whom you share a community of interests and activities. A good travel agent who specializes in selling cruises is aware of the differences and should be able to steer you to a ship that's right for you. But before you visit an agent or begin to cull the colorful and enticing brochures, here are some tips on the items affecting cost that can help you in making a selection.

Selecting a Cabin

The largest single item in the cost of a cruise is the cabin, also known as a stateroom. The cost of a cabin varies greatly and is determined by its size and location. Generally, the cabins on the top deck are the largest and most expensive; the prices drop and the cabins narrow on each deck down from the top. (Elevators and stairs provide access between decks.) But the most expensive cabins are not necessarily the best. There are other factors to consider.

Almost all cruise ship cabins have private bathrooms, but the size and fittings vary and affect cost. For example, cabins with full bathtubs are more expensive than those with showers only. Greater standardization of cabins is a feature of most new cruise ships.

Outside cabins are more costly than inside ones. There is a common misconception that inside cabins are to be avoided. It dates back to the days before air-conditioning when an outside cabin above the waterline was desirable because the porthole could be opened for ventilation. Today's ships are climate-controlled; an inside cabin is as comfortable as an outside one. What's more, on a Caribbean cruise particularly, you will spend very little time in your cabin; it is mainly a place to sleep and change clothes. An inside cabin often provides genuine savings and is definitely worth investigating for those on a limited budget.

For the most stable ride, the deck at water level or below has less roll (side-to-side motion) and the cabins in the center of the ship have the least pitch (back-and-forth motion). But these cabins also cost more than those in the front (fore) or the back (aft) of the ship. Fore (or the bow) has less motion and is therefore preferable to aft (or the stern), where sometimes there is vibration from the ship's engines.

A ship's deck plan shows the exact location of each cabin and is usually accompanied by diagrams of the fittings in the cruise line's brochures. It does not give the dimensions of the cabin, but you can have a reasonable estimate since beds are standard single size—about 3 x 6 feet. Some ships have double beds, but most have twin beds that can be converted to doubles on request.

A few ships have single cabins; otherwise, a passenger booking a cabin alone pays a rate that is one and a half times the price per person for two sharing a cabin. A few ships offer special single rates on certain cruises or reserve a few cabins for single occupancy at the same rate as the per person rate on a shared basis plus a small supplement. Your travel agent should be able to give you specific information about single rates.

Other Cost Factors

As might be expected, rates for the winter season in the Caribbean are higher than in the spring, summer, or fall. Cruises over Christmas, New Year's, and other major holidays are usually the year's most expensive, but often, real bargains are to be found on cruises immediately before or after a holiday season when demand drops and lines are eager to stimulate business.

The length of the cruise bears directly on its cost. Longer cruises provide more elegance and fancier dining and service. The cost also varies depending on the ship's itinerary. For example, it is more economical for a cruise line to operate a set schedule of the same ports throughout the year, such as the ships departing weekly from Florida to the Caribbean, than it is to change itineraries every few weeks.

Family Rates

If you are planning a family cruise, look for cruise lines that actively promote family travel and offer special rates for children or for third and fourth persons in a cabin. It means a bit of crowding but can yield big savings. Family rates vary from one cruise line to another. As a rule, children sharing a cabin with two paying adults get discounts of 50 percent or more of the minimum fare. Qualifying ages vary, too, with a child usually defined as two to twelve, and sometimes up to eighteen years. Some lines have teen fares, while at certain times of the year others have free or special rates for the third or fourth person sharing a cabin with two full-fare adults, regardless of age. Most lines permit infants under two years to travel free of charge.

Cruise Discounts

In today's highly competitive market, discounts have become a way of life. Cruise lines use them to publicize a new ship or itinerary, to attract families, younger passengers, singles, and a diversity of people. Some low fares are available year-round but may be limited to a certain number of cabins on each sailing; others are seasonal or may apply to specific cruises.

You can take advantage of fare discounts in two ways. If you book early, you can usually benefit from early-bird discounts, often up to 50 percent or more, and of course, you can be sure you have the cruise and cabin you want. On the other hand, if you are in a position to be flexible, you can wait to catch the last-minute "fire sales." To take advantage of this situation, you need to have maximum flexibility.

Remember, when you are buying a cruise, you will have already paid for all your accommodations, all meals (three meals a day is only the beginning; most ships have five or more food services daily), all entertainment, and all recreational facilities aboard ship, and in many cases, round-trip airfare to the ship's departure port, baggage handling, and transfers. It is this all-inclusive aspect of a cruise that makes it a good value—a particularly significant advantage for families with children and those who need to know in advance the cost of a vacation.

Shore Excursions

Sightseeing tours, called shore excursions by the cruise lines, are available for an additional cost at every port of call in the Caribbean. A pamphlet on the shore excursions offered by the cruise line is often included in the literature you receive before

sailing. If not, ask for one. However, more and more cruise lines now post their shore excursions on their Web sites and enable passengers to book their excursions in advance online. If not, you can buy them on board ship from the purser, cruise director, or tour office. Some people prefer buying them on board, since frequently their interests and plans change once the cruise is under way.

A word of caution: When I began this series in 1987, I found that there was very little difference between the cruise ships' prices for tours and those of local tour companies if you were staying in a hotel. However, since then, the situation has changed so dramatically that I must alert readers to the change. In their need to keep their cruise prices down in the face of intense competition and rampant discounting, many cruise lines have come to regard shore excursions (as well as other ancillary services such as shipboard shopping, bars, and spa facilities) as profit centers; some are selling their tours at exorbitant prices.

In a preliminary survey, I found prices jacked up 30 to 50 percent; some are even double the prices you would pay on shore. To help you in your selection and to gauge fair prices, each port of call in this book has descriptions of the main shore excursions offered by the majority of cruise lines, as well as some that you must arrange on your own. The approximate price of each excursion when you buy it directly from a tour company on shore is noted, where possible, along with the current price at which it is sold aboard ship. The prices were accurate at press time but, of course, they are not guaranteed.

Since tours vary from vendor to vendor and cruise ship to cruise ship, it is difficult to generalize. Therefore, when you check prices, it is important that you compare like items and, when necessary, factor in such additional costs as transportation from the pier to the vendor's office or starting point. The information and prices provided here are intended as guidelines. Even if they change, the increase is not likely to be more than a dollar or two. If you come across shore excursion prices that appear to be out of line in comparison with those found in this book, please write to me and enclose a copy of the tours with their descriptions and prices sold on your cruise.

Port Talks

All ships offer what is known as a port talk—a brief description of the country or island and port where the ship will dock as well as shopping tips. The quality of these talks varies enormously, not only with the cruise line but also with the ship, and can depend on such wide-ranging considerations as the knowledge and skill of the cruise director and the policy of the cruise line as to the true purpose of the information.

You should be aware that most cruise lines in the Caribbean have turned these port talks into sales pitches for certain products and stores with which they have exclusive promotional agreements and in which the cruise lines take commissions or are paid directly by the stores. You will receive a map of the port with "recommended" shops. What that really means is that the shop has paid the cruise line for being promoted in port talks and advertising in the ship's magazine that might appear in your cabin. Also, sometimes cruise directors receive commissions from local stores, even though they deny it. Hence, their vested interest could color their presentation and recommendations.

There are three ways to avoid being misled. If a cruise line, a cruise director, a guide, or anyone else recommends one store to the exclusion of all others, that should alert you to shop around before buying. The recommended store may actually be the best place to buy—but it may not. Second, if you are planning to make sizable purchases of jewelry, cameras, or china, etc., check prices at home before you leave, and bring a list of prices with you. Be sure, however, you are comparing like products. Finally, check the prices in shipboard shops, which are usually very competitive with those at ports of call.

Happily, because you have this book, you do not need to rely on port talks for information, but if you do attend your ship's port talks and find that they have been more sales pitch than enlightenment, please write and tell me about your experience.

Know Before You Go

Luggage and wardrobe There are no limits on the amount of luggage you can bring on board ship, but most staterooms do not have much closet and storage space. More important, since you are likely to be flying to your departure port, you need to be guided by airline regulations regarding excess baggage. Life on a cruise, especially a Caribbean one, is casual. It is needless to be burdened with a lot of baggage; you will spend your days in sports clothes—slacks, shorts, T-shirts, bathing suits. Men usually are asked to wear a jacket at dinner.

The first and last nights of your cruise and the nights your ship is in port almost always call for casual dress. At least one night will be the captain's gala party, where tuxedos for men and long dresses for women are requested but not mandatory. Another night might be a masquerade party; it's entirely up to you whether to participate.

A gentleman who does not have a tuxedo should bring a basic dark suit and white shirt. Add a selection of slacks and sport shirts, one or two sports jackets, and two pairs of bathing trunks. Women will find nylon and similar synthetics are good to use on a cruise because they are easy to handle, but these fabrics can be hot under the tropical sun. It largely depends on your tolerance for synthetic fabrics in hot weather. Personally, I find cottons and cotton blends to be the most comfortable. You will need two cocktail dresses for evening wear. A long dress for the captain's party is appropriate but not compulsory. Add a sweater or wrap for cool evening breezes and the ship's air-conditioning in the dining room and lounges. Take cosmetics and sun lotion, but don't worry if you forget something. It will most likely be available in shipboard or portside shops.

You will need rubber-soled shoes for walking on deck and a comfortable pair of walking shoes for sightseeing. Sunglasses and a hat or sun visor for protection against the strong Caribbean sun are essential. A tote bag comes in handy for carrying odds and ends; include several plastic bags for wet towels and bathing suits upon returning from a visit to a beach. You might also want to keep camera equipment in plastic bags as protection against the salt air and water and sand. And don't forget to pack whatever sporting equipment and clothes you will need. If you plan to snorkel, scuba, or play tennis, often you can save on rental fees by bringing your own gear.

Documentation Requirements for vaccinations, visas, and so on depend on the destinations of the ship and are detailed in the information you receive from the cruise lines. Among the Caribbean's many advantages is that normally no destination (except Cuba, which is not covered in this book) requires visas of U.S. and Canadian citizens arriving as cruise passengers. However, new U.S. government regulations soon will require all U.S. citizens to have a passport in order to reenter the United States. Actually, every traveler should have a passport—it's the best identification you can carry.

Mealtimes All but the most luxurious Caribbean cruise ships, adventure-type, small ships, and some mainstream lines (Norwegian Cruise Line, Princess, Carnival), which have recently introduced flexible plans, have two sittings for the main meals. Early-sitting breakfast is from 7:00 to 8:00 a.m., lunch is from 12:00 to 1:00 p.m., and dinner is from 6:15 to 7:30 p.m. On the late sitting, breakfast is from 8:00 to 9:00 a.m., lunch is from 1:30 to 2:30 p.m., and dinner is from 8:15 to 9:30 p.m. If you are an early riser, you will probably be happy with the early sitting. If you are likely to close the disco every night, you might prefer the late one. Of course, you will not be confined to these meals as there are usually a buffet breakfast, lunch on deck, a midnight buffet, and afternoon tea. Also, more and more ships, particularly the new ones, have added alternative dining for dinner, usually turning the lido restaurant into a casual evening dining venue; many ships have added small specialty restaurants. In another effort to provide flexibility, many ships now have introduced open seating for breakfast and lunch and assigned seats for dinner only.

Requesting a table Your travel agent can request your table in advance, if you want a table for two or for your family, as well as your preference for early or late seating. Some cruise lines will confirm your reservation in advance; others require you to sign up for your dining table with the maître d'hôtel soon after boarding your ship. In this day of computers, it's hard to understand why any cruise line would want to put a passenger through this unnecessary inconvenience, but some do.

Electrical appliances Cabins on almost all new ships have outlets for electric razors and have hair dryers or are wired for them, but older ships are not. Instead, rooms with special outlets are provided. Few ships allow you to use electric irons in your cabin because of the potential fire hazard. Electric current is normally 115–120 volts—but not always—and plugs are the two-prong, American-type ones. Check with your cruise line for specific information.

Laundry and dry cleaning All ships have either laundry service for your personal clothing (for which there is an extra charge) or coin-operated laundry rooms. Only a very few have dry-cleaning facilities. In the Caribbean, this is not an important consideration since the clothes required are cotton or cotton blends and should be easy to wash.

Hairdressing Almost all Caribbean cruise ships have hairdressers for both men and women. Prices are comparable to those at deluxe resorts.

Religious services All ships hold interdenominational services; many also have a daily Catholic mass. Services will be conducted by the captain or a clergyman. At ports of call you will be welcome to attend local services.

Medical needs All cruise ships are required by law to have at least one doctor, nurse, and infirmary or minihospital. Doctor visits and medicine are extra costs.

Seasickness First-time cruise passengers probably worry more about becoming seasick than about any other aspect of cruising. Certainly they worry more than they should, particularly on a Caribbean cruise, where the sea is calm almost year-round. Ships today have stabilizers, which steady them in all but the roughest seas. But if you are still worried, there are several types of nonprescription medicines such as Dramamine and Bonine that help to guard against motion sickness. Buy some to bring along—you may not need it, but having it with you might be comforting. Also, the ship's doctor can provide you with Dramamine and other medication that will be immediately effective, should you need it.

Sea Bands are a fairly new product for sea-sickness prevention. They are a pair of elasticized wristbands, each with a small plastic disk that, based on the principle of acupuncture, applies pressure on the inside wrist. I use Sea Bands and have given them to friends to use and can attest to their effectiveness. They are particularly useful for people who have difficulty taking medication. Sea Bands are found in drug, toiletry, and health-care stores and can be ordered from Travel Accessories, P.O. Box 391162, Solon, OH 44139, (216) 248-8432. They even make sequined covers in a dozen colors to wear over the bands for evening.

There are two important things to remember about seasickness: Don't dwell on your fear. Even the best sailors and frequent cruisers need a day to get their "sea legs." If you should happen to get a queasy feeling, take some medicine immediately. The worst mistake you can make is to play the hero, thinking it will go away. When you deal with the symptoms immediately, relief is fast, and you are seldom likely to be sick. If you wait, the queasy feeling will linger, and you run a much greater risk of being sick.

Caution against the Caribbean sun: You should be extra careful about the sun in the tropics. It is much stronger than the sun to which most people are accustomed. Do not stay in the direct sun for long stretches at a time, and use a sunscreen at all times. Nothing can spoil a vacation faster than a sunburn.

Shipboard shops There's always a shop for essentials you might have forgotten or that can't wait until the next port of call. Many ships—particularly the new ones—have elaborate shops competitive with stores at ports of call. It's another reason to pack lightly, since you are almost sure to buy gifts and souvenirs during the cruise.

Tipping Tipping is a matter of a great deal of discussion but much less agreement. How much do you tip in a restaurant or a hotel? Normally, the tip should be about $3.50 per person per day for each of your cabin stewards and dining room waiters. On some ships, particularly those with Greek crews and adventure-type cruises, the custom is to contribute to the ship's common kitty in the belief that those behind the scenes such as kitchen staffs

should share in the bounty. On some ships dining room staffs also pool their tips. Tipping guidelines are usually printed in literature your cruise line sends in advance, enabling you to factor the expense into your budget even before booking a cruise. The cruise director, as part of his advice-giving session at the end of the cruise, also explains the ship's policy and offers guidelines.

More recently, the cruise lines that have introduced flexible meal plans—Norwegian Cruise Line's *FreeStyle,* Princess's *Personal Choice,* and Carnival's *Total Choice*—now add the tip, particularly for the dining staffs, to your shipboard bill. The amount is established by the cruise lines, but you can elect to increase or decrease the amount.

Communications Most new ships have telephones in cabins with international direct dialing capability and fax facilities in their offices. Be warned, however, the service is very expensive—about $9 to $15 per minute. If someone at home or in your office needs to reach you in an emergency, they can telephone your ship directly. Those calling from the continental United States would dial 011 plus 874 (the ocean area code for the Caribbean), followed by the seven-digit telephone number of your ship. Someone calling from Puerto Rico should dial 128 and ask for the long-distance operator.

Instructions on making such calls, how to reach the ship, or whom to notify in case of an emergency are usually included in the information sent to you by your cruise line along with your tickets and luggage tags. If not, your travel agent can obtain it. You should have this information before you leave home.

Staying in touch when you are on a cruise is getting easier all the time as more and more ships have added Internet access, enabling passengers to send and receive e-mail almost around the clock. Now, the trend toward equipping ships with wireless capabilities is picking up steam, enabling passengers to use their wireless-enabled computers at sea—for a fee.

Regarding cell phones, there are no restrictions about using them on a cruise ship, but the range is currently very limited and useful only in or near port. Exceptions are Norwegian Cruise Line's ships, which are equipped with the technology to enable cell phone connection virtually anywhere the ships sail. Be aware, however, that you will be billed by your phone company at its long-distance or international rates, which are likely to cost as much as $5 per minute.

Over the next few years, we are likely to see major changes in the use of cell phones at sea. In 2005, SeaMobile, a provider of wireless voice and data communications at sea, and CapRock Communications, a global satellite communications company, joined forces to deliver communications facilities to cruise lines, enabling passengers throughout the world to use their cell phones, wireless PDAs, or wireless-enabled computers at sea in the same manner they use them on land. In November 2005, Silversea Cruises became the first cruise line to sign an agreement with SeaMobile, enabling passengers and crew aboard the ship to use their own cellular phones and wireless PDAs while at sea, just as they do on land. Charges for calls and data services appear on the customers' wireless bills from their home carriers. Meanwhile, many cruise lines have followed suit; ask your cruise lines for information on their cell phone service, or visit www.seamobile.com and www.caprock.com.

PART TWO

Caribbean Cruise Lines and Their Ships

A Guide

Every effort has been made to ensure the accuracy of the information on the cruise lines and their ships, their ports of call, and prices, but do keep in mind that cruise lines change their ships' itineraries often for a variety of reasons. Always check with the cruise line or with a travel agent before making plans. For specific information on the itineraries of ships cruising to the Caribbean, see the chart at the end of this book.

American Canadian Caribbean Line

461 Water Street, Warren, RI 02885; (401) 247-0955; (800) 556-7450; fax (401) 245-8303; www.accl-smallships.com

Ships (passengers): *Grande Caribe* (100); *Grande Mariner* (100)

Departure ports: Various ports

Types of cruises: 11 days of Bahamas; Virgin Islands; Turks and Caicos

Lifestyle tips: Family-style dining; mature and experienced passengers; light adventure; no frills; emphasis on natural attraction and local culture

If you are looking for tranquility, informality, and conversation with fellow passengers instead of floor shows and casinos, American Canadian Caribbean Line offers low-key cruises around the Bahamas archipelago and the Caribbean during the winter season.

In 1964, the late Luther Blount designed his first small ship for cruising Canada's inland waterways. By 1988 the line had expanded to the extent that it could add Caribbean to its name. In the intervening years, ACCL remained faithful to the concept that small, intimate ships with limited planned entertainment can be successful. The ships' innovative bow ramps and shallow drafts give passengers direct access to beaches, coves, and places that are inaccessible to larger ships.

ACCL's ships are popular with mature, well-traveled passengers who like hearty American menus and the informal atmosphere of family-style dining. It is an atmosphere for instant friendships and complete relaxation. The line's large number of repeaters would seem to indicate that passengers agree with its concept and appreciate the "in-close" facility the ships bring to the cruise experience.

Azamara Cruises

1050 Caribbean Way, Miami, FL 33132; (305) 539-6000; (800) 646-1456; fax (800) 437-5111; www.azamaracruises.com

Ships (passengers): *Azamara Journey* (710); *Azamara Quest* (710)

(See Celebrity Cruises)

Carnival Cruise Lines

3655 NW Eighty-seventh Avenue, Miami, FL 33178-2428; (305) 599-2600; (800) 438-6744; fax (305) 599-8630; www.carnival.com

Ships (passengers): *Carnival Conquest* (2,974); *Carnival Destiny* (2,642); *Carnival Dream* (3,652); *Carnival Freedom* (2,974); *Carnival Glory* (2,974); *Carnival Legend* (2,124); *Carnival Liberty* (2,974); *Carnival Magic* (3,652); *Carnival Miracle* (2,124); *Carnival Pride* (2,124); *Carnival Spirit* (2,124); *Carnival Splendor* (3,006); *Carnival Triumph* (2,758); *Carnival Valor* (2,974); *Carnival Victory* (2,758); *Celebration* (1,486); *Ecstasy* (2,052); *Elation* (2,052); *Fantasy* (2,056); *Fascination* (2,052); *Holiday* (1,452); *Imagination* (2,052); *Inspiration* (2,052); *Paradise* (2,052); *Sensation* (2,052)

Departure ports: Miami, Port Canaveral, Tampa, New Orleans, San Juan, Galveston, Jacksonville, Mobile, Fort Lauderdale, year-round. New York, Charleston, Norfolk, summer/fall

Types of cruises: 3, 4, and 5 days to Bahamas and Key West; 4 to 10 days to Western, Northern, Eastern, and Southern Caribbean, and the Panama Canal

Lifestyle tips: The "Fun Ships"; youthful, casual, action-filled; high value for money

Carnival Cruise Lines is the stuff of legends. In 1972 the late Florida-based cruise executive Ted Arison and an innovative Boston-based travel agency bought the *Empress of Canada,* which they renamed the *Mardi Gras,* to start a cruise line that would stand the stodgy old steamship business on its ear. But alas, the *Mardi Gras* ran aground on her maiden cruise. After staring at losses three years in a row, Arison took full ownership of the company, assuming its $5 million debt, buying its assets—i.e., the ship—for $1, and launched the "Fun Ships" concept that is Carnival's hallmark.

The idea was to get away from the class-conscious elitism that had long been associated with luxury liners and to fill the ship with so much action-packed fun that the ship itself would be the cruise experience. The line also aimed at lowering the average age of passengers by removing the formality associated with cruising and providing a wide selection of activity and entertainment to attract active young adults, young couples, honeymooners, and families with children at reasonable prices. In only a few months, Carnival turned a profit, and in the next two years, it added two more ships.

The line's next move was as surprising as it was bold. In 1978, when shipbuilding costs and fuel prices were skyrocketing—threatening the very future of vacations-at-sea—Carnival ordered a new ship, larger and more technologically advanced than any cruise ship in service. It changed the profile of ships and enhanced the "fun" aspects of cruises. But it was Carnival's next move that really set the trend of the 1980s and beyond.

In 1982, less than ten years after its rocky start, Carnival ordered three "superliners," *Holiday, Jubilee,* and *Celebration,* each carrying 1,800 passengers, with design and decor as far removed from the grand old luxury liner as could be imagined. The decor was so different, it was zany. The owners called it "a Disney World for adults." On the *Holiday,* the main promenade deck, called "Broadway," complete with boardwalk and a Times Square, had as much glitz and glitter as the neon on Broadway.

In the 1990s Carnival outdid itself with the Fantasy group, eight megaliners even more dazzling than the earlier superliners. A ship for the twenty-first century, the *Fantasy,* with its flashy decor and high-energy ambience, had at its heart an atrium, awash in lights, towering five decks high. Here and in the entertainment areas, 15 miles of computer-ized lights were programmed to change color—constantly, but imperceptibly—from white and cool blue to hot red, altering the ambience with each change. The ships have full-fledged gyms and spas and so many entertainment and recreation outlets that you need more than one cruise to find them all. Beginning in 2007 the eight Fantasy class ships are being renovated. Major new facilities, such as a water park for children and a "serenity" section for adults, are being added, and the decor will be toned down for a more upscale, less-Vegas, look. Renovations are expected to take two years to complete.

In 1996, the *Fantasy* class ships were followed by *Carnival Destiny,* the world's largest cruise ship when it was put in service. Since then, Carnival has added two new classes of ships—four 110,000-ton megaliners and four 88,500-ton superliners. It is also building another, even larger class of 130,000-ton ships carrying 3,652 passengers. Carnival's largest ships are called "post-Panamax," meaning that they are too large to transit the Panama Canal—at least until the new third channel opens in a few years. All Carnival ships have Internet cafes and are fitted for wireless connections.

Now headed by Arison's son, Micky, Carnival is directed by an energetic and aggressive team that seems determined to entice everybody—single; married; families; children; retirees; disabled; first-time cruisers; repeat cruisers; people from the North, South, East, and West; and from all walks of life—to take a cruise. To that end, the cruises are priced aggressively and offer among the best values in cruising.

Carnival has a 24-hour, toll-free hot line to help passengers who encounter a travel emergency, such as severe weather or an airline delay or strike, en route or returning from their cruise. The U.S. number is (800) 885-4856; outside the United States, call collect (305) 406-4779. The service is staffed by Carnival employees.

Do all these ideas work? You bet they do! Carnival has twenty-two cruise ships in service, carrying more than three million passengers a year and three more very large ships under construction. That's up from 80,000 passengers in its first year.

Carnival Cruise Lines is a public company and owns the long-established Holland America Line,

Costa Cruises, Cunard, Princess Cruises, and Seabourn Cruise Line. Altogether, Carnival Corporation operates eighty-three cruise ships, accounting for more than 49 percent of the U.S. cruise market. These lines operate under their own banners, but the combination makes Carnival one of the world's largest cruise lines and gives it enormous marketing clout across the widest possible spectrum.

Celebrity Cruises

1050 Caribbean Way, Miami, FL 33132; (305) 539-6000; (800) 646-1456; fax (800) 437-5111; www.celebrity.com

Ships (passengers): *Celebrity Century* (1,750); *Celebrity Constellation* (1,950); *Celebrity Eclipse* (2,850); *Celebrity Equinox* (2,850); *Celebrity Galaxy* (1,750); *Celebrity Infinity* (1,950); *Celebrity Mercury* (1,750); *Celebrity Millennium* (1,950); *Celebrity Solstice* (2,850); *Celebrity Summit* (1,950); *Celebrity Xpedition* (94)

Departure ports: Fort Lauderdale, San Juan, Jacksonville, Miami, Cape Liberty

Types of cruises: 2 to 5 nights to the Bahamas; 7 to 14 nights to Northern, Southern, Western, and Eastern Caribbean; Bermuda.

Lifestyle tip: Modestly deluxe cruises at moderate prices

In 1989 when John Chandris, the nephew of the founder of Chandris Cruises, announced the creation of a new deluxe midpriced cruise line, he said the goal was "to bring more luxurious cruises to experienced travelers at affordable prices." He was met with a great deal of skepticism; "deluxe" and "midpriced" seemed a contradiction in terms. But three years later, he had made believers out of all his doubters.

Not only did Celebrity Cruises accomplish what it set out to do, it did it better than anyone had imagined and in record-breaking time. A Celebrity cruise is not only deluxe; it also offers true value for the money.

Celebrity was a completely new product with a new generation of ships designed for the 1990s and beyond. It defined the ideal size of a cruise ship and the appropriate layout, cabins, decor, and ambience for its market and set new standards of service and cuisine in its price category.

Celebrity's ships are not as glitzy as some of the new megaliners, but they are spacious and have a similar array of entertainment and recreation. The once-standard one-lounge-for-all was replaced by small, separate lounges, each with its own decor, ambience, and entertainment, and a variety of bars to give passengers a range of options. They have stunning, stylish decor that brought back some of the glamour of cruising in bygone days, but with a fresh, contemporary look.

From its inception, Celebrity Cruises aimed at creating superior cuisine as one way to distinguish itself and engaged as its food consultant an award-winning master French chef with two Michelin three-star restaurants in England and other food enterprises. Celebrity set a new standard for other cruise lines. The food is high quality, sophisticated but unpretentious. Celebrity was launched with stylish, elegant ships that were classic and very contemporary at the same time. They have mostly outside staterooms equipped with television that carries daily programs of events, first-run movies, and world news; a piano bar; a nightclub; a duplex show lounge with state-of-the-art sound and lighting systems; a disco; a casino; and an observation lounge. There are shops, a sports and fitness center, two swimming pools, three Jacuzzis, and Internet cafes. In the suites, butler service is available. As a send-off on the last day of the cruise, all passengers may enjoy a classic high tea with white-glove service and classical music.

In 1992 Celebrity introduced three new megaliners even more spacious and luxurious than the first ships. In 2000 the line launched the millennium with the *Celebrity Millennium*, another new class of four ships, even larger, more spacious, and more elegant than the previous ones. In 2004 the line acquired the deluxe, 94-passenger *Celebrity Xpedition*, based year-round in the Galapagos. Three years later, Celebrity acquired two 710-passenger ships and created a small ship brand, Azamara Cruises, which is being marketed as deluxe—in cruise parlance that means between premium and luxury. Meanwhile, Celebrity has a new class of even larger ships under construction. The 118,000-ton *Celebrity Solstice*, the first of three ships to be introduced between 2008 and 2010, will carry 2,850 passengers.

Celebrity Cruises was bought by Royal Caribbean in 1997 but operates as a separate company.

Club Mediterranée, S.A.

40 West 57th Street, New York, NY 10019; (212) 977-2100; (800) CLUB-MED; fax (212) 315-5392; www.clubmed2.com/FR/clubdescroisires

Ships (passengers): *Club Med II* (392)

Departure port: Martinique

Type of cruises: 7 days to Eastern and Southern Caribbean

Lifestyle tip: Casual and sports oriented

Club Med, a name synonymous with all-inclusive vacations and an easy lifestyle, took its popular formula to sea in 1990 with the introduction of the world's largest sailboat and geared it to upscale, sophisticated, and active vacationers. But theirs was no ordinary sailing ship.

Longer than two football fields, she is 610 feet long and is rigged with five 164-foot masts. The $100 million ship was the last word in twenty-first-century technology, with seven computer-monitored sails. All 191 outside staterooms have a twin porthole and hand-rubbed mahogany cabinetwork. The spacious, 188-square-foot cabins are fitted with twin or king-size beds. All cabins have private bath, closed-circuit television, radio, safe, and minibar.

The ship has two restaurants: One, located on the top deck, offers casual dining and has an outdoor veranda for breakfast and luncheon buffets; the other, on the deck directly below, is a more formal dining room with waiter service and a la carte menu. Complimentary wine and beer accompany both luncheon and dinner, and an extensive wine list is available for an additional charge. Both restaurants have single unassigned seatings. Afternoon tea is served daily in the piano lounge with indoor and outdoor tables.

The ship has a fitness center with a panoramic view from the top deck, pine saunas and licensed massage therapists, tanning salon, two swimming pools, a discotheque, casino, 24-hour room service, and satellite telecommunications. Other facilities

include a boutique, theater, hair salon, and observation deck. Passengers can take aerobics, stretch, and other fitness classes.

In the stern the ship carries water-sports equipment and has a special sports platform that unfolds into the sea from which passengers can sail, windsurf, scuba dive, water-ski, and snorkel. There are qualified instructors to teach the fine points. Scuba-diving excursions, however, are reserved for certified divers who have their C-card.

During the winter season *Club Med II* is based in Martinique, from where she sails on five alternating itineraries that visit almost all the islands of the Eastern and Southern Caribbean, from the U.S. and British Virgin Islands on the north to Los Roques, off the coast of Venezuela, on the south.

Costa Cruise Lines

Venture Corporate Center II, 200 South Park Road, Suite 200, Hollywood, FL 33021-8541; (954) 266-5600; (954) 266-2100; (800) GO-COSTA; www.costacruise.com

Ships (passengers): *Costa Allegra* (1,000); *Costa Atlantica* (2,114); *Costa Classica* (1,356); *Costa Concordia* (3,300); *Costa Europa* (1,494); *Costa Fortuna* (2,720); *Costa Magica* (2,720); *Costa Marina* (1,000); *Costa Mediterranea* (2,114); *Costa Romantica* (1,356); *Costa Serena* (3,300); *Costa Victoria* (1,928)

Departure ports: Miami, Ft. Lauderdale, Guadeloupe

Types of cruises: 7 days to Western, Northern, and Eastern Caribbean

Lifestyle tip: More European atmosphere and service than similar mass-market ships

"Cruising Italian Style" has long been Costa Cruise Lines' stock in trade, with a fun and friendly atmosphere created by its Italian staff. The emphasis is on Italian food, which means pasta and pizza (there are other kinds of cuisine, too); European-style service, particularly in the dining room; and, not to forget the Italians' ancestry, a toga party, which is usually a hilarious affair, one night of the cruise.

Founded by the Genoa-based Costa family, which has been in the shipping business for more than one hundred years and in the passenger business for sixty years, Costa began offering one-week Caribbean cruises from Miami in 1959. It was the first to offer an air/sea program, introduced in the late 1960s.

Costa launched the 1990s with new ships, introducing interesting new features in its design, combining classic qualities with modern features and boasting unusually large cabins for their price categories. Among the ships' nicest features are canvas-covered outdoor cafes and pizzerias serving pizza throughout the day without additional charge. The ships also have Internet cafes.

Catalina Island is Costa's "private" beach off the southeast coast of the Dominican Republic featured on Eastern Caribbean cruises. The island is near the sprawling resort of Casa de Campo, which has, among its many facilities, three of the best golf courses in the Caribbean, a tennis village, horseback riding, and polo. With Casa de Campo's new marina and seaside village, Costa ships usually call at the island during the day and move to the marina for the nightlife. Costa's ships have fitness centers and spas (most services are extra), along with a health and fitness program to suit individual needs. Costa lets you combine two consecutive cruises into one fourteen-day cruise, at a price considerably less than that of two separate cruises. Another popular feature: During a Caribbean cruise a couple can renew their wedding vows in a special shipboard ceremony.

Costa is owned by Carnival Cruise Lines but operates as a separate entity.

Crystal Cruises

2049 Century Park East, Suite 1400, Los Angeles, CA 90067; (310) 785-9300; fax (310) 785-3891; www.crystalcruises.com

Ships (passengers): *Crystal Serenity* (1,080); *Crystal Symphony* (960)

Departure ports: Miami and worldwide

Types of cruises: 10- to 17-day Eastern/Western transcanal

Lifestyle tip: Ultra luxury for sophisticated travelers

The launching of Crystal Cruises in 1989 was one of the most anticipated in the cruising world. The owners spared no expense to ensure that the sleek *Crystal Harmony* (since transferred to a new sister company of her owners, Mitsubishi, in 2005) would live up to its advance billing. Its goal was to create luxury cruises that would return elegance and personalized service to cruising and be designed for an upscale mass market at deluxe prices.

The *Crystal Harmony* exceeded expectations and quickly became the ship by which others in its class—or trying to be in its class—are measured.

Crystal Symphony is essentially a copy of the *Crystal Harmony,* with some refinements and new features. For example, there are no inside staterooms. The *Crystal Serenity* has taken luxury to another level, with larger cabins, more cabins with balconies, a larger spa, and more dining options, including a specialty restaurant by famed master chef Nobu Matsuhisa. The ships are magnificent, with exquisite attention to detail. The food is excellent and the service superb, with the staff at every level smiling and gracious and always willing to go the extra mile.

These are spacious ships for experienced travelers with sophisticated lifestyles. The luxury is evident from the moment you step aboard. The atrium lobby, the ship's focus, is accented with greenery and hand-cut glass sculptures. The piano bar features—what else?—a crystal piano.

Staterooms have sitting areas, minibars, spacious closets, and such amenities as hair dryers, plush robes, VCRs, and 24-hour hookup with CNN and ESPN; more than half have verandas. The ships' penthouses have Jacuzzis and butler service. Facilities include spa and fitness centers and full promenade decks for jogging. The indoor/outdoor swimming pools have swim-up bars and lap pools with adjacent whirlpools. The ships have casinos.

The ships' most innovative feature was the choice of dinner restaurants—Japanese or Asian and Italian—at no extra cost, which set the trend for cruising. These restaurants are in addition to standard meal service in the main dining room and 24-hour room service.

Crystal's ships offer Computer University@Sea, with hands-on lab sessions. Laptop computers can be rented. Crystal also offers passengers individual e-mail addresses to use onboard.

Cunard

24303 Town Center Drive, Suite 200, Valencia, CA 91355-0908; (661) 753-1035; (800) 7-CUNARD; fax (661) 259-3103; www.cunard.com

Ships (passengers): *Queen Mary 2* (2,620); *Queen Victoria* (2,014)

Departure ports: New York, Fort Lauderdale

Types of cruises: 8 to 14 days for Caribbean on seasonal schedules

Lifestyle tips: Deluxe, and no mistaking the British touch; caters mostly to affluent travelers

The 150,000-ton *Queen Mary 2*, the largest cruise ship ever built, is heir to a family of transatlantic liners reaching back more than a century and a half and the only ship still on regular transatlantic service, from April to December.

The *Queens* set the standard of elegance at sea in times of peace and served their country with distinction in times of war. Today, *QM2*, which made her maiden voyage in January 2004, sets the tone for Cunard for the years to come. It is an ocean liner reminiscent of the great steamships and, in Cunard's words, was meant to "relaunch the golden age of travel for those who missed the first one."

Costing more than $800 million, the *QM2* is one of the world's fastest ships, with speeds up to 30 knots. She carries 2,620 passengers in a "quasi-class system," with cabin category determining assignments in each of three restaurants—one with a grand staircase similar to that seen by moviegoers in *Titanic*. Seventy-five percent of the cabins have balconies. The *QM2* also boasts the largest spa afloat, designed by the famous Canyon Ranch, which also operates it.

In 1998 Cunard was purchased by Carnival Cruises but operates as a separate company.

Even though Cunard is one of the oldest lines afloat, it has been an innovator, responding to today's changing lifestyles with gusto and recognizing the impact of the electronic revolution on peo-ple's lives—including their holidays. Its ships were the first to have a full-fledged spa at sea, a computer learning center, and satellite-delivered world news.

In 2007, *QE2* was sold and made her last voyage for the line in winter 2008. The *Queen Victoria* made her debut in December 2007 with a world cruise.

Disney Cruise Line

210 Celebration Place, Suite 400, Celebration, FL 34747-4600; (407) 566-3500; (800) 939-CRUISE; fax (407) 566-6910; www.disneycruise.com

Ships (passengers): *Disney Magic* (1,760); *Disney Wonder* (1,760)

Departure port: Port Canaveral

Types of cruises: 3-, 4-, 5, and 7-day Eastern and Western cruises combined with Disney World vacations

Lifestyle tip: Family oriented but designed for all ages

Disney Cruise Line was launched in July 1998, with its first ship, *Disney Magic*, followed by a sister ship, *Disney Wonder*, in 1999. Both ships have classic exteriors reminiscent of the great transatlantic ocean liners of the past, but inside they are up-to-the-minute in Disney innovation and family entertainment.

The line combines a three- or four-day stay at a Walt Disney World resort with a three- or four-day cruise aboard ship, sailing round-trip from Port Canaveral. The itinerary includes Nassau and a day at Castaway Cay, Disney's own private island. In 2000 the line introduced a seven-day itinerary combining the Bahamas with the Eastern Caribbean, and the following year, it added Western Caribbean cruises.

In addition to catering to families, *Disney Wonder* and *Disney Magic's* major innovations are three themed restaurants as well as an adults-only alternative restaurant, swimming pool, and night-club on each ship.

Nightly entertainment features Disney-produced shows with Broadway-quality entertainers, cabaret, and a comedy club.

The children's programs are the most extensive in the industry, with the largest children-dedicated space and age-specific activities and a large number of counselors. The ships have a separate pool, lounge, teen club, and game arcade for older kids.

The ships sport spacious suites and cabins, with 73 percent outside and almost half with small verandas.

Disney Cruises is building two new megaliners to be added to its fleet in 2011 and 2012.

Holland America Line

300 Elliott Avenue West, Seattle, WA 98119; (206) 281-3535; (800) 426-0327; fax (206) 301-5327; www.hollandamerica.com

Ships (passengers): *Amsterdam* (1,380); *Eurodam* (2041); *Maasdam* (1,266); *Noordam* (1,848); *Oosterdam* (1,848); *Prinsendam* (794); *Rotterdam* (1,316); *Ryndam* (1,266); *Statendam* (1,266); *Veendam* (1,266); *Volendam* (1,440); *Westerdam* (1,848); *Zaandam* (1,440); *Zuiderdam* (1,848)

Departure ports: Fort Lauderdale, Tampa, New York; Boston, Norfolk seasonally

Types of cruises: 5 to 11 days to Western and Eastern Caribbean; 10 days to Southern Caribbean; 10 to 23 days to Panama Canal

Lifestyle tip: Classic but contemporary

Begun in 1873 as a transatlantic shipping company between Rotterdam and the Americas, Holland America Line stems from one of the oldest steamship companies in the world. Through the years and two world wars, its ships became an important part of maritime history, particularly significant in the westward passage of immigrants to America. The line also owned Westours, the Seattle-based tour company that pioneered tours and cruises to Alaska in the 1950s. The following year the group was purchased by Carnival Cruise Lines, but each operate as separate entities.

Holland America now has one of the newest fleets in cruising, having added ten magnificent, brand-new ships in less than ten years. The ships combine the Old World with the New in decor and ambience and boast million-dollar art and antiques collections reflecting Holland's association with

trade and exploration in the Americas and Asia. Their Dutch officers and Indonesian and Filipino crews are another reminder of Holland's historical ties to Asia.

The ships have the space and elegance for long cruises of two weeks or more, for which they were designed. They feature a three-level atrium lobby with unusual sculpture, an elegant two-level dining room, small lounges and bars, disco, casino, a large state-of-the-art spa, a sliding-glass dome for the swimming pool, spacious cabins, and premium amenities. All suites and 120 deluxe cabins have private verandas, whirlpool baths, minibars, and VCRs. There are bathtubs in all outside cabins.

In 1997 Holland America bought the uninhabited 2,400-acre Bahamian island of Little San Salvador, located between Eleuthera and Cat Island, renaming it Half Moon Cay and developing it as a private island included on all its Caribbean itineraries. Ships anchor offshore and tender passengers ashore. The line's multimillion-dollar facility, covering forty-five acres along a gorgeous white-sand beach, has three areas—an arrival marina and plaza built to resemble the ruins of an old Spanish fort, a shopping area in the style of a West Indian village, and a food pavilion—all connected by walkways and a tram.

The market area has shops, an ice-cream parlor, coffee shop, bar, and art gallery. There is a children's playground, wedding chapel, and post office that sells Bahamian stamps and has its own postmark. The sports center offers snorkeling and diving on nearby reefs, Sunfish sailing and other water sports, volleyball, and basketball. Parts of the island were designated as a bird sanctuary by the Bahamian National Trust; nature trails lead to areas with the best bird-watching.

Signature of Excellence is a program that Holland America launched in 2004 to update its ships with new features—such as Internet cafes, extensive spa facilities, alternative dining venues, and expanded children's facilities—in order to make the ships more relevant to boomers and multigenerational families, which are markets that are becoming more and more important to cruise lines.

Life aboard the ships of Holland America proceeds at a leisurely pace. Traditionally the line has attracted mature, experienced travelers and families. During the winter the fleet sails on Caribbean and Panama Canal cruises, some departing from Tampa, a port Holland America helped to develop for cruise ships, and New Orleans to the Western Caribbean and the Panama Canal; others leave from Fort Lauderdale for the Eastern Caribbean.

6750 North Andrews Avenue, #605, Fort Lauderdale, FL 33309; (954) 772-6262; (800) 666-9333; fax (954) 776-5881; www.msccruises.com

Ships (passengers): *Lirica* (1,590); *Musica* (3,000); *Opera* (1,756); *Orchestra* (3,000)

Departure port: Fort Lauderdale

Type of cruises: 7, 10, and 11 days to Eastern and Western Caribbean and Panama Canal

Lifestyle tip: Classic but contemporary, Italian style

Part of a Swiss group operating a global fleet of container ships and fast ferries, Mediterranean Shipping Company (MSC) acquired three cruise ships in less than four years and added another six ships by 2007. (All but one or two ships sail primarily in Europe.) Its almost overnight expansion launched the line's bid to be a major player in Europe and North America.

With an Italian staff and ambience, the ships offer classic cruises with good food and service. MSC aims for a mix of 85 percent American and 15 percent international passengers when its Florida-based ships sail the Caribbean. Onboard, MSC made changes to appeal to American tastes, such as prices being in dollars rather than euros, cabin television with CNN and American movies, and breakfast and lunch buffets with choices that American passengers prefer.

The *Lirica* (or *Lyric* in English) made her debut in 2003, with actress Sophia Loren doing the christening honors. *Lirica* is powered by an advanced propulsion system that reduces engine noise and increases comfort levels. Among other amenities, she has two swimming pools, a gym and jogging track, two hot tubs and a sauna, a virtual-reality center, and an Internet cafe. The ship also has a disco and a theater with shows nightly, a supervised Mini Club for children, and a shopping

gallery. All cabins have satellite television, minibar, safe, radio, and 24-hour room service. Out of 795 cabins, 132 cabins have verandas, and 4 are designed for disabled passengers. *Lirica* has two restaurants as well as a grill and pizzeria that serve authentic Italian cuisine. The *Lirica* is the only ship of the fleet which will be sailing from U.S. ports for the 2008 winter season. In 2009, she will be joined by another, similar ship from the fleet.

7665 Corporate Center Drive, Miami, FL 33126; (305) 436-4000; (800) 327-7030; fax (305) 436-4120; www.ncl.com

Ships (passengers): *Norwegian Dawn* (2,240); *Norwegian Dream* (1,748); *Norwegian Gem* (2,376); *Norwegian Jewel* (2,376); *Norwegian Majesty* (1,462); *Norwegian Pearl* (2,376); *Norwegian Spirit* (1,966); *Norwegian Star* (2,240); *Norwegian Sun* (2,002)

Departure ports: Miami, New York, San Juan, Houston; Boston, Charleston, New Orleans seasonally

Types of cruises: 2, 3, 4, and 7 days to the Bahamas; Northern, Eastern, and Western Caribbean; Bermuda

Lifestyle tip: Mainstream of modern cruising

Norwegian Cruise Line (NCL) was started in 1966 by Knut Kloster, whose family has been in the steamship business in Scandinavia since 1906. Kloster is credited with launching modern cruising when he introduced year-round three- and four-day cruises from Miami to the Bahamas, thus creating the first mass-market packaging of cruises.

By 1971 NCL had added three new ships and pioneered weekly cruises to Jamaica and other Caribbean destinations. NCL introduced a day-at-the-beach feature in the Caymans and bought a Bahamian island to add a day-on-a-private-island to the line's Bahamas cruises. The idea has since been adopted by most cruise lines sailing the Bahamas and Caribbean.

Yet, in its history loaded with "firsts," nothing caused as much excitement as the entry of the *Norway* (now retired) in 1980. After buying the former *France* for $18 million, NCL spent $100 million to transform her from the great ocean liner she had been to the trendsetting Caribbean cruise ship she became.

The 2,000-passenger *Norway* was the largest passenger ship afloat. Her size enabled NCL to create a completely new environment on board with restaurants, bars, and lounges of great diversity; shopping malls with "sidewalk" cafes; full Broadway shows and Las Vegas revues in its enormous theater; full casino; and sports and entertainment facilities that could keep passengers in motion almost around the clock. These innovations set the pattern for all cruise ships that followed.

NCL is known for its entertainment—ranging from comedy clubs and cabaret stars to Broadway shows, and the line has an extensive youth and children's program.

In 2000 NCL was bought by Star Cruises, the largest cruise line in Asia, which stepped up NCL's expansion with seven new megaliners in five years, keeping its promise to add a new ship every year for the remainder of the decade. The newest ships reflect NCL's FreeStyle Cruising, one of the line's most significant innovations. The program aims at providing passengers with the utmost flexibility, enabling them to dine where, when, and with whom they choose, with up to ten restaurants, along with choice of attire, among other features. NCL was one of the first cruise lines to provide wireless capability on its newest ships.

Oceania Cruises

8300 Northwest Thirty-third Street, Suite 308, Miami, FL 33122; (305) 514-2300; (800) 531-5658; fax (305) 514-2222; www.oceaniacruises.com

Ships (passengers): *Insignia* (684); *Nautica* (684); *Regatta* (684)

Departure port: Miami

Type of cruises: 10 to 16 days to the Caribbean, Panama Canal, Central and South America in winter

Lifestyle tip: Casual country-club elegance without pretension

Formed in late 2002 by two well-known cruise industry veterans, Frank Del Rio and Joe Watters,

Oceania Cruises has carved out a niche between the premium and luxury categories similar to that of now-defunct Renaissance Cruises, using three of the former line's ships and appealing to discerning, sophisticated travelers.

The cruise line has created an outstanding product with its cuisine, service, and destination-oriented itineraries and offers it at reasonable prices. The relaxed onboard atmosphere is meant to resemble the casual elegance of a country club, neither stuffy nor pretentious. Formal wear is never a requirement for dining; passengers dress comfortably to enjoy their evenings.

The 30,277-ton ships—small compared with today's more typical megaships—provide an intimate atmosphere while, at the same time, having the facilities of larger ships. For example, each ship has four restaurants with open seating, enabling passengers to dine when, where, and with whom they choose.

Each restaurant offers a different type of cuisine and a different ambience. Menus have been crafted by master chef Jacques Pepin, the line's executive culinary director and one of America's best-known chefs as a host of numerous public television shows, food columnist, and cookbook author. He has also served as the personal chef to three French heads of state, including Gen. Charles de Gaulle.

Of the total 340 spacious cabins and suites, 92 percent are outside, and almost 70 percent have verandas. The Owner's and Vista Suites, each encompassing nearly 1,000 square feet, have floor-to-ceiling glass doors that lead to a veranda. The ships have spas where passengers can be pampered with aromatherapy massage and hot stone treatments, among other offerings. The fitness center has state-of-the-art equipment and an aerobic area; personal trainers are available. Oceania@ Sea, the 24-hour computer center, has Internet access, and there's a library, card room, medical center, self-service launderette, and four elevators. The ships have a high staff-to-guest ratio, with more than one crew member per cabin to provide a high degree of personal service.

The *Regatta*, inaugurated in July 2003, spends her winters in the Caribbean and her summers in Europe. Some itineraries have been tailored to include overnight port stays to allow passengers to immerse themselves in the history, culture, and local flavor of the region. *Insignia* sails in Central and South America. The third ship, *Nautica,* cruises in Asia and Europe. The cruise line is building two new ships to debut in 2010 and 2011. Passengers are registered in the line's Repeaters Club from their first cruise, making them eligible for travel rewards and other benefits.

Princess Cruises

24305 Town Center Drive, Santa Clarita, CA 91355; (800) 774-6237; fax (661) 284-4771; www.princess .com

Ships (passengers): *Caribbean Princess* (3,100); *Coral Princess* (2,000); *Crown Princess* (3,100); *Dawn Princess* (1,950); *Diamond Princess* (2,700); *Emerald Princess* (3,100); *Golden Princess* (2,600); *Grand Princess* (2,600); *Island Princess* (2,000); *Pacific Princess* (700); *Royal Princess* (700); *Ruby Princess* (3,100); *Sapphire Princess* (2,700); *Sea Princess* (1,950); *Star Princess* (2,600); *Sun Princess* (1,950)

Departure ports: Fort Lauderdale, San Juan, Acapulco, Los Angeles, New York (summer), Barbados (winter)

Types of cruises: 7 to 14 days, combining Western, Eastern, and Southern Caribbean, and Panama Canal

Lifestyle tip: Casually stylish and modestly affluent

Princess Cruises, a West Coast pioneer begun in 1965, is credited with helping to create the relaxed and casual atmosphere that typifies life aboard today's cruises. One of its ships, the former *Pacific Princess* (now retired), was the ship used in the popular television series *The Love Boat.* It's impossible to calculate, but that show probably did more to popularize modern cruising than all other cruise publicity combined. It was certainly a factor in dispelling cruising's elitist image and enabling people who might have never considered a cruise holiday to identify with it.

The *Royal Princess* (now retired), which was christened by the Princess of Wales, made her debut in 1983. The ship set new standards in pas-

senger comfort with all outside cabins, and refrigerators, televisions, and bathrooms fitted with tubs as well as showers in every cabin category. All suites, deluxe cabins, and some of those in lesser categories had private outside balconies—a first for cruising.

In 1995 and for the next decade, Princess launched two new classes of megaships. First came the *Sun Princess* in 1995, followed by her twin, *Dawn Princess,* and the *Grand Princess,* the largest cruise ship ever built when it was launched in 1998. These were followed by nine even larger ships.

Designed by Njal Eide, the architect of the elegant *Royal Princess,* the *Sun Princess* is one of the most beautiful large ships afloat, with exquisite interiors of the finest Italian workmanship. It introduced many new features, including two atrium lobbies and two main show lounges, a true theater at sea, and a restaurant offering 24-hour dining. About 70 percent of the outside cabins have verandas. *Grand Princess* and her sister ships have even more choices—three show lounges with different shows each night, three dining rooms, three alternative restaurants, and more. All have elaborate spas and Internet cafes.

With the new ships, the cruise line introduced a flexible dining program enabling passengers to dine when and with whom they wish as in a restaurant, along with traditional dining in the main dining room.

In recent years Princess has had one of the strongest presences in the Caribbean in the winter season. The line has a private beach, Princess Cays (on south Eleuthera in the Bahamas), where the ships call. The facility has just about every water sport a passenger could want, nature trails with guided walks, games, kiosks for local crafts, and a large dining pavilion where passengers are served lunch.

In 2003 Princess Cruises was purchased by Carnival Corporation, outbidding Royal Caribbean Lines for this prize. Princess continues to operate as a separate company.

Princess caters to a modestly affluent clientele from thirty-five years of age plus, with a median age of fifty to fifty-five. It is very aggressive with promotional fares and seasonal savings.

600 Corporate Drive, No. 410, Fort Lauderdale, FL 33334; (954) 776-6123; (800) 477-7500; fax (954) 772-3763; www.rssc.com

Ships (passengers): *Paul Gauguin* (320); *Seven Seas Mariner* (729); *Seven Seas Navigator* (490); *Seven Seas Voyager* (708)

Departure ports: Fort Lauderdale and worldwide ports seasonally

Types of cruises: 7 to 14 days; transcanal, Eastern Caribbean

Lifestyle tip: Luxury for affluent travelers

Diamond Cruises, a joint venture of Finnish, Japanese, and U.S. interests, formed a partnership with Radisson Hotels International, and in 1995 Radisson Diamond joined with Seven Seas Cruises to form a new company, Radisson Seven Seas, renamed Regent Seven Seas in 2006.

In the years that followed, the cruise line built four new, ultraluxurious ships that sail the world. They are among the most spacious ocean liners afloat. The *Seven Seas Mariner* and *Seven Seas Voyager* were cruising's first all-suite-with-balcony ships. Throughout the fleet, the decor is one of understated elegance. The ships have several lounges and bars, a spa, and a fitness center with a gym sauna and jogging track. The dining rooms and alternative restaurants serve as fine cuisine as one finds in top restaurants in New York or Paris.

Only one of the newest ships sails in the Caribbean, and only for a limited time in winter. These cruises are usually combined with the Panama Canal or South America. The cruises are expensive and cater to affluent passengers who are accustomed to the best.

1050 Caribbean Way, Miami, FL 33132; (305) 539-6000; (800) 659-7225; (800) 722-5329; fax (305) 373-4394; www.royalcaribbean.com

Ships (passengers): *Adventure of the Seas* (3,114); *Brilliance of the Seas* (2,000); *Empress of the Seas* (1,602); *Enchantment of the Seas* (1,950); *Explorer of the Seas* (3,114); *Freedom of the Seas* (3,600); *Grandeur of the Seas* (1,950); *Independence of the Seas 2008* (3, 634); *Jewel of the Seas* (2,100); *Legend of the Seas* (1,808*); Liberty of the Seas* (3, 634); *Majesty of the Seas* (2,354); *Mariner of the Seas* (3,114); *Monarch of the Seas* (2,354); *Navigator of the Seas* (3,114); *Radiance of the Seas* (2,000); *Rhapsody of the Seas* (2,000); *Serenade of the Seas* (2,100); *Sovereign of the Seas* (2,276); *Splendor of the Seas* (1,800); *Vision of the Seas* (1,950); *Voyager of the Seas* (3,114)

Departure ports: Miami, San Juan, Fort Lauderdale, Port Canaveral, Bayonne, Philadelphia, Baltimore, Boston, Tampa, Galveston, New Orleans

Types of cruises: 3 to 10 days to the Bahamas and Western, Eastern, and Southern Caribbean

Lifestyle tip: Active, wholesome ambience

Royal Caribbean Cruise Line (RCCL), launched in the early 1970s, was the first line to build a fleet of ships designed specially for year-round Caribbean cruising. The ships were established so quickly that within five years RCCL needed more capacity and did so by "stretching" two of the vessels. They were literally cut in half, and prefabricated midsections were inserted. Although the method had been used on cargo and other vessels, RCCL's work was the first for cruise ships.

For the 1980s it added superliners with unique design features, and in 1988 it got a head start on the 1990s with the *Sovereign of the Seas,* the first of the new generation of megaliners and the largest cruise ship afloat at the time. Few ships in history have received so much attention.

Over the next decade, RCCL added a new group of six megaliners. The first ship, *Legend of the Seas,* introduced the first miniature golf course at sea and a spectacular "solarium"—an indoor/outdoor swimming, sunning, and fitness facility. The cruise line entered the new millennium with another new group of ships, dubbed Eagle class. The *Voyager of the Seas,* first of the three ships, at 142,000 tons, was the largest ship ever built when it made its debut in 1999. It came with such unusual features as a rock-climbing wall, a skating rink, cabins overlooking the atrium, and more. These were followed by four smaller Radiance-class ships, the most beautiful of the fleet, noted particularly for their walls of glass. Next came the 158,000-ton Freedom class, with the largest cruise ships ever built. The first one, *Freedom of the Seas,* arrived in May 2006, followed by two sister ships in 2007 and 2008. And now, an even larger ship of 220,000 tons for 5,400 passengers is under construction and is scheduled to enter service in 2009. Known as Project Genesis, it will be the largest cruise ship ever built. Her sister will follow in 2010.

It would be impossible for even the most active passenger to participate in all the daily activities offered on an RCCL ship. Fitness folks have a ⅓-mile outside deck encircling the vessel and one of the best-equipped health clubs at sea, complete with ballet bars, sophisticated computerized exercise equipment, and a high-energy staff to put them through their paces. The sports deck has twin pools and a basketball court.

For those with something less strenuous in mind, there are small, sophisticated lounges for drinks, dancing, and cabaret entertainment. Enrichment programs run the gamut from napkin folding to wine tasting. The library resembles a sedate English club, with its wood paneling and leather chairs. Two feature films run daily in twin cinemas; the shopping boulevard has a sidewalk cafe; the show lounge, a multitiered theater with unobstructed views, runs two different Las Vegas–style revues and variety shows.

Somewhere there's music to suit every mood, from Big Band, steel band, Latin, country, rock, or strolling violins to classical concerts. The Schooner is a lively piano bar; Music Man has entertainers from blues to country; and the disco projects holograms on the mirrored walls and music videos around the dance floor. Casino Royale offers blackjack, 216 slot machines, and American roulette. The chic Champagne Bar is a quiet corner where fifty people clink flutes and scoop caviar.

Designed as they are for Caribbean cruising, RCCL ships have acres of open sundecks and large pools. The line offers low-fat, low-calorie fare and has a ShipShape program on all ships in the fleet. It is often combined with sports in port. Golf Ahoy! enables passengers to play golf at courses throughout the Caribbean.

The cabins are compact—in fact, they are small, but they are functional and spotless. A top-deck lounge cantilevered from the funnel provides fabulous views from twelve or more stories above the sea. These lounges are RCCL's signature.

RCCL blankets the Caribbean year-round. It has cruises year-round on the West Coast and Mexico, and in Alaska and Europe in the summer. CocoCay, a small island in the Bahamas, is used for the ships' day at the beach. Labadee, RCCL's private resort on the north coast of Haiti, is very popular.

Founded in 1969 as a partnership of three prominent Norwegian shipping companies, RCCL went public in April 1993. In 1997 RCCL purchased Celebrity Cruises, which it operates as a separate company.

RCCL caters to a moderately upscale market. The atmosphere is friendly and casual, and the activities are so varied that there is something for everyone at almost every hour of the day. All RCCL ships have programs for children and teenagers because the line believes that a happy kid on a cruise now will still be a customer in 2020.

Seabourn Cruise Line

6100 Blue Lagoon Drive, Suite 400, Miami, FL 33126; (305) 463-3000; (800) 929-9391; fax (305) 463-3010; www.seabourn.com

Ships (passengers): *Seabourn Legend* (214); *Seabourn Pride* (214); *Seabourn Spirit* (214)

Departure ports: Fort Lauderdale, Barbados, Aruba, San Juan, Antigua, St. Thomas

Types of cruises: 3 to 21 days in Eastern and Southern Caribbean and Panama Canal in winter; worldwide schedules year-round

Lifestyle tip: The ultimate luxury cruise

When Seabourn was formed in 1987, it set out to create the world's most deluxe cruises on the most elegant, luxurious ships afloat. Despite very high per diem rates, Seabourn quickly won enough fans to add more ships.

The ships and cruises were designed with a certain type of person in mind—one who normally stays in the best rooms at a luxury hotel and books a deluxe suite on a luxury liner. The staterooms are luxuriously appointed in soft, warm colors and have television with CNN, CD and DVD players, stocked bars, refrigerators, walk-in closets, and large marble bathrooms with tub and shower. Each has a roomy sitting area beside a large picture window with electrically manipulated shades and outside cleaning mechanisms. In 2000 French balconies replaced the picture windows in thirty-six suites of each of the Seabourn trio, along with an expanded spa and computer learning center and other improvements.

Passengers dine on gourmet cuisine served on Royal Doulton china and have open seating. They may also dine from the restaurant menu in their suites, and there is a 24-hour room service menu with a wide selection and a choice wine list.

Seabourn's ships have sleek profiles that resemble the most modern of yachts. A water sports platform at the stern has a "cage" that can be lowered into the water for passengers to swim in the open sea without fear. The ships carry sailboards, snorkeling and dive equipment, and two high-speed boats. The ships' itineraries take them to all parts of the world, but at least one spends some of the winter in the Caribbean.

Seabourn is building two new 32,000-ton ships to be delivered in 2009 and 2010. The company is owned by Carnival Cruise Lines but operates as a separate entity.

SeaDream Yacht Club

2601 South Bayshore Drive, Penthouse 1B, Coconut Grove, FL 33133-5417; (305) 631-6100; (800) 707-4911; fax (305) 631-6110; www.sea dreamyachtclub.com

Ships (passengers): SeaDream I/SeaDream II (110)

Departure ports: San Juan, Barbados, St. Thomas, St. Maarten

Types of cruises: 7-day Caribbean, seasonally

Lifestyle tip: Luxury but casual

SeaDream Yacht Club, a venture of two cruise-industry veterans, began operating in late 2001 with the luxury twin ships SeaDream I and II (formerly Sea Goddess I and II). The handsome twins, which the line calls megayachts, are meant to provide a totally different experience from

today's typical cruise, one that more closely resembles yachting. Like yachts, the ships offer an open, unstructured ambience for passengers to move at their own pace. "No clocks, no crowds, no lines, no stress" could be the company's motto.

According to SeaDream, what make its cruises different are flexible schedules and itineraries: SeaDream's yachts depart their first port and arrive at their last port as scheduled, but the port calls in between are not run by a strict timetable. Captains have the authority to adjust for local opportunities. For example, they might make an unscheduled visit to an island fish market so the chef can pick up the day's catch. Also, while most cruise ships arrive at ports of call at about 8:00 a.m. and sail at 5:00 or 6:00 p.m. the same day, SeaDream yachts overnight at popular ports where the action doesn't get started until late evening.

While the ship is in port, passengers may visit a small-town pastry shop with the chef, go snorkeling with the captain, or go hiking, biking, or golfing with the officers. What better guides to have.

The ships have alcoves for sunning on double sun beds, a private massage tent on deck, a large-screen golf simulator that also can be used to watch sports events or movies, and a water sports marina at the stern equipped for kayaking, water-skiing, windsurfing, snorkeling, and Sunfish sailing. Tai chi, yoga, and aerobics classes are also offered.

Indoors, passengers have an Asian-style spa and fitness center. The ships also have a Main Lounge, a piano bar, casino, and a library with books, CDs, DVDs, and computer outlets. Laptop computers are available. Passengers are given their own onboard e-mail address.

Of the fifty-five cabins, thirty-eight are 195 square feet; sixteen are 390 square feet with his and her bathroom facilities and a dining area accommodating four. The 450-square-foot Owner's Suite has a bedroom, bathroom with a tub and separate shower with a view of the sea, a living room/dining area, and a guest bathroom. Bathrooms have multiple-jet massage showers and lighted magnifying mirrors. All cabins are Internet ready and have an entertainment center with a flat-screen television, CD and DVD systems with movies and other selections, and a personal jukebox with more than one hundred digital music programs.

SeaDream has no dress code; rather it stresses the casual nature of yachting.

Silversea Cruises

110 East Broward Boulevard, Fort Lauderdale, FL 33301; (954) 522-4477; (800) 722-6655; fax (954) 522-4499; www.silversea.com

Ships (passengers): *Silver Cloud* (306); *Silver Shadow* (388); *Silver Whisper* (388); *Silver Wind* (306)

Departure ports: Fort Lauderdale, Barbados

Type of cruise: Caribbean, seasonally

Lifestyle tip: Ultraluxurious surroundings in a relaxing, friendly—not stuffy—atmosphere

Silversea Cruises was launched in late 1994 with the luxurious all-suite *Silver Cloud,* designed by Oslo-based Petter Yran and Bjorn Storbraaten, the architects of the Seabourn ships. Its twin, *Silver Wind,* made its debut the following year.

The Silversea ships mirror Seabourn's in many ways but carry 306 passengers (100 more than Seabourn's), and 107 of the Silversea's 155 suites have verandas.

Silversea's large suites, averaging 300 square feet, have a spacious sitting area, walk-in closet, fully stocked bar, hair dryer, TV with VCR, direct-dial telephone, and marble-floored bathroom with tub. Passengers are welcomed to their staterooms with fresh flowers, a bottle of champagne, a basket of fruit replenished daily, personalized stationery, and plush terry robes for use during their cruise.

There is open seating in the dining room and 24-hour room service. The ship has a tiered show lounge spanning two decks, with a nightclub at the upper level, plus a casino, a spa, and a library.

In 2000 and 2001 the line added two new, slightly larger, and even more spacious ships, *Silver Shadow* and *Silver Whisper,* but almost identical in style to the earlier ships. Silversea's newest build is again, slightly larger at 36,000 tons, and will be launched in late 2009.

The ships sail on worldwide itineraries throughout the year, but at least one is in the Caribbean for transcanal, Central, and South American itineraries

in winter. The co-owners of the line are passenger and shipping veterans Francesco Lefebvre of Rome and the Vlasov Group of Monaco. Silversea sails under the Italian flag, with Italian officers and a European staff.

Star Clippers, Inc.

7200 Northwest Nineteenth Street, Suite 206, Miami, FL 33126; (305) 442-0550; (800) 442-0551; fax (305) 442-1611; www.starclippers.com

Ships (passengers): *Royal Clipper* (224); *Star Clipper* (180); *Star Flyer* (180)

Departure ports: St. Maarten; Barbados

Type of cruises: 7 to 14 days on alternating itineraries in the Eastern Caribbean

Lifestyle tip: For active travelers looking for the romance of sailing to out-of-the-way places

Star Clippers is the brainchild of Swedish shipping entrepreneur Mikael Krafft, whose passions for sailing and building yachts and his love of the clipper ship (which he says is one of America's greatest inventions) led him to create a cruise line with clipper ships. Launched in 1991, the cruises are priced to fit between budget-conscious cruises and pricey yachtlike ships.

Star Clippers is truly distinctive. The *Star Clipper* and *Star Flyer*—each accommodating 180 passengers in ninety staterooms—are direct descendents of the fast, sleek clipper ships that ruled the seas in the mid-1800s. Built in Belgium, the vessels are 357 feet long with four masts and square-rigged sails in the forward mast—a Barguentine configuration—with a total of seventeen sails (36,000 square feet of sail area). They are manned, not computerized, and capable of attaining speeds of 19.4 knots. At 208 feet tall, they are among the tallest of the tall ships.

Today's clippers retain the romance of sailing under canvas coupled with the excitement of participating in the sailing of an authentic square rigger. They are further enhanced by the out-of-the-way Caribbean destinations that the cruises visit. Passengers quickly get to know the youthful crew, who double in their duties as deckhands, as sports instructors, and in other capacities.

Responding to a changing preference among some vacationers for a deemphasis on ostentatious food and the crowds of big ships, the cruises focus on an active, casual, and even educational experience, so it's more like being on a private yacht. The food is good but not gourmet. Dress is very casual, with shorts and deck shoes the uniform of the day, and only slightly less casual in the evening. Fellow passengers will be kindred souls—you hope—and 50 percent or more might be Europeans, depending on the time of the year. The cruises are also a great environment for families with children ages seven to seventeen.

All cabins have air-conditioning, carpeting, and private bathrooms with showers. Most cabins are outside-facing and fitted with twin beds that can be converted to a bed slightly larger than the standard queen size. Eight inside cabins are furnished with upper and lower beds, and eight cabins can accommodate three passengers. The top staterooms on the main deck have marble bathrooms with bathtubs and hair dryers. Cabins are equipped with multichannel radio and video players. Videotapes are available from the ship's library. There is storage for luggage, golf clubs, scuba gear, and other such items.

Facilities include a small piano bar, located midship on the main deck. It has brass-framed panoramic windows, carved paneling, and cushioned banquettes. The unusual lighting comes from the skylight overhead—it's actually the transparent bottom of the sundeck pool, one of the ship's two small pools. The piano bar is on the landing of a double staircase leading into the Clipper Dining Room on the deck below. All passengers dine at one seating, although when the ship is full the room can be very crowded. In addition to regular meal service, the dining room converts into a meeting room with screen projectors and video monitors.

Adjoining the aft end of the Piano Bar is the Tropical Bar, protected from the elements by a broad canvas awning, under which is found the bar, a dance, floor, and the stage where the captain holds his daily talks, and where much of the entertainment takes place during the cruise. Breakfast and lunch buffets are occasionally served here, too. Also on the main deck is a library that resembles an English club with large brass-framed windows,

carved paneling, and a marble fireplace. It doubles as a reception desk and is used for small meetings.

The line's newest 5,000-ton ship, *Royal Clipper,* is the largest sailing vessel in the world— more than twice the size of its sister ships but with a capacity for only 224 passengers, compared to their 180 passengers. Built for more than $75 million, the ship is 439 feet in length with a 54-foot beam and has five masts with thirty-nine sails.

The *Royal Clipper* is also more upscale. It has three small swimming pools, one with a glass bottom that allows light into the three-deck atrium below; an observation lounge with wraparound windows on the deck below the bridge; and a dining room, accommodating all passengers at a single seating, which is built on two connecting levels. The ship also has a water-sports platform and an inflatable floating raft for swimmers.

Cabins are larger than those on the sister ships, and some have a third fold-down bed. The suites have private verandas and bathrooms with whirlpool tubs. *Royal Clipper* sails the Caribbean in winter from Barbados. The *Star Clipper* is based in St. Maarten in winter, sailing on alternating seven-day cruises in the Eastern Caribbean. An unduplicated fourteen-day itinerary is possible with back-to-back cruises. The clippers can anchor in bays that large cruise ships cannot reach. Launches take passengers to isolated beaches and scuba and snorkeling spots or to enjoy other water sports. Snorkeling gear, water skis, sailboards, and volleyballs are carried on board.

In September 2007, Star Clippers announced plans to build a five-masted, 7,400-ton ship—the world's largest sailing vessel—for delivery in 2010. The new ship, 518 feet long with 37 sails, will be 48 percent larger than *Royal Clipper* and carry 30 percent more passengers—296 passengers and 140 crew. She will have an 8,200-square-foot sundeck area among other new amenities.

Windstar Cruises

300 Elliot Avenue West, Seattle, WA 98119; (206) 281-3535; (800) 258-7245; fax (206) 281-0627; www.windstarcruises.com

Ships (passengers): *Wind Spirit* (148); *Wind Star* (148); *Wind Surf* (308)

Departure ports: Barbados, Puerto Caldera, St. Thomas

Types of cruises: 7 days to the Eastern and Southern Caribbean, Costa Rica, Belize, and Panama Canal

Lifestyle tips: Combination of sailing yacht and deluxe cruise ship; for active people

Imagine a deck one and a half times the length of a football field and half its width. Now, look up to the sky and imagine four masts in a row, each as high as a twenty-story building and each with two enormous triangular sails. If you can picture these dimensions, you will have a mental image of the windcruiser, which was, when she debuted, the most revolutionary vessel since the introduction of the steamship in the last century. The six great sails are controlled by computers instead of deckhands. The computer is designed to monitor the direction and velocity of the wind to keep the ship from heeling no more than six degrees. The sails can be furled in less than two minutes.

The windcruiser marries the romance and tradition of sailing with the comfort and amenities of a cruise ship. The ship has seventy-five identical, outside 182-square-foot staterooms (so they are comparable in size to those on regular cruise ships). The well-designed cabins make optimum use of space and are fitted with twin- or queen-size beds, minibar, color television, VCR, satellite phone communications, and individual safes.

Cabins, gym, and sauna are on the bottom two of four passenger decks. The third deck has a main lounge and dining salon; both are handsome rooms that have the ambience of a private yacht. The dining room, which has open seating, serves sophisticated gourmet cuisine. The ship has a tiny casino, boutique, and beauty salon. The top deck has a swimming pool, bar, and veranda lounge used for lunch during the day and a disco at night. Through the overhead skylight of the lounge, passengers can have a dramatic view of the majestic sails overhead.

The vessel has a shallow 13½-foot draft that enables it to stop at less-visited ports and secluded beaches and coves. The ship is fitted with a water sports platform that gives passengers direct access to the sea. Sailboats and windsurfing boards are carried on board, as are Zodiacs (inflatable boats) to take passengers snorkeling, scuba diving, water-skiing, and fishing. The gear for these activities is available for use without additional charge. Any passenger lucky enough to hook a fish can have it cooked to order by the ship's chefs.

In 1997 Windstar Cruises bought *Club Med I,* one of two identical ships in the Club Med fleet that are large versions of Windstar's ships. It was remodeled and renamed *Wind Surf.* Among *Wind Surf*'s renovations, thirty-one deluxe suites were created, and a 10,000-square-foot spa was added. Both moves were intended to enhance the ship's appeal and offset its larger size and capacity, more than double the number of passengers carried on the Windstar ships. In addition to the standard amenities, the suites boast his-and-hers bathrooms with shower, complete with teak flooring, plush terry towels and robes, and vanity lighting.

More recently, the ship added a computer center, an outdoor barbecue station, and improved gangway and access to the ship. The ship also offers a complimentary water-sports program off its marina deck and a fully equipped conference center.

Windstar's cruises are planned to be partly cruise, partly yacht charter. They are geared to working professionals who can afford to take a cruise and like the luxury of a cruise ship or resort but who want a more active and unusual vacation than that associated with traditional cruises; thus they attract experienced cruise passengers and boat owners as well as people who may have shunned cruise ships in the past.

In 2007 Windstar Cruises was purchased by Majestic America Cruises, which specializes in cruises on U.S. rivers. Windstar, however, continues as a separate entity with its own special type of cruises.

PART THREE

Gateways to Points East and South

Three of the islands covered in this section—Puerto Rico, St. Thomas, and St. Maarten—are bases, or home ports, from which many ships depart en route to destinations in the Eastern and Southern Caribbean. These, together with their neighboring islands—St. John, St. Croix, the British Virgin Islands, Saba, St. Eustatius, and Anguilla—form a bridge between the Northern and Eastern Caribbean. We have, therefore, grouped them as the Gateways to Points East and South.

Puerto Rico
San Juan, Ponce

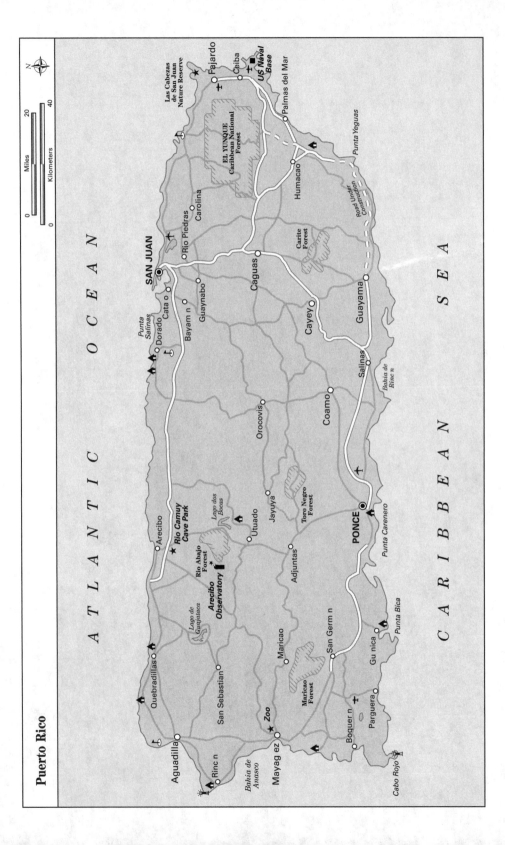

Puerto Rico

ATLANTIC OCEAN

CARIBBEAN SEA

N

Miles
0   20

Kilometers
0   40

Aguadilla
Rincón
Bahia de Añasco
Mayagüez
Zoo
Cabo Rojo
Boquerón
Parguera
Punta Bica
Güanica
Punta Carenero
San Germán
Maricao
Maricao Forest
Adjuntas
San Sebastián
Quebradillas
Lago de Guajataca
Arecibo Observatory
Rio Abajo Forest
Río Camuy Cave Park
Arecibo
Lago dos Bocas
Utuado
Maricao
Jayuya
Toro Negro Forest
Orocovis
Coamo
PONCE
Salinas
Bahia de Rincón
Guayama
Cayey
Carite Forest
Caguas
Guaynabo
Bayamón
Cataño
Dorado
Punta Salinas
SAN JUAN
Río Piedras
Carolina
EL YUNQUE Caribbean National Forest
Humacao
Road Under Construction
Punta Yeguas
Palmas del Mar
Ceiba
US Naval Base
Fajardo
Las Cabezas de San Juan Nature Reserve

The Complete Island

Cruise passengers sailing into San Juan Bay have a breathtaking view of Puerto Rico. From afar the green peaks of the thickly wooded Cordillera Central, rising to 4,398 feet, are outlined against the blue Caribbean sky. By the sea, palms etch miles of white-sand beaches. As the ship approaches the harbor, it passes the colossal fortress of El Morro to dock in Old San Juan, the oldest city now under the American flag. Beyond the ramparts of the fortress, the skyline of new San Juan is juxtaposed against the Old World grace of the colonial city.

Puerto Rico, the easternmost island of the Greater Antilles, has been under the American flag since 1898. Before that it was under Spanish rule for almost four centuries. From the intermingling of the two cultures comes modern Puerto Rico. It offers visitors the best of both worlds—the familiarity of home in a setting that is distinctly foreign. And it offers a great deal more.

Rectangular in shape, Puerto Rico is only 110 miles long and 35 miles wide, yet it has the range of scenery and geographic features of a country fifty times its size. From the quiet, palm-fringed beaches on the east, the land rises to two rugged mountain ranges that fall off in an ocean of rolling surf on the west. The mountainous spine of the island peaks toward the center at more than 4,390 feet, separating the north coast on the Atlantic Ocean from the south coast facing the Caribbean Sea. The slopes are thick with rain forests; the foothills are covered with breadfruit, mango, and coffee trees and rolling hills planted with sugar and pineapple.

The island has desert, salt flats, mangroves, and three phosphorescent bays that glow in the night. On the west end is the Maricao State Forest, one of the island's ten forest reserves; near the east end is the 28,000-acre Caribbean National Forest, known locally as El Yunque, the only tropical rain forest in the U.S. National Forest Service system.

Puerto Rico has long been a popular port of call. Among the many reasons for its popularity is the variety of activities and attractions it offers.

Sports enthusiasts can enjoy Puerto Rico's miles of beaches for swimming, windsurfing, kite sailing or kiting, sailing, and even surfing. Anglers can try to beat one of the three dozen sportfishing world records previously set in Puerto Rican waters. Golfers have seventeen courses to test; tennis buffs can choose from one hundred courts in and near San Juan. A dozen or more places around Puerto Rico and its offshore islands are suitable for snorkelers and divers. There are caves to explore, hikes in the rain forest, and horseback riding and racing. Puerto Rico even has its own special breed of horses, Paso Fino.

In a country whose culture spans more than five hundred years, attractions for history buffs are abundant. Shoppers can be diverted at street markets and boutiques in the Old City, arcades in hotels, or the Texas-size shopping centers of the suburbs. But what will interest them most are the crafts made in Puerto Rico.

Entertainment and nightlife offer so much variety, you could stay in Puerto Rico a month, try a

At a Glance

Antiquities	★★★★
Architecture	★★★★★
Art and artists	★★★★
Beaches	★★
Colonial buildings	★★★★★
Crafts	★★★★
Cuisine	★★★★
Culture	★★★★★
Dining/Restaurants	★★★★
Entertainment	★★★★
Forts	★★★★★
History	★★★★
Monuments	★★★★★
Museums	★★★★
Nightlife	★★★★★
Scenery	★★★★
Shopping	★★★
Sightseeing	★★★
Sports	★★★★★
Transportation	★★★★

Fast Facts

Population: 3.9 million

Size: 3,421 square miles

Main Cities: San Juan, Ponce, Mayagüez, Caguas, Arecibo

Government: Following the Spanish-American War, Puerto Rico was formally turned over to the United States in 1898. Puerto Ricans were made U.S. citizens and given the right to vote in local elections in 1917, and the island was made a commonwealth in 1952. It is represented in the U.S. Congress by a resident commissioner with a voice but no vote, except in the committees on which he or she may serve.

Currency: U.S. dollar

Customs Regulations: Cruise passengers who disembark in San Juan to return to the United States by plane after visiting other islands and countries must go through U.S. customs here.

Departure Tax: None

Language: Spanish. English widely spoken.

Postal Service: Same as U.S. mainland

Public Holidays: January 1, New Year's Day; January 6, Three Kings Day; January 11, Patriot de Hostos; January 20, Martin Luther King Day; February, Presidents' Birthday; March 23, Emancipation Day; Good Friday; April 16, Patriot de Diego Day; May, Memorial Day; July 4, U.S. Independence Day; July 17, Muñoz Rivera Day; July 25, Constitution Day; July 27, Barbosa Day; September 1, Labor Day; October 14, Columbus Day; November 11, Veteran's Day; November 19, Discovery of Puerto Rico (by Columbus); November, Thanksgiving; December 25, Christmas.

Smoking Ban: Effective March 2007, a comprehensive smoking ban prohibits smoking in all food establishments, cultural centers, casinos, bars, shopping centers, public and government buildings, and schools.

Telephone Area Code: 787 and 939. All local calls in the San Juan area must be preceded by 787; those outside are preceded by 1-787 or 939. When dialing from a land line that does not have the same area code as the number you are calling, it is necessary to dial a "1." If you have dialed incorrectly, a phone message will tell you when you are wrong.

Airlines: From the United States mainland: American, Continental, Delta, JetBlue, Northwest, Spirit, United, and U.S. Airways. Regional: Air Sunshine, American Eagle, Cape Air, LIAT. Local: Isla Nena Air Service, Vieques Air Link.

Information: www.gotopuertorico.com

In the United States:

Puerto Rico Tourism Company:

New York: 666 Fifth Avenue, 15th Floor, New York, NY 10013; (800) 223-6530; (212) 586-6262; fax: (212) 586-1212.

Los Angeles: 3575 West Cahuenga Boulevard, No. 405, Los Angeles, CA 90068; (800) 874-1230; (323) 874-5991; fax: (323) 874-7257.

Miami: Peninsula Building, 901 Ponce de Leon Boulevard, No. 101, Coral Gables, FL 33134; (800) 815-7391; (305) 445-9112; fax: (305) 445-9450.

In Canada:

230 Richmond Street West, Suite 902, Toronto, Ontario M5V 1V6; (800) 667-0394 (Canada only); (416) 368-2680; fax: (416) 368-5350.

In San Juan:

La Casita: Puerto Rico Tourism Information Center (PRTC), Comercio Street, Old San Juan; (787) 722-1709; fax: (787) 722-5208. Hours: Monday to Wednesday 8:30 a.m. to 8:00 p.m.; Thursday and Friday 8:30 a.m. to 5:30 p.m.; Saturday and Sunday 9:00 a.m. to 8:00 p.m. *Que Pasa* is the free quarterly official tourist guide.

Paseo de la Princesa #2, Old San Juan, San Juan, PR 00901; (787) 721-2400; fax: (787) 722-1093.

---

different restaurant and nightclub every night, and still have plenty left for your next visit. There are discos, cabarets, casinos, and the Puerto Rican specialty—lobby bars with salsa and other Latin beats, where you can catch the beat in the afternoon and dance the night away.

The variety of arts and cultural attractions is equally impressive. No week goes by without art exhibits in galleries and museums. The performing arts calendar is filled year-round with concerts, opera, ballet, and theater and highlighted by the annual Casals Festival in late February/early March.

For those planning a stay before or after their cruise, Puerto Rico offers a large variety of hotels in San Juan and around the island to suit any lifestyle or pocketbook. Remember, too, that it's part of the United States, so you can use your U.S. dollars, credit cards, and driver's license.

A ten-million-square-foot mixed-use urban plan to reshape the San Juan waterfront was announced in 2007. This project will include a convention center, hotels, retail stores, residences, an aquarium, and a mega yacht marina in Puerta de Tierra. The first phase will take six years to complete, with a cost of up to $19.5 million from the Port Authority and an additional $137 million from the private sector.

New pier facilities include the Pan American Pier in Isla Grande, managed by Royal Caribbean International and a completely renovated Pier #4, managed by Carnival Cruise Lines. Ponce's Port of the Americas welcomed its first ship in January 2007, and the Port of Mayaguez greeted its first cruise ship in December 2006.

Budget Planning

Costs in Puerto Rico are similar to those on the mainland. In San Juan they are comparable to those in a large metropolitan area, such as New York City or Chicago; those in the Puerto Rico countryside, to small-town America. The best way to save money is to walk, which is delightful in Old San Juan, and to use public transportation, which is inexpensive and plentiful. All but the most deluxe restaurants are reasonably priced. Outside of San Juan they are cheap by any standard.

Port Profile: San Juan

Location/Embarkation One of the biggest attractions of San Juan for cruise passengers is the location of the port. Quite literally, you step off your ship into the oldest, most interesting part of town. All ships pull in dockside unless there is an unusually large number in port. The piers are within walking distance of the city's main sightsee-

ing, shopping, dining, and transportation to other parts of the city. In recent years the port and its surrounding area have been extensively renovated and beautified.

The ride from the airport to the pier takes twenty-five to forty minutes, depending on traffic. Taxis Turísticos, a program in the San Juan tourist area, is sponsored by the Puerto Rico Tourism Company. Participating taxis are white and have the Taxis Turísticos logo on the door. They follow set fares: Airport to Isla Verde $10; to Condado/Miramar $14; to Old San Juan/piers $19; to Plaza Las Américas $20. From piers to Old San Juan $7; to Condado/Miramar $12; to Isla Verde $19. These rates apply only from Luis Muñoz International Airport or the cruise ship piers in Old San Juan. There is a charge of 50 cents each for the first three pieces of luggage, $1 each for the fourth and up. Between and beyond the tourism areas, taxi rates are metered. If you are arriving as part of an air/sea package, your cruise line arranges the transfer. Tourist police (wearing white hats) are available to help visitors.

Local Transportation Fleets of taxis are on hand to meet all ships. Taxis operate on meters and are comparable in price to those in stateside cities. You can hire them by the hour or half day, but settle the price in advance. A taxi dispatcher is available at the port to help passengers.

City buses to Condado and all parts of San Juan leave frequently from the bus station near Pier 3. A list of bus routes can be found in *Que Pasa*. Free motorized trolleys, sponsored by the Old San Juan Merchants Association, operate on two routes: from in front of the bus depot in Cavadonga to Plaza de Armas via San Francisco and Fortaleza Streets; and to Calle del Cristo and Fortaleza via Boulevard del Valle and Calle Norzagaray.

Roads and Rentals Puerto Rico has an excellent network of roads. You can drive around the entire island on a road that skirts the coast; drive through its mountainous center on the Panoramic Highway, one of the Caribbean's most scenic routes; and detour to rural mountain-town or seaside fishing villages along the way.

All major U.S. rental firms are represented in San Juan, but none has offices at the port. The nearest offices are in Condado, ten minutes from the port. There are also many local companies with lower rates. A list appears in *Que Pasa*.

Ferry Service Ferries leave frequently from San Juan pier to Cataño across the harbor. Cost is 50 cents. On Sunday sightseeing ferries operate cruises around the harbor.

Urban Train/Tren Urbano The new rail system, primarily above ground, connects Bayamón with eastern Santurce near Sagrado Corazón University via Guaynabo, Centro Médico, University of Puerto Rico at Río Piedras, and the financial district of Hato Rey. It has sixteen stations and air-conditioned cars. The train operated free of charge while it was being inaugurated in summer 2005. When fully operational, it will run daily from 5:30 a.m. to 11:30 p.m. and cost $1.50 per ride with one transfer to a local bus; 75 cents for students and seniors. With a special permit, bicycles will be allowed on trains. For information, (866) 900-1284; www.ati.gobierno.pr.

Domestic and Regional Air Service
American Airlines/American Eagle (800-981-4757) flies to Mayagüez, Vieques, and throughout the Eastern Caribbean. Air Flamenco (787-724-1818) Isla Nena Air Service (787-863-4447) and Vieques Air Link (787-741-8331) serve Vieques and Culebra. Air service to Ponce is very limited.

Emergency Numbers
General emergency: 911
Medical service: (787) 343-2550
Ambulance: (787) 343-2550

Police: (787) 343-2020; Tourist Zone Police, 24 hours, emergencies, (787) 726-7015 (Old San Juan to Ocean Park); (787) 726-2981 (Isla Verde)
Alcoholics Anonymous: (787) 723-4187; (787) 786-8287

Shore Excursions

The first tour listed is available on almost all cruise ships, but the second might not be or may vary in length and price. Both sites are described elsewhere in the chapter.

City Tour—Old and New San Juan: 2–4 hours, $25–$40. San Juan is a large, sprawling metropolis; a brief tour can be a useful introduction on a first visit.

El Yunque Rain Forest and Luquillo Beach: 7–8 hours, $40–$60. A drive in El Yunque is combined with a stop at palm-fringed Luquillo Beach, the most popular *balneario*, or public beach.

Rum Distillery and Old San Juan: Half-day, $40. A guided tour of the Barcardi rum distillery followed by a tour of Old San Juan.

These and other tours are available from Rico Suntours, (787) 722-2080, www.ricosuntours.com; Castillo Tours & Watersports, (787) 791-6195, www.castillotours.com; Tour Co-op of Puerto Rico, (787) 762-7475; and United Tour Guides Co-op, (787) 723-5578.

San Juan on Your Own

San Juan, the air and cruise hub of the Caribbean, with a population exceeding one million, has the bustle of a large American city, the grace of its Spanish heritage, and the beat of the Caribbean. It also has a wonderful variety of big-city activity and attractions, yet it is only a stone's throw from quiet fishing villages and quaint mountain hamlets.

Beautifully restored Old San Juan is a living city bursting with activity from morning to night and ideal for walking. (For more than 350 years, it was a walled and fortified city.) Then, beginning in the 1900s with growth and expansion to new areas along Condado and Isla Verde beaches, the old part of San Juan became seedy. It might easily have been lost to the bulldozers had it not been for some farsighted Puerto Ricans who banded together to save it, by first getting it made a protected historic zone in 1949. In 1955 the Society for the Development and Conservation of San Juan got a ten-year tax exemption for those restoring Spanish colonial buildings, and the Institute of Puerto Rican Culture designed a twenty-year plan to guide the preservation effort.

The renovations sparked a renaissance that has recaptured the town's old charm and ambience. Along streets paved with the blue cobblestones and in lovely old Spanish houses with flower-filled balconies and colonnaded courtyards, you can browse in shops, museums, and art galleries, enjoy lunch or refreshments at restaurants and cafes, and visit some of the oldest monuments in the Western Hemisphere.

An Old San Juan Walkabout

Old San Juan was laid out in typical Spanish colonial fashion as a grid and built on a hill, which slopes from El Morro and San Cristobal fortresses on the north to the port on the south. With the exception of the perimeter roads that follow the contour of the Old City walls, streets run north-south and east-west, making it easy to find your way. Colonial Adventure (888-774-9919; 787-793-2992) conducts two- to three-hour-long walking tours for groups of ten or more. Legends of Puerto Rico (787-605-9060; fax: 787-764-2354; www.legendsofpr.com) is a tourist guide service company specializing in innovative and entertaining heritage and nature tours, including a nighttime walking tour of Old San Juan, an arts and crafts tour, rain-forest walks, and more. You can book online as well as by phone or fax.

From your ship the twenty-five-minute walk west-northwest along the Old City walls to El Morro is a lovely introduction to Old San Juan and the way visitors in olden times had to approach it. If you want to conserve time and energy, take a taxi to El Morro ($6) and start your walking tour from there. Upon leaving the **piers (1)** turn left (west) to Plaza de Hostos, passing **La Casita (2),** where the Puerto Rico Tourist Office is located. On certain weekends, Festival La Casita, combining miniconcerts and street theater with an arts fair,

takes place here. Some places observe summer hours, closing earlier than during the winter months.

The Arsenal (3) South of Calle La Princesa is the eighteenth-century building known as the Arsenal, which houses the **Institute of Puerto Rican Culture,** with changing art exhibits. Here in 1898 the last Spanish general, Ricardo Ortego, turned over Puerto Rico to the United States. Hours: Wednesday through Sunday, 9:00 a.m. to 4:30 p.m.; (787) 724-5949.

La Princesa (4) At the west end of Calle La Princesa is a former jail, built in 1837. It was restored to house the offices of the Puerto Rico Tourism Company. The beautiful building is also used as a gallery for contemporary Puerto Rican art. Calle La Princesa rounds the corner along the massive **City Walls,** which rise to 70 feet above the sea and once completely surrounded the city.

Gate of San Juan (5) Walking north along the walls, you come to the small park and the Gate of San Juan, one of the four original gates to the city, built in 1639. On the south is **La Fortaleza (16),** the residence of the governor of Puerto Rico for almost five hundred years. Originally it was the fort where the early Spaniards stored their gold and silver.

La Rogativa (6) After you pass through the Gate of San Juan, turn left to the Plaza de La Rogativa. The spectacular sculpture of *La Rogativa* is one of the most forceful, inspired works in iron ever conceived. It was done by Lindsay Daen to mark the city's 450th anniversary in 1971. *La Rogativa,* meaning the Procession, commemorates the saving of San Juan in 1797, after the British had laid siege to it from the sea. As the saga goes, after two weeks city leaders thought their defeat was imminent and asked the bishop to lead a night vigil in honor of St. Catherine, the governor's patron saint. Marchers bearing torches started from San Juan Cathedral at the top of the hill above *La Rogativa,* proceeded through the streets, and returned to the church for mass. The British commander, seeing the torchlights and hearing the ringing of church bells, thought reinforcements had arrived by land from the east. Rather than face an uncertain battle, he hoisted anchor and quietly slipped away under the cover of night. The next morning the townspeople found their prayers had been answered.

A path north of *La Rogativa* leads directly to El Morro.

El Morro (7) A magnificent fortress begun in 1539, El Morro was part of the Spanish defense system that stretched from Puerto Rico on the Atlantic to the coast of South America. It was built to protect the ships carrying gold and silver from Mexico and South America to Spain.

El Morro is built on a promontory, or *morro,* in the shape of a head of a longhorn steer. The fortress was built with such strength that it withstood all attempts to take it from the sea for more than 350 years. During the Spanish-American War, the U.S. Navy bombarded El Morro; after the war, when the Spaniards left Puerto Rico, the U.S. Army occupied the site for several years.

El Morro was a living citadel, with seven levels of tunnels, storage rooms, barracks, and artillery emplacements, plus kitchens, a chapel, and foundry. Be sure to go up to the level of the lighthouse for splendid views. The fort has been beautifully restored and is maintained by the U.S. National Park Service; it is listed on the National Register of Historic Sites. El Morro and its companion fort, San Cristobal; San Juan Gate and the City Walls; and La Fortaleza have been designated by UNESCO as landmarks on the World Heritage List. Orientation is available in English and Spanish; there is a museum and bookshop. Hours: daily 9:00 a.m. to 5:00 p.m. June to November, and until 6:00 p.m. December to May. Entrance: persons age sixteen and older, $3 per fort or $5 for both forts; age fifteen and younger, free. (787) 729-6960; www.nps.gov/saju.

Ballaja Barracks and Casa de Beneficencia (8) As the centerpiece of San Juan's Quincentennial effort, the Ballaja district was transformed by the $60 million restoration of the buildings and grounds that once constituted Fort Brooke (decommissioned in 1967). The district covers the 5 blocks from the Dominican Convent and Church of San José on the east to Casa Blanca, the ancestral home of the Ponce de Leon family, on the west. Now part of the San Juan National Historic Site, Ballaja contains some of Old San Juan's largest, most historically significant buildings.

Most of the buildings date from the nineteenth century, but Ballaja was the name of the *barrio,* or district, as early as the eighteenth century. In 1857, after the construction of the Ballaja Military Barracks (El Cuartel de Ballaja) as the headquarters of the Spanish Army, the barrio became more integrated with its contingent areas, and the Dominican Convent (1523), Conception Hospital (1774), and other nearby buildings were taken over by the military. After the Spanish-American War, the U.S. Army occupied the buildings and added three small structures. All were turned over to the Commonwealth in 1976.

The Barracks, the largest, most imposing of the buildings, is used by the University of Puerto Rico and houses the **Museum of the Americas,** created by Ricardo Alegria, the founding director of the Institute of Puerto Rican Culture. Facing the Barracks, another huge building, dating from 1861, **Casa de Beneficencia,** is the home of the Institute of Puerto Rican Culture (www.icp.gobierno.pr). The facades of the two buildings define a triangle that has a small plaza and park. Here, the street leads directly to El Morro, which is in full view. Museum hours: Tuesday to Friday 10:00 a.m. to 4:00 p.m.; Saturday and Sunday 11:00 a.m. to 5:00 p.m. (787) 724-5052; www.museolasamericas.org.

Casa Blanca (9) The first structure, a modest wooden house, was built in 1521, but after it was partially destroyed by fire, Ponce de Leon's son-in-law built a stone-and-masonry structure, which also served as a fort against Indian attacks. In 1540, when La Fortaleza was completed, Casa Blanca became the Ponce de Leon family home and so remained until 1779, when it was sold to the Spanish government as a residence for the army engineer corps. After the Spanish-American War, Casa Blanca was occupied by the U.S. military until 1967. The following year the house was declared a National Historic Monument and is used for exhibits. Hours: Tuesday to Sunday 9:00 a.m. to noon and 1:00 to 4:00 p.m. Entrance: $3; $2 seniors and children. (787) 725-1454.

Plaza of Five Centuries (10) The historic and symbolic centerpiece of the Ballaja restorations is the Plaza of Five Centuries, a three-tiered urban park highlighted by a monumental commemorative sculpture. Beneath the plaza is an underground parking lot for 500 cars.

Old San Juan

0 Yards 500
0 Meters 500

N

Punta del Morro

ATLANTIC OCEAN

City Wall

CALLE DE MORRO

City Wall

AVENUE TIBURICO REYES

CALLE LUCILA

SILVA

City Wall

CALLE NORZAGARAY

CALLE NORZAGARAY

CALLE SAN SEBASTIAN

CALLE SOL

CALLE DEL CRISTO

CALLE SOL

CALLE DE LA CRUZ

CALLE SAN JUSTO

CALLE LUNA

CALLE DE O DONELL

CALETA LAS MONJAS

CALLE SAN JOSE

CALLE SAN FRANCISCO

CALLE TANGA

CALETA SAN JUAN

CALLE FORTALEZA

CALLE TETUAN

RECINTO SUR

CALLE COMERCIO

City Wall

CALLE LA PRINCESA

CALLE MARINA

BAHIA DE SAN JUAN

Pier 3 Cruise Ship

Pier 2 Ferry

CALLE PRESIDIO

CALLE PUNTILLO

Pier 1

BAHIA DE SAN JUAN

1. San Juan Pier and Plazoleta del Puerto
2. La Casita
3. Museum of Puerto Rican Culture (The Arsenal)
4. La Princesa Jail and City Walls
5. Gate of San Juan
6. Plaza de La Rogativa
7. El Morro Fortress
8. Ballaja Barracks (Museum of the Americas) and Casa de Beneficencia
9. Casa Blanca
10. Plaza of Five Centuries
11. Church of San José and Dominican Convent
12. San Juan Museum
13. San José Plaza and Casals Museum
14. Hotel El Convento
15. San Juan Cathedral
16. La Fortaleza
17. Pigeon Park and Christ Chapel; La Casa del Libro
18. Department of State and Provincial Deputation Building
19. City Hall
20. Plaza Colón, Tapia Theatre, and Old Casino of Puerto Rico
21. Fort San Cristobal
22. Municipal Bus Station

Church of San José and Dominican Convent (11)

The east side of the plaza is bordered by the Church of San José and Dominican Convent. The church is the second-oldest Roman Catholic church in the Americas and one of the purest examples of Gothic architecture in the world. Built in the early sixteenth century as a chapel of the Dominican monastery on land donated by Ponce de Leon's family, it was used as a family church until the last century. Ponce de Leon was buried here after his remains were brought from Cuba in 1559; his body was moved to San Juan Cathedral in 1908. The Church of San José has undergone lengthy renovation to strip away centuries of coatings on the walls and reveal the beautiful apricot stone and magnificent cross-vaulting of the ceiling.

Next to the Church of San José is the convent, which dates from 1523. It was one of the first buildings to be constructed after Ponce de Leon moved from Caparra, the site of his original settlement, to establish San Juan. The convent was converted into a barracks for the Spanish Army and later became the U.S. Antilles Command headquarters. It now houses the Center for Popular Arts.

San Juan Museum (12)

Next to the convent, but facing Calle Norzagaray, is a large structure originally built in 1855 as a marketplace. Restored in 1979, it is used as a cultural center, with an exhibit about San Juan and changing art and cultural events staged in its large courtyard. An audiovisual show on the history of San Juan is available. Open Tuesday to Sunday 9:00 a.m. to 4:00 p.m., admission is free. (787) 724-1875.

San José Plaza and Casals Museum (13)

On the south side of the church is San José Plaza, with a statue of Ponce de Leon. Made in 1882, the statue is said to have been cast from the melted-down cannons used by the British during their attack on San Juan in 1797. On the east side of the plaza, a town house holds the Casals Museum, devoted to the great Spanish cellist who made his home in Puerto Rico for more than twenty years. Pablo Casals spearheaded the founding of the performing arts festival that bears his name. The island's leading cultural event, the festival is held annually in late February. Hours: Tuesday to Saturday 9:30 a.m. to 4:30 p.m.; 787-723-9185. Admission: $1.06 adults, 53 cents seniors and children.

Next door is the **Museum of Our African Roots,** highlighting Puerto Rico's African heritage. Open Tuesday to Saturday 8:30 a.m. to noon and 1:00 p.m. to 4:20 p.m. Entrance: $2, seniors and children $1. (787) 724-4294.

The plaza, Calle San Sebastian, and adjacent streets are the setting for the *Festival of San Sebastian,* an annual art and music show in mid-January. Walk west on Calle San Sebastian to a set of stone steps, **Calle del Hospital,** leading to Calle Sol and a second set of stairs, **Stairway of the Nuns,** leading directly to Hotel El Convento.

Hotel el Convento (14) Built in 1646 as a convent for the Carmelite nuns, it was first made into a deluxe hotel in the 1970s, but altered several times in the 1980s. Now after extensive renovation, the hotel has reopened under new ownership. The first two levels have boutiques and restaurants; third to fifth floors house the deluxe hotel. The lovely colonial architecture was retained, and furnishings throughout are antiques or authentic reproductions from the seventeenth and eighteenth centuries. The project was directed by Jorge Rosello, the architectural genius behind the El San Juan and El Conquistador hotels.

On the west side of the pocket park in front of the hotel is the **Museo del Nino** (Museum of the Child), which features fun and educational hands-on exhibits and a staff of youth counselors to help kids get the most out of their visit. Hours: Tuesday to Thursday 9:00 a.m. to 3:30 p.m.; Friday 9:00 a.m. to 5:00 p.m.; Saturday and Sunday 12:30 to 5:00 p.m. Entrance: $7 children (age one through fifteen), $5 adults. (787) 722-3791; www.museo delninopr.org.

San Juan Cathedral (15) Facing El Convento on Calle del Cristo, San Juan Cathedral enjoys a commanding position at the top of the hill leading up from San Juan Gate. It was from here that the procession commemorated by *La Rogativa* set out in 1797 and miraculously saved the city. The present nineteenth-century structure stands on the site of the first chapel built soon after the city was founded. Ponce de Leon's tomb is on the north wall. Open daily 8:00 a.m. to 5:00 p.m. (787) 722-0861.

La Fortaleza (16) Continuing south on Calle del Cristo, you'll pass some of the best shops and art galleries in the city; turn west on Calle Fortaleza.

La Fortaleza, the official residence of the governor of Puerto Rico, is said to be the oldest executive mansion in continuous use in the Western Hemisphere. Hours: daily, 8:30 a.m. to 5:00 p.m.; Sunday to 2:00 p.m. Tours in English through the lovely grounds are available weekdays, every hour. Visitors must be properly dressed. (787) 721-7000.

Pigeon Park (17) From Fortaleza, return to Calle del Cristo, and turn right at the corner onto the pretty little street with outdoor cafes leading to Pigeon Park (Las Palomas), where you can get a great view of San Juan Harbor and spot your ship at the pier. **Christ Chapel,** with a silver altar, is said to have been placed here after a horseman racing down the hill from El Morro missed the turn in the road and was thrown over the wall to the sea below to seemingly certain death. Miraculously, he did not die, according to the legend. On the east side of the street, adjoining eighteenth-century buildings house **La Casa del Libro** (787-723-0354), a rare book museum, and **Centro Nacional de Artes Populares y Artesenias** (787-722-0621; open Wednesday to Sunday 10:00 a.m. to 5:00 p.m.) with exhibits of island crafts. At press time this building was being remodeled; offices are temporarily relocated at San Sebastion #1, with exhibits being show at the Museo de Las Américas in the Ballajá Building.

Department of State (18) At Calle San José, turn left (north) for a stop at the Department of State, whose interior courtyard is one of the loveliest examples of colonial architecture in San Juan. Note especially the staircase on the right of the entrance. Across the street is the **Provincial Deputation Building,** so called because it served for eleven days as the headquarters of Puerto Rico's first representative body, formed in 1897 when Puerto Rico gained autonomy from Spain.

City Hall (19) Across Plaza de Armas is City Hall, dating from 1602 and the site of many important events in Puerto Rico's history, including the abolition of slavery in 1873.

Here on the square, you can pick up the trolley to return to the port or walk east 2 blocks to Calle Tanca, which leads south directly to the pier where you started. One block farther east on Fortaleza is Plaza Colon.

Plaza Colón (20) The plaza is dominated by the statue of Christopher Columbus (whose Spanish name is Colón) placed here in 1893 to mark the 400th anniversary of Columbus's discovery of Puerto Rico. On its south side is the **Tapia Theatre,** built early in the nineteenth century. It has been renovated many times, but claims to be the oldest theater in continuous use in the Western Hemisphere. The theater has a year-round schedule of concerts and drama. Check *Que Pasa,* or call (787) 722-0407.

On the east side of the plaza is the **Old Casino of Puerto Rico,** built in 1915 to be the most elegant social hall in the Americas. Because of the war, however, the building never realized its potential and came to be used for many purposes, deteriorating all the while. It was renovated in 1985, its magnificent drawing rooms restored to their former elegance. Renamed the Manuel Pavia Fernandez Government Reception Center, it is used mainly by the Puerto Rico State Department for special occasions and receptions. Hours: weekdays 8:00 a.m. to 4:00 p.m.

Fort San Cristobal (21) Northeast of Plaza Colón is the entrance to Fort San Cristobal, part of the defense structure begun in 1633. The impressive fortress is larger than El Morro, with several levels of ramparts, moats, tunnels, and storerooms, and is considered a masterpiece of strategic military design. It, too, is maintained by the U.S. National Park Service. Hours: daily 9:00 a.m. to 5:00 p.m. Orientation is available in English and Spanish. Entrance: $3 adults; age fifteen and younger free. (787) 729-6960.

Museum of Puerto Rican Art (Museo de Arte de Puerto Rico) (300 De Diego Avenue, Santurce; 787-977-6277; www.mapr.org). The museum is not within walking distance of the port, but it is accessible by taxi and certainly worth a visit.

Located in Santurce, near the Condado hotel district, the world-class museum is housed in two wings. The west wing, the main entrance, is a neo-classical structure built in the 1920s as part of the Municipal Hospital. Now restored, it houses the permanent collection in eighteen exhibition halls and showcases Puerto Rican artists, with paintings, drawings, sculptures, ceramics, printmaking, and photography reflecting the history of Puerto Rican culture through its art.

The east wing is a modern, five-story structure, designed by well-established Puerto Rican architects Otto Reyes and Luis Gutierrez. It has a three-story atrium, an interactive family gallery called ActivArte, a computer learning center, studios and workshops, a 400-seat theater, a museum shop, and Pikayo, a restaurant directed by well-known Puerto Rican chef Wilo Benet. There are two large galleries for local and international exhibitions.

The works of fourteen Puerto Rican artists are displayed in the museum's five-acre sculpture garden, complete with a lake, trails, and gazebos where visitors can sit and reflect. The museum is a private, nonprofit corporation whose $55 million development and construction was financed by the Puerto Rican government. Hours: Tuesday to Saturday 10:00 a.m. to 5:00 p.m.; Wednesday to 8:00 p.m.; Sunday 11:00 a.m. to 6:00 p.m. Admission: $6 adults, $3 children, students, and seniors. For special tours, contact the Education Department (787-977-6277, ext. 2230).

For those who wish to view contemporary Puerto Rican art, visit the **Museum of Contemporary Art** in its new location (Ponce de León Avenue, corner R. H. Todd, Parada 18; 787-977-4030; www.museocontemporaneopr.org; open Tuesday to Saturday 10:00 a.m. to 4:00 p.m., Sunday noon to 5:00 p.m.) in a lovely two-story brick building.

Shopping

Old San Juan with its pretty boutiques and specialty shops is the best area of the city for shopping. The Condado hotel area also has a large selection of stores. You'll find the high fashion boutiques of Ferragamo, Chanel, Gucci, and Jill Sanders on Ashford Avenue as well as Texas-style shopping centers, such as Plaza Las Americas, in Hato Rey. Most are open Monday to Saturday from 9:00 a.m. to 9:00 p.m., Sunday from 11:00 a.m. to 5:00 p.m.

Because cruise passengers frequently visit duty-free ports, such as the U.S. Virgin Islands, they are often understandably confused about Puerto Rico's status. Puerto Rico is not a duty-free port. Imported goods such as gold jewelry and Scottish cashmeres have the same duties levied on them here as in New York or Miami. Advertisements for "duty-free" merchandise mean only that you will not have to pay additional customs duties upon your return home, and, of course, you save state and local taxes. The best buys are for art, crafts, clothing, and rum made in Puerto Rico. And for those last-minute needs, there's a Walgreens (Plaza de Armas) a short walk from the port.

Art and Artists On a walk in Old San Juan, you will see art galleries where you can discover many fine Puerto Rican and other artists living and working here. Gallery nights are held on the first Tuesday of the month during February to May and September to December, when twenty or more art galleries and museums remain open from 6:00 to 9:00 p.m. and there's a festive atmosphere throughout the Old City. For information: (787) 723-7080.

Galeria Botello in Old San Juan (208 Calle del Cristo; 787-723-9987; www.botello.com) showcases fine international artists and represents the estate of the gallery founder, Angel Botello, one of Puerto Rico's best-known artists with a very distinctive style, along with a younger generation of local artists. The gallery is now owned by Botello's family.

Galeria San Juan (204 Boulevard del Valle; 787-722-1808) is set in three restored seventeenth-century buildings. The gallery is the home and studio of American-born artist Jan D'Esopo, known for her Old San Juan street scenes.

Galeria Arte Espinal (304 Calle San Francisco), the gallery of artist Santiago Espinal, has changing exhibits of high quality Puerto Rican, Caribbean, and South American artists.

Amparo Porcelain Inn (53 Calle de Cristo, 787-722-1777) Artist Amparo Cuillar is known as the Porcelain Lady. Her exquisite porcelain paintings fit all budgets; the studio—and her home—is open only on Wednesday from 11:00 a.m. to 5:00 p.m. or by appointment.

The Butterfly People (257 Calle de la Cruz; 787-723-2432; www.butterflypeople.com) is in a beautifully restored Spanish colonial mansion, where all artwork on display features butterflies in the design.

Cigars Cigar stores, as well as cigar bars, have proliferated. Near Pier 3, opposite the Sheraton San Juan Hotel in the Covadonga building near the trolley station, is **Cigarros Antillas,** where you can watch a Dominican craftsman roll tobacco into shape and purchase the product. One cigar costs $2.50; a box of twenty-five cigars, $55.00.

Clothing A Ralph Lauren outlet is at the corner of Calle del Cristo and San Francisco Street (787-722-2136). Just up the street is **Coach** (158 Calle del Cristo; 787-722-6830), the **Dooney & Bourke Factory Store** (200 Calle del Cristo; 787-289-0075), and **the Polo Ralph Lauren Factory Store** (201 Calle del Cristo; 787-722-2136). **Big Planet** (205 Calle del Cristo; 787-725-1204) carries good quality sportswear. Farther along Calle del Cristo there is **Guess** (213 Calle del Cristo; 787-977-1550).

T-shirt shops are everywhere. The most attractive have designs adapted from Taino Indian petroglyphs. Hand-painted T-shirt dresses and bathing cover-ups are also popular.

Not to be overlooked are Puerto Rican designers. **Nono Maldonado** (787-721-0456), a former fashion editor of *Esquire,* has a boutique on Ashford Avenue and **David Antonio** has a shop (69 Avenida Condado) in Condado. **Lisa Cappelli** (206 Calle O'Donnell, Old San Juan; 787-724-6575) is a young designer who creates fun, fresh, funky outfits that are sold at several shops around town.

Crafts An Artisan's Market is held next to La Casita Information Center in Old San Juan on weekends and during the week when cruise ships are in, from noon to 6:00 p.m. The carving of *santos*—small wooden figures representing a saint or depicting a religious scene—is considered Puerto Rico's most distinctive craft. The *santeros'* style and techniques have been passed from father to son for generations.

Musical instruments and masks are two of the oldest crafts. The *cuatro* is a five-double-string guitar inherited from the Spaniards; the *guiro,* or gourd, comes from a tradition that goes back to the Taino Indians. Mask making is found mainly in Loiza, a town east of San Juan that has maintained its African heritage. Papier-mâché masks, a Spanish tradition, are used in Carnival, particularly in Ponce. Hammocks are another skill that was taught

to the early Spaniards by the Taino Indians. *Mundillo,* handmade bobbin lace, came with the Spaniards and Portuguese.

Aguadilla en San Juan (205 Calle de la Cruz) and **Puerto Rican Art & Crafts** (204 Calle Fortaleza; 787-725-5596; www.puertoricanart-crafts .com) specialize in Puerto Rican crafts. Calle Fortaleza has a tiny lane known simply as **La Calle,** with a variety of attractive shops selling jewelry, leather handbags and belts, and other accessories, masks, and crafts.

Jewelry Calle Fortaleza has so many jewelry stores, especially for gold, you might think they were giving it away! (A check of stateside prices will convince you they are not.) Some cruise directors and guides direct passengers to certain stores, where they have something to gain. The practice is no different here than in other places around the world, so a good dose of skepticism on your part is healthy. If you plan to buy expensive jewelry, become familiar with prices at home, and do not buy in San Juan or any other Caribbean port without looking around and comparing prices. **Boveda** (209 Calle del Cristo; 787-725-0263) has unusual, one-of-a-kind mod jewelry, accessories, and women's clothing.

Leather Several shops in Old San Juan import leather goods from Spain and South America. Prices are often much less than those in the United States. The best buys are in the small shops of **La Calle,** a-cul-de-sac near Calle del Cristo and Fortaleza. **Coach** (158 Calle del Cristo; 787-722-6830) has fine leather goods. Most cost about 20 percent less than mainland ones, but some go up to 40 percent.

Dining and Restaurants

Puerto Rico has a cuisine of its own, which you can enjoy at pretty restaurants set in town houses of Old San Juan. Some dishes you might find on menus are black-bean soup; *asopao,* a spicy chicken stew; *pionono,* ripe plantain stuffed with ground beef; *mechada,* stuffed eye of round beef; *pernil,* roast pork; *arroz con gandules,* rice with pigeon peas; and *tostones,* fried plantain.

Entries range from moderate (less than $10) to

moderately expensive ($10 to $25) to expensive (more than $25).

Old San Juan

Amadeus (106 Calle San Sebastian; 787-722-8635) was one of the first to offer nouvelle Puerto Rican cuisine, sophisticated creations based on local products. Moderately expensive.

Aguaviva (364 Calle Fortaleza; 787-722-0665) offers seafood with Latin pizzazz and even has a ceviche bar. Expensive.

Baru (150 Calle San Sebastian; 787-977-7107) offers Mediterranean/Caribbean cuisine in one of the most beautiful settings in the Old City, with a spectacular inner courtyard. Especially popular on weekends. Moderately expensive.

Cafe Berlin (407 San Francisco/Plaza Colón; 787-722-5205) is a pastry shop and sidewalk cafe with light fare and vegetarian specialties. Great people-watching spot. Moderate.

Dragonfly (364 Calle Fortaleza; 787-977-3886) is the best of trendy Asian/Latin fusion cuisine eateries. Expensive.

El Patio de Sam (102 Calle San Sebastian; 787-723-1149) is perfect for a snack or light meal of Puerto Rican and other cuisine during your walking or shopping tour. Moderate.

Il Perugino (105 Calle del Cristo; 787-722-5481) has a wide selection of veal dishes and fresh fish. Moderately expensive.

La Mallorquina (207 Calle San Justo; 787-722-3261), in operation since 1850, claims to be the oldest restaurant in Puerto Rico. Its menu has the most typical Puerto Rican dishes, along with Spanish and Cuban ones. Moderate.

The Parrot Club (363 Calle Fortaleza; 787-725-7370; www.parrotclub.com) offers an eclectic menu with spicy Caribbean cuisine. Moderately expensive. (*NOTE*: The Parrot Club was the first of the culinary enterprises belonging to Emilo and Gigi Figueroa. The Figueroa restaurants are among the best and most popular in Old San Juan. In addition to Aguaviva and Dragonfly [described above], there are **Sonne** [364 Calle Fortaleza], a new steakhouse with live jazz six nights weekly; **Toro Salao** [367 Calle Tetuan], a new tapas bar; and **Sofia** [355 San Francisco], an Italian restaurant offering live jazz Thursday through Saturday.)

Condado—Isla Verde

BLT Steak at the Ritz-Carlton (Ritz-Carlton, San Juan Hotel, 787-253-1700) is the first Caribbean member of the rapidly expanding BLT Steak restaurants of French chef Laurent Tourondel. BLT (which stands for Bistro Laurent Tourondel) has a raw bar and a selection of seafood entries, but the specialty is steak, particularly Kobe beef and Wagyu Skirt, the American version. There's also a selection of fifteen scrumptious desserts and a kid's menu. Dinner only. Expensive

Chayote (603 Avenida Miramar, Olimpio Court Hotel; 787-722-9385) features fresh local fruits, vegetables, and fish. Moderately expensive.

Marisqueria Atlantica (2475 Loiza Street, Ocean Park; 787-726-6654) offers seafood as its specialty. You can select your fish fresh from the display and have it cooked to order. Its sister restaurant (7 Lugo Viñas Street; 787-722-0890) is located at the entrance to Old San Juan. Moderately expensive.

Pikayo (Museum of Puerto Rican Art, 300 De Diego Avenue, Santurce; 787-721-6194; www.pikayo.com). Museum dining has been elevated to an art form by Puerto Rico's well-known chef Wilo Benet. Expensive.

Ramiro's (1106 Magdalena; 787-721-9049), set in a house across from the Condado Plaza Hotel, features *la nueva cocina criolla* along with Spanish cuisine. Expensive.

Sports

Puerto Rico has some of the best sports facilities in the Caribbean, near enough to the pier for cruise passengers to use them with ease. You should contact the hotel or sports operator in advance to make arrangements, particularly during the peak season. And don't overlook spectator sports, especially baseball. In the winter season, from October through February, all six of the local professional teams have major league players in their lineups. Check newspapers or the **Professional Baseball League of Puerto Rico** (Box 1852, Hato Rey, San Juan 00919; 787-765-6285).

Horse races are held on Monday, Wednesday, Friday, Saturday, Sunday, and holidays at **El Commandante** (787-724-6060). Buses leave from Plaza

Colón, timed for the starting race, and return according to the racing schedule. Horse shows are often held when a village celebrates a saint's day or festival. The local breed, Paso Fino, is a small, spirited horse noted for its gait. Shows are held year-round; check *Que Pasa.*

Beaches/Swimming All beaches are public, including hotel beaches. Those operated by the government or municipality have *balneario* facilities (lockers, showers, and parking) at nominal fees. Hotels on or near Condado Beach are the closest to the port; Caribe Hilton and Condado Plaza are the most popular. Isla Verde Beach, where El San Juan Hotel and Ritz-Carlton Hotel are located, is 1 mile from the airport.

Deep-Sea Fishing San Juan is one of the world's favorite sportfishing spots. Half- or full-day and split-boat charters with crew and equipment are available; expect to pay about $550 and up for a half day and $900 and up for a full day for up to six people. Contact **Benitez Fishing Charters** (Club Nautico San Juan, Miramar; 787-723-2292; www.mikebenitezfishingpr.com) or **Caribbean Outfitters** (787-396-8346; www.fishinginpuerto rico.com).

Golf The quartet of Robert Trent Jones championship courses at the **Dorado Beach Resort & Club** (formerly Hyatt) (787-796-1234) are not only among the best in the Caribbean, but in the world. Located at Dorado 15 miles west of San Juan, these courses are famous for their layouts and natural settings. East and West greens fees for nonguests: $160 morning, $90 afternoon, $40 after 4:00 p.m. in the low season; Sugar Cane and Pineapple: $120 morning, $70 afternoon, $13 after 4:00 p.m. Reserve in advance.

Rico Suntours (800-844-2080) can make arrangements to play the Dorado Beach Club courses as well as other courses in Puerto Rico.

Rio Mar Beach Resort & Spa, a Wyndham Grand Resort (787-888-7060; www.wyndhamriomar .com) east of San Juan (a forty-minute drive from the port), has two 18-hole courses: one designed by Tom and George Fazio and another by Greg Norman, his first in the Caribbean. Both are dotted with lakes and have El Yunque as a backdrop and a palm-fringed beach in the foreground.

The **Bahia Beach Golf Course,** the first in Puerto Rico by Robert Trent Jones Jr, opened in fall 2007. Water will be a strong component of this course overlooking the Atlantic Ocean; the three finishing holes play directly along the ocean and beach. To make reservations, call (787) 957-5800. The course is part of a planned 483-acre residential and vacation enclave anchored by the St. Regis Resort & Residences (www.bahiabeachpuertorico.com).

Hiking The best trails are in the rain forest of the Caribbean National Forest of El Yunque and range from an easy fifteen-minute walk to arduous eight-hour treks. Information and maps are available from El Portal, the visitor and interpretive center that opened in 1996. Hours: daily 9:00 a.m. to 5:00 p.m. Admission: $3.00 adults, $1.50 seniors; children younger than age 15 are free. For hiking information call Caribbean National Forest (787-888-1810; www.fs.fed.us/r8/caribbean). See El Yunque section for more information.

A list of companies that offer hiking excursions is available from the Puerto Rico Tourism Company. The following are samples:

* AdvenTours (Luquillo; 787-889-0251; www .adventourspr.com). Excursions with environmental and cultural focus, bird and wildlife observation, hiking, biking, kayaking. Reservations required.

* Aventuras Tierra Adentro (San Juan; 787-766-0470; www.adventurespr.com). Rappelling, caving, rock climbing, canyoning, body rafting.

* Copladet Nature & Adventure Travel (San Juan; 787-765-8595; www.copladet.com). Nature and adventure excursions with environmental education: bird-watching, rappelling, caving, hiking, body rafting, trips to Mona Island.

* Encantos Ecotours (San Juan; 787-272-0005). Historic, cultural, and nature tours; kayaking, snorkeling, biking, hiking, and sailing lessons and gear rental. Also custom design excursions.

Horseback Riding East of San Juan near Luquillo Beach, **Hacienda Carabali** (787-889-5820) offers group riding along the coast and foothills of El Yunque. Reservations are required. The Caribe Hilton (787-721-0303) sells a riding excursion for the hacienda.

Rico Suntours (800-844-2080) offers a half-day guided riding excursion for $85.

Kayaking Kayaks are available at the **Condado Plaza Hotel** water-sports center, where they can be rented by the hour. **Yokahú Kayak Trips** (Fajardo; 787-863-5374) offers eco-adventure kayak tours to the bioluminescent bay and lagoon, with licensed guides and equipment included. Also see companies under "Hiking."

Scuba and Snorkeling Puerto Rico's best snorkeling and diving are found on the east coast around the coral-fringed islands facing Fajardo. Boats operated by water-sports centers at San Juan resort hotels depart daily for these locations. Equipment is available for rent for certified divers, and the centers offer diving courses. Several catamarans offer full-day picnic sails with snorkeling to Icacos for $60 per person. Check *Que Pasa.*

Caribe Aquatic Adventures (Park Plaza Normandie in Condado; 787-281-8858; www.diveguide.com/p2046.htm) is one of the oldest dive operations on the island and a member of the Puerto Rico Water Sport Federation. It has daily dive trips and arranges kayaking, sailing, windsurfing, and the newest aquatic craze, kite sailing or kiting. An outstanding scuba location, dubbed the Puerto Rican Wall and as exciting for divers as the Cayman Wall, is off the south coast at La Parguera. A list of dive operators is available in *Que Pasa.*

Tennis Courts and full-time pros are available at more than a dozen San Juan hotels. Nearest the port is Caribe Hilton, with three night-lit courts. El San Juan Hotel (Isla Verde) has one, while nearby, the Ritz-Carlton (787-253-1700) has two night-lit courts. San Juan Central Park (Cerra Street; 787-722-1646) has more than a dozen public courts with night lighting. Hours: open daily.

Entertainment/Cultural Events

San Juan has a full calendar of seasonal concerts by the Puerto Rico Symphony Orchestra, San Juan Opera Company, several ballet and theater groups, Broadway productions, and performances by visiting artists. Most are given at the **Fine Arts Center** (El Centro de Bellas Artes; 787-620-4444; www.cba

.gobierno.pr), also known as the Performing Arts Center, a multiauditorium complex and one of the best-equipped facilities in the Caribbean. Another venue is the **Tapia Theatre,** in Old San Juan.

The year's biggest cultural event is the **Casals Festival of the Performing Arts** in late February/early March, but there are many art and music festivals throughout the year. *Que Pasa* lists all major cultural and sporting events.

The **LeLoLai Festival** offers weekly shows highlighting Puerto Rico's folklore with song, dance, and crafts. Each show has a different theme to reflect Puerto Rico's long and rich culture and blends the island's Spanish, African, and Taino Indian heritages. The festival, staged at participating hotels, is sponsored by the Puerto Rico Tourism Company and is usually available to cruise passengers as part of a shore excursion.

You also have a choice of small bars with Spanish guitars or jazz in the Old City or nightclubs, discos, cabarets, and casinos in Condado or Isla Verde. Some of the liveliest action is at lobby bars that have combos playing salsa and other Latin and disco beats, and there's even a **Hard Rock Cafe.**

Small-scale **Carli Café Concierto** (206 Tetuan Street; 787-725-4927; www.carlicafeconcierto.com) in Old San Juan is the place to hear jazz. Some other night spots:

- **Nuyorican Café** (312 San Francisco Street; 787-977-1276; www.nuyoricancafepr.com) is a cafe theater with live music, theatrical performances, and poetry readings; live *salsa* Friday and Saturday nights, *Charanga* on Saturday after 10:30 p.m. Mick Jagger and other celebrities use it as an after-concert hangout.

- **Parrot Club** (363 Fortaleza Street; 787-725-7370; www.parrotclub.com) offers background jazz and live Latin music Tuesday, Thursday, and Saturday.

- **Borinquen Grill & Brewing Company** (800 Av. Isla Verde, San Juan; 787-268-1900; www.borinquenbrewing.com) is the island's first and only microbrewery, offering hard-to-find draft beer.

- **Brick House Bar & Grill** (359 Calle Tetuán, Old San Juan; 787-724-3359) offers great burgers and wings and is open until 3:00 a.m.

Casinos All of San Juan's casinos are in hotels, and some, like the Condado Plaza and El San Juan, are practically in the lobby.

San Juan's Environs

Catano and Palo Seco Across the bay from San Juan in Catano is the home of the **Bacardi Rum Distillery,** the largest single producer of rum in the world. There are a gift shop and open-air patio bar with beautiful views across manicured grounds and the bay to Old San Juan. At the plant's visitor center, Casa Bacardi (www.casabacardi.com), you wander through interactive exhibits chronicling the Bacardi family and its rum with the help of individual audio guides. About a mile from the distillery is the fishing village of Palo Seco, noted for its waterfront seafood restaurants.

The ferry for Catano (787-788-0940; www.prpa.gobierno.pr) departs every fifteen minutes on weekdays and every half hour on Saturday and Sunday from 5:45 a.m. to 9:45 p.m. from a small dock situated between Pier 1 and Pier 2. The ride takes about twenty minutes. On the opposite side of the bay, you can get a *publico* (shared minibus) to the Bacardi Rum Distillery. Open Monday to Saturday, 8:30 a.m. to 5:30 p.m. (the last tour is at 4:15 p.m.), and Sunday, 10:00 a.m. to 5:00 p.m. (last tour at 3:45 p.m.).

Botanic Gardens In the San Juan suburb of Rio Piedras, about a thirty-minute drive from the port, are the Agricultural Experiment Station Botanical Gardens, which is part of the University of Puerto Rico, and the Institute of Tropical Forestry (787-766-5335; www.tropicalforestry.net), which is part of the U.S. Forest Service. Spanning both sides of a stream and a series of ponds, the gardens cover an area of 270 acres, 45 of which are developed in a park setting, providing a delightful introduction to the enormous variety of plants, flowers, and trees of Puerto Rico and the Caribbean. At Casa Rosada (787-767-1710, open weekdays), the headquarters, an orientation and a leaflet guide in Spanish are available.

East of San Juan

El Yunque In the Luquillo Mountains, about thirty minutes east of San Juan, is the Caribbean National Forest, more commonly known as El Yunque—the only tropical rain forest in the U.S. Forest Service system. Long a research center on tropical flora and fauna, El Yunque has 240 species of trees, more than 200 types of fern, and 60 species of birds. One of its most important projects has been the effort to save the Puerto Rican parrot, decimated from an estimated million birds at the time of Columbus to only twenty-two in 1975. Now the bird's numbers are slowly being rebuilt.

You can drive through El Yunque on a tarmac road (No. 191) that goes into the heart of the rain forest, passing waterfalls, lookouts, and picnic areas. At the northern boundary of the forest, you'll find the office of the Caribbean National Forest and **El Portal,** the new visitor and interpretive center, open daily. Maps—essential for hiking—and an orientation are available. Look for *Where Dwarfs Reign: A Tropical Rain Forest in Puerto Rico* by Kathryn Robinson (University of Puerto Rico Press, 1997). Written in readable layman language, it is the most comprehensive book available on El Yunque.

La Mina/Big Tree Trail, a paved path leading to La Mina Falls, takes about an hour, round-trip. It runs along the Mina River and passes through a forest of stately tabonuco trees, one of the four types of forest found in the reserve.

Las Cabezas de San Juan In the northeastern corner of the island, about a thirty-minute drive from El Yunque, is **Las Cabezas de San Juan Nature Reserve,** a 316-acre peninsula of forest land, mangroves, lagoons, beaches, cliffs, cays, and coral reefs, marked by a nineteenth-century lighthouse, **El Faro,** which serves as the visitor center. Opened in 1991 by the Conservation Trust of Puerto Rico, there are nature exhibits in the lighthouse and walkways through the mangroves. Guided tours on trolleys introduce visitors to the peninsula's ecology. Reservations (787-860-2560) are required. A spectacular view from the lighthouse extends 40 miles east to the Virgin Islands and west over El Yunque and the Caribbean.

Fajardo South of the reserve on the coast is Fajardo, home to Puerto Rico's largest marina and an occasional port for small cruise ships. Nearby is **El Conquistador Resort and Golden Door Spa** (787-863-1000; www.elconresort.com), a large elaborate resort with a championship golf course and excellent tennis and water-sports facilities.

West of San Juan

Rio Camuy Cave Park The Camuy Caves are the largest on the island, with a surface area of 268 acres. Seven miles of passageways have been explored, including chambers as high as a twenty-five-story building. The Camuy River, the third-largest underground river in the world, passes through the complex system.

At the visitor center a film provides an orientation. At the cave entrance visitors accompanied by bilingual guides board a tram for the tour. The tram winds through a ravine with rain-forest vegetation to the first of sixteen chambers, where passengers begin a forty-five-minute walk. The room is illuminated by natural light that penetrates the entrance. It leads to another huge chamber, tall enough to hold a 17-foot-high stalagmite. The trail winds along a path from which the Camuy River, 150 feet below, comes into view. The park (787-898-3100) is open Wednesday to Sunday and on holidays. Entrance: $10 adults, $7 children, $5 seniors. From Old San Juan it is a 1.5-hour drive west via Arecibo and inland on Route 129. Not far from the park, you can detour to the small mountain town of Lares, which is famous for its ice-cream parlor (Heladería de Lares; Plaza de Recreo, Lecaroz Street; 787-897-3290), where you can sample any of the sometimes bizarre flavors, such as tomato, garlic, cabbage, chickpea, celery, and beer. Not to worry, there are the customary flavors: chocolate, strawberry, and many more as well.

Arecibo Observatory Nearby, the Arecibo Observatory (www.naic.edu) is the largest radar/radio telescope in the world—a twenty-acre dish set in a sinkhole equal in size to thirteen football fields—where scientists listen for signs of intelligent life in the universe. Many exciting discoveries have been made here, including the mapping of one of the largest structures in the universe—a cluster of galaxies—and observations from which scientists determined the true rotation of the planet Mercury. Here, too, the first planets outside the solar system were found.

Operated by Cornell University, the observatory has the wonderful Arecibo Observatory Visitor and Educational Facility. It makes the research being undertaken here more accessible to the nonscientific community. The building houses interactive exhibits, a theater, meeting rooms, work space, and a science-related book and gift shop. A variety of exhibits and video displays in English and Spanish introduce visitors to the basics of astronomy, the radio telescope, and more. A second level is devoted to the work being done at Arecibo. Hours: Wednesday to Friday noon to 4:00 p.m.; weekends and holidays 9:00 a.m. to 4:00 p.m. Admission: $5 adults, $3 seniors, students, and children younger than age twelve.

The Panoramic Route Crossing the center of Puerto Rico is a spine of tall green mountains, Cordillera Central, with peaks that are often concealed by clouds. The Panoramic Route, a 165-mile road made up of forty different routes, winds through the mountains, from Yabucoa on the southeast to Mayagüez on the west coast, providing spectacular panoramas through forests and rural landscapes—light-years away from the bustle and glitter of San Juan. The route divides into three sections, each requiring a day to cover with stops along the way. There are trails, picnic areas, a spring-fed swimming hole, and man-made lakes—reservoirs created in the 1930s to harness the island's water resources.

Ponce

Puerto Rico's second-largest city, Ponce, was founded in 1692 by a great-grandson of Ponce de Leon, for whom it was named. The site is thought to be an ancient one, since a huge Indian burial ground lies a short distance north of town.

Ponce is a treasure of architecture, with streets of colonial houses with balconies and wrought-iron railings reminiscent of Savannah and New Orleans. Other houses are turn-of-the-twentieth-century Victorian gems, with gingerbread trim reminiscent of Key West; still others built in the 1930s and 1940s are straight off the drawing boards of art deco architects.

On the main square, the Old Firehouse is painted bright red and black, Ponce's colors. It's all the more startling, standing as it does next to the classic Cathedral of Our Lady of Guadaloupe, which dates from 1670. The firehouse has a collection of memorabilia pertaining to the history of the building.

Ponce is especially proud of its **Museo de Arte de Ponce** (2325 Avenue Las Americas; 787-848-0505; www.museoarteponce.org), housed in a building designed by Edward Durrell Stone. The collection, one of the largest in the Caribbean, has more than one thousand paintings and four hundred sculptures representing all periods of Western art from ancient to contemporary. Hours: daily 10:00 a.m. to 5:00 p.m. The Visitor's Information Center (Cristina and Mayor Streets) is directly across from La Perla Theatre, where plays, concerts, and other events are held throughout the year.

Castillo Serralles, the former mansion of a wealthy local rum-producing family, sits high on a hillside overlooking the city and has been converted into a museum. Open Tuesday to Sunday. (787-259-1774; www.castilloserralles.org).

Indian Ceremonial Park One of the oldest, most important burial grounds ever discovered in the Caribbean is the Tibes Indian Ceremonial Park, 2 miles north of town. Here, seven ceremonial plazas belonging to the Igneri culture, dating from A.D. 600 to 1000, were found. The museum has displays pertaining to the Taino Indians and other pre-Columbian cultures. A film on the first Puerto Ricans is shown every forty-five minutes as an orientation to the site. Guides are available. Open Tuesday to Sunday.

Hacienda Buena Vista In the foothills of the Cordillera Central north of Ponce is an old estate that was once one of the largest working plantations in Puerto Rico, growing coffee and other cash crops. Now a property of the Puerto Rico Conservation Trust, it has been extensively renovated as an interpretive center and museum. A footpath through the pretty woods leads to waterfalls along an aqueduct that once carried water to a huge waterwheel supplying the estate with its power. Multilingual guides lead visitors through the grounds. Reservations are required. (787) 722-5882 (San Juan); (787) 284-7020 (Buena Vista).

The Virgin Islands

U.S. Virgin Islands

**Charlotte Amalie, St. Thomas; Cruz Bay, St. John;
Frederiksted, St. Croix; Christiansted, St. Croix**

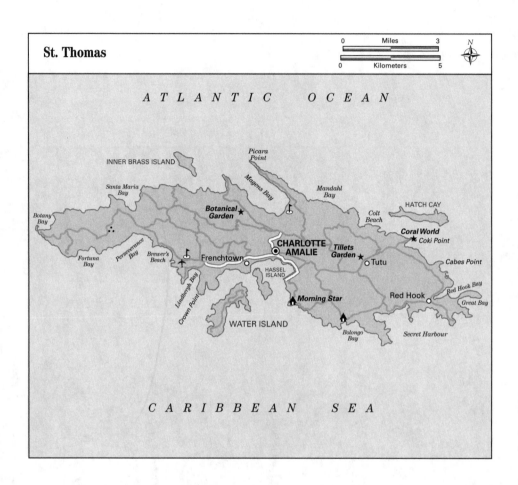

St. Thomas

0 Miles 3

0 Kilometers 5

N

ATLANTIC OCEAN

INNER BRASS ISLAND

Picara Point

Santa Maria Bay

Magens Bay

Mandahl Bay

HATCH CAY

Botany Bay

Botanical Garden ★

Colt Beach

Coral World ★
Coki Point

Fortuna Bay

Perseverance Bay

Brewer's Beach

CHARLOTTE AMALIE

Tillets Garden ★

Tutu

Cabes Point

Frenchtown

Lindbergh Bay

Crown Point

HASSEL ISLAND

Morning Star

Red Hook

Red Hook Bay

Great Bay

WATER ISLAND

Bolongo Bay

Secret Harbour

CARIBBEAN SEA

U.S. Virgin Islands

The American Paradise

Their license plates say "American Paradise." They are our corner of the Caribbean, and, topside or beneath the sea, you will not find a more beautiful place under the American flag. Every turn in the road reveals spectacular scenes of white beaches washed by gentle turquoise water, backed by forest-green hills, and colored by a rainbow of flowers with such marvelous names as Catch-and-Keep and Jump-Up-and-Kiss-Me. Easy breezes carrying the light scent of jasmine cool the air.

The Virgin Islands are divided between the United States and Britain into two groups of about fifty islands and cays each. They are situated in the northeastern Caribbean adjacent to the Anegada Passage, a strategic gateway between the Atlantic Ocean and the Caribbean Sea, 40 miles east of Puerto Rico, where the Lesser Antilles begin.

The U.S. Virgin Islands constitute a "territory" rather than a state. Only four islands are inhabited: St. Croix, the largest, lies entirely in the Caribbean and is the easternmost point of the United States; St. Thomas, the most populated and developed, is 40 miles north of St. Croix, between the Caribbean and the Atlantic Ocean; and neighboring St. John, the smallest, is 3.5 miles east of St. Thomas. The islands are so close together that they can be visited in a day, yet no three in the Caribbean are more different from one another than our American trio.

Columbus first sighted the Virgin Islands on his second voyage in 1493. He arrived at an island native Carib Indians called Ayay and named it Santa Cruz, or Holy Cross (we call the island by its French name, St. Croix). There Columbus sailed into the Salt River estuary on the island's north coast to replenish his ships' supply of fresh water. (Hence, St. Croix's claim: that it is the first land now under the American flag to have been visited by the great explorer.)

But the fierce Caribs did not welcome Columbus as the peaceful Arawaks had done elsewhere. Columbus made a hasty withdrawal and continued north through the archipelago. The admiral, like all those who have followed him, was dazzled by the islands' exquisite beauty. Seeing so many clustered together, he named the group after the ancient legend of St. Ursula and the eleven thousand virgins.

Columbus claimed the islands for Spain, but the Spaniards paid little attention to them for a century or more. Sir Francis Drake, the dashing corsair of English history, was among those who sailed the Virgins' waters—long enough to form the basis of England's claim to them. The islands' jagged coastlines, good harbors, and proximity to major shipping lanes made them natural havens for pirates and privateers. By 1625 the English and Dutch had recognized the islands' strategic location and began colonizing St. Croix.

The Danes took possession of St. Thomas in 1672, adding St. John in 1717 and St. Croix in 1733. Two decades later Denmark declared the islands a crown colony and subsequently made St. Thomas a free port that flourished as the center of

At a Glance

Antiquities	★
Architecture	★
Art and artists	★★
Beaches	★★★★★
Colonial buildings	★★★★★
Crafts	★
Cuisine	★★
Culture	★
Dining/Restaurants	★★
Entertainment	★★
Forts	★★★★
History	★★★★
Monuments	★
Museums	★★
Nightlife	★
Scenery	★★★★★
Shopping	★★★★
Sightseeing	★★★
Sports	★★★★★
Transportation	★★★★

Fast Facts

Population: St. Croix, 60,000; St. John, 3,504; St. Thomas, 50,000.

Size: St. Croix, 27 miles long, 82 square miles; St. John, 9 miles long, 19 square miles; St. Thomas, 13 miles long, 32 square miles.

Main Towns: Christiansted and Frederiksted, St. Croix; Cruz Bay, St. John; Charlotte Amalie, St. Thomas.

Government: Executive power is vested in the governor, who appoints the heads of his twelve departments. Residents were granted the right to vote for their governor in 1970. The legislature, which has convened since 1852, is a single body of fifteen senators from the three islands, elected for two-year terms. Residents vote in local elections and, since 1972, have sent a representative to Congress. They pay federal income tax but cannot vote in national elections, and their congressperson does not vote on the floor of the House of Representatives.

Currency: U.S. dollar

Customs Regulations: Cruise passengers who disembark in the U.S. Virgin Islands and plan to return to the mainland by plane pass through customs here. The U.S. Virgin Islands have a special status, enabling U.S. residents to bring back up to $1,600 worth of goods—twice that of other islands in the Caribbean—free of customs tax. Persons over twenty-one years old are allowed five fifths of liquor, plus a sixth one of a Virgin Islands spirit (such as Cruzan Rum) and five cartons of cigarettes or one hundred cigars. You can also mail home gifts (other than perfume, liquor, or tobacco), each valued up to $100.

Departure Tax: None

Language: English. But don't be surprised if you have trouble understanding some Virgin Islanders. The local dialect is an English-Creole, which has had a profound influence on their speech. If you have trouble with the dialect, ask the person to speak slowly—and you should do the same.

Public Holidays: January 1, New Year's Day; January 6, Three Kings Day; third Monday in January, Martin Luther King's Birthday; February, Presidents' Day; Easter Thursday, Good Friday, Easter Sunday and Monday; March 31, Transfer Day (from Denmark to United States); May, Memorial Day; July 3, Emancipation; July 4, Independence; September, Labor Day; October 14, Columbus Day; October 21, Hurricane Thanksgiving; November 1, Liberty Day; November 11, Veteran's Day; November, Thanksgiving Day; December 25, 26, Christmas. Banks and stores are closed on the major holidays; stores remain open on local ones.

Telephone Area Code: 340

Airlines: From the United States mainland: American, Continental, Delta, Spirit Airlines, U.S. Airways, and United Airlines. Intraregional: Air St. Thomas, Air Sunshine, American Eagle, Cape Air (USVI/San Juan), LIAT, Seaborne Seaplane (340-773-6442; www.seaborne airlines.com).

Information: www.usvitourism.vi www.stcroixhotelandtourism.com

In the United States:

U.S. Virgin Islands Tourist Information: (800) 372-USVI.

Atlanta: 245 Peachtree Street NE, Marquis One Tower, Suite MB-05, Atlanta, GA 30303; (404) 688-0906; fax: (404) 525-1102; usviatl@aol.com.

Chicago: 500 North Michigan Avenue, No. 2030, Chicago, IL 60611; (312) 670-8784; fax: (312) 670-8788; usvichgo@earthlink.net.

Los Angeles: 3460 Wilshire Boulevard, Los Angeles, CA 90010; (213) 739-0138; fax: (213) 739-2005; usvila@aol.com.

Miami: 2655 LeJeune Road, No. 907, Coral Gables, FL 33134; (305) 442-7200; fax: (305) 445-9044; usvimia@aol.com.

New York: 1 Penn Plaza, Ste. 3525, New York, NY 100119-0002; (212) 502-5300; fax: (212) 465-2324; usviny@aol.com.

Washington: 444 North Capital Street, No. 305, Washington, DC 20001; (202) 624-3590; fax: (202) 624-3594; usvidc@sso.org.

In Canada:

2810 Matheson Boulevard E, Suite 200, Mississauga, ON L4W 4X7; (416) 622-7600; fax: (416) 622-3431; jsintzel@travmarkgroup.com.

In St. Croix:

P.O. Box 4538, Christiansted, USVI 00822; (340) 773-0495; fax: (340) 773-0598.

In St. John:

P.O. Box 200, Cruz Bay, USVI 00830; (340) 776-6450.

In St. Thomas:

P.O. Box 6400, Charlotte Amalie, USVI 00804; (340) 774-8784; fax: (340) 774-4390.

contraband for the entire Caribbean, while St. Croix and St. John became rich with sugar plantations.

In 1917 the United States, concerned about protecting the Panama Canal, bought the Virgin Islands for $25 million—or about $300 an acre—a high price at the time. Island residents were made U.S. citizens in 1927; the present structure of territorial government was established by the U.S. Congress in 1954. In December 1996 the U.S. Department of the Interior transferred ownership of fifty acres of Water Island, a former World War II military installation, to the Virgin Islands government. Located a quarter mile off St. Thomas's Charlotte Amalie Harbor, the island's remaining 440 acres will be transferred as agreements with homeowners are finalized.

Although the islands are American—with fast-food shops and supermarkets, direct dial and cable television—they have retained enough of their past to give visitors a sense of being in a foreign yet familiar place.

Budget Planning

Prices for sports and tours in St. Thomas and St. John generally are typical for the Caribbean; St. Croix is slightly lower. The largest expenses for visitors are taxi fares and fancy restaurants. On the other hand there is an ample selection of moderately priced, attractive restaurants serving local dishes; public transportation is plentiful and inexpensive; and beaches are free or have minimal charges.

Port Profile: St. Thomas

St. Thomas is the ideal cruise port. The green mountainous island rises dramatically from the deep turquoise sea to peaks of 1,550 feet that frame an irregular coastline of fingers and coves, idyllic bays, and white-sand beaches. Steeped in history, St. Thomas is as up-to-date as Fifth Avenue; it is small enough to see in a day, yet it has the diversity and facilities to offer cruise passengers a wide choice, with every kind of warm-weather sport a visitor could want. There are inviting restaurants—some in historic settings, others with lovely views—and enough colonial buildings, old homes, forts, and monuments for history buffs easily to fill their day.

Location/Embarkation Set on a deep horseshoe bay, Charlotte Amalie (pronounced Ah-*mahl*-ya) is the busiest cruise port in the Caribbean—a role it played for two hundred years during the colonial era as a major trading port on the sea-lanes between the Old and New Worlds.

The heart of town—both historic and commercial—hugs the shore and climbs the mountainsides overlooking the port. The harbor has three docks; the size of your ship usually dictates which one is used. On the east, about 1.5 miles from downtown, is the West Indian Company Dock, where the majority of ships arrive. Six cruise ships can berth here at one time. **Yacht Haven Grande,** a new $160 million megayacht marina complex, is next to the cruise ship piers. Phase One includes a marina that accommodates fifty yachts, three restaurants, and 80,000 square feet of retail space with high-end shops; a hotel and other facilities will be completed in the next phase.

Small ships (fewer than two hundred passengers) often sail directly to the waterfront in town a few steps from the Virgin Islands Tourist Bureau (Territorial Building, Veterans Drive; 774-8784). On the west side is Crown Bay Dock, about 1.5 miles from town. Since more cruise ships call at St. Thomas than at any other port in the Caribbean, it is not surprising to find the port crowded. The system operates more or less on a first-come, first-served basis; the number of ships in port will determine whether your ship draws dockside or tenders.

At the West Indian Company Dock, you can find telephones for local and long-distance calls, an Internet cafe, a U.S. post office, a tourist information center where you can get maps and information, and a large shopping complex, Havensight Mall, where many of the Main Street stores have branches. Crown Bay Dock's facilities are more limited.

Local Transportation The transportation system at the ports is well organized and convenient. You will find taxis, minibuses, and open jitneys (locals call them safaris) for twenty passengers lined up by the dozens for transportation from the port to Emancipation Square in downtown Charlotte Amalie. Average cost is $6 per passenger one-way, $5 if more than one person is traveling; prices vary depending on location. The square is located at the head of Main Street, the central shopping street. It is also the ideal place from which to start a walking tour. To return to your ship, jitneys and taxis leave frequently from the square to the docks; you can almost always share a taxi with other returning passengers. Be sure to give yourself ample time to return to your ship, particularly around the noon hour and from 4:00 to 6:00 p.m., when local traffic is extremely heavy and moves at a snail's pace. It can take forty-five minutes to drive the 1.5 miles between town and the West Indian Company Dock.

Taxi rates, set by the government, are based on destination rather than mileage; a copy of the rates should be available from the driver. Rates for most locations beyond town are $6 to $18 one-way. Coki Beach is $17 for one person and $9 per person for two or more. Taxis are available for island tours. Drivers, who act as guides, are usually informed on the basics, but some are definitely better than others—be prepared to take potluck. Cost is $30 for two persons for a two-hour tour, $12 for each additional passenger.

Buses Regular bus service connects Charlotte Amalie with Red Hook, at the eastern end of the island, where ferries leave for St. John and Bordeaux at the west end. Buses run about hourly, with the last returning to town about 10:00 p.m.; cost is $1. The open-sided "safari" buses, or jitneys, from Market Square to Red Hook leave hourly

Roads and Rentals Roads on St. Thomas are generally well marked with route signs, but pay close attention because the roads are very winding and frequently branch onto small roads. In addition, driving is on the left side of the road, and it is very easy to get distracted by the views.

Route 38 traverses the island east-west from Charlotte Amalie to the eastern end, forking northeast to Coki Point and southeast to Red Hook. Route 40, known as Skyline Drive, runs parallel along the north side of the mountains, affording magnificent views, and leads to Mountain Top, the highest accessible point on St. Thomas.

You need a valid U.S. driver's license to rent a car here. Expect to pay about $55 to $70 per day for a compact with unlimited mileage from an international chain and about $50 from independent dealers. Jeep rentals cost about $65, but unless you have had experience with driving on the left and on mountain roads, you may be wiser to rent a car. Some car-rental companies have agreements with local merchants offering discounts on rentals and/or merchandise. Some also have free pickup and delivery service at the port, but during the winter season, when demand is greatest, availability of cars is uneven and pickup service unreliable.

A list of rental firms is available in *St. Thomas This Week*, a free booklet widely distributed in tourist offices and elsewhere. Among them are **Amalie Car Rental** (774-0688; www.amaliecar.com); **Budget** (776-5774; 800-626-4516; www.budgetstt.com); **Dependable Car Rental** (774-2253; 800-522-3076; www.dependablecar.com); and **Discount** (776-4858; www.discountcar.vi).

Ferry Service Ferries between downtown and Marriott Frenchman's Reef Hotel leave every half hour 9:00 a.m. to 4:00 p.m., daily except Sunday; and from the downtown waterfront, 8:30 a.m. to 4:30 p.m. Cost is $5. St. John is connected by hourly service from Red Hook from 6:30 a.m. to midnight; the trip takes twenty minutes. Another ferry, less frequent but more convenient for cruise passengers, leaves from the downtown waterfront several times daily, beginning at 9:00 a.m.

SeaTrans (776-5494; caribbean.fastferry@ gmail.com) is a new service between St. Thomas and St. Croix that takes ninety minutes one-way and costs $50 one-way, $90 round-trip for adults. It runs Friday through Monday, departing Charlotte Amalie at 9:30 a.m. and 6:30 p.m.

Ferries to Tortola, B.V.I.—**Smith's Ferry** (775-7292; www.smithsferry.com) and **Native Son** (774-8685)—leave from Charlotte Amalie frequently and take forty-five minutes; some continue to Virgin Gorda. You need a passport to reenter the United States. Schedules are printed in *St. Thomas This Week*.

Interisland Air Seaborne Airlines (773-6442; www.seaborneairlines.com) flies seaplanes between St. Thomas and St. Croix almost hourly during the day. It also has service between St. Thomas and Old San Juan, Puerto Rico, as well as from St. Thomas to Virgin Gorda. **American Eagle** connects St. Thomas and St. Croix with Puerto Rico. **Cape Air** (800-352-0714; www.flycapeair .com) flies almost hourly between San Juan, St. Thomas, and St. Croix.

Emergency Numbers
Medical: St. Thomas Hospital, 776-8311
Ambulance, Fire, Police: 911
Recompression Chamber: 776-2686
Alcoholics Anonymous: 776-5283

Shore Excursions

What to do in St. Thomas largely depends on your personal interest—the choices are plentiful. Be sure to plan some activity: Despite all you have heard about the wonderful shopping here, most people complete their shopping within two hours and then are disappointed if they have not planned something else, too.

St. Thomas Island Tour: 2.5 hours, $30–$40. Drive to Bluebeard's Castle for the view; Mafolie Hill and Drake's Seat for scenic panorama of Magens Bay and British Virgin Islands; and return to town. Same drive available by taxis for $30 for two.

St. John Safari: 4.5 hours, $50–$60. Recommended for those who have visited St. Thomas before or who prefer outdoor activity to shopping.

The excursion goes by ferry to Cruz Bay, tours St. John, and visits Trunk Bay for a swim and snorkel. Bring a towel and plastic bag for swimsuits.

Underwater life: 3 hours, snorkelers, $39; introductory dive lesson, $75. Some cruise ships send snorkelers and divers in separate groups; others combine them. They are accompanied by an instructor. For sightseeing or hiking and snorkeling combination, see **Captain Nautica, Inc.** (www .captainnautica.com) in the Sports section.

Sailing: 3.5 hours, $50–$65; full day $75–$90. Your yacht (with crew) sails to nearby uninhabited islands to anchor while you swim and snorkel. It has an open bar, and light snacks are served.

Horseback riding and kayaking: See Sports section later in this chapter.

Golf: See Sports section and Mahogany Run Golf Course (777-6250; 800-253-7103; www .mahoganyrungolf.com).

Accessible Adventures (344-8302; www .accessvi.com), a company launched in 2002, provides tours on St. Thomas for those with restricted mobility. Each of its vehicles has a lifting device, four-point tie-down system, and flip-up seats to accommodate up to three wheelchairs. Tours begin at $34 for adults, $24 for children.

Day Pass: Bolongo Bay Beach Resort (775-1800; 800-766-2840; www.bolongobay.com) offers a Day Pass for a full day's use of the resort's facilities—1,000 feet of palm-lined beach; swimming pool with swim-up bar; tennis, basketball, and volleyball courts; a room to shower and change; use of the resort's non-motorized equipment including kayaks, Sunfish, paddleboats, and snorkel equipment. Cost: $60 adult; $30 children age twelve and younger or $150 for a family of four (two adults/ two children).

Walk Through Old St. Thomas: (714-1672; www.st-thomas.com/walktour) Two hours, $20 per person: student with ID, $15, children younger than age fifteen free when accompanied by parent. Two-person minimum. Monday to Friday, rain or shine. Saturday on request. Participants meet guide Cindy Burn at 9:30 a.m. at Fort Christian main entrance; tour ends on waterfront near Hard Rock Cafe. 12:30 p.m. tour upon request.

St. Thomas on Your Own

The historic district of Charlotte Amalie is listed in the National Register of Historic Places. Most restorations were done by private owners who gave the old structures new life as stores, business and government offices, hotels, restaurants, and residences—uses not far removed from their original purposes. A walk through these streets is a chance to learn something about the island's history and shop in lanes made charming by the past. The St. Thomas Historical Trust (642-4074; www.st thomashistoricaltrust.org) can provide information.

A Charlotte Amalie Walkabout

Historic Charlotte Amalie is a grid of 3 blocks deep from the waterfront on the south to the hillsides on the north, intersected by long east-west streets extending from old Hospital Gade on the east to just below General Gade on the west. A walk takes two to three hours, depending on your pace. Taxis from the cruise ports discharge passengers at or near Emancipation Garden at the head of Main Street.

Emancipation Garden (1) A small park that was originally the town square was named to commemorate the abolition of slavery on July 3, 1848. It has a bandstand and an open-air market where T-shirts and souvenirs are sold. There is a bust of the Danish king Christian IX and a small replica of the Philadelphia Liberty Bell. At the southwest corner is the USVI Welcome Center (777-8827). The lounge has restrooms, telephones, and information on St. Thomas.

Grand Galleria (2) The building on the north side of the park, built in 1839 as the Commercial Hotel, was the town's leading accommodation for more than a century and known as the Grand Hotel. Originally the Greek Revival structure occupied an entire block overlooking the square. The complex, now a commercial building, has recently undergone a six-year, multimillion-dollar reconstruction in its interiors, which includes more shops; local arts and crafts; **Lillian's Caribbean Grill** (774-7900), a restaurant serving local cuisine; a two-floor, centrally air-conditioned atrium; and new interior

courtyard with a sushi bar and an outdoor cafe and deli. An ATM and public toilets are available.

Fort Christian and Museum (3) East of the park, Fort Christian is the oldest building in the Virgin Islands and a National Historic Landmark. The red-brick fortress, built between 1666 and 1680, was named for Denmark's King Christian V and was the center of the community for three centuries, housing the colony's first governors and later serving as a church, garrison, surgeons' quarters, shipwatch, prison, police station, and local courthouse. It now houses a small museum (776-4566), and a gift and bookshop. Hours: weekdays 8:30 a.m. to 4:30 p.m.

Legislative Building (4) The lime-green Italian Renaissance structure on the waterfront is the home of the Virgin Islands Legislature. Here in 1917 the Danish flag was lowered for the last time, transferring ownership to the United States. Built in 1874 as barracks for the Danish police, it served as a U.S. Marine Corps barracks from 1917 to 1930 and as a public school until 1957. Open weekdays.

Frederick Lutheran Church (5) Built in 1820 to replace an earlier one destroyed by fire, it is the oldest church on the island. The church was originally established in 1666, the year Erik Nielson Smith took formal possession of St. Thomas in the name of the Danish West India Company. The charter that the royal government granted to the company stockholders included a provision for the Lutheran church, the state church of Denmark. When St. Thomas became a Crown colony in 1754, the church quickly expanded its role, increasing the number of schools it operated and adding a hospital.

The **Parsonage** (23 Kongen's Gade) behind the church is more than 250 years old and is one of the oldest structures in continuous use on the island. The original walls, partially exposed in several rooms, consist of bricks and stones brought from Denmark as ballast for sailing ships and exchanged for cargoes of sugar, cotton, and rum.

Moravian Memorial Church (6) Farther east on Norre Gade is another nineteenth-century church. The two-story structure is built of local volcanic rock called blue-bitch stone and beveled sandstone cornerstones. Atop the hip roof is a bell tower with a delicate wooden cupola dating from

1882. Inside, the church has balconies supported by columns on three sides.

Government House (7) Built from 1865 to 1867 for the Danish Colonial Council, Government House is the official residence and office of the governor of the U.S. Virgin Islands. The first two floors are open to the public and have paintings and objets d'art relating to the islands' history and works by the French Impressionist Camille Pissarro, who was born in St. Thomas in 1830. Hours: weekdays 8:00 a.m. to noon and 1:00 to 5:00 p.m. Closed holidays.

A short detour east of Government House is the **Seven Arches Museum** (774-9295), a private residence open to the public as a lived-in museum. It is a modest example of Danish West Indian architecture; some rooms are furnished with antiques. A thick vine growing on the wall of the garden is full of iguanas. Hours: daily except Sunday and Monday, 10:00 a.m. to 3:00 p.m.

The 99 Steps (8) The steep hills made it difficult to build roads; instead, access between the higher and lower parts of town was gained by a series of stone stairs. Two of the best preserved ones, built by the Danes in the mid-eighteenth century, are west of Government House—one immediately west of the mansion and a second, known as the 99 Steps, a short walk beyond.

Fort Skytsborg (9) Both passageways lead to Fort Skytsborg, a five-story conical watchtower known as Blackbeard's Tower, built by the Danes in 1678. Legend has it that the infamous pirate used the tower to scout his prey and hide his treasures. The view from here is reward enough for climbing the 99 Steps.

Haagensen House (10) Built in the early 1800s by Hans Haagensen, a Danish banker, the Haagensen House (774-5541) has been renovated and furnished with regional antiques. Situated just above Hotel 1829, the main salon and terrace command a magnificent view of Charlotte Amalie. The lower level, which is used for parties and receptions, has a small craft and gift shop selling items made in the Virgin Islands. Hours: 9:00 a.m. to 4:00 p.m. Admission: $8 adults, $4 children and seniors.

Hotel 1829 (10) At the foot of the 99 Steps on Kongen's Gade is Hotel 1829, formerly known as Lavalette House after its builder, a French sea cap-

tain. The initial L of the original owner can still be seen in the wrought-iron grillwork at the entrance. The two-story stucco town house, begun in 1819, was designed by an Italian architect in a Spanish style. It has had extensive restoration down to the two-hundred-year-old Moroccan tiles in the main dining room. The bar is in the original Danish kitchen, and there is a pleasant courtyard.

Continue to Garden Street, and turn west onto Crystal Gade.

St. Thomas Dutch Reform Church (11) The Greek Revival building, constructed in 1846, has such classical features that it looks more like a temple than a church. Its two-story facade is surmounted by a large triangular pediment supported by four Doric columns. Its doors are framed by columns with classical cornices and moldings.

Synagogue Hill (12) Farther along, Beracha Veshalom Vegemilith Hasidim Synagogue, built in 1833 on the site of two earlier structures, is one of the oldest synagogues in North America. (As early as 1684 Gabriel Milan, a member of a prominent European Jewish family, was appointed governor by the Danish Crown.) The synagogue marked its 200th anniversary in 1996. In 2000, following a year's restoration, the synagogue was designated a National Historic Landmark.

The synagogue is a freestanding, one-story structure of cut stone and brick. A wrought-iron fence encloses a small patio. Marble steps lead to its unusual entrance: the front doorway, a high pointed arch, which is covered by a porch supported by four columns from which plaster has been removed to expose its red-brick composition. Similar columns are repeated at the entrance, and matching bricks frame the arched windows on either side.

Inside, the exposed walls are composed of native stone with a mortar made of sand and molasses. Mahogany pews face the center of the sanctuary; the *mechitzah* that once separated the men and women can be seen behind the fourth row. The furniture and many of the fixtures and ornaments date from 1833. On the east wall the Holy Ark contains scrolls of the Torah, three of which are more than two hundred years old; one set of *rimonim* (handles of the scrolls) were saved from a fire in 1831; and the old mahogany doors

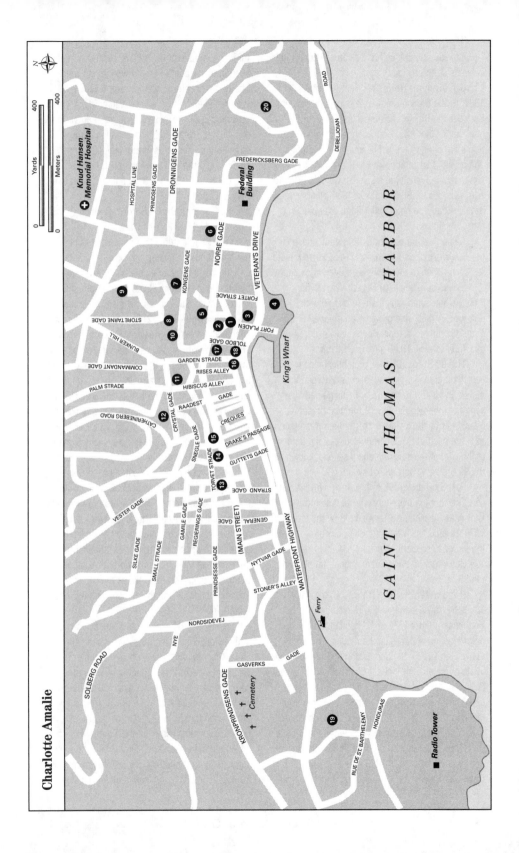

Charlotte Amalie

1.	Emancipation Garden	11.	St. Thomas Dutch Reform Church
2.	Grand Galleria	12.	Synagogue Hill
3.	Fort Christian and Museum	13.	Market Square
4.	Legislative Building	14.	Enid M. Baa Public Library
5.	Frederick Lutheran Church	15.	Pissarro's Birthplace
6.	Moravian Memorial Church	16.	Riise Alley
7.	Government House	17.	Post Office
8.	The 99 Steps	18.	Virgin Islands Tourist Information Office
9.	Fort Skytsborg or Blackbeard's Tower	19.	Frenchtown
10.	Haagensen House and Hotel 1829	20.	Bluebeard's Castle Hotel

have ivory insets. Above the Ark are the blue-and-gilded Tablets of the Decalogue; the lamp of eternal light hanging in front can be raised and lowered with a counterweight. Overhead in the center of the dome is a Magen David encircled with designs; from it hangs an eighteen-armed candle chandelier with Baccarat crystal hurricane shades.

There are four corner columns with Doric capitals, said to represent the four mothers of Israel: Sarah, Rebecca, Rachel, and Leah. Several interpretations are given for the sand floors, but according to the synagogue's historian, Isidor Paiewonsky, they are meant as reminders of the time when the Jews of Spain were forced to pray in unfinished basements. Hours: weekdays 9:30 a.m. to 4:30 p.m. Docent-led thirty-minute tours begin at 10:30 a.m. weekdays. For information, call 774-4312, or e-mail brewcong@islands.vi.

The *Weibel Museum* (at rear of synagogue; 774-4312) covers the three-hundred-year-old history of the Jews of St. Thomas; gift shop sells ritual items and Judaic arts and crafts. Hours: weekdays 10:00 a.m. to 4:00 p.m.; weekends 12:30 to 4:00 p.m.

Market Square (13) Continuing west on Backstreet, Market Square is the site of the notorious slave market, one of the biggest in the West Indies. Today it is covered by an iron market shed built in the early twentieth century and used as the town's open-air fruit-and-vegetable market, and it's now called the Sanderilla Thomas Bungalow, after a woman who sold produce there for fifty years. It reopened in July 2007 following a $1 million rebuilding project. Saturday is market day. One

block west on Main Street is the Cathedral of St. Peter and St. Paul, built in 1844.

Public Library (14) East of Market Square on Main Street is the Enid M. Baa Public Library, built around 1800 as the Lange residence. The library is named for one of the island's first female university graduates, who served as librarian for many years and was instrumental in creating the von Scholten Memorial Collection with books, prints, and documents on the Virgin Islands and the West Indies.

Pissarro's Birthplace (15) No. 14 Dronningens Gade (Main Street) is the birthplace of Camille Pissarro (1830–1903), a Sephardic Jew who lived here until he went to Paris to study at the age of twelve. Pissarro lived in Paris most of his life, but he is known to have returned to St. Thomas at least once. The building is marked by a small oval sign. On the second floor is the **Camille Pissarro Gallery** (774-4612), directed by Debra Wombold and featuring local artists. On both sides of Main Street, small lanes have been made into palm-shaded shopping plazas where shops are housed in eighteenth-century buildings that were houses of the old port; some are recent structures made to look old.

Riise Alley (16) One of the first old structures to be renovated, helping to spark the renaissance of the historic district, was **A. H. Riise Store and Alley,** belonging to the Paiewonsky family, whose patriarch is the island's leading historian and historian of the synagogue. In olden days each warehouse had its own lift to haul cargo from the ships at the waterfront and load it onto a flatbed car that ran on rails through the alleyway to Main Street.

The sample here is the only one remaining. At the end of Riise Alley, the eighteenth-century building was the **Danish Harbor Office.**

At the end of Main Street by the Emancipation Garden is the **post office (17),** with murals by illustrator Stephen Dohanos. They were painted in the 1940s as a WPA project, before he gained his reputation as an illustrator for the *Saturday Evening Post.* Next to the post office, the Continental Building is the old Danish Customs House. Next door is the Territorial Building, housing the Tourist **Information Office (18).**

Frenchtown (19) At the west end of town is the old fishing village of Frenchtown, settled by French immigrants fleeing the Swedish invasion of St. Barts in the late eighteenth century. Some of their descendants continue to speak a Norman dialect. While many of the old structures have given way to new houses and buildings, Frenchtown has retained a community feeling, and fishermen can often be seen bringing in their catches to sell on the dock. This small area has a concentration of restaurants popular with islanders and a pretty village church, the Church of St. Anne. Frenchtown is known as Cha Cha Town for the pointed straw hat called cha cha, woven by the town's women.

Paradise Point Tramway Directly behind the West Indian Company Dock is the station (774-9809; www.paradisepointtramway.com), where a cable car whisks passengers up a steep mountainside in four minutes to Paradise Point, the summit. There are spectacular views of Charlotte Amalie and St. Thomas. Cost is $18 for adults, $9 for children round-trip. The restaurant/bar at the peak is a popular spot for cocktails at sunset. Paradise Point can also be reached by road from the harbor. At the summit, there is a nature trail of 1 mile for hiking. The tramway station now has a pretty gazebo where couples can be married and from where there are fantastic views. Information is available on the Web site.

Driving Tour of St. Thomas

Remember: KEEP TO THE LEFT. East of Charlotte Amalie the waterfront boulevard, called Veterans Drive (Route 30), forks and leads up to **Blue-**

beard's **Castle Hotel (20),** high on a hill from which you can enjoy a spectacular view of Charlotte Amalie and spot your ship at the West Indian Company Dock directly below. The hotel is set in gardens of tropical plants, and its seventeenth-century Danish watchtower, for which it is named, is the honeymoon suite. Look closely among the hibiscus and you might see an iguana, a reptile that looks like a miniature dinosaur. Unlike other Caribbean islands, where the iguana is elusive and endangered, it is something of a pet on St. Thomas and will often remain still for a photograph.

From Bluebeard's, Routes 35/40 lead to **Drake's Seat,** a small lookout named for the British sea captain Sir Francis Drake, who is said to have used this vantage point to watch for the Spanish treasure galleons on which he preyed. You may not see any treasure ships, but you will be richly rewarded with a magnificent view of Magens Bay and neighboring islands; off to the east is Drake's Passage, a sea channel first explored by Drake in 1580. On Route 40, the **Estate St. Peter Greathouse and Botanical Garden** (St. Peter Mountain Road; 774-4999 or 690-4499; www.greathouse-mountaintop.com) was once part of an eighteenth-century plantation. It is now a twelve-acre landscaped spread 1,000 feet above Magens Bay Beach. The estate's modern West Indian–style house is furnished with works by fifty local artists. Self-guided nature trails are also offered. Hours: daily 9:00 a.m. to 5:00 p.m.; $10 adults, $5 children.

Crown Mountain Road (Route 33 west) circles Crown Mountain at 1,550 feet, the highest peak. Solberg Hill Road (Route 40 south) returns to Charlotte Amalie, providing extensive views of the town, harbor, and Hassel Island in the foreground and Water Island beyond.

West of Charlotte Amalie, Veterans Drive passes Frenchtown and the airport, continuing to the **University of the Virgin Islands,** situated on 175 acres. Not far from the entryway to Botany Bay, the Bordeaux Farmer's Market is held the last Sunday of every month on the tennis courts and fairgrounds. The market is sponsored by a growers' co-op founded in 1993. In addition to delicious prepared dishes and organic fruits and vegetables, there is live music by steel drummers and reggae musicians.

Shopping

Main Street and side lanes such as newly renovated Palm Passage have pretty stores and smart boutiques housed in renovated old warehouses from its heyday as a trading post. You will find top-brand watches, jewelry, cameras, electronic equipment, china and crystal, designer clothes and accessories, perfumes, and other gift items—all at prices ranging from 15 percent and more off those on the mainland. Stores are open Monday to Saturday 9:00 a.m. to 5:00 p.m. Some stores in Havensight Mall (777-5313; www.havensightmall.com) remain open until 6:00 p.m. Stores close on Sunday unless a cruise ship is in port, when some may open for half a day. The Havensight Mall's Web site has a diagram and a list by location of all its stores and services. Check out also "Port of $ale," a complex of colorfully painted boutiques at the western end of the West Indian Company Dock, next to the Havensight Mall.

Duty-free Shopping The matter of "duty-free" needs some explanation. All stores in the U.S. Virgin Islands are duty-free. Even so, the goods they sell are not entirely without import taxes. Local merchants pay taxes on the merchandise they import, but the levies are lower in the U.S. Virgin Islands than on the mainland.

A Word of Caution Merchandise in St. Thomas is not always the bargain that is claimed. The proliferation of discount houses in the United States, particularly for cameras and electronic equipment, has cut into the traditional savings on duty-free merchandise. The only way to know a real bargain is to come prepared with prices from home and to do some comparative shopping before you buy. Cigarettes and liquor have the lowest prices and represent the greatest savings.

Art and Artists A. H. Riise Gifts and Art Gallery (Main Street; 800-524-2037; www.ahriise.com) has a collection by local as well as Haitian artists. In late March, August, and November, Tillett's Gardens (Route 38, Tutu; 775-1929; www.tillettgardens.com), where some artists and jewelry designers work and sell their products year-round, holds an arts fair, **Arts Alive,** with more than fifty local artists and artisans. The colorful

Mocko Jumbies, clowns, acrobats, and folkloric dancers are part of the entertainment. Admission is free. **Tillett's** also offers a series of musical concerts in the winter season and there is wireless Internet service in the garden. **Mango Tango** (777-3060) is one of the best places in St. Thomas to buy quality art by local artists. **Jonna White Gallery** (Main Street; 774-1201) is the gallery of the artist who has a distinctive style, using Caribbean colors on handmade paper. **Gallery St. Thomas** (2A-2C Garden Street and Government Hill; 777-6363; www.GalleryStThomas.com) was opened in 2003 by owner Claire Ochoa to promote art from or inspired by the Virgin Islands. She carries a variety of artists and mediums, creating an interesting showcase for local art. For antiques, check out the **Carson Company** (Royal Dane Mall; 774-6175), where you can find unusual antiques and ethnic artifacts. **Blue Turtle Art Gallery** (Emancipation Gardens; 774-9440), in a white building with blue trim, is owned and operated by well-known local artist Lucinda Schutt and features a range of Caribbean painters, sculptors, and photographers. Lucinda is artist-in-residence at the Ritz Carlton St. Thomas and offers art classes to locals as well as visitors.

Books Dockside Bookshop (Havensight Mall; 777-8786; www.havensightmall.com) has the largest selection of books and carries stateside newspapers—costing $2 or more. Hours: Monday through Thursday and Saturday, 9:00 a.m. to 5:00 p.m., Friday to 6:00 p.m., Sunday, 11:00 a.m. to 3:00 p.m.

Cameras/Electronics All leading makes are available, but bring stateside prices for comparison. The largest selections are at **Boolchand's** (31 Main Street and Havensight Mall; www.boolchand.com). Prices are comparable to those of discount houses in New York.

China/Crystal Little Switzerland (Main Street; www.littleswitzerland.com) carries a wide selection of English china, French crystal, and similar high-quality goods. You can get a catalog by calling (800) 524-2010. **A. H. Riise Gifts** (Main Street) is something of a department store with a collection of boutiques for gifts, jewelry, perfume, china, silver, and crystal, as well as liquor.

Clothing You can find boutiques with designer fashions in the narrow passageways between Main Street and the waterfront. **Fendi, DKNY, Nicole Miller, Tommy Hilfiger,** and **Polo Ralph Lauren** (Palm Passage) have their own stores. **Local Color** (Hibiscus Alley) has handpainted T-shirts, dresses, and sportswear. Look for the label **Sloop Jones** (www.sloopjones.com), which is based at Hansen Bay, St. John.

Zora's of St. Thomas (34 Norre Gade; 774-2559; www.zorasofstthomas.com) has custom-made sandals and leather goods and a wide variety of canvas bags, backpacks, and travel bags. The **Doubloon Company Store** (www.boatshirt.com) sells boat merchandise from both of their boats, the *Doubloon* and the *Dancing Dolphin,* including flags and shirts with the Jolly Roger design. **Caribbean Marketplace** (Havensight Mall; 776-5400) sells a wide selection of crafts from the region. The new **Yacht Haven Grande** (9100 Port of Sale, 774-5030; YHGST@igymarinas.com) houses a variety of famous-label stores, including **BeBe, BCBG Max Azria, Caché, Coach,** and **Louis Vuitton.**

Crafts Don't overlook locally made products, especially for gifts and souvenirs. You do not have to count these products in your $1,600 customs allowance. Products you will find include straw hats, mats, and baskets; candles with scents of local herbs and spices; candies and preserved fruits and spices; pottery and ceramics; folkloric dolls; macramé and scrimshaw; and perfume and suntan lotions made from native flowers and herbs.

Down Island Traders (on the waterfront) sells preserves, herbs, and spices as well as imported teas and coffees. The **Native Arts and Crafts Cooperative** (Tolbod Gade; 777-1153; adjacent to the visitor center) and the **Haagensen House** shop specialize in island-made art and other crafts from ninety different craftspeople. **Caribbean Chocolate** (15 Main Street; 774-6675) sells handmade chocolates as well as Virgin Islands rum cake.

Jewelry Stores such as **Cardow, Cartier,** and **H. Stern** (all on Main Street) have international reputations; **A. H. Riise Gifts** has a large jewelry department and is the exclusive Mikimoto dealer

and official Rolex retailer. The **Caribbean Bracelet Company** (A.H. Riise, Main Street; www.caribbeanbracelet.com) sells the popular hand-crafted bracelet of the same name. Many smaller jewelry stores on Main Street and adjacent malls sell gold jewelry. Look around before you buy.

Leather/Luggage Royal Dane Mall has several shops with high-quality Italian and Spanish handbags. **Cuckoo's Nest** (International Plaza; 776-4005) specializes in men's clothing.

Linens Table linens are among the best bargains here. Most come from India and China. **Linen House** (774-8117) and **Mr. Tablecloth** (Palm Passage; www.mrtablecloth-vi.com) have large collections, and you might also check out some of the general stores on Main Street.

Liquor Prices are very competitive, but **Al Cohen's** near the port claims to have the best prices in St. Thomas. Check *St. Thomas This Week* and other free pamphlets distributed for tourists. The centerfold or back page usually has a list of current liquor prices.

Perfumes Tropicana Shop (Main Street) has nothing but perfume. **West Indies Bay Company** (Estates Thomas; 800-422-9786; www.stjohns bayrum.com) makes St. Johns Bay Rum for men, J'Ouvert for women, and other fragrances packaged in bottles with handwoven palm fronds in a traditional design used by Caribbean fishermen for their fish pots. The company offers factory tours.

Dining and Nightlife

The Virgin Islands did not gain their reputation as Paradise in the kitchen. It's not that innkeepers and restaurateurs don't try. They try very hard, perhaps too hard, to create gourmet havens. But for myriad reasons (Herman Wouk's hilarious *Don't Stop the Carnival* was written from his trials and tribulations in trying to operate a hotel in St. Thomas), they are unable to maintain a consistently high level. Aspiring places can quickly become pretentious disappointments at very high prices instead.

With this caveat, the selection here is based less on the great gourmet experience you are unlikely to have than on the aesthetic one you are sure to experience, either thanks to a view, a historic setting, or both. Some of the best establishments are open for dinner only. Expensive means more than $30 per person. If wine is added, the bill can quickly climb to $50 per person and more. Most are open daily, but check locally.

With a View or Historic Setting

Hervé Restaurant and Wine Bar (Government Hill; 777-9703; www.herverestaurant.com), one of the island's most popular restaurants, is set in a renovated eighteenth-century building with a panoramic view of Charlotte Amalie. "Hervé" is Herve Paul Chassin, a St. Thomas restaurateur for more than thirty years. You lunch and dine in an informal atmosphere on contemporary American and classic French selections, all touched by a bit of Caribbean. The bar serves wines by the glass. Closed Sunday. Expensive.

Hotel 1829 (Government Hill; 776-1829; www .hotel1829,com) is a historic landmark with a long-established reputation for its classic international selections in a pretty setting. Very expensive.

Light and Local

Beni Iguana (Grand Hotel Courtyard; 777-8744; www.beniiguanas.com) is a sushi bar in an old Danish courtyard with umbrella tables. There are cooked dishes and daily specials, as well. The bar serves domestic and Japanese beer and sake. Live classical and jazz guitar on Friday evenings. Closed Sunday. Moderate.

Café Amici (Riise's Alley; 776-5670), a sidewalk cafe in the heart of town, is perfect for lunch or a refreshment break during a shopping expedition. The menu offers pasta, salads, and other light fare and usually a specialty of the day. Moderate.

Craig and Sally's (Frenchtown; 777-9949; www.craigandsallys.com) is a family-run restaurant/bar with owners Craig at the door and Sally in the kitchen. The bar, open daily 11:30 a.m. to 1:00 a.m. except Monday, serves wine by the glass. The restaurant offers an eclectic menu that's changed daily. Closed Saturday and Sunday lunch. Moderately expensive.

Cuzzin's Caribbean (7 Backstreet; 777-4711) is a lively restaurant-bar in the heart of Charlotte Amalie featuring West Indian dishes, sandwiches, and pasta. Moderate.

Gladys' Cafe (Royal Dane Mall; 774-6604) is a charming cafe in town that serves lunch plus dinner on Friday with jazz, 6:00 to 9:00 p.m. Lunch offers fresh fish, hamburgers, salads, and local specials. Gladys's own hot sauce, attractively packaged for gifts, is on sale for $6 a bottle. Moderate.

Havana Blue (MorningStar Beach Resort; 715-2583; www.havanabluerestaurant.com) offers Pacific Rim and Cuban- and Latin American–inspired dishes with exotic spices and tangy sauces. Favorites include grouper encrusted with red chile and avocado, seared Thai tenderloin, and duck lettuce cups. Moderate.

Randy's Bar & Bistro (Al Cohen's Plaza; 775-5001) is a wine and gourmet shop that doubles as an eatery with a creative menu that changes daily and includes fresh seafood and a large selection of wines. Moderate.

The Old Stone Farmhouse (Mahogany Run Golf Course, 777-6277; www.oldstonefarmhouse .com) is situated in a 200-year-old restored field house. Executive chef Ric Aide offers a range of internationally inspired, eclectic cuisine, such as upside-down spinach "martini" and "calypso" seafood hot pot. Expensive.

W!kked (Yacht Haven Grande; 775-8953) a hip waterfront shack offering island fare and favorites like wings and tacos. Open 7:00 a.m. to midnight. Moderately expensive.

XO Bistro (Red Hook Plaza, behind Duffy's Love Shack and by the Grateful Deli; 779-2069) is a wine and champagne bar popular with locals but little known to tourists. Open daily with different theme or specialty each evening, some with live music. Some say it's the place to be on Friday nights. Moderate.

Evening Entertainment

Nightlife is small-scale—steel bands, combos, discos—and mostly revolves around hotels and restaurants. Check local newspaper and tourist publications such as *St. Thomas This Week* for what's happening.

A terrace at **Paradise Point** and **Room with a View** (Bluebeard's Castle; 774-1600) provide a good perch for cocktails at sunset and offer a fabulous view of Charlotte Amalie.

Duffy's Love Shack (Red Hook Plaza; 779-2080; www.duffysloveshack.com). Nightly, a parking lot is transformed into a popular local watering hole. The rustic, thatch-roofed bar serves up exotic concoctions like the Love Shack Volcano and Revenge of Godzilla (in a big green Godzilla you can take home). For lunch and dinner, you can grill your own meat or fish. After 9:00 p.m. on "Taco Tuesday," tacos are $1.25; "Chicks Rule" on Wednesday is ladies' night with free drinks and $2.00 beer; and Friday is dancing under the stars. Open daily from 11:30 a.m. to 2:00 a.m. No credit cards.

Marriott Frenchman's Reef Hotel features entertainment, music, and dancing several nights a week. On Monday, the Ritz Carlton stages Caribbean Night with steel band music from 8:30 to 10:00 p.m., and various hotels have entertainment on different nights of the week.

St. Thomas This Week (774-2500; www.st thomasthisweek.com) has a full page of the island's entertainment, from steel band to calypso to guitar and jazz.

Sports

St. Thomas boasts good facilities for almost every warm-weather sport—fishing, golf, tennis, parasailing, waterskiing, windsurfing—and those for sailing and diving are outstanding.

Beaches/Swimming The coves and bays that sheltered pirates in the old days are among St. Thomas's biggest attractions for tourists today. The most celebrated—and the most crowded—beach is at Magens Bay on the north side of the island. Beaches closest to Charlotte Amalie are Morningstar, Limetree, and Bolongo on the south/southeast. Tranquil Honeymoon Beach on Water Island, which is slowly—very slowly—getting a face-lift, is open for visitors and can be reached by a short ferry ride from town. You'll find a list of beaches and facilities in *St. Thomas This Week.*

Biking Water Island Adventures (714-2186; www.waterislandadventures.com) offers a bike tour and swim on Water Island.

Boating Calm seas and year-round balmy weather have made the Virgin Islands a boating mecca. Every type of craft is available for chartered, bare boat, or crewed, and with all provisions. Many charter operators have stateside offices and toll-free numbers for information and reservations. **Yacht Haven Marina** is the home port for the V.I. Charter Yacht League (774-3944) and the venue for the league's annual boat show in mid-November. On the east end at Red Hook are **American Yacht Harbor** (775-6454; www.ayh marina.biz) and **Charter Boat Center** (Piccola Marina; 775-7990; www.charterboat.vi), among others. Cost is about $90 for a full day.

Several dozen boats operate day sails that take passengers to pretty beaches for swimming and snorkeling. Some boats hold only six people, whereas party boats can take several dozen. Among them are *Daydream* (www.daydreamervi .com), *Independence* (www.independence44.us), and *True Love* (www.sailtruelove.com).

Deep-Sea Fishing Experts say the Virgin Islands are among the best places in the world for blue marlin, and the records set here support the claim. Other fish—maho, kingfish, sailfish, wahoo, tuna, and skipjack—are plentiful, too. American Yacht Harbor, St. Thomas Sports Fishing Center (775-7990), and a dozen or more boat operators offer half- and full-day trips; they provide bait, tackle, ice, and beer. Half-day trips cost $400 to $500; full-day, $650 to $900 for up to six people. The time of year makes a difference in the prices; the marlin season is mainly July and August. The **Virgin Islands Game Fishing Club** (775-9144) has a Web site (www.vigfc.com) with information on tournament schedules and other competitions in the Virgin Islands and nearby islands, social events, and other information. The club, a pioneer in conserving fish resources by banning the use of double hooks in competition, was the winner from clubs worldwide of the Billfish Foundation's Inaugural Club Conservation Challenge. At **Deep Sea Fishing** (775-6147; red@sportfishvi.com) a half-day starts at $650.

Golf Mahogany Run Golf Course (777-6006 for tee-off times; www.mahoganyrungolf.com) is St. Thomas's only 18-hole course. The championship layout is one of the Caribbean's most challenging. It was completely renovated in 1996, and a new watering system was installed to ensure optimum conditions year-round. Located about twenty minutes from Charlotte Amalie, the spectacular course (6,100 yards, par 70) by George and Tom Fazio extends over verdant hills and rocky cliffs overlooking the north coast. It has a pro shop, driving range, and practice green. Greens fees: $140 including cart fee for 18 holes; $65 for 9 holes. After 1:30 p.m., twilight fee, $100; all include shared cart. Call for tee time. Ship golf package may cost $150 or more, but will include transportation from the port.

Hiking Captain Nautica, Inc. (715-3379) offers hiking, sightseeing, and snorkeling excursions. The snorkel package combines two hours of sightseeing and two hours snorkeling at two locations; $58 per person with snorkel equipment, snacks, and beverages. Snorkeling/hiking excursion, 4.5 hours, combines several snorkeling trips with a 1.3-mile hike in the national park on St. John; $100 per person.

Magens Bay Trail: Guided hikes on a nature trail on seventy-five acres above Magens Bay are now available. Created by the Nature Conservancy with environmental experts, the trail runs downhill from 450 feet elevation and passes through forests and dense vegetation to the beach. The sixty- to ninety-minute hike is moderately strenuous. Virgin Island Ecotours (779-2155; www.viecotours.com), an ecotour operator, has a guided three-hour tour that begins with exploring the mangrove ecosystem by kayak followed by a hike in Cas Cay, a fifteen-acre wildlife sanctuary, with stops at a natural whirlpool and blowhole, followed by snorkeling in the protected reserve; cost is $75. For honeymooners, the outfitter provides pick-up and drop-off service for a day of secluded fun. Children can celebrate their birthday with a treasure hunt party and swim at Cas Cay.

Kayaking Virgin Island Ecotours (779-2155; www.viecotours.com) offers 2.5-hour guided kayak tours of the Virgin Islands Marine Sanctuary Mangrove Lagoon, led by marine biologists and naturalists from the University of the Virgin Islands. It uses single- or two-person ocean kayaks that are easy to paddle. No motorized vessels are allowed in the lagoon, so kayakers can enjoy quiet waters.

Tours start from the Holmberg Marina and cost $65, with a fifteen-minute orientation and slide show to introduce kayakers to local flora and fauna. Kayaks may also be rented for individual exploration.

Snorkeling and Scuba Diving The Virgin Islands are rated by dive experts among the best in the world for both novice and experienced divers. Visibility ranges up to 150 feet, water temperatures average 82 degrees Fahrenheit in summer and 78 degrees Fahrenheit in winter, and there's great variety plus excellent facilities. Three dozen of the Virgin Islands' one hundred dive sites lie within a twenty-minute boat ride of St. Thomas. Most dive operators have their own tanks and boats and offer packages ranging from half-day to weeklong certification. A list of operators is available from the V.I. tourist offices. Many cruise ships offer a half-day course as an introduction to scuba diving.

If you don't swim, you might opt for the *Atlantis 15* (776-5650; www.atlanticadventures .com), a recreational submarine that departs from its station next to the West Indian Company Dock for Buck Island (not to be confused with Buck Island off St. Croix,) a twenty-minute boat ride away. The 50-foot-long, air-conditioned ship with all systems duplicated to ensure safety, dives up to 80 feet. The dive lasts about an hour and costs $84 for adults, $45 for children.

Coral World Ocean Park (775-1555; 888-695-2073; www.coralworldvi.com), an underwater observatory and park at Coki Point and St. Thomas's most popular attraction, was purchased in spring 1997 by a group of local investors, who spent $8 million renovating, expanding, and greatly improving the facility with more beautiful landscaping, an improved aquarium, a semisubmarine, and other attractions. Admission: $18 adults, $9 children age three to twelve years, and $52 for families (two adults and up to four children). Hours: daily 9:00 a.m. to 5:00 p.m. Daily talks and feeds.

Coral World's newest attraction is the **Lorikeet Garden,** a 1,600-square-foot walk-through aviary that's home to a collection of lorikeet parrots. Visitors can purchase a cup of nectar to feed them by hand. Also not to be missed is **Sea Trekkin',** where you can walk on the floor of the Caribbean Sea and enjoy its incredible marine life.

Participants (eight years of age and older) wear a special helmet and are led by a guide along a trail equipped with a handrail, 12 to 30 feet deep into the crystal-clear water. The helmet provides air and allows communication with the guide while keeping your head dry. The 2.5-hour tours are offered from 9:00 a.m. to 4:00 p.m. daily; in summer, usually closed on Friday and Sunday. Rates: $68 adults, $59 children, including park admission.

The more adventurous will want to try the **Shark Encounter** at Coral World. There are no cages or barriers, just you and your guide in the Shark Shallows Pool, home to more than a dozen juvenile lemon, blacktip, and nurse sharks. Cost: $42.95 adults and $33.95 children, including Coral World admission. Participants must be a minimum of 54 inches tall.

If you are not quite ready for diving, there's an alternative called **Snuba** (693-8063; www.visnuba .com), a cross between scuba diving and snorkeling. It, too, is available at Coral World. Cost: $65, including your Coral World pass. Participants must be at least eight years old.

Homer's Scuba and Snorkel Tours and Berry Charters (Hull Bay; 774-7606; www.night snorkel.com) offers boat diving, kayak dives, snorkel trips for small groups, and fishing, as well as surfboard, kayak, dive, and snorkel gear rentals. Hull Bay, on the north side of St. Thomas, is the island's best-kept secret with great snorkeling, fishing, and diving on reefs little touched by crowds. Kayak/scuba and snorkel trips use two-person inflatable Diveyaks, which are stable and easy to maneuver, in groups of eight with never more than four divers, accompanied by a dive master. Kayak scuba $60; kayak snorkel $40. Morning trips only, departing at 9:30 a.m., returning about 1:30 p.m.

Tennis About three dozen hotels here have tennis courts. Those closest to the West Indian Company Dock and open to nonguests are at **Frenchman's Reef & Morning Star Marriott Beach Resort** (776-8500), two courts, $10 per hour. Courts nearest to Crown Bay Dock are two public ones, lighted until 10:00 p.m.

Windsurfing Morningstar Beach is nearest the West Indian Company Dock, but the eastern end of the island has the best windsurfing. **Sap-**phire Beach (775-6100) offers instruction on a simulator and instruction in the water. **West Indies Windsurfing** (775-6530), on the beach in Red Hook, has the best rentals.

On the southside of Red Hook, Vessup, known locally as **Bluebeard's Beach,** is a popular venue for windsurfing contests.

Cultural Events and Festivals

The Virgin Islands observe all the U.S. national holidays, plus a few of their own. Leading the list is **Carnival,** which on St. Thomas is held during the last two weeks of April. It begins officially with a weeklong calypso competition for the coveted title of the Calypso King; followed by a week of festivities with the crowning of a Carnival Queen and an elaborate all-day parade featuring the Mocko Jumbi Dancers.

Reichhold Center for the Performing Arts (693-1559; www.reichholdcenter.com) offers a year-round schedule of concerts, opera, ballet, Broadway musicals, jazz, gospel, and plays at its wonderful outdoor theater.

St. John: A Gift of Nature

www.stjohnisland.com
www.gotostjohn.com

Serene St. John, the least developed of the U.S. Virgin Islands, is truly America the Beautiful. Almost two-thirds of the heavily forested, mountainous island—9,485 acres—is covered by national park on land donated in 1956 by Laurance Rockefeller. The island is edged by lovely coves with pristine, white-sand beaches and some of the most spectacular aquamarine waters in the Caribbean. Beneath these waters is a tropical wonderland, also protected by the park.

Development is restricted; it has occurred mainly in the area of the lilliputian port of Cruz Bay and in the southwest corner. On the north coast is the superdeluxe Caneel Bay, set on an old sugar plantation in the magnificent gardens fronting seven—yes, seven—of the prettiest beaches in the Caribbean. The tennis facilities are great, too.

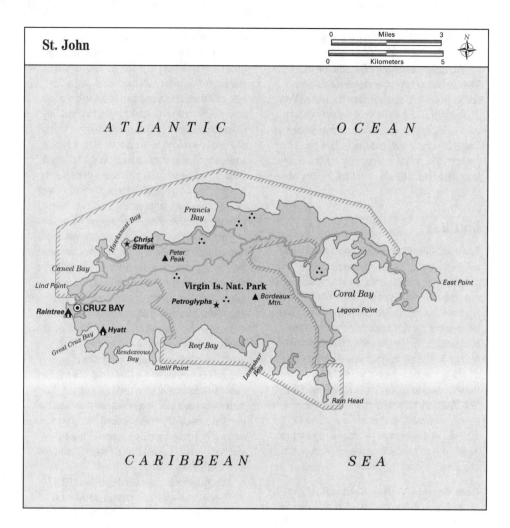

St. John map showing locations including Francis Bay, Hawksnest Bay, Christ Statue, Peter Peak, Caneel Bay, Lind Point, Raintree, CRUZ BAY, Hyatt, Great Cruz Bay, Rendezvous Bay, Dittlif Point, Reef Bay, Virgin Is. Nat. Park, Petroglyphs, Bordeaux Mtn., Coral Bay, Lagoon Point, East Point, Lameshur Bay, Ram Head, with the Atlantic Ocean to the north and Caribbean Sea to the south.

Several cruise ships call at St. John, but the majority of its visitors come on day trips from St. Thomas; it is one of the most delightful excursions available for cruise passengers, whether as an organized tour, a day sail, or on your own. The day's target for most visitors is a circle route along North Shore Road (Route 20) and Centerline Road (Route 10), the two main roads, with stops for a swim, picnic, and short hikes.

Ferry Service Ferries depart Red Hook hourly from 6:30 a.m. to midnight for Cruz Bay and return from 6:00 a.m. to 11:00 p.m. One-way fare is $5. Others depart from the Charlotte Amalie waterfront at two-hour intervals from 9:00 a.m. to 5:30 p.m. Cost is $11 one-way and takes forty-five minutes.

There is also ferry service from St. John to Jost Van Dyke and Tortola, B.V.I.

Transportation Taxis with driver/guides can be hired in Cruz Bay at the pier, or you can rent a car or jeep for about $55 per day. A two-hour island tour costs $45 for one or two persons, $16 per person for three or more. Several St. Thomas tour companies provide service in St. John and combine the two islands into one package. Drivers take and return you to the ferry docks on both islands. After a tour of St. John, your driver leaves you at a beach to fetch you later. St. John has new buses, including a van for disabled passengers and senior citizens. The service operates hourly from Cruz Bay and Coral Bay from 5:30 a.m. to 8:30 p.m. Fares are

$1 for the bus, $4 to $24 for the van, depending on location. Call 776-6346.

St. John Community Foundation (693-693-9410; www.sjcf.org) offers tours for mobility restricted visitors, sponsored by the United Way St. Thomas/St. John and Virgin Islands Department of Human Services. They operate weekdays from 8:30 a.m. to 4:30 p.m. Rates: $18 per person per hour, $12 per person per hour for groups of four. The accessible van has space for two wheelchairs.

Cruz Bay

Tiny, yacht-filled Cruz Bay hugs a narrow strip of land between the harbor and the mountains. Most of the buildings and houses are West Indian–style in architecture and painted a medley of pastel colors. Until recently the structures were small and blended into the landscape as naturally as the bougainvillea. Regretfully, new construction is drastically altering the character of the town by crowding the space around the harbor and turning the once-natural setting into a tacky T-shirt and fast-food mall. Nonetheless, the town—three streets wide and four streets deep—is worth exploring and easy to do on foot. Facing the pier is a park, and on its north are the Taxi Association and Tourist Information Center.

Park Service Visitor Center Northwest of the harbor is the Virgin Islands National Park Service Visitor Center (www.nps.gov), open from 8:00 a.m. to 4:30 p.m. The center is well organized and offers a variety of activities, including ranger-led tours, hikes, snorkeling trips, cultural and wildlife lectures, and film presentations. A schedule is available in advance from the park service (776-6201, ext. 238). Reservations during the winter season are strongly recommended. The park's user fee is $4 per person. Information is also available from **Friends of the Park** (779-4940; www.friendsvinp .org), which holds a variety of interesting workshops and educational excursions during the winter season.

Hikes and Tours *Trail Guide for Safe Hiking* is a park brochure outlining twenty-one trails with a map and tips on preparations. Most trails are designed in clusters of two or three contiguous paths to be taken in segments as short as ten minutes, or, when strung together, as long as two to four hours. The most popular is Reef Bay, a 2.5-mile trail that takes about two hours to cover in a downhill direction. The park ranger–led Reef Bay hike is available at 10:00 a.m. on Monday, Thursday, and Friday for $15 per person. Hikers must arrange their own transportation to the trailhead. Taxis ($7 per person) can take hikers there; local buses, too. At the end of the trail, the Park Service ferries hikers back to its dock in Cruz Bay. Reservations required: 776-6201, ext. 238.

Among the historic programs is the Annaberg Cultural Demonstrations (three hours), which visits the partially restored ruins of the Annaberg Plantation, where you can learn about tropical food, plants, weaving, baking, charcoal making, and other skills islanders once needed to subsist.

Cruise-ship excursions usually stop at Trunk Bay, a lovely beach on the north shore, about twenty minutes from town and the site of an underwater trail laid out for snorkelers by the Park Service. Unfortunately, the reef is now badly deteriorated from overuse. Snorkelers and divers on their own have many other reefs around St. John to explore. At Honeymoon Beach, one of the palm-studded coves of Caneel Bay, snorkelers can swim with spotted eagle rays.

Thunderhawk Trail Guides (774-1112; 774-1030), specializing in hiking tours, provides two-hour guided tours of St. John's nature trails from Cruz Bay to Lind Point, Honeymoon Beach, and the Caneel Hill spur trail. Guides provide information on history and culture of the Taino Indians, the island's ancient inhabitants.

The National Park Service (776-6201) offers a Culture Walk at Cinnamon Bay Tuesdays from 9:30 a.m. to 10:30 a.m. and a Waters Edge Walk every Wednesday from 10:30 a.m. to noon that meets at Leinster Bay trailhead. The snorkeling trip at Trunk Bay operates every Monday from 9:30 a.m. to 10:30 a.m.; bird watching at the Francis Bay trailhead goes on every Sunday from 7:30 a.m. to 9:00 a.m.; and a full-day, guided Reef Bay hike occurs from 9:30 a.m. to 3:00 p.m. on Mondays and Thursdays.

Shopping

St. John's beauty and tranquility have made it something of an artists' community. Several artists have stores in town sandwiched between the T-shirt and junky-merchandise shops.

The **Pink Papaya** (Lemon Tree Mall; 693-8535; www.pinkpapaya.com) is the gallery and gift shop of Virgin Islands artist Lisa Etre, whose distinctive style reflects her West Indian environment in a sophisticated way. In addition to original paintings and prints, elements from her drawings are used in designs on tableware, greeting cards, and lovely gifts.

Mongoose Junction (www.mongoosejunction stjohn.com), a ten-minute walk north of the pier, is a shopping plaza designed as an artist's enclave with rustic wooden buildings incorporating the trees in a natural setting. You will probably want to browse, as each shop is different. Among the boutique/studios of local artists and transplanted mainlanders, **Donald Schnell Studio** (800-253-7107) features ceramics of natural materials—coral sand, woods—by an American artist who comes originally from Michigan. **The Clothing Studio** (776-6210; www.clothingstudio.com) has handpainted tropical wear from $6 T-shirts to $150 dresses. **Fabric Mill,** belonging to interior designer Trisha Maize, carries unusual fabrics and accessories. **Bajo El Sol Gallery/Under the Sun** (Reef Building, 2nd Level, 866-593-7070; 593-7070; www .bajoelsolgallery.com) is one of St. John's largest galleries, featuring Caribbean-inspired original art, prints, jewelry, and crafts. **Sea Leathers & Antique Jewels** (777-6850) carries an unusual array of goods made from skins such as salmon and eel.

South of the pier, **Wharfside Village** (www .wharfsidevillage.com) is a multilevel mall of West Indian–style structures awash in cool pastels, with more than forty shops and restaurants. **Freebird Creations** (693-8625; www.freebirdcreations.com), one of the island's longest-established businesses, sells unusual and many one-of-a-kind jewelry crafted by Caribbean artists. **The Balcony at Cruz Bay** (774-8470) (formerly Pusser's Landing) offers a Euro-Caribe fusion menu with fresh seafood from local waters.

The **Marketplace** (Cruz Bay; 776-6455) is a shopping center with a variety of stores and services. Built in native stone and mahogany, with verandas and courtyards, the center is anchored by the **Starfish Market** (779-4949) and **St. John Hardware** (693-8780). Other stores include the **Artists' Association of St. John Gallery** (774-2275; www.stjohnarts.org), **Surf da Web Cyber Cafe, Baked in the Sun, Chelsea Drug Store** (776-4888), and **Book & Bean** (779-2665), among others.

The **Kareso** (Cruz Bay; 714-5511) art gallery exhibits local art, including paintings by owner Karen Samuel, whose contemporary style features island landscapes and people. The gallery also has her brother's turn-wood pieces, such as bowls, vases, and other decorative items made from exotic tropical hardwoods. The gallery sells local handmade baskets, painted clothing, photography, watercolors, prints, and furniture. Open daily.

Dining

Asolare (Cruz Bay; 779-4747; www.stjohn restaurants.com) is an island favorite for Pacific Rim cuisine, which can be enjoyed along with spectacular views. Moderately expensive.

Chilly Billy's Lumberyard Café (Lumberyard Shopping Center, Boulon Center Road; 693-8708), a sandwich shop by day, gets transformed in the evening into an intimate French restaurant, seating only twenty-four people, at 6:00 and 8:00 p.m. Open Monday to Saturday, reservations recommended. Moderately expensive.

Happy Fish (The Marketplace; 776-1717) is a new popular sushi and martini bar open for lunch Monday through Friday 10:30 a.m. to 2:00 p.m. and for dinner daily 5:00 to 10:00 p.m. Nightly music entertainment as well as kung fu movies. Moderately expensive.

The Lime Inn (Lemon Tree Mall, Cruz Bay; 776-6425) serves lunch and dinner in a tropical setting and features fresh fish, charcoal steaks, and creative specials. Moderate.

Panini Beach Trattoria (Wharfside Village; 779-9119; www.paninibeach.com). Evening dining on homemade pastas and Northern Italian specialties. Bar opens at 3:00 p.m.; Sunday brunch. Moderately expensive.

Stone Terrace (Cruz Bay; 693-9370; www .stoneterrace.com), a restaurant housed in a beautiful stone building by owners of the popular **Fish Trap** (693-9994; www.thefishtrap.com) restaurant (Raintree Court), serves international cuisine. The menu features seasonal specialties. Diners are seated along a covered archway and awning-covered side terrace with harbor views.

Tage (Cruz Bay; 715-4270; www.tagestjohn .com). The restaurant (formerly Patios) belongs to Ted Robinson, one of the island's best-known chefs, long associated with Paradiso. His ambitious fusion menu (posted on his Web site) includes such creations as pan-seared yellowfin tuna; roasted day-boat scallops; pear-fennel-arugula breast stuffed with Black Forest ham and basil; and more. Open Monday to Saturday 6:00 to 9:30 p.m. Moderately expensive.

Sports

Horseback Riding Carolina Corral (693-5778; www.st-john.com/trailrides) offers horse and donkey rides by the hour or half-day with guide. Little instruction is given, and trails are steep and narrow. Cost: $75 for ninety-minute ride; $55 for children age twelve and younger. Carriage rides are also available.

Kayaking The sport of kayaking is very popular in St. John and available from several operators, who for $50 offer guided tours of the beautiful coastal waters with time for swimming, snorkeling, and exploring isolated beaches accessible only by boat. **Low Key Watersports** (800-835-7718; 693-8999; www.divelowkey.com) will tailor the trip to your interest.

Arawak Expeditions (P.O. Box 853, Cruz Bay, St. John; 800-238-8687; 693-8312; www.arawak exp.com) offers guided kayaking and mountain-biking excursions to remote parts of St. John and nearby islands. No previous experience is necessary. Full-day (six hours) kayaking excursion leaves from Cruz Bay at 10:00 a.m. to Henley Cay for snorkeling and to Lovango Cay for lunch and more snorkeling. Cost is $90 per person including lunch. Half-day (three hours) excursions depart at 9:00

a.m. and 2:00 p.m. for Henley Cay or other snorkeling spot; $50.

Biking tours on front-suspension Cannondale mountain bikes offer several routes. Half-day (three hours) 9:00 a.m. and 2:00 p.m., $50, is good for beginners who will see beautiful scenery, historic ruins, and learn about St. John's flora and fauna, plus enjoy swimming at a beach along the way. Full-day (six hours) departs at 10:00 a.m., $90, with stops for snorkeling and picnic lunch.

Water Sports Low Key Watersports (Cruz Bay, St. John; 800-835-7718; 693-8999; www .divelowkey.com) offers reef and wreck dives departing daily at 8:30 a.m. Cost is $88, including gear, for a two-tank dive. Resort course is $85. The operator offers a customized package for minimum of four people. The day sail is $110 with lunch; sportsfishing charter, $495 for half day; $895 for full day. **Cruz Bay Watersports** (Box 252, St. John 00830; 776-6234; www.divestjohn.com) has similar programs as well as day sails with snorkeling, drinks, and lunch for $120. For information: www .divestjohn.com. For a new experience, try snuba. It's something like scuba without the serious gear. Snuba of St. John (Trunk Bay; 693-8063; www. visnuba.com) has daily guided tours, starting at 9:30 a.m., for $65 plus the $4 National Park entrance fee.

St. Croix: The Sleeping Virgin

www.gotostcroix.com

St. Croix, 40 miles south of St. Thomas, is the largest of the U.S. Virgin Islands and served as the capital for more than two hundred years, but today it is less developed and generally less known to tourists than St. Thomas.

St. Croix has much to offer: scenery, sightseeing, sports, shopping, historic towns, pretty beaches, good restaurants, and some attractions that not even St. Thomas or St. John can boast. It has two 18-hole golf courses, a "rain forest," botanic gardens, wildlife refuges for birds and leatherback turtles, and three parks, including the only underwater park in the U.S. National Park Service.

A low-lying island of gentle landscape and

rolling hills, St. Croix is vastly different from its mountainous sisters. From the time Columbus sighted the island in 1493 to the United States' purchase in 1917, it saw seven flags fly over the land. Whereas St. Thomas prospered on trade, St. Croix became a rich sugar producer and developed a plantation society that prevailed long after the abolition of slavery. Today many of the sugar mills and plantation homes have been restored as hotels and restaurants; and the colonial hearts of Christiansted, the main town, and Frederiksted, the old capital, are on the National Historic Registry.

Frederiksted, on the west coast, has a deep-water harbor used by most cruise lines and is convenient to popular attractions included on most shore excursions. Christiansted, 17 miles east of Frederiksted on the north shore, has a pretty yacht-filled harbor trimmed by a colorful, historic waterfront anchored by a grand fort—all beautifully restored. Although Christiansted is more developed than Frederiksted for shopping, restaurants, and water sports, unless the harbor is dredged, it is limited to receiving small, shallow draft ships—a situation many local people prefer.

St. Croix has good roads and transportation, and travel is easy regardless of which port is used. Your ship's port of call can, however, influence your selection of activities by its proximity and convenience to certain attractions. A more serious limitation is the length of time your ship is in port. Often ships calling at Frederiksted arrive about 7:00 or 8:00 a.m. and depart by 1:00 or 2:00 p.m. Such brief stopovers restrict tours to 3 or 3.5 hours and limit the range of possibilities.

Most ships offer **St. Croix Island Tour** (3.5 hours, $31; or by taxi, $60) and a **Buck Island Tour** ($60 to $90, depending on the boat and duration of the excursion).

In addition to sailing ($49), beach party ($33), shopping ($11), and diving for certified divers ($74), passengers can snorkel or learn to snorkel ($23 and $32) or get initiated to diving ($40), take a 12-mile guided bike tour ($49), a walking tour of Frederiksted and the Botanical Gardens ($36), or a nature hike in the western, forest-clad mountains ($40).

For those on their first visit who prefer to travel on their own, we recommend an island tour, preferably by taxi with a driver/guide. It is not worthwhile renting a car unless your ship remains in port for a full day. A shuttle bus is usually available between the Frederiksted pier and Christiansted; a taxi between the two towns is $20. The average charge for a three-hour tour for one to four persons is $100.

Taxi and tour prices are posted at the Visitor's Bureau office by the pier. **The St. Croix Combined Taxi and Tour Association** (Box 2439, Frederiksted, USVI 00841; 772-2828; fax: 772-3718) has more than seventy-five members, who must take tourism/guide refresher courses every six months. Maurice Hamilton (772-1180) drives a minivan and makes a particularly pleasant and knowledgeable guide.

St. Croix Safari Tours (773-6700; www.goto stcroix.com/safaritours) offers rides in colorful open-air safari buses with a covered top and visits to the island's main heritage sites. Sweeny is probably the best-known guide in the Virgin Islands, with extensive knowledge of St. Croix. **Tan Tan Tours** (473-6446; www.stxtantantours.com) and owner Wave Phillip take you off the beaten path by Jeep to parts of St. Croix only accessible with four-wheel drive.

St. Croix Environmental Association (773-1989; www.stxenvironmental.org) offers nature hikes into the rain forest, snorkel trips, bird-watching tours, turtle nesting and hatchling watches, and stargazing.

Caribbean Tour Services (776-3650; www .caribbeantourservices.com) takes you biking through Frederiksted and along the western beaches, stopping to admire a sugar mill and several great houses and to hear about the island's history. **AirVentures in Paradise** (277-1433; www.airventuresinparadise.com) can take you flight-seeing.

Frederiksted

A Williamsburg in the Making

Frederiksted was an almost deserted town in the 1970s, but federal legislation granting tax benefits to historic preservation galvanized community action, and many old buildings were renovated. Despite the setback of Hurricane Hugo in 1989, city fathers dream of someday making Frederiksted a

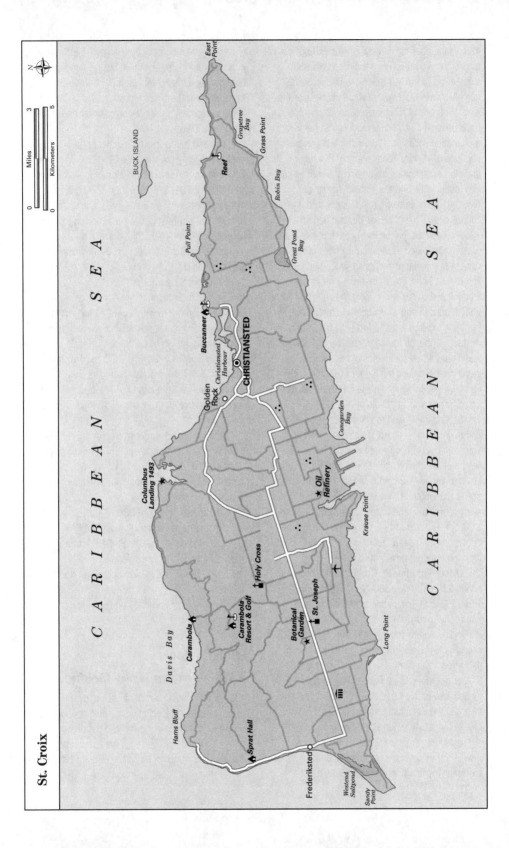

Williamsburg of the Caribbean. But more recently Frederiksted has had another setback—when most of the cruise lines pulled out, saying passengers preferred to visit St. Thomas. Some small ships still do call occasionally in Frederiksted, and the Cruzans hope the large ships will return in the future. Cruise passengers have a choice of staying close to town to enjoy the beach and stroll through its historic center, taking an island tour, or enjoying a specific sport—diving, horseback riding, golf, or hiking.

The old district of Frederiksted, directly in front of the pier, is laid out in a grid running 7 blocks from Fort Frederik and the Customs House on the north, to the Library and Queen Cross Street on the south, and 5 blocks deep from the waterfront (Strand Street) east to Prince Street. **Fort Frederik,** which dates from 1752, was the site of the emancipation of the slaves in 1848. Other important buildings include **Government House,** built in 1747; **St. Paul's Anglican Church,** 1817; and **St. Patrick's Roman Catholic Church,** 1848. Many historic homes and commercial buildings line the old streets.

Sandy Point National Wildlife Refuge Just 3 miles south of Frederiksted is a protected area that is one of only two nesting grounds for the leatherback turtle in the United States. From March through June the enormous turtles—up to 6 feet in length and 1,000 pounds in weight—come ashore to dig holes where each lays as many as eighty eggs. Afterward they cover the eggs with sand for protection and lumber back to the sea, returning to repeat the ritual as many as six times during nesting season. After about two months the hatchlings emerge from the sand pits and dash to the sea under the cover of night. Earthwatch, a U.S.–based, nonprofit research organization, and the St. Croix Environmental Association (773-1989; www.stx environmental.org) maintain a turtle watch in which visitors can participate from April through June and in August. Reservations must be made in advance. Inquiries should be made to the association. The group also conducts guided environmental tours.

St. Croix Heritage Trail (713-8563; www .stcroixheritagetrail.com), a self-guided tour of the island's historic and cultural heritage, is entertaining as well as enlightening. Named one of fifty national Millennium Legacy Trails by the White House Millennium Council, the St. Croix Heritage Trail traverses the entire 28-mile length of St. Croix, from Frederiksted on the west end to Point Udall, the easternmost point of the United States, and links the history of the island's diverse inhabitants, and agricultural and historic attractions.

The Heritage Trail traces St. Croix's evolution, which was influenced by a variety of nationalities—European planters and merchants, African slaves, free people of color, Caribbean immigrants, and American settlers—that have lived here during the past 350 years and have profoundly shaped the island's history and culture.

With a trail map, and following the Heritage Trail road signs, travelers can explore the island on a self-guided driving tour, stopping at places of interest. They can also learn about the island's oral traditions, music, and food. Some sites charge an admission fee. Trail brochures with maps are available at the U.S. Virgin Islands Department of Tourism offices and select island locations. The St. Croix Heritage Trail, supported by the USVI Department of Tourism, the St. Croix Landmarks Society (www.stcroixlandmarks.com), and many St. Croix businesses, also has trail maps and highlights on its Web site.

Christiansted
The Picture-Perfect Port

Christiansted is one of the Caribbean's prettiest little towns. In an area of about 5 square blocks, you will find some of the best-preserved and most interesting landmarks in the Virgin Islands. Alongside them are shops, making it easy to combine a walking tour with a shopping excursion.

Scalehouse Scalehouse, once part of the Customs House where goods were weighed for tax purposes, now houses an information office connected to the national park. The building is thought to date from 1855. In 1989 the winds and sea surge of Hurricane Hugo were so powerful they lifted the base of the heavy scales out of the ground. Hours: weekdays 8:00 a.m. to 5:00 p.m.

Fort Christian Overlooking the harbor is the best preserved of the five Danish forts in the West

Indies. Built in 1749, Fort Christian is now under the supervision of the U.S. National Park Service. You can get a brochure for a self-guided tour, and park rangers who know their history well are on hand to answer questions and provide fascinating tidbits not available in brochures. For one thing, they'll show you the cell where Alexander Hamilton's mother was jailed for her "improprieties." Tut tut! New interpretive exhibits have been installed in some of the rooms to demonstrate life in the fort in the mid-eighteenth century. Hours: weekdays 8:00 a.m. to 4:45 p.m.; weekends and holidays 9:00 a.m. to 4:45 p.m.

Between the fort and Scalehouse is the old Customs House and Post Office, built in 1751. It is used now as a library.

Government House One block west on King Street, an imposing eighteenth-century town house that was built as a private home was later used as the residence and offices of the Danish governor. A handsome outside staircase leads to a beautiful ballroom on the first floor. In 2000 a six-year restoration project was completed, adding air-conditioning, elevators, and other modern conveniences.

Steeple Building The first church the Danes built after acquiring St. Croix in 1733 stands at the corner of Church and Company Streets. Completed in 1750, it was a Lutheran church until 1831, and afterward served as a school, hospital, and storehouse. It now has a small museum with Amerindian and other types of artifacts.

Nearby, the new **St. Croix Archeological Museum** (Company Street; 692-2365) has exhibits of ritualistic, ceremonial, and utilitarian artifacts found on St. Croix that date back to 2000 B.C. and continue up to the Taino culture (A.D. 1200–1492) at the time of Columbus. Shell and stone tools, ceramics, hammer and polishing stones, and chisels are but some of the items on display. Entrance: $4.

Buck Island The Buck Island Reef National Monument (www.nps.gov/buis), 3.5 miles northeast of St. Croix, is a volcanic rock of about 300 acres surrounded by 550 acres of underwater coral gardens of unusual beauty and scientific interest. The reef around Buck Island makes up the only underwater park in the U.S. National Park Service. A Park Service pamphlet explains the reef and pic-

tures some of the fish that swimmers are likely to see; it is usually distributed to participants of snorkeling excursions.

Glass-bottom boats, catamarans, and motorboats with snorkeling equipment operate daily from King's Wharf in Christiansted to Buck Island. (See snorkeling in the Sports section.) The ride to Buck Island takes about thirty minutes. The time spent at the reef is usually an hour, but it can be longer, depending on your interest.

A Drive around St. Croix

A driving tour by bus or car is usually made in a circular fashion from Frederiksted to Christiansted via Mahogany Road (Route 76), a scenic east-west road through the rain forest, a stretch of lush tropical vegetation very different from the rest of the island. The return uses Centerline Road, the island's main east-west highway, convenient for stops at three of St. Croix's main attractions. In the I-have-to-see-it-to-believe-it department, you can watch the world-famous beer-drinking pigs at the **Mt. Pellier Hut Domino Club** (722-9914), a restaurant/bar on Mahogany Road in the forest. The original beer-drinker has passed on to pig heaven, but her siblings and offspring are carrying on the family tradition without missing a can.

St. George Village Botanical Garden On the north side of Centerline Road, about 5 miles east of Frederiksted, are sixteen acres of tropical gardens, landscaped around the ruins of a Danish sugar-plantation workers' village dating from the eighteenth and nineteenth centuries. The garden began in 1972 as a cleanup project of the local garden club, but when the debris was cleared away, the members recognized the site as one of historic significance. Archaeologists excavated the area and found beneath the colonial ruins an Arawak settlement dating from A.D. 100 to 900. It is believed to have been the largest of the ninety-six Indian villages that existed on St. Croix at the time of Columbus.

Designed to incorporate the colonial ruins, the garden combines natural growth, landscaped plantings, and open land. The standout is the cactus garden.

Among the restored ruins you will see the bake oven, which is operating again, and the blacksmith's shop, where volunteer smiths using original tools produce items sold in the gift shop. An excellent map is available, and walkways are signposted for self-guided tours. The garden is open daily. Admission is $8 adults, $6 seniors, $1 children. The garden (127 Estate, St. George; 692-2874; www.sgvbg.org) is privately supported and volunteer managed.

Cruzan Rum Distillery At the pavilion of the Virgin Islands' leading rum maker, visitors are offered a free tour, rum cocktails, and recipe booklets. Tours run weekdays from 9:00 to 11:30 a.m. and 1:00 to 4:00 p.m. Call 692-2280 or visit www.cruzanrum.com.

Whim Greathouse St. Croix's pride is Whim Greathouse, a restoration project of the St. Croix Landmarks Society (www.stcroixlandmarks.com). The beautifully restored plantation house, built in 1803, is furnished with lovely antiques; and the old kitchens, mill, and other buildings give visitors a good picture of life on a sugar plantation in the eighteenth and nineteenth centuries. You will also see the cook house, bathhouse, apothecary, 1856 steam engines, animal mill, windmill, boiling shed, rum still, and sugar factory. It has a museum, gift shop, and furniture showroom. Hours: daily 10:00 a.m. to 4:00 p.m. For information, call 772-0598. Admission with guided tour: $10 adults, $4 children. The society offers tours of historic homes annually in February and March. In March it stages an annual antiques auction.

Lawaetz Museum Another of the St. Croix Landmarks Society's project is **Estate Little La Grange,** where an exhibit of St. Croix life in its sugar production heyday can be seen in the eighteenth-century estate house. The manor is furnished with antiques and heirlooms of the Lawaetz family, who have lived on the estate since the family arrived in St. Croix from Denmark in 1890. The grounds also have the remains of a windmill, mill, and the only aqueduct on the island. Guided tours: Tuesday to Saturday 10:00 a.m. to 3:00 p.m. Tours cost $8 adults, $4 children. For information: 722-1539. A 2-mile walking trail has been added and is part of the St. Croix Heritage Trail. With the help of interpretive signs, brochures, and an information kiosk, visitors can learn about the cultural significance of the trees and other vegetation along the trail. Concurrently, the Museum Tree Documentation Project is making an inventory of the trees at both the **Lawaetz Museum** and **Estate Whim Plantation.**

Cramer Park and Point Udall The eastern end of St. Croix with Point Udall is covered by Cramer Park, a dry, low-lying area that is a marked contrast to the western end. The park has a public beach with changing rooms and bathrooms. Point Udall is also the easternmost extension of the United States in the Western Hemisphere.

St. Croix East End Marine Park (773-3320; www.viczmp.com; www.stxeastendmarinepark.org.) In 2003 the Virgin Islands Department of Planning and National Resources created a new marine park to protect a 60-square-mile area along St. Croix's easternmost tip. Legislative approval recently made the area an official (and the first) territorial park, encompassing a magnificent barrier reef less than .5 mile offshore and home to a great array of fish, sponges, coral heads, and patch reefs. The park covers one of St. Croix's few remaining mangrove systems located at Great Pond, and it includes a turtle preserve that protects a variety of endangered species that nest on its beaches. Leatherbacks and green and hawksbill turtles populate the remote beaches throughout the year. The park will be open to the public for swimming and diving; fishing will be allowed in select areas only. An Interpretive Center at Cramer Park is planned.

Casino On the southeastern shores of St. Croix at Grapetree Bay, the **Divi Carina Bay Beach Resort,** which opened in mid-1999 after extensive renovation, has St. Croix's and the Virgin Islands' first casino. The 15,400-square-foot gaming room, operated by Treasure Bay Corp., a Mississippi casino company, has 386 slot machines and 20 table games, as well as two restaurants and three snack bars, gift shop, live entertainment, and complimentary high-speed Internet service.

Columbus Landing Site and the Salt River Bay National Park On the north shore at the mouth of the Salt River, Salt River Bay is an estuary, an important Arawak Indian site, a major dive location, and the site of Columbus's landing. The site was designated a national park in 1992 to commemorate the Columbus Quincentennial. Southeast of the estuary at Triton Bay, the Nature Conservancy has a twelve-acre preserve.

Shopping

St. Croix's best shopping is in Christiansted, where eighteenth- and nineteenth-century warehouses have been made into attractive, palm-shaded shopping plazas. The streets paralleling King Street—Company Street on the east, Strand Street on the west—also have attractive shops. The historic buildings around Market Square, between Company and Queen Streets, have been renovated and house many smart shops. Shopping in Frederiksted is limited, but a few Christiansted stores have branches there. Cruzans, as the people of St. Croix are called, maintain that their prices are better than those in St. Thomas because they do not have to pay St. Thomas's high rents or the high commission demanded by some cruise directors.

Art and Artists St. Croix has an active art community of local artists and mainlanders who live there part of the year. But since artists and galleries come and go, you should consult *St. Croix This Week* (773-9864; www.stcroixthis week.com) for a current list of artists and galleries. The **Yellow House** (3A Queen Cross Street; 719-6656; www.judithkingart.com) is the studio-gallery of artist Judith King, who works in bright, colorful acrylics. The shop also has handmade jewelry and a small collection of works by other local artists. Hours: Monday to Saturday 10:00 a.m. to 5:00 p.m. **Danica Art Gallery** (54 King Street; 719-6000; www.danicaartvi.com) is owned by St. Croix–born artist Danica David and showcases original art, including jewelry, pottery, clocks, tiles, and mahogany sculptures by David and several other local artists. Hours: Monday to Friday 11:00 a.m. to 5:00 p.m. **Maria Henle Studio** (55 Company Street; 773-0372; www.maria henlestudio.com) in the historic inn upstairs above Indies Restaurant, has a permanent exhibit of the late owner/artist's paintings and a display of photographs by her famous father, the late Fritz Henle, a leading recorder of Caribbean scenes. Hours: Monday to Saturday 10:00 a.m. to 5:00 p.m.

Some artists can be visited at their studio by appointment: **Campen Gallery** (Estate Pearl; 719-2246; www.betsycampen.com) features the work of photo-realist artist Betsy Campen, who portrays the St. Croix scene, particularly its flora. **Mitchell–Larsen Studio** (Company Street; 719-1000; www .janmitchellcollection.com) is the home of the delightful artistry in glass by Jan Mitchell. Visitors can watch the work in progress and shop for gifts in the setting of a historic building. Upstairs, in a historic town house, the **Christiansted Gallery** (1 Company Street; 773-4443) is a showcase for local art, including original works and prints, along with paintings by artist/gallery owner Marjorie P. Robbins. Hours: Monday to Friday 10:00 a.m. to 4:00 p.m.; Saturday 11:00 a.m. to 2:00 p.m.

Akin Studio (713-8419) showcases watercolors by St. Croix resident Jane Akin. The artist's depiction of tropical flora and architectural subjects captures the elegant essence of the Caribbean. By appointment. Local artist **Mark Austin**'s creations include handpainted furniture and buckets, sculpture, original paintings, prints, and more. He works from home.

In Frederiksted, **Island Webe** (across the pier; 772-2555) is the permanent home of the colorful works of Caribbean-born artist Joffre George. The gallery features works in various media by other local artists as well. You may also want to visit the **Caribbean Museum Center** (10 Strand Street; 772-2622; www.cmcarts.org). Hours: Thursday to Saturday 10:00 a.m. to 4:00 p.m.

And don't forget, original works of art are exempt from customs duty and do not count in your $1,600 exemption.

Books/Maps The Bookie (3 Strand Street) sells books and periodicals. **Church Street General Store** has cards and a bit of everything, as does **St. Croix Landmark Museum Store** (6 Company Street).

China/Crystal Baci (55 Company Street) has quality English china, French crystal, Swiss watches, Hummel figurines, and other gift items.

Clothing/Sportswear Quiet Storm (1108 King Street; www.quietstormshop.com) specializes in Tommy Banana and Lily Pulitzer fashions, but don't expect cheap prices. **PacifiCotton** (Strand Street) features sportswear of 100 percent cotton for women and children. **The Gecko Boutique** (1233 Queen Cross Street; 778-9433; www.fromthe gecko.com) features hand-crafted jewelry, accessories, and exclusive clothing lines for the whole family, including the handpainted Sloop Jones Collection made on St. John.

Crafts Many Hands (Pan Am Pavilion; 773-1990; www.manyhands-gifts.com) displays handcrafts by three hundred artisans living in the Virgin Islands. The products range from jewelry and ceramics to sculpture and paintings. The **St. Croix Landmarks Society Museum Store** (52 Estate Whim Frederiksted; 772-0598; www.stcroixlandmarks.com) has a wide selection of West Indian crafts, art prints, teak furniture reproductions, maps, and home furnishings. Open Monday to Saturday 10:00 a.m. to 4:00 p.m. **St. Croix Leap** (Mahogany Road, Route 76; 772-0421) is a great place to stop if you are touring the eastern end of the island. You can watch crafters make bowls, vases, and other practical home products from native woods. The items can be purchased. Crafts and original art are duty-free upon your return through U.S. Customs.

Tesoro (36C Strand Street; 773-1212) carries a wide range of Haitian art and crafts from the Dominican Republic. **Gone Tropical** (5 Company Street; 773-4696) is stuffed floor to ceiling with interesting crafts and art from Indonesia, India, the Philippines, Africa, and other exotic places, which the owner, Margot Meacham, selects herself. **The Royal Ponciana** (1111 Strand Street; 773-9892) stocks crafts and locally made soaps, herbs, and spices. Not to be overlooked is the **Whim Plantation Museum** gift shop, which has a very good selection of fine gifts and crafts.

Jewelry Sonya Ltd. (1 Company Street; 773-8924; www.sonyaltd.com) specializes in hand-wrought gold and silver jewelry, as does **Crucian Gold** (Strand Sreet; www.cruciangold.com).

If you need a watch repaired, stop by **Patrick's Watches** (King's Alley Walk; 773-7882). **The Caribbean Bracelet Company** (King's Alley Walk; 773-9110) specializes in silver bracelets with a horseshoe clasp that has come to be known as the "St. Croix" design, though it was not originated

here. The bracelets, which make nice gifts to take home, come in all sizes, from those small enough for a child to those for a large adult, and vary in price from $20 and up. An explanation of the design is included with every purchase.

Perfume Violette Boutique (Caravelle Arcade; 773-2148) has as complete a selection as any store in town—and at competitive prices. You can call ahead for a price list: (800) 544-5912.

In the shopping plazas and at the King Christian Hotel facing the waterfront, there are car-rental firms and water-sports operators who make excursions to Buck Island and offer diving and other sports.

Dining

In Frederiksted Le St. Tropez (Limetree Court, 67 King Street; 772-3000) is a pleasant outdoor bistro whose French owner offers tasty fare with a Mediterranean flavor. Moderate.

In Christiansted In addition to the longtime favorite **Kendrick's** (773-9199; www.gotostcroix .com/kendricks), **The Avocado Pitt** (on the boardwalk; 773-9843), is a casual addition to the downtown restaurant scene and offers a diverse menu for breakfast and lunch. Burgers, sandwiches, and vegetarian selections are also available, as are takeout and boxed lunches. Open 8:00 a.m. to 5:00 p.m. daily. Moderately expensive. **Bacchus** (Queen Cross; 692-9922), upstairs in a historic town house in the heart of town, offers fine dining daily from 6:00 to 10:00 p.m. and stocks a large selection of fine wines. The menu emphasizes hand-carved prime cuts of beef, fresh local seafood, lobster, and vegetarian selections. Reservations recommended. Expensive. **Cafe Christine** (6 Company Street; 713-1500), located in the back of a small courtyard, is open Monday to Friday for lunch only from 11:30 a.m. to 2:30 p.m. and serves the best food in St. Croix. The blackboard menu changes daily and includes excellent salads with unusual combinations and freshly baked pies by a great chef. Inexpensive. **Off the Wall** (778-4771; www.offthe wall.com) is a beach bar serving seafood, pizza, sandwiches, and snacks. Open daily. **Rum Runners Steaks & Seafood** (Hotel Caravelle; 773-

6585; www.RumRunnersStCroix.com), the water-front bar and cafe in the heart of town and next to the Seaplane landing, is a delightful setting for lunch or a break from shopping and sightseeing. In addition to Caribbean specialties and seafood, Rum Runners serves hand-rolled sushi and sashimi, and you can choose your own live lobster from the island's only tank. Moderately expensive.

Sports

Beach/Boating Frederiksted has a pretty public beach only a few minutes' walk from the pier and, south of town at Sandy Point, one of the most beautiful stretches of sand in the Caribbean.

Golf and Tennis Equidistant between Frederik-sted and Christiansted, on the north side of the island, is **Carambola Beach Resort and Golf Club** (6,856 yards, par 72), a lovely, 18-hole layout designed by Robert Trent Jones. It has a clubhouse and pro shop. Call in advance for tee-off times (778-5638; www.golfvi.com); greens fee 18 holes May–November, $65, 9 holes $35; 18 holes December–April $95, 9 holes $55.

A mile east of Christiansted, **Buccaneer Hotel** (714-2100; www.thebuccaneer.com) sprawls over 240 landscaped acres with great views, beaches, spa, and water-sports facilities. It has an 18-hole golf course, and its eight Laykold courts are the largest complex on the island. Greens fee including cart: 18 holes $95 winter; $55 summer; 9 holes $65 winter, $40 summer.

Hiking and Biking In the northwest corner of St. Croix, an area known as the **Rain Forest** has winding roads with light traffic and paths in the woods that lead to seasonal streams and water-falls. The most scenic route, Western Scenic Road, begins (or ends) at Hams Bay on the northwest coast. The coastal road (Route 63) north passes Butler Bay, where a nature preserve of the St. Croix Landmarks Society is popular for bird-watching. Caledonia Valley, on the south side of the ridge, has the island's only year-round stream and is also popular for bird-watching.

Caribbean Adventure Tours (778-1522; www.stcroixkayak.com) offers kayaking and hiking to Salt River National Park, learning about the island's history and ecology along the way; moon-light kayaking, with a guide sharing local folk tales and ghost stories; sunset kayaks along the north shore; and hikes along Annaly Bay or Jack and Isaac's Bay.

Ay-Ay Eco Hike and Tours (772-4079), owned by Ras Lumumba, a gardener and herbalist who came to St. Croix from Dominica in 1964, offers two- to four-hour ecotours to such locations as Salt River Bay, Annaly Bay, and Caledonia Rain Forest, focusing on the island's environment and history.

The St. Croix Hiking Association (778-2076) offers a hiking tour of Castle Nugent, a 300-acre working farm established in the 1730s on the island's south shore. The hike of about 4 miles over moderate to strenuous terrain covers the area's cul-tural, historical, agricultural, and ecological signifi-cance. From the 1700s to 1800s, the farm grew cotton, sugarcane, and indigo and raised Senepol cattle. Today, it continues to raise Senepol cattle and operates a bed-and-breakfast. The great house, listed in the National Historic Register, is surrounded by historic buildings, including the for-mer slave quarters and a small chapel. Cost: $10; hikers should bring water and snacks and wear long pants and sturdy shoes. The hiking association conducts other tours; for information, contact 778-2076 or 778-9087.

Horseback Riding Paul and Jill's Equestrian Stable (772-2880; www.paulandjills.com), next to Sprat Hall Estate 2 miles north of Frederiksted, is operated by a member of the family that has owned Sprat Hall, one of the island's most historic inns, for more than two hundred years. The stable offers two-hour scenic trail rides for about $75. Buccaneer Hotel (near Christiansted) has riding over trails on its property. Both facilities require advance reservations. **Kerry's Northshore Horse-back Riding** or **Equus Rides** (778-0933; www .stcroixlink.com) offers tours through the mountains along the north shore to enjoy the spectacular views and along the beaches. Cost: $20 per person, per hour. Each tour lasts a minimum of two hours. All-day tours including lunch and beverages are also available. Reservations should be made at least one day in advance.

Kayaking Caribbean Adventure Tours (800-532-3483, 778-1522; www.stcroixkayak.com) offers kayaking excursions of Salt River National Park as well as the north shore. Departures are daily at 9:00 a.m. and 2:00 p.m.; tours are approximately 2.5 hours. See the Hiking and Biking section. **Virgin Kayak Company** (778-0071) offers guided north shore tours and rentals.

Kiting Kite St. Croix (643-5824; www.kitestcroix .com) rents equipment and offers lessons to get students airborne.

Snorkeling and Scuba Diving St. Croix is almost completely surrounded by coral reefs. In addition to Buck Island, there are forty-seven dive sites near St. Croix. The greatest variety of coral and fish is found along 6 miles of the north shore where the reef is only 500 yards from the coast in water about 35 feet deep. It is most accessible from Christiansted, which is also the location of **Caribbean Sea Adventures** (773-2628; www .caribbeanseaadventures.com), which has several daily excursions to Buck Island: A powerboat or glass-bottom boat leaves at 9:30 a.m. and returns at 1:30 p.m., cost is $50 adult, $35 child; catamaran or trimaran for twenty passengers runs from 10:00 a.m. to 3:00 p.m., $85 adult, $55 child includes lunch.

Cruzan Watersports & Tours (across from Christiansted Boardwalk at Protestant Cay; 773-7060; www.cruzanwatersports.com) offers Jet Ski and kayak rentals as well as two-hour open water rides with snorkeling and beach stop.

On the south of St. Croix, **Anchor Dive Center** (778-1522; www.anchordivestcroix.com), in the Salt River National Park, has daily dives to what it calls the "seven wonders of St. Croix."

The Salt River Dropoff at the mouth of the river is a prime diving location made up of two sites: the east and west walls of a submerged canyon, which shelve and plunge more than 1,000 feet. The walls are encrusted with corals, sponges, and forests of black coral and attract large schools of fish. Frederiksted is not without interest, particularly for shipwrecks and the abundance of tiny seahorses around the harbor.

The Virgin Islands

The British Virgin Islands

Tortola, Norman Island, Jost Van Dyke, Virgin Gorda, Anegada

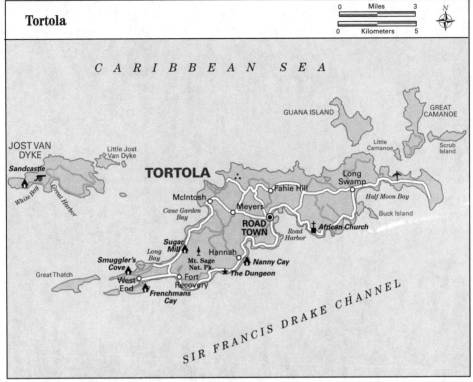

Tortola

CARIBBEAN SEA

JOST VAN DYKE
Little Jost Van Dyke
Sandcastle
White Bay
Great Harbor

GUANA ISLAND

GREAT CAMANOE
Little Camanoe
Scrub Island

TORTOLA

Long Swamp
Fahie Hill
Half Moon Bay
Buck Island

McIntosh
Meyers
Cane Garden Bay
ROAD TOWN
Road Harbor
African Church

Sugar Mill
Long Bay
Hannah
Mt. Sage Nat. Pk.
Nanny Cay
Smuggler's Cove
The Dungeon
West End
Fort Recovery
Great Thatch
Frenchmans Cay

SIR FRANCIS DRAKE CHANNEL

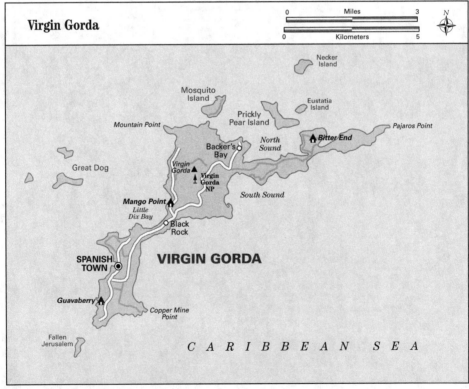

Virgin Gorda

Necker Island

Mosquito Island
Mountain Point
Prickly Pear Island
Eustatia Island
Pajaros Point

Great Dog
Backer's Bay
North Sound
Bitter End

Virgin Gorda
Virgin Gorda NP
South Sound

Mango Point
Little Dix Bay
Black Rock

SPANISH TOWN
VIRGIN GORDA

Guavaberry
Copper Mine Point

Fallen Jerusalem

CARIBBEAN SEA

The British Virgin Islands

Yachtsman's Haven

The British Virgin Islands, an archipelago of about fifty green, mountainous islands, cays, and rocks, are spread over 59 square miles of sapphire waters along the Anegada Passage between the Caribbean Sea and the Atlantic. Mostly volcanic in origin and uninhabited, they have scalloped coastlines and idyllic little coves with white-sand beaches. In olden days their strategic location made them a favorite hiding place of pirates who plundered ships carrying treasures and cargo between the Old and New Worlds. Today the islands of this British Crown Colony are favorite hideaways for yachtsmen drawn by the good anchorage, vacationers drawn by the beaches, and a growing number of cruise ships determined to get away from the crowd.

The largest and most populated islands are Tortola, the capital; Virgin Gorda; and Anegada. Others such as Peter Island and Guana Island have become popular after being developed as private resorts, but for the most part the British Virgin Islands are almost as virgin as the day Christopher Columbus discovered them.

The BVI, as the aficionados call them, say frankly that they do not appeal to everyone. They have no golf courses or casinos, and what little nighttime activity exists is low-key. But what these islands lack in flashy entertainment is more than made up for in facilities for boating, scuba diving, deep-sea fishing, and windsurfing.

The British Virgin Islands are next-door neighbors of the U.S. group, and without a map it's hard to tell the difference. On the other hand, when you ask someone from the BVI if there is a difference between their islands and ours, they will delight in answering, "Yes, the British Virgins are still virgin."

Arriving in the British Virgin Islands

Most visitors arrive in the BVI on a cruise ship, ferry, or private yacht—their own or one they have chartered. Frequent ferry service connects Tortola with St. Thomas and St. John in less than an hour.

Round-trip fare is $40. Less frequent service is available between either St. Thomas or Tortola and Virgin Gorda.

Tortola is the home of the largest yacht charter fleet in the Caribbean, where boats with or without crew can be chartered for a day or a year. Lying in close proximity astride Drake's Passage, the islands create a sheltered waterway that is one of the world's prime sailing locations. From their base in Tortola, boats crisscross the passage to visit Peter and Norman Islands directly across from Road Town, Virgin Gorda to the east/northeast, and Jost Van Dyke on the northwest. These are also the stops made most often by cruise ships.

In only the last few years, after the new pier in Road Town was complete, has Tortola become a cruise port of some significance, growing in the availability of services and activities to meet the needs of cruise passengers.

At a Glance

Antiquities	★
Architecture	★
Art and artists	★★
Beaches	★★★★★
Colonial buildings	★
Crafts	★
Cuisine	★
Culture	★
Dining/Restaurants	★
Entertainment	★
Forts	★
History	★★★
Monuments	★
Museums	★
Nightlife	★
Scenery	★★★★★
Shopping/Duty-free	★★
Sightseeing	★
Sports	★★★★★
Transportation	★★

Fast Facts

Population: Anegada, 173; Tortola, 14,000; Virgin Gorda, 3,000.

Size: Anegada, 15 square miles; Tortola, 21.5 square miles; Virgin Gorda, 8.5 square miles.

Main Towns: Road Town, Tortola; Spanish Town, Virgin Gorda.

Government: British Crown Colony

Currency: U.S. dollar is the official currency

Departure Tax: $20 by air; $5 by boat; $7 by cruise ship.

Language: English

Public Holidays: January 1, New Year's Day; March 4, Commemoration of H. Lavity Stoutt Day; March 11, Commonwealth Day; April, Good Friday, Easter Monday; May 20, Whit Monday; June, Sovereign's Birthday; July 1, Territory Day; August, Festival Monday, Tuesday, Wednesday; October 21, St. Ursula's Day; December 25, Christmas Day; December 26, Boxing Day.

Telephone Code: 284

Airlines: *From North America:* via Antigua, Puerto Rico, St. Maarten, St. Thomas connecting to Air Sunshine, American Eagle, Cape Air, Fly BVI, LIAT, or Winair. Seaborne Airlines (www.seaborneairlines.com) offers scheduled seaplane service on Fridays from San Juan to Virgin Gorda via St. Thomas.

Smoking Policy: A law passed recently by the Legislative Council bans smoking in public places including bars, restaurants, nightclubs, airports, offices, and sports facilities. It also bans smoking within 50 feet of any public space.

Information: www.bvitouristboard .com; www.bviwelcome.com; www .britishvirginislands.com

In the United States:

British Virgin Islands Tourist Board

Atlanta: 1275 Shiloh Road, Suite 2930, Kennesaw, GA 30144; (770) 874-5951; fax: (770) 874-5953.

Los Angeles: 3450 Wilshire Boulevard, Suite 1202, Los Angeles, CA 90010; (213) 736-8931; fax: (213) 736-8935; bvila@bvitouristboard .com.

New York: 1270 Broadway, Suite 705, New York, NY 10001; (212) 696-0400; (800) 835-8530; fax: (212) 563-2263; ny@bvitouristboard.com.

In Tortola:

BVI Tourist Board, Akara Building, 2nd Floor, DeCastro Street, Road Town, Tortola; (284) 494-3134; fax: (284) 494-3866; info@bvitourism .com

Local Transportation Tortola's three entry points—Road Town, the main town on the south coast, the Soper's Hole West End ferry landing, and the airport on Beef Island at the east end—are linked by paved roads. Beef Island is connected to Tortola by a bridge. Paved roads wind over the mountains to Brewers Bay, Cane Garden Bay, and other resort areas on the northwest coast. More remote areas are accessible by dirt roads, some requiring four-wheel drive. Taxis are plentiful in Tortola; they use fixed rates, based on distance.

Sightseeing Taxis and travel agencies offer half-day tours by minivan and open-air safari buses. Major car-rental firms, as well as independent ones, have offices in Tortola and on Virgin Gorda; no service is available on the other islands. Remember: In this British colony, driving is on the left.

Cruise ships calling at Tortola offer a limited number of shore excursions; the following are samples.

Snorkeling Tour: 2.5 hours, $59. View colorful corals and exotic fish on a guided snorkel tour of Norman Island. A similar four-hour excursion ($69) by yacht sails across Sir Francis Drake Channel for snorkeling and swimming at Norman, Cooper, Salt, or Peter Islands.

Tortola Sightseeing and Cane Garden Bay Beach: 3.5 hours, $59. While in Road Town, visit the Botanic Gardens, a four-acre oasis of colorful plants and tropical foliage; then drive to Skyworld, from where you can see Puerto Rico on a clear day. The scenic journey across mountainous Tortola has many heart-stopping views along the winding route. End at Cane Garden Bay for swimming at this beautiful white-sand beach.

Virgin Gorda Tour: 4 hours, $69. An excursion launch picks you up shipside and cruises along Sir Francis Drake Channel to Spanish Town, Virgin Gorda, where an open-air safari bus takes you on a short drive to the famous Baths at Spring Bay for swimming, snorkeling, and sunning amid the mammoth boulders and sea caves. After a short tour you return to the launch and your ship.

Dolphin Swim: 2 hours, $159. Participants are transferred by bus to Dolphin Lagoon for a thirty-minute introductory talk followed by a thirty-minute swim session with the dolphins.

X BOB: 3.5 hours, $109. BOB is an underwater bike tethered to the surface on a floating buoy, allowing a maximum depth of less than 7 feet. A safety briefing is followed by thirty minutes of underwater fun. The BOBs are led and followed by the diving team throughout the underwater trail.

If you prefer to make your own arrangements, these are some resources and local vendors to contact in advance.

On Tortola

National Parks Trust (61 Main Street, Road Town; 284-494-2069; www.bvinationalparkstrust.org) has maps of parks and hiking trail tours.

B.V.I. Taxi Association (284-494-2322), Quality Taxi Association (284-494-8397), and Romney Associates Consultants (284-494-2872)—all at Wickham's Cay 1, Road Town—offer guided open-air safari bus tours or air-conditioned vans for sightseeing and trips to the beach.

Travel Plan Tours (Waterfront Drive, Tortola and Spanish Town, Virgin Gorda; 284-494-2872; 284-494-4000; www.aroundthebvi.com) provides tours by glass-bottom boat, island tours by vans and buses, and snorkel and scuba day sails.

Island Helicopters International (Beef Island Airport; 284-495-2538; www.helicoptersbvi .com) offers half-hour flight-seeing, day trips to other islands, and other services.

On Virgin Gorda

Andy's Taxi and Jeep Rental (284-495-5252; fischers@candwbvi.net) and Mahogany Taxi Service (284-495-5469; www.mahoganyrentals.puzzle piece.net)—both at the Valley—have guided island tours by safari buses and vans.

Fly BVI (284-495-1747; info@flybvi.com) provides bird's-eye views of the BVI and trips to Anegada.

Virgin Gorda has an open-air jitney bus that shuttles between Spanish Town, the Baths, and some resort areas. With it you can see most of the island on your own in less than three hours.

Tortola and Its Neighbors

In the past, Tortola was a sleepy little place with not a great deal of activity, but with its development as a cruise port and the bustle that accompanies hundreds of cruise passengers roaming the island almost daily, particularly during the winter season, its character is beginning to change. New, modern buildings are replacing the colorful West Indian ones; new cars and buses are crowding the roads; and more and more people, attracted by jobs and business opportunities, are swelling the island's population. Road Town is still the only sizable residential center. It has shops, hotels, restaurants, and bars with local bands. Most are located along the south shore road and on Main Street.

If you want to know more about the BVI, visit the Virgin Islands Folk Museum, operated by the Virgin Islands Historical Society.

For shoppers, the first stop is likely to be Crafts Alive, the government-funded crafts village of local craftspeople and artists in Road Town. Here, an array of locally made goods are housed in small, colorful wooden buildings meant to resemble an island village of the past. The center is only a short walk from the cruise ship pier and was motivated, in part, by the ready market cruise passengers bring.

At the BVI Handicrafts Association, all the crafts are handmade by ten women who make up the group. Among their crafts are the dancing "Mocko Jumbie" dolls of acting president Frances Springette. Colorful batik fabrics of original designs, hats, baskets, and prints are available. Next door, BVI Social Development Department, a government-sponsored shop, carries crochet work, rag rugs, and straw hats made by elderly craftspeople of the islands. A specialty to note are handmade Afro-Caribbean dolls with two heads—two dolls each skillfully hidden under the skirt of the other. Turn one over, and you see another doll with a completely different costume.

Joan Wilson's Creative Crafts displays her one-of-a-kind banana leaf dolls; she uses the contours of scorched banana leaves to fashion the dolls' clothing. **Caribbean Essence,** in an African-style hut, has nicely packaged beauty products produced in the BVI, and the **Bush Tea Doctor,** Ashley Nibbs, brews up hot sauce, guavaberry liquor, and gooseberry syrup from family recipes under the label A. Nibbs Sons & Daughters.

The effort to keep local crafts alive is reflected elsewhere in other ventures: **Bamboushay,** a pottery studio and art shop located at the Nanny Cay Hotel and Marina, features the work of English artisan Val Anderson as well as a large selection of locally made cards, paintings, prints, photographs, and baskets; Pat Faulkner of **Pat's Pottery** on Anegada, known for the whimsical dancing crabs and seascapes that decorate her work, has a shop at Nutmeg Point. Aragorn Dick-Read, a local sculptor, has **Aragorn's Studio** (284-495-1849; www .aragornsstudio.com), a Caribbean arts and crafts shop at Trellis Bay, and gives lessons in pottery, woodcarving, and basketry. The studio's Art Centre provides an outlet for the crafts of the Carib Indians. Aragorn's connection to local agricultural communities has led to the creation of a line of Island Spices as well as a Fruit Depot where local farmers come to sell their organic produce. Among the island's master weavers, ninety-two-year-old Estelle Dawson, who has been weaving straw hats since she was a child, continues to work in her small house by the sea on the East End. She uses a palm known locally as broom teyer palm (*Cocothrinix alta*) that grows in shallow, rocky ground by the sea. **Sunny Caribbee Spice Shop** (284-494-2178; www.sunnycaribbee.com), one of the best-known Caribbean labels, displays the work of master basket weaver Darwin "Gun" Scatliffe, who uses the local hoop vine in his creations.

J.R. O'Neal Botanic Gardens One of Road Town's most prized attractions is the tropical Botanic Gardens, created on a neglected site formerly occupied by the BVI Agricultural Station. The four-acre spread, opened in 1987, is the work of the BVI National Parks Trust and volunteers from the Botanic Society and Garden Club. The garden is divided into about twenty collections of rare and indigenous tropical plants.

Mount Sage National Park In the 1960s Sage Mountain, on Tortola, and Virgin Gorda's Spring Bay and Devil's Bay were donated to the BVI government by Laurance Rockefeller. The gift led to the creation of the BVI National Parks Trust (www .bvinationalparkstrust.org) and the start of a land- and sea-conservation program with eleven of twenty-three proposed areas under management.

The ninety-two-acre Mount Sage National Park (www.b-v-i.com/Nature/MtSage.htm) is located on the peaks of the tall volcanic mountains that cross the center of Tortola, reaching 1,780 feet, the highest elevation in either the U.S. or the British Virgin Islands. Its vegetation, characteristic of a rain forest, is thought to be similar to that of the island's original growth. A road leads to the park entrance, where you will find panoramic views. Two graveled, signposted trails, each about an hour's hike, wind through the forest past huge elephant ears, hanging vines, lacy ferns, and a variety of trees common to the Caribbean, such as kapok, mahogany, and white cedar.

Norman Island Across Drake's Passage from Tortola is uninhabited Norman Island (www.norman island.com), said to be the "Treasure Island" of Robert Louis Stevenson's novel. The island has old ruins, a salt pond with abundant bird life, and footpaths. One path is a thirty-minute hike up Spy Glass Hill, from which you can get a fabulous 360-degree view. In olden days pirates used this vantage point to watch for Spanish treasure ships; hence its name. The island is apparently still a convenient base for illegal activity; BVI authorities have seized boats smuggling drugs here. At Treasure Point partly submerged caves can be enjoyed by snorkelers as well as divers.

Norman Island was purchased by the owners of Guana Island and is slated for development with million-dollar homes in a fashion similar to Mustique Island in the Grenadines.

Rhone National Marine Park (www.bvi marineguide.com/programs) Southeast of Tortola at Salt Island lies the wreck of the *Rhone,* the most famous—and popular—shipwreck dive in the Virgin Islands, if not the entire Caribbean. The movie

The Deep was filmed here. The wreck, lying at 20- to 80-foot depths west of Salt Island, has been made into a marine park covering 800 acres. Along with nearby reefs and caves, the park includes Dead Chest Island on the west, where seabirds nest on the tall cliffs.

The 310-foot Royal Mail Steamer *Rhone* sank in 1867 during a terrible hurricane. Anchored in calm seas off Peter Island, the ship was loading passengers and stores for its return trip to England when a storm blew in suddenly. The ship lost its anchor when its cable broke, and, no longer safe at anchor, with her rigging torn by the winds, she steamed at top speed for open water to ride out the storm. But the hurricane struck again from another direction, forcing the *Rhone* onto the rocks at Salt Island. She split apart and sank. Parts of the ship can be seen by snorkelers.

Salt Island has a few residents who still tend the salt ponds, trails that lead up a hill to a wonderful view, and a good beach.

Jost Van Dyke Off the northwest coast of Tortola and directly north of St. John, Jost Van Dyke's good anchorage and beautiful beaches make it a popular stop for yachts and small cruise ships that sail regularly through the Virgin Islands. Most anchor at yacht-filled Great Harbour, the main settlement surrounded by green hills. Two of the best-known beach bars in these parts are **The Soggy Dollar** (284-495-9888; www.soggydollar.com) at the Sand Castle Hotel and **Foxy's Tamarind Bar and Restaurant** (284-495-9258). They are favorites of the yachting crowd, where a beach party with calypso music is the order of the day—any day.

Sports

Biking In recent years, cycling has become a major sport in the BVI. It's a great way to explore the islands. **Last Stop Sports** (Nanny Cay, Tortola; 284-494-1120; www.laststopsports.com), a fully equipped cycle and water-sports shop, recommends that you bring cycling shoes for mountain biking or casual cycling. Helmets (mandatory), locks, and racks are provided at no extra charge.

Boating Experienced yachtsmen consider the waters of the BVI to be among the finest sailing in the world. Little wonder that it's home to five sailing schools. As noted earlier, Tortola is also the base for the largest yacht charter fleet in the Caribbean. A complete list of charter companies is available on the BVI Tourist Board's Web site and its publication *Welcome,* available from the board's U.S. offices.

In July 2007, The Mooring, one of the Caribbean's largest yacht charter companies, announced plans for a $10 million expansion of its flagship operations base in Road Town. When completed in 2008 the new facilities will include a bar and restaurant, spa facilities, conference area, new oceanfront hotel suites, and retail shops.

Diving and Snorkeling Few places in the Caribbean match the BVI for the clarity of the water, the variety and accessibility of marine life and shipwrecks, the quality of the dive operations, and the ease, particularly for beginners, for enjoying snorkeling and diving. A complete list of dive operations, along with their services and rates, can be found at www.bvitouristboard.com and www.bviscuba.org. These are a few sample prices: One-tank dive, $80 to $85; two tanks, $110 to $120; resort course, $120; lesson and excursion, $120; snorkeler/rider, $40. **UBS Dive Center** (Harbour View Marina, East End, Box 852, Road Town, Tortola; 284-494-0024; www.scubabvi.com) is somewhat unusual in that it offers private diving services: your own boat for the day; your schedule, instruction, and tours. No groups mixed. Rate: two persons full day, $175 per person.

Fishing Avid anglers the world over come to the BVI to test their skill, particularly in the deep waters off Anegada. Fishing charters range from $350 to $650 for half-day excursions and $650 to $990 for full-day trips and are offered by **Blue Ocean Adventures** (284-499-2837; fax 284-495-5820; blueocean@hotmail.com), among others. You must have a permit from the Fisheries Division (284-494-3429).

Hiking Sage Mountain on Tortola and Gorda Peak on Virgin Gorda are the most popular hikes. Both are part of BVI's National Parks System and have maintained trails. **National Parks Trust** (Fishlock Road, Road Town; 284-494-2069; ww.bvinational parkstrust.org; bvinpt@caribsurf.com) has park maps and hiking trail tours.

Horseback Riding Shadows Stables (Ridge Road; 284-494-2262) will take you through the rain forest on Sage Mountain or down to Cane Garden Cay.

Kayaking The BVI's warm, protected waters and unspoiled nature are ideal for kayaking, especially for beginners and intermediates, in the mangroves or the bays; experienced kayakers can venture farther out to Drake Channel. Rental companies offer advice on where to kayak and what conditions to expect. They stock a range of kayaks and supply life vests. Those named here are on Tortola and are open from 8:00 a.m. to 5:00 p.m. daily.

Boardsailing BVI Shop (Trellis Bay, Beef Island, Box 537, Long Look; 284-495-2447; fax: 284-495-1626; www.windsurfing.vi) has surfboards and single and double kayaks. Hourly rentals; rates on request. Two-hour lessons available.

Last Stop Sports (Nanny Cay and The Moorings, Box 3208, Road Town; 284-494-0564; fax: 284-494-0593; www.laststopsports.com) offers sailboards, kayaks, surfboards, laser sailboats, water skis, and body boards. Rentals from $28 per day.

Windsurfing The northwest coast of Tortola is one of the prime windsurfing locations in the Eastern Caribbean. See **Boardsailing BVI Shop** mentioned above.

Virgin Gorda

Virgin Gorda is known for the **Baths,** an extraordinary grotto created by toppled gigantic rocks that have puzzled geologists for years. They are completely different from any other rock formation of the area. Worn smooth by wind and water over the millennia, the enormous rocks have fallen in such a way as to create labyrinths and caves that are fun to explore, although they are not real caves, of course. Where the sea rushes in and out, the formations near the shore catch the water, creating pools of crystal-clear water shimmering from the sunlight that filters between the rocks. They are delightful for a refreshing splash—hence their

name. The area can be reached by land or sea, and the reefs fronting the Baths are popular for snorkeling.

Virgin Gorda rises from its boulder-strewn coast and sandy beaches on the south in a northerly direction to 1,370-foot Gorda Peak near the island's center. The top of the mountain is protected by the **Virgin Gorda Peak Park,** which covers 265 acres of forests. The park has a self-guided hiking trail leading to an observation point; it is actually the end of a paved road leading to Little Dix Bay—one of the Caribbean's famous resorts and the sister resort to Caneel Bay on St. John. Equally as expensive, exclusive, and low-key, the resorts were begun by Laurance Rockefeller as Rockresorts and were among the Caribbean's first ecologically designed hotels, encompassing the natural environment in which they are set and harmonizing their architecture with it.

On the south end of the island is the Devil's Bay National Park, a secluded coral-sand beach, which can be reached by a scenic trail in a fifteen-minute walk from the area of the Baths.

Virgin Gorda's other famous spots are **Bitter End,** a hotel/restaurant/bar that is probably the most popular watering hole in the Caribbean for the yachting crowd; and Necker Island, across the bay from Bitter End, which belongs to English entrepreneur Sir Richard Branson, who built his sumptuous nest on its summit. This ten-bedroom perch is available for rent at a mere $32,000 and up per day!

Anegada

Unlike the other BVI, which are green and mountainous, Anegada is a flat, dry coral atoll fringed by miles of sandy beaches and horseshoe-shaped reefs. The most northerly of the BVI, it was once a pirates' lair, where the low-lying reefs caught pursuers unaware. An estimated three hundred ships are thought to have gone down here. Today those wrecks and the reefs attract divers, and the fish attracted to the reefs make the island's waters a prime fishing location.

In addition to sailing, the BVI's healthy and abundant reefs are popular for snorkeling and scuba diving. The BVI waters are also popular for live-aboard dive boats, which carry passengers in cruise ship–style comfort. Some are based in Tortola year-round, whereas others visit from time to time. Dive operators, based in Tortola, offer a full range of excursions. Glass-bottom boat tours are available, too.

Tortola Fast Ferry, operated by Smith's Ferry Service (284-494-4454; www.smithsferry.com), offers a special excursion to Anegada on Monday, Wednesday, and Friday that departs from Road Town at 7:00 a.m. and returns at 3:30 p.m. Cost: $50 round-trip, adults; $35 children younger than age 12.

The BVI waters teem with fish, and the islands are adjacent to the 50-mile Puerto Rican Trench. But surprisingly, deep-sea fishing has only recently been developed here. Sportfishing boats are available for charter in Tortola and Virgin Gorda, which are both a forty-five-minute boat ride from the trench.

You can get windsurfing equipment at most resorts. Experienced surfers say the northwest coast of Tortola, where the swells roll in from the Atlantic and break against the north end of Cane Garden Bay, is the Virgin Islands' best surfing location.

St. Maarten/St. Martin

and Neighbors

Philipsburg, St. Maarten; Marigot, St. Martin; Fort Bay, Saba;
Oranjestad, St. Eustatius; Sandy Ground, Anguilla

St. Martin, St. Maarten, and Neighbors

Miles 0 — 2
Kilometers 0 — 4

N

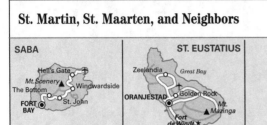

SABA

Hell's Gate
Mt. Scenery ▲ Windwardside
The Bottom
St. John
FORT BAY ◉

ST. EUSTATIUS

Zeelandia · Great Bay
ORANJESTAD ◉ ○ Golden Rock
Mt. ▲ Mazinga
Fort de Windt ★

ATLANTIC OCEAN

Eastern Point

Bell Point
Anse Marcel
Grand Case Bay
Grand Case
French Cul-de-Sac
Orient Beach

Arago Point
St. Louis
ST. MARTIN
▲ Pic Paradis
Poison Lake
L'Embouchure Bay

Marigot Bay
Rouge Bay
○ La Belle Creole
○ Colombier
Orleans ○
Oyster Pond

MARIGOT ◉
○ Sandy Ground

Mullet Bay
Simpson Bay Lagoon
○ Point Piroutte
Monument ★
○ Dutch Cul-de-Sac
ST. MAARTEN

Simpson Bay
Guana Bay

Pelican Key ○
Cole Bay
Great Salt Pond
PHILIPSBURG ◉

Little Bay ★
Fort Amsterdam
Great Bay
○ Point Blanche
Cruise Ship Dock

CARIBBEAN SEA

The Dutch Windward Islands

And Their Neighbors

Centered at a cluster of lovely hideaways in the northeastern Caribbean are three of the most distinctive islands in the entire region. They share their seas with a neighbor that recently became the most talked-about gem in the ocean.

Sint Maarten (commonly written as St. Maarten), the capital of the Dutch Windward Islands and the major cruise-ship port of the group, is an island of green mountain peaks that swoop down to scalloped bays and stretches of powdery white-sand beaches and the shimmering, turquoise sea. Situated on an island of only 37 square miles, Sint Maarten shares more than half of the land with French St. Martin. Their split personality—Dutch on one side, French on the other—enables visitors to dine, tour, sail, and play tennis in two languages, under two flags, without ever leaving the island.

Saba (pronounced *SAY*-ba), another member of the Dutch group, is unique. The 5-square-mile volcanic peak, 28 miles southwest of St. Maarten, rises straight up from the sea. Its history reads like a fairy tale.

St. Eustatius, known as Statia, is the third of the Dutch Windwards and is ten minutes by plane south of Saba. This island of 8 square miles was once the richest free port in the Americas, though today it takes some imagination to picture it.

Anguilla, a British colony 5 miles north of St. Martin, was the best-kept secret in the Caribbean until the addition of some highly publicized superdeluxe resorts brought trendsetters flocking to this spot of tranquility. You can easily discover Anguilla for yourself on a day trip from St. Maarten.

Before Concordia

Before Columbus got to St. Maarten in 1493 and claimed it for Spain, the island was inhabited by the Carib Indians. More than a century later—after the island had bounced among the Dutch, French, and Spanish—a young Dutchman of later New York fame, Peter Stuyvesant, tried to wrestle it from Spain. He lost a limb instead—only to see the

Spaniards abandon their claim to the island to the Dutch just four years later, in 1648.

When the Dutch sent their commander from St. Eustatius to take possession, they found the French waiting to do battle. But the Dutch and French soon agreed to stop fighting over the island and split the spoils instead. Legend says the accord has lasted more than three centuries; in fact, the island changed hands another sixteen times. The place where the agreement was reached is known as Mt. Concordia, nonetheless, and the old accord is celebrated as an annual holiday. More important: The two sides have no real border between them. The only way you know you are crossing from one country to the other is by a welcome sign on the side of the road.

Yet the two sides of this island are noticeably different, beginning with the spelling of the names: Sint Maarten and Saint Martin. Signs are in Dutch

At a Glance	
Antiquities	★
Architecture	★
Art and artists	★★
Beaches	★★★★★
Colonial buildings	★
Crafts	★
Cuisine	★★★★★
Culture	★
Dining/Restaurants	★★★★★
Entertainment	★★★★★
Forts	★
History	★
Monuments	★
Museums	★★
Nightlife	★★★★★
Scenery	★★★
Shopping	★★★★★
Sightseeing	★★★
Sports	★★★★★
Transportation	★★

St. Maarten

Population: St. Maarten, 39,000; Saba, 1,090; St. Eustatius, 2,089.

Size: 16 square miles

Main Town: Philipsburg

Government: The three Dutch Windward Islands, together with Bonaire and Curaçao in the South Caribbean, make up the Netherlands Antilles. The government is a parliamentary democracy, headed by a governor who is appointed by and represents the queen of the Netherlands. The central government is in Curaçao; each island has its own representative body called the Island Council.

Currency: Netherlands Antilles guilder, written NAf. US $1 equals NAf 1.80.

Departure Tax: US $30 airport (this departure tax might be already included in the airfare of certain airlines) and US $12 port departure tax on boat trips to neighboring islands; $20 adults, $10 children, $5 day trippers to Anguilla. For islands within the Netherlands Antilles, the departure tax is US $10.

Electricity: St. Maarten and St. Martin have separate systems: the Dutch side uses 110–120 volts AC, 60 cycles.

Language: Dutch is the official language, but English is a common second language.

Public Holidays: January 1, New Year's Day; Good Friday; Easter Monday; April 30, Coronation Day (Dutch); May 1, Labor Day; Whit Monday; Ascension Thursday; November 11, St. Maarten's Day; December 25 and 26, Christmas.

Telephone Area Code: St. Maarten and St. Martin have separate telephone systems, and that's where the island's two-country quaintness can lose some of its charm. A call between the two is an international phone call; sometimes it's easier to call New York from Philipsburg than to call Marigot, less than 8 miles away. So much for Concordia! To make matters even more confusing, the telephone numbers on the Dutch side have seven numbers rendered as 344-4444; while those on the French side have six, written as 22-22-22 or 22.22.22, the traditional French way. To call St. Maarten from the United States, dial 011-599-54 plus the five-digit local number. To call from the Dutch to the French side, dial 00-590-590 plus the local number.

Wireless: In January 2005 Philipsburg became the first Caribbean town to go wireless, allowing residents and visitors alike to use their enabled computers or other mobile devices anywhere in town. SMITCOMS (St. Maarten International Telecommunications Services) teamed up with Lucent Technologies and BelAir Networks to provide a Wi-Fi network for the St. Maarten capital.

Airlines: *From the United States:* American, Continental, Delta, JetBlue, Spirit, United, USAir; American Airlines. American Eagle from San Juan to St. Maarten. *Interisland:* from Princess Juliana International Airport (www.pjae.com) in St. Maarten, Winair (Windward Islands Airways) has daily service to Montserrat, Saba, St. Eustatius, Anguilla, St. Barts, St. Kitts, and Tortola; Air Caraibes flies frequently to St. Barts and Guadeloupe. Caribbean Airlines (www.caribbean-airlines.com) also has service to neighboring islands. Check out AirStMaarten (www.airsxm.com), an online search and reservation site for airlines serving St. Maarten.

Information: www.st-maarten.com; www.mrstm.com; www.saint-martin-online.com

In the United States:

St. Maarten Tourist Office, 675 Third Avenue, No. 1807, New York, NY 10017; (212) 953-2084; (800) STMAARTEN; fax: (212) 953-2145.

In Canada:

St. Maarten Tourist Board, 2810 Matheson Boulevard E, Suite 200, Toronto, Ontario, L4W 4X7; (416) 622-4300; fax: (416) 622-3431.

In Port:

St. Maarten Tourist Bureau, Vineyard Office Park, W. G. Buncamper Road 33, Philipsburg; 011-599-542-2337; fax: 011-599-542-2734; info@st-maarten.com.

and French (also in English), and the people speak Dutch or French (also English). Two currencies—guilders and euros—circulate, but everyone takes dollars (even vending machines on the Dutch side take U.S. coins). There are two governments, two flags, and two sets of stamps—which your philatelic friends will love. Most important, each side has a distinctive, unmistakable ambience.

Small as it is, St. Maarten has as many diversions as places ten times its size. The beaches are gorgeous, the water spectacular, and the sports facilities excellent. There's golf, scuba, tennis, windsurfing, fishing, riding, sailing, snorkeling, and biking. St. Maarten has bouncing showplaces and quiet corners, fancy restaurants, discos, and twelve casinos.

Located in the heart of the Caribbean between the Virgin Islands and the French West Indies, St. Maarten is an air- and sea-transportation hub for the northeastern Caribbean. Its central location enables cruise passengers to explore the neighboring islands—Anguilla, Saba, and Statia—by air or boat in a day.

Note to readers: This chapter is oriented to St. Maarten for practical reasons. An estimated 80 percent of all cruise ships arrive in Philipsburg; hence most passengers are likely to want information on the facilities and services convenient to it. Separate entries for French St. Martin have been made when it seemed pertinent and clearer to do so.

Budget Planning

If you choose the beachcomber's St. Maarten, costs are reasonable. You can take advantage of the beaches near the pier, snack at one of the modest places in town, and do your shopping on Frontstreet, where you will find bargains galore. If you choose the elegant side, however, for haute cuisine and shops with designer clothes, you will find St. Maarten/St. Martin to be expensive. Top French restaurants cost US $200 or more for dinner for two persons; chic shops with fashions by Armani, Valentino, and other top designers may be 20 percent lower than U.S. prices, but they are still expensive. It pays to look around, and do not be shy about asking the price. You should know that some restaurants have two sets of prices—one for local clientele and one for tourists.

Taxis, unless you share with others, are expensive. If you plan to tour on your own, a car rental is the best deal.

Shore Excursions

Cruise lines usually offer several excursions, but St. Maarten is easy to see and enjoy on your own.

Island tour: 3 hours, $25–$30 by bus (or by taxi, 2 hours, $45–$50 for two people; each addi-

tional person is $10). For first-time visitors reluctant to drive, a bus tour is a quick look at the island.

America's Cup 23 Metre Challenge: 3 hours, $75–$95 per person, depending on the cruise line. Experience the fun and thrill of racing an authentic Americas Cup 12-meter yacht in an actual race. It's the most popular excursion in St. Maarten. You don't need experience, but you do need to be in good physical condition.

Diving or snorkeling package: 3 hours, single tank, $50–$65; snorkeling, $30–$50 per hour. Most cruise ships offer a variety of snorkeling and dive packages; some include an island tour, and others include sailing around the island to the uninhabited islets off the northeast coast.

Port Profile: Philipsburg

As your ship approaches St. Maarten, the tall green mountains make the island seem much larger than it is; and when you walk down the streets of Philipsburg, its capital, the crowds make it seem larger than it is, too.

Philipsburg, situated on a crest of land facing Great Bay, was founded in 1733 as a free port and named for John Philips, who served as the commander from 1735 to 1746. It is still a free port. Frontstreet and the lanes leading to Backstreet are lined with trendy boutiques and air-conditioned malls selling duty-free goods from around the world. The Dutch side, which saw its first hotel open in 1947, developed sooner than its French counterpart. In addition to the international airport and cruise-ship port, the Dutch side has the majority of hotels, banks, and stores.

St. Martin

Population: 34,037

Size: 21 square miles

Main Towns: Marigot and Grand Case

Government: St. Martin is a sub-prefecture of Guadeloupe. Along with Guadeloupe, Martinique, and St. Barts, it is part of the French West Indies, whose nationals are French citizens with the same rights and privileges as their countrymen in France. St. Martin has a town council elected by the people and headed by a mayor; the subprefect is appointed by the French government.

Currency: Euro. US$1.00 equals about € 0.50, or 1 € equals about U.S.$1.50. Check exchange rate before leaving home and locally at a bank as the dollar has been dropping considerably against the euro recently.

Electricity: St. Martin's electricity system is separate from the Dutch side and is 220 volts AC, 50 cycles.

Language: French is the official language; English, although widely used, is often not spoken by French people with the same fluency as those with a Dutch language background.

Public Holidays: January 1, New Year's Day; Good Friday; Easter Monday; May 1, Labor Day; Whit Monday; July 14, Bastille Day; Ascension Thursday; November 11, St. Martin's Day; December 25 and 26, Christmas.

Telephone Area Code: St. Martin and St. Maarten have separate telephone systems. To call St. Martin from the United States, dial 011–590–590 plus the six-digit local number. To call from the French to the Dutch side, dial 00–599–54 plus the local number. (See page 102 St. Maarten Fast Facts, for further explanation.)

Airlines: *From the United States and intrersland:* See St. Maarten Fast Facts. *From Esperance Airport,* a small domestic airport in St. Martin, Air St. Barts and St. Barth Commuter fly daily to St. Barts. Air Caraibes and Air Antilles fly several times a day to Guadeloupe and Martinique.

Information: www.st-martin.org

In the United States:

St. Martin Tourist Board, 675 Third Avenue, New York, Suite 1807, NY 10017; (212) 475–8970; fax: (212) 260–8481.

In Canada:

French Government Tourist Board, 1981 Avenue McGill College, No. 490, Montreal, P.Q. H34 2W9; (514) 288–4264; fax: (514) 844–8901.

In Port:

St. Martin Tourist Office, Route de Sandy Ground 97150, Marigot; 0590–87–57–21; fax: 0590–87–56–43.

Location/Embarkation St. Maarten's cruise facility at Pointe Blanche (www.portofstmaarten.com) on the eastern tip of Great Bay includes a $40 million shopping and entertainment complex called Harbor Point Village. The dock can accommodate up to four ships at a time. The terminal has a tourist information kiosk, post office, deli, ATM machines, Internet access, pay phones, gift shop, and conference space for rent. There are four covered taxi stands and space for up to sixteen tour buses.

All the shops, the open-air market, restaurants, bars, and entertainment areas adhere to the same theme and color scheme as the terminal building: yellow walls with red and purple roofs, and gray and red cement block walkways. To go to the center of town, cruise passengers have the option of walking or taking a taxi or St. Maarten Tender Ser-

vices, a water taxi ($3 one-way, $5 round-trip unlimited access) that departs every fifteen minutes from the pier to Capt. Hodge's Wharf in Wathey Square, directly in front of the Frontstreet shopping area where ships dropped passengers in the past.

When you walk, you will pass Great Bay Marina and Bobby's Marina, where you can sign up for diving or a picnic sail to a secluded beach or a day sail to a neighboring island. Most boats leave about 9:00 or 9:30 a.m.

In August 2007, the St. Maarten government and the Port of St. Maarten finalized an agreement with Carnival Corporation for the latter to provide $34.5 million funding for the construction of a new two-berth cruise-ship pier. Carnival Corporation also guaranteed a certain number of passengers and will enjoy preferential berthing rights for twenty years. Eight Carnival ships and its ten brands, including three European ones, will call on St. Maarten. The new pier will accommodate two post-Panamax cruise ships. Construction was scheduled to begin in December 2007 and completed by 2009.

Local Transportation Taxis do not have meters; rates, which must have government approval, are based on destination for two passengers per trip. A charge of $4 is added for each additional person. There is a 25 percent surcharge after 10:00 p.m. and 50 percent between midnight and 6:00 a.m. Always ask for the fare in advance. Cab drivers usually quote prices in U.S. dollars, but to avoid misunderstandings, be sure to ask which currency is quoted. Your driver will expect a 10 to 15 percent tip.

Approximate fares in U.S. dollars from Philipsburg: west to Little Bay, $7; airport/Pelican Resort, $12; Maho, $16; Mullet Bay, $18; La Samanna, $16; east to Oyster Pond and Dawn Beach, $15; north to Marigot, $15; Grande Case, $25; or Orient Beach, $18.

For budget-minded travelers, public buses run between Philipsburg and Marigot throughout the day. The fare is $1.50. Other buses run every half hour between Mullet Bay, Simpson Bay, Cole Bay, and Grand Case; every hour to Mullet Bay; and every fifteen to twenty minutes to the French Quarter. Bus stops on the Dutch side are marked "Bushalte"; on the French side, "Arret"; or you can usually stop an approaching bus by waving to it.

Roads and Rentals St. Maarten's narrow, winding roads are barely adequate for the traffic around town and the airport. Driving is on the right. Most companies have pickup and delivery service and offer unlimited mileage. You should book in advance, particularly in high season, and don't be surprised if your confirmed reservation is not fulfilled. As we have noted many times in this book, although intentions are good, execution often falls short of them. Expect to pay about $40 for a standard shift and $50 for automatic with air-conditioning.

Among the rental companies are **Budget** (545-4030), which has cars and jeeps; Alamo, Avis, Hertz, National, and Thrifty are also represented.

Motorbikes Harley-Davidson Rental (544-2704, www.h-dstmartin.com); **Rodale Rental** (scooters; 542-5155); **TriSports** (mountain bikes; 545-4384; www.trisportsxm.com). **Rent-A-Scoot** (87-20-59; www.l2r-rentascoot.com), on the French side, has scooters from $28, motorbikes from $35, and Harleys from $100. We do not recommend bikes even for experienced, careful drivers, however, because St. Maarten's roads are narrow, hilly, and replete with potholes and blind curves. You are likely to have to stop dead for a cow or goat that has strayed onto the road, particularly in the rural northeast side—and animals have the right of way.

Ferry Service High-speed ferries to St. Barts (forty to sixty minutes): The new *Rapid Explorer* (542-9762; 27-66-33; www.rapidexplorer.com) departs up to four times daily. Current schedules are posted on its Web site. *The Edge,* operated by Aqua Mania Adventures (544-2640/2631), departs daily (9:00 a.m.) from Pelican Marina, Simpson Bay; $55 round-trip adult, $25 child. *Voyager* (87-10-68) departs from Captain Oliver's Marina at Oyster Pond daily at 12:30 and 4:00 p.m. with additional departures on Wednesday and Sunday (9:00 a.m. and 6:45 p.m.), $72 round-trip, $61 one-way. To Saba: *The Edge* departs (9:00 a.m.) Wednesday to Sunday from Pelican Marina and returns by 5:00 p.m.; $65.00 round-trip adults, $32.50 child; port fee $12.00 per person when departing St. Maarten. Ferries have a start-and-stop history here. Always check in advance before making plans.

Interisland Air Service See St. Maarten Fast Facts.

Emergency Numbers
Medical: Philipsburg Hospital, 543-1111
Ambulance: 542-2111
Police: St. Maarten, 542-2222 and 111

Marigot: A French Delight

Marigot is less than a twenty-minute drive from Philipsburg, but the differences make it light-years away. Marigot is so unmistakably Gallic you don't need the language, the signs, the food, the wine, or the khaki-clad gendarme to tell you so. The ambience is St. Tropez in the tropics—complete with sidewalk cafes, fishing boats, and a topless beach or two. You will find boutiques with French perfumes and fashionable sportswear, and gourmet shops and grocery stores where you can stock up on French products.

The little French capital is definitely worth a stroll. Despite modern incursions from new hotels, stores, and a marina with a large shopping and restaurant complex, the town retains its old character thanks to many West Indian–style houses, colonial buildings, and the main streets beautified with flowers.

At the harbor filled with fish and ferry boats, there are outdoor markets for fruit and vegetables and souvenirs. The waterfront has recently been expanded by landfill, adding a larger market area and parking space. Outdoor cafes offer delicious croissants and *pains au chocolat* to be enjoyed with espresso or cappuccino.

In Marigot a taxi service is located at the port near the ferries. Sample fares from Marigot: to Grand Case Beach Club, $12 to $15; to Philipsburg, $15. A 25 percent surcharge is added after 9:00 p.m. and 50 percent after midnight.

Ferries From Marigot Harbor, service to Anguilla leaves approximately every half hour, takes fifteen minutes, and costs $10 one-way plus $2 departure tax. You can buy tickets at a kiosk by the dock. The ferry dock in Anguilla is on the south side of the island. Don't forget to bring your passport or travel identification documents. Also from Marigot to St. Barts, *Voyager* (87-10-68; www.voyager-stbarths .com) departs Monday and Tuesday and Thursday through Saturday twice a day (9:15 a.m. and 6:45 p.m.); $72 round-trip, $61 one-way.

Interisland Air Service See St. Martin Fast Facts.

Emergency Numbers
Medical: Marigot Hospital, 29-57-57
Gendarmerie (police): 17
Fire, accident, ambulance: 18

Information St. Martin Tourist Information Bureau, Route de Sandy Ground, south of Marigot; 87-57-21; www.st-martin.org; info@st-martin.org.

St. Maarten on Your Own

Philipsburg sits on a thin crest of land hemmed in by two bodies of water: Great Bay on the south and Great Salt Pond on the north, and anchored by high hills at both ends of the crest. As a result, the downtown is only 2 blocks deep with two main streets: Frontstreet (Vorstraat, in Dutch) with traffic one-way east; Backstreet (Achterstraat), one-way west. Recently Frontstreet has been made into a pretty pedestrian mall and is being closed to traffic when cruise ships are in port. On the waterfront a new boardwalk has been laid in patterned brick and is gradually attracting new restaurants and shops, becoming the center of the action for Philipsburg.

With growth, two new roads—Cannegieter Street and Walter Nisbet Road (better known as Pondfill Road)—were added through landfill of Great Salt Pond in order to relieve the downtown traffic congestion. They have barely kept up with the pace. The pond once provided the island with its major source of income: salt, once an important commodity in world trade.

A stroll around town takes less than an hour unless you get sidetracked with shopping. Frontstreet and the little lanes, or *steegjes,* that connect it to Backstreet have boutiques, restaurants, air-conditioned shopping malls, and small hotels.

Courthouse On the north side of Wathey Square, a white clapboard building with green trim is the old Courthouse, built in 1793 and rebuilt in 1825. Originally the house of the colony's commander, in subsequent years it was used as the council chambers, courts, fire hall, and jail. Today the upper floor is still used by the courts, and the building serves as the town hall.

Guavaberry Emporium (599-542-2965; www .guavaberry.com) St. Maarten liquor made from rum and a local fruit, guavaberry, can be purchased from a shop at the east end of Frontstreet housed in a historic building dating from the late eighteenth century. Once the home of a St. Maarten governor, it is said to occupy the former site of a synagogue. The shop sells many flavors, any of which you can sample before you buy.

Royal Guest House Across the street is the **Pasanggrahan Hotel** (542-3588; www.pasanhotel .com), once the Royal Guest House, which hosted Queen Wilhelmina of the Netherlands when she was en route to exile in Canada after the Nazi invasion of her country. The modest inn, hidden behind its tropical gardens, was the favorite of those who discovered St. Maarten before the boom. The front porch and restaurant are directly on Great Bay Beach.

Museum of St. Maarten At the east end of Frontstreet is the Museum of St. Maarten, created in 1989 by the St. Maarten Historic Foundation. Located on the second floor of a small shopping complex, the modest museum has displays from excavations on the island and artifacts donated by residents. Next door is the gallery-museum of Mosera, one of St. Maarten's leading artists. Hours: Monday to Saturday from 10:00 a.m. to 4:00 p.m. Admission is $1; 542-0554.

Sint Maarten Nature Foundation Established in 1997 to preserve St. Maarten's environment, the foundation (599-542-0267; www.nature foundationsxm.org) is creating two nature parks accessible to the public with $306,000 in funding from the World Wildlife Fund—Holland. The **Sint Maarten Marine Park** (Great Bay Marina, #3 P.O. Box 863, Philipsburg; 599-542-0267) focuses on the eastern and southeastern areas of Dutch St. Maarten, protecting coastal waters and some adjacent coastline from Oyster Pond to Cupecoy Beach, including four small islands that serve as breeding grounds for birds and fish. The first step was to install moorings along the reefs so that dive operators and other vessels no longer had to anchor directly to the reefs. Now there are more than twenty-five moorings and a large area designated for local fishermen, as well as areas for diving sites and other water sports. The foundation negotiated with both the island's Dutch and French governments to pass laws to create the park.

The foundation's second effort is being aided by a group in Holland and the local government to purchase and restore Emilio Wilson Estate, the home of Commander John Philips, the island's first governor under British rule, and the adjacent Mary's Fancy Estate, two historical estates in the Cul-de-Sac area. Phase One, which entailed developing the Emilio Wilson Historical and Cultural Park, called Doctor's Yard, opened in 2002 with the first structure, a wood and guinea—grass thatched slave watch house. Located on L. B. Scott Road in Dutch Cul-de-Sac, the interesting property was originally a sugar plantation where slaves worked and lived. In 1851 part of the estate was sold to a medical doctor; that part became known as the doctor's yard.

The estate changed owners many times until 1954, when it was sold to Emilio Wilson, the son of a former slave. Wilson died in 2001, leaving an arrangement that enabled the foundation to establish the park. Now more structures can be visited, and the park has a restaurant and visitor facilities. Hours: daily 10:00 a.m. to 5:00 p.m. Donations are welcomed.

The foundation has also been involved in a mangrove planting program at Little Bay and Fresh Bay Ponds, organized a Sea Turtle Club with volunteers to help identify and safeguard nesting sites, and started an environmental awareness program in the local schools.

Fort Amsterdam Philipsburg does not have any "must see" historic sites, but a pavement at the foot of Frontstreet goes over the hill to Little Bay to the ruins of Fort Amsterdam, on the finger of land separating Great Bay and Little Bay. The fort dates from the seventeenth century.

A Drive around the Island

The best way to see and enjoy St. Maarten is to rent a car and drive around the island on your own. When you find a pretty beach or a scenic view, stop for a swim, a photo, or a picnic. One road circles the island, and secondary ones go inland or to secluded beaches. You can leave Philipsburg by the Ring Road, which runs west along Great Salt Pond and over Cole Bay Hill.

Cole Bay Hill Cemetery The Scottish adventurer John Philips is buried on the hill overlooking the town he founded. The hill separates Philipsburg from the west end of the island, where its best-known resorts are located. From an observation platform at the summit, you can see neighboring Saba, St. Eustatius, St. Kitts, and Nevis. The valley below overlooking Cay Bay was where Peter

Stuyvesant unsuccessfully battled the Spaniards in 1644.

Simpson Bay Lagoon After several winding miles the road intersects with Welfare Road, where you can turn north to Marigot or continue west along Simpson Bay Lagoon, the island's main setting for water sports. The road parallels the airport on the south; at the end of the runway is Maho Bay, the smart "suburb" of St. Maarten with attractive shops, good restaurants, and entertainment.

The main road west continues to Cupecoy and the French side, where secondary roads lead to La Samanna, a very expensive luxury resort on Long Beach, one of the island's most magnificent stretches of sand. The western end is hilly and provides good views of the island and coastline. West of Cupecoy is the dividing line between the two parts of the island.

Marigot The little French capital, even with its modern incursions, is definitely worth a stroll. For the most part the town has retained its character, with many Creole or West Indian–style houses and colonial buildings. Most now house chic little boutiques, perfume shops, restaurants, or the occasional sidewalk cafe, where the croissants are as tasty as in Paris.

At the harbor, filled with fishing and ferry boats, there is a daily outdoor arts and crafts market on the landfill-widened seafront promenade and a major fresh fruit, vegetable, and seafood market under its own roof on Wednesday and Saturday from 7:00 a.m. to 1:00 p.m. The **Marina Fort Louis** offers dock space, a landscaped area, and extended parking, and the **West Indies Mall** has very high-end shops (don't look for bargains here) and one of the town's best dinner restaurants, Le Gaiac (51-97-66). Bordering the harbor square on three sides are restaurants and sidewalk cafes. Those on the south side are tiny stalls, popular with townsfolk and tourists at lunchtime.

Branching out from here are the three main shopping streets—rue de la République, rue Kennedy, and rue General Charles de Gaulle—lined with shops in balconied buildings, some trimmed with gingerbread and wrought iron, reminiscent of New Orleans.

The town's most delightful spot is the yacht-filled Marina Royale, which you pass on your way into town. It is lined with seafood restaurants and sidewalk cafes—the best people-watching spots in town—where you really do feel you are in St. Tropez. Marigot has several supermarkets, where you can buy French cheese, wine, and other picnic supplies.

Louis Fort Built in 1776 on a strategic hilltop above Marigot Harbor, the fort is St. Martin's largest colonial fortification and at one time had fifteen cannons. Under the guidance of the St. Martin Historic and Cultural Foundation, the fort has been made more accessible and is being restored. Steps from the car park of the Sous-Prefectus lead up the hill; from here there are grand views south, across the islands to Simpson Lagoon and the leeward coast, and north, across the sea to Anguilla. The best time for a visit is early morning or late afternoon.

St. Martin Museum At Sandy Ground on the south side of Marigot is the St. Martin Museum, also called "On the Trail of the Arawaks." Three permanent exhibits are on view. The first displays artifacts from the archaeological excavations in St. Martin over the past decade, some dating from 1800 B.C.; a second display covers early explorers and colonization; and the third presents the island from 1900 to the 1960s. The exhibits are labeled in French and English. There are also changing exhibits of works by local artists. Hours: Monday to Friday, 9:00 a.m. to 1:00 p.m. and 3:00 to 6:00 p.m., Saturday to 1 p.m. Entrance: $5. Historic tours of St. Martin can be reserved through the museum: phone/fax: 29-22-84; museestmartin@power antilles.com; tours depart at 9:00 a.m. and return at 11:00 a.m. Cost is US $30.

Paradise Peak After Marigot en route to Grand Case, country roads on the east lead to the village of Colombier and Paradise Peak, the island's highest mountaintop. There is a short trail at the top, from which there are panoramic views. Look for the sign for **Loterie Farm** (Pic Paradise; 87-86-16; www.loteriefarm.net), a former sugar plantation whose long-hidden structures were uncovered when Hurricane Luis swept away the vegetation in 1995. This private nature reserve's 150 acres of untouched farmland, tropical forest, and hills provide excellent hiking trails as well as a unique setting for musical events and theme evenings around its rustic Hidden Forest Café. An informative 1.5-hour guided ecotour begins at 10:00 a.m. some mornings for $25. A canopy tour, which the Californian owner of the farm calls "fly the trees," has two levels: a higher and more challenging tour for adults and a lower, easier one for children at least 4 feet tall. For information and reservations for the treetop tour, call 87-86-16, visit www.loterie farm.com, or e-mail visit@loteriefarm.com.

Grand Case Five miles north of Marigot is Grand Case, a small town with an international reputation as a gourmet haven that now counts more than thirty dining establishments, including half a dozen that rank among the island's best. In the middle of all the haute cuisine are the *lolos* (seaside barbecue shacks) serving fresh West Indian fare, from Creole dishes to lobster, with lots of local atmosphere and down-to-earth prices. At the north end of town a dirt road west leads to Grand Case Beach Club, an American-operated beachfront hotel.

French Cul-de-Sac From Grand Case the road cuts east across the north tip of the island, the most mountainous part, to French Cul-de-Sac and the eastern side of the island fronting the Atlantic Ocean. A very hilly road continues north to Le Habitation, on one of St. Martin's prettiest beaches.

Orient Beach From the main east-coast route, secondary roads lead to Orient Beach. The long stretch of beautiful white sand is now densely populated with restaurants and beach clubs. The beach and swimming are free, but you will have to pay if you want to use one of the beach lounges and any other amenities or sports equipment. (There is a nudist beach at its eastern end.) Several of the water-sports operators here offer boat trips to the nearby islands that face the beach.

Continuing south, you will pass through the most rural part of the island. A side road takes you into the interior to Orleans.

The Butterfly Farm On Le Galion Beach Road (about a thirty-minute drive from Philipsburg) is **La Ferme des Papillons** (87-31-21; www.thebutterfly farm.com; info@thebutterflyfarm.com). In 1,000 square meters of tropical gardens fenced with wire mesh like an aviary, you can see hundreds of rare exotic butterflies flitting about freely. The gardens have a montage of blossoms to provide nectar for the butterflies and special plants to feed the caterpillars.

A guide leads visitors through the exhibit area, identifying species, pointing out courtship and mating displays, and relating interesting facts and stories about these beautiful creatures. Visitors also see the stages of the butterflies' life cycle, from laying their eggs to caterpillars hatching, growing, and forming their chrysalis. Visitors may wander through the gardens to take photos and video film or sit in the shaded areas to absorb the tranquil atmosphere, watch the butterflies, and listen to the soothing pan music heard quietly in the background. Guests are warmly welcomed by English owners William and Karin Slayter, general manager John Coward, and a staff that is always on hand to answer questions. They also can provide information on butterfly gardening, the unique farming techniques used at the Butterfly Farm, and tips for photographers. Hours: 9:00 a.m. to 3:00 p.m. Admission US $12 adults, US $6 children, which includes a complimentary pass for the duration of one's vacation. Visitors from cruise ships receive a $2 discount in lieu of the pass. A shop sells unusual butterfly gifts.

The Old House (87-32-67) Just beyond the entrance to Le Galion Beach is a rambling, traditional-style house with a green roof. A prominent family, the Beauperthuys, have occupied this hilltop structure for six generations. The present owner, Pierre, recently converted his ancestral home into a rum museum, where he displays many of his family's treasures and personally recounts their fascinating history. The rum-related poster collection and rums from around the world are as amusing as they are unusual. Hours: 10:00 a.m. to 4:00 p.m. daily except Monday. Admission: $10.

Oyster Pond/Dawn Beach Immediately after crossing the Dutch/French border, the road takes a sharp turn to the east, and after another mile it forks east to the Dawn Beach and Oyster Pond resort areas. (The return to Philipsburg can be made via Naked Boy Hill Road, a winding road south along Great Salt Pond.)

This drive can easily be taken in the reverse direction. If it is an afternoon drive, time your return to the western side for late afternoon to watch a St. Martin sunset. Don't miss it!

Shopping

On this half-Dutch, half-French island with its duty-free goods and smart boutiques, shopping is as much an attraction as are its restaurants and sports. You can buy delftware and Gouda cheese as easily as Limoges and Brie, not to mention Japanese cameras, Italian leather, Chinese linens, Colombian emeralds, and a host of other quality products from around the world. Savings range from 20 to 40 percent off U.S. prices, but, as we always emphasize, the best way to know if you are getting a good buy is to come with prices from home. St. Maarten shopkeepers are very competitive; it pays to shop around. Yet even the most ardent shoppers will probably find they can check out the best in either Philipsburg or Marigot in an hour or two.

Attractive shopping complexes with quality stores are also in the resort areas west of Philipsburg. The Maho Bay shops are centered around Maho Beach Hotel, and the attractive Cinnamon Grove Plaza is designed around an outdoor courtyard with boutiques in low-rise buildings of colorful West Indian–style architecture.

Stores named below are on Philipsburg's Frontstreet unless otherwise indicated. Some close for lunch from noon to 1:00 p.m. When cruise ships are in port on Sundays and holidays, some shops—not the best—open briefly.

Art and Artists Greenwith Galleries (542-3842) specializes in fine art of the Caribbean and represents thirty-six artists living in St. Maarten and nearby islands. **Simpson Bay Art Gallery** (Airport Road; 544-3464), situated in a lovely stone-and-wood "dollhouse," features the fanciful and sometimes whimsical works of Mounette Radot, a French artist who has lived on St. Maarten for many years. She also shows the work of local artists. Open daily, including Sunday.

Mosera Fine Arts Gallery (7 Speetjens Arcade, Frontstreet; phone/fax: 542-0554; www .speetjens.com/mosera; mosera@speetjens.com) is the gallery of Mosera Henry, one of St. Maarten's most talented artists, who is originally from St. Lucia. In addition to his works, exhibits of other artists are shown and poetry readings and plays are held from time to time. Hours: weekdays 10:00 a.m. to 2:00 p.m. and 3:00 to 5:00 p.m.

Among other St. Maarten artists are Ria Zonneveld, who creates unusual clay busts with a touch of whimsy; Ruby Bute, Joe Dominique, and Cyrnic Griffith, are some of the best-known painters of local scenes.

The French side is particularly active, with several dozen galleries. Most are located in Marigot or Grand Case; many show French or other Europeans and Americans living in St. Martin for part or all of the year. Many restaurants show local artists throughout the year. *Ti Gourmet,* a local guide to dining and restaurants, has a list of galleries and artists who show at their homes, along with their phone numbers. **Roland Richardson Gallery** (6 rue de la République, 87-84-08; 87-32-24; www .rolandrichardson.com) is the gallery of Roland Richardson, the island's best-known artist, situated in a handsome, renovated nineteenth-century Creole house next door to the house where he was born.

In Grand Case members of an artist family from New York have a gallery in their home (87-77-24). They include Gloria Lynn, a painter of local scenes; husband, Martin Lynn, a sculptor; and son, Robert, also a painter.

On the main road at Orient is **The Potters,** where you can watch master potters and their apprentices at work and buy their products.

Books/Maps In addition to crafts, **Shipwreck Shop** carries books, magazines, maps, postcards reproduced from paintings, prints by island artists, and stamps.

Cameras/Electronics Boolchand's (www .Boolchand.com) has three downtown stores where you will find the leading names in Japanese cameras and electronic equipment. Bring prices from home for comparison. The shops also carry linens, jewelry, and Bally and Adidas shoes.

China/Crystal Little Switzerland, a familiar name throughout the Caribbean, carries only the highest-quality English china, French crystal, Swiss watches, Hummel figurines, and other gift items. You can request a catalog in advance by calling (800) 524-2010. **Dutch Delft Blue Gallery** is a specialty shop for delftware.

Clothing Liz Claiborne, Ralph Lauren, and Tommy Hilfiger are the most familiar name-labels with their own stores here. The **Sint Rose Shopping Mall** in the heart of town has a variety of shops facing Frontstreet and restaurants, bars, an art gallery, and other attractions on the other side along the boardwalk and the beach. The **Fashion District Italian Outlet** (Maho Village; 545-3573) is the first in the Caribbean and offers wall-to-wall Italian designer labels such as Prada, Armani, Versace, and more at 50 percent off or more. They offer free delivery to cruise ships. **Endless Summer** (27 Frontstreet; 542-1510; endlesssummer sxm@hotmail.com) has an impressive selection of international beachwear, particularly bathing suits in all shapes and sizes.

Crafts Impressions (Promenade Arcade) specializes in authentic native arts and crafts from the Caribbean, folklore, occult artifacts, and herbs and spices. The best craftwork comes from Moro of Haiti, whose artisans make carved and painted wood pieces that are original and distinctive. Another unusual craft, bread and fruit baskets made from fired coconut shells, comes from Nevis. **Seabreeze** (Promenade Arcade) carries hand-painted T-shirts by Ruby Bute as well as her postcards. **The Shipwreck Shop** and **American West Indian Company** carry quality Caribbean crafts and souvenirs.

Food Specialties The Antilles Spice Clipper (542-5358; www.lordandhunter.com; info@shipwreckshops.com) line of sauces and Caribbean condiments carried at **Lord & Hunter** and a dozen other stores, including **Shipwreck, Cabana,** and **Boardwalk,** are perfect small carry-home gifts. The stores also carry island clothing, souvenir items, and gifts.

Jewelry H. Stern is known from New York to Rio for fine jewelry of original design. Its merchandise comes with an international one-year exchange guarantee. **Little Switzerland** also has a full line of quality brands. If emeralds are your passion, **Colombian Emeralds** has the largest collection, and the staff is quick to remind you that unmounted emeralds can be brought into the United States free of customs duty. The merchandise also carries a guarantee honored by the company's Miami office. The best selection of high-end watches is found at **Oro de Sol** (Cartier, Chopard, Ebel, and Harry Winston), along with exclusive jewelry, and **Goldfinger's,** which is also the island's Rolex agent. **Pearl Gems** has the Caribbean's largest selection of cultured and freshwater pearls; **Artistic** is the Mikimoto specialist. For more modest shopping, **Treasure Cove,** in a restored West Indian house, has gold jewelry and semiprecious stones.

Leather/Luggage Several stores, such as **Maximo Florence** and **MCM** (Simpson Bay; 545-5470), carry high-quality Italian-leather handbags and accessories.

Linens New Amsterdam (you'll recognize it by the brightly painted tulips on the facade) specializes in hand-embroidered linens, quality gifts, and jewelry. The second floor features large selections of men's and women's sportswear, bathing suits, and shoes.

Liquor Philipsburg Liquor Store and Rum Jumbie Liquor (Point Blanche; 542-3587; www.rumjumbie.com) adjacent to the cruise-ship dock is hard to miss. It's St. Maarten's best, with a full line of liquors and wine. And don't overlook the **Guavaberry Tasting Shop** (described earlier in the Philipsburg walking tour). Their attractively bottled liqueurs made from a local fruit, guavaberry, make unusual, inexpensive gifts to take home. Don't miss **Ma Doudou's** flavored rums and spices in their unique handpainted bottles found in the better souvenir shops and markets on both sides of the island.

Perfumes The Yellow House (west of the post office), **Lipstick,** and **Penha** have large stocks of cosmetics and French perfumes. The latter store also carries sportswear and fashion jewelry.

Marigot

Shops along rue de la République, rue Kennedy, rue General Charles de Gaulle, and around the Marina Royale feature French and Italian designer clothes at designer prices, including such prestigious names as Armani, Chloe, Jean-Paul Gaultier, Hermes, Max Mara, and Versace. The craft market has expanded into more spacious waterfront stalls, and shopping is now as good as in Philipsburg. The better shops have branches on both sides.

The area around and beyond the Ferry Dock has been upgraded with the addition of the Marina Fort Louis, with space for mega-yachts, and Le West Indies Mall, a glossy trilevel structure providing luxury shopping, wining, and dining in air-conditioned comfort with twenty-two boutiques (Lancel, Newman, Lacoste, among others), a piano bar, and two restaurants, including a rooftop gourmet gathering place, **Le Gaiac,** with 180° views and a chef from Michel Guerard. Store hours are Monday to Saturday from 9:00 a.m. to 1:00 p.m. and 3:00 to 7:00 p.m. Some stores open when ships are in port on Sundays and holidays.

For those interested in art, many resident artists show their works in several galleries and at-home studios. Among the best known are Roland Richardson, the late Alexandre Minguet at Morne O'Reilly, Francis Eck in Concordia, Antoine Chapon in Cul-de-Sac, and Marie Moine and Donna Bryhiel in Oyster Pond.

Dining and Restaurants

The number and variety of good restaurants on this small island are astonishing. The best gourmet selections, which have won the island international recognition, are on the French side, particularly in the tiny village of Grand Case. But be prepared for the bill. Many are as expensive as top French restaurants in New York. The restaurants listed below in Philipsburg are located on Frontstreet unless otherwise indicated. Moderate means less than $20 per person, expensive means $35 or more, and very expensive means $50 or more per person. Expensive gourmet restaurants close one day during the week, usually Sunday or Monday, but it is best to check in advance, as opening hours and days vary.

St. Maarten

Cheri's Cafe (Maho Shopping Center; 545-3361) is a lively open-air cafe and bar, with music and dancing every evening. Food is served from 11:00 a.m. to midnight; the varied menu has salads, fresh fish, steaks, and hamburgers. Moderate.

Kangaroo Court (Frontstreet; 542-4278), a cafe/deli in a historic building across from the courthouse, serves big salads, hearty sandwiches on home-baked bread, fresh-squeezed lemonade, and scrumptious cakes and pastries in a lovely hidden garden, a true oasis in the middle of Philipsburg's bustle. Moderate.

Oualichi (Boardwalk; 542-4316), a restaurant on the new boardwalk, offers air-conditioned inside seating or outdoor seating on the terrace for pizza, pasta, lobster, and a variety of other selections. Huge portions. Moderate.

Saratoga (Simpson Bay; 545-2421) was created by a Culinary Institute of America graduate who creates contemporary American cuisine with a Pacific Rim touch. It has a delightful terrace setting overlooking the bay. Expensive.

Taloula Mango's (Boardwalk; 542-1645), an early newcomer to the boardwalk, serves burgers, ribs, and seafood. Jazz on Sunday. Moderate.

Temptation (Atlantis Casino Courtyard; 545-2254) is the restaurant of the well-known local chef Dino Jagtiani, who is St. Maarten's first native-born graduate of the Culinary Institute of America. His menu is French–Caribbean fusion and has garnered rave reviews. In the same location, he also has **Rare** (545-5714), an American-style steakhouse. Expensive.

Turtle Pier Bar (Simpson Bay Lagoon; 545-2562; www.turtlepier.com), in a delightful setting on the lagoon, has its own boat dock and sundeck, where you can enjoy light fare or nightly entertainment. Moderate.

St. Martin
Marigot and Beyond

Bar de la Mer (on the waterfront; 87-81-79; bardelamer@powerantilles.com), a casual, friendly cafe and bar serving salads, pizzas, and steak, is a great people-watching and rendezvous place. They lend backgammon sets, too! Moderate.

Mini Club (87-50-69) is an old-time rustic favorite, especially on Wednesday and Saturday evenings for the large buffet ($35). Moderate.

Tropicana (Marina Royale; 87-79-07) has terrace tables overlooking Marigot's popular marina, which are much in demand at both lunch and dinner and require a reservation. The small brasserie-style menu is creative, the daily specials are always excellent, the ambience is convivial, and the prices just can't be beat for the consistently high quality. Moderate.

Grand Case and Environs

L'Alabama (87-81-66) is a local favorite for French cuisine. (This is despite its unlikely name; one owner, Karin, is from Austria and the other, Pascal, is from France.) Fish and steak dishes with wonderful sauces and great desserts are served for very reasonable prices. Closed Monday.

L'Auberge Gourmande (Grand Case; 87-73-37; www.laubergegourmande.com) offers the best value of the town's leading dozen restaurants. Moderately expensive. The owner's other restaurant, Le Tastevin (across the street; 87-55-45) has a contemporary French menu. Expensive.

Captain Oliver's Restaurant & Marina (Oyster Pond; 87-30-00; www.captainolivers.com) has a delightful waterfront setting where you—and its loyal local patrons—can enjoy French and Continental cuisine. Moderate.

Rainbow (176 Boulevard de Grand Case; 87-55-80). Many St. Martin cognoscenti consider this airy beachfront restaurant the best on the island for contemporary French cuisine. It's expensive but worth the price. Open for dinner daily except Sunday.

Sunset Cafe (Grand Case Beach Club; 87-37-37; www.gcbc.com), extending out over the water, is a great relaxing and informal location to enjoy excellent seafood. Moderate.

Sports

In most cases you should contact the hotel or sports operator in advance to make arrangements, particularly during the peak season, when demand is likely to be high.

Beaches/Swimming St. Maarten is famous for its beaches—more than three dozen lovely white-sand stretches and coves where you might easily spend the day. Some are busy with people, facilities, and concessioners; others are quiet and secluded. Some of the beaches on French St. Martin are nude or topless, but none are on St.

Maarten. If you take a taxi to one of the more secluded beaches, arrange with the taxi driver a specific time to return, and agree in advance on the price of the round-trip fare. The Web site www.sint-maarten.net has photographs and descriptions, beach by beach, of those on both the Dutch and French coasts.

The beaches are listed here by their proximity to Philipsburg. A taxi to west-side beaches costs about $10 to $15; those to the east side about $15; and north to Orient Bay, $20.

Great Bay, a mile-long strand directly in town on Great Bay, has calm and generally clean water, and now, with the new boardwalk and renovations and the cruise port having been moved to Pointe Blanche, the beach is once again an attractive and convenient place to enjoy a beach day. Little Bay, west of town within walking distance of town, is a smaller beach with lovely water; there are several hotels on the beach with water sports. Simpson Bay and Maho Bay, by the airport, have hotels with concessioners handling water-sports activities. Farther west, Cupecoy Beach—with sandstone cliffs as a backdrop—is quiet and less accessible. There are no facilities other than a beach bar on the cliffs, where you can rent snorkel gear. The far end of the beach is used for bathing in the buff.

Long Beach, at the far western end of the south shore, is one of the Caribbean's most beautiful beaches, and rounding the point are Plum Bay and Rouge Beach, two secluded beaches more easily reached by boat. Rouge Beach has a beach bar. Both are topless beaches.

On the east side of St. Maarten, Oyster Pond and Dawn Beach constitute a long, wide stretch along Guana Bay where the Atlantic washes the shore. The south end is popular for surfing. Orient Beach, on the northeast, is another very long beach that has been built up with condos and beach bars in recent years. The southeastern end of the beach is a nudist beach.

Boating St. Maarten offers excursions on two types of boats: large catamarans, holding up to twenty-five or more passengers, which go to Anguilla, Prickly Pear, and Tintamarre, or small sailboats for six to ten passengers, which sail to a secluded beach for a swim, snorkel, and picnic or sunset cruise. Boats leave from **Bobby's Marina** (542-4096; www.bobbysmarina.com) or **Pelican Marina** (544-2640) about 9:00 or 9:30 a.m. and return about 5:00 or 5:30 p.m. Prices are $70 to $80 per person plus $5 departure tax.

The America's Cup Regatta (542-0045, www.12metre.com) is St. Maarten's most popular excursion for cruise passengers. Participants do actually sail in a race as crew on a boat that has been an America's Cup contender. The price for the excursion can range from $85 to $99, depending on your cruise ship. The price is $78 if you buy the excursion directly from the America's Cup operator, but departures are not guaranteed. Booking through your ship's excursion desk gives you a guarantee to sail, so you are better advised to buy your ship's excursion and to book it at your earliest opportunity, because it sells out quickly. There are four sails a day, every day of the year except Christmas.

Deep-Sea Fishing Charters with tackle, bait, sandwiches, and drinks cost approximately $600 for half-day, $900 for full-day, and are available from **Bobby's Marina** and **Blue Water Sport Fishing** (Simpson Bay; 545-3230); on the French side, **Samaco Sportfishing** (61-81-61) and **Luxe Caraibes** (29-51-93; www.luxecaraibes.com). The season for dolphin, mahimahi, and kingfish is December to April; tuna, year-round.

Golf Mullet Bay Golf Course (545-2801) is the island's only golf course. It's open daily but only minimally maintained.

Hiking There are 25 miles of hiking trails, and *Nature*, an impressive local magazine published annually, has brief descriptions of them, including length and level of difficulty. Paradise Peak, on the French side, is the highest point on the island and can be reached partway by vehicle, but eventually must be approached by foot. Contact the Association Action Nature (87-97-87) or the Dutch Hiking Club (542-4917). TriSports (545-4384; www .trisportsxm.com) offers hiking, mountain bikes, and kayaking. On the French side try **Authentic French Tours** (Rue de Hollande, Marigot, 87-05-11). Other

sources are **Loterie Farms-Colombier** (87-86-16; see description earlier in this chapter; **Oliver Borensztejn** (0690-62-79-07, oliviersxm@ yahoo.fr); St. Maarten National Heritage Foundation (599-542-4917); and St. Maarten Road Runners Club (599-556-7815).

Horseback Riding Bayside Riding Club (Le Galion Beach; 87-36-64; www.baysideridingclub .com) takes small groups with a guide on rides. Reservations must be made in advance. At the north end in French St. Martin, **OK Corral** (Coralita Beach; 87-40-72) offers similar excursions. On the Dutch side is **Lucky Stable** (Cay Bay; 544-5255; cell 555-7246; www.luckystable.com), which offers one-hour ($45) and two-hour ($65) trail rides, along with a dip in the ocean.

Kayaking TriSports (Simpson Bay; 545-4384; 599-545-4385; www.trisportsxm.com) rents kayaks for exploring the lagoon. It also has mountain bikes for rent for exploring the island. On the French side there's **Wind Adventures** (29-41-57) and **Tropical Wave** (87-37-25).

Kiteboarding The new craze sweeping the water-sports world is popular in St. Martin. Orient Bay and Le Galion Beach are considered to be good places to start. The island's kitesurfing school, located between Kakao and Kontiki on Orient Beach, is operated by **Club Nathalie Simon** (29-41-57). Classes are limited to two persons and are taken off from nearby Green Cay. **Wind Adventures** (Orient Bay Resort, 29-41-5; www.wind-adventures.com) offers a three-hour lesson of kiting basics for €100.

Snorkeling/Scuba St. Maarten is a good place to learn to snorkel, because there are reefs near shore in shallow water so clear that visibility to 150 feet is normal. It is also a good place to try your first scuba dive. A one-day resort course is available from **Ocean Explorers Dive Center** (Simpson Bay; 544-5252; www.stmaartendiving .com), $70. On the Dutch side are **Aqua Mania Adventures** (Pelican Bay Marina; 544-2640), **Dive Safaris** (Bobby's Marina; 542-9001; www.divest maarten.com), and **Scuba Fun** (Divi Little Bay; 542-2333; www.scubafun.com); on the French side, **The Scuba Shop** (Oyster Pond; 87-48-01; www

.thescubashop.net) and **Scuba Fun** (Anse Marcel; 87-36-13).

Experienced divers will enjoy St. Maarten's wrecks, as well as a variety of reefs characterized by a descending series of gentle hills and valleys and a rich display of colorful fish. Near the entrance to Great Bay Harbor lies the British man-of-war the HMS *Prostellyte,* sunk in 1801. The hull is gone, but divers can see coral-encrusted anchors, cannons, and other of the ship's fittings.

Off the northeast coast, **Ilet Pinel** offers shallow diving; **Green Key** is a barrier reef rich in sea life; **Flat Island,** also known as Tintamarre, has sheltered coves and a sunken tugboat. The area comprising Flat Island, Ilet Pinel, Green Key, and **Petite Clef** is protected in the Underwater Nature Reserve. The water-sports operator at Orient Beach has snorkeling trips to Green Key island, two hours, for $30.

Windsurfing The best windsurfing is at Le Galion Beach, where **Tropical Wave** (87-37-25) rents boards for $25 to $30 per hour and has a lesson package, too. Orient Beach is another popular location. **Wind Adventures** (Orient Bay Resort, 29-41-57; www.wind-adventures.com) offers a private one-hour lesson for €40. Windsurfing boards are also available at most beachside resorts.

Entertainment

St. Maarten's very lively nightlife offers music varying from piano bars to discos and calypso bands at large resorts and restaurants specializing in Caribbean cuisine. Small as it is, the Dutch side has thirteen casinos. Most are in or connected with a hotel and open at noon. Those closest to the Philipsburg pier are on Frontstreet: **Beach Plaza** (Frontstreet; www.beachplazasxm.com); **Rouge et Noir** (www.casinorougeetnoir.com) at Seaview Hotel and the Coliseum Casino, with a gallery of slot machines and a shopping arcade; and **Jump Up** (Emmaplein; www.jumpupcasino.com), with its Carnival theme. The Maho area is the center of the action, although that's beginning to change somewhat with the new attractions on the new boardwalk in town.

On the French side, Marina Royale and the waterfront by Marigot's market draw the crowds.

Clubs start at midnight and go until dawn. Some names to note are **Q Club** and **The Sopranos** at the Sonesta Maho Beach Resort & Casino, **Bamboo Bernies** (www.bamboobernies.com) at Caravanserai Resort, and the **Havana Too** in Marigot.

Festivals The year's major festival is Carnival, beginning mid-April and ending with Coronation Day, April 30, a public holiday.

Saba: The Storybook Isle

Saba (pronounced SAY-ba), located 28 miles southwest of St. Maarten, is the most curious island in the Caribbean. It is a cone-shaped volcanic peak rising straight up from the sea to 3,000 feet. It has no flat land and no beaches.

When Dutch engineers surveyed the island's steep mountainous terrain in the 1930s, they concluded that construction of a road would be impossible. Undeterred, a local resident, Lambertus Hassell, decided to prove them wrong even though he had no technical training. He sent away for and studied an engineering correspondence course, organized the island's citizens, and in 1943 completed the first .75-mile of road up the mountain face to the capital, The Bottom.

Twenty years later, in 1963, the last stretch was finished. The road drops 1,312 feet in twenty hairpin turns ending at the island's airport, which was cut out of the mountainside, too. It looks something like the deck of an aircraft carrier at sea. Landing here in one of Winair's STOL aircraft is an experience you will never forget.

But then, everything about Saba is unusual and unforgettable. The population of about 1,090 is made up mostly of the descendants of Scottish, Irish, and Dutch settlers. And what a hardy bunch they must have been! Before the airport and road were built, people and goods were hoisted up the side of rock cliffs. The alternative was to climb the steep mountain paths to reach the island's several villages.

Hell's Gate and Windwardside Today the hand-laid road that zigzags up the mountain from the airport leads first to Hell's Gate and continues to Windwardside, a lilliputian village of gingerbread houses with white picket fences. Were it not for the tropical gardens surrounding them, you could imagine yourself on the set of *Hansel and Gretel* rather than on a Caribbean island. One of the homes, a sea captain's house built in the mid-nineteenth century, is the **Saba Museum,** which has a display of pre-Columbian artifacts found on Saba. It is open Monday to Friday from 10:00 a.m. to noon and 1:00 to 3:30 p.m. There is a small donation for admission.

Mount Scenery From Windwardside a series of 1,064 steps rise through the misty rain forest rich in flora and fauna to the summit of 2,855-foot Mount Scenery—well named for the magnificent panoramas of the Caribbean and neighboring islands that are there to reward hikers. Most trekkers take a picnic lunch and make a day of the climb to enjoy the views and lush vegetation along the way. If you have less time and energy, you can hike to one of several other locations on trails that have been developed by the **Saba Conservation Foundation** (Box 18, Fort Bay, Saba, N.A.; 416-3295; fax: 416-3435; www.sabapark.org).

The most popular stop for lunch or dinner is **Brigadoon Restaurant** (416-2380) in Windwardside. The menu has selections of seafood and Creole specialties that have been given a sophisticated touch and are served with fruits, vegetables, and herbs from local farms. **My Kitchen** (Windwardside; 416-2539; caru@unspoiledqueen .com) is located near the Mount Scenery trailhead; you can pick up lunch to carry on your hike. It features an open deck in a tropical setting for lunch or dinner and serves steaks, seafood, freshly baked bread, and European-Caribbean fusion dishes. **Scout's Place** (Windwardside; 416-2205) restaurant and bar is newly renovated and offers a variety of dishes, such as Saba lobster, spit-roasted chicken, and the catch-of-the-day at reasonable prices.

Rainforest Restaurant (416-3888; www .ecolodge-saba.com), the restaurant of the Ecolodge, changes its menu daily depending on what can be gotten fresh from its garden and the sea. Moderate.

The Bottom From Windwardside the road descends to The Bottom, another doll-like village of white clapboard houses with red gabled roofs and neat little gardens. The former **Government Guesthouse,** one of the town's most historic buildings, is Antique Inn.

Saba Artisans' Foundation At the Saba Artisans' Foundation (416-3260) you can find needlework, silk-screened fabrics, beachwear, and other island specialties. Open 8:00 a.m. to noon. and 2:30 to 5:00 p.m.

Saba Marine Park Saba's steep volcanic cliffs drop beneath the sea as vertical walls encrusted with a fantastic variety of reefs and other marine life. To protect this treasure, the Saba Marine Park was developed with the help of the Netherlands Antilles National Park Foundation, the World Wildlife Fund of the Netherlands, and others. The park comprises the entire shoreline and seabed from the high-water mark to a depth of 200 feet and two offshore seamounts. It has twenty-six self-guided underwater trails and areas designated for recreation. The park was developed under the guidance of Tom van't Hof, who also directed the marine parks in Bonaire and Curaçao and has written a guidebook to the park. The main dive areas are on the west coast. **Ladder Bay** to **Torrens Point** is an all-purpose recreational zone and includes Saba's only "beach," a stretch of pebble shore with shallow water. The most frequented sites are at Tent Bay to the southwest, where the wall drops to 80 feet and is covered with colorful tube sponges and black coral. The reef is a long, shallow ledge at 50 feet with overhangs where snorkelers and divers can see huge barrel sponges, barracudas, French angelfish, and more.

Saba Deep Dive Center (416-3347; fax: 416-3397; 888-DIVE-SABA; www.sabadeep.com), **Saba Divers** (Scout's Place; 416-2740; www.sabadivers .com), and **Sea Saba** (416-2246; 800-883-SABA; www.seasaba.com) are the island's fully equipped dive operators with their own dive boats. Each offers several dive trips daily and arranges fishing excursions. The Saba Bank, 3 miles southwest of Saba, is a 32-mile region of shallow water where fishing is terrific. Sea Saba's Web site publishes a newsletter with information on the dive operators' PADI/National Geographic program, a link to its "Sea & Learn" program, and updates and calendar of events of interest to divers and environmentalists.

Sightseeing Taxis with driver/guides are available at the airport for tours of the island, or, for those who arrive by boat, at Fort Bay, the port on the southwest corner of the island. Guided nature tours of Mount Scenery and other locations can be arranged through the Saba Tourist Office in Windwardside.

Ferry Service From St. Maarten, *The Edge,* a high-speed ferry, departs Wednesday to Sunday at 9:00 a.m. from Pelican Marina and returns by 5:00 p.m.; $65 round-trip adults, $32.50 children. *Dawn II* (www.sabactransport.com) leaves from Dock Maarten Tuesday, Thursday, and Saturday, $80 round-trip adult, $35 child age two through twelve, same day return.

Telephone Area Code To phone Saba from the United States, dial 011-599-41 plus the local number.

Information www.sabatourism.com

From the United States: Saba and St. Eustatius Tourist Information Office, P.O. Box 527, Windwardside, Saba, N.A.; iluvsaba@unspoiledqueen.com.

In Saba: Saba Tourist Office, Windwardside, Saba, N.A.; 416-2231, 416-2322; fax: 599-416-2350; iluvsaba@unspoiledqueen.com; holmglen@hotmail.com

St. Eustatius: A Cruel Twist of Fate

Statia, as St. Eustatius is known, is ten minutes by plane south of Saba. You may need all the imagination you can summon to believe it today, but this island of only 8 square miles was once the richest free port in the Americas, with a population of 8,000 (it has 2,089 today), where everything from cotton to contraband from around the world was traded. In the first two hundred years after Columbus discovered it, the island changed hands twenty-two times!

Fort Oranje During the American Revolution the neutral position of Holland, which had claimed the island in 1640, was suspect to the British because St. Eustatius was used as a transit point for arms and goods destined for the rebels. On November 16, 1776, after the island's garrison saluted the *Andrew Doria* flying the American flag—the first foreign port to do so after the United States declared its independence—the gesture so enraged the British that they sacked the town and destroyed the harbor. (The late Barbara Tuchman's book *The First Salute,* published in 1988, is based on this incident.)

In one of history's saddest cases of overkill, the British navy left the Dutch flag up long enough to lure 150 merchant ships into the harbor, then confiscated their cargo, burned the town to the ground, and, as the coup de grâce, destroyed the harbor's breakwater. The grand houses and warehouses tumbled into the sea. The island never recovered.

(More recent research debunks this version of the events, which has become the embellished truth of local lore.)

Under President Franklin D. Roosevelt, the United States expressed its belated thanks, and the fort and other buildings dating from the eighteenth century were restored with U.S. help. Although we can wonder why, Statia-America Day, celebrated on November 16, is one of the island's main events.

Oranjestad The little town of Oranjestad is divided into two parts. Upper Town, a pretty little community of palm-shaded, cobblestoned streets lined with West Indian gingerbread-trimmed houses and flowering gardens, grew up around the old fort atop a 150-foot cliff overlooking the sea. Lower Town, the site of the famous old harbor, is the docking area today, and to the north is the island's main beach. Only a few feet beneath the sea rests centuries-old debris that has led researchers to call Statia "an archaeologist's nightmare and a scuba diver's dream." The two parts of town are connected by the cobblestoned pedestrian walk and a paved road.

St. Eustatius Historical Foundation Museum (Simon Doncker House, Oranjestad, 318-2693, www.steustatiushistory.org, secar@hotmail.com) A colonial house near the fort contains the town's museum, which displays artifacts from Indian settlements dating from A.D. 300, as well as seventeenth- and eighteenth-century artifacts found in the underwater ruins of warehouses, wharfs, and shipwrecks. You can get a brochure with a map for a self-guided tour of the fort and surrounding historic buildings. These include the old Government House, a Dutch Reform church, a synagogue that was probably the second or third created in the Western Hemisphere, and other ruins from the eighteenth century.

The Quill The crater of an extinct volcano that dominates the south end of the island, the Quill can be seen distinctively in the island's silhouette. A series of eight signposted trails has been developed, enabling you to hike up to and around the crater's rim, down into the cone, and around the outside of the cone at about midgirth. The hikes were designed as a series of contiguous trails that can take from one hour up to a full day.

The most popular trail leads from town up the western slope of the crater to the rim in about an hour. It meets another trail, which is a steep path down to the floor of the crater, passing through steamy thick foliage where trees, protected from winds and hurricanes, grow tall. Their trunks and branches are entwined with enormous elephant ears, other vines, and sometimes tiny orchids. The crater's interior is planted with bananas, but over the years it has been cultivated with coffee, cacao, and cinnamon trees, which now grow wild.

Stenapa (St. Eustatius Marine and National Parks Foundation), a nongovernmental organization for conservation and protection of the natural and cultural heritage of St. Eustatius, manages the national parks. In 1997 the island council adopted the Protection of Flora and Fauna ordinance, which gave particular areas of the island protective status, including the higher parts of the Quill and certain plant and animal species. Hunting the Antillean iguana is prohibited, as is collecting and trading the Statia morning glory and fifteen species of orchid. For information: STENAPA, Gallowsbay, P.O. Box 59, St. Eustatius, N.A.; 599-318-2814; fax: 599-318-2913; www.statiapark.org.

St. Eustatius Marine Park The Marine Park (www.statiapark.org/parks/marine), opened in January 1998, is currently being developed east of St. Eustatius. Scuba divers have a heyday exploring the ruins of the houses and warehouses in the old harbor that have lain undisturbed for two hundred

years. Farther out the sea bottom is littered with hundreds of shipwrecks, some dating back three hundred years. Atop this jumble corals grow, attracting a great variety of fish and marine life. That combination of coral reefs, marine life, and historic shipwrecks, all untouched by commercial development, is what makes Statia extraordinary and so exciting to divers. Most diving is in 20 to 80 feet of crystal-clear water, which makes it accessible to snorkelers, too.

Sixteen sites have been charted to date—a descriptive map is available on the park's Web site. The most popular, dubbed the Supermarket, is located about .5 mile off the coast from Lower Town at a 60-foot depth. It has two shipwrecks less than 50 yards apart, with patches of beautiful coral and colorful sponges growing over them. There are also rare fish here; the flying gurnards are the most intriguing. About 12 inches long, these fish are black with white spots and iridescent blue pectoral wings, and they move through the water like hovering birds. The park maintains twelve yacht moorings in the bay (yellow buoys) and charges a yacht fee, $10 per night or $30 per week. Snorkelers wishing to use the moorings must buy a dive tag: $3 for a single dive or $15 for an annual pass. Fees go toward maintenance, cleaning, and rope replacement of the moorings.

In 2002 the St. Eustatius government acquired the 300-foot *Charles L. Brown,* a vessel used for cable-laying by AT&T, and is preparing it to be an artificial reef. The vessel crossed many oceans to arrive in Statia. Information is available from www.statia park.org/artreef/charlesbrown.html. The Web site also provides links to the St. Eustatius Office of Tourism and to Statia's three local dive operators: **Dive Statia** (Lower Town; 318-2435; 866-614-3491; U.S. 405-843-7846; www .divestatia.com), the island's first water-sports operator, with its own boats making two or three dives daily; **Golden Rock Dive Center** (P.O. Box 93; Lower Town, St. Eustatius; 800-311-6658; 318-2964; www.goldenrockdive.com), which offers one-tank dives for $45, two-tank for $75, and snorkeling for $25; and **Scubaqua** (Blue Bead Restaurant; 318-2160; www.scubaqua.com), operated by a professional Swiss group. All three operators can handle from beginners to advanced divers.

Interisland Air Service St. Eustatius is a ten-minute flight south of Saba or seventeen minutes from St. Maarten. Winair has five flights daily; round-trip airfare is about $100. The airport is located midisland, about 1.5 miles from town. There you can arrange a tour by taxi or rent a car. Donkeys can be hired for climbing up to the crater.

Telephone Area Code To phone St. Eustatius from the United States, dial 011-599 plus the local number.

Information www.statiatourism.com

In St. Eustatius: St. Eustatius Tourist Bureau, Fort Oranjestraat 3, Oranjestad, St. Eustatius, N.A.; 318-2433 or 318-2213.

Anguilla: Tranquility Wrapped in Blue

Anguilla is a British colony that has the distinction of rebelling to remain a colony. Until its super-deluxe resorts were spread across the pages of slick travel and fashion magazines in the 1980s, Anguilla was the best-kept secret in the Caribbean. The small coral island 5 miles north of St. Martin is especially noted for its three dozen gleaming white-sand beaches—which you can have practically to yourself—and the clear, blue-green waters surrounding it.

Known to its original Arawak Indian inhabitants as *Malliouhana,* the island takes its name from the French word for eel, *anguille,* or the Spanish, *anguilla*—they were both here—because of its shape. In the past, when it had only a few tiny hotels and guesthouses, the tranquil island appealed to true beachcombers who cared little for social conveniences. Yachtsmen, too, have long been attracted to the spectacular waters around Anguilla, as have snorkelers and scuba divers from neighboring islands. Two large reefs with huge coral formations growing to the surface of the sea lie off the island's shores.

Even with all the attention, the island's unspoiled quality remains. But then, the Anguillans are as appealing as their island. Until the tourism boom began, most were fishermen supplying the restaurants in St. Martin. The 16-mile-long island got its first golf course in 2006, but it still has no casinos, and there may still be as many goats and sheep as people.

Several of the superdeluxe hotels attracted much of the attention. **Cap Juluca,** a sybaritic fantasy in Moorish design, graces one of the most magnificent powdery white-sand beaches in the Caribbean. **Malliouhana,** on the island's northwest coast overlooking two spectacular beaches, is Mediterranean in design with graceful interiors by Larry Peabody, known for his stylish decor in other Caribbean resorts. The resort has three terraced swimming pools, three tennis courts, a full range of water sports, and a new 15,000-square-foot spa. If you want to do any more than look—perhaps have a meal—you will need to make arrangements in advance and be prepared to spend US $100 for lunch.

For such a small island, Anguilla has an extraordinary number of good restaurants; there were eighty at last count. Some of the best are in the top hotels: Altamer, Cap Juluca, CuisinArt, and Malliouhana, but these are also the most expensive ones. There are some outstanding independent ones, however.

Hibernia (Island Harbour; 497-4290; www.hiberniarestaurant.com) is one of the best restaurants in Anguilla. The French owner is a serious chef who smokes his own fish and knows how to combine Asian flavors with fine French cuisine—all to be enjoyed on a terrace overlooking the Caribbean. Entrees range from US $29. Its only drawback is its location in Island Harbour at the eastern end of Anguilla, which is not convenient to major hotels that are mainly in the west.

Oliver's Seafood Grill (Long Bay, 497-8780; www.olivers.ai), set on a double deck by the beach, serves seafood and a refined version of West Indian specialties.

Overlook (South Hill, 497-4488), set on a hillside overlooking Sandy Ground, offers fresh fish and Caribbean selections.

Anguilla has two PADI dive centers: **Shoal Bay Scuba** (497-4371; www.shoalbayscuba.com), directly on Shoal Bay East, and **Anguillan Divers** (497-4750; www.anguillandivers.com), at Meads Bay in the west. Both offer instruction and dive packages.

Concerned about the phenomenal growth in the 1980s, Anguilla created a National Trust with a permanent staff to oversee the preservation of the island's cultural and national heritage and direct already-active volunteer organizations. These include the Archaeological and Historical Society, which organized in 1979 the first scientific survey of the island, which unearthed thirty-three sites of antiquity; the Horticultural Society, which organizes periodic cleanup and beautification drives; the Marine Heritage Society, the driving force behind the creation of marine parks; and various cultural groups working to preserve Anguilla's folklore, music, and other traditions.

In 1990 the Anguillan government took its first major step at marine-resource management. Six wrecks resting by Anguilla's shores were towed to sea and sunk to create artificial reefs that have become nurseries for fish and new sites for divers. Their removal also eliminated a potential boating and marine hazard in Road Bay, the island's main harbor.

Transportation American Airlines/American Eagle has daily service from San Juan to Anguilla, and Winair has several flights daily making the five-minute trip from St. Maarten to Anguilla. LIAT (497-5000; www.liatairline.com) provides service to neighboring islands.

Ferries from St. Martin take fifteen minutes and cost US $20 one-way plus US $4 port tax. They leave almost every thirty minutes during the day from Marigot harbor. Last ferries of the day leave at 6:15 p.m. from Anguilla and 7:00 p.m. from Marigot Bay. The ferry dock in Anguilla is located on the south side of the island, where you can hire a taxi or rent a car, essential for touring the island because there is no regular bus service.

Telephone Area Code 264

Information www.anguilla-vacation.com

In the United States: Anguilla Tourist Information Office, (877) 4-ANGUILLA; 246 Central Avenue, White Plains, NY 10606; (914) 287-2400; fax (914) 287-2404; mwturnstyle@aol.com.

In Anguilla: Anguilla Tourist Board, Coronation Avenue, The Valley, Anguilla, B.W.I.; (264) 497-2759; (800) 553-4939; fax: (264) 497-2710; atb-tour@anguillanet.com

Anguilla Life, a quarterly published by veteran Caribbean writer Claire Devener, is a valuable source of information. Contact P.O. Box 1622, Anguilla, B.W.I.; 497-3080; Anguillalife@anguilla net.com; www.anguilla-beaches.com.

PART FOUR

The Eastern Caribbean

Antigua

St. John's, Falmouth, English Harbour, Antigua; Codrington, Barbuda

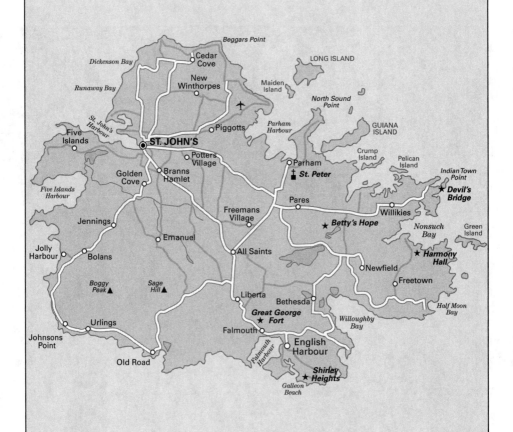

Antigua

	Miles	
0		3
0	Kilometers	5

N

ATLANTIC   OCEAN

Dickenson Bay

Beggars Point

Cedar Cove

New Winthorpes

Runaway Bay

LONG ISLAND

Maiden Island

North Sound Point

St. John's Harbour

Piggotts

Five Islands

ST. JOHN'S

Parham Harbour

GUIANA ISLAND

Potters Village

Golden Cove

Branns Hamlet

Parham
✝ **St. Peter**

Crump Island

Pelican Island

Indian Town Point

★ **Devil's Bridge**

Five Islands Harbour

Freemans Village

Pares

Willikies

Jennings

Emanuel

All Saints

★ **Betty's Hope**

Nonsuch Bay

Green Island

Jolly Harbour

Bolans

★ **Harmony Hall**

Newfield

Freetown

Boggy Peak ▲

Sage Hill ▲

Liberta

Bethesda

Half Moon Bay

Great George Fort ★

Willoughby Bay

Urlings

Falmouth

Johnsons Point

Old Road

Falmouth Harbour

English Harbour

★ **Shirley Heights**

Galleon Beach

CARIBBEAN   SEA

A Beach for Every Day of the Year

Relaxed and quietly sophisticated, Antigua is a mecca for those who love the sea. Shaped roughly like a maple leaf, the protruding fingers provide Antigua's coastline with sheltered bays, natural harbors, and extra miles of beautiful beaches—one for every day of the year, the Antiguans say. The coral reefs that fringe the island are a magnet for snorkelers and scuba divers. Together these assets have made Antigua one of the most popular beach and water-sports centers in the Caribbean. As a bonus, low humidity coupled with year-round trade winds create a wonderful climate for tennis, golf, horseback riding, and a variety of other sports—and, of course, for sightseeing.

Antigua (pronounced An-TEE-ga) is the largest of the Leeward Islands. Barbuda, its sister island 30 miles to the north, is largely undeveloped; the third member, Redonda, 36 miles to the southwest, is uninhabited. Located at the heart of the Caribbean, east of Puerto Rico and the Virgin Islands between the French and Dutch West Indies, Antigua is a transportation hub of the region.

Settled by the British in 1632, Antigua was Britain's most strategic Caribbean colony for two centuries due to her protected harbors and position on the trade routes, with the winds blowing almost year-round from the east. The island's historic character is most evident at English Harbour, where the buildings of the old wharf, known as Nelson's Dockyard, have been restored. The British legacy is also seen in the island's passion for cricket, afternoon tea, and driving on the left side of the road.

Of the eighty or more archaeological sites found here, the oldest dates back more than four thousand years to the Ciboney, a Stone Age people about whom little is known. The most extensive excavations have been those of the Arawak Indians, who arrived in Yarumaqui, as they called Antigua, about A.D. 500. They remained about five centuries and moved north, probably to flee pursuing Carib Indians, a warlike people after whom the Caribbean is named.

Wadadli, the Carib name for the island, was sighted by Columbus in 1493. He did not come ashore, but he did name the island Santa Maria de la Antigua, after the virgin saint of the Cathedral of Seville in Spain. Attempts by the Spaniards, and later the French, to settle the island were unsuccessful. Then in 1632 English settlers from St. Kitts, led by Edward Warner, the son of Thomas Warner, who founded the first settlement on St. Kitts, came ashore near Old Road on the south coast, where they established a colony. Except for a brief French occupation in 1666, Antigua remained British for the next three hundred years.

The first settlers cleared the land and planted tobacco, a crop they learned from the Arawaks. But in time tobacco was replaced by sugar, and slaves were imported from Africa to work the cane fields. The island was divided into estates, and a plantation society developed that lasted well into the twentieth century. Much of this history is reflected today in village, family, and location names.

In 1784 Horatio Nelson, who later became one of Britain's most celebrated admirals, took command

At a Glance

Antiquities	★★
Architecture	★★
Art and artists	★★
Beaches	★★★★★
Colonial buildings	★★★
Crafts	★
Cuisine	★★
Culture	★
Dining/Restaurants	★★
Entertainment/Nightlife	★
Forts	★★★
History	★★★
Monuments	★
Museums	★★
Scenery	★★
Shopping	★★
Sightseeing	★★★
Sports	★★★★★
Transportation	★

Population: 66,000

Size: Antigua, 108 square miles; Barbuda, 62 square miles.

Main Town: St. John's

Government: Antigua has a parliamentary government headed by a prime minister and is a member of the British Commonwealth. The queen is represented by a governor general.

Currency: Eastern Caribbean (EC) dollar. US$1.00 equals EC$2.70. Major credit cards and U.S. dollars are widely accepted. Since both currencies are rendered in "dollars," be sure to determine which currency is being discussed whenever you negotiate the price of a service or commodity.

Departure Tax: EC$53 (US$20). A US$10 passenger facility charge is added to tickets at the time of purchase for airport improvement. The departure tax is expected to be increased soon.

Language: English has been the language of Antigua for three centuries and adds to the ease of getting around.

Public Holidays: January 1, New Year's Day; Good Friday and Easter Monday; Labor Day, first Monday in May; Whit Monday; Queen's Official Birthday, second Saturday in June; Carnival, first Monday and Tuesday in August; November 1, Independence Day; December 25, Christmas; December 26, Boxing Day. Although not a public holiday, Sailing Week in late April is one of the biggest events of the year and commands the attention of most people.

Telephone Area Code: 268

Airlines: *From North America,* American Airlines, Continental Airlines, Delta Airlines, and US Airways; American Eagle flies from San Juan. Antigua's airport is headquarters for LIAT (Leeward Islands Air Transport), offering frequent service to the neighboring islands of the Eastern Caribbean. Caribbean Sun (www.flycsa.com) announced plans to re-launch in late 2007 as a charter carrier. Carib Aviation operates flights to Barbuda, a trip of ten minutes. For schedules and information, call (268) 481-2403, or e-mail reservations@carib-aviation.com. Ask about day trips to Barbuda.

Information: www.antigua-barbuda.org

In the United States:

Antigua and Barbuda Department of Tourism, 305 East 47th Street, Suite 6A, New York, NY 10017; (212) 541-4117; fax: (212) 541-4789; info@antigua-barbuda.org.

25 Southeast Second Avenue, No. 300; Miami, FL 33131; (305) 381-6762; fax: (305) 381-7908.

In Canada:

Antigua and Barbuda Department of Tourism, 60 St. Clair Avenue East, Toronto, ON M4T 1N5; (416) 961-3085; fax: (416) 961-7218; info@antigua-barbuda-ca.com.

In Antigua:

Antigua Tourist Board, Ministry of Tourism, Queen Elizabeth Highway, Box 363, St. John's, Antigua, W.I.; (268) 462-0029, (268) 462-0480; fax: (268) 462-2483. There's also an information office at the Heritage Quay by the port in St. John's. Antigua Historical and Archaeological Society, Museum of Antigua and Barbuda, P.O. Box 103, Market Street, St. John's, Antigua; (268) 463-1060. National Parks Authority, Box 1283, St. John's, Antigua; (268) 463-1053.

---

of the Leeward Islands Squadron in which the future king, William IV, served as captain of the HMS *Pegasus*. Antigua became the New World headquarters for the Royal Navy, and English Harbour, as it is known today, was strongly fortified.

After the abolition of slavery in 1834, the sugar-based economies of the Caribbean declined, and the introduction of the steamship changed the course of trade between the Old and New Worlds. For the next century Antigua, like so much of the Caribbean, was largely ignored by its colonial masters. During World War II, the island became a U.S. military base, and the impact was immediate. It brought jobs, new roads, piers, an airport, and technicians, who helped to train Antiguans in skills that served the local population well after the war.

In 1958 Britain granted Antigua and its other colonies semiautonomous status in the West Indies Federation. In 1967 Antigua, with Barbuda and Redonda, became an Associated State within the Commonwealth, governing its own internal affairs. Finally in 1981 full independence was achieved.

After two decades on its own, Antigua was transformed from an agricultural economy to a service one, with tourism the major source of jobs and revenue.

Budget Planning

Taxi fares are high, and unless you have others with whom to share them, sightseeing by taxi is expensive. Car rental is more reasonable and recommended. Aside from taxis, prices in Antigua are moderate, and restaurants serving local or West Indian cuisine are inexpensive.

Port Profile: St. John's

Location/Embarkation St. John's, the capital, is located on the island's northwest Caribbean coast at the head of a deepwater harbor. A pier at the foot of town enables passengers to walk off their ships directly into Heritage Quay, a shopping, food, and entertainment complex. Antigua Deepwater Harbour, another pier on the north side of the harbor about a mile from town, is used for large ships and when there are more ships than the town pier can accommodate. Yachts and some small cruise ships often arrive at English Harbour, one of the prettiest yacht basins in the Caribbean, or at neighboring Falmouth Harbour, both on the southeastern coast.

Local Transportation The distance from the pier at Deepwater Harbour to St. John's is short enough to walk, but most visitors prefer to take a taxi because the only place to walk is in the road. Taxis are plentiful and cost US$11; they can be shared by up to four people for the ride into town. From St. John's to the airport or to Nelson's Dockyard costs about US$21 to US$25 one-way. A new bus route called "Coolidge" runs from St. John's to the airport area. A taxi with the driver acting as guide can be hired for touring. Rates are set by the government and tend to be expensive, costing US$24 per hour for up to four persons, negotiable for more, or about US$80 to US$90 and up for an island tour. Be sure to set the price in advance and to confirm whether the price quoted is in U.S. or EC dollars. Local buses are not useful for cruise passengers.

Roads and Rentals If you have an adventurous spirit, the ideal way to tour the island is by self-drive car. Antigua has an extensive network of roads, but driving can be a bit difficult due to narrow, winding roads that are not well marked. Also, traffic in this former British colony moves on the left. A good map is essential, but even with it, roads can be confusing: Expect to get lost several times. Happily, the Antiguans are friendly and helpful, although not very precise in giving directions; you might need to ask for directions several times. Basically, the road system fans out from St. John's on major arteries that loop around each area of the island—north, southeast, southwest—making it easy to leave from the capital by one route and return by another.

Rental cars and jeeps are reasonably priced, costing from about US$55 per day for a small car with unlimited mileage plus a set insurance rate of US$10 daily. During the winter season demand is often greater than supply, and cars can be difficult to obtain; reservations are recommended. Avis, Budget, Dollar, Hertz, National, Thrifty, and some local companies are represented. You'll need a local driver's license, but the car-rental agency will obtain it for you upon presentation of a valid U.S. or Canadian one; the fee is US$20. Before starting out be sure to have a full tank of gasoline; there are few gas stations on some roads outside of St. John's.

Interisland Air Service See Fast Facts.

Emergency Numbers
Medical: Holberton Hospital, Hospital Road, St. John's; 24-hour service, 462-0251
Ambulance: 462-0251
Police: 462-0125

Shore Excursions

With advance arrangements, local travel companies can tailor a tour to your specifications by using a private car with a driver/guide. But whether on an organized tour in a minibus or by car, local guides are not well trained and cannot be depended upon for much commentary. The shore excursions most often available on cruise ships follow; prices are per person and may vary from ship to ship. Details on the sites are described later in this chapter.

Historic Antigua: 3 hours, US$54 (US$70 for up to four persons by car with driver/guide). Drive across the heart of the island to English Harbour, Clarence House, and Shirley Heights.

Scenic and historic Antigua: 4 hours, US$40–$45 (US$90 for up to four persons by car). The above tour with the addition of a drive along the southwest coast via Fig Tree Road.

Antigua by Sea: 6 hours, US$94. A coastline sail on a luxury catamaran with views of Jumby Bay, Bird Island, and Devil's Bridge. Stop at Green Island for lunch and snorkeling; then explore Nelson's Dockyard.

Antigua Canopy Tour: 3.5 hours, US$99. A series of ziplines, suspension bridges, and optional parachute jump offer a bird's-eye view of the rain forest.

Flight-seeing: For a bird's-eye view of Antigua and the nearby islands, Caribbean Helicopters (460-5900; www.caribbeanhelicopters.com), which operates out of Jolly Harbour, offers trips from about US$85 per person for a half-island tour and US$150 for a full-island tour. Arrangements should be made in advance. Flight-seeing tours to Montserrat are available for US$220.

Barbuda day excursion: Adventure Antigua operates a day excursion to the island via powerboat that takes about 1.5 hours from Antigua. For reservations and information, call 726-6355; www.adventureantigua.com.

Some new active excursions are being offered by most cruise lines. (See Sports section later in this chapter for descriptions.)

Kayak and Snorkel Eco-adventure: 4 hours, US$69.

Catamaran/snorkel: 3 hours, US$52.

Cedar Valley Golf: 5 hours, US$96.
Stingray Swim and Snorkel: 3 hours, US$69.
Hiking safari: 3 hours, US$49.

Antigua on Your Own

Antigua's capital was a sleepy West Indian town that was transformed into a new town by the tourist boom over the past decade.

A St. John's Walkabout

One of the island's oldest ports, settled in the early seventeenth century, St. John's was once a scruffy town of hard-drinking sailors and traders and an unsavory reputation to match. It was laid out formally in 1702 and given city status in 1842. Through the centuries the town suffered destruction by fires, hurricanes, and earthquakes, yet enough of its historic buildings and West Indian architecture remain to give it character. The most historic and interesting area is a grid of 6 blocks in the heart of town, best seen on foot in an easy hour's walk.

Redcliffe Quay (1) On the waterfront on the west side of town is a group of former warehouses and other buildings that have been restored and made into attractive boutiques, restaurants, and offices. To the west is pretty **Heritage Quay (2)**, a shopping, food, and entertainment center of two stories built around an open-air plaza. Although modern in design, its architecture incorporates colonial and West Indian elements that blend into the old town. **The Tourist Information Office and the post office (3)** (Thames Street) are a block to the north.

Museum of Antigua and Barbuda (4) The oldest structure in use in St. John's now houses the Museum of Antigua and Barbuda (Market and Long Streets; (462-1469; www.antiguamuseum .org). An eighteenth-century courthouse built from white stone quarried from an island off the northeast coast, the building has been repaired and rebuilt many times over the centuries. It housed the island's parliament until 1974, when the building was damaged by an earthquake. The renovations were undertaken by the Antigua Historical and

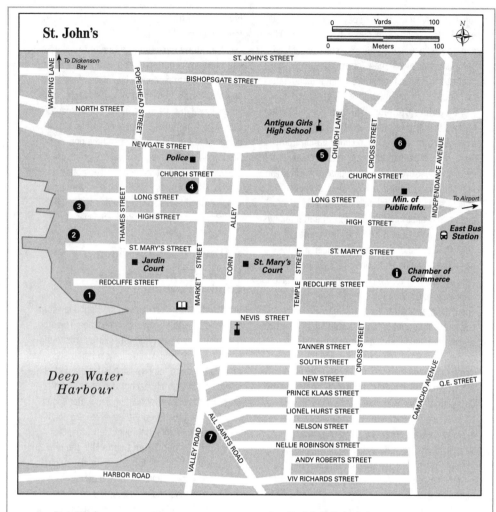

St. John's

1. Redcliffe Quay	5. St. John's Cathedral
2. Heritage Quay and town pier	6. Government House
3. Tourist Information Office and Post Office	7. Public Market
4. Museum of Antigua and Barbuda	

Archaeological Society with the aid of Canada, UNESCO, and private donors, to create the museum. The museum underwent an extensive renovation in 2001, following damage by a hurricane. Additional exhibits have been opened on the second floor for arts and crafts, carnival display, and art shows. There is no admission fee, but a US$2 donation is suggested. Hours: Monday to Thursday 8.30 a.m. to 4:00 p.m.; Friday 8.30 a.m. to 3:00 p.m.; Saturday 10:00 a.m. to 2:00 p.m.

The collection includes Arawak and pre-Columbian artifacts found in Antigua; other displays interpret Antigua's history from the colonial period to independence. The museum's main purpose is to educate the island's children about their history, but it is very much worth a visit for others, too. Hours: Monday to Thursday 8:00 a.m. to 4:00 p.m.; Friday 8:30 a.m. to 3:00 p.m.; Saturday 10:00 a.m. to 2:00 p.m.; 462-1469; museum@candw.ag. The Historical and Archaeological Society, which operates the museum, sponsors cultural and natural history tours and invites membership.

St. John's Cathedral (5) On the highest rise of town stands the Cathedral of St. John the Divine (Newgate Street and Church Lane), dating from 1847. It is on the site of an earlier church, built in 1745 and destroyed by an earthquake in 1843. The first church, dedicated in 1683, was a wooden structure built by the island's largest plantation owner, Sir Christopher Codrington. The iron railings at the entrance date from 1789. The figures of John the Baptist and John the Evangelist at the south gate, originally destined for Dominica, were the spoils of war for an English man-of-war, taken from a French ship in the early nineteenth century. The church has two towers, topped with silver cupolas; the interior is faced with pitch pine, a type of pine that yields pitch and is intended to strengthen the structure to withstand hurricanes and earthquakes.

Behind the church is Government House (6), dating from the seventeenth century. Originally two houses, one of which was the residence of the minister for the parish of St. John's, it was bought as a residence by Lord Lavington of Carlisle Estate in 1801. Today it is the official residence of the governor general of Antigua and generally is not open to the public.

Public Market (7) By the waterfront on the south end of Market Street is the Public Market, a particularly lively, colorful scene on Fridays and Saturday mornings and a good place for an introduction to Antigua's local produce and some of the exotic fruits and vegetables of the Caribbean. Next door is the Industrial School for the Blind, where a limited selection of handcrafts is on sale.

St. John's Point, the tip of a 2-mile scenic headland on the north side of the harbor, has the remains of Fort James, built in the early eighteenth century, with ten of its original thirty-six cannons. Its counterpart, Fort Barrington, crowns a promontory known as Goat Hill, on the south side of the harbor. The forts were part of the extensive British military installations to protect the main

harbors and attest to the island's strategic importance in colonial times.

Sea View Farm Village One of Antigua's oldest traditions is pottery making, dating back to the early eighteenth century, when slaves fashioned cooking vessels from local clay. Today folk pottery is fashioned in several locations, but the center is Sea View Farm Village, west of St. John's. The clay is collected from nearby pits, and the pottery is fired in an open fire under layers of green grass in the yards of the potters' houses. The pottery can be purchased at outlets in the village as well as in shops around the island. Be aware, however, that this pottery can break easily in cold climates.

A Drive around Antigua

South to Falmouth and English Harbour

Southwest of St. John's along the Caribbean coast are some of Antigua's prettiest beaches. The most immediate road west from St. John's leads to the Royal Antiguan, the island's largest hotel. Secondary roads take you to the Five Islands area, a part of the island with beautiful beaches and reefs and offshore islets popular for boating and water sports.

The main road from St. John's to the southwest coast runs inland through Jennings, the turnoff to 595-foot Green Castle Hill, the remnant of a volcano with rock formations whose origin is unknown. A trail climbs to the top, from which there is a grandstand view over the south end of the island. Immediately before Johnson's Point on the southwest tip are Jolly Beach, with a large resort, and Dark Wood Beach, an exquisite stretch of white sand on the quiet Caribbean, popular with cruise ships for their crews on R&R.

Boggy Peak The small village of Urlings sits on the southern flank of Boggy Peak, the highest point on the island (marked by a communications tower), and overlooks Cades Bay. A road inland leads to the top of the hill. The area is famous for the Antigua black pineapple, an unusually sweet, delicious variety cultivated here. Offshore is the 2.5-mile-long Cades Reef, part of which is a marine park.

Old Road The hamlet of Old Road, at Carlisle Bay, marks the site of the first English settlement in 1632. Curtain Bluff Hotel, perched on a small bluff overlooking two lovely beaches, is one of Antigua's most attractive resorts, embraced in magnificent flowering gardens.

Fig Tree Drive At Old Road the main route turns inland onto Fig Tree Drive (fig is the Antiguan name for the banana plant) and winds through the hills between Old Road and the village of John Hughes. The 3-mile, sometimes bumpy stretch, overhung with tropical vegetation, is called "The Rain Forest" locally, because the area is more lush than the dry landscape typical of most of Antigua.

Antigua's hilly south coast between Old Road and Falmouth is popular for hiking on footpaths leading to hilltops and cliffsides for panoramic views and to beautiful, secluded beaches, otherwise accessible only by boat.

Liberta and Monks Hill At the tiny village of Swetes en route to Falmouth, the main road bends southeast to Liberta, one of the first settlements founded by freed slaves after the emancipation in 1834. The church of **St. Barnabas,** the parish church, dates from the nineteenth century. East of Liberta a road leads to Monks Hill and remnants of **Fort George,** built by the British in the seventeenth century primarily as a place of refuge for women and children in times of attack. The road— used for walking or driving—is marked with a sign to the village of **Table Hill Gordon,** a steep hike of about an hour to Monks Hill. The rough road, best negotiated by jeep, rewards you with a fabulous view of the island.

Falmouth The port of Falmouth, set on a pretty bay, was once Antigua's capital. It is surrounded by former sugar plantations whose old mills dot the landscape here as they do throughout Antigua. The restored **St. George's Church,** dating from the seventeenth century, is one of the island's oldest churches. The Antigua Yacht Club is located here, too.

English Harbour A small inlet on the southeast coast barely visible from the sea is one of the best natural harbors in the Caribbean, deep enough for oceangoing ships. Thanks to its deep water, hidden opening, and protective hills sheltering it from hurricanes and providing strategic positions for defense, the harbor became the main base of the British Admiralty in the West Indies. Throughout the eighteenth and nineteenth centuries, it was used as a base of operations by such famous British admirals as Nelson and Rodney and played a major role in helping to establish British naval superiority over the French.

The naval base, constructed between 1725 and 1746, occupied a narrow promontory that juts into the bay and separates English Harbour from Falmouth Harbour. A series of fortifications were added at the harbor and on the ridge surrounding it. The hills on the east are known as **Shirley Heights,** named for the governor of the Leewards who built the hilltop installations. After the Battle of Waterloo and peace in 1815, English Harbour's strategic importance began to decline. It was formally closed as a royal dockyard in 1889 and fell into decay until 1931, when an effort was launched to preserve the site.

Nelson's Dockyard English Harbour (www .antiguamuseums.org/nelsonsdockyard), today one of the busiest yacht basins in the region, is obviously still appreciated by sailors. Serious reconstruction of the old dockyard, now called Nelson's Dockyard after the British admiral, began in 1951. The first phase took a decade, and the harbor was officially reopened in 1961, but another decade was needed to complete the task. The beautifully restored historic buildings house charming shops, museums, inns, restaurants, and a marina. **The Admiral's House,** Nelson's former residence, contains a museum of colonial history (Hours: 8:00 a.m. to 5:00 p.m. year-round, Sundays and holidays included). **Admiral's Inn** is a hotel with a terrace restaurant overlooking the harbor. The old **Copper and Lumber Store** is also a hotel furnished in colonial style. An entrance fee includes a guided tour of the dockyard, which is now part of the national park.

Clarence House The eighteenth-century residence of Prince William Henry, Duke of Clarence and later King William IV, who was based here as commander of the HMS *Pegasus* in 1787, stands on a hill overlooking English Harbour. The Georgian manor, furnished with antiques loaned by the British National Trust, is now the country house of the governor of Antigua and can be visited. A guide is on duty.

Dow's Hill Interpretation Centre Operated by the national park, the center is a must stop for those interested in the island's history, culture, and natural attractions. "Reflections in the Sun," a multimedia presentation, traces the history of Antigua and Barbuda from prehistoric times to the present. The center is on a hilltop above Nelson's Dockyard en route to Shirley Heights.

Shirley Heights The military installations on the hillside east of the harbor also have been restored and contain a small museum and a restaurant. The main attraction, though, is the magnificent view overlooking English and Falmouth Harbours, the hills, and south coast of Antigua. On a clear day you can see as far away as Redonda and Montserrat, 32 miles to the southwest. The Heights is a popular place to watch a fabulous Antiguan sunset. Jammin' at the Heights has become a Sunday tradition, when half the island is on hand to dance, hang out, and watch the sunset.

The **Lookout Trail,** a nature walk created by the National Parks Authority (268-460-1379; www .antiguamuseums.org), leaves from Galleon Beach Hotel on the east side of English Harbour. A descriptive pamphlet for a self-guided hike, available from the Parks Authority, explains the traditional uses of the trees and plants you'll see along the way. The hike is not difficult and takes about forty minutes to go up and fifteen minutes to descend. Wear sneakers or similar shoes.

A secondary road winds over the heights to **Dow's Hill,** a site used by NASA for a tracking station during the Apollo program. The former NASA building now houses the **Antigua University of Health and Sciences.** Here a footpath leads to Bat's Cave, a small cavern with hundreds of bats.

The fastest return to St. John's from English Harbour is across the center of the island via All Saints, a pretty little village where pottery making is a traditional craft.

North of St. John's

Antigua's main resort center is north of the capital, along the Caribbean coast. The stretch of sand closest to St. John's, known as Runaway Beach, is often used by cruise ships for their "day-at-the-beach" excursions. At the south end, you will find **Miller's by the Sea** (462-9414), a beachside restaurant, water-sports, and entertainment center.

In recent years, it has become the most popular location for cruise-ship beach excursions, but you can easily go on your own. There's live music at lunch and in the evenings with a different band each day and a beach barbecue on Thursday. Dickinson Bay and Hodges Bay, farther north, have the largest concentration of hotels. Water sports are available from vendors at resorts along the beach. You'll find good snorkeling here and in the pristine waters of the uninhabited islets offshore.

Parham Directly east of St. John's on the northeast coast, the little settlement of Parham was the first capital of Antigua. **St. Peter's Church,** built in 1840 to replace an earlier church destroyed by fire, was designed by Thomas Weekes, a famous architect of the time, who was brought from Britain for the purpose. About a mile northeast of Parham is **Crabbs Slipway and Marina,** a boating center and a port of entry for yachts. The area is popular for biking tours.

Great Bird Island National Park (www .antiguamuseums.org/Natural.htm) An uninhabited islet offshore, with a pretty little beach, the park is popular for day-sailing excursions. The limestone cliffs of Great Bird Island are home to the red-billed tropic bird that can be seen gliding on the wind currents blowing in from the Atlantic. Bird Island and nearby cays have good snorkeling. There is a trail up to a great view of the Atlantic Ocean from the 100-foot-high cliffs. Some cruise lines offer a sailing excursion for about US$79, including lunch. Local tour companies also can arrange the trip as a private excursion. Contact **Antigua Vacations,** Box 1026, St. Mary's Street, Jardine Court; 460-7383; fax: 463-8959; **Kiskidee Travel & Tours,** Briggins Road, Box 185, St. John's; 462-4801; fax: 462-4802; or **Nicholson's Travel Agency,** P.O. Box 185, St. John's; 463-7391 or 562-2065; fax: 462-4802.

East to the Atlantic Coast

From St. John's, two roads lead east to the Atlantic coast. The more northerly one passes through the villages of Pares and Willikies to Indian Town Creek, a national park on the northeast corner of Antigua. En route feeder roads and tracks extend to the north coast, an area sheltered by cays and reefs that provide calm waters for sailing, snorkeling, and fishing.

Betty's Hope (www.antiguamuseums.org/bettyshope.htm) Near Pares a signposted road turns inland to the ruins of the first large sugar plantation in Antigua, Betty's Hope, founded in the 1650s and granted to Sir Christopher Codrington, a prosperous planter from Barbados, in 1668. Codrington is credited with introducing large-scale sugar cultivation and innovative processing methods in Antigua. The success of Betty's Hope, named for Sir Christopher's daughter, is said to have led other planters to turn from tobacco and indigo to sugarcane as their main crop.

Codrington and his son served as governor-general of the Leeward Islands, developing the plantation as the seat of government. The estate remained in the Codrington family until 1944. The ruins include two windmill towers and arches of the boiling house, among other structures.

In 1990 a $10 million restoration project was launched to restore Betty's Hope for use as a cultural center and historic attraction. The fund-raising activities are spearheaded jointly by the government, business and civic leaders, Partners of the Americas (Rochester, New York, Antigua's sister city), and Antigua Historical Society. There is an interpretive center in the old stables. Hours: Tuesday to Saturday 10:00 a.m. to 4:00 p.m. Donation suggested: US$2. Call 462-1469. Some cruise ships offer a combination half-day tour of Betty's Hope and time at the beach for about US$55. If you hire a taxi or rent a car, you can easily do this program on your own.

Indian Town National Park The main road beyond Willikies ends at Allegro Pineapple Beach, an all-inclusive resort on Long Bay. Tracks branch out across the northeastern peninsula to pretty coves. In a deep cove known as Indian Town Point is Devil's Bridge, a natural bridge that has been carved out of the rocks by the relentless waves of the Atlantic. Alongside it, "blowing holes" send jets of water high into the air. The south side of the peninsula overlooks Nonsuch Bay, one of the prettiest bays on the Atlantic coast, protected by coral reefs. Offshore Green Island is a nature preserve. The reef between Green Island and tiny, uninhabited York Island is a popular area for day-trippers.

The southerly of the two roads from St. John's to the east coast skirts Potworks Reservoir for almost 2 miles. The largest of Antigua's numerous man-made catchments and one of the largest bodies of freshwater in the Eastern Caribbean, it has a pretty wooded setting, popular for bird-watching.

Shopping

The best shopping is found in the heart of St. John's along St. Mary's, High, Redcliffe, and Market Streets, the oldest thoroughfares, where many shops are housed in colorful historic buildings of West Indian architecture. Here you will find a variety of locally made clothing, straw products, pottery, paintings, batiks, and jewelry with local semiprecious stones. Locally made rum and liquor prices are some of the lowest in the Caribbean. The downtown area is relatively small, and shops are within easy walking distance of one another. Stores are open daily (except Sunday) 9:00 a.m. to 5:00 p.m. Many take an hour's noontime lunch break.

Heritage Quay, a shopping and entertainment complex located directly at the pier, was built with cruise-ship passengers in mind. The center has more than forty stores with high-quality merchandise such as English bone china, French crystal and perfumes, Italian leather, and Swiss watches at duty-free prices.

Art and Artists Harmony Hall (Brown's Bay; 460-4120; www.harmonyhallantigua.com), until its recent sale, was a branch of the well-known art gallery in Jamaica. It stocks work by quality Jamaican, Antiguan, and other Caribbean artists and holds exhibitions on the first Sunday of every month, seeking out the best local artists and artisans. The gallery has a delightful setting on an old sugar plantation and now has a great outdoor restaurant. It's almost an hour's drive from St. John's, but worth a stop, if you plan to spend a day rambling about the island. Normally, the gallery closes for the summer months.

Among other galleries are **Elvie's Pottery** (Seaview Farm; 463-1888), which exhibits authentic Antiguan terra-cotta–colored clay pottery; **Fine Art Framing** (Redcliffe Quay; 562-1019), which carries an interesting range of original art and photography by local and regional artists; **Hide Out Restaurant & Art Gallery** (Picadilly Mamora Bay; 460-3666;

fax: 460-3667); and **Rhythm of Blue Gallery** (English Harbour; 562-2230; arawakart@yahoo.com) with pottery by Nancy Nicholson, scrimshaw by Michael Strzalkowski, as well as paintings, photographs, and sculpture by other leading local artists. Open November to April.

Island Arts (Heritage Quay; 462-2787; www.yodaguy.com) is the gallery of artist and filmmaker Nick Maley and specializes in Caribbean art and handcrafts; original oils and prints by Katie Shears, who specializes in wildlife; and other local artists. Signed limited editions, pretty silk-screened gifts, and handpainted T-shirts are other specialties.

Books/Maps The Map Shop (St. Mary's Street; 462-3993; fax: 462-3995) stocks maps of Antigua and the Caribbean and reproductions of antique maps, as well as postcards and stationery. It also sells British Admiralty charts. **BB, the Best of Books Bookshop** (Redcliffe Quay; 562-3198; bestofbooks@yahoo.com) carries a wide range of books as well as newspapers.

China and Crystal Little Switzerland (Heritage Quay; www.littleswitzerland.com) offers fine china and crystal, jewelry, and perfumes. **The Lady Hamilton** (Redcliffe Quay) specializes in English crystal and ceramics, antique maps, souvenirs, collector's stamps, and swimwear.

Clothing Benetton (Heritage Quay; 462-3273; www.benetton.com), the well-known Italian clothing and accessories chain, has sportswear in bright coordinated colors. **Sun Seekers** (Heritage Quay, 462-3618) stocks a large selection of swimwear.

Island Woman Boutique (7 Redcliffe Quay; 462-4220) carries locally designed leisure wear for men and women, jazzy swimwear from Jamaica and Brazil, fun design T-shirts, and stuffed batik animals for children. **Noreen Phillips Couturiere** (Redcliffe Quay; 462-3127) designs a full line from elegant casual wear to sophisticated evening wear, which the shop claims can be made in two hours. **The Galley Boutique** (English Harbour; 460-1525), the shop of designer Janie Easton, stocks casual clothes and sportswear by the owner and others. Particularly attractive are the fashions by John Warden, a designer from St. Kitts. **Thousand Flowers** (Redcliffe Quay; 462-4264) carries great

cottons, accessories, and footwear, ideal for island travel.

Crafts and Souvenirs The Pottery Shop (Redcliffe Quay; 462-5503) carries mugs, vases, plates, and other pottery made in Antigua. If you are traveling around the island, check out **Cedars Pottery** (Buckley Road), where a team of potters makes brightly decorated tableware and sculptures. **Jacaranda** (Upper Redcliffe Quay; 462-1888) stocks island spices, herbs, teas, and cosmetics, along with prints by Bajan artist Jill Walker. **Shipwreck Shop** (Heritage Quay, 2nd floor; 562-4625) specializes in gifts indigenous to Antigua and the Caribbean, local art, books, and magazines.

Sugar Mill Boutique (St. Mary's Street; 462-4523) specializes in silk-screened originals with designs of flowers, fish, and shells of the Caribbean by Antiguan artists. It also carries swimwear.

Jewelry The Goldsmitty (Redcliffe Quay; 462-4601) makes fine, handcrafted gold jewelry of original design, often using local stones. **Colombian Emeralds** (Heritage Quay), a major gem dealer, has stores throughout the Caribbean.

Leather and Luggage Millennium (Heritage Quay; 462-3076) sells top name-brand leatherwear as well as jewelry.

Linens The Linen Shop (Heritage Quay; 462-3611) specializes in imported hand-embroidered tablecloths, table mats, sheets, towels, and bedspreads at low prices.

Perfumes Lipstick (Heritage Quay; 562-1130) offers an excellent selection of French perfumes as well as cosmetics and skin care products. There is a similar store in St. Martin. **Scent Shop** (High Street; 462-0303) has perfumes along with Cartier watches, jewelry, pens, and leather goods; Baccarat, Waterford, and other crystal.

Smokes La Casa de Habana (Heritage Quay; 562-0376) has a large selection of Cuban cigars, kept in a walk-in humidor. **The Cigar Shop** (Airport; 462-6854) has an even wider variety.

Dining and Restaurants

Antigua is an island of many different lifestyles, reflected in its variety of restaurants—from rustic taverns by the beach, English pubs, and unpretentious establishments for West Indian food to elegant dining rooms where jacket and tie are required. Seafood is a specialty, with fresh local lobster and conch at the top of the list. Exotic Caribbean vegetables include christophene (a type of squash), dasheen (a leafy plant similar to spinach), plantains, and breadfruit. The Antigua black pineapple is one of the sweetest, best-tasting kinds anywhere; mangoes, papayas, and coconuts are abundant. Rum turns up in many recipes and drinks. Normally restaurants open daily for lunch and dinner, unless noted otherwise. This being the laid-back Caribbean, however, it is always wise to check in advance.

St. John's and Environs

The Beach Restaurant (Dickenson Bay, 480-6940; www.bigbanana-antigua.com) offers great international cuisine by the beach. Antigua's hot spot on Friday evenings. Moderate.

Big Banana Holding Company/Pizza's in Paradise (Redcliffe Quay; 480-6985; www.big banana-antigua.com) serves pizza and sandwiches on a garden terrace. There's live music on Thursday at lunchtime. Open Monday to Saturday 8:30 a.m. to midnight. Moderate.

Coconut Grove (Siboney Beach Club, Dickinson Bay; 462-1538; www.coconutgroveantigua .com). Pretty, romantic beachfront setting, specializing in seafood. Live music during the winter season. Reservations advised. Moderate.

Chez Pascal (Galley Bay; 462-3232; www .chezpascalantigua.com) Chef-owner Pascal Milliat, assisted by his Brittany-born wife, Florence, serves classic French dishes ranging from freshly cooked seafood to rack of lamb, the house specialty. Open Tuesday to Saturday 11:30 a.m. to 3:00 p.m. and from 6:30 p.m. for dinner.

Hemingways (St. Mary's Street; 462-2763). Second-floor bar and restaurant is situated in one of the oldest houses of West Indian gingerbread, with an attractive veranda overlooking the town center. Great variety of tropical drinks are featured, along with salads, seafood, and sandwiches. Moderate.

Home (Gambles Terrace, Luther George Place; 461-7651; www.thehomerestaurant.com), made famous by CNN, which featured owner-chef Carl Thomas for his seafood and local dishes. Dinner only.

Julian's Alfresco (Runaway Beach; 562-1545), now in a new location, has long been considered one of Antigua's best, serving a modern version of classic French cuisine, touched by Caribbean influences. Expensive.

Papa Zouk (opposite Princess Margaret School, 464-6044; 463-7383) is called the best fish and rum restaurant in Antigua by those in the know. Moderate.

Cocos (Valley Church, 460-2626; www.cocos hotel.com), on a hillside on the south coast with a stunning view of the Caribbean, has a great wine list and a menu of fresh-caught fish and spicy local dishes that make this a popular spot for locals as well as guests. Moderately expensive.

The Pavilion (480-6800, www.thepavilion antigua.com) offers fine dining in posh surroundings. An extensive temperature-controlled wine cellar, with a timber oak ceiling, handmade bricks, and limestone floors, is home to more than 8,000 bottles. Jacket for men mandatory. Expensive.

Sticky Wicket (No. 20 Pavilion Drive; 481-7000; www.thestickywicket.com) is Valhalla for cricket fans with a Hall of Fame and memorabilia. The pub features special sports events: Super Bowl, cricket, etc. Moderate.

English Harbour

Admiral's Inn (Nelson's Dockyard; 463-1027; www .admiralsantigua.com). Built in 1788 as offices for the naval engineers, the inn's tree-shaded dining terrace overlooking the harbor provides one of Antigua's most pleasant settings for seafood and light lunches. The soups are especially good. Moderate.

OJ's (Crabbe Hill Beach; 460-0184). A beachside setting offering amazing sunsets makes this beach bar and restaurant the perfect place to kick back island-style. OJ is famous for his grilled red snapper, and if you have to wait it's only because they're catching it. The lobster salad is great, and the rum punch is terrific. Open for lunch and dinner with live entertainment on Sundays. Moderate.

HQ2 Restaurant and Bar (Nelson's Dockyard; 562-2563; www.hq2antigua.com) offers inside/ outside dining on French Caribbean cuisine and a piano bar in the evening. Closed Monday. Expensive.

Nightlife

Nightlife revolves around hotels, small bars, and discos. Almost any evening there will be a barbecue, with steel band music, at one of the hotels.

The casinos are **King's Casino** (Heritage Quay; www.kingscasino.com); **Grand Royal Antiguan,** south of St. John's on Deep Bay; **Grand Princess Casino** (Jolly Harbour; www.grandprincess entertainment.com); and the **St. James's Club,** on the southeast coast at Mamora Bay. The **Coast Night Club, Bar and Restaurant** (Heritage Quay; 562-6278; www.coast.ag) is the hot late-night party spot and in addition to live music and local DJs, the club offers free WiFi access in both the bar and restaurant.

Sports

Antigua has some of the best sports facilities in the Caribbean for swimming, sailing, and tennis. In most cases you should contact the sports operator or hotel in advance to make arrangements, particularly during the peak season, when demand is likely to be high.

Beaches/Swimming Many people would say the best reason to visit Antigua is its beaches— frequently ranked by Caribbean aficionados as the best in the region—and there are plenty of them. Antigua's maple leaf shape gives it extra miles of shore, with beaches in little coves hidden between rocky fingers and long, powdery white sands that often stretch for a mile. Some beaches can be reached only by hiking or from a boat; others have bars, restaurants, music, and facilities for water sports.

The beaches closest to the port are at **Runaway** and **Dickinson Bays** on the north, **Deep Bay** and **Hawksbill** on the south (where one of Hawksbill's four beaches is clothing optional). All are on the Caribbean, or leeward, side, where the sea is calm and gentle. The beaches on the Atlantic, or windward, coast often have wave action and surf, but many coves are protected by reefs and have calm water.

Biking Bike Plus (St. John's; 462-2453) has bicycles for US$15 per day. **Paradise Rentals & Charters** (Jolly Harbour; 460-7125; www.paradise boats.com) rents mountain bikes and kid's bikes for US$15 per day. Also rents scooters. **Cheke's Scooter & Car Rental** (562-4646; cell: 773-3508; chekescooter@hotmail.com) has scooters for US$30–$35 per day. Drivers must be at least eighteen years old and have a valid driving license and temporary Antiguan driving license (cost: US$20).

Boating Trade winds blowing 90 percent of the year from the east, the spectacular water surrounding the island, the variety of anchorages and sheltered coves with pretty beaches and reefs, plus splendid facilities all have made Antigua one of the major boating centers of the Caribbean. You can choose from among day trips to offshore islands or longer charters. There are daily cruises around Antigua and picnic sails to nearby islands. The large boats have steel-band music and make quite a party of it. **Excellence** (480-1225; www .tropicalad.com) is among the most popular and likely to be sold as an excursion by your cruise ship.

English Harbour is the main marina and headquarters for **Nicholson's Yacht Charters** (www .nicholsonsyachts.com), one of the Caribbean's oldest, most respected operations, with an international reputation. Its founders spearheaded the renovation of Nelson's Dockyard. The Yacht Club is on the southeast corner of Falmouth Harbour.

Regattas are held year-round, but for true salts Antigua is the place to be in late April or early May when the island hosts **Sailing Week,** the Caribbean's most prestigious annual yachting event, attracting sailing greats and would-be greats from around the world. Since its inception in the 1960s, Sailing Week has become to sailing what Wimbledon is to tennis.

Offering day sailing or power catamaran trips is **Wadadli Cats** (462-4792; www.wadadlicats .com); **Jabberwocky Yacht Charters** (764-0595; www.adventurecaribbean.com) offers a 50-foot yacht with crew for two to ten, from US$85 per person with skipper, chef, gourmet lunch and wine, and snorkeling. **Capt. Nash Sailing Cruises** (560-0014; nash@caribbean-marketing.net) caters to small groups.

Fishing Overdraft (464-4954; www.antigua fishing.com) has a fully equipped 40-foot sportfishing boat available for four- to eight-hour charters. Rates include boat, captain, mate, bait and tackle, and soft and alcoholic beverages for up to six persons. **Antigua & Barbuda Sport Fishing Club** (460-7400; cell: 726-4700; www.antiguabarbuda sportfishing.com) held its forty-first Annual Sport Fishing Tournament in 2007. Contact: Phillip Shoul, chairman.

Golf The Cedar Valley Golf Club (462-0161; www.cedarvalleygolf.ag), located 3 miles from St. John's, has an 18-hole course (6,077 yards, par 70). Greens fees are US$40 for 18 holes; golf cart, US$35; rental clubs, US$23. There is a pro shop and snack bar. **Jolly Harbour Golf Course** (462-7771) is the island's newest layout. The 18-hole course was designed by golf course architect Karl Litton of Florida. The course (6,001 yards, par 71) is open to visitors on a daily fee basis.

Hiking The Historical and Archaeological Society organizes monthly hikes. Inquire at the Antiquities Museum in St. John's. Antigua has a web of dirt roads and tracks that wander from main roads to beaches, where you can swim, or into woodlands and along ponds for bird-watching. The only marked trails on the island are those leading to the heights above English Harbour and a 7-mile marked trail system in the area of Wallings Reservoir (462-1007). There are short hikes in the hills of the south coast between Old Road and Falmouth that take 30 minutes or an hour to reach lovely beaches accessible only by hiking or by boat. If you bring a picnic lunch, you can make a day of it with time for swimming and snorkeling. Rendezvous Bay, one of the island's most spectacular beaches, can be reached from Falmouth by four-wheel-drive vehicles or a hike of about forty-five minutes.

Horseback Riding Spring Hill Riding Club (Falmouth; 460-7787; www.springhillridingclub .com) is home to the Antigua Horse Society. The stable offers a two-hour trail ride to Rendezvous

Bay, which can be reached only by boat, jeep, or on foot. Another very steep trail leads to Monks Hill, from which there are magnificent views. **Reliable Stables** has a dozen Antiguan-bred horses and offers trail rides to Runaway Beach and to Cedar Valley Golf Course.

Kayaking Look for turtles and other surprises of nature in bays and coves near Willikies and Seatons. **Tropical Adventures** Antigua (480-1225; www.tropicalad.com) also offers kayaking, sailing, and jeep safari tours. **Antigua Paddles Kayak Eco Trips** (463-1944; www.antiguapaddles .com) include kayaking, swimming, snorkeling, and nature walks on an uninhabited island. From the fisherman's cottage clubhouse at Seatons Village, participants go by motorboat through Mercer's Creek to a long raft where kayaks are moored. After a safety briefing, guides lead the group to tiny islands and fish spawning areas and explain mangrove ecosystems. After kayaking and refreshments, motorboats whisk the group across to North Sound National Park to Bird Island and snorkeling over coral reefs. The company is a member of the Antigua Environmental Eco Awareness Group.

Kitesurfing One of Antigua's fastest growing sports was a natural development for an island long known for excellent windsurfing. **KiteAntigua Kitesurfing Center** (Jabberwock Beach; 720-5483; www.kiteantigua.com) is affiliated with the International Kiteboarding Organisation (IKO), and adheres to industrywide teaching standards. Lessons, conducted by certified instructors, are an absolute requirement for this extreme sport. All courses from beginners to advanced are taught in two-hour sessions, at 9:00 a.m. and 1:00 p.m. daily. Two weeks advance booking is recommended. Open full-time December to August; closed September to November (open weather permitting and upon request).

Antigua Adventures (726-6355; www .antiguaadventures.com) offers quad biking, fishing, kitesurfing, and an Xtreme visit to Stingray City Antigua.

Snorkeling/Scuba Diving Antigua is surrounded by coral reefs in crystal-clear, shallow water, ideal for snorkelers. Almost all beaches and offshore islands have reefs within swimming distance or a short boat ride from shore. With a few exceptions diving is in shallow water at sites of less than a 60-foot depth, where colorful reef fish are abundant. North of St. John's above Dickinson Bay is **Paradise Reef,** a popular area for snorkeling. Fronting the palm-fringed beaches on the east coast are miles of reefs that break Atlantic waves and provide calm waters for snorkelers.

South of the capital along the west coast at **Hawksbill Rock,** there is a cave in 15 feet of water. **Sunken Rock,** which drops to a depth of 122 feet, is a deep dive for experienced divers. Along the drop-off divers see sting rays, barracudas, and occasional dolphins.

Cades Reef, a 2.5-mile-long reef about a mile off Cades Bay on the south coast, is typical of the reefs around Antigua. It is dominated by staghorn and elkhorn coral in the shallow areas and rich with colorful reef fish, such as parrotfish and blue tang. Visibility ranges from 80 to 150 feet. The reef is one of Antigua's main dive sites; part of it has been designated a marine park. Antigua and Barbuda are only now becoming known for wreck diving. The most popular of the six wrecks close to Antigua is the *Andes,* a three-masted, fully rigged merchant vessel that sank in 1905. It is located south of St. John's harbor by Deep Bay in only 20 feet of water.

Among the half-dozen dive shops belonging to the **Antigua Dive Operators Association** (http://divetravel.netfirms.com), the most convenient to the port is **Dive Antigua Rex** (Rex Halcyon Cove Hotel; 462-3483; www.diveantigua.com). Some other members are **Deep Bay Divers** (463-8000; www.deepbaydivers.com), with several locations, and **Jolly Dive** (Jolly Beach Resort; 462-8305; www.jollydive.com).

Stingray City Antigua Located in the lee of a barrier reef on the eastern (Atlantic) side of Antigua, the area has been dubbed **Stingray City Antigua** (562-7297; fax: 560-2118; stingray@candw.ag; www.stingraycityantigua.com). Here southern stingray have lived for centuries. On tour you are taken from the fishing village of Seatons by powerboat to the barrier reef, where guides who are former fishermen take you swimming in the clear water with the rays. You will discover they are like big puppies. Departure times: 9:00 and 11:00 a.m., 1:00 and 3:00 p.m. $40. Snorkeling gear is provided, but not ground transportation.

Tennis and Squash Antigua's low humidity makes it suitable for tennis, a sport very popular here. More than a dozen hotels have courts. **Curtain Bluff** often hosts Tennis Week in January, when tournaments feature top-seeded players. **Temo Sports** (Falmouth Bay; 460-1781) is a tennis and squash complex. It has locker rooms and showers, snack bar, and pro shop. Courts must be reserved.

Windsurfing The same trade winds that made Antigua a haven for ships of yesteryear and attract yachts today have made it a windsurfing mecca, too. Most beachside hotels have boards for rent. The quiet seas and gentle breezes along the Caribbean shores are ideal for beginners. Strong winds varying from 12 to 25 knots and seas with 2- to 3-foot chops on the Atlantic side attract experienced enthusiasts. Antigua has several internationally known windsurfing schools. **Windsurfing Antigua Week,** the annual international competition, is usually held in January. The **Lord Nelson Hotel** on the northeast coast is the favorite center for experienced windsurfers. **Windsurf Antigua** (Jabberwock Beach; 461-WIND; www.windsurf antigua.com) offers instructions and rentals.

Festivals and Celebrations

Antigua Sailing Week in late April or early May is the most important annual yachting event in the Caribbean and attracts sailors from around the world. More than one hundred top-class racing yachts take part, and, for a week or so, English Harbour is crammed with boats and people who come to be part of the activities. Along with racing, the week is full of frolic and festivities and topped off with a fancy-dress ball at Admiral's Inn—the social event of the season.

Carnival in Antigua began two decades ago as festivities to celebrate the visit of Queen Elizabeth II. The Antiguans had so much fun doing it, they repeated the celebration the following year, and the next, until it grew into an annual event. In 2007 Antiguans celebrated a Golden Jubilee, fifty years of heart-throbbing music, bright costumes, and energetic spirit. Since independence in 1981, Carnival has become an eleven-day arts festival highlighting the island's culture and heritage with parades and other competitions. It is held in late July and early August before Emancipation Week, which begins the first Monday in August.

Barbuda

Barbuda, Antigua's sister island, is a nature lover's paradise. Scalloped with miles of pink-sand beaches and fringed by reefs, the coral island is a sparsely settled wilderness interspersed with lagoons, marshes, and mangroves, which are home to the largest frigate-bird sanctuary in the Eastern Caribbean. Located 30 miles north of Antigua, the largely undeveloped island is only 143 feet above sea level at its highest point. Codrington, where most of the island's 1,500 people live, is the only village.

Codrington Lagoon A large estuary along the west coast is the mating ground for thousands of magnificent frigate birds. During the mating season, from late August to December, the sight is fantastic. Every bush appears to have a dozen or more females on it, and a few feet overhead dozens of males with wingspans up to 8 feet glide through the air in display, ballooning their red throat pouches to get the attention of the flapping females.

Boats are available in Codrington for the short trip to the middle of the lagoon, where you can watch and photograph the birds within a few feet of the bushes. In addition to the frigate bird, Barbuda is said to have 170 bird species. Other wildlife includes white-tailed deer and boar.

South of Codrington in the area of Palmetto Point are the island's most beautiful pink-sand beaches. Offshore, Palaster Reef is a marine reserve established in 1972 to protect the reef, its pristine waters, and historic shipwrecks. George Jeffries (Barbuda; 460-0143) takes up to three people on a four-hour tour, including the frigate bird sanctuary, for US$90 or US$25 per person for four or more. If you cannot contact him, **Paradise Tours Barbuda** (772-0661) operates the same tour for US$25 per person, for a maximum of eight persons to a boat (by law). The company is run by Linton Thomas, the executive chairman of Barbuda's Tourist Board.

Barbuda Ferry On Wednesday, Thursday, Saturday, and Sunday, the *Barbuda Express* (560-7989; www.antiguaferries.com), an 85-foot power catamaran, departs St. John's for Barbuda at 8:30 a.m. and returns by 5:00 p.m. for US$50 round-trip. The ferry also offers a day tour from St. John's to Barbuda on Wednesday, Thursday, and Sunday, 8:15 a.m. to 4:00 p.m., for $120. The boat makes the Atlantic crossing to Barbuda in about an hour.

St. Barthélemy (St. Barts)
Gustavia

St. Barts

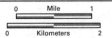

0	Mile	1
0	Kilometers	2

N

ATLANTIC   *OCEAN*

ÎLE CHEVREAU

Anse de
Colombier   *Anse Paschal*   *Pointe*
                                 Etages
              Anse des
              Flamands
Île de
la Petite
Jean   ○ Colombier   *Anse de*
                                    Cayes

              ○ Corossol   *Anse de*
Anse à   *Baise de*   *Lorient*   *Pointe Lorient*
Corossol   *Jean*
                                                          ○ Lorient
Anse de Public   Vitet ○
Les Islettes   ○ St. Jean
                                                                    Morne
Les Saintes   ● **GUSTAVIA**   *du Vitet* ▲

                    ○ Lurin   *Grande*   *Morne de*
                                     Saline   *Grand Fond* ▲

Les Grenadiers ○
                                                          La Tortue

Anse de Marigot
                    Marigot ○   *Anse de Grand*
                                       Cul-de-Sac
                                                    ○ Grand
                                                    Cul-de-Sac
                                                    Anse de Petit
                                                    Cul-de-Sac

                                                    Anse de
                                                    Toiny

                         Anse de
                         Grand Fond

                    Anse de
                    Grand Saline
         Anse du
         Gouverneur
Grande Pointe

CARIBBEAN   *SEA*

The Darling of the Jet Set

A seductive paradise of scenic beauty at first sight, serendipitous upon acquaintance, St. Barthélemy—or St. Barts, as it is better known—is a stylish hideaway, 15 miles southeast of St. Maarten. The smallest of the French West Indies, St. Barts is a tiny Eden of green mountains and miniature valleys overlooking two dozen gorgeous white-sand beaches and turquoise water.

Discovered four decades ago by the Rockefellers and Rothschilds, it is something of a St. Tropez-in-the-Tropics, attracting jet-setters and a host of show-biz celebrities and all those who follow in their wake. But the lot of them are mere Johnny-come-latelies. The island was probably inhabited first by the Arawaks. Christopher Columbus came upon the island in 1493 and named it for his brother's patron saint, Bartolomeo. The first French colonists arrived in 1648 from St. Kitts and were followed by the Knights of Malta. After raids by the fierce Carib Indians, the island was abandoned until 1673, when it was again settled by Frenchmen from Normandy and Brittany.

In 1784 the French sold St. Barts to Sweden in exchange for trading rights elsewhere. The Swedes renamed the harbor Gustavia in honor of their king, declared it a free port, and profited handsomely from the enterprise. France repurchased the island in 1878, retaining its free port status to this day.

In addition to being the only Caribbean island the Swedes ever possessed, St. Barts has other features that make it different. Too dry and rocky to be coveted for agriculture, the little island attracted only small farmers who had to scratch for a living. It was never converted to a sugar economy as was most other Caribbean islands, slaves were never imported, and the plantation society typical of the colonial Caribbean never developed here.

Rather, St. Barts is a minuscule remnant of ancient France, with neat little villages surrounded by meadows marked with centuries-old stone fences, and fair-skinned farmers and blue-eyed fishermen who speak a dialect of their seventeenth-century Norman ancestors that even French-men cannot understand. Against this background of a conservative, closely knit society with Old World traditions, St. Barts has become a modern playground of worldly French sophistication for the rich and famous from both sides of the Atlantic.

Budget Planning

St. Barts offers the best that money can buy—and you will need plenty of it. It is one of the most expensive islands in the Caribbean, particularly so for its restaurants, which are comparable to top New York ones and often cost US$100 or more per person for lunch or dinner. On the other hand, day-sailing excursions and car rentals are reasonable. French products are slightly less than in the United States but, generally, more than on the neighboring St. Martin.

At a Glance

Antiquities	★
Architecture	★★
Art and artists	★
Beaches	★★★★
Colonial buildings	★
Crafts	★★
Cuisine	★★★★★
Culture	★★
Dining/Restaurants	★★★★★
Entertainment	★
Forts	★
History	★
Monuments	★
Museums	★
Nightlife	★
Scenery	★★★★
Shopping	★★
Sightseeing	★★
Sports	★★★★
Transportation	★

Population: 7,000

Size: Approximately 10 square miles

Main Town: Gustavia

Government: St. Barts and neighboring St. Martin officially broke away from Guadeloupe on July 15, 2007, becoming Overseas Collectivities. Considered French territories, the residents have full French citizenship like those on the mainland. St. Barts will be run by a territorial council with a president and executive council.

Currency: Euro. US$1.00 fluctuates at about € 0.50, or 1 euro equals about US$1.50. U.S. dollars are widely accepted, and prices are often quoted in dollars. Be sure to check locally as the dollar has been dropping considerably against the euro recently.

Departure Tax: € 4.55

Firearms: Yachts are permitted to have firearms aboard, but they must be declared. Otherwise visitors are not allowed to bring them into St. Barts.

Language: French is the official language; the local dialect stems from old Norman speech and is hard to understand, even for Frenchmen.

Public Holidays: January 1, New Year's Day; May 1, Labor Day; May, Ascension Thursday; May, Pentecost Monday; July 14, Bastille Day; August 15, Assumption Day and St. Barts/Pitea Day, which commemorates the twinning in 1977 of St. Barts and Pitea, Sweden; November 1, All Saints Day; November 2, All Souls Day; November 11, Armistice Day; December 25, Christmas.

Telephone Area Code: 590. To call St. Barts from the United States station-to-station, dial 011-0590 plus the St. Barts number; person-to-person, dial 01-0590 plus the St. Barts number. To call St. Barts from other French West Indies islands, dial direct. To call Dutch St. Maarten from St. Barts, dial 00-599-54 plus the St. Maarten number. To call the United States from St. Barts, dial 00-1, followed by the code for the state. To call within the island or Guadeloupe, dial 0590, plus the phone number. For Martinique dial 0596 plus the phone number. There are no coin-operated phones; major credit cards can be used, and telephone cards (Télécartes) are available for purchase.

Airlines: *From the United States to St. Barts* there are no direct flights. Travelers fly to St. Maarten, San Juan, and other gateways to connect with Winair (599-545-4237; fax: 599-542-2002; www.fly-winair.com), Air Caraibes (0590-27-61-90), St. Barth Commuter (27-54-54; www.st-barths.com/stbarth-commuter; st-barth.commuter@wanadoo.fr), Air St. Martin (www.airsxm.com) or Carib Aviation (264-497-2719) for a shared charter from Antigua. The flight from St. Maarten takes ten minutes. St. Barts's small airport and short landing strip can handle nothing larger than twenty-seat STOL aircraft. It is not equipped for night landing.

Information: www.st-barths.com

In the United States:

New York: French West Indies Tourist Board, 825 Third Avenue, 29th Floor, New York, NY 10022; (212) 745-0950

French Government Tourist Offices:

Chicago: 205 North Michigan Avenue, Chicago, IL 60601; (312) 327-0290; fax: (312) 327-5207; nancy.anderson@franceguide.com

Los Angeles: 9454 Wilshire Boulevard, Suite 210, Beverly Hills, CA 90212; (310) 271-6665; fax: (310) 276-2835; christophe.carvenant@franceguide.com.

In Canada:

French Government Tourist Board:

Montreal: 1981 Avenue, McGill College #490, Montreal, PQ H3A 2W9; (514) 288-2026; fax: (514) 845-4868; (800) 361-9099.

In Port:

Office du Tourisme, Quai General de Gaulle, Gustavia, 0590-27-87-27; fax: 0590-27-74-47. Mailing: St. Barts Tourist Office, B.P. 113, Gustavia, 97098 Cedex, St. Barthélemy, F.W.I. Hours: weekdays 8:00 a.m. to 6:00 p.m., and 9:00 a.m. to noon on Saturday.

Port Profile: Gustavia

Embarkation/Location The pretty, yacht-filled harbor of Gustavia is located on the south side of the island. Small cruise ships usually steam directly into the harbor but do not dock; instead, they tender passengers the short ride to the wharf. Larger ships remain outside the harbor and tender passengers to the dock. Bordering the harbor on three sides are fashionable boutiques and outdoor cafes with an unmistakable French ambience.

Local Transportation There is no public bus system, but since the island is so small—only 25 miles of road—you can walk to many locations. There is a taxi station on rue de la République and another at the airport. You can also call for a taxi (0590-27-66-31). Taxi fare for up to three persons per car from Gustavia to St. Jean Beach is about € 5 for rides up to five minutes long and € 4 each additional three minutes. After 8:00 p.m. and on Sundays and holidays, fares have a 50 percent surcharge.

Roads and Rentals The best way to tour St. Barts is by car, which can be rented for about € 55–65 per day in winter and € 45–55 in the summer with unlimited mileage. Gas is extra and costs about € 1.28 per liter. Advance reservations are necessary, especially during the winter season, but be aware that some agencies require a two- or three-day minimum rental. The island has two gas stations; neither is open on Sunday. Not all car-rental companies take major credit cards. The most popular vehicles are open-sided Mini-Mokes, Gurgles, and Volkswagen Beetles—all well suited for the narrow, winding roads and hilly terrain—but drivers of these vehicles need to know how to operate a stick shift. Driving is on the right side of the road. The speed limit is 28 mph, which suits the roads and terrain—but not the French drivers from the mainland who race around St. Barts as if they were practicing for the Grand Prix.

Motorbikes, mopeds, scooters, and 18-speed mountain bikes are available from **Rent Some Fun** (0590-27-54-83). You'll need to show a motorbike or driver's license, and French law requires drivers to wear helmets. Rentals cost about € 35 a day in high season and include helmet and insurance.

Most car-rental firms are located at the airport. There are independent dealers and major names. **Avis/St. Barth Car** (0590-27-71-43; www.avis-stbarth.com); **Budget/Jean-Marc Greaux** (0590-27-66-30; budgetstbarth@wanadoo.fr); **Hertz/Henri's Car Rental** (0590-27-71-14; hertz.stbarth@wanadoo.fr); and **Tropic'All Car Rental** (0590-27-64-76; tropicallrent@saint-barths.com).

Ferry Services *Rapid Explorer* (Gustavia 0590-27-60-33; St Maarten 599-542-9762; www.rapidexplorer.com), a new deluxe high-speed catamaran, offers three departures daily between St. Barts and

St. Martin/St. Maarten. The trip takes forty-five minutes; schedules and prices are found on its Web site. Two others: *Voyager* (0590-87-10-68; www.voyager-st-barths.com) departs twice daily from St. Martin for a seventy-five-minute trip; *The Edge* (599-544-2640), a high-speed ferry, leaves once daily, Tuesday to Saturday from Pelican Marina, St. Maarten, and takes forty-five minutes to Gustavia. Fares range from € 50–55 one-way; € 62–75 round-trip. You can also charter a high-speed boat to pick you up in St. Maarten. Contact **Marine Service** (0590-27-70-34) or **Master Ski Pilou** (www.masterski-pilou.com), who offers a 24/7 St. Maarten water taxi service.

Interisland Air Service See Fast Facts.

Emergency Numbers
Medical: Gustavia hospital, 0590-27-60-00 or 0590-27-60-35
Police: 0590-27-66-66

Shore Excursions

Island tours are operated by minibus or by taxi, with the driver acting as guide.

Island Paradise Introduction: 1 hour, US$39. Introductory drive by taxi-van, which goes to La Tourments, St-Jean, the Côte au Vent, and Grand Fond.

Snorkeling Adventure: 2 hours, US$66. A catamaran cruise to Colombier Bay for snorkeling, including equipment and refreshments.

Semi-Submersible: 1 hour, US$99. In addition to seeing marine life while traveling in the unique *Sea Discoverer,* you'll also pass over the wrecks of the 50-foot freighter *Marginan* and the multimillion-dollar, 110-foot yacht *Non-Stop.*

Trekking in St. Barts: 2 hours, US$94. After a short ride to Petite Anse in Flamands, a guided hike begins to Anse de Grand Colombies, also known as Rockefeller Beach, where there is time for a swim in the secluded bay before the return trip.

St. Barts ATV Adventure: 2 hours, US$169. Explore both the windward and leeward sides of the island following expert guides. The tour passes through the fishing village of Corossol and travels on to Colombier, where a turn-off-road provides breathtaking views of the north shores. The return route heads up Morne Tourtertelle, with views of the area's salt ponds and a stop for a swim at Gouverneur's Beach. The Office du Tourisme can provide a list of independent driver/guides and sailboat operators that provide excursions.

St. Barts on Your Own

The delightful little town of Gustavia with its lilliputian port has a pretty setting: yachts bobbing in the harbor and red-roofed houses climbing the surrounding green hills. Only 3 blocks deep, the town has no must-see historic sites and can be explored easily on foot in an hour, stopping now and then to check out the boutiques and to enjoy refreshments at one of the sidewalk cafes that lend a French air to the setting. A few street signs in Swedish are reminders that the Swedes were here, too.

A Gustavia Walkabout

Old fortifications are located on both sides of the harbor. On the south a five-minute walk passes Fort Karl en route to Petite Anse de Galet, also known as Shell Beach, where there is good shelling. On the north Fort Gustave offers a nice view of the harbor.

The **Town Hall (Mairie de St. Barth)** and some restaurants are housed in old buildings dating from the eighteenth century. **St. Barth Municipal Museum (Musee Municipal de St. Barthélemy)**, on the south side of the harbor, depicts the island's history through photographs, documents, costumes, and antiques. It is open daily. Entrance: about € 2.

A steep road by the landmark clock tower on the east side leads over the hill, where a rough road continues to Anse du Gouverneur, a cove with one of the island's most beautiful, secluded beaches bracketed by jagged cliffs. You can see Saba, St. Eustatius, and St. Kitts in the distance.

A Drive around the Island

The quickest way to get into the St. Barts mode is to rent a Mini-Moke (a canopied jeep) and wander about following your whim. Stop at a beach for a swim or in a village to sip an aperitif, ramble down a country lane, or turn up a road to a hillside for a view. St. Barts can be easily toured by car in half a day. The narrow roads—yesterday's donkey tracks—twist and turn through tiny villages and along rocky shores to secluded, picture-book beaches.

West of Gustavia

On the north side of town, the road forks northeast to the airport and northwest to Corossol, the most traditional of the island's tiny fishing villages, where the old Norman dialect can be heard. Some of Corossol's elderly women still wear long blue-and-white-checkered dresses and the *caleche,* a stiff-brimmed bonnet derived from seventeenth-century Breton style. It is sometimes called *quichenotte,* meaning "kiss me not." The women are very shy and disappear at the first sign of strangers who might try to take their pictures. If you put away your camera and take an interest in the straw hats they want to sell you, you will find the reception quite different. The straw—the finest, most supple in the Caribbean—is hand-woven from the fan-shaped fronds of latania palms. Also in Corossol is the **Inter Oceans Museum** (0590-27-87-27; 27-62-97), a private collection of shells, open daily 10:00 a.m. to 4:00 p.m. Admission: about € 4.

Farther along, the road winds its way to Anse des Flamands on the north coast, where you will see another of the island's beautiful coves with a wide, half-mile stretch of white sand fringed by latania palms and framed by weather-worn rocks washed by intensely turquoise seas. It is home to several small resorts, Hotel St. Barth Isle de France, and a popular celebrity-watching spot, Taiwana (0590-27-65-01; www.hoteltaiwana.com), a beach club-hotel and popular restaurant.

Anse de Colombier on the northwest end is a pretty cove accessible only by foot or boat.

The North Coast and East End

From Gustavia a hilly, twisting road heads northeast, passing the airport and skirting St. Jean Bay on its way to the eastern end. The bay, rimmed by white-sand beaches and bathed by calm, reef-protected turquoise waters, is divided about midpoint by a small promontory topped by tiny Eden Rock (www.edenrockhotel.com), the island's first hotel, which was renovated and expanded by its new owners in 1997 and quickly reestablished its premier position as the best place to enjoy fabulous views and absorb something of the St. Barts legend, in the place where it began. The bay is the hub of St. Barts's resort and water-sports activity.

Lorient, at the eastern end of St. Jean Bay, is the site of the first French settlement in 1648. Its palm-fringed beach is used by local families, and its long rolling waves make it popular with surfers and windsurfers. Jutting out to sea between Lorient Bay and Marigot Bay on the east are the jagged cliffs of Milou and Mangin, where Atlantic waves crash against rock. Pointe Milou, almost barren a decade ago, is now a fashionable residential area of elegant homes and resorts.

Rising behind Lorient are the island's highest peaks: 898-foot Morne de Grand Fond on the west and 938-foot Morne du Vitet on the east. One road passes between the mountains to the south coast, another loops around Morne du Vitet via Grand Cul-de-Sac and the south coast, and a third winds up Morne du Vitet. They all pass centuries-old rural landscapes of farmhouses, grazing cattle, and patchwork fields outlined by stone fences.

Grand Cul-de-Sac, a large bay on the northeast, is another resort and water-sports center, where shallow, reef-protected waters are ideal for novice windsurfers and snorkelers. Another road passes over the mountain to Anse de Toiny, with wild landscape that reminds people of the Normandy coast.

Shopping

St. Barts is a duty-free port. Perfumes and famous-brand crystal, silver, china, jewelry, liquor, and tobacco are sold for about 20 percent less than U.S. prices. But as we have said earlier, St. Barts is not a place for bargains. As in most of France, stores close for lunch.

Art and Artists Pompi (Petit Cul de Sac; 0590-27-75-67) is the local boy who made good. Pompi is an intuitive artist who has his atelier, gallery, and restaurant under one roof. **Anchor Art Gallery** (rue Jeanne d'Arc; 0590-52-93-66) carries contemporary Caribbean and international art. A list of artists and art galleries is found in *Ti Gourmet Saint-Barth,* a local publication issued annually.

Other products on sale include exquisite straw work, woven from latania palm, by the older women in the fishing village of Corossol; lovely jewelry by Annelisa Gee, who also sells it at her boutique **Made in St. Barth** (0590-27-56-57), in St. Jean; and paintings by artists living in St. Barts.

Books and Maps For books in French and English, try **Librairie de Oasis** (Lorient).

China/Crystal Several shops around the island carry French china, crystal, and silver; convenient to the port is **Carat** (Quai de la République), which has Baccarat, Lalique, Christofle, and other high-quality brands.

Clothing and Accessories Boutiques of **Hermés, Gucci, Donna Karan,** and other famous designers are found in Gustavia, St. Jean, and the **La Savane Commercial Center** opposite the airport. A variety of somewhat less expensive stores housed in colorful cottages make up **Villa Creole,** a small shopping mall on St. Jean beach. A canvas tote bag stamped "Loulou's Marine," sold at the well-known nautical supply shop in Gustavia, is a popular cognoscenti take-home souvenir. **Lolita Jaca** (Gustavia; 0590-27-59-98) is best known for straw, leather, or beaded handbags and unusual, sophisticated jewelry; silk and cotton clothing; and Lolita's new perfume, which comes in a fabric pouch filled with pearls perfumed with the same fragrance, to be used as a sachet. **Laurent Eiffel** (0590-27-54-02) has especially attractive, light-weight men's linen shirts in a rainbow of colors. For some specialty shops, **Black Swan** (Gustavia and Villa Creole; 0590-27-65-16) has active sportswear; **C. Demours** (0590-251-14-60) and **Maryvonne & Gerard** (0590-252-37-68), both on rue de la République in Gustavia, have original, one-of-a-kind jewelry designed and crafted in St. Barts.

Crafts and Souvenirs The women of Corossol and Colombier are famous for their hand-woven baskets, broad-brimmed hats for men and women, and handbags, made of delicate, supple straw with designs that resemble old lace. Other locally crafted products include sandals and shell jewelry.

Groceries If you want to take home some French products, **Match** (St. Jean; 0590-27-68-16) is a useful stop. **Foodland** (Gustavia port; 0590-27-68-37), a grocer-caterer, is patronized by locals and boat people.

Liqueurs and Wine Fine French vintages stored in temperature-controlled rooms are found at **La Cave du Port Franc** (Gustavia). The store also sells contemporary paintings and antique objets d'art. **Cellier du Gouverneur** (Gustavia; 0590-27-99-93) is the place for wines, rums, and passionfruit punch.

Perfumes and Cosmetics The well-known French labels are available in boutiques, but more unusual are the locally made perfumes, lotions, and suntan oils of natural products. Beauty lotions and suntan oils made from island plants and other natural materials also make unusual gifts. One line, **La Ligne de St. Barth** (0590-27-82-63; fax: 0590-27-70-93; www.lignestbarth.com), is produced and sold by Brigit and Hervé Brin, whose ancestors settled on St. Barts hundreds of years ago. Their boutique and laboratory in Lorient are well worth a visit.

Another local face and body product with all natural ingredients is made by **Belou's P d'Helene Muntal**. It includes three body oils named after St. Barts's beaches and a mosquito repellent that nourishes skin as it repels the insects. It is available at Mandarine (www.shopmandarine.com) in Gustavia.

Dining and Restaurants

St. Barts is the gastronomic capital of the Caribbean, where dining is one of the main attractions. Renowned chefs from France frequently visit the island, and some teach classes here during the winter season. Young chefs trained in France's best restaurants come to work in St. Barts, bringing with them a high standard and creativity. By combining local ingredients, Gallic traditions, and modern trends, they have created a new French Caribbean cuisine.

Restaurants are small, and each has something special, either in food, setting, or atmosphere. About half of the ninety or so restaurants are open only for dinner or only during the winter season. Most close on Sunday. For three courses without wine, expect to pay about US$25 per person for a modest meal, $40 per person for a moderate one, and $60 per person and up for an expensive one. Some restaurants do not accept credit cards; inquire in advance.

Gustavia and Environs

La Marine (rue Jeanne d'Arc; 0590-27-68-91). Picnic-style tables and benches on a waterside terrace. Seafood is a specialty. Moderate.

La Route des Boucaniers (on the port; 0590-27-73-00; fax: 0590-27-73-05; boucaniers@wanadoo.fr). Lively brasserie overlooking the harbor. Moderately expensive.

Le Bete a Z'ailes (Gustavia port; 0590-29-74-09; bazbar@wanadoo.fr). Sit inside or outside to enjoy the harbor setting, with sailboats bobbing in the water at the shore of the little town, and feast on fresh fish, sushi, sashimi, and pasta salad. Jazz some evenings. Moderately expensive.

L'Esprit Salines (on road to Saline beach; 0590-52-46-10; lesprit3@wanadoo.fr) is in a pretty garden cottage where brothers Guillaume and Christophe prepare refined French fusion cuisine, beautifully presented, in a friendly ambience. Fresh fish specialties are available daily. Moderately expensive.

Maya's (Public Beach; 0590-27-75-73; mayas restaurant@wanadoo.fr). Just around the bend from Gustavia, overlooking the sea, it's the favorite of St. Bart cognoscenti and good for celebrity watching as well as dining. Maya is from Guadeloupe, which is famous for its chefs; her husband is from Nantucket. Menu changes daily and is always fresh. Dinner only; sunset drinks from 4:00 p.m.; closed Sunday. Informal. Expensive.

Wall House Restaurant (Quai du Wall House; 0590-27-71-83; fax: 0590-27-69-43). Located in a quiet corner of the harbor, owners

Franck and Denis prepare light menus for lunch and more elegant gourmet specialties for dinner to be enjoyed overlooking the water. Moderate.

West of Gustavia

François Plantation (Colombier; 0590-29-80-22; info@francois-plantation.com). Now under new owners, the hillside villa hotel houses one of St. Barts's brightest dining stars. A long arbor covered with blooming vines leads to a plant-filled bar and elegant, terraced dining room with a wine cellar that is partly under a decorative waterfall. The cuisine is French and Mediterranean, and the ambience sophisticated. Dinner only. Expensive. Closed April 15–November 1.

La Case de L'Isle (Hotel Isle de France; 0590-27-61-81; isledefr@saint-barths.com). This intimate beachside eatery of the hotel on Anse des Flamands is one of the island's best. Managed by American Evelyn Weber, the chef de cuisine is Bruce Domain. Moderately expensive.

New Born (en route to the Manapany Hotel at Anse des Cayes; 0590-27-65-11; www.newborn stbart.com). Authentic Creole dishes such as *accras* (codfish fritters), *boudin* (sausage), *blaff* (poached fish), and *calalou* are served a stone's throw from the beach in simple, pleasant surroundings. Moderate.

St. Jean and Beyond

Club Lafayette (Grand Cul-de-Sac; 0590-27-62-51; gnlabau@yahoo.fr). Fun fashion shows with clothes from the Club Lafayette boutique are part of the weekend entertainment. For a table between 12:30 and 2:00 p.m., reservations are suggested. No credit cards. Very expensive. Closed May–November.

Eden Rock (0590-29-79-99; www.edenrock hotel.com). This completely renovated landmark—St. Barts's first hotel—is worth a visit for the beautiful view, to have a drink at the harbor bar, and to dine in the original bar perched over St. Jean Bay. In its short reincarnation, the Eden Rock acquired its neighboring hotel, Filao, which it replaced with new beachside villas, and is once again the heart of St. Barts. **The Sand Bar,** especially popular at lunch, serves grilled fish (and other selections) in a manner reminiscent of the French Riviera and is moderately expensive. The elegant **On The Rocks,** on the terrace of the original building, is watched over by chef de cuisine Jean-Claude Dufour from Bordeaux, well known to St. Barts's cognoscenti for his tenure at Hotel Isle de France. Expensive.

Hostellerie des Trois Forces (Vitet; 0590-27-61-25; 3forces@st-barths.com). Grilled shrimp, lobster in basil sauce, fish with fennel, and other dishes are turned out from a wood-burning fireplace and served in the cozy atmosphere of a rustic country inn. The proprietor is an amateur astrologer and yoga practitioner; hotel rooms are named for the signs of the zodiac. Moderate to expensive.

K'fe Massai (L'Orient; 0590-29-76-78; kfmassai@hotmail.com). Done up like an African safari camp, the restaurant offers French cuisine that is high quality, but you might want to go only for drinks at the bar unless you don't mind noise. Expensive.

Le Gaiac (Hotel le Toiny; 0590-27-88-88; letoiny@saint-barths.com). If you happen to be on the far eastern side of St. Barts at lunchtime or on a Sunday, you can't do better than the lovely outdoor restaurant setting of this hotel perched high above the sea. Many rate it as the best restaurant on St. Barts. Very expensive.

L'Indigo (Guanahani Hotel; 0590-27-66-60; guanahani@wanadoo.fr). Since Guanahani's famous Le Bartolomeo serves only dinner, you might try L'Indigo, its poolside cafe. It's a good choice for casual daytime dining in an air of relaxed sophistication. Expensive.

Nightlife

Leisurely dining is the main evening pastime. St. Barts has no movie houses or casinos. Young locals and visitors gather at such popular hangouts in Gustavia as **Bar de l'Oubli** (across from Loulou's Marine; 0590-27-70-06), where the open porch is a great people-watching spot reminiscent of Saint-Tropez. Its neighbor, **Le Select** (0590-27-86-87), is a long-standing local hangout for snacks, drinks, and people watching. The garden restaurant, **Cheeseburger in Paradise,** is next door; it's named for Jimmy Buffett, an island habitué. *St. Barth Magazine,* a lively French/English publication, is the best source of information on current nighttime attractions.

Sports

St. Barts has good facilities for water sports. You should always contact the hotel or sports operator in advance to make arrangements, particularly during the peak season. There are about a dozen tennis courts but no golf course.

Beaches/Swimming St. Barts is scalloped with more than two dozen pearly beaches bathed by calm turquoise waters—and few are ever crowded, even in peak season. Signs prohibiting nudism are all around the island, but the teensiest monokini is the fashion. All beaches are public and free.

Anse du Gouverneur, near the port, and **Anse de Grande Saline,** also on the south coast, are the most secluded beaches; **St. Jean** on the north coast and **Grand Cul-de-Sac** on the northeast are the most developed ones, with hotels, restaurants, and water sports.

The **Nikki Beach** (0590-27-64-64; www.nikki beach.com) has brought a little South Beach and St. Tropez to St. Barts. The beach club, the place to see and be seen, is located on St. Jean beach next to Eden Rock, which certainly doesn't hurt it for attracting a cool crowd. Light lunch and dinner menus include sushi. Moderately expensive.

Boating St. Barts's popularity for yachting is due in part to its location midway between Antigua and Virgin Gorda, two major sailing centers. Gustavia's harbor, which runs 13 to 16 feet in depth, has mooring and docking facilities. **Loulou's Marine** (Gustavia; 0590-27-62-74) is known throughout Caribbean yachting circles as one of the best-stocked marine supply stores in the Leeward Islands. The staff speaks English, and its bulletin board is something of a message center.

Sunfish sailing is especially pleasant in St. Barts, because most of the bays have gentle waters. Boats can be rented at St. Jean, Grand Cul-de-Sac, Public, and Colombier beaches.

Ocean Must (0590-27-62-25) and **La Marine Service** (0590-27-70-34) have half-day sails and other excursions to nearby beaches and islets. Bare-boat rentals, with gas and ice, cost about € 170 for a half day to € 400 for a full day at Marine Service. Full-day sailing excursions to Colombier or Ile Fourchue, a desolate island of wild moonscape terrain off the northwest coast, depart Gustavia at about 9:00 a.m. and return about 5:00 p.m. The cost is about € 110 per person (minimum of four) and includes swimming, snorkeling, cocktails, open bar, and picnic lunch. The island is interesting to explore but hot; bring a generous supply of water, sun protection, and sturdy shoes for hiking. A half-day cruise with swimming, snorkeling, and open bar departs at 9:00 a.m. and 1:00 p.m. and costs about € 65.

Deep-Sea Fishing Fishing charters can be arranged through **Ocean Must** (0590-27-62-25) and **Marine Service** (0590-27-70-34). The latter charges € 700 for a half day to € 1200 for a full day, including fishing gear, open bar, and sandwiches for four persons. Popular catches are tuna, bonito, dorado, marlin, and barracuda. Check with local fishermen before eating your catch; not all fish in these waters are edible. **Patrick Laplace** (0590-27-61-76) is a professional deep-sea fishing guide.

Golf Golfers, don't get your hopes up, but St. Barts now has a small driving range: **Golf Driving Range** (Cul de Sac; 0590-37-46-45), open in the afternoons. Located by the water, golfers hit balls into the water and the wind sends the balls back. One basket of balls, € 6; 12 baskets, € 60.

Hiking St. Barts's pretty landscapes and country roads with light traffic make walking and hiking popular pastimes. Almost any location is within easy reach, although the hilly terrain and hot sun make distances deceiving.

Horseback Riding Ranch des Flamands at Anse des Flamands. Contact Laure Nicolas (0590-27-13-87). A two-hour-long excursion that departs at 9:00 a.m. and 3:00 p.m. costs € 55. Another is St. Barth Equitation (Flamands, 0690-62-99-30).

Snorkeling/Scuba Diving St. Barts is almost completely surrounded by shallow water reefs, better suited for snorkeling than diving, and often within swimming distance of shore. St. Jean Bay has the most accessible reefs. Equipment can be purchased at **Loulou's Marine** (0590-27-62-74) or rented from **La Marine Service** (0590-27-70-34).

The best dive locations are on the west coast at about 50- to 60-foot depths within easy reach of Gustavia. Immediately outside the harbor is Gros Ilet, a rock poking about 75 feet above the sea, where you can see grouper, snapper, moray eel, lobster, and large schools of reef fish.

Dive operators run boat trips daily. **La Marine Service** (0590-27-70-34; fax: 0590-27-70-36; www.st-barths.com/marine.service) offers PADI and French certification. Dive trips cost about € 75 to € 99 per person, gear included. **St. Barth Plongee** (Gustavia, 0590-41-96-66; www.st-barth plongee.fr; birdy.dive@wanadoo.fr) and **Plongee Caraibes** (Quai de la République; 0590-27-55-94; www.plongee-caraibes.com) also offer PADI certification. The staffs, certified as instructors by their French federation, are familiar with American methods and standards, and the shops maintain American as well as French tanks and regulators. **Ouanalao Dive St Barth** (Grand Cul de Sac beach, (0690-63-74-34; www.ouanalao-dive.com, ouanalao-dive@gmail.com) is PADI certified and has three daily diving excursions, at 9:00 and 11:00 a.m and 2.30 p.m., for all skill levels. Also offers snorkeling excursions and private outings upon requests. Gift shop has snorkels, fins, masks, and kayaks for rent.

Surfing Lorient, east of St. Jean Bay, is the most popular surfing area. You can rent boards at water-sports centers and get advice about water conditions at the same time.

Windsurfing/Kiteboarding Shallow waters and gentle winds make conditions at St. Jean and Grand Cul-de-Sac ideal for learning to windsurf. Rentals are available at beachside water-sports centers. **Carib Water Play** (St. Jean; 0690-61-18-81) and **Wind Wave Power** (St. Barth's Beach Hotel; 0590-27-82-57) offer rentals and lessons. Rentals average about € 20 an hour. Both also offer kayaking. Lorient is the most popular site for experienced sailboarders. Kiteboarding, or Kitesurf, has come to St. Barts, as it has to all the Caribbean. Contact **Kitesurf** (Grand Cul de Sac, 0690-69-26-90; enguerrand7@voila.fr).

Festivals and Celebrations

St. Barts celebrates **Mardi Gras** in the French tradition and has some festivals and events special to the island.

The **St. Barts Music Festival** (www.stbarts musicfestival.org/), under the direction of Frances DeBroff, president of the Pittsburgh Symphony Association, is an annual affair in mid- to late January/early February featuring chamber music, dance, and other arts. Artists from the United States and Europe perform in the church of Lorient and at the wharf in Gustavia.

The **Festival of St. Barthélemy,** August 24, is the colorful feast day of the island's patron saint. Similarly, the **Feast of St. Louis,** August 25, is celebrated in the village of Corossol.

St. Kitts and Nevis

Basseterre, St. Kitts; Charlestown, Nevis

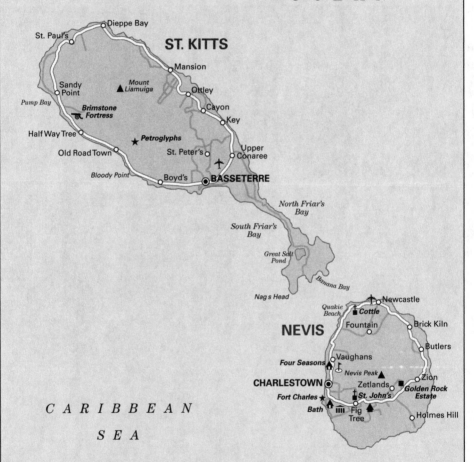

St. Kitts and Nevis

0   Miles   4
0   Kilometers   6

N

A T L A N T I C

O C E A N

Dieppe Bay

St. Paul's

ST. KITTS

Mansion

Sandy
Point

Mount
▲ Liamuiga

Ottley

Pump Bay

Cayon

*Brimstone
Fortress*

Key

Half Way Tree

★ *Petroglyphs*

Old Road Town

St. Peter's

Upper
Conaree

Bloody Point

Boyd's

● **BASSETERRE**

*North Friar's
Bay*

*South Friar's
Bay*

*Great Salt
Pond*

Banana Bay

Nags Head

*Quakie
Beach*

✈ Newcastle

■ *Cottle*

NEVIS

Fountain

Brick Kiln

Butlers

Four Seasons ▲

Vaughans

Nevis Peak ▲

Zion

CHARLESTOWN ●

Zetlands

*Golden Rock
Estate*

† *St. John's*

Fort Charles ★

C A R I B B E A N

Bath

Fig
Tree

Holmes Hill

S E A

The Secret Caribbean

Graceful islands of gentle beauty, St. Kitts and Nevis (pronounced NEE-vis) enchant visitors with their lovely landscapes and unspoiled qualities. Christopher Columbus, who came upon the islands in 1493, selected St. Kitts from all his discoveries to name for his patron saint, St. Christopher. Located in the Leeward Islands west of Antigua, St. Kitts and Nevis call themselves "The Secret Caribbean," being discovered only now by tourists and cruise ships. The irony is that these islands were the first the English settled, and St. Kitts—as St. Christopher came to be known—had the title of the "mother colony" throughout its colonial history.

Here the British gained great wealth from the land that produced the highest-yielding sugar crop in the world. Little wonder that the native Carib Indians called the island Liamuiga (Lee-a-MOO-ee-ga), meaning "fertile land." To protect their valuable possession, the British built their most massive fortress in the Eastern Caribbean. From their base in St. Kitts, the British settled Nevis, Antigua, and Montserrat.

Shaped like a paddle, St. Kitts rises from a grassy coastal skirt through intensively cultivated green hills to a central spine of mountains covered with rain forests. Mount Liamuiga, a dormant volcano whose peak, at almost 4,000 feet, is usually hidden under a cap of white clouds, dominates the north. Different in climate and terrain from the main body of St. Kitts, the Southeastern Peninsula, a hilly tongue of land forming the "handle of the paddle," is covered with dry woodlands and salt ponds and scalloped with the island's best beaches.

After a century as a Spanish possession, the first English settlers arrived in St. Kitts in 1623 to stake a claim for Britain. They established a colony near the place known today as Old Road Town. The following year the French arrived and claimed the northern and southern parts of the island. Like the British, they used it as a base for further colonization, laying claim to Guadeloupe, Martinique, St. Martin, and St. Barts—the islands that make up the French West Indies today.

For more than a century Britain and France fought over St. Kitts for possession of this rich prize, but they first had to battle the Carib. It was not until 1783, under the Treaty of Versailles, that the British finally got St. Kitts and Nevis for themselves. The islands remained British colonies until 1983, when full independence was established.

Budget Planning

St. Kitts and Nevis are among the least expensive islands in the Caribbean. If you can share the cost, a taxi is the best way to tour in the short time usually available to cruise passengers. Restaurants (with local cuisine) are moderately priced. As for shopping, the island compares favorably in price with St. Thomas for duty-free goods, but you are likely to find the locally made products of more interest.

At a Glance

Antiquities	★
Architecture	★★
Art and artists	★★
Beaches	★★
Colonial buildings	★★★
Crafts	★
Cuisine	★★★
Culture	★
Dining/Restaurants	★★
Entertainment	★
Forts	★★★★★
History	★★★
Monuments	★
Museums	★
Nightlife	★
Scenery	★★★★
Shopping	★★
Sightseeing	★★★★
Sports	★★★
Transportation	★

Population: St. Kitts, 31,880; Nevis, 9,423.

Size: St. Kitts, 68 square miles; Nevis, 36 square miles.

Main Towns: Basseterre, St. Kitts; Charlestown, Nevis.

Government: St. Kitts and Nevis, officially known as the Federation of St. Christopher and Nevis, belong to the British Commonwealth. They are governed by a parliamentary government headed by a prime minister. Each island has a legislature and assembly. The queen is represented by a governor-general.

Currency: East Caribbean (EC) dollar. EC$2.70 equals US$1.00. U.S. dollars are widely accepted.

Departure Tax: US $22, including an environmental tax.

Language: English

Public Holidays: January 1, New Year's Day; Good Friday; Easter Monday; Labor Day, first Monday in May; Whit Monday; Queen's Birthday, second Saturday in June; August Monday, first Monday in August; September 19, Independence Day; December 25, Christmas; December 26, Boxing Day; late December, Carnival Day at the end of the two-week festivities that begin a week before Christmas.

Telephone Area Code: 869. From the United States and Canada, dial 869-465 for St. Kitts and 869-469 for Nevis, followed by the four-digit local number. International telex service is operated by Skantel; international collect calls can be made from their office in Basseterre.

Airlines: *From the United States and Canada:* St. Kitts is served directly by American Airlines /American Eagle, and Delta from Air Canada, LIAT, USAirways via San Juan; Continental, and Winair. *Interisland:* Other international carriers connect with regional ones via St. Maarten, and Antigua to St. Kitts. Nevis is served by American Eagle from San Juan, LIAT from Antigua, and Winair from St. Maarten.

Information: www.stkittstourism .kn; www.nevisisland.com

In the United States:
St. Kitts Tourism Authority, 414 East 75th Street, Ste. 5, New York, NY 10021; (212) 535-1234; (800) 582-6208; newyork@stkittstourism.kn.

In Canada:
St. Kitts Tourism Authority, 133 Richmond Street West, Suite 311, Toronto, ON M5H 2L3; (416) 368-6707; fax: (416) 368-3934; canada@ stkittstourism.kn.

In Port:
St. Kitts: St. Kitts–Nevis Department of Tourism, Pelican Mall, P.O. Box 132, Basseterre, St. Kitts, W.I.; (869) 465-2620/4040; fax: (869) 465-8794; ceo@stkittstourism.kn.

Nevis: Nevis Tourist Authority, Main Street, Charlestown, Nevis, W.I.; toll free: (866) 556-3847; (869) 469-7550; fax: (869) 469-7551; info@ nevisisland.com.

Port Profile

Location/Embarkation Cruise ships arrive in St. Kitts at Basseterre, the capital, on the southwest side of the island. Most ships are now using Port Zante, the new facility in town where land reclamation extended Basseterre's waterfront from the shore behind Pelican Mall about 800 feet into the bay. The twenty-six acres of new land has an arrival center and shopping mall, yacht club and marina, and other businesses in a park setting.

All the buildings must conform to the Victorian-colonial-style of Basseterre's historic town center, after which the port's architecture has been adopted. Unfortunately, before the project could be finished, the new pier and buildings were badly damaged by a hurricane, and much of the construction has had to be done all over again. When the entire project is completed, cruise passengers should find the arrival in St. Kitts to be one of the most delightful in the Caribbean. Meanwhile, some ships may continue to use the old port, Deep Water Port, on the south end of a wide bay about a mile or so from the town center.

In Nevis cruise ships and ferries from St. Kitts arrive in Charlestown, the main town. Its waterfront has been renovated, too. The pier for cruise ships to dock or tender has been rehabilitated, and the historic Cotton Ginnery has been renovated to house small arts-and-crafts shops, a small museum, and other facilities. Land reclamation has provided parking areas and passenger gazebos in a parklike setting.

Local Transportation On St. Kitts, private buses operate between villages, but generally they are not used by cruise-ship passengers due to the short time their ships are in port. Taxis, operating on set rates, are available for touring on both islands. Drivers are a loquacious lot and likely to sprinkle their commentary with local lore. Sample rates: one-way from Basseterre to Frigate Bay, EC$27.00 (US$10.00)) or US$2.50 per person for five or more passengers; Deep Water Port, EC$22.00 (US$8.00) or US$2.00 per person for five or more; to Half Way Tree (near Brimstone Hill), EC$37.00 (US$14.00) or US$3.50 per person for five or more; Sandy Point EC$44 (US$16); Brimstone Hill US$50 for a maximum of two hours for one to four people or US$12.50 per person for five or more, to Dieppe Bay, EC$60.00 (US$22.00) or US$5.50 per person for five or more; Ottley's Village, EC$38.00 (US$14.00) or $3.50 per person for five or more; Ottley's Plantation Inn, EC$54.00 (US$20.00) or US$5.00 per person for five or more. For a taxi from one point to another within Basseterre, EC$13.50 (US$5.00), US$1.25 per person for five or more. Waiting time charged for every fifteen minutes, EC$5 (US$2). Taxi rates are published in Tourism Department pamphlets.

Roads and Rentals A good road circumnavigates the main body of St. Kitts, hugging the coast all the way; and a wonderful scenic road, opened in 1989, crosses the Southeast Peninsula to the tip, a stretch of about 7 miles. The coastal road makes it easy to drive—or bike—around the island and provides access to the mountainous interior, where you'll find splendid hiking. There are no cross-island roads through the central mountains, but there are footpaths. Maps are available from the Tourism Department.

Nevis has about 20 miles of narrow, winding roads that encircle the island, but not always along the coast; some cut across the foothills of Mount Nevis. The south side of the island is honeycombed with country lanes and footpaths, ideal for rambling. Local people use the roads for walking as much as for driving, since traffic is light.

To drive, you must obtain a local driver's license by presenting your valid U.S. or Canadian license and paying a fee of EC$64.80 (US$24.00) at the Traffic Department (Central Police Station, Cayon Street, Basseterre, or the police station in Charlestown). Normally the transaction takes only a few minutes. Driving in this former British colony is on the left.

Car-rental rates are comparable to U.S. ones. Some agencies require that drivers be at least twenty-five years of age. Most offer pickup and delivery service. Some agencies have Mini-Mokes or jeeps, mopeds or motorbikes, as well as popular Japanese and European cars.

In St. Kitts: **Avis** (South Independence Square St.; 465-6507; www.avis.com); **Delisle Walwyn Auto Rentals** (Liverpool Row, 465-8849; www.delislewalwyn.com); and **Thrifty/T.D.C.** (Central Street; 465-2991; www.thrifty.com). The latter two as well as **Island Moped & Auto** (Sprott Street) have mopeds and bicycles.

In Nevis: **Hertz** (Nelson's Spring; 469-7467); **Thrifty/T.D.C.** (Main Street; 469-5430). **Meadville Bike Rental** (Craddock Road; 469-5235) and **Mountain Bike Rentals** (Oualie Beach; 469-9692) have bicycles and scooters.

Ferry Service Four ferry companies—M & M Transportation (*Carib Breeze/Carib Surf;* 466-6734), **Wesk Agency** (*Sea Hustler/Mark Twain;* 469-0403), **St.Kitts & Nevis Fast Ferries** (*Geronimo Express;* 662-8930) and **F & F Transportation** (*Carib Queen*) run frequent service Monday through Saturday and limited Sunday services between Basseterre and Charlestown. It takes forty-five minutes. Fares from EC$20 (US$8) round-trip. Schedules are available from the Tourist Office on both islands. For information, call 466-INFO.

Emergency Numbers

Medical: Joseph N. France General Hospital, Basseterre; 465-2551; Alexandra Hospital, Nevis, 469-5473

Police: 911

Fire: 333; Nevis Fire Services 469-3444.

Shore Excursions

Scenic Railway Tour: 3.5 hours, US$109 adults, US$54 children. The old sugar railroad tracks are used by a train built especially for the popular tour. See description later in this chapter.

Island/Brimstone Hill Tour: 3 hours, US$54, US$39 child. The most frequent shore excursion is an island tour that takes in the scenic west coast with a stop at Caribelle Batik and Brimstone Hill. You could take a similar route on your own, with a stop at **Rawlins Plantation Inn** on the north coast for lunch or a swim. A two-hour tour in a private taxi for up to four people costs US$50.

Mount Liamuiga Rain Forest: 5–6 hours, US$69. You can take a guided hike to the crater rim of Mount Liamuiga through local companies; make arrangements in advance. Half-day rain-forest hikes can also be arranged here and in other areas of St. Kitts.

Sea Kayaking: 3 hours, US$89. A scenic transfer by coach to White House Bay, where participants paddle along the rugged coastline to Friars Bay. There they break for refreshments and a transfer back to the ship.

Snorkel Adventure: 3 hours, US$79 adult, $49 child. A snorkel safari along St. Kitts's southeast peninsula stops at White House Bay to explore a sunken Spanish galleon, and then to Ballast Bay and Green Point.

St. Kitts on Your Own

The capital of St. Kitts is unmistakably British, despite its French name. Hard by the sea along a wide bay, Basseterre, which means "lowland" in French, is considered one of the best remaining examples of a traditional West Indian town in the Eastern Caribbean. Despite fires, hurricanes, and earthquakes, many examples of Georgian and Victorian architecture have survived and give the town its historic character.

A Basseterre Walkabout

The historic town center, laid out in a modified grid, is easy to cover on foot and to combine with a shopping tour.

The Circus (1) One block inland from the waterfront, the palm-shaded Circus is a small replica of Piccadilly Circus in London, with a Georgian clock tower and a memorial to Thomas Berkely, a former president of the Leeward Islands Legislative Council. The roundabout is in the heart of the business district at the intersection of Fort and Bank Streets and Liverpool Row—all with shops, car rentals, tour companies, and restaurants.

Independence Square (2) East of the Circus at the end of Bank Street is Independence Square, a public park with flowering gardens and a central fountain. The square was the site of the slave market in the eighteenth century and is surrounded by some of the town's best-preserved colonial buildings, many with balconies and gingerbread trim. Its side streets have shops, the island's best art gallery, and restaurants. On the east side stands the **Church of the Immaculate Conception.**

St. George's Anglican Church (3) Originally built as Notre Dame by the French in 1670, the church was destroyed by fire in 1706 by the British,

1.	The Circus	5.	Treasury Building and Post Office
2.	Independence Square	6.	Market
3.	St. George's Anglican Church	7.	Fisherman's Wharf and Pelican Cove Marina
4.	St. Kitts and Nevis Tourist Office	8.	Port Zante

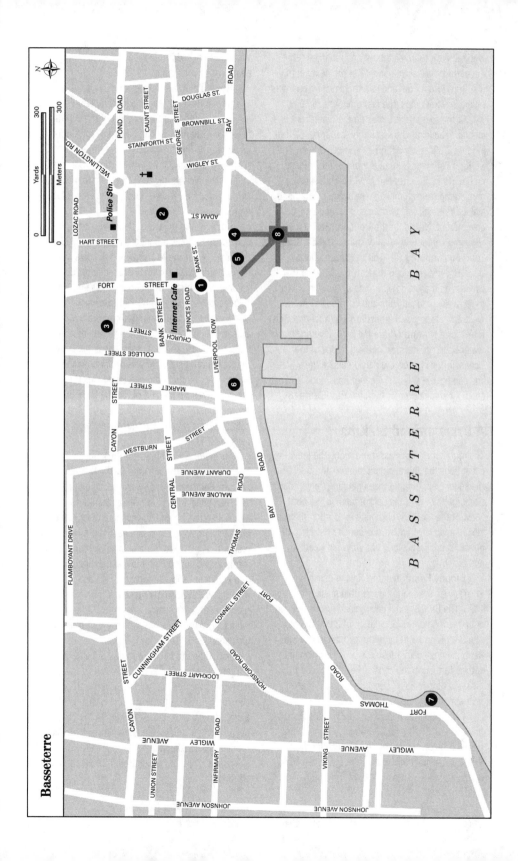

who rebuilt it four years later and renamed it for the patron saint of England. Over the next century it suffered from fires and natural disasters and was rebuilt several times (the last time was in 1869).

At the foot of the Circus on the waterfront is a landmark building known as the **Treasury (5)**, dating from 1894; the post office is located here. The St. Kitts Philatelic Bureau is west of the Treasury on Bay Road. St. Kitts and Nevis each issues its own stamps, which make them prized by stamp collectors—and a nice source of revenue for the government. Next door the **Pelican Mall** is a small shopping center with quality shops. The **St. Kitts Tourism Authority (4)** is on the second floor.

Farther west along the bay, the **Market (6)**, liveliest on market day (Saturday), is a good place to learn about local fruits and vegetables. At the west end of the bay, **Fisherman's Wharf** and **Pelican Cove Marina (7)** are the main dive and water-sports centers. From the gardens of the Ocean Terrace Inn on the hillside above the wharf, you can have a splendid view of Basseterre and see your ship docked at the new **Port Zante (8)**.

A Drive around St. Kitts

The road north from Basseterre along the leeward coast hugs the shoreline and borders the tracks of the sugar train fringing the sugarcane fields; Mount Liamuiga towers in the background on the north. Most of the coast is rockbound except for an occasional small cove with a tiny beach or stretch of golden sand, particularly between Old Road Town and Half Way Tree.

Bloody Point Stonefort Ravine, north of Boyd's, was the scene of a terrible massacre in 1626. The British and French joined forces to wipe out almost an entire population of 2,000 Caribs, after receiving word of an attack planned by the Carib Indians against the new colonists who had settled farther up the coast. The site is known today as Bloody Point, because it is said that the ravine ran with blood for three days.

Old Road Town On the shores of Old Road Bay in 1623, Sir Thomas Warner, his family, and fourteen followers landed to establish the first British settlement in the West Indies. It served as the capital of St. Kitts until 1727. The tomb of

Warner, who died in 1648, lies in a churchyard nearby at Middle Island.

Romney Manor Inland from Old Road Town en route to Romney Manor and Wingfield Estate, former plantations in the foothills of the central mountains, there are small boulders with Carib petroglyphs. The land of Wingfield Estate once belonged to a Carib tribe whose chief, Tegreman, befriended Warner and permitted him to make a settlement on St. Kitts—much to the chief's later regret.

Romney Manor, a seventeenth-century plantation house partially rebuilt after a fire in 1996, is the home of **Caribelle Batik** (465-6253; www.caribellebatikstkitts.com), surrounded by lovely gardens and shaded by an enormous saman, or rain tree, as it is known locally, said to be more than 350 years old. At Caribelle Batik you can watch artisans—mostly girls from the surrounding villages—at work, re-creating drawings taken from the Carib petroglyphs, scenes of Caribbean life, and West Indian motifs. Caribelle Batik uses the ancient Javanese method of making batik; its sole concession to the twenty-first century is the use of colorfast dyes rather than traditional vegetable dyes, which fade.

Brimstone Hill National Park Begun in 1690 by the French, and completed by the British over a century, Brimstone Hill (www.brimstonehillfortress.org) has been dubbed the Gibraltar of the West Indies. Perched on an 800-foot spur of Mount Liamuiga overlooking the west coast, the fortress covers thirty-eight acres. It's one of the most massive fortifications built during the colonial era. Made into a park in 1965, the fort has been beautifully restored with British assistance; it has three redoubts, officer's quarters, hospital, ordnance stores, kitchen, and drainage system. A museum was added in 1982.

In addition to being beautiful, the view from the ramparts brings into focus St. Kitts's strategic location to the colonial powers. Beyond the green cultivated fields on the north lie the islands of Saba, St. Eustatius, and St. Barts. On the south beyond the sugarcane fields that cover the hills forming the backbone of St. Kitts are the peaks of Nevis and Montserrat. Admission: US$8 adult, US$4 child.

Mount Liamuiga The brooding volcano known in colonial times as Mount Misery rises behind Brimstone's gray stone walls. From its rain-forested peaks, the mountain slopes down through a quilt of green cultivated hills to a sapphire sea. The rim of the crater, at 2,625 feet, is not the actual peak, which is located east of the crater, but it is the area that can be climbed.

The trail is a gradual ascent along deep ravines under a dense canopy of trees more than 50 feet high and dangling with curtains of vines, ferns, and philodendron. There are magnificent views down the coast and across St. Kitts to the surrounding islands. At the rim you have the unusual opportunity to walk down (crawl is more accurate) into the crater of a dormant volcano, but it is an arduous trek requiring stamina and agility.

Hikers usually approach the volcano from the north, at Belmont Estates, where a dirt road leads to the trailhead at about 1,500 feet elevation. The hike to the crater rim takes about 2.5 hours on the ascent and about 1.5 on the descent. There are no facilities whatsoever on the trail. If you want to go down into the crater, it is essential to have a local guide, because it is easy to become disoriented and lost.

Black Rocks On the northern tip of St. Kitts at Dieppe Bay, the coast is fringed by coral stone and black-sand beaches.

Beaumont Park Racetrack As part of the multimillion-dollar Whitegate Development in the Deippe Bay area, a racetrack for horse and greyhound races is under construction. Another future development in the northernmost area, known as **Kittitian Hill** (www.kittitianhill.com), is described as a contemporary Caribbean community founded on sustainable development principles. Set on a 400-acre site in the foothills of Mt. Liamuiga, it is designed as a village with villas, apartments, a cottage hotel, a center for the creative arts, a destination spa, and a championship golf course.

At Belle Vue, on the windward coast, huge boulders of molten lava from prehistoric volcanic eruptions rest at the edge of the sea, where the pounding surf has shaped and weathered them into spectacular, wild scenery. You can return to Basseterre along the east coast via Conaree and the international airport. Use Ottley's, a plantation acquired in 1989 by an American family and converted into a hotel using the 1832 greathouse, as the centerpiece. **Ottley's Plantation Inn** (800-772-3039; 465-7234; fax: 869-465-4760; www.ottleys.com).

Scenic Railway Tour (465-7263; scenicreservations@sisterisles.kn; www.stkittsscenicrailway.com). When the St. Kitts Scenic Railway National Tour began service in 2002, it made history on two counts. It's the first luxury train tour in the Caribbean, and the train itself travels over the essence of St. Kitts's history—sugar.

From the early 1700s, sugar plantations were located near the coast and in the foothills of the mountains rising in the center of the island. The scenic train uses the same rail lines built in 1912 to deliver the cane from the plantations to the sugar mill in Basseterre.

The tour, which encircles about two-thirds of the island, departs from the Needsmust Station in Basseterre and heads north, counterclockwise across the coastline, passing small villages and providing passengers with great views of the sea and countryside. The conductor narrates the tour, describing the scenery: old sugar estates with abandoned windmills and chimneys; slave quarters that housed Africans imported to work the plantations; Brimstone Hill Fortress; Old Road Town, where Thomas Jefferson's great-grandfather is buried; and other historic villages and sites. Because of the deep canyons, or *ghuts,* that run from St. Kitts's mountainous center to the coast, the train travels over twenty-three bridges. The trip takes less than three hours and when offered as a cruise ship excursion, passengers return via the coast by motor coach.

The scenic railway has ten 28-passenger double-decker railway coaches, built especially for the tour. Every passenger has two seats—one on the first level in the air-conditioned cabin with 6-foot-wide vaulted windows and another on the open-air observation deck. The coaches are equipped with water coolers, restrooms, and a sound system. Car attendants are on board to assist passengers.

The railway tour schedule varies according to demand, e-mail scenicreservations@sisterisles.kn to confirm schedule. Price: US$89.00 adults,

US$44.50 children, including beverages and musical entertainment. Tickets can be purchased at the Needsmust train station or the St. Kitts Scenic Railway office in Basseterre. The tour is designed to coordinate with cruise-ship arrivals. Cruise passengers may buy tickets on board most ships; round-trip transportation from the pier is included.

Frigate Bay and the Southeastern Peninsula

On the south side of Basseterre, a narrow strip of land stretches southeasterly in a series of knolls, ponds, and coves with St. Kitts's prettiest white-sand beaches. In the late 1970s the first phase of a long-range resort development of the peninsula began with the first mile or so in an area known as Frigate Bay. The remaining 7-mile strip was accessible only on foot or by boat until the completion of the first road through the area in 1989. The road affords lovely views throughout the drive and ends at the peninsula's most beautiful beaches.

Marine World St. Kitts is under construction on South Friar's Bay Beach. When it opens, the four-acre Marine World will have a stringray lagoon, dolphin encounters, an educational program on marine life, a nature trail, an aviary with tropical birds and butterflies, and a beach bar/grill. The $16 million park will also offer water sports compatible with the marine life.

Majors Bay, a horseshoe cove, has a half-mile crest of white sand, Banana Bay, and Turtle Beach, home of the Turtle Beach Bar (469-9086; www.turtlebeach1.com), a rustic seaside restaurant/bar with a full array of water sports that reopened in February 2008 under Auberge management. These beaches front the island's best snorkeling reefs.

Shopping

The development of tourism and the island's growing economy is reflected in the increasing number of shops in Basseterre, particularly those offering island crafts and duty-free gifts. Generally, store hours are from 8:00 a.m. to noon and 1:00 to 4:00 p.m. daily except Sunday. Most shops of interest to visitors are found in a compact area, from the waterfront near the Nevis ferry pier to the Circus,

Pelican Mall by the port, and Independence Square. Some stores are situated in renovated historic buildings, others in new shopping plazas like Palms Arcade at the Circus and the small, pretty TDC Mall on lower Fort Street, where shops and a restaurant are set around an open courtyard.

Art and Antiques Spencer-Cameron Art Gallery (10 North Independence Square; 465-1617; www.spencercamerongallery.com). Located in a restored colonial building dating from the 1860s, the art gallery and workshop of artist Rosey Cameron-Smith has works by artists from St. Kitts/Nevis and around the Caribbean. Rosey arrived in St. Kitts in 1977, en route to South America to visit friends, and never left. Finding herself in demand as an artist, she created collections for several hotels and then went into business producing silk-screened fabrics with island-inspired designs.

Carla Astaphan (Camps; 465-5947; www.thepottershousestkitts.com), one of St. Kitts' best-known artisans and potters, uses selected blends of local and specially imported clays and glazes to create unique ceramics and masks. She has recently converted her studio-home into a gallery for other local artists whose paintings and photographs are shown along with her own works.

Books and Records Mini Wall's (Princes Street) and Harpers (Fort Street, above the Circus) have local guidebooks, stationery and greeting cards, cookbooks, magazines, and Caribbean music.

China/Crystal Ashbury's (Liverpool Row) and Ram's Duty Free (Pelican Mall and Frigate Bay; 466-RAMS; www.ramstrading.com) carry fine china, crystal, famous name watches, and jewelry.

Clothing and Accessories Brown Sugar (Bay Road; 466-4664; www.mybrownsugar.com) is the store, gallery, and label of Judith Rawlins. Her fashion designs are simple yet stunning, ranging from comfortable day-wear to sophisticated looks for evening. Island Hopper (the Circus) carries a variety of tropical wear and souvenirs. Glass Island (corner of Princes and Fort Streets; 466-

6771) sells jewelry as well as colorful, handblown vases, bowls, and plates.

Crafts Caribelle Batik (Liverpool Row at the Circus; 465-6253; www.caribellebatikstkitts.com) is the in-town outlet for the batik maker at Romney Manor. The shop features colorful, handmade, and original wall hangings and fashionable sportswear, all on fine sea-island cotton. **The Crafthouse** (Shoreline Plaza, Bay Road; 465-7754; www.stkitts crafthouse.com) is a government-sponsored center for local craftspeople to work and improve their skills as well as to display their wares. In addition to crafts and souvenirs, they sell perfume, gold jewelry, and fashion accessories. **Palm Crafts** (Fort Street) features island crafts of shell, straw, and coconut as well as homemade jams and local spices and potpourri.

Jewelry Linen and Gold (Pelican Mall) offers handcrafted items in gold and other jewelry and accessories. **Objects of Art** (the Circus) is a store and factory where jewelry is created from local shells, corals, and volcanic rock.

Perfume Ashbury (Liverpool Row) sells perfumes as well as watches and jewelry, china, crystal, and leather goods at duty-free prices that claim to beat those in St. Maarten.

Dining and Restaurants

St. Kitts has a delicious local cuisine that reflects the Caribbean melting pot as well as any place in the region. Carib, African, European, Asian, and Middle Eastern influences are found in the taste and variety of dishes, which use exotic vegetables such as breadfruit and christophene (a type of squash), eggplant and okra, herbs, and fresh seafood. Peter Mallalieu, a fifth-generation Kittian and food specialist, says such dishes as pepperpot, a meat stew, was learned from the Caribs; konki, a cassava, yam, and coconut bread steamed in banana leaves, came with the African slaves; paelau, a rice-and-peas dish served for celebrations, mingles Spanish and East Indian traditions; and kibbe and rolled grape leaves arrived with the Lebanese traders at the turn of the nineteenth century.

Restaurants are open daily except Sunday, unless otherwise noted. Not all take credit cards; inquire in advance. For dinner, not including wine, inexpensive means less than US$15 per person; moderate, US$15–25; expensive, more than US$25. Lunch is generally US$5 less.

The Ballahoo Restaurant (the Circus; 465-4197). A good place to relax after shopping, it is popular with locals and tourists for seafood and local fare and for its location, which offers seating on a second-floor balcony overlooking the town. Moderate.

Bobsy's (466-6133; bobsy@caribsurf.com) features fresh lobster as well as local and international dishes in a Caribbean atmosphere. Open for lunch and dinner daily. Karaoke, dancing, and entertainment. Moderately expensive.

Dolce Cabana (Frigate Bay; 465-1569; www .dolcecabanaclub.com) serves traditional Italian dishes. Beach bar, live music, dancing. Moderate.

Mr. X's Shiggidy Shack Bar & Grill (Frigate Bay, 663-3983; mrx_watersports@hotmail.com) serves grilled fish, lobster, and chicken in traditional Kittian style. Open bar, live music. Their water taxi is available to transport passengers from the Port Zante Cruise Terminal for US$10 round-trip. Inexpensive.

Oasis Sports Bar and Grill (Frigate Bay; 466-6029) has eight large television screens where you can watch major American sports telecasts while enjoying burgers, barbecues, salads, and sandwiches. Open daily, afternoon to wee hours; closed Tuesday. Moderate.

The Pizza Place (Central Street; 465-2546). In addition to pizza, you can get rôti, chicken, and fried conch to enjoy in its courtyard or to take out. Inexpensive.

Rawlins Plantation (465-6221; www.rawlins plantation.com). The dining room of this small plantation inn is famous for its luncheon buffets of West Indian cuisine. The inn is in a magnificent setting at the foot of Mount Liamuiga. Moderately expensive.

Royal Palm (Ottley's Plantation Inn; 465-7234; www.ottleys.com). Innovative cuisine by chef Pamela Yahn, who creates Caribbean-inspired dishes with Asian flavors, can be enjoyed in a spectacular al fresco setting. Expensive.

StoneWalls Tropical Bar and Eating Place
(Princes Street; 465-5248; www.stonewallstropical
bar.com) enjoys an international reputation as a
bar, thanks to *Newsweek* magazine, but you can
also dine in a tropical garden setting with selections as varied as jerk chicken and sushi. Moderate.

Nightlife

St. Kitts is very low-key. Nighttime entertainment
takes the form of live dance music by a small
combo on the patio of one of the main hotels, bars,
or discos. There is a casino at Jack Tar Village at
Frigate Bay.

Sports

Beaches/Swimming Beaches are open to the
public, but access may be private along some
stretches. St. Kitts's best beaches are on the southeastern peninsula.

The northern Atlantic coast has stretches of
black sand, which are more of a natural curiosity
than good bathing beaches. On the east coast
south of Black Rock, swimmers should be cautious,
because there are strong currents and undertow.
Conaree Beach, on the east coast, has surf.

Biking St. Kitts, with a good road on the lowland
skirt of the mountains, reasonably light traffic, and
friendly people, is well suited for biking. Inquire in
advance through the Tourist Board about the availability of equipment. **Fun Bikes** (Cayon Street;
662-2088) has quad bike tours, call a half-day
ahead for reservations.

Boating Several boats offer day trips, but boating as a sport is not well developed in St. Kitts.
Blue Water Safaris (466-4933, fax: 466-6740;
www.bluewatersafaris.com) and **Leeward Island
Charters** (465-7474; fax: 465-7070) offer a day
excursion to secluded Friar's Bay for a swim, snorkeling, and fine view of Nevis. **Tropical Tours**
(Cayon Street; 465-4039; fax: 465-6400; www
.tropicalstkitts.com) has boat charters, sightseeing,
and dive excursions. These companies arrange
deep-sea fishing charters, too.

Although the waters around St. Kitts are rich
in fish, sportfishing is not developed. Local fishermen catch mackerel, barracuda, kingfish, snapper,
grouper, and marlin, among others.

Golf The **Royal St. Kitts Golf Club** (466-2700;
www.royalstkittsgolfclub) reopened in 2004 after
being renovated and redesigned by Canadian architect Thomas McBroom. It features two holes on the
Caribbean Sea and three on the Atlantic Ocean
with water hazards on 10 holes and 80 bunkers.
The course plays as an 18-hole, par 71 course at
6,900 yards from the back tees. The course is
located at Frigate Bay adjacent to the **St. Kitts
Marriott Resort**. Greens fees: $180 from Novem-
ber to April; $140 May to October.

Hiking The variety of hiking on St. Kitts ranges
from easy rambling on country lanes to arduous
trekking on volcanic peaks. With a map you can
easily find your way in the lowlands and foothills.
In the rain-forested mountains, however, you
should have a local guide, as vegetation often
obscures trails. Guided hikes are available from
Greg's Safaris (465-4121; www.gregssafaris.com).

Horseback Riding Plantation roads through
lush sugarcane and banana fields in the shadow of
brooding volcanic peaks are ideal for horseback riding. **Trinity Stables** (Frigate Bay; 465-9603; 662-
3098; fax: 465-9464; trinity@caribsurf.com) offers
half-day excursions in the rain forest departing
daily at 9:00 a.m. Cost $55, call a day in advance to
reserve. **Royal Stables** (West Farm; 465-2222; fax:
465-4444) has similar 2.5- to 3-hour excursions
departing at 8:45 a.m. and 1:30 p.m. for a minimum
of four persons and a maximum of eight persons.
Cost: US$60 adult; children half price.

Snorkeling/Scuba Diving Under the sea St.
Kitts remains largely unexplored. It has extensive
reefs and a diversity of sites offering walls,
canyons, and caves and drift diving in some locations. But the biggest attraction is wrecks. Of 350
unexplored wrecks known to be in St. Kitts waters,
only 12 have been identified. Historic records show
that approximately one hundred ships were lost in
Basseterre harbor in one hurricane alone.

The reef in front of Banana Bay is in about 15 feet of water and is one of the island's best snorkeling locations. It has star coral, elkhorn and brain corals, and a large variety of colorful reef fish.

A long barrier reef, known as the Grid Iron, stretches for more than 6 miles from Conaree on the east coast of St. Kitts to Newcastle Bay on Nevis at depths varying from 6 to 50 feet. It helps protect the Narrows, the shallow seabed connecting St. Kitts and Nevis. Here, a large circular reef spread over an area of about a half mile ranges from 18 feet to 50 feet. On the south side of the reef, an area known as Monkey Shoals is thick with black coral at 35 feet. It also has a few nurse sharks, rays, and lobsters.

Facilities for diving and other water sports can be found at **Dive St. Kitts** (Bird Rock Beach Hotel; 465-1189; brbh@sisterisles.kn). Daily 9:00 a.m. departures for nearby reefs and shipwrecks return at 12:30 p.m. Lunch and beverages are served at Rocky's Beach Bar.

Tennis Tennis courts are available at most resorts. The largest complex in the Frigate Bay area is at **St. Kitts Marriott Resort** (466-1200).

Windsurfing The best locations on St. Kitts are Frigate Bay and Banana Bay. Equipment is available from water-sports operators and beachfront hotels.

Nevis

Separated from St. Kitts by a 2-mile channel and linked by ferry, Nevis appears to be a perfect, dark-green cone rising with graceful symmetry from the sea. Mount Nevis, at more than 3,000 feet, is usually crowned with white clouds, as though the mountain were covered with snow. Apparently the illusion was enough to inspire Columbus to name it Las Nieves, after a range of snowcapped mountains in Spain.

After its discovery by Columbus in 1493, little happened to Nevis until 1627, when it was granted to the Earl of Carlisle. The following year Thomas Warner sent one hundred settlers from St. Kitts to establish a settlement at Jamestown. After it was destroyed by a tidal wave in 1680, the capital was

moved 2 miles south to Charlestown, where it is today. Although the colony started with tobacco as its first export, by the eighteenth century sugar had become the main crop, bringing with it large plantations and great wealth.

The rich plantation society soon made Nevis the social hub of the Caribbean, with an international reputation as the "Queen of the Caribbees." The Bath House Hotel, built in 1778 immediately south of Charlestown amid elaborate gardens, was said to be the finest building in the Caribbean: It had a casino, where planters and traders won and lost fortunes and made big deals, and a tiny brothel for the officers of visiting ships. It became the most fashionable spa in the region, attracting English and other European aristocrats, who came to its mineral springs to cure their rheumatism, gout, and similar ailments. But even before the Europeans, the Carib must have appreciated the waters, too, because their name for Nevis was Oualie (pronounced WAL-lee), meaning "land of beautiful water."

The springs still flow, and tourists still come to Nevis, but not for the old spa, a historic ruin that awaits renovation, but for the former plantation houses that are now some of the finest small resorts in the Caribbean. Nevis is ideal for travelers who like to wander about, curious to learn what lies down an unnamed lane or over the next hill, stopping to chat with folks they meet along the way. It's what the West Indians call "limin'," or doing nothing in particular. The best way to see the small island is on a stroll around Charlestown, where cruise ships and the ferry from St. Kitts arrive, followed by a drive around the island by taxi, or on a hiking excursion.

Charlestown Located on the west side of the island, Charlestown is a West Indian colonial village so perfectly caught in time it could be a movie set. Only 2 blocks deep and about 4 blocks long, its streets are lined with a medley of pretty old buildings, many with gingerbread trim, and only a few modern intrusions. You step off your ship onto a pier with facilities built specifically to attract more cruise ships. The **Cotton Ginnery,** a small complex of ten shops designed in traditional architecture,

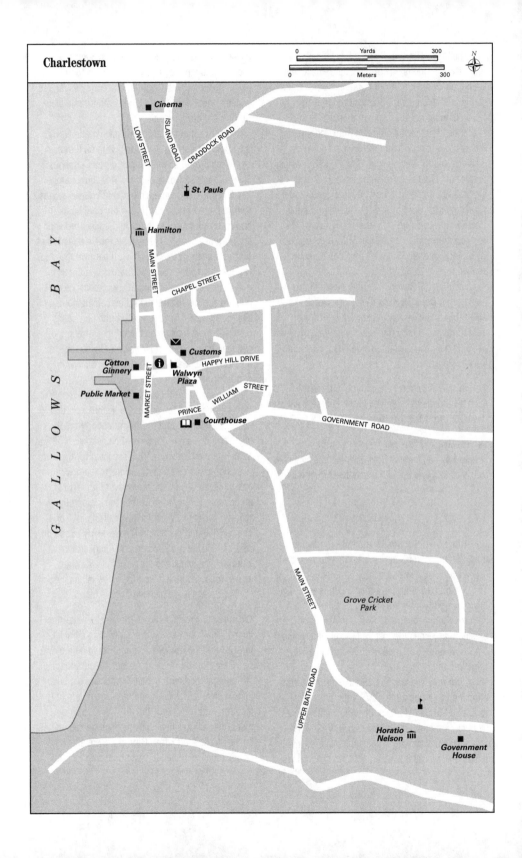

Charlestown

0 — Yards — 300
0 — Meters — 300

N

GALLOWS BAY

Cinema

LOW STREET

ISLAND ROAD

CRADDOCK ROAD

† St. Pauls

🏛 Hamilton

MAIN STREET

CHAPEL STREET

✉

■ Customs

Cotton Ginnery ■

ⓘ

HAPPY HILL DRIVE

Walwyn Plaza

Public Market ■

MARKET STREET

PRINCE

WILLIAM STREET

📖 ■ Courthouse

GOVERNMENT ROAD

MAIN STREET

Grove Cricket Park

UPPER BATH ROAD

Horatio Nelson 🏛

♪ ■

Government House ■

was the historic site where farmers came to sell their products and cotton was ginned, baled, and made ready for shipping. Check out the recently expanded **Nevis Craft House** (469-5505) for locally made handicrafts and souvenirs.

On the south side of the pier is the Market, best on Saturday morning, market day, when folks from all around the island come to town to buy and sell. A few steps away are the Tourist Board Office, which has maps and books on Nevis for sale, and the **Nevis Philatelic Bureau,** one of the busiest places in town.

The street directly in front of the pier leads to Main Street, with the **Nevis Handicraft Cooperative** (469-1746) on the south, and the post office and landmark Treasury building, dating from the eighteenth century, on the north. A turn south on Main Street leads past shops to the courthouse and public library, a handsome stone building dating from the late nineteenth century; the original eighteenth-century building was destroyed by fire in 1873. In front is a memorial to the fallen sons of Nevis in World Wars I and II. Farther along, at the corner of Government Road, an old Jewish cemetery has tombstones dating from the seventeenth century and the ruins of what may be the oldest synagogue in the Eastern Caribbean.

You can visit Nevis's small galleries and see artists and craftspeople at work on a tour led by Gillian Smith and Ceri Whitfield, owners of **Cafe des Arts** (Main Street; phone/fax: 469-7098), a gallery/cafe in Charlestown. The half-day trip ends at the cafe, where you are treated to lunch and can browse the artwork of Kittian and other Caribbean artists.

North on Main Street you pass some attractive shops, particularly the **Island Hopper** (469-0873), known for its batik clothing; and **Island Fever** boutique (469-0887), with a good selection of beach-wear, and island fashions. Also check out **Nevis Craft House** for local crafts. On the west side of Main Street is the **Museum of Nevis History** (www.nevis-nhcs.org), the home of Alexander Hamilton, the first U.S. secretary of the treasury, who was born here in 1755. Hours: Monday to Friday, 9:00 a.m. to 4:00 p.m., Saturday to noon; cost US$5 adults, $2 children.

Horatio Nelson Museum (Belle Vue, next to Government House east of town; 469-0408) contains memorabilia of the famous admiral. **Knick Knacks Boutique** (469-5784; knickknacks@sister isles.kn), newly relocated to Henville's Plaza on Samuel Hunkins Drive, sells some of the most delightful, fun crafts by local artists to be found in the Caribbean. Best of all are cloth and carnival dolls by owner Jeannie Rigby.

Pinney's Beach North of Charlestown, the road to Newcastle, where the airport is located, skirts the coast along 4-mile-long Pinney's Beach, an idyllic, palm-fringed stretch of golden sand where the well-known Four Seasons Nevis Resort is located. At Cades Point a steep road leads to a hilltop high above Tamarind Bay, from which there are breathtaking views of St. Kitts and the Caribbean. It is the best place on the island to watch a spectacular Caribbean sunset. Have sunset cocktails at the top of the hill after 4:30 p.m., November to mid-July.

Nevis's coast is sprinkled with springs and seasonal lagoons that fill after heavy rains, often catching fish when the waters spill over to the sea. At Nelson's Spring, a freshwater pond on the north end of Pinney's Beach, cattle egrets flock in the late afternoon to roost. This area had not been developed until 1991, when the **Four Seasons Nevis Resort** opened Nevis's first international deluxe resort. Located 3 miles north of Charlestown, its most outstanding feature is its golf course. Another mile north is **Oualie Beach Resort,** an attractive beachfront resort with cottages in West Indian style, which has one of the island's main dive and water-sports centers.

Newcastle On the north coast Nisbet Plantation, once the estate of Frances Nisbet, the wife of the famous British admiral Lord Nelson, is now an antiques-filled plantation inn, **Nisbet Beach Resort** (www.nisbetplantation.com), with a magnificent lawn that flows to the beach between double rows of stately palms and flowering gardens. With a little imagination you can easily envision the opulent life here in Nevis's heyday.

Nearby at **Newcastle Pottery,** you can watch pottery made from Nevis's rich red-clay soil being shaped and fired in traditional ways. The pottery is available for sale.

Bath Stream On the south side of Charlestown are the ruins of the famous Bath spa and stream whose waters supply the spa. There is a small bathhouse still in use by local people. Plans to renovate and rebuild the spa have been discussed often but languish for lack of funds.

Fig Tree Village The main road turns inland to Fig Tree Village and St. John's Church, where the book of records is open to the page that recorded the marriage of Lord Nelson and Frances Nisbet in 1787. Admiral Nelson, who was headquartered at the British naval base in Antigua, was first attracted to Nevis for its fresh water to supply his ships. Then he discovered Frances Nisbet, a widow of a wealthy plantation owner. The best man at their wedding—the Duke of Clarence—later became King William IV of England. The marriage took place at the Montpelier great house, which belonged to Frances Nisbet's uncle at the time. It is now restored as an inn (www.montpeliernevis.com), set in beautiful gardens. It's also a delightful place for lunch, which is served on the open-air terrace of the main building.

Gingerland Beyond Morning Star, the area known locally as Gingerland has **Hermitage Plantation, Croney's Old Manor Estate,** and **Golden Rock Estate**—former plantations whose great houses or sugar mills have been converted into inns. All are situated at about 1,000 feet elevation, on the southern slopes of Mount Nevis.

Rainforest Trail A trail through the rain forest on the side of Mount Nevis leaves from Stonyhill, above Golden Rock Estate, and winds north through groves of cacao, breadfruit, and nutmeg trees and overlooks the Atlantic coast. Vervet monkeys can be seen frequently on the walk. **Golden Rock Estate** has a map for a self-guided walk.

Mount Nevis Dominating the landscape in every direction is cloud-covered Mount Nevis. Dormant since its last eruption in 1692, it continues to emit hot sulfurous gases. The crater is a half-mile wide and almost 800 feet deep. A very difficult trail of about 2 miles leads to the crater rim—for experienced hikers only. New, less strenuous trails are being developed, though, at a lower level on the mountainside. (See Hiking section.)

Botanical Gardens of Nevis (Mount Pelier Estate; 469-3509; www.botanicalgardennevis.com) is an eight-acre spread of tropical gardens, divided into sections: cactus, bamboo, lily pools, fruit, and more. A rain-forest conservatory, Mayan temple, and waterfalls are part of the attraction. There is a gift shop and a teahouse/bar. Hours: Monday to Friday, 10:00 a.m. to 3:00 p.m. Admission: US$10 adults, $7 children age six to twelve, younger than age six free.

Saddle Hill Battery Built by the British with slave labor in the eighteenth century, at about 1,700 feet, the fort is the only fortification on Nevis that is not on the coast. Recently, the site was converted by the Nevis Historical and Conservation Society (www.nevis1.com/nevis-museum-history) into a tourist attraction with a trail and interpretive markers explaining the history of the fort and its strategic significance. Along the way, hikers enjoy the panoramic view of St. Kitts, Statia, Montserrat, Redondo, and Antigua. **Saddle Hill** has an observation center with a telescope at about 1,200 feet above sea level. The telescope was given to the island by Greenpeace to use for watching migrating whales.

Plantation Carriage Rides Hermitage Plantation Inn (469-3477; nevherm@caribsurf .com) has authentic, classic Creole adaptations of Victorian-style carriages, crafted of West Indian mahogany, and offers 2- to 3-mile trips that wind through historic Gingerland or scenic back roads where you can see everyday West Indian country life.

Sports

Four Seasons Nevis Resort on Pinney's Beach has the best facilities, but they are expensive.

Beaches/Swimming All beaches are open to the public, and the 4-mile stretch of reef-protected **Pinney's Beach** is the standout. **Oualie Beach,** north of Pinney's Beach, is another fine, more open strand of golden sand with surf and is popular for windsurfing and kayaking.

Deep-Sea Fishing Mount Nevis Beach Club (800-756-3847; 469-9373; www.mountnevishotel .com) and **Oualie Beach Resort** (469-9735; fax: 469-9176; www.oualie.com) arrange sportfishing trips. **Deep Venture** (469-5110, mattlloyd@ caribsurf.com), with professional fisherman Matt Lloyd, offers half- and full-day charters. Catch belongs to the boat captain, who offers generous portions to those who come fishing or want to sample the catch at his restaurant, Le Bistro (469-5110). On **Venture II** (469-9837) champion fisherman Claude Nisbett gives half- and full-day trips on a 28-foot sportfishing boat (with a bar on board). **Nevis Water Sports** (Oualie Bay, 469-9060; www.fishnevis.com) offers full- and half-day charters with tackle and drinks.

Golf The 18-hole championship layout by Robert Trent Jones is part of the **Four Seasons Nevis Resort** (800-332-3442; www.fourseasons.com/ nevis). Greens fee for 18 holes: US$195. Considered one of the best—and certainly one of the most beautiful—courses in the Caribbean, it overlooks Pinney's Beach and the Caribbean, with lofty Mount Nevis as a backdrop. **Cat Ghaut Chip'n Putt** (469-9826), a 9-hole course in Newcastle operated by Roger and Peggy Staiger, also has a nature trail on the property.

Hiking and Biking Nevis's web of country lanes and footpaths provides a delightful variety of hiking for ramblers. With a map it is easy to find your way. **Rainforest Trail** on the slopes of Mount Nevis can be covered without a guide. **The Nevis Historical and Conservation Society** (469-5786), with help from the U.S. Peace Corps, developed six easy to strenuous trails on Mount Nevis accessible from various locations and has a brochure describing them. In recent years the interest in hiking and the availability of trails has increased greatly. Among the newest trails is **Upper Round Road**, a 9-mile road constructed in the 1600s being developed for hiking, horseback riding, and off-road mountain biking. It was part of an extensive road system built to provide access to the sugarcane fields and communities that once surrounded Mount Nevis. The road connects Golden Rock Plan-

tation Inn on the east side of Nevis with the Nisbet Plantation Beach Club on the northern tip. It passes through local villages with quaint West Indian houses, a seasonal rain forest, orchards, and vegetable gardens. Hikers are likely to see monkeys frolicking and mongoose scampering by. Organized by the Nevis Historical and Conservation Society, with a grant from RARE, Center for Tropical Conservation, the project has received an ecotourism award from *Islands* magazine.

Golden Rock Nature Trail, behind the Golden Rock Plantation Inn (469-3346; info@golden-rock .com; www.golden-rock.com), is an easily accessible trail that runs along a ridgeline and meanders down a gentle sloping ravine bed with huge rainforest plants, fruit trees, and flowers. Here a troop of African green, or vervet, monkeys make their home and are seen often peering from behind the trees. Trail maps are available at the inn.

Expert guides can make your trip more meaningful with their knowledge of the flora, fauna, and history. It's also safer than hiking on your own. At **Top to Bottom**, biologists Jim and Nikki Johnson (469-9080; walknevis@caribsurf.com) offer seventeen different educational hikes, from a walk in the "green ghaut" to climbing Mount Nevis. Michael Herbert, **Heb's Nature Tours**, (469-3512, heb nature@hotmail.com) is known as the "bush doctor" for his knowledge of local bush remedies, which he shares on his rain-forest hikes. Earla Liburd (469-2758; info@nevisnaturetours.com; www.nevisnaturetours.com), a local teacher, leads moderately challenging hikes to little-known areas and three waterfalls with **Sunrise Tours**.

Horseback Riding Nevis's lush countryside and hills are a wonderful setting for horseback riding. Inquire at the **Nevis Equestrian Centre** (Cole Hill; 469-8118).

Snorkeling/Scuba Diving Nevis's underwater world is even less explored than that of St. Kitts. The island is completely surrounded by reefs, some within swimming distance of shore. The best snorkeling locations are off **Pinney's Beach.** The **Grid Iron,** the barrier reef that stretches across the Narrows between Nevis and St. Kitts, starts at

Newcastle Bay on the north coast of Nevis. **Scuba Safaris** (Oualie Beach; 469-9518; www.scubanevis.com) has PADI and NAUI instructors and offers diving trips for US$65 for one-tank and US$95 for two-tank excursions. It also has glass-bottom boat cruises and kayaks.

Under the Sea, Sealife Education Centre (469-1291; cell 662-9291; www.undertheseanevis.com) offers guided snorkel trips led by owner Barbara Whitman, a marine biologist and educator, who gives lessons at her colorful seaside aquarium on Oualie Beach.

Tennis Four Seasons Nevis Resort's tennis complex is one of the largest in the Eastern Caribbean.

Windsurfing The best location is the northwest coast from Cades Bay to Newcastle. Equipment can be rented from the **Oualie Beach Resort** (469-5329; fax: 469-9176). You can also rent mountain bikes and kayaks here, as well as arrange for guided excursions. For lessons at all levels, contact champion windsurfer Winston Crooke (469-9682; windsurf@caribsurf.com) located on Oualie Beach.

Montserrat

Plymouth

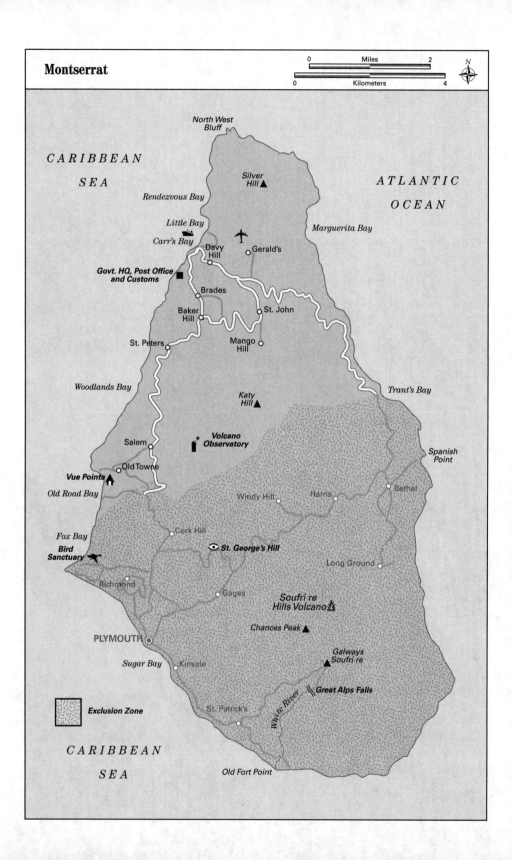

A Quiet Corner of the Caribbean

Note to readers: For a decade beginning in July 1995, volcanic eruptions in the southern half of the island plagued Montserrat, and the area south of the Belham Valley has been declared off-limits to both visitors and residents. The residents and businesses that were in this area, including those in the capital of Plymouth, had to leave and move north. Most resettled north of Plymouth in the area of Salem, where life continues as normally as can be expected.

The good news is that the volcano seems to have calmed down, and people, who have shown remarkable resilience, hope the worst is behind them. A new airport was completed in spring 2005 when Princess Anne came to Montserrat to dedicate it, and air service by Winair was launched. The Montserrat Tourist Board has a promotional campaign to attract visitors. Indeed, for naturalists, environmentalists, and adventurous travelers, now is probably the most interesting time of all to visit Montserrat. In May 2007, Montserrat's new $2 million Cultural Centre (www.montserratcultural centre.com) opened, a big step in the long-term strategy to develop Little Bay, on the west coast, as the country's new urban area.

Known as the Emerald Isle of the West, Montserrat has the distinction of being the only place in the Caribbean settled by the Irish. The title also comes from the island's physical resemblance to Ireland, as velvet green as ever a place could be. The early settlers also left their mark in the names of people and places, evident throughout the island. And to honor them all, a shamrock was mounted on the governor's mansion, visitors' passports are stamped with a shamrock, and St. Patrick's Day is a public holiday.

This quiet corner of the Leeward Islands, 27 miles southwest of Antigua, promotes itself as "The Caribbean as It Used to Be," in praise of its uncommercialized ambience and natural environment. Mostly of volcanic origin, pear-shaped Montserrat rises quickly from a narrow belt of lowlands and foothills to mountains formerly covered with tropical rain forests dominated by 3,002-foot Chance's Peak, the highest point.

Montserrat was sighted by Christopher Columbus in 1493, and, according to tradition, he gave the island its name because its serrated peaks reminded him of the mountain range surrounding Santa Marie de Monserrate, a monastery near Barcelona. The Spaniards apparently had no interest in the island, and the hills and forests were left to the Carib Indians until the middle of the seventeenth century, when the first European settlers arrived.

The Irish came to Montserrat in 1632, fleeing religious persecution on nearby St. Kitts. The French and British subsequently fought over the island until 1783, when Montserrat was ceded to Britain in the Treaty of Versailles. It remains a British crown colony.

At a Glance

Antiquities	★
Architecture	★
Art and artists	★
Beaches	★★
Colonial buildings	★
Crafts	★
Cuisine	★★
Culture	★
Dining/Restaurants	★
Entertainment	★
Forts	★
History	★
Monuments	★
Museums	★★
Nightlife	★
Scenery	★★★★★
Shopping	★
Sightseeing	★★
Sports	★★
Transportation	★

Fast Facts

Population: 4,482

Size: 11 miles long and 7 miles wide; 39 square miles.

Main Town: Salem

Government: Montserrat is a British crown colony, whose governor is appointed by the Queen.

Currency: Eastern Caribbean (EC) dollar. US$1.00 equals EC$2.70. U.S. dollars are used widely, but credit cards are not.

Departure Tax: US$21

Language: English

Public Holidays: January 1, New Year's Day; March 17, St. Patrick's Day; Good Friday; May, Labour Day; Whit Monday; June 9, Queen's Birthday; August Monday (first Monday); December 25, Christmas Day; December 26, Boxing Day; December 31, Festival Day.

Telephone Area Code: 664. When calling from the United States, dial 491 plus the local four-digit number.

Airlines: Blackburne Airport on the east coast was destroyed by the volcano's eruption. However, a new airport located at Geralds (between Sweeneys and St. John's) was inaugurated in spring 2005 and Winair (www.fly-winair.com), which was awarded a two-year contract, began operating scheduled flights between Montserrat, Antigua, and St. Maarten on nineteen-seater Twin Otter aircraft. Reservations can be made online.

Montserrat can also be reached by ferry and helicopter from Antigua and by an occasional cruise ship. The 300-passenger *Opale Express* (Carib World Travel, Lower Redcliffe Street, St. John's, Antigua; 268-460-6101, fax: 268-480-2995; Montserrat Aviation Services, phone/fax 664-491-2362) operates twice daily, except Sunday, departing from St. John's, Antigua, at 6:30 a.m. and 4:30 p.m. and from Little Bay, Montserrat, at 8:00 a.m. and 5:50 p.m. The trip takes approximately one hour and costs US$75 round-trip. An eight-seat helicopter (Carib Aviation, 268-462-3147, fax: 268-462-3125, caribav@candw.ag; Montserrat Aviation Services, phone/fax: 664-491-2362) departs from Bird International Airport, Antigua, daily, except Wednesday and Saturday, at 8:00 a.m. and 5:00 p.m.; and from Gerald's Park, Montserrat, at 8:30 a.m. and 5:30 p.m., except Wednesday and Saturday. The flight takes twenty minutes and costs US$112 round-trip. You must reserve and/or confirm seats in advance.

Information: ww.visitmontserrat .com

In the United States:

Montserrat Tourist Board, c/o Caribbean Tourism Organization, 80 Broad Street, New York, NY 10004; (212) 682-0435.

In Port:

Montserrat Tourist Board, & Farara Plaza, Buildings B&C, P.O. Box 7, Brades, Montserrat; (664) 491-2230, fax: (664) 491-7430; info@montserrat tourism.ms.

Montserrat National Trust, Salem Main Road, Salem, Montserrat; (664) 491-3086; mnatrust@candw .ms.

Sugar and a plantation society based on the labor of African slaves dominated the island throughout the eighteenth century. Limes and, later, cotton were introduced after emancipation in the early nineteenth century. Today bananas are the main crop, with some production of limes and cotton, but farming has been severely disrupted by the volcanic eruptions.

Port Profile

www.visitmontserrat.com

Location/Embarkation The cruise-ship port of entry was Plymouth, on the west coast, but for now, cruise ships and private boats anchor offshore and tender passengers to Little Bay on the northwest coast, where a new commercial port is operating. For information, contact Montserrat Port Authority, Little Bay, P.O. Box 383 (664-491-2791; fax: 664-491-8063).

Local Transportation Taxis and car rentals are available from the Vue Pointe Hotel, the major hotel and base of most tourist activity. A list of taxi and van operators and car-rental agencies is available from the Montserrat Tourist Board. If you hire a taxi, settle the cost in advance and be sure to determine whether the agreed amount is U.S. or EC dollars. If you rent a car, you'll need a temporary driver's license, which can be obtained for US$19 (EC$50) from police headquarters in Salem (664-491-2555), open twenty-four hours a day, Monday to Friday.

Roads and Rentals Montserrat has a network of paved roads that serve most parts of the island. The main road winds north around hillsides that skirt the island's main beaches. Driving is on the left.

Given the difficult nature of the driving, if you're unfamiliar with the narrow mountain roads and left-handed driving, you might prefer to hire a taxi. This way you are free to enjoy the beautiful scenery and listen to the driver, who is likely to be an animated storyteller as well as a guide.

Emergency Numbers
Medical: Hospital, 664-491-2552
Operator Assistance: 411
Emergencies: 664-491-2802
Police: 999
Fire: 911

Shore Excursions

Sightseeing excursions are available by taxi, for four persons, or by small minibuses for up to eight people, or you might prefer to enjoy a sport—sportfishing, kayaking, diving, or hiking—because sights such as the **Great Alps Waterfalls** and **Galways Soufrière** are covered by volcano ash in the region where travel is prohibited.

Montserrat on Your Own

Montserrat Museum (P.O. Box 393, Salem Main Road, Olveston, 664-491-3086, fax: 664-491-3046) Housed in the mill of a former sugar plantation, the museum covers Montserrat's history from pre-Columbian times to the present. There are natural-history exhibits as well. The museum, operated by the Montserrat National Trust with a volunteer staff, is also responsible for the renovation of historic sites around the island; excavation of pre-Columbian sites; conservation programs that have established the Woodlands Beach Picnic Area and the Fox's Bay Bird Sanctuary; and flora and fauna research that brings scientists and other experts to the island. **Oriole**, a shop located in the museum, carries T-shirts, local crafts, postcards and volcano photos, local books, and videotapes. Visitors can obtain a map of Montserrat here. Hours: Monday to Friday 8:30 a.m. to 4:00 p.m., Saturday 9:00 a.m. to 1:00 p.m.

Fox's Bay Bird Sanctuary On the coast 3 miles northwest of Plymouth is a fifteen-acre protected wildlife area established by the trust in 1979. The sanctuary is a mangrove and bog with a central pond that is the nesting area for coots, gallinules, and other waterfowl. There are several species of heron, of which the cattle egrets number more than one thousand. The sanctuary is encircled by a nature trail that ends at the beach, where there are facilities for swimming and picnicking. The endemic black-and-yellow Montserrat oriole, the national bird, dwells in mountainous areas. Among the island's thirty breeding species are three species of hummingbirds. (Check locally to learn if the area is off-limits.)

Castle Peak Up the hill from the Vue Pointe Hotel, which has a great view of the rumbling volcano, is the volcano's scientific observatory. Travelers interested in volcanoes are welcome to visit and speak to the experts who man the center twenty-four hours a day.

Castle Peak is also the name of the island's newest volcano. It seems to be teasing the islanders with its capricious behavior. Indeed, volcano watching has become a full-time pastime for both visitors and residents.

Garibaldi Hill Located behind Fox's Bay on the west coast, Garibaldi Hill is the best location to look across to deserted Plymouth and to view Soufrière Hills Volcano, whose growing summit now makes it the island's highest point. **Richmond Hill,** behind Fox's Bay on the west coast, is another place to see the sharp contrast between the barren flanks of the mountains to the south and the lush rain-forested hills in the north. Only a few vertical struts jutting from rocks and other debris are all that can be seen of the Belham Valley Bridge, but the effect is dramatic and gives a clue as to how deep beneath the surface lies the bridge, now concealed by the mud flows from the volcano. From **Jack Boy Hill,** near the east coast, you get a panoramic view of the coastline and the airport, abandoned after the volcanic eruptions.

Volcano Observatory The **Montserrat Volcano Observatory** (664-491-5647; www.mvo.ms), established in 1996 following volcanic eruptions in the Soufrière Hills, has a new location 3 miles northwest of the still active peak, providing visitors with a safe, front-row seat to the continuing spectacle. The new facility has sophisticated visual and seismic equipment to monitor volcanic activity, and has played an important role in attracting scientists and scholars as well as visitors. Tours of the observatory by the staff are available Monday to Saturday at 3:30 p.m. Fee: EC$10 (US$4) for those age twelve and older; there is a small gift shop.

Southern Montserrat

Montserrat's most popular attractions in the southern third of the island are no longer accessible, and travel in the region is prohibited to visitors and even for residents without special permission. Nonetheless, we have retained the information for those interested in reading about the area and in the hope that someday people will be able to visit some of the places again.

Galways Estate Three miles south of Plymouth are the ruins of a sugar plantation that was started in the mid-seventeenth century and operated more than 250 years. Selected in 1990 by the Smithsonian Institute as a preservation project for the Columbus Quincentennial, excavations had been under way for almost a decade, under the auspices of the Montserrat National Trust, aided by specialists from the University of Tennessee and Boston University, as well as Earthwatch and Partners for Liveable Places, among others.

Before excavation began in 1981, the foliage, allowed to run wild after the plantation was abandoned, had become so dense that structures could no longer be recognized. The ruins include a sugar mill and boiling house, windmill tower, cattle mill, great house, cisterns, and other structures, many of them built of beautifully cut stone.

Galways Soufrière The southern third of Montserrat is dominated by the Soufrière Hills, several of whose peaks were covered with rain forest before the volcanic eruptions. Galways Soufrière, an active boiling volcanic fissure at 1,700 feet, known as the **Devil's Playground,** was a treacherous field of unstable rocks with a witch's brew of boiling mud, hissing steam, and the strong smell of sulfurous vapors. It was the main area of volcanic eruption from 1995 to 1999. Just when it seemed to be settling down, the volcano erupted again in the summer of 2001. In August 2005, the current phase of dome growth began with renewed activity. Dome growth continues, and the volcano is being monitored very closely.

Dining and Restaurants

Montserrat's native cuisine is West Indian with British and French influences. The most popular dish is mountain chicken, or frogs' legs, as we know them. Known locally by its Creole name, crapaud, the large frog is hunted at night after rainy spells. Also hunted for its meat is the agouti, a rabbit-size, tailless rodent that was once abundant in the Lesser Antilles and is now extinct on most islands. Goat Water, another popular dish, is an adaptation of Irish stew substituting goat meat for beef and seasoned with rum and cloves.

One to try is the **Jumping Jack** (Old Beach Road, 664-491-5645), which serves "pub grub" like fish and chips and burgers. Fisherman Danny Sweeney catches the fish and his partner, Margaret, does the home cooking. An average meal costs about US$15, including dessert and a drink. Open Wednesday to Sunday.

Others to try are the **Gourmet Garden** in Olveston and the **Attic Restaurant** (664-491-7859). Ask a resident and you'll find **Alla** (known to one and all for her famous rôtis). Seek out, too, **John Watts Ice Cream,** which specializes in tropical flavors such as mango, coconut, and passion fruit.

Sports

Beaches/Swimming Vue Pointe (www.vue pointe.com), the main hotel and base of most tourist activity is currently closed . It has a freshwater pool, shuffleboard, and access to scuba diving and windsurfing. The island's best and most accessible beaches stretch north along the Caribbean coast. Most are secluded strands of black or gray sand bracketed by rock cliffs with calm, clear water for swimming and snorkeling.

None have been developed commercially: They are **Woodlands Beach,** where the National Trust has a picnic site; **Carrs Bay,** and **Little Bay,** where the sand is a butterscotch color.

The only white-sand stretch, **Rendezvous Beach,** is surrounded by steep cliffs and is usually reached by boat from Little Bay, directly to the south. Alternatively, you can hike on an inland path from Little Bay to Rendezvous in about forty minutes, or make a steep thirty-minute climb over the bluff separating the two bays.

Biking Imagine Peace Bicycles (Brades, 664-491-8809; ghbikes@hotmail.com), named in tribute to John Lennon, has aluminum frame, front suspension, 21- and 24-speed bicycles for rent at its shop in the BBC Building in Brades and at Gingerbread Hill Guest House and Tropical Mansions. Rates: US$10 to $15 per day. Helmets, tail lights, and bells are provided. Guide service is available. Owner/operator James Naylor, who has operated bicycle shops in New York and Florida, is familiar with Caribbean cycling conditions, having lived in the British Virgin Islands.

Hiking The Montserrat National Trust, together with the Forestry Department and Montserrat Tourist Board, has cleared several new trails: **Runaway Ghaut Trail** has a variety of bird species as well as the dwarf gecko; a trail from Duck Pond to Duberry Estate offers superb views of Plymouth, the island's sputtering volcano, and surrounding environs; the **Forgathy to Cassava Ghaut Trail** has a profusion of flowers and offers a possible

glimpse of the rare Montserrat oriole, the national bird, the shy bridled quail dove, and the rarely seen galliwasp (part lizard, part snake).

Blackwood Allen Trail, about 1.5 hours to traverse, takes hikers from Baker Hill near the west coast to Mango Hill in the center of the island. Visitors can see a broad spectrum of island flora, a lovely spring filled with crayfish, and, maybe, agoutis. From a viewing platform, hikers can see Lookout Village and out to sea to neighboring Antigua. Interpretive signs on all trails are planned.

Scuba Diving/Snorkeling Sea Wolf Diving (664-491-6859, cell 664-496-7807; www.seawolf divingschool.com), owned by South African Bryan Cunningham (an experienced, PADI-trained dive operator), is operating from the Vue Pointe Hotel beach and offers a range of instruction and excursions. For those interested in underwater photography, contact David Graham (dgraham@candw.ms).

Festivals and Celebrations

The **Christmas Festival** is Montserrat's version of Carnival and begins officially on December 20. But actually it starts in November with preview activities, when masqueraders begin rehearsing their quadrilles and polkas. There are calypso contests and performances by bands, groups, and schools. Once an adult art rooted in African folklore, masquerading is now done by children, who perform on holidays and for arriving cruise ships. Competitions, concerts, pageants, and parties keep revelers on the go during the festival until New Year's Day.

Guadeloupe

Pointe-à-Pitre, Guadeloupe; Basse-Terre, Guadeloupe; Iles des Saintes; Marie-Galante

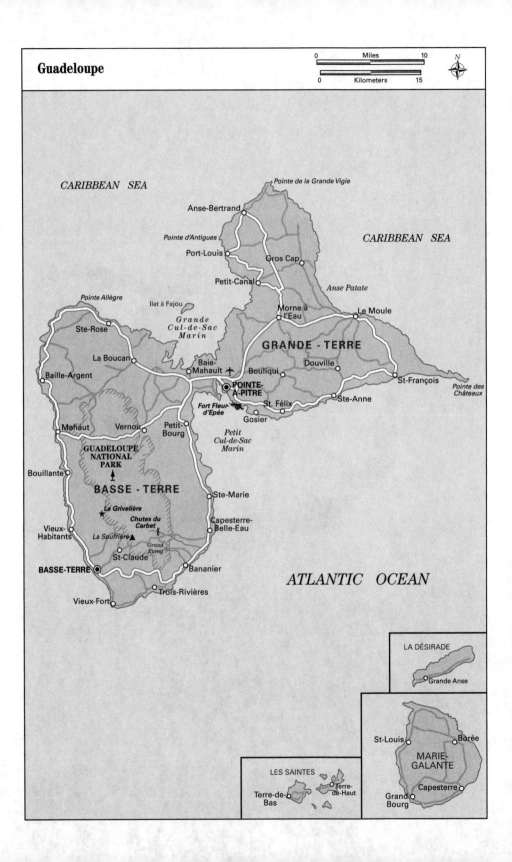

The Caribbean in Miniature

Guadeloupe is actually two islands shaped like butterfly wings. The two parts—Basse-Terre and Grande-Terre—are separated by a narrow channel and connected by a short bridge. No two islands in the Caribbean are more different.

Guadeloupe is also a small archipelago composed of Marie-Galante, Les Saintes, and La Désirade. Together they make up a Caribbean in miniature with the full range of natural features and beauty for which the region is known, along with good facilities to enjoy them.

Grande-Terre, the eastern wing of Guadeloupe, is a flat, dry limestone island, densely populated and developed. It has Guadeloupe's largest town, Pointe-à-Pitre, the business and commercial capital and main cruise port. The south coast is the main resort area, with long strands of white-sand beaches along its quiet Caribbean shores, where many cruise passengers often elect to spend their day.

In contrast, Basse-Terre, the western wing, is a volcanic island dominated by a spine of steep, forest-green mountains climbing to 5,000 feet and mostly covered by the 74,100-acre National Park. From their lofty peaks, where up to 400 inches of rain falls annually, spectacular waterfalls rush over rocky cliffs, crash through canyons, and careen through the mountains, forming the rivers and streams that irrigate an emerald skirt of sugarcane and banana fields along Basse-Terre's east coast. Basse-Terre is the name both of the island and of its main town, which is also the capital of Guadeloupe, on the southwest coast. Offshore are the Iles des Saintes, or Les Saintes, also of volcanic origin.

When Christopher Columbus came upon the islands in 1493, he sailed north from Dominica to the island he named Marie-Galante for his flagship, which had brought him there. He arrived in Guadeloupe at the place known today as Sainte-Marie de la Capesterre, on the east coast of Basse-Terre, and claimed the island for Spain. Several attempts by the Spaniards to settle Guadeloupe were repulsed by the fierce Caribs, and a permanent European settlement was not established until after France took possession of the island in the early seventeenth century. Under the patronage of Cardinal Richelieu, French entrepreneurs formed La Compagnie des Iles d'Amérique to develop Guadeloupe.

In 1635 it sent two noblemen, Charles Liénard de l'Olive and Jean Duplessis d'Ossonville, and a group from Normandy and Touraine to make a settlement.

For the next five years they fought the Caribs and drove them away to neighboring islands. The French cleared the land, introduced sugar and other crops, and imported slaves from Africa to work the land. In 1674 Guadeloupe was officially annexed by France, but for the next century it continued to be the scene of intense rivalry between France and Britain.

During the French Revolution Guadeloupe was occupied by Britain, but it was reconquered in 1794 by Victor Hugues, who abolished slavery. When Napoleon came to power, however, he reinstituted slavery. Through the efforts of Victor Schoelcher, a

At a Glance

Antiquities	★★
Architecture	★★
Art and artists	★★
Beaches	★★
Colonial buildings	★★
Crafts	★★
Cuisine	★★★
Culture	★★
Dining/Restaurants	★★★★
Entertainment	★★
Forts	★★★
History	★★
Monuments	★
Museums	★★★
Nightlife	★★
Scenery	★★★★★
Shopping	★★
Sightseeing	★★★★
Sports	★★★★
Transportation	★★★

Population: 435,000

Size: 583 square miles

Main Towns: Basse-Terre, Pointe-à-Pitre

Government: Guadeloupe is a *région* of France with a prefect appointed by the French Minister of the Interior.

Currency: Euro. US$1.00 fluctuates around €0.50. One euro equals about US$1.50. U.S. and Canadian currency are widely accepted. Banks are open Monday to Friday from 8:00 a.m. to noon and 2:00 to 4:00 p.m.

Departure Tax: None

Firearms: Yachts are permitted to have firearms on board, but they must be declared.

Language: French and Creole. English is spoken in hotels by the manager and front-desk staff, but the personnel in stores, restaurants, and other tourist facilities are likely to speak French only. Non-French speakers should carry a French phrase book and a pocket dictionary when they strike out on their own.

Public Holidays: January 1, New Year's Day; Easter Monday; May 1, Labor Day; Ascension Thursday; Pentecost Monday; May 27, Slavery Abolition Day; July 14, Bastille Day; July 21, Schoelcher Day; August 15, Assumption Day; November 1, All Saints Day; November 11, Armistice Day; December 25, Christmas.

Telephone: To phone station-to-station from the United States, dial 011-590-0590 plus the six-digit local number; for person-to-person, dial 01-590-0590 plus the six-digit local number. Guadeloupe telephone/fax numbers now have a total of ten numbers. To phone from Guadeloupe, *Télécartes* (sold at post offices and outlets marked *télécarte vente ici*) are used in special booths marked *Télécom* throughout the island. Visa and MasterCard may also be used.

Airlines: American Airlines/American Eagle from U.S. cities via San Juan. Other carriers make connections through St. Maarten. LIAT (0590-21-42-93) provides scheduled service between Guadeloupe and major islands in the Eastern Caribbean. Air Caraibes (Air Guadeloupe-Air Martinique; 0590-82-47-00), serves the French West Indies islands daily and flies to Puerto Rico, St. Maarten, and Santo Domingo. Caraibes Air Tourisme flies to Les Saintes twice daily.

Information: www.antilles-info-tourisme.com; www.lesilesde guadeloupe.com

In the United States:

New York: French Government Tourist Board, 825 Third Avenue at 50th Street, 29th floor, New York, NY 10022; (212) 838-7855; fax: (212) 838-7855.

Also French Government Tourist Offices:

Chicago: 205 North Michigan Avenue, Chicago, IL 60601; (312) 327-0290, fax: (312) 327-5207 nancy.anderson@franceguide.com

Los Angeles: 9454 Wilshire Boulevard, No. 210, Beverly Hills, CA 90212; (310) 271-6665, fax: (310) 276-2835 christophe.carvenant@franceguide.com.

In Canada:

Montreal: 1981 Avenue McGill College, No. 490, Montreal, PQ H3A 2W9; (514) 288-2026; (800) 361-9099; fax: (514) 844-8901.

In Port:

Guadeloupe Tourist Office (Office Departmental du Tourisme), 5 Square de la Banquet, 97163 Cedex Pointe-à-Pitre, Guadeloupe, FWI.; (0590) 82-09-30; fax: 83-89-22; office.tourisme.guadeloupe@wanadoo.fr. Maps, magazines, and brochures are available.

Les Iles de Guadeloupe Office du Tourisme (0590-82-09-30; www.les ilesdeguadeloupe.com; info@lesiles deguadeloupe.com).

National Park of Guadeloupe Habitation Beausoleil, Monteran, F97120 Saint-Claude, Guadeloupe; (0590) 80-8600; fax: (0590) 80-0546; www .guadeloupe-parcnational.com.

---

national hero today, slavery was abolished permanently in 1848. In the following years indentured workers from India were imported to work the cane fields.

In 1946 Guadeloupe was officially designated a French *département* with the same status as a *département* of metropolitan France, in the way that the Hawaiian Islands are a state of the United States. In 1974 Guadeloupe and its satellite islands, along with St. Barts and French St. Martin, were given the further status of *région*. Martinique is a separate *région*. Together they form the French

West Indies, whose people are culturally French and citizens of France in all respects.

Budget Planning

Guadeloupe is an expensive island, particularly for taxis and restaurants. An average meal for one person in an ordinary restaurant can cost US$25, and in one of the better establishments, it will be US$40 and up. All service charges—taxes and tips—are included in the prices. You do not need to add more tip unless you want to. If you speak French and have the time to use local buses, you can travel economically. Otherwise you should plan to take one of the shore excursions offered by your cruise line, or if you can share with others, hire a taxi or rent a car for touring.

Port Profile

Location/Embarkation Pointe-à-Pitre, Basse-Terre, and the offshore islands of Les Saintes are regular cruise ports; Marie-Galante is an occasional one. Pointe-à-Pitre has four berths and can accommodate the largest liners; Basse-Terre has two. Most cruise ships use Pointe-à-Pitre, where they dock directly in the heart of downtown only a block from the shopping district and the Tourist Office. The port complex, St. John Perse Center, has a hotel, restaurants, bars, several government ministries, and shops. In the last few years, Pointe à Pitre has suffered with the development of the new, very large commercial center of Baie Mahault, located west of Pointe à Pitre, where many of the downtown shops have moved their business and now, where people do their shopping. In an effort to revitalize the city's economy, a new law was passed recently making Pointe à Pitre a tax-free area.

Local Transportation Inexpensive easy-to-use public buses linking the main towns of Guadeloupe operate from 5:30 a.m. to 7:30 p.m. In Pointe-à-Pitre buses for Gosier and the south coast depart from Dares Station, near the dock and Tourist Office; those to the north and central regions depart from Moreno Station. Buses connecting Grande-Terre with Basse-Terre leave from the Bergevin Station on the north side of town. Buses stop at signs marked arrêt-bus, or you can wave to the driver to stop. Few drivers—very few—speak English.

Due to their short time in port, cruise passengers usually prefer to use taxis, but they are expensive. They are plentiful at the port upon the arrival of cruise ships. Most drivers are looking for cruise passengers they can take on island tours, so expect a certain amount of hustling. (Do not count on them to speak English.) Half-day tours about €70; full-day €120.

The taxi stand closest to the St. John Perse Center terminal is Place de la Victoire near the Tourist Office. From Pointe-à-Pitre to the airport is about US$30, and to Gosier hotels US$35. A 40 percent surcharge is added from 9:00 p.m. to 7:00 a.m. and all day Sunday and holidays. For radio cabs, call 90-70-70; 20-74-74; 83-89-98.

There is helicopter service on demand for sightseeing and to Les Saintes, Marie-Galante, and other neighboring islands. For information, check www.helio-guadeloupe.com.

Roads and Rentals Guadeloupe has a network of excellent roads covering 1,225 miles. You can make a complete loop around Basse-Terre or Grande-Terre and explore their interiors, except for certain parts of Basse-Terre. But due to the nature of the terrain, distances can be deceiving and often take double the amount of time you are likely to plan.

A self-drive car is the best way to tour the island; rates for car rentals are comparable to those in the United States and Europe. A valid driver's license is needed. Driving is on the right, and traffic regulations and road signs are like those in Europe. Drivers here tend to speed.

Car-rental companies in Pointe-à-Pitre are open weekdays from 8:00 a.m. to noon and 2:30 to 5:00 p.m.; Saturday to noon or 1:00 p.m. Among the major car-rental companies is **Rent-a-Car** (21-13-62; 22-74-14; www.rentacar-caraibes.com); at the Pole Caraibe International Airport and major hotels, the major companies are **Budget** (21-13-49) and **Europcar** (21-13-52; http://car-rental.europcar.com). There are also independent companies such as **Antilles Voitures** (85-00-00); you can get a list from the Tourist Office. There's also an online rental service: http://guadeloupe.rentalcargroup.com.

Bicycles and motorbikes can be rented from Dingo (Place de la Victoire, 2 blocks from the port; 83-81-19). Vespas cost about US$20 to $30 per day with unlimited mileage.

Ferrry Services From Pointe-à-Pitre to Les Saintes, **Express des Iles** (83-12-45; www.lex pressdesiles.net), **TMA Archipel** (83-19-89), and **Brudey Freres** (90-04-48) operate daily; fare is about €58 round-trip. To Marie-Galante, ferries leave most days at 8:00 a.m. from Pointe-à-Pitre; fare is about €39 round-trip for the two-hour crossing. (Both locations have daily air service from Pointe-à-Pitre.)

From Trois-Rivières on Basse-Terre (1.5 hours' drive from Pointe-à-Pitre), ferries leave twice daily at 8:00 a.m. and 4:00 p.m. for Les Saintes; the trip takes about thirty minutes. They also depart from the town of Basse-Terre to Les Saintes.

Emergency Numbers

Medical: Centre Hospitalier de Pointe-à-Pitre, 89-10-10. The Tourist Office can assist in locating English-speaking doctors.

Ambulance/SOS service: 24 hours a day, 87-65-43, 91-39-39

Police: Pointe-à-Pitre, 17; 82-00-89; Basse-Terre, 81-11-55

Shore Excursions

If you enjoy spectacular scenery, hiking in a rain forest, and picnicking in the woods, Basse-Terre will be your first choice. If beaching and biking are preferences, you will have the best of both in Grande-Terre. A Tourist Office booklet entitled *Guadeloupe Excursions* maps out six itineraries for self-drive tours. Similar tours can be made by taxi,

and some are available as motorcoach tours. From my experience, guides in Guadeloupe score the best in the Caribbean for knowledge about their island. Tours begin in Pointe-à-Pitre; prices and duration will vary, depending on the cruise line and tour company. Places mentioned here are described later in the chapter.

Basse-Terre to the Carbet Falls/Grand Etang: 4 hours, about US$100 as a cruise ship excursion by bus. After skirting the east coast of Basse-Terre to St-Sauveur, you turn inland to Carbet Falls. Longer versions include Grand Etang, an inland lake, or the town of Basse-Terre.

Basse-Terre to the Soufrière Volcano: 8 hours, about US$200. Same as above tour but instead of turning inland to Carbet Falls, it continues to Basse-Terre and winds up the mountains to the Soufrière Volcano.

National Park/Southern Basse-Terre: 8 hours, about US$200. The route crosses the National Park from east to west, where there are trails and picnic sites. On the west coast it turns south to Vieux-Habitants, along the magnificent scenery of the Grande Rivière to La Grivelière, a coffee plantation. The return is via Basse-Terre, Archaeological Park, and east coast.

Grand Tour of Grande-Terre: 4–5 hours, about US$140. From the resort town of Gosier, the drive follows the south coast to Pointe-des-Châteaux; east coast to Le Moule; and around to the west coast at Petit-Canal and Morne-à-l'Eau.

Le Petit Train: 1.5 hours, about US$20. Discover the heart of Pointe-à-Pitre in a caboose-drawn tram, departing frequently from the St. John Perse Center by the port (83-21-82).

Discover the Mangroves: Clarisma Tour (3 Chemins Gros Cap 97131, Petit-Canal; 22-51-15; fax: 20-11-86) has a two-hour boat excursion in the bird-rich mangroves between Grand-Terre and Basse-Terre, with departures at 9:00 a.m. (cost: €25) and 4:00 p.m. (cost: €16).

Jungle Safari Adventure (56-17-03; jungle safariadventure@wanadoo.fr). Explore off the beaten track in daylong four-wheel-drive tours.

Le Attelages du Comté (Ste. Rose; 56-61-12; fax: 28-71-70) offers horse-driven wagon rides. Per person €12 for one hour; €32 for half-day.

Guadeloupe on Your Own

Pointe-à-Pitre is the main city of Guadeloupe. As early as the mid-eighteenth century, its value as a well-protected, deep-water harbor was recognized by the English and the French, who took turns at building the city and fortifying the nearby hills. It thrived despite fires, earthquakes, and hurricanes. Today the city has a slightly tatty look, with an architectural diversity of wooden houses with wrought-iron balconies in the small narrow streets of the old town juxtaposed against modern commercial and government buildings.

A Pointe-à-Pitre Walkabout

Pointe-à-Pitre can be explored easily on foot. The **St. John Perse Center (1),** a hotel and shopping complex at the port, was designed with cruise pas-

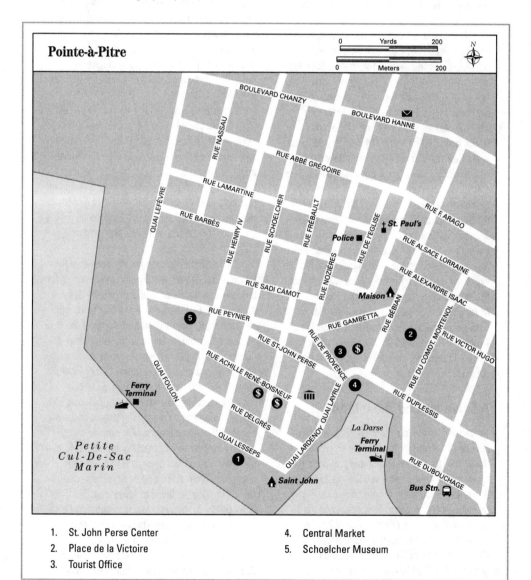

Pointe-à-Pitre

1. St. John Perse Center
2. Place de la Victoire
3. Tourist Office
4. Central Market
5. Schoelcher Museum

sengers in mind. The center is accessible to local citizens as well.

A short walk will put you in the heart of Pointe-à-Pitre at **Place de la Victoire (2)**, a garden square shaded by royal palms and sandbox trees. They were planted in 1794 by Victor Hugues on the day after his victory against the British. The square is bordered by colonial-style houses that lend an Old World atmosphere to the town. Many have been renovated to house boutiques and sidewalk cafes. Among them: DeliFrance, Caraibes Cafe, and La Bella Vita.

The Tourist Office (3) is on the southwest corner of the square. One of the town's several markets, a lively vegetable-and-fish market, is on the south by the harbor front. Walking west along rue Peynier, you will cross the main shopping streets of rue Nozières, rue Frébault, and rue Schoelcher, where boutiques stock perfume, china, and other French goods. At the corner of Peynier and Frébault is the **Central Market (4)**, a large town plaza where vendors sell tropical flowers, fruits and vegetables, spices, and crafts. West of the market, in a pink ornate colonial building on rue Peynier, is the **Schoelcher Museum (5)**. It is dedicated to the leading French abolitionist of his time, who led the fight to end slavery in the French West Indies. Nearby on rue René-Boisneuf, a plaque at No. 54 marks the birthplace of Nobel Prize–winning poet St. John Perse and the **Saint-John Perse Museum,** which opened for his centennial in 1987. For a guided walking tour, contact **Pointe Pitre Tour** (90-04-71; fax: 90-05-23), which offers tours for four to eight persons, for about US$10 per person.

A Drive around the Island

To Basse-Terre: From Pointe-à-Pitre, you cross Pont de la Gabare, the bridge over the Rivière Salée, the channel separating the two parts of Guadeloupe. After 2 miles you'll come to the Destrellan traffic circle, where you can turn south on highway N 1 to Basse-Terre town and the Soufrière Volcano; or turn north on N 2 to Le Lamentin, Ste-Rose, and the beaches and fishing villages of northern Basse-Terre. A third option is to go to the N 1/D 23 intersection at Versailles and turn west on Route de la Traversée, the east-west highway that crosses the heart of the National Park.

Southern Basse-Terre

Basse-Terre's southeastern coast, from Petit-Bourg to Capesterre-Belle-Eau and Bananier, stretches in green fields of banana plantations from the sea, bordered by small villages and pretty beaches, to the brooding peaks of the Soufrière Mountains. The coast south of Petit-Bourg is popular for swimming and scuba diving; offshore, tiny Ilet Fortune is a nudist beach. Farther along, Ste-Marie has a monument commemorating Columbus's landing in 1493. At Changy a Hindu temple is one of several reminders of the multiracial makeup of the French West Indies.

Capesterre-Belle-Eau has a cassava-processing plant where you can watch cassava flour and bread being made. Cassava was a staple of the Amerindians, who taught early European explorers to use it, and it continues to be a basic food of the West Indies. En route from Capesterre to St-Sauveur, the road passes through Allée Dumanoir, one of the most photographed settings of Guadeloupe, where the route is lined with stately century-old royal palms.

Carbet Falls (Chutes du Carbet) A detour inland at St-Sauveur takes you to the imposing Carbet Falls and the Grand Etang, an inland lake whose tranquil waters mirror the lush landscape surrounding it. From the eastern slopes of the Soufrière Volcano, waters cascade more than 800 feet in three stages, forming the tallest falls in the Caribbean and creating the Grand Carbet River that empties into the sea at Capesterre-Belle-Eau.

Grand Etang (Grand Pond) Situated at 1,312 feet altitude, Grand Etang is the largest of several ponds in the area, covering fifty acres in a hot, humid atmosphere and creating a greenhouse that nurtures giant philodendron and ferns, orchids, anthurium, bromeliads, and other rain-forest vegetation not normally found at lower altitudes. The quiet pond—a striking contrast to tumbling Carbet Falls—was created when lava from a volcanic eruption blocked the St-Sauveur River.

Archaeological Park (Parc Archéologique des Roches Gravées) Near Trois-Rivières on the road to the ferry for Les Saintes, there is an outdoor museum with petroglyphs of the Carib Indians, the pre-Columbian inhabitants of Guadeloupe. The drawings date from about A.D. 300 and depict animal and human figures. A footpath is bordered with cassava, cacao, calabash, pimiento, and other plants the Indians cultivated.

All along the drive of southern Basse-Terre, the dark green Soufrière Mountains loom high on the western landscape. To go directly to the Soufrière Volcano, turn north on D9 via Choisy, a hamlet surrounded by vast banana plantations, to St-Claude and La Savane à Mulets, a plateau and parking area where the hike to the volcano's summit begins.

Basse-Terre The capital of Guadeloupe, which sits at the foot of the Soufrière Mountains, is one of the best-kept secrets in the Caribbean. A delightful town almost untouched by tourism, it was founded in the early seventeenth century and occupied several times by the British during the two centuries of rivalry between France and Britain over the Caribbean. To the south on a promontory was Fort St-Charles; the Gallion River, which originates on the slopes of La Soufrière, runs under the fort's ramparts on its way to the sea. The fort was surrounded by the Carmel quarter, the traditional military and government section. Today it has the Palais d'Orléans with the Prefecture, the Palace of Justice, and the General Council building—all handsome examples of colonial architecture.

To the north was St-François parish, the commercial district with the streets laid out in a grid. It is still the commercial section, and behind the Town Hall on avenue Général de Gaulle are the main downtown streets. Rue du Docteur Cabre leads to the **Cathedral of Our Lady of Guadeloupe,** with a facade that's been classified as a historical monument.

St-Claude The drive from Basse-Terre town to La Savane à Mulets, at 3,747 feet at the base of La Soufrière, takes thirty minutes and passes through the pretty hillside town of St-Claude. A wealthy residential community, its West Indian houses are set in flowering gardens against rain-forest greenery and cascading streams. A visitor center, **La Maison du Volcan,** has displays relating to La Soufrière and the other volcanic regions of the

Eastern Caribbean, as well as on volcanology throughout the world. Nearby is Habitation l'Esperance, an eighteenth-century coffee plantation whose estate house is now home to the restaurant **Ti Café de la Bonifierie** and a boutique with local products.

Soufrière Volcano The forest green, deeply creviced mountains that dominate southern Basse-Terre are part of the National Park and take their name from the highest peak, La Soufrière, the brimstone-belching volcano at 4,813 feet. It is surrounded by other volcanic peaks more than 4,000 feet—all with waterfalls, hot springs, rain and cloud forests, and trails.

Although rumblings had been recorded since the fifteenth century, La Soufrière had been dormant for centuries when it began to erupt in 1975. Warnings had come as early as 1956, when tremors sent up rocks and ash and caused new fractures. La Soufrière continues to boil and bubble, but it is quiet enough to be climbed. A visit to the summit of an active volcano, the center of nature's most awesome force, is a rare and fascinating opportunity.

You can go by car as far as the base of the cone at La Savane à Mulets, from which four marked trails—Red, Yellow, Green, and Blue—lead to the summit. When combined the trails take 3.5 hours to cover. One trail (Red) leads from the La Savane parking lot directly to the top in a series of switchbacks that gain 1,000 feet in forty-five heart-pounding minutes. Composed of solidified lava, the crown has a deep split through the center, where continuing volcanic action can be seen. It is an eerie landscape of weird-shaped rocks, bubbling mud, and jagged fumaroles emitting hot gases and steam.

You should wear sturdy shoes and protection against the rain and wind, and be extremely cautious walking around fumaroles at the summit. Some parts of the trails are very difficult; mist and clouds often make it difficult to see your way. If you do not have the time or stamina to go to the summit, you can choose from several easy walks in the La Savane area.

Matouba Two miles northwest of St-Claude, the town of Matouba, at 2,234 feet in altitude, was settled by the East Indians brought to the French

West Indies as laborers in the mid-nineteenth century after the abolition of slavery. The hot springs of Matouba are well known for their therapeutic properties.

Vieux-Fort At the southern tip of Basse-Terre, where the Atlantic Ocean meets the Caribbean Sea, is an old town that takes its name from the fort that once guarded the strategic point. Today the town is known for a delicate embroidery art made by the women of the village. The volcanic Carib Mountains rise behind the town.

National Park of Guadeloupe (Parc National de Guadeloupe) The spine of forested mountains that run almost the length of Basse-Terre constitute the 74,100-acre National Park. You'll find exhibits throughout on particular aspects—volcano, forest, coffee, sugarcane, archaeology, and wildlife—of the park, but explanations are in French only. The exhibits are intended as learning centers as well as outdoor museums. The centers are accessible on paved roads and are usually the starting point for one of the park's 200 miles of signposted trails.

Route de la Traversée The highway through the center of the park starts from the banana and sugarcane fields on the east coast at Versailles and climbs to 600 feet at Vernou, a fashionable residential district of pretty villas with tropical gardens overlooking the serpentine Lézarde River Valley. After Vernou the highway winds through the park to a pass, **Col des Deux Mamelles,** where it crosses the ridge to the west coast. The scenic drive provides access to more than a half-dozen walks and hikes from a ten-minute stroll to a 10-mile trek.

Ecrivisses Falls (The Falls of the Crayfish) About a mile from the park entrance on the south side of the Route de la Traversée, a path along the Corossol River leads in a ten-minute walk to the **Cascade aux Ecrevisses.** The pretty waterfall is the most accessible one in the park and is usually included on motorcoach tours of eastern Basse-Terre. It is also popular for swimming and picnicking. (Do not leave valuables unattended. Young boys, finding tourists easy prey here, sometimes sneak out from the woods to grab a handbag or camera and disappear into the foliage.)

The Forest House and Bras David Tropical Park About halfway on the Route de la Traversée is the Forest House (**La Maison de la Forêt;** Hours: 9:00 a.m. to 4:30 p.m.) in the Bras David Tropical Park, which takes its name from a nearby river. It has picnic grounds, trails, and a nature center with outdoor displays. Three short trails start south of the highway.

Les Mamelles When the Route de la Traversée crosses over the main ridge, it passes several peaks where there are roads or footpaths for hiking. On the south are the Deux Mamelles: Petit-Bourg, 2,349 feet; and Pigeon, 2,526 feet. The latter has a path of forty-five minutes with a lookout at 1,969 feet that takes in a grandstand view of the mountains and the coasts. From the pass of the Deux Mamelles, the Route de la Traversée winds down to the coast under a 2-mile umbrella of flamboyant trees that are magnificent when they are in bloom, from May to October.

At Mahaut on the west coast, you can turn north to Pointe-Noire and Deshaies or south on the scenic road known as the Golden Corniche, which winds along pretty little coves between cliffs and gorges to Basse-Terre town.

Pigeon Island/Cousteau Underwater Nature Park At Malendure Beach you can take a five-minute boat ride to Pigeon Island or a glass-bottom boat excursion to the Underwater Park of Pigeon Island, also known as the Cousteau Underwater Reserve, Guadeloupe's main diving location.

Maison du Cafe Inland from Vieux-Habitants, a scenic drive winds along the Grande Rivière through the wooded mountains with magnificent views of the park, Soufrière Volcano, and the coast. It ends at the Maison du Cafe, one of the interpretive centers of the park, and La Grivelière, a small coffee plantation that has been in the same family for more than a century. A tour is available. Vieux-Habitants, one of the island's oldest villages, has the oldest parish church in Guadeloupe (1650), which was recently restored. South of the village and at Rocroy are two of the nicest beaches on this coast.

Northern Basse-Terre

You can approach northern Basse-Terre from either the east or west coast. On the east coast the drive skirts miles of banana and sugar plantations and mangroves; on the west coast the wooded high-lands of the park fall almost directly to the sea. The fishing villages of the north coast are popular for their Creole and seafood restaurants. **Domaine de Séverin** (28-91-86; fax: 28-36-66; domaine.de.severin@wanadoo.fr) in Ste-Rose and Grosse-Montagne in Lamentin are long-established rum makers where guided tours are offered.

From Mahaut at the western end of Route de la Traversée, the road north passes Pointe-Noire, a town known for its wood craftsmen. Here the **House of Wood** (98-16-90; www.guadeloupe-parcnational.com) is a display center and forestry museum. Another attraction in the vicinity is the eighteenth-century coffee plantation, located on a hillside above Point-Noire, with a restaurant, **Cafeiere Beausejour,** and boutique of local products (98-10-09; fax: 98-12-49; www.cafeiere beausejour.com). Farther north Deshaies has a marina and **Le Jardin Botanique de Deshaies** (Botanical Garden of Deshaies; 28-43-02; fax: 28-51-37; www.jardin-botanique.com), with walkways, birds, and waterfalls. Entrance fee: €13.50 adults, €9.00 children, ages five through twelve. Hours: 9:00 a.m. to 4:30 p.m. A restaurant serves Creole dishes. Nearby, Grande-Anse, a long crescent of golden sand, has a campground. About a mile west is Plage de Cluny, a nudist beach.

Around Grande-Terre

Grande-Terre, Guadeloupe's eastern wing, is flat in comparison to Basse-Terre and is as popular for biking as Basse-Terre is for hiking. From Pointe-à-Pitre the highway east passes Bas du Fort, with its large yacht-filled marina and the **Guadeloupe Aquarium** (Place Creole; 90-92-38; www .guadeloupeaquarium.com; aquarium-guadeloupe@ wanadoo.fr). Here you can see exhibits of Carib-bean marine life and walk through the glass tunnel of a 21,000-gallon tank with sharks. There is a bou-tique and restaurant. Admission: €8.50 adults, €5 children age five through twelve. Hours: 9:00 a.m. to 7:00 p.m. daily.

After passing the campus of the university, the road continues along the south coast to Guade-loupe's main resort centers—Gosier, Ste-Anne, and St-François—which are set on attractive beaches or on hillsides overlooking the sea; they offer the

full range of water sports. Petit-Havre, between Gosier and Ste-Anne, and Raisins-Clairs Beach at St-François are public beaches. St-François, a fish-ing village, is known for its seafood restaurants.

Pointe des Châteaux The easternmost point of Grande-Terre at Pointe des Châteaux, which is marked by a large white cross, has a dramatic set-ting with big Atlantic waves rolling in from the north and smashing against the cliffs of the rocky headlands. Immediately before the point a short track crosses to the north side to Tarare Beach, a nudist enclave. Offshore the uninhabited islets of Iles de la Petite-Terre are popular destinations for yachts. On La Désirade, inhabitants live a simple life as fishermen and boat builders.

Le Moule Once the capital of Guadeloupe, Le Moule was the site of fierce fighting between the early French settlers and the Caribs. Today it is the main town on the Atlantic coast with a horseshoe beach and a picturesque church that is a historic monument. The neighboring village, La Rosette, has the **Edgar Clerc Archaeological Museum** (Musee d'Archéologie Precolombienne Edgar Clerc), where Amerindian artifacts gathered from the islands of the Eastern Caribbean are displayed. Hours: daily except Tuesday 10:30 a.m. to 6:30 p.m.; 23-57-57. Admission is free.

The region around Le Moule is covered with cane fields and dotted with sugar mills, some with their original machinery, as well as the ruins of old plantation houses. There are several rum distiller-ies in the area. The contrast between the pastoral landscape of Grande-Terre and the brooding peaks of Basse-Terre is particularly noticeable here.

At **Rhum Damoiseau,** the old windmill, com-plete with its arms and together with the mill works, was restored in 1996 and can be visited (Distillerie Bellevue, 97160 Le Moule, Guadeloupe, FWI; 23-55-55; fax: 23-48-50; www.damoiseau.net; rhum@damoiseau.com). Hours: Monday to Satur-day 7:30 a.m. to 2:00 p.m.

Les Grands Fonds Across central Grande-Terre, between Pointe-à-Pitre and Abymes on the west and Le Moule on the east, is the roller-coaster terrain of *mornes* and *fonds,* the hills and valleys that characterize this region, known locally as *montagnes russes.* Les Grands Fonds is inhab-ited by the descendants of the Blancs Matignon, a small group of white settlers who retreated here after the abolition of slavery in 1848. They formed a unique ethnic and social group, but today they are distinguishable from the rest of the population only by race.

Morne-â-l'Eau South of Abymes in the town of Morne-à-l'Eau is one of the island's best-known landmarks, an amphitheater-shaped cemetery in checkerboard black and white. It is a place of pilgrimage on All Saints Day, November 1, when people from all over the island—as well as visitors—come to light candles for their deceased loved ones.

Petit-Canal The **Monument to Liberty** in the small village of Petit-Canal is one of the most poignant sites in the Caribbean. It stands on a hillside at the head of fifty-three steps—one for each plantation that once flourished in Guadeloupe. During slavery, plantation owners punished their rebellious slaves by putting them in barrels with spikes driven into the sides and rolling them down these steps.

North of the fishing villages of Port-Louis, the inviting beaches are all but deserted on weekdays.

Exploring the Offshore Islands

Iles des Saintes (Les Saintes) Off the south coast of Basse-Terre is an archipelago of eight tiny volcanic islands with quiet bays and rocky coves etched with white-sand beaches. These idyllic hideaways, where time seems to have stood still, have been discovered in recent years by day-trippers from Guadeloupe and a few small cruise ships.

Only Terre-de-Bas and Terre-de-Haut, the largest of the group, are inhabited, and only the latter has tourist facilities. Most inhabitants are descended from the settlers from Brittany, who were often the pioneers of the French West Indies. Many are fishermen who still wear the salako, a broad-brim, flat straw hat covered with white cloth, which they inherited from their seagoing ancestors.

Mountainous Terre-de-Haut, usually called Les Saintes, has one village, Bourg des Saintes, and one road, a flower-filled lane that runs from one end of the 3-mile-long island to the other. From the harbor situated on the north side of the island, the walk in either direction is delightful. On a hilltop

overlooking the village is **Fort Napoleon,** built in the seventeenth century to defend Pointe-à-Pitre harbor. The fort has a botanic garden and, surprisingly, contains a museum of modern art. South of town, 1,020-foot Le Chameau is the island's highest hill, where a track zigzags up to an old watchtower and a panoramic view of Terre-de-Haut and its neighbors, Basse-Terre and La Soufrière.

West from the harbor the road leads up a hill along a row of small, colorful houses with gingerbread trim and flowering gardens to delightful beaches with small hotels, good restaurants, and water-sports facilities. On the east end of the island, pretty St-Pierre Bay has a white-sand beach; there is an entrance fee. On the south side of the island where the small airport is located, the beach is usually too windy and rough for swimming, but there is a path to a cliff with a beautiful view of the coast.

The island has taxis; daily ferry service from Trois-Rivières and Basse-Terre takes thirty minutes, from Pointe-à-Pitre about an hour. There is also air service from Pointe-à-Pitre.

Marie-Galante Located 27 miles south of Grande-Terre, Marie-Galante is an occasional cruise port of call. Similar in appearance to Grande-Terre, the slightly pear-shaped island has green rolling hills and long, reef-protected white-sand beaches along the west and south coast. The east side is mostly rockbound. Historic Marie-Galante is called the island of a hundred windmills. Some of the old mills that dot the landscape still produce cotton and sugar, the island's mainstay. Château Murat, an old plantation manor house, is now a museum.

The three main towns—St-Louis on the west, Grand-Bourg on the southwest, and Capesterre on the southeast—are connected by good roads. Each town has narrow streets with tiny stores and pastel houses. The good roads, low terrain, and light traffic make biking a delightful mode of travel for the island.

One of the main roads crosses the southern third of the island from St-Louis and the beaches of the west coast over rolling hills to the eastern part of the island. About midway the road branches to **Trou à Diable,** a grotto of stalactites. From St-Louis and Anse-Canot on the northwest coast, there are scenic routes along **La Grande Barre,** a high green ridge dividing the northern half of the island into two plateaus. Anse-Canot and Vieux-Fort have beautiful beaches with reefs.

Marie-Galante is the most populous of the off-shore islands and has restaurants and small hotels. Daily flights from Pointe-à-Pitre take fifteen minutes; ferries take 1.5 hours.

Now, after years of languishing in the backwaters, Marie-Galante is being discovered by tourists, particularly French and other Europeans, with the opening of the island's first resort of international standard. And more are on the way. Perhaps it's too early to call Marie-Galante the next "in" spot, but that may be coming, too. Stay tuned.

Shopping

Perfumes, china, crystal, leather goods, cosmetics, clothing and accessories, fine wines, and liqueurs are some of the French products' famous labels that will attract your immediate attention, but don't overlook local products. You will find rum, coffee, spices, handcrafted pottery, straw, gold jewelry, madras dolls and shell figurines, and much more. French perfumes are about 20 percent lower in price here than in the United States. When you pay in U.S. travelers' checks, 20 percent is sometimes deducted on certain luxury items in specialized shops.

The main downtown shopping streets run about 6 blocks deep from the port between rues Frébault, Nozières, and Schoelcher. All are picturesque with colorful old, balconied houses between the chic boutiques with fashions from Paris and the trendsetting Côte d'Azur. Don't expect much English to be spoken.

In the last few years, Pointe-à-Pitre has suffered with the development of the very large commercial center at Baie Mahault to the west, where people now do their shopping and to where many of the downtown shops have moved their business.

Ideally situated on a spit of land between Grande-Terre and Basse-Terre, **Destreland** (www.destreland.com/) with Creole-style architecture, is the largest commercial center in Guadeloupe with more than one hundred boutiques, services, and restaurants. It is open daily except Sunday.

Recently, in an effort to revitalize the downtown economy, a new law was passed making Pointe à Pitre a tax-free area. Shops in town are open on weekdays from 8:30 or 9:00 a.m. to 12:30 or 1:00 p.m. and from 2:30 or 3:00 to 5:30 or 6:00 p.m.; on Saturday to 1:00 p.m. There are also two large commercial areas at Bas-du-Fort where stores remain open until 7:00 p.m. during the week and on Saturday afternoons.

Even more fun than chic boutiques is a visit to the open-air markets. The main market is found at **Place du Marché,** north of rue Peynier. Here in the mélange of colors, sounds, and aroma, Creole-speaking market women in madras dress sell exotic flowers and fruits, vegetables, and fresh spices, and they know how to drive a hard bargain.

Books and Maps Espace St. John Perse (3 rue Boisneuf) and **Librairie Générale** (46 rue Schoelcher) are main outlets for books in French. For books on Guadeloupe and the French West Indies in English, try the gift shops in hotels.

Cheese and Groceries Cora Supermarket on the east side of Pointe-à-Pitre is a large supermarket where you can find pâtés, cheese, canned delicacies, liquor, wine, and kitchen gadgets, as well as inexpensive beachwear and boutiques for jewelry, shoes, and more.

Clothing and Shoes As noted earlier the **Destreland Shopping Center,** on the west side of Pointe-à-Pitre, is the island's largest shopping center with more than one hundred shops, including designer labels and well-known fashion brands, jewelry, shoes, accessories, and fancy leather goods, plus banks, a drugstore, **Roger Albert** (perfume accessories), **Continent Department Store** (food, liquor, wine, cheese, and sports wear), and restaurants, including Subway, McDonald's, and a pizzeria. A fashionable boutique in town is **Paul et Virginie** (rue Schoelcher). Stylish sandals and inexpensive shoes are found at **Bata** and **100,000 Chaussures** (both on rue Frébault).

Crafts and Souvenirs Handicrafts such as dolls dressed in madras, known as *doudou* dolls; madras table linens; aprons; cards with colorful collages; straw hats and bags; baskets of spices;

shells; and wooden carvings can be found at various shopping centers. **Galerie de l'Artisanat** (Destreland Center; 25-45-15; fax: 25-02-04; espace.art@wanadoo.fr) has the Craft Gallery, a boutique with crafts by local artisans. **Grain d'Or** (47 rue Frebault) sells costume jewelry and unusual gifts. **Oceans** (25 bis Rue Lamartine) does also, and Espace Mod has creations by local fashion designers.

Music Zouk is the French West Indies' answer to calypso or *soca*. Kassav is the best-known group of the zouk artists. Two locations of **Debs** (27 and 116 rue Frébault) sell their records. Although the selection of zouk recordings is greater here, the prices are higher than in New York.

Perfume Phoenicia (rue Frébault) has a wide selection of perfumes and cosmetics, as well as ties, scarves, and small accessories.

Dining and Restaurants

Although other French islands are becoming famous for their gourmet restaurants, Guadeloupe has traditionally been the culinary capital of the French West Indies—and it is the only island in the Caribbean with an annual feast honoring the patron saint of cooking. The island's distinctive Creole cuisine reflects its multifaceted heritage: the French interest in careful preparation of fine cuisine, the ingredients inherited from the Arawaks, and the spices and traditions introduced by Africans, Indians, and Asians. Fresh seafood is an important element, as are conch and stuffed land crabs. To start your meal the traditional way, try a ti-punch, a small but potent mixture of rum, lime juice, and sugarcane syrup that is meant to stimulate the appetite.

Cruise-ship passengers normally do not have the luxury of spending two or three hours over a meal as the French traditionally do, but if trying new and exotic cuisine is high on your list of priorities, you might want to spend part of your day enjoying a Creole meal. It is easy to combine sightseeing with lunch in an out-of-the-way place, since some of the best restaurants are rustic establishments on the south coast of Grande-Terre, the north coast of Basse-Terre, and in small villages

along the way. Prices are on the high side. An inexpensive three-course meal for one person, without wine, costs less than US$30; moderate, US$30 to $45; and expensive, US$45 and higher. Inquire in advance about the use of credit cards and serving hours.

Pointe-à-Pitre/Gosier Area

Auberge de la Vieille Tour (Montauban, Gosier; 84-23-23). The newly renovated hotel has one of the best restaurants in Guadeloupe and specializes in French cuisine and seafood with a Creole flair. Moderately expensive.

Côte Jardin (7 La Marina; 90-91-28). This restaurant quickly went to the head of the list of Guadeloupe's movers, shakers, and gourmets for its excellent cuisine and service in a lovely indoor garden setting. Expensive, but worth it for those who appreciate fine dining.

Lollapalooza (Gosier; 84-56-18). Part Latin bar with live DJ, part restaurant, it introduced a new concept to Guadeloupe's dining and dancing scene and quickly became a meeting place for locals and French expatriates. The European menu features grilled lobster, seafood, and meats flavored with hints of local produce and spices. Expensive.

Quatre Épices (25 Général-de-Gaulle Boulevard; 84-76-01), situated in a 200-year-old Creole house, serves high quality French Creole cuisine. Flan of red snapper and boeuf à l'antillaise with seasonal vegetables are specialties.

Villa Fleur d'Epée (rue du Fort Fleur d'Epée, 97190 Gosier; 90-86-59; fleurdepee@wanadoo.fr). Fine French cuisine with a Creole touch. Nice garden. Expensive.

St-François Area

Iguane Cafe (route de la Pointe des Chateaux, St-François; 85-03-09). Fine, innovative cuisine served in a renovated Creole house. Moderately expensive.

Northern Basse-Terre

Chez Clara (Ste-Rose; 28-91-86). Charming rustic restaurant facing small fish port of Ste-Rose, specializing in Creole cuisine. Moderately expensive.

Domaine de Severin (Cadet Ste-Rose; 28-34-54). Colonial house nestled in a magnificent tropical garden. French and Creole cuisine with fish and ouassous (crayfish) specialties. Moderately expensive.

Le Karacoli (Deshaies; 28-53-40). Open-air terrace in the shadow of coconut trees, facing Grand-Anse. Excellent authentic Creole cuisine. Moderately expensive.

Southern Grand Terre

La Paillotte de Pêcheur (Grande Anse, Trois-Rivières; 92-94-98) is a family-run "fisherman's hut" that specializes in seafood, particularly fresh lobster. Open daily for lunch and dinner except Sunday. Moderate.

La Rocher de Malendure (Bouillante, Basse-Terre; 98-70-84). Enjoy views of Pigeon Island and the sea from a rustic terrace setting amid tropical gardens while you lunch on fresh seafood. This provides an ideal stop on a day tour of Basse-Terre. Moderately expensive.

Le Caprice des Iles (Baillif; 81-74-97). Dining room and covered terrace overlooking the sea, offering fish and chicken specialties. Moderately expensive.

L'Orangerie (Desmarais Basse-Terre, behind Hôtel des Imports; 81-01-01). Situated on slopes of the Soufrière Volcano in an authentic Creole house built in 1823. Its talented chef, Christophe Moreau, serves genuine traditional and modern Creole cuisine; quiet ambience; garden. Lunch: Monday to Friday and Sunday. Dinner: Thursday, Friday, Saturday. Moderate.

Ti Cafe (route de Petit-Paris, Morin 97120 St-Claude; 80-06-05; fax: 80-31-63). Situated in an eighteenth-century estate house of a coffee plantation, the cafe specializes in Creole cuisine made from fresh local products and fresh fish. Moderately expensive.

Nightlife

In addition to hotel discos and nightclubs, there are nightspots for zouk, the pop music craze. Guadeloupe has two casinos: one in Gosier and the other in St-François. The legal age is twenty-one, and proof of identity (passport or driver's license with photo) is required. Jacket and tie are not required, but dress is fashionable.

Sports

Beaches/Swimming Guadeloupe has a great variety of beaches, from long stretches of white sand and sheltered coves to black-sand beaches and surf-washed Atlantic shores. Public beaches are free, though some may charge for parking. Unlike hotel beaches, they have no facilities. Generally, hotels welcome nonguests but charge for the use of facilities. There are several officially designated nudist beaches, the most popular being Pointe Tarare near Pointe des Châteaux. Topless is common at hotel beaches, but less so on village beaches.

Biking Cycling is a national sport whose popularity gets an annual boost from the Tour de la Guadeloupe, a ten-day international race in August that is as hotly contested as the Tour de France on the mainland. For visitors biking is best in Grande-Terre and Marie-Galante. **Cyclo-Tours** (84-11-34) and **Dingo** (83-81-19) in Pointe-à-Pitre have bikes for rent.

Boating Strong winds and currents make yachting a challenging sport in Guadeloupe. Boats of all sizes are available for charter by day, week, or month, with crew or bareboat. Safe anchorages and pretty beaches make Les Saintes and Marie-Galante popular destinations for day excursions. Full-day picnic sails are organized by local travel companies.

Guadeloupe has three good marinas: **Port de Plaisance Marina** (Bas-du-Fort; 90-84-85), the largest, is located ten minutes from Pointe-à-Pitre and is considered in yachting circles to be one of the best in the Western Hemisphere for its facilities. **The Capitainerie** (harbormaster) is open weekdays 8:00 a.m. to 1:00 p.m. and 3:00 to 5:00 p.m., and Saturday to 11:30 p.m. (82-54-85).

Canyoning/Rappeling Canopée (Plage de Malendure, Bouillante; 26-95-59; www.canopee guadeloupe.com); **Mangofil** (St.Claude; 81-10-43; mangofil1@wanadoo.fr). Sequence of fifty crossings from tree to tree on Tyrolean traverses and rope bridges.

Deep-Sea Fishing Sportfishing boats are based at **Port de Plaisance Marina** (Bas-du-Fort;

82-74-94), the **Fishing Club Antilles** (Bouillante; 90-70-10), and **Guadeloupe Marlin Club** (98-70-10).

Golf Golf International (St-François, (88-41-87; fax: 88-42-20) on the southeastern end of Grande-Terre is within walking distance of several hotels. The 18-hole course, designed by Robert Trent Jones, has a clubhouse with pro shop, lockers, and restaurant and an English-speaking pro.

Hiking Basse-Terre's National Park, with its spectacular scenery and good trails, offers some of the best hiking in the Caribbean. The 200 miles of sign-posted trails range from easy walks through tropical rain forests to arduous treks through wild mountain terrain. Many short hikes lead to pretty picnic spots, waterfalls, and mountain pools. The Tourist Office in Pointe-à-Pitre has brochures on the park. Guided hikes can be arranged through the **Bureau des Guides de Moyenne Montague,** Maison Forestière, Matouba 97120; 81-24-83.

Jacky Action Sport (Baie Malhaut, 14 res Louverture, La Jaille 97122; 26-02-34; jacky.noc@wanadoo.fr). Mountain guides, hiking, acrobatic canopy tours, equestrian sports. **Vert Intense** (Basse-Terre, Marine Rivière Sens; 99-34-73; www.vert-intense.com). Hiking La Soufrière and rivers in the heart of the national park; mountain biking; canyoning.

Horseback Riding Le Criolo (St-Félix; 84-38-90), a riding school with horses and ponies, offers tours and picnic excursions. Other stables in Grande-Terre are **Le Cheval Vert** (Ste-Anne; 88-00-00), **Le Grand Morne** (Port Louis; 22-84-19), and **La Boisviniere** (Abymes; 20-14-52). In Basse-Terre, **Poney Club** (Deshaies; 28-46-76) and **La Manade** (81-52-21; fax: 81-90-73), with a horseback-riding facility at St-Claude on the northern flank of Soufrière Mountain, offer rides on trails in the tropical forest.

Kayaking/Canoeing The lagoons and mangroves of Grand Cul-de-Sac Marin on the north-west of Basse-Terre are ideal for kayaking. Guided excursions are available from **Nature Passion Ecotourisme** (Ste-Rose; 28-98-73; fax: 68-47-55; nature-passion-ecotourisme@wanadoo.fr) and Guadeloupe-Adventure (35-45-78; www

.guadeloupe-adventure.com) which also offers canyoning and hiking.

Sports & Adventure (Gosier; 38-00-25; www.sport-adventure.com, sportdav@wanadoo.fr). Excursions in four-wheel-drive vehicles and sea kayaking. **Tam Tam Pagaie** (Ste-Rose; phone/fax: 28-13-85; tamtam-pagaie@wanadoo.fr). Offers kayak trips.

Snorkeling/Scuba Diving The snorkeling locations nearest to the port in Pointe-à-Pitre are the reefs fronting Gosier and the offshore island, Ilet du Gosier. Equipment is available from water-sports operators based at beachside hotels in Grande-Terre.

The most popular dive area is Pigeon Island off the west coast of Basse-Terre. It is actually two tiny volcanic islands with abundant marine life. Each dive location is different in character. The west side has a wall that begins at the surface, drops to 25 feet, slopes to 40 feet, and drops again. Here soft corals, large brain coral, seafans, and sponges and colorful fish are abundant, making it interesting for undersea photographers and popular with snorkelers.

The north side has a reef beginning in shallow water suitable for novice divers; it drops off to small canyons and walls, interesting for experienced divers. On the northeast side, a wall begins at the surface and drops to 40 feet. It is rich in sponges, pillar corals, and a great variety of fish. Ilet à Fajou, off the north coast of Basse-Terre, is another location visited on day trips from Grande-Terre.

Individual dives range from about US$50 to $75, depending on distance to dive sites. Dive operators in Grande-Terre usually take groups to Pigeon Island. On Malendure Beach, facing Pigeon Island, there are four dive operators: **Les Heures Saines** (98-86-63); **Plaisir Plongee Karukera** (98-82-43); **UCPA** (Bouillante, 98-89-00; ucpa.bouillante@wanadoo.fr), which also offers hiking excursions and windsurfing, and **Archipel Plongee Guadeloupe** (Malendure, Basse Terre, 98-93-93; www.archipel-plongee.fr), with departures at 10:15 a.m. and 12:45 p.m. Cost: Snorkeling, €16; novice dive from €40; two dives €85. Nondivers can take a glass-bottom boat operated by **Antilles Vision** (Plage de Malendure, Bouillante; 98-70-34; fax: 98-97-05), which departs daily at 10:30 a.m., noon, and 2:30 and 4:00 p.m. The eighty-minute ride passes over the Cousteau Marine Reserve, a protected area just off the coast at Malendure. On Les Saintes, Centre Nautique des Saintes is located on Terre-de-Haut.

American visitors should be aware that the French, who pioneered the sport of diving, use a system for dive tables and apparatus that is different from the American one. As a safety matter, divers (including certified ones) are checked on the use of the equipment before they are permitted to don tanks. Courses for certification by CMAS (Confédération Mondiale des Activités Subaquatique), the French national scuba association, are rigorous.

Tennis Most hotels have courts. Those closest to Pointe-à-Pitre are **La Creole Beach** in Gosier and **Novotel Fleur d'Epée** and **Marissol** near Bas-du-Fort. Each has two courts.

Windsurfing/Kitesurfing Guadeloupe was a pioneer of windsurfing in the 1970s, and it is a frequent venue for international meets. Lessons and rental equipment are available from most beachfront hotels. **Loisirs Nautiques** (Callinago; 84-25-25) and **Nauticase** (Salako Hotel) rent boards for about US$15 to $20 per hour. Beginner's lessons cost about US$25. Ecole de Voile (88-12-32). Now, kitesurfing has become the new attraction. Contact **Sports & Adventure** (Gosier; 38-00-25; www.sport-adventure.com; sportdav@wanadoo.fr).

Festivals and Celebrations

Fête des Cuisinières (Festival of the Women Cooks), one of the Caribbean's most colorful festivals, takes place on the second weekend in August. It is the feast day of St. Laurent, the patron saint of cooking. But this is no ordinary feast. For days the women cooks of the island prepare their specialties and make their costumes for a special parade. The celebration begins with a High Mass at the Cathedral in Pointe-à-Pitre to bless the food, which is placed at the altar. Afterward the women promenade through the streets in their Creole finery, carrying their elaborately decorated plates of island specialties and gaily decorated baskets of fruits and vegetables trimmed with miniature kitchen utensils. The parade ends at a local school for a ceremony attended by the mayor and other dignitaries, followed by a feast and dancing. Visitors are invited to participate.

Other celebrations include Carnival, held in the traditional pre-Lenten period. For the last five days of Carnival, all business stops, and by Shrove Tuesday, or Mardi Gras, festivities reach a frenzy with parades of floats, costumed red devils, and dancing in the streets of Pointe-à-Pitre. In the French West Indies Carnival continues through Ash Wednesday, when participants dress in black and white, King Carnival is burned on a funeral pyre, and a night parade with torches is held to bury Vaval.

Dominica
Roseau, Portsmouth/Prince Rupert Bay

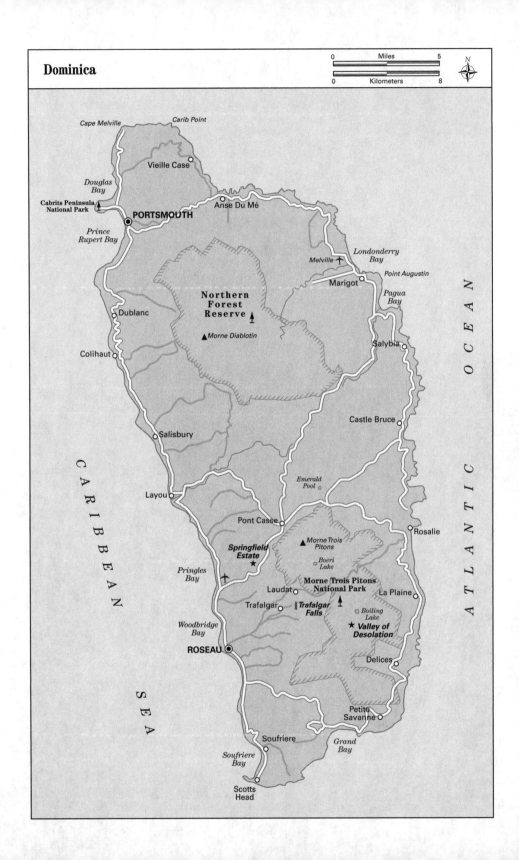

The Gift of Nature

Covered from end to end with towering volcanic mountains and spectacular tropical scenery, Dominica is the gift of nature. Mists rise from the green valleys and fall softly over the blue-green peaks densely carpeted with rain forests and exotic plants that host more than 135 species of birds. Natural wonders hide in the mountain vastness, and rivers and streams cascade over cliffs and rush down steep mountains.

Located in the heart of the Eastern Caribbean between Guadeloupe and Martinique, Dominica—not to be confused with the Dominican Republic—bridges the Leeward and the Windward Islands. The most mountainous of the Lesser Antilles, the land rises steeply from the shore to peaks that reach almost 5,000 feet. The native Carib Indians called their island by the descriptive name of *Wai'-tukubuli,* meaning "tall is her body." Moisture-laden trade winds from the east hang over the mountains, where they condense and release 250 inches of rain per year.

Dominica does not fit the usual image of a Caribbean island. Tourism's role is secondary in the economy. The island has no large resorts or shopping centers and does not want them. There are only a few beaches, and except for a stretch on the north coast, they consist mostly of black, volcanic sand—a matter of little importance, since the exquisite beauty of Dominica's interior more than compensates for the absence of beach-scalloped shores.

Columbus came upon Dominica on a Sunday in 1493 and named it for the day. The French and British fought over the island but in 1686 agreed in a treaty to recognize Dominica as a neutral territory to be left to the Caribs forever. But neither honored the agreement, and in practice Dominica became a sort of no-man's land of endless battles, with the French and British encroaching increasingly on Carib lands.

In 1805 Britain took possession of Dominica, and after almost two centuries of more turbulence, the island became independent in 1978. The French influence on the culture lingers to this day almost as much as that of the British. It is particularly apparent in the Creole speech, the cuisine, and the names of people and places.

Budget Planning

In some ways Dominica is one of the least expensive islands in the Eastern Caribbean, but it is also one of the least developed for tourism. Restaurants serving locals are cheap; some catering to tourists are outrageously expensive. Outside of the capital and Portsmouth, tourist facilities are extremely limited or nonexistent. If the shore excursions offered by your cruise ship do not suit your interests, it is best to arrange a tour or hike with one of the local travel companies rather than go on your own.

Port Profile

Location/Embarkation Dominica has three ports. Roseau, the capital on the southwest coast, has a new passenger port in the heart of town. (The exit gate is directly in front of the museum.)

At a Glance

Antiquities	★
Architecture	★
Art and artists	★
Beaches	★
Colonial buildings	★★
Crafts	★★★★
Cuisine	★★★
Culture	★★★
Dining/Restaurants	★★
Entertainment	★
Forts	★★
History	★★★
Monuments	★
Museums	★★★
Nightlife	★
Scenery	★★★★★
Shopping	★★
Sightseeing	★★★
Sports	★★★★
Transportation	★

Fast Facts

Population: 75,000

Size: 29 miles long and 16 miles wide; 290.8 square miles.

Main Towns: Roseau, Portsmouth

Government: Dominica is a democratic republic headed by a president. The constitution provides for seven ministers, including a prime minister who is the leader of the party with a majority in the House of Assembly. The cabinet, comprising the prime minister, ministers of government, and attorney general, is the chief policy-making body.

Currency: Eastern Caribbean (EC) dollar. US$1.00 equals EC$2.70. Credit cards are accepted at major hotels but are not widely used.

Departure Tax: US$20

Language: English is the official language, but Creole, a French-based patois, is spoken widely.

Public Holidays: January 1, New Year's Day; Carnival, Shrove Monday and Tuesday; Good Friday; Easter Monday; May 1, Labor Day; May/June, Whit Monday; first Monday in August, August Monday; November 3 and 4, National Day Celebrations; December 25, Christmas; December 26, Boxing Day.

Telephone Area Code: 767. Direct telephone and fax services to all parts of the world are operated by Cable and Wireless Ltd.

Airlines: There is no direct service from the U.S. mainland to Dominica. Rather, you must fly to San Juan, Antigua, or another of the Caribbean's main gateways, and transfer to American Eagle, Dominica Air Taxi, LIAT, or other local airlines that fly to Dominica.

Dominica has two airports: Canefield, 3 miles north of Roseau, accommodates aircraft up to a nineteen-seater twin otter; and Melville Hall on the northeast coast, 29 miles from Roseau and 20 miles from Portsmouth, takes larger aircraft. LIAT operates daily flights to both airports.

Information: www.dominica.dm; www.visit-dominica.com

In the United States:

In lieu of an office, the Discover Dominica Authority (DDA) has a new toll-free number (866-522-4057) for callers from the United States and Canada to assist with tourism-related inquires. The number is answered by tourism representatives from the DDA, Monday to Friday between 9:00 a.m. and 5:00 p.m.

In Port:

Discover Dominica Authority, Valley Road, Roseau, Commonwealth of Dominica, W.I.; (767) 448-2045; fax: (767) 488-5840; tourism@discover dominica.com.

Forestry Division, (767) 448-2401.

A second, deepwater harbor and commercial port is at Woodbridge Bay, about 1 mile north of town, which is sometimes used by cruise ships. The third port is Portsmouth, the second-largest town, and is located 25 miles north of Roseau on Prince Rupert Bay, a wide bay adjacent to the historic Cabrits Peninsula National Park.

Dominica built the port in an effort to develop Portsmouth and the Cabrits as a tourist attraction. A $7 million dock and modern terminal, designed in West Indian architecture typical of the eighteenth century, was added. Here passengers disembark directly into the national park.

Local Transportation Dominica's public transport is provided by private taxis and minivans in Roseau and between towns and villages.

Roads and Rentals Dominica has more than 300 miles of excellent roads that were built in the mid-1980s with the help of the United States. They connect Roseau with the main towns and villages of the country in a few hours' drive, making many of the island's most scenic parts—heretofore almost inaccessible—easy to reach. No highway completely encircles the island, but it is possible to loop around the northern end. Three highways connect Roseau on the west coast with the main east-coast villages of Rosalie, Castle Bruce, and Marigot.

And now for the bad news. The secondary roads and tracks feeding from the tarmac roads range from passable to terrible, and none are well marked. You must have a good map to find your way, but even detailed maps do not show all the important places. To see the most beautiful parts of Dominica, you need to leave your car and hike into the interior to the forests, lakes, waterfalls, and mountain heights.

Cars are available for rent; you need a visitor's driving permit, which can be obtained upon presentation of a valid driver's license to the Police Traffic Department (High Street, Roseau) and select car-rental agencies, and payment of EC$30 (US$12). Rental rates start at about US$40 per day; a deposit, payable by credit card, is sometimes required. Driving in this former British colony is on the left. And, be aware, driving here is hazardous. Some car-rental firms in Roseau are **Island Car Rentals** (448-0737; fax: 448-0737; www.islandcar .dm), **Garraway Rent-a-Car** (17 Old Street, Roseau; 448-2891; fax: 448-0541; www.avirtual dominica.com/garrawaycarrental.htm), and **Valley Rent-a-Car** (448-3233; www.valleyrentacar.com).

Ferry Service L'Express des Iles (448-2181; www.lexpressdesiles.net) provides high-speed catamaran services between Dominica and Guadeloupe on the north and Martinique on the south. Since ferries have a start-and-stop history in the Caribbean, you should check with the ferry company before making plans.

Emergency Numbers

Medical: Harlsbro Medical Centre, Hillsborough Street; contact through local operator, or dial 999
Police: 999

Shore Excursions

Dominica has good, reasonably priced tour companies, and their tours are recommended for first-time visitors. You can waste a great deal of time trying to find your way in Dominica's mountainous terrain, where distances are very deceiving, routes often taking two or three times the normal amount of time to cover. Descriptions of sites mentioned here are provided elsewhere in the chapter. All rates are per person.

City/Trafalgar Waterfalls: 4 hours, US$40–$58. Drive to Morne Bruce for a spectacular view of Roseau and harbor, visit the Botanic Gardens, and continue to Trafalgar Falls and a short walk in the rain forest.

Trafalgar/Emerald Falls/Carib Reserve: Full-day, US$45–$60. The Trafalgar Falls, Emerald Falls Trail, and a drive on the scenic Imperial Road to the Carib Indian Reservation. Return via the Layou River Valley to Layou, a town on the Caribbean coast.

Trafalgar/Freshwater Lake/Emerald Falls: Full-day, US$50–$60. The first tour described above combined with a hike to Freshwater Lake can be followed by a drive through the central mountains to Emerald Falls Trail and return via the Layou Valley.

Whale watching (see Sports).

Rain forest aerial tram excursion (see description later in this chapter).

Hiking safaris: 6 hours, US$50; US$200 for four people. To hike in the rain forest, you must have a guide. They can be obtained through the Dominica Tourist Office or from tour companies listed below. Most local companies specialize in safari-type excursions with nature guides who convey passengers in minivans or jeeps to points in the mountains from where hikes begin.

In Roseau, **Dominica Tours** (Box 34; 448-2638; fax: 448-5680); **Ken's Hinterland Adventure Tours** (Box 447; Roseau; 448-4850; fax: 448-8486 www.kenshinterlandtours.com); **Nature Island Dive** (449-8181; fax: 449-8182; www.nature islanddive.com); **Rainbow Rover Tours** (Box 3, Roseau; 448-8650; fax: 448-8650); **Wilderness Adventure Tours** (79 Bath Road; 448-2198; fax: 448-3600). Arrangements must be made in advance. **WRAVE, Wacky Rollers Adventure Vacations and Expeditions** (786-440-4FUN; fax: 786-513-7638; www.wackyrollers.com) has a fleet of six former military vehicles, colorfully hand-painted by Dominica's leading artist, Earl Etienne, that are used for tours. WRAVE also has a river tubing tour.

Dominica on Your Own

Dominica's capital is situated on a flat river delta at the mouth of the Roseau River on the site of a former Indian village. It takes its name from a wild reed, roseau, that once grew here in abundance. The French, the first Europeans to settle here, built a fort around which their colony developed. When the British took control of the island, they expanded the French fort and renamed it Fort Young, for the first British governor.

A Roseau Walkabout

A typical West Indian port, Roseau sprawls along the waterfront and climbs Morne Bruce and the other steep hills that frame it. The town has retained much of its old character, despite the devastation caused by Hurricane David in 1979. The oldest part is laid out in a modified grid of about 10 blocks and can be covered easily in an hour or so.

Museum and Market At the waterfront in front of the cruise dock (1) is the **Museum of Dominica (2)** (448-8923), with a small, beautifully displayed collection that traces the island's history from pre-Columbian times to the present. Admission: $3. Next door is the tourist information office, and directly behind it is an outdoor market of Dominican crafts on the spot that was once the island's slave market.

The **fruit-and-vegetable market (3)** at the north end of Bay Street is a wonderful place to visit, particularly on Saturday mornings, when it is jammed with people from the countryside selling exotic fruits and flowers in a kaleidoscope of colors.

Fort Young South of the museum on Victoria Street is Fort Young, constructed in 1770 to replace the original fort built by the French. It served as the main defense of the town and the harbor; some of its cannons can be seen at the entrance. In more recent times the building was used as the police headquarters and later was made into a hotel.

Government House Across from the Fort Young Hotel is Government House, built in the 1840s to replace an earlier building on the same site. It was altered and improved over the years as the official residence of the queen's representative. After independence it became the residence of the president of Dominica.

Also opposite the Fort Young Hotel is the nineteenth-century St. George's Anglican Church and the public library, one of several built in the Caribbean by the Andrew Carnegie Foundation in 1905.

The Cathedral East of Old Market Square on Virgin Lane, the Roman Catholic Cathedral of Our Lady of Fair Haven was built in 1854 to replace an earlier church and cemetery on the site. The side walls have old stained-glass windows; behind the main altar are modern ones. One of the old windows in the west wall depicts Columbus's discovery of the New World.

The town center has a number of wooden houses with second-story balconies and gingerbread trim. One of the oldest was once the home of novelist Jean Rhys.

Dominica Botanic Gardens (www.da-academy.org/dagardens) Originally laid out in 1890 on 110 acres at the foot of the wooded cliffs of Morne Bruce, the Dominica Botanic Gardens have been reduced to forty acres. Despite urban growth, they are still the largest area of open space in town. Near the entrance to the gardens, which were devastated by Hurricane David in 1979, is a poignant reminder of David's visit: a yellow school bus crushed by a toppled African baobab tree. The wreck now supports new life; in 1985, after the tree had sprouted new branches, it began to flower again.

The gardens retain about 150 of the original 500 species of trees and shrubs; a replanting program has been in progress for many years. Among the significant trees is Carib Wood, whose red blossom is Dominica's national flower; it blooms from March to May. Others to note are the pretty orchid trees near the entrance and two unusual bottle palms, whose name comes from the shape of the trunk, which is similar to the shape of the original Coca-Cola bottle. The gardens' most curious tree is the no-name tree, so called because specialists have not been able to identify it.

Spectacular views of Roseau and the coast can be seen from Morne Bruce, an elegant residential hillside above the gardens.

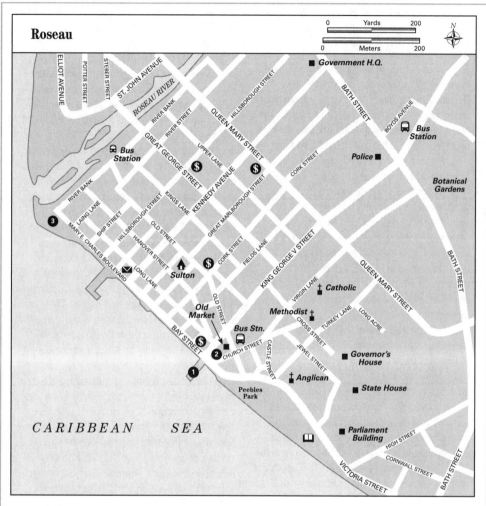

Roseau

CARIBBEAN SEA

1. Dock
2. Museum of Dominica
3. Market

A Drive around the Island

Roads east and north of Roseau lead to the edge of the national park, from which hiking trails ascend the mountains through rain forests to the lakes and waterfalls. Information on trail conditions and brochures prepared by the Park Service are available from the Dominican Tourist Board. Seven of the following nature sites are being developed with access roads, forest trails, interpre-tive centers, restroom facilities, picnic shelters, and ancillary services: Soufrière Sulfur Springs, east of Soufrière; Fresh Water Lake; Middleham Falls and nature trails; and Emerald Pool (work has been completed), all located within the Morne Trois Pitons National Park. Similar improvements have been made at Trafalgar Falls, and Morne Dia-blotin National Park is under development. The Sulfur Springs suffered damage due to flooding

*caused by Hurricane Dean in August 2007 and was
closed until further notice at press time.*

Dominica National Park (www.natureisland.com)
Established in 1975 on seventeen thousand acres
in the central and southern highlands, Dominica
National Park has magnificent scenery and a great
variety of plant and animal life. Known also as the
Morne Trois Pitons National Park after the highest of four peaks in the park, it has hiking trails
ranging from a comfortable thirty-minute walk to
Emerald Pool to a tortuous four-hour trek to Boiling
Lake. On the north side of Roseau, a road inland
winds through the lush Roseau River Valley to the
tiny village of Laudat on Mount Micotrin and the
"gateway" to the main attractions in the park's
central region. In 1998 the park was declared a
World Heritage Site by UNESCO. It covers five
major peaks as well as Boiling Lake, Freshwater
and Boeri Lakes, and associated waterfalls and a
thermal area.

Trafalgar Falls One of the most beautiful,
accessible sites in the park is also the one closest
to Roseau. Spectacular Trafalgar Falls are actually
three separate cascades, which tumble down the
steep sides of Mount Micotrin into pools several
hundred feet below. The falls are quite far apart.
The trail is an easy fifteen-minute walk and provides a good introduction to tropical rain forests.

At the base of the cliff and the entrance to the
trail at a 1,000-foot elevation is the Papillote Inn, a
wilderness retreat and nature sanctuary with a
rain-forest garden. Begun in 1969 by former New
Yorker Anne G. J. Baptiste, the proprietor of the
inn, the garden follows the natural contour of the
mountainside, although some terraces were added.
More than fifty species of nesting birds can be
seen from the inn's terrace or nearby. The rustic inn
organizes guided nature walks and trail hikes.

Freshwater and Boeri Lakes Laudat is also
the start of hikes to Freshwater Lake at 2,779 feet
and Boeri Lake at 2,800 feet. The two bodies of
water were once a single lake in the crater of an
ancient volcano until Morne Micotrin, a young
cone, formed in the crater and separated the
water. Freshwater Lake, the largest of Dominica's
five lakes and the source of its hydroelectric
power, is surrounded by dense forests. Hummingbirds are seen often. The walk from the Laudat

trailhead to Freshwater Lake takes about forty minutes. The views across the park as you approach
are wonderful.

North of Freshwater Lake, a steep, narrow trail
of about one hour's hiking winds up the mountain
along the ridge separating the two lakes to Boeri
Lake. It passes through different types of forests
with giant tree ferns and many types of plants, and
along small streams and hot and cold springs.
Throughout the hike there are sweeping views
across the island to the Atlantic coast. Boeri Lake
has a magnificent setting between Morne Micotrin
on the south and Morne Trois Pitons on the north,
where it is difficult to believe you are in the
Caribbean. The lake and its wooded surroundings
look more like Vermont than the tropics.

Rainforest Aerial Tram (www.natureisland
.com/AerialTram) One of Dominica's newest attractions is an aerial tram, located near Laudat village,
about a thirty-minute drive from Roseau. The tram
starts in the wooded area at the end of a road and
returns to the same location. On the ride up, the
tram, a modified ski lift, travels up a steep slope on
the side of Mount Micotrin and over a spectacular
ravine where passengers see waterfalls, and then it
passes through the lower canopy of the forest. Passengers, accompanied by a naturalist guide, discover plants and life-forms that are usually hidden
from view in the forest treetops. Halfway through
the tour, passengers get off the tram for a ten-
minute walk across a suspension bridge spanning
the Breakfast River Gorge and through the forest
understory. On the return, the tram goes through
and over the canopy, with spectacular views of the
forest-covered hills and the Caribbean Sea beyond.
The price is US$74 adult, $62 child and student.

For cruise-ship passengers who have booked a
shore excursion or a tour through a local tour company, transportation to the tram is included. If you
go on your own, you will need to arrange your own
transportation. At the site there are restroom facilities, a nature walkway that leads over an aerial
bridge, a juice bar, and a gift shop. The tram own-
ers/operators are Rainforest Aerial Trams (2250
Southwest Third Avenue, Suite 301, Miami, FL
33129; 866-759-8726; 448-8775; www.rainforest
aerialtrams.com), which also operates aerial trams
in Costa Rica.

Titou Gorge—Valley of Desolation—Boiling Lake South of Laudat, the Titou Gorge, a narrow, deep, water-filled defile, is the start of the trail to the Valley of Desolation and Boiling Lake, the world's second-largest solfatara lake. Boiling Lake is 6 miles east of Roseau as the crow flies, but to reach it on the ground takes four hours over a 6-mile roller-coaster trail. Some of the most difficult hiking in the Caribbean, this is an undertaking for experienced hikers and then only with a guide. As an alternative, you can go as far as Titou Gorge or go halfway on the trail to the edge of the Valley of Desolation, a hike of three hours round-trip.

First studied by British scientists in the 1870s, Boiling Lake resembles a huge cauldron of bubbling gray-khaki water smothered in mist. It is thought to be a flooded fumarole, or hole in a volcanic region, that releases hot gases and boiling vapors from the molten lava below.

Soufriere On the south end of Dominica, 5 miles from Roseau, is the fishing village of Soufriere. It is situated on a wide scenic bay that ends at Scotts Head, a promontory that offers great views of the Martinique Channel where the Atlantic and Caribbean collide. Martinique is in view on the south. Scotts Head has some of the island's main dive sites. According to local legend, the cliffs above Soufriere Bay were used by Carib men to punish unfaithful wives—they threw them into the sea.

Soufriere takes its name from the Sulfur Springs that can be found less than a mile east of the village. A road continues to the east coast and, at about halfway, a track south takes you to **Petit Coulibri** (446-3151), a rustic cliffside lodge with fabulous views of Martinique and the sea. The property is not opened at present.

From Soufriere, the road west takes a wide swing around the bay along a narrow stretch of road to Scotts Head village, where you can see fishermen mending their nets and repairing their boats. On Friday nights the area is transformed into a street fair attracting Dominicans from the capital and all over the area coming for a raucous good time.

At Pointe Michel, a village between Roseau and Soufriere settled by survivors of the catastrophic 1902 eruption of Mount Pélé in Martinique, farmers grow the grass used to make Dominica's distinctive rugs. The tough grass, khuskhus, is put on the road for cars to run over in order to make it more pliable to weave. In Jamaica the roots of this plant are used to make a perfume.

Soufriere/Scotts Head Marine Reserve (www.natureisland.com/Scuba) Dominica has established its first marine reserve on the island's southwest coast to protect the area's important marine resource and to manage its use by traditional as well as recreational users. The Soufriere/Scotts Head Marine Reserve is under the Local Area Management Authority (LAMA), made up of community groups, private sector operators, the Fisheries Department, and the Dominica Watersports Association. LAMA is charged with developing a system to avoid conflict among users and enable visitors to enjoy the reserve now and in the future and with training wardens for beach and shore patrol. The reserve starts at the impressive "Champagne," a dive site named for its champagnelike bubbles, as the northern limit and runs through Scotts Head/Soufriere Bay, along the south shore of the Scotts Head peninsula to "Lost Horizons," another dive site, as the southern limit. There are four user zones: diving, fishing, general recreation, and research. Among other popular dive sites in the reserve are the pinnacles at Soufriere and Scotts Head, Dangleben's Reef, and L'Abym (also called "the Wall"). For information: National Development Corporation, 448-2045; fax: 448-5840.

Middleham Trails North of Roseau the road to Pont Casse, a junction in the center of the island, winds east along hairpin curves through the steep mountains. It passes Springfield Estate, an old plantation at 1,200 feet, and now a rustic, ecotourist inn, and skirts the Middleham Estate on the northwest edge of the national park. Here a 950-acre tract was donated to the park in 1975 by John D. Archbold, the American owner of Springfield Plantations. It has some of Dominica's finest rain forests with trails. One trail begins in Providence near the village of Laudat; the other, at the village of Cochrane. Both lead, in about a one- to two-hour hike, to the waterfalls, where you rejuvenate in the freshwater pool at the base of the falls.

Emerald Pool Nature Trail At the north end of the national park near the Pont Casse junction, a sign on the road to Castle Bruce marks the turnoff for Emerald Pool Nature Trail, the national park's most accessible trail. An easy thirty-minute walk on a good half-mile footpath, it passes through lush forest to a beautiful cascade that drops 20 feet into a grotto of black rock with emerald walls of ferns, orchids, and dense foliage. (The pool is large enough for a swim. Bring a towel; there are no facilities.)

The trail has lookouts over the magnificent Belle Fille Valley, an area of banana groves backed by jungle-thick mountains, and a stretch of the wild east coast at Castle Bruce. A short paved section of the trail is part of the old road—an ancient Indian trail—to Castle Bruce used by the Caribs before the main road was built in the 1960s.

The Imperial Road The 20-mile stretch known as the Imperial Road, between Pont Casse and Marigot on the northeast coast, crosses the heart of the Central Forest Reserve, one of two reserves in northern Dominica. The other, the enormous Northern Forest Reserve, is dominated by the island's highest peak, Morne Diablotin, at 4,748 feet. The northern reserve is the last refuge of the rare imperial parrot, known locally as the sisserou, and its smaller relative, the red-necked parrot, or jacquot. In 2000, 842 acres of Morne Diablotin were set aside as a national park. You can climb to the summit of the morne on a trail classified as moderate to difficult.

The Central Forest Reserve protects a small gommier forest with gigantic trees up to 120 feet in height. The gommier is a beautiful hardwood used to make furniture, but for centuries it has been used by the Amerindians to make oceangoing canoes. The top branches of the gommier are the principal nesting places for Dominica's endangered parrots. Before strong conservation measures were put in place, commercial logging was destroying the forests at an alarming rate. The trend has been stopped, but poaching of trees and birds does continue.

From the gommier forest the road drops into lime and banana plantations laced with ferns along the Pagua River. At Pagua Bay a wide crest of golden sand bracketed by rocky cliffs is washed by the crashing waves of the Atlantic, where wind-sheared vegetation clings hard to the cliffs. The bay is the north boundary of the Carib Indian Reservation.

The Carib Indian Reservation (www.centre link.org) Dominica is the only place in the Caribbean where the Carib, after whom the Caribbean is named, have survived. In 1903 approximately 3,750 acres, including eight hamlets in the northeastern part of Dominica from Castle Bruce to Pagua Bay, were set aside as a reserve for the Caribs. The land is held in common by the 3,202 descendants of the Caribs who inhabited the island at the time of Columbus. To be eligible, claimants must have at least one parent of Carib origin and must reside on the reservation. About 10 percent of the descendants are considered predominantly of Carib stock, but there are probably no pure-blooded Caribs today. Those who survived the wars or were not hunted down by the earlier settlers eventually intermingled with other people who came to the island. Today the Caribs you meet usually have rather distinct Asian features and straight black hair and bear some resemblance to the Amerindians of South America. Until recently some lived in traditional thatched huts, but those dwellings have been replaced by modern houses.

Visitors are often misled by descriptions in brochures and some guidebooks and go to the Carib reserve expecting to see a Stone Age people living as they did when Columbus arrived five hundred years ago. The Carib villages, as well as most of the people themselves, are indistinguishable from others on the island. A few Carib traditions that link them with their past have survived nevertheless. The Carib straw craft is instantly recognizable by its design and fabric and is different from any other straw woven in the Caribbean.

Another legacy—but one that is getting harder to find—is the oceangoing canoe that the Indians make from the trunk of the gommier tree. On the beach at Castle Bruce, you can sometimes see boatmen making dugout canoes in the same method used by the Indians since before Columbus. A modified version is still made and used as fishing boats in other Eastern Caribbean islands.

The **Kalinago Barana Autê** (Carib Cultural Village by the Sea; Old Coast Road, Crayfish River;

445-7979; www.kalinagobaranaaute.com), opened in February 2006, provides a unique opportunity to learn and appreciate the heritage of the Carib people. This cultural destination includes an arts and crafts gallery where Kalingo artisans use the Larouma plant to weave functional items like bottles, mats, and baskets, create crafts from calabash, make pottery, and build canoes. They harvest plants and herbs for medicine. A cassava mill is used to grind this dietary staple, which is converted into bread and farine. Beautiful Kalingo structures, including the "karbet" that serves as the center for daily performances of traditional dance, drama, and song. Hours: daily, 10:00 a.m. to 5:00 p.m.; October 15 to April 15, closed Monday; April 16 to October 14, closed Wednesday and Thursday. Admission: US$8, $4 child.

Portsmouth The small, sleepy village of about 2,000 people overlooks Portsmouth Bay, known in history as Prince Rupert Bay. This wide natural harbor has a freshwater source, Indian River, on the south end. Behind the town rises Morne Diablotin, Dominica's highest peak. The natural harbor, a freshwater supply, and a defensive headland—the Cabrits Peninsula on the north side of the bay—were reasons enough for the area to be strategically important to the British and French and heavily fortified during their colonial wars. Indeed, one of the most decisive naval battles of the colonial wars was fought here in 1782. The British victory helped Britain establish its sea supremacy over the French and, hence, the trade routes and wealth of the West Indies.

Portsmouth has a few modest beachfront hotels and a rustic restaurant on the beach. Windsurfing and snorkeling are the main water sports to enjoy here.

Cabrits Historical and Marine Park The silhouette of the 260-acre Cabrits Peninsula can be recognized by its two steep hills, remnants of ancient volcanoes. The peninsula, a freshwater swamp that joins it to the mainland, and an 800-acre marine reserve in adjoining Douglas Bay make up the Cabrits Historical and Marine Park, which is part of the Dominica National Park. *Cabrit* is said to come from the word meaning "goat" in several European languages. Early exploration ships had

the habit of leaving goats here to graze so that they would have fresh meat to eat on future visits.

From 1770 to 1815, on a promontory of the peninsula, the British built Fort Shirley, one of their most impressive military installations in the Caribbean. Since 1982 the extensive ruins have been under restoration following the original plans, which were found preserved in England. In addition to the battlements, there is a museum in the former powder magazines and trails—one leading to the ghostly remnants of the commander's house, now choked by enormous roots of ficus and sandbox trees.

When restoration began, the growth all but obscured the ruins. Before the area became a national park, the Forestry Division had planted trees on an experimental basis; even earlier, orchards of tropical fruit trees were cultivated here, so that now the park has an interesting variety of Caribbean flora. The adjoining swamp hosts a variety of plants and birds; and on the park's beaches, two species of sea turtles nest here from April to September. The marine park of Douglas Bay is a popular snorkeling area.

In the terminal reception hall, passengers are introduced to the attractions with audiovisual displays. (The Cabrits project was the 1990 winner of the Caribbean Heritage Award, a grant given by American Express to encourage historic preservation.)

The Indian River South of Portsmouth at the mouth of the Indian River, a rowboat with a nature guide can be rented for a trip upriver. The tranquil estuary is so thick with tropical vegetation, it forms a tunnel over the river so dense only slim rays of light filter through the foliage, dancing on the leaves and water, creating a hauntingly beautiful setting. About thirty minutes up the river, your boatman stops at a clearing, where he leads his group on a hike, identifying the birds and flora along the way. Fee: half-day US$40.

Gingerette Nature Sanctuary This sanctuary (440-3412; rastours@cwdom.dm) is the first phase of a thirty-five-acre ecological preserve along the Layou River. Intended as a model agrotourism project, the sanctuary is a showcase for native vegetation such as cocoa trees, breadnuts, avocados, sugarcane, and bananas. There is a waterfall and a mineral-water spring; river bathing, bird-watching, nature walks, and guided tours are available.

Shopping

Dominica is not a place for duty-free shopping for designer fashions and fancy electronics, but it is definitely worthwhile if you are interested in handcrafts. Dominica's crafts are not only good but distinctive, particularly the products of the Carib Indians and grass rugs. In recent years, crafts in Dominica have been flourishing, with many shops specializing in art and crafts by local artists. *Destination Dominica,* a free tourist brochure sponsored by the government division of tourism, lists the local art and crafts shops with a brief description of their specialties: batiks, jewelry, tie-dye, pottery, and more.

An outdoor market next to the museum (facing the cruise-ship pier) has crafts and souvenirs; however, they are not always the best available. Before buying, if you are interested in quality crafts, visit some of the specialty stores in Roseau, such as **Dominica Handcrafts** (Hanover Street); **Caribana Handcraft** (Cork Street; 448-4838), which specializes in products made by the Caribs; **Shanice's Craft Centre** (Hanover Street; 225-1429; sharon-joyn@hotmail.com); and **Tropicrafts Ltd.** (Queen Mary Street). The latter is the factory and shop for grass rugs made of verti-vert, as the khuskhus plant is known here. The craft was started in a Catholic convent by Belgian nuns, who taught their students to make straw rugs using the designs they copied from traditional lace. Other good buys include soaps made locally from fresh coconut oil, leather crafts, cigars, and cassette recordings of traditional "jing-ping" folk music.

Crazy Banana (Duty Free Emporium, Dame Eugenia Charles Boulevard; 449-8091; archipelage@cwdom.dm) specializes in quality artwork and souvenirs; and next door, **Land** (Duty Free Emporium, Dame Eugenia Charles Boulevard; 448-3394; land@archip.com) sells leather products. Among the duty-free shops for luxury goods, **Asbury's** and **Colombian Emeralds** are located in the Fort Young Hotel, within walking distance of the cruise-ship dock.

Dining and Restaurants

Dominica has a Creole cuisine incorporating a great array of locally grown vegetables, fruits, and herbs that reflects its African and French heritage more than its British one. The most popular specialty is mountain chicken, or frogs' legs, known locally by its Creole name, crapaud; crayfish, or river shrimp, and stuffed land crabs are others. Among the common vegetables are bananas, plantains, and dasheen, a root vegetable with green heart-shaped leaves, which can be seen growing throughout the country. The root is used like potatoes, and the young spinachlike leaves are used to make callaloo, a thick soup.

Evergreen Hotel Terrace Restaurant (Castle Comfort; 448-3288; evergreen@cwdom.cm). In a delightful terrace setting overlooking the Caribbean, you can enjoy well-prepared local specialties at reasonable prices as well as a magnificent view. Moderate.

La Robe Creole (3 Victoria Street, Roseau; 448-2896; www.larobecreole.com). The Dominican cuisine turned out by Erica Burnett-Biscombe is reason enough to visit Roseau. Particularly outstanding is the callaloo and crab soup and the mountain chicken. Fish and meats are grilled over charcoal. Expensive.

The Orchard (King George V and Great George Streets, Roseau; 448-3051). The menu has Creole favorites like black pudding, rôti, crabbacks, conch, and lobster. No credit cards. Moderate.

The Sutton Place Grill (25 Old Street; 449-8700). Set in one-hundred-year-old stone walls, the restaurant is part of the family-run Sutton Place Hotel and offers traditional West Indian cooking with international inspiration. (Be sure to see one of the hotel's guest rooms—they may just be the prettiest hotel rooms in the Caribbean.) Moderately expensive.

Sports

Beaches/Swimming Except for the golden strands of the northeast, most of Dominica's beaches are steel-gray volcanic sand. But the best swimming in Dominica is not always at seaside beaches. Lakes, rivers, and waterfalls of the interior provide some of the most pleasant spots. On the west coast at Layou, a ten-minute walk along the lush banks takes you to a spring-fed pool popular for swimming.

Biking Mountain biking is available from **Nature Island Dive** (449-8181) and other tour operators, but you'll need to be in top physical condition with lots of stamina to negotiate the island's steep mountains and rugged trails.

Fishing Sportfishing is a relatively new tourist attraction, although fishing has been a livelihood for people as long as they have lived in Dominica. Fishing charters are arranged by **Rainbow Sportsfishing** (Castaway Beach Hotel; 448-8650; fax: 448-8834; rollei@cwdom.dm). The operator also offers whale-watching excursions for US$40 per person, minimum of four.

Hiking The best and sometimes the only way to see Dominica's attractions is hiking. The easiest short walks are the Emerald Pool Nature Trail, Trafalgar Falls near Roseau, and Cabrits National Park. Longer, more strenuous hikes go to Freshwater Lake, Boeri Lake, and Middleham Falls. For hiking in the rain forest, you must have a guide; fast-growing vegetation often obscures trails, and it is easy to get disoriented and lost.

Horseback Riding Highride Nature Adventures (New Florida Estate, P.O. Box 467, Roseau; 448-6296; highriders@cwdom.dm) is one of the last remaining estates in Dominica to maintain a family tradition of horsemanship. For more than fifty years, horses have been an integral part of estate operations, both for pleasure riding and farming activities.

Kayaking Nature Island Dive (449-8181; fax: 449-8182; www.natureislanddive.com) and other dive and water-sports operators also provide kayaking excursions, and some combine kayaking and snorkeling. Costs range from US$25 per person per hour; $55 half-day double kayak. Also available through **Castaways Beach Hotel and Dive Center** (449-6244); **Wacky Rollers** (449-8276; fax: 513-7638; www.wackyrollers.com), which offers river to ocean kayaking; and **Cobra Tours** (Portsmouth; 445-3333; www.cobratours.dm), which offers kayaking and snorkeling, including lessons and rentals, as well as windsurfing, surfing, and bodyboarding.

Snorkeling/Scuba Diving Dominica has only recently been discovered as a dive location. It has reefs on the north and west coasts. Hodges Beach, a white-sand beach on the northeast coast, faces three small offshore islands with banks of brain corals and an abundance of tropical fish. On the northwest shore the best snorkeling is found in Douglas Bay, where there is a large reef about 180 feet from shore in 20 to 50 feet of water.

On the south side of Roseau and about 300 feet north of the Anchorage Hotel, a reef approximately 180 feet from shore starts at about a 45-foot depth. Wall diving at Pointe Guignard, less than a mile north of Soufriere, holds the greatest interest for divers due to the variety of attractions: caves, lobsters, black and brown coral, sponges, and diverse marine life.

On the south end of the island, Scotts Head has a variety of diving locations from the Caribbean around to the Atlantic side of the promontory. These are mainly drop-offs and reef dives with characteristics similar to those of Pointe Guignard. The beach on the north side of Scotts Head is rocky, but it is popular for snorkeling, as the coral is within swimming distance. The area is small and features mostly finger corals, but it has a large variety of small, colorful reef fish.

Dive Dominica (448-2188; www.dive dominica.com) is a qualified dive operation offering a full range of services, including PADI instruction and a ten-passenger dive boat. Deep-sea fishing can also be arranged. Dive Dominica charges US$50 for a single-tank dive and US$80 for two tanks. Participants must show a certification card. The operator also has snorkeling excursions for US$27.

Whale Watching Twenty-one species of whales and four dolphin species have been identified in waters off Dominica. Although whale watching is available year-round, the best months are from October to April, when sperm whales cavort only 3 to 8 miles offshore.

Whale-watching excursions are well organized and readily available from **Castle Comfort Diving Lodge/Dive Dominica** (P.O. Box 2253, Roseau;

888-414-7626, 448-2188; fax: 448-6088; www.dive dominica.com), **Anchorage Hotel and Dive Center** (448-2638; www.anchoragehotel.dm), and other local companies that offer daily tours. The cost for a 3.5-hour excursion is US$50 per person. Tours are Wednesday and Sunday at 2:00 p.m.

Windsurfing The best areas for windsurfing are Hodges Beach on the north coast, Douglas Bay on the northwest, the west coast south of Roseau, and Soufriere Bay.

Festivals and Celebrations

Creole Day, which coincides with Dominica's Independence Day, is the year's main celebration. Schoolchildren, teachers, and other adults don the traditional, colorful madras costume for a day filled with parades, competitions, and other festive activities. The **World Creole Music Festival** takes place the last weekend in October. The annual event brings together Creole bands from the English-, French-, and Spanish-speaking islands, as well as West Africa.

Martinique
Fort-de-France

Martinique

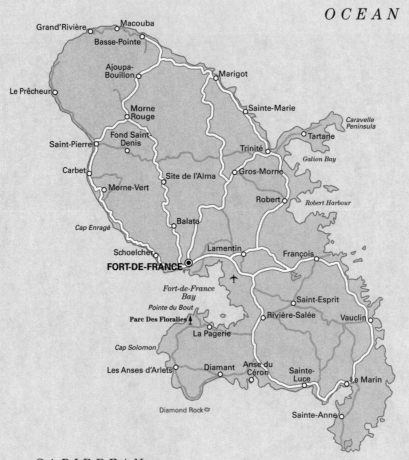

ATLANTIC

OCEAN

Grand'Rivière
Macouba
Basse-Pointe
Ajoupa-Bouillon
Marigot
Le Prêcheur
Sainte-Marie
Morne Rouge
Caravelle Peninsula
Fond Saint-Denis
Saint-Pierre
Tartane
Trinité
Galion Bay
Carbet
Site de l'Alma
Gros-Morne
Morne-Vert
Robert
Robert Harbour
Cap Enragé
Balata
Schoelcher
Lamentin
François
FORT-DE-FRANCE
Fort-de-France Bay
Pointe du Bout
Saint-Esprit
Parc Des Floralies
Rivière-Salée
Vauclin
La Pagerie
Cap Solomon
Les Anses d'Arlets
Diamant
Anse du Céron
Sainte-Luce
Le Marin
Diamond Rock
Sainte-Anne

CARIBBEAN

SEA

The Isle of Flowers

Beautiful and beguiling, Martinique is a paradox of razorback ridges and undulating meadows, steep peaks and soft hills, and possesses the diversity of a continent rather than a small Caribbean island. Its three distinct regions of greatly varied terrain leave visitors with the impression that it is a much larger island.

Volcanic mountains, their peaks hiding under a hood of clouds, dominate the northern end of the island, where windswept cliffs hang high above the sea and the land climbs steeply along deeply creviced mountain slopes to the cone of Mount Pelée, an active volcano more than 4,500 feet high. From these rain-forested slopes, the land drops to skirts of fertile green fields of banana and pineapple plantations. The central region rises in spiked peaks and ridges carved by rivers and streams that fall quickly to meadows with grazing cattle and sugarcane fields. Even greater in contrast is the dry, flat south end with parched lowland and saline flats bordered by white-sand beaches.

Some authorities say that when Columbus first sighted the island in 1493, he named it for a saint, as was his usual custom. Others claim that the name derives from a Carib word, madinina, meaning "isle of flowers"—a theory that's easy to believe, since masses of flowers color the landscape in every direction.

Columbus is believed to have come ashore at Carbet, on the Caribbean coast, on his fourth voyage, in 1502. The first settlers did not arrive until 1635, however, under Pierre Belain d'Esnambuc, a French nobleman from Dieppe. For the next quarter of a century, many other settlers arrived, and battles with the native Carib Indians were frequent. So too were skirmishes with the British and Dutch for control of the island. Then in 1763 Louis XV, in the Treaty of Paris, gave up Canada—which he reportedly called "a few snowy acres"—rather than his territory in the West Indies. The decision was later to be as pivotal for the young United States as it was for France, which used Fort-de-France as a supply base to aid the Americans during the American Revolution.

By the early nineteenth century, the voices of emancipation had grown strong. Through efforts led by Victor Schoelcher, an Alsatian deputy and one of the leading French abolitionists of the time, slavery in the French West Indies was abolished in 1848. Soon after, indentured workers from Asia were imported to work the sugar plantations. Some of this ethnic diversity—French, African, Asian—remains, but for the most part it has blended into an exotic combination, creating Martinique's character today—which is as distinctive as its landscape.

Budget Planning

Taxis and leading restaurants are expensive. Collective taxis and the ferry to Pointe du Bout are cheap. Sports facilities are comparable to prices in other popular Caribbean locations. The most economical way to tour the island is on an organized motorcoach tour or on your own, by rented car, if

At a Glance

Antiquities	★
Architecture	★★
Art and artists	★★★
Beaches	★★★
Colonial buildings	★★
Crafts	★★
Cuisine	★★★★
Culture	★★★
Dining/Restaurants	★★★★
Entertainment	★
Forts	★
History	★★
Monuments	★★
Museums	★★★★
Nightlife	★
Scenery	★★★★★
Shopping	★★★
Sightseeing	★★★★
Sports	★★★
Transportation	★★

Fast Facts

Population: 392,000

Size: 50 miles long and 22 miles wide; 425 square miles.

Main Town: Fort-de-France

Government: In 1946 Martinique was made a French *département* with representation in the French Parliament. More recently it was made a *région*. Martinique, along with Guadeloupe, St. Barts, and St. Martin, make up the French West Indies. Its people are French citizens sharing the same culture and privileges as those in mainland France. The electorate sends four deputies and two senators to the French Parliament. It is governed by two elective bodies: the Conseil Général, with thirty-six representatives, and the Conseil Régional, with forty-one members.

Currency: Euro. US$1.00 fluctuates around €0.50, or I € equals US$1.50. U.S. and Canadian traveler's checks and credit cards are readily accepted.

Departure Tax: None

Electricity: 220 A.C.; 50 cycles. U.S. and Canada appliances require French plug converters and transformers.

Language: French and Creole. English is spoken in most tourist facilities, but a French phrase book and pocket dictionary are useful.

Public Holidays: January 1, New Year's Day; Easter Monday; May 1, Labor Day; Ascension Thursday; Pentecost Monday; May 22, Slavery Abolition Day; July 14, Bastille Day; August 15, Assumption Day; November 1, All Saints Day; November 11, Armistice Day; December 25, Christmas Day.

Telephone Area Code: 596. To phone station-to-station from the United States, dial 011-596-596 plus the local number. In Martinique, *Télécartes,* sold at post offices and outlets indicating *télécartes en vente ici,* are used in special booths marked Télécom and make local and international calling easier and less expensive. Visa and MasterCard can also be used.

Airlines: Air France via Miami; Air Canada from Montreal; LIAT, Air Caraibes, and Take Air Lines from neighboring islands. American Airlines/American Eagle nonstop service from New York via San Juan to Fort-de-France four times weekly. Delta weekly from Atlanta.

By Sea: *l'Express des Iles* (596-596-42-04-05; fax: 63-34-47; www.express-des-iles.com; info-reservations@express-des-iles) and *Brudey Frères* (90-04-48; fax: 70-53-75; www.brudey-freres.fr) provide high-speed catamaran services between Guadeloupe and Martinique for about $130 round-trip. Since ferries have a start-and-stop history in the Caribbean, you should check with the ferry company before making plans.

Information: www.martinique.org

In the United States:

(800) 391-4909

New York: Martinique Promotion Bureau, 825 Third Avenue, 29th Floor, New York, NY 10022; (212) 838-6887; (800) 371-4909; fax: 838-7855; www.martinique.org; info@martinique.org

Also, French Government Tourist Offices:

Chicago: 205 North Michigan Avenue, Chicago, IL 60601; (312) 327-2090; fax: (312) 327-5207; nancy.anderson@franceguide.com

Los Angeles: 9454 Wilshire Boulevard, Suite 210, Beverly Hills, CA 90212; (310) 271-6665; fax (310) 276-2835; christophe.carvenant@franceguide.com.

In Canada:

Office du Tourisme de la Martinique au Canada

Montreal: 1981 McGill College, Suite 490, Montreal, H3A 2W9; (514) 288-2026; (800) 361-9099 (Canada only); fax: (514) 845-4868

In Port:

Office Départemental du Tourisme (Martinique Tourist Office), Immeuble Beaupré, Pointe de Jaham, 97233 Schoelcher, Martinique, F.W.I.; 596-61-61-77; fax: 596-61-22-72; www.touristmartinique.com; info.cmf@martiniquetourism.com. Hours: weekdays 7:30 a.m. to 12:30 p.m. and 2:30 to 5:30 p.m. (Friday to 5:00 p.m.); Saturday 8:00 a.m. to noon. The office has maps, literature, and an English-speaking staff.

you can share the expense with others. Don't over-look the many walking excursions to be taken in Fort-de-France and the endless hiking opportunities around the island.

Port Profile

Location/Embarkation The main commercial harbor of Fort-de-France is located on the south side of the bay, a few minutes' drive from the city center. The newest passenger port, Pointe Simon, is on the north side within walking distance of town. Sometimes the largest ships anchor in the bay and tender passengers to the pier at the foot of town. Small ships sometimes dock at Pointe du Bout, the main resort area on the south side of the bay.

Two ships, regardless of the size, can pull dockside at Pointe Simon. The terminal building has an information desk to help arrange island tours, public phones that accept credit and phone cards, and restrooms.

A team of young English-speaking Martini-quais members of the Welcome Brigade (Brigade d'Accueil) circulate in town to provide visitors with information and assistance. They are easily recog-nizable by their uniforms: white polo shirts, blue vests, and jeans, Bermuda shorts, or skirts. Mem-bers report regularly to fixed posts—near Pointe Simon dock, the old cruise-ship terminal, and south edge of La Savane—and are on duty from 8:00 a.m. to noon (Tuesday 12:30 to 4:30 p.m.); sched-ules are also adjusted to coincide with cruise-ship arrivals.

Local Transportation Taxis are plentiful but tend to be expensive. There are taxi stands at the port, in town, and at major hotels. Sample fares from the port terminal: to Fort-de-France, about €13; to Pointe du Bout, about €44. Between 8:00 p.m. and 6:00 a.m., there is a surcharge of 40 per-cent. **Cooperative Martinique Taxis** (0596-63-63-62). Collective taxis, eight-seat limousines with the sign TC, are less costly and are used widely by tourists, particularly those who speak some French. The collectives depart frequently from the main ter-minal, on the waterfront at Pointe Simon, to outly-

ing areas, discharging passengers en route. Public buses serve all parts of the island.

Roads and Rentals Martinique has some of the best roads in the Caribbean, although those over the mountainous interior are very winding. Essentially the network fans out from Fort-de-France and intersects with cross-island highways.

The Tourist Office has seven "Circuits Touris-tiques" for self-drive tours, which depart from Fort-de-France and vary in driving time from a half to a full day. They use one road on the outbound and a different one for the return, covering the north of the island in three circuits, the central in one, and the south in three. Each is named—North Caribbean, North Atlantic, and so on—with a color-coded map to match the route's road signs.

With a valid driver's license you can rent a car for up to twenty days. There are many car-rental companies, and most have French-made cars such as Peugeot, Citröen, and Renault. Those in Fort-de-France are **Avis** (42-11-00; www.avis .fr); **Budget** (30 rue Ernest Deproge; 70-22-75; www.budget-antilles.com); **Hertz** (51-01-01; www .hertzantilles.com). They are open weekdays 8:00 a.m. to noon and 2:30 to 5:00 or 5:30 p.m.; Satur-day to noon.

Bicycles and motorbikes can be rented from **Discount** (Pointe du Bout; 66-54-37) and **Funny** (80 rue Ernest Deproge, Fort-de-France; 63-33-05). The Regional Natural Park of Martinique in cooperation with local bicycle organizations has designed off-the-beaten-track biking itineraries. For information, call 70-54-88.

Ferry Service Fort-de-France is linked to Pointe du Bout, the main resort center, by frequent ferries that run daily from early morning until after midnight. Between Fort-de-France and Pointe du Bout costs €7 round-trip, adults, €4 children age two to eleven. In Fort-de-France all ferries (known locally as *vedettes*) depart the Quai d'Esnambuc, the pier at the foot of the town center.

Interisland Air Service See Fast Facts.

Emergency Numbers
Medical: 15.
La Meynard (Quartier La Meynard; 55-20-00) on the east side of Fort-de-France is one of the main hospitals. The Tourist Office can assist in locating English-speaking doctors.
Police: 17 or 63-00-00
Fire: 18

Shore Excursions

Any of the seven self-drive circuits designed by the Tourist Office could be made by taxi, and local tour companies offer some by motorcoach. Taxis charge $50 per hour for up to four passengers. The most popular are likely to be sold as shore excursions on your ship. Sites mentioned here are described later in the chapter.

To Saint-Pierre along the West Coast: 2.5 hours, US$125. The classic island tour runs north 18 miles along the Caribbean coast through picturesque fishing villages to Saint-Pierre, known as the "Paris of the West Indies" until 1902—when Mount Pelée erupted and turned it into the Pompeii of the New World. Return via the volcanic observatory to the Route de la Trace or **Leyritz Plantation, St. James Rum Distillery,** and **Balata Gardens.** The tour is made in the reverse direction.

To Trois-Ilets and La Pagerie: 3 hours, US$150. South of the capital, a westbound circuit follows the expressway on a wide swing around Fort-de-France Bay to Rivière-Salée, where a detour west leads to Trois-Ilets, Pointe du Bout, and the Caribbean coast beaches. Visit **Pagerie**

Museum and a fish barbecue at **Les Salines Beach.**

Martinique on Your Own

The pretty capital of Martinique stretches from the Bay of Fort-de-France to the foothills of the Pitons du Carbet, rising more than 3,500 feet in the background. A natural port and commercial center, Fort-de-France did not become the capital until 1902, after the old capital, Saint-Pierre, was buried under volcanic ash from Mount Pelée.

A Fort-de-France Walkabout

Fort-de-France is a delightful place to explore on foot. Its narrow streets, reminiscent of the French Quarter in New Orleans, are lined with pastel-colored houses and lacy wrought-iron balconies housing boutiques with fashions from Paris. The main business and shopping district is a 6-block area bounded by rue de la Liberté and rue de la République, from rue Victor Hugo to rue Perrinon—all to the west of La Savane.

La Savane (1) A large public square by the bay is the heart of the city, with spacious lawns shaded by royal palms, flamboyant, and other flowering trees. The houses, hotels, and cafes around the square are in buildings dating from the nineteenth century that help give the city its colonial character. The square, a good people-watching spot, serves both as a playground and promenade often used for parades and other events on special occasions and public holidays.

The park has a statue of Marie Josephe Rose Tascher de la Pagerie, better known in history as Napoleon's Josephine. The white Carrara-marble statue by Vital Dubray shows her in the flowing high-waisted dress of the First Empire and looking across the bay to Trois-Ilets, where she was born (looking, that is, before someone made off with her head). A relief on the base depicts Josephine's coronation. At the southeast end of the park, the seventeenth-century Fort Saint-Louis, surrounded by water on three sides, commands the harbor. Closed to visitors.

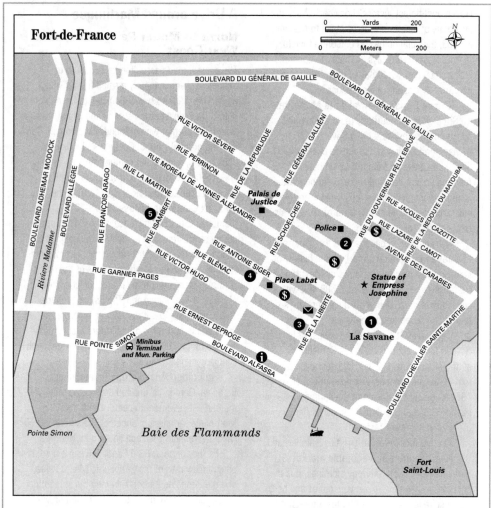

Fort-de-France

0 Yards 200
0 Meters 200

N

BOULEVARD DU GÉNÉRAL DE GAULLE
BOULEVARD DU GÉNÉRAL DE GAULLE

RUE VICTOR SEVERE
RUE PERRINON
RUE MOREAU DE JONNES ALEXANDRE
RUE LA MARTINE
RUE DE LA RÉPUBLIQUE
RUE GÉNÉRAL GALLIÉNI

BOULEVARD ADHEMAR MODOCK
BOULEVARD ALLÉGRE
RUE FRANÇOIS ARAGO
RUE ISAMBERT

Rivière Madame

Palais de Justice ■

RUE SCHOELCHER

Police ■

RUE DU GOUVERNEUR FÉLIX ÉBOUÉ
RUE JACQUES CAZOTTE
RUE LAZARE CARNOT
RUE DE LA REDOUTE DU MATOUBA

5

2 $

$

AVENUE DES CARABIES

RUE ANTOINE SIGER
RUE BLÉNAC
RUE VICTOR HUGO
RUE GARNIER PAGES

4

Place Labat ■

$

Statue of
★ Empress
Josephine

✉

RUE DE LA LIBERTÉ

3

1

RUE ERNEST DEPROGE

La Savane

RUE POINTE SIMON
🚌 Minibus
Terminal
and Mun. Parking

BOULEVARD ALFASSA

ℹ

BOULEVARD CHEVALIER SAINTE-MARTHE

Pointe Simon

Baie des Flammands

⛴

Fort
Saint-Louis

1. La Savane
2. Schoelcher Library
3. Musée Départemental de la Martinique
4. Cathédral St-Louis
5. Open-air vegetable market

The southwest corner also has a lively open-air market where you can find madras-costumed dolls, ceramics, shell figures, and wicker and straw products, as well as inexpensive costume jewelry and Haitian paintings. **Centre des Métiers d'Art,** west of the park beyond the Tourist Office, also has a small selection of local crafts, particularly bright patchwork tapestries, a Martinique specialty.

Schoelcher Library (2) On the northwest corner of La Savane is the city's architectural showpiece, the Schoelcher Library (rue de la Liberté; 72-45-55). A Romanesque-Byzantine gem built for the Paris Exposition of 1889, it was dismantled and shipped piece by piece to Fort-de-France, where it was reconstructed on the site of the old Hotel du Petit Gouvernement, where the Empress Josephine once resided. Named for the

French abolitionist Victor Schoelcher, who donated his library of nine thousand volumes to Martinique in 1883, the building has an elaborate fanciful facade. Hours: weekdays 8:30 a.m. to noon and 2:30 to 6:00 p.m.; Saturday to noon. Unfortunately, it's currently closed for renovations.

Musée Départemental de la Martinique (3) Situated in a beautifully restored colonial house on the west side of La Savane, the Archaeological Museum (9 rue de la Liberté; 71-57-05) has artifacts from pre-Columbian Amerindian cultures and representations of the island's everyday life and folklore in literature, art, music, clothing, and crafts. Unfortunately, it's currently closed for renovation.

Two companion galleries are the **Musée de l'Esclavage** (Route de Didier), on the history of slavery, and **Archival Services of Martinique** (Tartenson; rue St-John Perse; 63-88-46), with a collection of maps and engravings from the sixteenth and seventeenth centuries.

Cathedral St-Louis (4) Also west of La Savane, rue Blenac leads to the Cathédral St-Louis, on the site of previous churches destroyed by war or natural catastrophes. The present church, built in 1978 following the design of the earlier nineteenth-century church, is earthquakeproof. Its fine stained-glass windows were restored.

Another block west at the rues Isambert and Blenac is the **open-air vegetable market (5),** particularly lively on Saturday mornings. It is the best place to see the exotic vegetables and herbs that inspire island cooks to the taste treats of Creole cuisine.

Walking Tours: **Azimut Tourisme Urbain** (74 Route de la Folie, 97200 Fort-de-France; 60-16-59; fax: 63-05-46) has four walking excursions of Fort-de-France accompanied by multilingual guides. (Azimut also has a kiosk in the craft market at La Savane.) *Traces* is a 2.5-hour historic/architectural tour; *Verso* reveals the unknown heart of the city; *Ship-Shop* is a shopping/sightseeing excursion designed for cruise-ship passengers; and *Bet Afe* (Creole words for "firefly") is Fort-de-France-by-night with dinner and entertainment.

A Drive around Martinique

North to Mount Pelée along the West Coast

The coastal road passes the large suburb of Schoelcher—once merely a small fishing village named for the French abolitionist—to Case-Pilote, one of the oldest settlements on the island, named after a Carib chief who befriended the French. Carbet, the probable site of Columbus's landing in 1502, has an eighteenth-century church.

Nearby at Anse Turin, a village where Paul Gauguin lived for four months in 1887, is the **Gauguin Art Center and Museum** (78-22-66), a small memorial to the noted French painter. The contemporary structure is in a rustic setting designed to encompass the natural surroundings that inspired Gauguin and contains reproductions of the dozen pictures he painted on the island, including *Two Women of Martinique* and *The Bay of St-Pierre*. There are books about the painter, biographical information, and some of his letters. Hours: daily 10:00 a.m. to 5:00 p.m. Admission: about €4 adult; children younger than age eight, €1.

Habitation Anse Latouche, at Carbet's Botanical Garden, is situated among the ruins of the earliest seventeenth-century settlements of Martinique. Admission: about €5.50 adults, €2.50 children; younger than age seven admitted free.

Farther north at Fond Capot you can enjoy panoramic views of the Caribbean, Mount Pelée, and the Pitons du Carbet. All along the serpentine coast, roads climb inland to pretty mountain villages and trails on the Pitons du Carbet. The landscape and cool climate has earned it the name of Little Switzerland.

Saint-Pierre The once-fashionable capital, Saint-Pierre was totally devastated by the eruption of Mount Pelée on May 8, 1902, when a cloud of burning gas with temperatures higher than 3,600 degrees Fahrenheit, ash, and stones rained down onto it. In minutes the entire population of 30,000 perished, except for one survivor, a prisoner named Cyparis, who was protected by the walls of his underground cell. The town never recovered. Today Saint-Pierre is only a village.

The eruption was not a total surprise. An increase in Mount Pelée's volcanic activity had been observed for several years before the tragedy. In early April of 1902, tremors and steam were observed, and later in the month, ash fell over the mountain during five days of rumblings. In early May ash fell on the town itself for the first time. Nearby rivers and streams swelled, and birds fled. Yet no one heeded the warnings, least of all the municipal authorities, who were preparing for an election on May 8.

Saint-Pierre Museum (Musée Volcanologique; 78-15-16), created by American volcanologist Franck A. Perret, is a poignant memorial to the fatal eruption. A number of clocks on display—all stopped at the same time—mark the historic moment. Photographs and documents of the old town and exhibits of molten glass and twisted metal reveal its ferocity. Among the bizarre relics are petrified spaghetti, teapots fused with lava, and twisted musical instruments, melted by the heat. Hours: Monday to Friday 9:00 a.m. to noon and 3:00 to 5:00 p.m. Admission is about €2.50.

The **Cyparis Express,** known as the Little Train of Saint-Pierre, offers tours of the historic town. On weekdays the tour lasts one hour. Price is €8 adult, €2 children. Resting on the seafloor in Saint-Pierre Bay are twelve ships that were destroyed in the harbor at the time of Mount Pelée's eruption. Because the bones of survivors were found, the site is a memorial grave kept intact. Jacques Cousteau headed the team that researched the site and made a film of it.

Le Prêcheur North of Saint-Pierre the coastal road skirts the spectacular scenery of Mount Pelée's western flank. Le Prêcheur, one of the oldest villages on the island, is a base for climbing the mountain. Beyond Le Prêcheur a secondary road twists along the coast to Anse Céron, a beautiful beach with heavy surf and a tiny offshore island, La Perle, a dive site.

Inland, **Habitation Céron** (Anse Céron, Le Prêcheur; 52-94-53; habitation.ceron@wanadoo.fr), the manor house of a seventeenth-century sugar plantation in a beautiful park setting by a stream, has impressive remains of its ancient mill. Surrounded by fields where coffee, cocoa, tapioca, and bananas once flourished, the principal crop today is avocados. Céron, historically, is connected to Françoise d'Aubigue, the celebrated Madame de Maintenon, who secretly wed France's King Louis XIV. Individuals are welcome, and day trips for small groups can be organized by bus or boat from Fort-de-France. The outing includes a Creole luncheon, a swim, and a guided tour of the estate by the English-speaking owner, Madame Laurence des Grottes. The estate also offers horseback riding.

From Saint-Pierre two routes cross the island. One passes the **Observatoire du Morne des Cadets,** the observatory that monitors Mount Pelée's activity, and the village of Fond St-Denis, where the slopes on both sides of the road are covered with gardens. Fond St-Denis is a frequent winner of an annual, islandwide contest for the village with the most beautiful flowers. After Fond St-Denis, the cross-island highway joins the Route de la Trace.

North of Fort-de-France over the Pitons

Behind Fort-de-France are the Pitons du Carbet, traversed by the most scenic route on the island, Route de la Trace, known simply as the Trace, a central highland road that winds through the rain forests of the Regional Natural Park of Martinique (PNRM) to the foot of Mount Pelée. As the narrow road leaves Fort-de-France and snakes up the mountains, you can enjoy sweeping views of the city and the bay. In the distance on the north is **Sacre-Coeur de Balata,** a miniature of Montmartre in Paris, set, incongruously, in the tropical landscape of the Pitons.

Balata Botanical Gardens On a hillside at 1,475 feet, overlooking the capital, is a private botanical park created by its owner, an artist and landscape designer. It is centered by a restored Creole house furnished with antiques and has more than a thousand varieties of tropical plants. At the entrance are hedges of brilliant magenta bougainvillea, a flower that grows profusely in Martinique in many colors and named for Louis de Bougainville, who imported it from Brazil in 1768. Walkways through the gardens have lookouts that take advantage of the fabulous views of Fort-de-France and Cap Solomon; one path leads to a lily pond framed by a dramatic view of the Pitons. Along the way, look closely, and you probably will see hummingbirds flitting about the hibiscus.

Hours: daily 9:00 a.m. to 6:00 p.m. Admission: about €6.50 adult; €2.50 children age seven to eleven; signs and literature are in French. 64-48-73; fax: 64-73-40.

Absalon Mineral Springs On the west side of the Trace, the Absalon Mineral Springs are the starting place of trails through the central mountains. In the immediate vicinity of the springs is a loop trail of about three hours' hiking.

A mile north of the springs, the Trace reaches its highest altitude at 2,133 feet. A tunnel on the north side of the Pitons, Deux Choux, marks a junction of the Trace with D1, a major east-west artery. The road west runs through a deep gorge known as the Porte d'Enfer, or Gate of Hell, to Fond St-Denis and Saint-Pierre, on the coast.

Trace des Jésuites East of the Trace and the cross-island highway is the Jesuits' Trail (Trace des Jésuites), one of the most popular rain-forest hikes in Martinique. The signposted trail, maintained by the Forestry and Parks departments, starts less than a mile north of Deux Choux and passes through beautiful forest under a canopy of giant hardwoods, such as mahogany and gommier, typical of the Eastern Caribbean. The gommier, also known as white gum, has a tall, straight trunk whose sap the early Jesuit missionaries used in making incense—hence the trail's name. The Amerindians used the trunks of the gommier for their dugout canoes. Today a boat called gommiers, or gomye, used by local fishermen, derives from the tradition.

It is about an hour's walk to the Lorrain River, which is a pleasant spot for a picnic. The complete hike takes about three hours and is ideal if you have limited time or want a relatively easy hike to see a tropical rain forest up close. Scheduled hikes led by park guides are available.

Mount Pelée Towering over the northern part of Martinique from almost any location is cloud-capped Mount Pelée, the island's highest peak, at 4,584 feet. The outward signs of volcanic activity have subsided, but the volcano is still boiling and belching. The hike to the summit takes a strenuous five hours round-trip.

At Morne-Rouge you can turn west to Saint-Pierre and return to Fort-de-France via the Caribbean coast. Or turn east to continue to Grand'Rivière on the north coast.

Ajoupa-Bouillon The route east snakes through a beautiful part of the highlands under a canopy of tall tree ferns, bamboos, and palms to Ajoupa-Bouillon. It is a delightful mountain hamlet, dating from the seventeenth century, where flowering hedges and colorful gardens border the highway. A narrow dirt road and trail marked GORGE DE LA FALAISE leads to a trail to a narrow river canyon with a beautiful waterfall. Guide, €7 adult, €4 children age five to eleven.

Les Ombrages On the east side of Ajoupa-Bouillon is one of the island's most beautiful attractions, Les Ombrages—tropical gardens and rain-forest trail in a magnificent natural setting. Heliconia and other colorful flowers natural to the rain forest have been added along a signposted footpath, which follows the natural contours of the land, winding beside a brook under a canopy of enormous trees and stands of bamboo that reach more than 60 feet in height. The privately maintained park provides a map for the forty-five-minute self-guided hike. There is an admission fee of about €5.00 for adults, €2.50 for children five to eleven years. (53-31-90; fax: 53-32-04)

Basse-Pointe From Ajoupa-Bouillon the highway winds through green hillsides of banana, sugarcane, and pineapple plantations to Basse-Pointe, the main town on the northern Atlantic coast. Basse-Pointe (which means "low point") is situated at the base of windswept cliffs that plunge into the sea. They are covered with heavy foliage sheared by the alizés, or northeast winds, that blow off the Atlantic. Basse-Pointe has a high concentration of East Indians brought to Martinique to work the cane fields after slavery was abolished. There is a Hindu temple in the area.

Musée de Poupées Végétales (Plantation Leyritz; 78-53-92), created by resident artist Will Fenton, has a display of fifty or so elegantly dressed miniature dolls of celebrated women, such as Madame de Pompadour and Josephine Baker. The dolls are made from six hundred different natural fibers and plants. Hours: daily 8:00 a.m. to 5:00 p.m. Fee: about €5; children younger than age twelve admitted free with visit to the Leyritz gardens and plantation house, which dates from the eighteenth century.

Farther north, Macouba has one of the oldest

churches of the island, and from there the road weaves north through banana, coffee, and tobacco fields to Grand'Rivière, crossing some of the most spectacular scenery on the island. Big volcano rocks that have tumbled down the mountains from Mount Pelée rest at the edge of black-sand beaches, where huge white-capped waves crash against the vertical-sided cliffs carpeted with wind-sheared foliage.

Grand'Rivière On the isolated north coast is an old fishing village where time has stood still. Grand'Rivière is set against the deep green, wind-sheared cliffs of Mount Pelée under palms and giant breadfruit trees. Village fishermen returning with the day's catch must perform a feat of great skill by riding the swells and, with split-second timing, pulling their boat onto the beach to avoid being slammed against the rocks by the crashing waves. From Grand'Rivière a trail through the forests of Mount Pelée's northern flank rounds the coast.

East of Fort-de-France to the Atlantic Coast

Fort-de-France is separated on the south and east by a wide savanna, grazed by cattle and oxen and edged by a landscape of tumbling hills. The region is watered by the Blanche River and other streams that flow from the Pitons into the Lézarde River, Martinique's longest river, which empties into Fort-de-France Bay at Lamentin.

Robert, a fishing village on the Atlantic, is connected to Fort-de-France by an expressway. François is one of the prettiest spots on the east coast, with offshore islets and shallow, calm water; boat excursions are available. Two islets have plantation houses that have been converted into inns.

Caravelle Peninsula and Nature Reserve Jutting into the Atlantic directly east of Fort-de-France at La Trinité is Presqu'ile de la Caravelle, a peninsula with a nature reserve on the eastern half. A road of about 5 miles crosses the peninsula to the ruins of Château Dubuc, a seventeenth-century plantation house, where there are trails to the easternmost point of the peninsula, marked by a nineteenth-century lighthouse. The chateau museum is open weekdays 8:30 a.m. to 12:30 p.m. and 2:30 to 5:30 p.m. Admission: about €3 adults,

€1 children ages six to twelve. Call 58-09-00.

La Trinité, once one of the island's most prosperous towns, sits in the elbow of the Caravelle Peninsula on a sheltered bay with beaches for safe swimming, overlooking the rockbound north coast. Between Sainte-Marie and Marigot at Pointe Ténos, there is a wooded park with a picnic area and marked trails overlooking a beautiful bay with wild windswept scenery.

At Sainte-Marie, the **Rum Museum** at the St. James Distillery (69-30-02; 69-39-29) is set on a sugar plantation in an old Creole plantation house. It has displays of engravings, artifacts, and machinery on the history of sugar and rum production from 1765 to the present; visitors can sample St. James products. Hours: weekdays 9:00 a.m. to 5:30 p.m.; weekends 9:00 a.m. to 1:00 p.m. Recently added is a ride on the Plantation Train through the sugarcane and banana fields surrounding the distillery. Admission: €3 adult, €2 child.

Nearby, the **Banana Museum** (Sainte Marie, Habitation Limbe, 69-45-52; www.lemuseedela-banane.com) is the first of its kind in the Caribbean. Located on Habitation Limbe, an authentic seventeenth-century banana plantation, the exhibits cover the history, cultivation, and medicinal properties of the banana and its importance to the island's economy. Banana beverages and pastries are available. Admission: €7.50 adult, €4.00 children ages five to twelve. Hours: daily 9:00 a.m. to 5:00 p.m. Call 69-45-52.

Farther north, **Fonds Saint-Jacques** is one of the best-preserved estates on Martinique. Built by Dominican Fathers in 1658, it was the home from 1693 to 1705 of Père Labat, the French Dominican priest who was an explorer, architect, engineer, historian—and even warrior against the British. The chapel, windmill, and workshops remain, and there is a museum, **Musée du Père Labat.** Hours: daily 9:00 a.m. to noon. Admission is free; guided tours are available.

South of Fort-de-France along the Caribbean

The Caribbean coast south of the capital bulges with a peninsula that stretches west to Cap Solomon and is scalloped by pretty coves and white-sand beaches. Although there are good roads to the area, the quickest and most direct way to get there from Fort-de-France is the twenty-minute ferry ride across the bay to Pointe du Bout, a small finger of land with luxury hotels and a marina. Small cruise ships dock here occasionally, and boats sail from here daily on excursions down the coast for swimming and snorkeling. Some of Martinique's main attractions are only a few miles from Pointe du Bout.

Les Trois-llets On the bay, halfway between Pointe du Bout and Rivière-Salée, is the historic town of Les Trois-llets, one of the prettiest villages in Martinique. In its heyday the town prospered from the nine refineries that served the nearby sugar plantations. Much of that history has been preserved in nearby attractions.

Maison de la Canne (Pointe de la Vatable; 68-32-04). Opened in 1987, the House of Sugar is a modern museum in the ruins of an old distillery, with exceptionally good exhibits on sugar and rum in a park setting, labeled in French and English for a self-guided tour. Hours: daily except Monday 9:00 a.m. to 5:00 p.m. Admission: about €3.00 adults, €0.75 children ages five to twelve.

Pottery Center (Centre Artisasnal de la Poterie) East of Les Trois-llets a pottery-making center, established in the eighteenth century, was restored in 1987 to serve as an artisan's center. Using the rich terra-cotta–colored clay of the area, potters make a mixture of three types of clay, which they fashion on hand-thrown wheels into objects such as carafes, bowls, ashtrays, and copies of pre-Columbian artifacts.

La Pagerie South of Les Trois-llets is La Pagerie, the former sugar plantation where Empress Josephine was born. The remaining stone structures of the estate house now contain the **Musée de La Pagerie** (68-38-34; fax: 68-33-96), set in landscaped gardens. The museum has a collection of furniture (including the bed that Josephine slept in until her departure for France at age sixteen), portraits of her and of Napoleon, invitations to great balls in Paris, medals, bills attesting to her extravagance as the empress, and letters—notably a passionate one from the lovelorn Napoleon. Hours: daily except Monday from 9:00 a.m. to 5:30 p.m. Admission: about €5 adults, €2 children.

The Caribbean coast from Pointe du Bout south to Sainte-Anne has a series of pretty coves and beaches. Anse (or cove) Mitan is one of the island's main restaurant, bar, and water-sports centers.

The road winds south over hilly terrain to Les Anses d'Arlets, a large bay with mile-long, palm-shaded white-sand beaches cupped by Cap Solomon, the westernmost point of Martinique's Caribbean coast. Popular weekend yacht havens today, these idyllic coves inspired Paul Gauguin, who lived here in 1887. Grande Anse, a fishing village, has colorful gommiers, fishing boats made in the traditional manner of the Amerindian dugouts.

Diamond Rock Two miles off the south coast, at Diamond Bay, is a steep-sided volcanic rock jutting from the sea to 590 feet. The multisided rock has the shape of a cut gem, hence its name, Diamond Rock. It is the only known rock in history to be declared a warship. In the early nineteenth century, during the endless battles between Britain and France, the British landed two hundred sailors with cannons and arms on the rock, declaring it the HMS *Diamond Rock*. For eighteen months, they were able to hold the French at bay, bombarding any French vessel that came within range. When the French learned—through an "indiscretion"—that the British defenders had grown weary of their isolation, they devised an ingenious scheme to regain the rock. They loaded a boat with rum and caused it to run aground on the rock. As expected, the British garrison quickly consumed the rum, and the French took the rock without difficulty.

Two miles of tree-shaded beach stretch along the bay overlooking Diamond Rock, and at the eastern end is Le Diamant, one of the island's oldest villages. You can rent a boat to go to the rock, but the crossing is often rough. Diamond Bay is one of Martinique's main windsurfing locations. From Le Diamant you can return on the expressway to Fort-de-France, or continue south to Sainte-Luce, a fishing village and popular resort. The route south of Sainte-Luce to Sainte-Anne passes Le Marin, a picturesque old village with a large, yacht-filled marina.

Do not miss the Slave Memorial at Le Diamant, fifteen larger-than-life statues (each more than 8 feet tall) looking out to sea. They were erected in 1998 to commemorate the 150th anniversary of the abolition of slavery. The group immortalizes an incident in the nineteenth century when a ship carrying slaves sank off Martinique. Eighty-six of the captives were saved, mostly women and children, but their fate is unknown. Although the slave trade was outlawed in 1815 by the Congress of Vienna, it was still legal to own slaves in Martinique until 1848.

Sainte-Anne An idyllic colonial village with a tree-shaded square anchored by an eighteenth-century stone church, the popular resort of Sainte-Anne has good seafood restaurants and water-sports facilities, as well as a pretty beach. At the south tip of the island, **Grande Anse des Salines** is a mile-long crescent of powdery white sand shaded by coconut palms that bow to the sea. The beach is trimmed with almond and white pear trees and huge sea grape with bent, knotted trunks. A similar tree, the manchineel, is marked with bands of red paint as a warning: Its small green apples are poisonous. Do not sit under the tree, particularly while it is raining, because the water washes sap from the leaves and bark that can cause a rash and severe blisters. The Caribs used its sap to coat their arrowheads.

Shopping

French perfume, crystal, jewelry, sandals, leather goods, designer scarves, and liqueurs, as well as locally made dolls, patchwork tapestries, and other crafts and rums, are among the good buys. At the time of purchase, when you pay with traveler's checks or certain credit cards, shops selling duty-free items to tourists deduct the 20 percent tax on perfumes and other luxury items that local residents must pay. Downtown stores are open week-days from 8:30 a.m. to 6:00 p.m.; Saturday to noon. La Galeria (www.galeria.mq), one of the largest shopping centers in the Caribbean, is a five-minute drive from the airport and about twenty minutes from the port, depending on the traffic. Many of the best stores that were formally in the downtown area have moved to La Galeria (50-66-63; www.galleria.mq; galleria@galleria .mq). Another popular shopping area, particularly for tourists, is the Village Creole (www.village creole.com) at Pointe du Bout next to the casino. It

has mostly small, specialty shops—some funky, most expensive.

Art and Artists Galerie Artibijoux (89 rue Victor Hugo) specializes in Haitian painting and some local artists. It stocks a few French and English art books and has a small costume-jewelry section. The Gold Dolphin (7 boulevard Chevalier, Sainte-Marthe) is a gallery with an exposition salon. Paintings by native-born Martiniquais and other artists who live on the island are shown year-round in some hotels.

Caribbean Art Center (Savane Park) has colorful patchwork tapestries that are considered original works of art; the best carry such artists' names as Réné Corail and Balisier. Prices range from €135 and up. **Boutique Tam Tam** (60 rue Victor Hugo) has tasteful, inexpensive crafts from Haiti, South America, and Bali. **Artisanat and Poterie des Trois-Ilets** (Les Trois-Ilets; 68-18-01) is the shop of the Pottery Factory, where you can watch artisans at work.

China and Crystal Cadet Daniel (72 rue Antoine Siger) stocks Christofle silver, Limoges china, and crystal from Baccarat, Lalique, and others. Roger Albert (rue Victor Hugo) is another long-established emporium for crystal.

Clothing In fashion-conscious Martinique a new crop of boutiques blossoms each season. Here are a few that carry stylish pret-à-porter (ready-to-wear): **La Chamade** (38 rue Victor Hugo) and **Georgia** (56 rue Victor Hugo). For the hottest new look in sportswear from Paris and Côte d'Azur, try **Parenthése** (6 rue Schoelcher). **Samourai** (rue Antoine Siger) and **New Borsalino** (27 rue Blenac) are exclusive men's shops. The latter has handsome Italian-made linen sports shirts in a variety of fashion colors for US$75 to $100.

Mounia (rue Perrinon) carries top French designers including Claude Montana, Dorothée Bis, and Yves St. Laurent. It is owned by Mounia, a beautiful Martiniquaise who was one of the top models for St. Laurent. Shows presenting collections by young Martinique designers are held in Fort-de-France hotels in spring and fall. Among the prominent names are Yves Gérard, Daniel Rodap, and Gilbert Basson, whose ready-to-wear label is

Gigi, and Paul-Herve Elizabeth, who returned from Paris and opened his elegant **Le Showroom** in a Fort de France suburb.

The streets alongside the cathedral and open-air vegetable market are lined with shoe stores. Most carry reasonably priced shoes of mediocre quality for men and women, but a terrific buy are stylish, inexpensive summer sandals, averaging €13 to €25. Try **Sergio Valenti** (corner of rues Isambert and Blenac) and **Vankris** (46 rue Lamartine).

Jewelry Gerbe d'Or and L'Or et L'Argent sell pretty island-made 18-karat gold baubles, including the beaded collier chou, or "darling's necklace," the traditional ornament for the Creole costume. You can find great costume jewelry for low prices at **Cleopatre** (72 rue Victor Hugo) and in some of the stalls at the craft market (La Savane). **Cadet Daniel** carries the work of Emile Mothie, a top designer of both classic and modern Creole jewelry.

Leather and Luggage Roger Albert (rue Victor Hugo) has moved its leather goods department to the Galeria Shopping Center, but the best, most attractive selections can be found at **La Calèche** (41 rue Victor Hugo).

Liqueur and Wine Martinique rum is some of the Caribbean's best and least expensive—about €8 a fifth for light, €9 for dark; aged rums are higher and can go to €800 and more. **La Case à Rhum** (rue de la Liberté) has a good selection. The dozen or so members of Le Comité de Défense du Rhum welcome visitors at their distilleries from January to July to see the processing and sample their products.

Music Records and tapes from folk music to zouk, the French West Indies answer to calypso, are found at **Georges Debs, Hit Parade,** and other downtown shops, but prices are often higher than at record/video shops in New York.

Perfumes Martinique boasts that it has the lowest prices for French perfume in the Caribbean, but prices are now so standardized by French suppliers, I have found little difference. The best savings are to be found on quantities of an ounce or more. The exchange rate fluctuates, however, so check prices in advance at home to know how much of a bargain you can get. **Roger Albert** (rue Victor Hugo) has the largest selection but the least helpful staff.

Spices and Groceries Gourmet chefs can have a field day here buying spices in the open-air markets and pâté or canned quail at local supermarkets. **Galeries Lafayette,** a department store, sells shredders, graters, and other culinary collectibles. French wines and champagnes are sold in grocery stores. One of the best products is fruit preserved in rum, attractively packaged in glass jars and sold at the St. James Distillery in Sainte-Marie (69-30-02).

In the village of Bezaudin, near Sainte-Marie, **Ella,** a "boutique gourmande," specializes in exotic homegrown spices, preserves, and syrups. Another homemade delicacy, rillettes landaises au foie gras, is prepared at Habitation Durocher, a duck farm near Lamentin. At Christmas its specialty is a terrine de foie gras made with Armagnac and packaged in attractive crockery made by Pottery Center of Les Trois-Ilets.

Dining and Restaurants

Martinique has excellent restaurants, most offering traditional French and Creole cuisine. Fresh seafood is always on the menu, prepared in Creole style or in a more sophisticated French manner. Classic French dishes are often served with exotic tropical fruits and vegetables, such as guava, soursop, cassava, christophene, and breadfruit. Specialties vary according to the morning's catch. Typical are *soudons* (small clams), *z'habitants* or *cribiches* (freshwater crayfish), *lambi* (conch), *oursin* (sea urchin), and *langouste* (clawless Caribbean lobster). Prices for a three-course meal for one person, without wine, can be inexpensive (less than US$30) to moderate (US$30–$45) to expensive (US$45 and up). Most restaurants include tax and service charges in the menu prices. Restaurants close one day each week, but there is no uniformity about it. Check in advance, and also inquire about the use of credit cards.

Fort-de-France

La Belle Epoque (Route de Didier; 64-41-19). Nine tables on a spacious terrace of a pretty turn-of-the-twentieth-century house is the setting to enjoy light, creative dishes by chef Yves Coyac. Elegant and excellent. Open Tuesday to Saturday. Expensive.

La Cave à Vin (118 rue Victor Hugo; 70-33-02). Fine French cuisine along with excellent wines. Lunch and dinner daily except Sunday. Expensive.

La Plantation (Lamentin, near the airport; 50-16-08). The dining room of the eight-unit Martinique Cottages is one of Martinique's best restaurants for its French and Creole specialties. Its country garden setting, so near to town, is delightful. Expensive.

Le Mareyeur (183 Blvd de la Point des Nègres; 61-74-70). Lobster and other seafood specialties. Moderate.

South of Fort-de-France

Au Poisson d'Or (12 rue des Bougainvilliers, Anse Mitan; 66-01-80). Creole cuisine in attractive surroundings. Moderate.

La Langouste (by the ferry jetty, Plage de l'Anse Mitan; 66-04-99). Dine on seafood and Creole specialties on the veranda by the water. Moderately expensive.

Manoir de Beauregard (Sainte-Anne; 76-73-40). Several years ago, the old manor house/hotel was badly damaged by fire, but it has been restored and its restaurant, well-known for its good food, is back in business. Open daily for lunch and dinner. Moderately expensive.

North of Fort-de-France

Auberge de la Montagne Pelée (52-32-09). Dine on good French cuisine under the volcano, with a magnificent view of the Atlantic coast. Moderate.

Le Colibri (Morne-des-Esses; 69-91-95). Clotilde Palladino's small home is the setting of a family restaurant. English is limited, but the Creole food is so good and the atmosphere so pleasant you won't notice. Take one of the seven back terrace tables, relax, and enjoy the view and a ti punch while your meal is prepared to order. Phone ahead. Moderate.

Nightlife

Although popular as a base and departure port for chartered yachts, only one or two cruise ships use Martinique as a departure port. However, several ships arrive in the afternoon and remain for the evening, providing time for passengers to enjoy some early-evening nightlife. Fort-de-France has more than a half-dozen little night spots with zouk or jazz, in addition to the nightclubs and discos in the larger hotels. There are also several piano bars.

Les Grands Ballets de la Martinique, the island's leading folkloric troupe, performs at different hotels each night and often comes on board cruise ships to perform. Under the direction of Jean-Pierre Bonjour, the group is one of the best in the Caribbean. Dancers in traditional costume perform a spirited mazurka brought to the islands from the ballrooms of Europe; the exotic beguine, born in the French West Indies; and an erotic calenda, danced to the beat of an African drum. Shows often end with the traditional song of farewell in the French West Indies, "Adieu Foulard, Adieu Madras," a bittersweet melody that tells of a Creole girl's hopeless love for her French naval officer, who must sail away.

The **Casino Bateliere Plaza,** north of Fort-de-France near the Bateliere Hotel, is housed in a handsome building with a gaming room at one end and slot machines at the other. Hours: daily 9:00 p.m. to 3:00 a.m. Entrance for gaming room, about US$15. No fee for slots, which open at 11:00 a.m. The casino at **Trois-Ilets** (Pointe du Bout near the Village Creole) is open nightly. Photo identification is required. Dress code is casual. The legal gambling age is eighteen.

Sports

Beaches/Swimming The beaches south of Fort-de-France are white sand, while those of the north are mostly gray and black sand. The best beaches are found on the south Caribbean coast with the mile-long crest at Grand Anse des Salines, the standout. Swimming on the Atlantic coast is generally not recommended except at coves protected by coral reef, such as Cap Ferré. Public beaches do not have changing cabins or showers, and hotels normally charge nonguests for use of facilities. You won't find any nudist beaches here, but large hotels generally permit topless bathing.

Biking V T Tilt (Anse Mitan, Les Trois-Ilets; 66-01-01; cell: 60-69-64; www.vttilt.com) has a fleet of specialized bicycles and a nine-seat vehicle that can accommodate nine bicycles. The company organizes trips that highlight Martinique's diverse landscape, explore places not visited by most tourists, and offer contact with the Martiniquais. Tours with guide cost about €35–45 per person.

Boating Close to shore, Sunfish and Hobie Cats can be rented from hotel beach vendors. Yachts, bareboat or with crew, can be chartered for the day or week. Day-sailing excursions on large catamarans and schooners leave from Pointe du Bout and other marinas for Saint-Pierre in the north and Diamond Rock in the south, stopping for snorkeling and picnic; cost is about €90–115 with lobster lunch.

Martinique's irregular coastline and many coves have long made it a favorite of yachtsmen. Fort-de-France Bay is a popular departure point for yacht charters sailing to the Grenadines. Yacht-club members (showing membership cards) may use the facilities of the **Yacht Club de la Martinique** (Sainte-Marthe; 63-26-76). *A Cruising Guide to Martinique* is a French/English publication designed for experienced yachtsmen.

The Martinique Tourist Office can provide information on boat rental and charter companies in Fort-de-France, including trips on Martinique fishing yawls.

Canyoning An unusual experience—canyoning in the rain forest—awaits with **Aventures Tropical** (14 Chemin bois Thibault; 64-58-49; aventures-tropicales@wanadoo.fr). The company also offers kayaking and hiking.

Deep-Sea Fishing Deep-sea fishing must be arranged a day or two in advance. The most popular catches in Martinique waters are tuna, barracuda, dolphin, kingfish, and bonito. A full-day charter for up to six persons costs approximately €500 to €800. **Caribtours** (50-93-52) arranges sportfishing trips. For an unusual adventure, contact the **Association Coup de Senne** (phone/fax: 55-03-88) if you would like to fish in typical island manner with local fishermen.

Golf Golf de l'Impératrice Josephine (Les Trois-Ilets; 68-32-81; fax: 68-38-97; www.golf martinique.com), a five-minute drive from the Pointe du Bout ferry, is an 18-hole course (par 71) designed by Robert Trent Jones. Set on 150 landscaped acres of the rolling terrain overlooking the sea, it has a clubhouse, pro shop, and restaurant. Greens fees are about €60, cart about €40, and club rentals about €20. A David Leadbetter Golf Academy provides personalized training. It also has three tennis courts with night lights. Cruise ships often have golf packages for this course.

Hiking Thirty-one marked trails, most designed as self-guided hikes, laid out by the Regional Natural Park of Martinique (PNRM), National Forestry Office (ONF), and Le Club des Randonneurs (Hiking Club), are detailed (in French) in a guide, with maps, available from the Tourist Office. For information on trail conditions, call PNRM (73-19-30). Sunday hikes with PNRM guides are organized year-round on a published agenda. They are mainly intended to acquaint local people with the natural environment, but visitors are welcome (commentary is in French).

Guided hikes are also organized by **Aventures Tropicales** (75-24-24; aventures-tropicales@wanadoo.fr) and **Maison du Tourisme Vert** (9 boulevard General de Gaulle, Fort-de-France; 73-19-30).

Horseback Riding Ranch Jack (near Les Anses d'Arlets; 68-37-69), **Black Horse Ranch** (Les Trois-Ilets near La Pagerie; 68-37-80; fax: 68-40-87), and **Centre Equestre du Diamant** (Le Diamant; 76-29-41) offer riding excursions along scenic beach routes and through tropical hillsides. A one-hour ride costs about €25 per person; a half-day ride with guide, about €40–50 per person.

Kayaking There are several locations, but Belle Fontaine, about 10 miles north of Fort-de-France, is one of the best. Equipment is available there from **Aventures Tropicales** (64-58-49; www.adventures-tropicales.com; aventures-tropicales@wanadoo.fr), **Fun Kayak** (Ducos; 56-00-60), and **Madinina Tours** (70-65-25) in Fort-de-France; also **Caraibes Coast Kayak** (Sainte-Anne; phone/fax: 90-95-74) and **Kayaks du Robert** (Robert; 65-70-68).

Snorkeling/Scuba Diving Martinique is surrounded by reefs, but take the advice of local experts before snorkeling or diving on your own—many places have rough seas and tricky waters. There is a great variety of sea life, with walls, caves, and reefs with colorful sponges and corals.

In the south Pointe du Bout, Anse Mitan, the small bays around Les Anses d'Arlets, and Sainte-Anne offer super snorkeling, most directly from the beach. Area hotels have glass-bottom boats and equipment for rent. Les Anses d'Arlets is for novice divers, Diamond Rock for advanced ones.

North of Fort-de-France, Cap Enragé, near Case Pointe, is popular for walls and caves where there are large schools of soldierfish, triggerfish, and lobster. La Perle Island, north of Le Prêcheur, a site for experienced divers, has moray eels, lobsters, groupers, and other fish.

Dive operators are located in the main tourist centers and serve the hotels of a particular area. The Pointe du Bout operators have American and French licensed instructors and provide instruction for beginners. A list of operators is available from the tourist office.

Tennis Hotels with tennis facilities nearest the port are the Bakoua with two courts, on the south, and La Batelière, with six courts, north of the capital.

Windsurfing Beachfront hotels have windsurfing equipment, and many offer lessons. Beginners start in the calm coves of the Caribbean southwest coast; advanced ones find Diamond Bay challenging. Boards rent for about €14–18 per hour; a half-hour private lesson costs about €14–20. Martinique is a frequent venue for international windsurfing competition.

Festivals and Celebrations

Carnival is a five-day celebration when all business comes to a halt and the streets are filled with parades and revelers costumed as "red devils." Carnival continues to Ash Wednesday, when more devils, costumed in black and white, jam the streets for King Carnival's funeral procession and burial at La Savane.

In July the annual **Festival de Fort-de-France** is a monthlong celebration of the arts that attracts major names in theater, art, music, and dance from the Caribbean and around the world. The festival is organized by SERMAC (Service Municipal d'Action Culturelle, Place José-Marti; 71-66-25).

In the first week in December of alternating years, the **International Jazz Festival** (odd years) and **International Guitar Festival** (even years) attract international artists. The festivals are sponsored by the Centre Martiniquais d'Animation Culturelle (70-79-29).

The new **Atrium Cultural Center** (60-78-78), the premier facility in Martinique, offers a yearlong schedule of the performing arts and features international artists. Generally, performances are in the evening.

St. Lucia

Castries, Soufrière, Pigeon Point/Rodney Bay

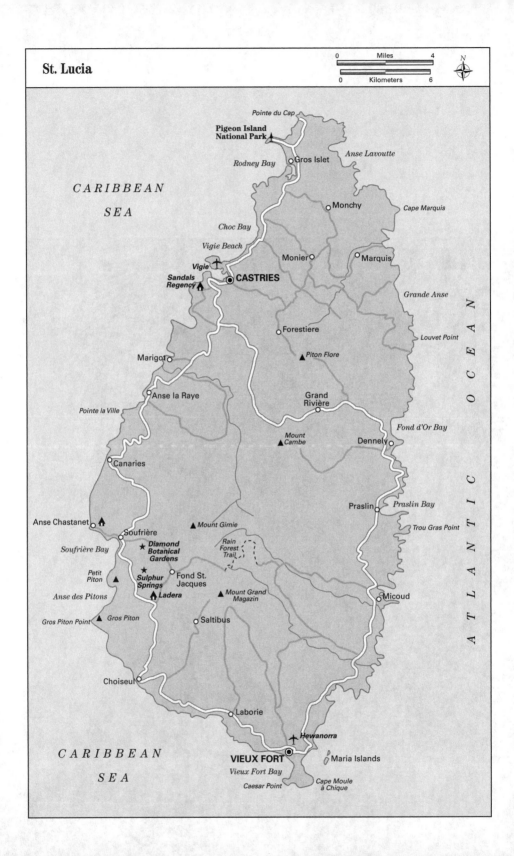

St. Lucia

Miles 0 — 4
Kilometers 0 — 6

N

Pointe du Cap

Pigeon Island National Park

Rodney Bay · Gros Islet

Anse Lavoutte

Cape Marquis

○ Monchy

CARIBBEAN SEA

Choc Bay

Vigie Beach

Vigie

● CASTRIES

Sandals Regency

Monier ○

○ Marquis

Grande Anse

● Forestiere

▲ *Piton Flore*

Marigot ○

○ Anse la Raye

Pointe la Ville

Grand Rivière

Louvet Point

Fond d'Or Bay

Mount Cambe ▲

Dennely ○

○ Canaries

A T L A N T I C   O C E A N

Praslin ○

Praslin Bay

Anse Chastanet ○

▲ *Mount Gimie*

Soufrière ○

★ **Diamond Botanical Gardens**

Rain Forest Trail

Trou Gras Point

Soufrière Bay

Petit Piton ▲

★ **Sulphur Springs**

○ Fond St. Jacques

▲ **Ladera**

▲ *Mount Grand Magazin*

Anse des Pitons

○ Micoud

Gros Piton Point ▲ *Gros Piton*

○ Saltibus

○ Choiseul

○ Laborie

✈ *Hewanorra*

VIEUX FORT ○

) *Maria Islands*

Vieux Fort Bay

CARIBBEAN SEA

Caesar Point

Cape Moule à Chique

The Bali Hai of the Caribbean

An island of surprises with scenic wonders on a grand scale, St. Lucia is a nature lover's dream, where every turn in the road—and there are many—reveals spectacular landscapes of lushly covered mountains and valleys colored with tropical fruits and flowers. Among its most celebrated natural attractions are a drive-in volcano and the ultimate postcard image of the tropics: the magnificent Pitons, sugarloaf twins that rise dramatically at the water's edge.

St. Lucia, mostly volcanic in origin, is the second largest of the Windward Islands. From the north, where the hills are up to about 1,640 feet, the terrain rises to a central mountain range with peaks more than 3,000 feet and quickly drops south to rolling hills and a coastal plain. In some places on the coast, cliffs rise almost directly from the sea, hiding tiny coves bathed by quiet Caribbean waters; in others rocky fingers bracket long stretches of white-sand beaches where Atlantic rollers wash the shores.

St. Lucia was inhabited by the Arawaks about A.D. 200 and the Caribs about A.D. 800. It has traditionally commemorated December 13, 1502, as the date of Columbus's discovery of the island on his fourth voyage. Some historians say Columbus was never there, however, and that it was Juan de la Cosa, Columbus's navigator, who actually made the discovery in 1499.

The first European colonists to arrive here were sixty-seven English settlers who were blown off course on their way to Guyana in 1605. They landed near Vieux Fort, on the south coast. Within a few weeks the Caribs had massacred most of them but allowed the nineteen survivors to leave the island in a canoe. Thirty years later the English tried again but failed. Then in 1650 two Frenchmen purchased St. Lucia, along with Martinique and Grenada, for the grand sum of £1,660 from the French West India Company, which had come to possess them. The following year French settlers arrived, and for the next 150 years the English and French fought over St. Lucia. By 1815, when the British finally won, St. Lucia had changed hands fourteen times.

Their constant presence in St. Lucia gave birth to a fascinating blend of English and French traditions, which, in turn, were overlaid by the African ones that came with the slaves who were imported to work the sugar plantations. Today the language, feasts, festivals, and cuisine of this richly textured society reflect the curious cultural mix.

After slavery was abolished in 1838, sugar production declined. Britain reorganized its colonies of St. Lucia, Barbados, Grenada, St. Vincent, and Tobago into one administrative unit, called the Windward Islands Government. During World War II the United States established a military base on the island and built an airport at Vieux Fort, which is now the international jetport. St. Lucia got its independence in 1979. Although sugar has long since been replaced by bananas as the main crop, St. Lucia remains an agricultural country. Over the last two decades tourism has gained steadily.

At a Glance

Antiquities	★
Architecture	★★
Art and artists	★★
Beaches	★★★
Colonial buildings	★★
Crafts	★★★★
Cuisine	★★★★
Culture	★★
Dining/Restaurants	★★★
Entertainment	★
Forts	★★★
History	★★★
Monuments	★
Museums	★
Nightlife	★★
Scenery	★★★★★
Shopping	★★★
Sightseeing	★★★★★
Sports	★★★★★
Transportation	★

Population: 150,000

Size: 27 miles long and 2 to 14 miles wide; 238 square miles.

Main Towns: Castries, Vieux Fort

Government: St. Lucia, a member of the British Commonwealth, has a parliamentary government with two chambers: the seventeen-member House of Assembly, whose members are elected for a five-year term, and a Senate, whose members are nominated. The prime minister is the leader of the major political party in the Assembly. The head of state is the governor-general, appointed by the queen on the advice of the prime minister.

Currency: Eastern Caribbean (EC) dollar. US$1.00 equals about EC$2.70. U.S. and Canadian dollars, traveler's checks, and most major credit cards are accepted by stores, restaurants, and hotels.

Departure Tax: EC$54 (US$22)

Language: English is the official language, but Creole, a French-based patois, is the common language; many people also speak French.

Public Holidays: January 1–2, New Year's holiday; February 22, Independence Day; Carnival; Good Friday; Easter Monday; May 1, Labour Day; late May/early June, Whit Monday; May 25, Corpus Christi; August 7, Emancipation Day; October 2, Thanksgiving; December 13, National Day; December 25, Christmas; December 26, Boxing Day.

Telephone Area Code: 758. From the United States, dial 758 plus 45, plus the five-digit local number. International direct-dial telephone, fax, and telex services are available at the cruise-ship terminal.

Airlines: St. Lucia has two international airports: George Charles (Vigie) Airport at Castries served by American Eagle from San Juan, Air Caraibes, and LIAT; and Hewanorra International at Vieux Fort for widebodied aircraft and served by Air Canada, Air Jamaica, American Airlines, Delta, and USAirways from North America. Martinique-based Take Air Lines, in an arrangement with Air Caraibes, has daily flights between Hewannora International and Martinique. The service is timed to connect with international flights arriving from the U.S. mainland.

By Sea: *Caribbean Express* (L'Express des Isles; www.lexpress desiles.net) offers high-speed ferry service to Martinique in one hour and twenty minutes. It also has service to Dominica and Guadeloupe. Cost: EC$235 adults age twenty-six and older, $170 adults younger than age twenty-six plus departure tax.

Information: www.stlucia.org

In the United States:
St. Lucia Tourist Board, 800 Second Avenue, New York, NY 10017; (212) 867-2950; (800) 456-3984; fax: (212) 297-2795; stluciatourism@aol.com or slutour@candw.lc.

In Canada:
St. Lucia Tourist Board, 65 Overlea Boulevard, Suite 250; Toronto, ON M4H 1P1; (416) 362-4242; fax: (416) 362-7832; sltbcanada@aol.com.

In Port:
St. Lucia Tourist Board, Pointe Séraphine, P.O. Box 221, Castries, St. Lucia, W.I.; (758) 452-4094; slutour@candw.lc.

St. Lucia National Trust, P.O. Box 525, Castries, St. Lucia, W.I.; (758) 452-5005; fax: (758) 453-2791; tours: (758) 453-7656; natrust@candw.lc.

St. Lucia gained attention when one of its native sons, poet and playwright Derek Walcott, won the Nobel Prize in literature in 1992 (he was the second Nobel Prize winner from St. Lucia, Sir Arthur Lewis having won for economics in 1979). More recently, St. Lucia was the film location for the Disney production *Pirates of the Caribbean.*

Budget Planning

In recent years St. Lucia has become an expensive island for tourists. Taxi and tour prices, particularly, seem to be out of line when compared to some other islands of the Eastern Caribbean. Shopping and restaurants (except those in deluxe hotels) are moderate. Restaurants may add a service charge or tax of about 10 percent to the bill.

Port Profile

Location/Embarkation The busy port of Castries, the capital, is located on the northwest coast overlooking a deep natural harbor with a narrow neck and sheltered by an amphitheater of green hills. In colonial days this anchorage was of immense strategic value. Today's cruise ships sail into the pretty harbor to an attractive facility, Pointe Séraphine (758-452-2036). It has berths for two cruise ships and a jetty for tenders, a shopping plaza with duty-free shops, and an outdoor cafe. The Tourist Board's information desk (758-452-7577; Soufrière, 758-454-7419) can arrange sports activities. Numerous tour and car-rental agencies, as well as taxi and minibus operators, also have desks where passengers can make arrangements. There is shuttle-bus service to town. Pointe Séraphine is close to Vigie Airport.

Some of the largest ships dock on the south side of the harbor at the commercial port. While this location is not as attractive as Pointe Séraphine, it has the merit of being directly at the foot of town, within walking distance of shops and Derek Walcott Square.

Cruise ships also stop at Soufrière, a small picturesque port at the foot of the Pitons on the southwest coast and at Rodney Bay, the main tourist center of the northern part of St. Lucia. The stop also enables passengers to visit Pigeon Island on the north side of Rodney Bay. Some ships stop in both ports.

Local Transportation Public transportation is operated privately rather than by the government. A popular (though not comfortable) mode of travel are jitneys (wooden-seat buses) that connect Castries with other towns and villages. They leave from the Castries Market on Jeremie Street in the town center.

Taxis are plentiful, but expensive. Rates are not fixed, but they are fairly standard. (Always agree on the fare with the driver before departure.) The one-way fare from Pointe Séraphine to Castries is US$10; from Castries south to Caribelle Batik, US$14; Hewanorra Airport, US$60 for up to four persons; and north to Rodney Bay Marina, US$16.

Roads and Rentals No roads encircle the island completely, but you can make a loop around the southern half, which has the main attractions. A new road that winds along the west coast from Castries to Soufrière offers some of the Caribbean's most spectacular scenery. Another new road, built in time for the Cricket World Cup in spring 2007, cuts north from the cross-island highway and gives access to the

northern part of St. Lucia without having to pass through Castries.

An alternative is a forty-five-minute motorboat trip, available daily from Castries to Soufrière, which provides wonderful views from the sea. South of Soufrière there is a west-coast road to Vieux Fort that takes about forty-five minutes.

You might enjoy your sightseeing more if you do not have to concentrate on those narrow, winding roads, particularly since driving in this former British colony is on the left. Local travel companies offer well-organized tours for small groups to the main attractions. Or, if you have others with whom to share costs, you could hire a taxi to tour. Be sure to set duration, in addition to the price, in advance. The cost is about US$180 per day for up to four people.

If you prefer to do your own driving, you will need a temporary driver's license, which can be arranged by your rental company. The cost is EC$54 (US$20). Car-rental companies in Castries include **Avis** (758-452-2700; www.avisstlucia.com); **Budget** (758-452-9887; www.budget-stlucia.com), which has Suzukis for US$50 and jeeps for US$80 per day with unlimited mileage and free pickup; and **Hertz** (758-452-0680; www.sunfuntoursltd .com). Rental cars cost US$55 and up per day plus insurance ranging from US$15 to $22 per day.

Emergency Numbers

Medical: Victoria Hospital in Castries has 24-hour emergency service. Dial the operator from any island location to be connected with the nearest medical facility or police.
Ambulance: 911
Police: (758) 452-2854

Shore Excursions

St. Lucia divides conveniently for touring into a southern circuit and a west/north-coast tour. The following tours may be offered as shore excursions by your cruise ship, but their length and cost will vary, depending on the port—Castries, Soufrière, or Rodney Bay—from which your tour commences.

Often Caribbean cruise ships northbound from the Panama Canal or Barbados stop at Soufrière

★ View of the Pitons from Ladera

★ Sailing into Soufrière

★ Hiking on the Rain Forest Trail

long enough to tender passengers to shore to pick up their tour and return overland. Meanwhile their ships sail on to Castries, where they dock, and the passengers on tours rejoin their ships there. The reverse procedure may be followed on southbound cruises.

Soufrière and Drive-in Volcano: 3 hours, US$100 round-trip for up to four persons in taxi; or US$30 per person for six hours, plus US$5 for air-conditioning. From Castries the tour drops south along the west coast to Soufrière, with views of the Pitons, visits the drive-in volcano, Diamond Falls, and returns to Castries via the east coast.

Day sail to Soufrière: Full-day, US$100. Sail down the west coast from Castries to Soufrière on a yacht or party boat, such as the Brig *Unicorn,* a miniature clipper ship (seen in the film *Pirates of the Caribbean*), with a stop for swimming and snorkeling.

After a city tour with stops at Walcott Square, Bagshaw's Art Studio, and views from Morne Fortune, the tour heads north to Pigeon Island National Park. Some tours allow time for a swim.

Rain Forest Walk: 5 hours, US$55 via east coast; full-day, US$85 via west coast from Castries (shorter and less expensive when originating from Soufrière). See later in this chapter for descriptions.

Flight-seeing: Contact **St. Lucia Helicopters** (758-453-6950; fax: 758-452-1553; www.stlucia helicopters.com).

Special Excursions: In the past few years, many new, interesting excursions have become available, some by jeep or horseback, that enable visitors to hike on new trails and visit working plantations and out-of-the-way villages. **Sunlink Tours** (758-452-8232; www.sunlinktours.com)

offers a large number of excursions, all described in an attractive four-color brochure. Sunlink is a division of St. Lucia Representative Services (758-456-9100). **St. Lucia Tours** (www.stlucia.com) has an extensive list of tours with descriptions, including some that are specifically designed for cruise-ship passengers. Also, **St. Lucia Naturalist's Society** (c/o St. Lucia National Trust; 758-452-5005; tours: 758-453-7656; natrust@candw.lc; www.slunatrust.org) conducts regular field trips.

Canopy Tour: See description in the section titled The East Coast.

Rhythm of Rum: Tours are available to the **Roseau Sugar Factory** (758-451-4258; fax: 758-451-4221; www.sludistillers.com/tour) in the Roseau Valley set amid a vast banana plantation, about twenty minutes from Castries, near Marigot Bay. The tour takes visitors through the history of rum and the distillery. There's a short video on the rum industry and a 3D display on sugarcane. You climb to a viewing platform to see the distilling columns, fermentation tanks, and a pot still, as the distillation process is explained. You can sample rums and liqueurs and make a purchase.

St. Lucia on Your Own

Castries dates from the mid-eighteenth century, but it is now a fairly new town, rebuilt in 1948 after a fire destroyed many of its historic homes and churches, including 80 percent of its old wooden houses.

A Castries Walkabout

Derek Walcott Square The square in the center of the city, formerly known as Columbus Square, was renamed in honor of St. Lucia's native son Derek Walcott, who won the 1992 Nobel Prize in literature. It is shaded by an enormous saman, or rain tree, said to have been planted by Governor Sir Dudley Hill in 1833. (Some sources claim the tree is more than three hundred years old.) The square, which was the Place d'Armes under the French, has a cenotaph, or monument, to the fallen of two world wars. On November 11, Remembrance Day, wreaths are laid in an official ceremony. Recently, the square was renovated and the bust of Derek

Walcott added, as well as the bust of Sir Arthur Lewis, the first Nobel Prize winner from St. Lucia, who won for economics in 1979.

On the east side is the **Cathedral of the Immaculate Conception,** one of the largest churches in the West Indies, built in 1897 and consecrated in 1931. It became a cathedral in 1957, when the Castries diocese was established. Facing the square on the south side, Brazil Street has several nineteenth-century buildings, the best known being a white-and-green Victorian building with gingerbread trim. It is one of the few colonial houses to have survived the 1948 fire. The building is said to have been a setting in Sinclair Lewis's *Arrowsmith,* which takes place on a fictitious

Caribbean island, "St. Huberts," that was, in reality, St. Lucia. Farther east at Brazil and Chisel Streets is the **Anglican Holy Trinity Church,** dating from the early nineteenth century. West of the square on Bourbon Street is the **Central Library,** built in 1925 by the Andrew Carnegie Foundation.

Castries Market One of the most interesting places in town is Castries Market (Jeremie Street), with a bright red facade and a clock over the entrance. Built in 1894 by engineers from Liverpool, the structure has had only minor repairs over the years and is virtually unchanged architecturally. The clean, well-organized market is a feast for the eyes as well as the table, with its colorfully dressed vendors selling an array of exotic fruits,

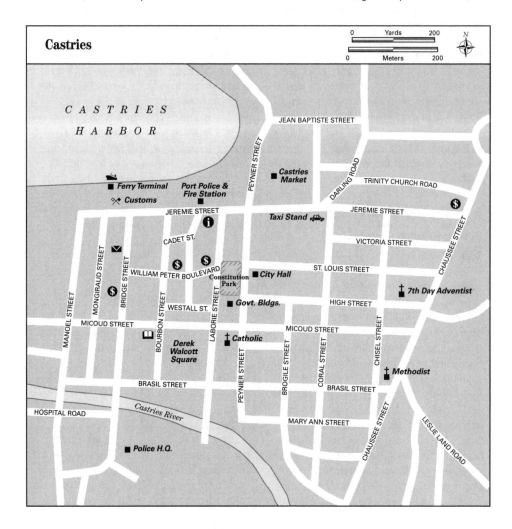

vegetables, and spices. Saturday is market day, when farmers bring their produce to sell, crowding into the market and spilling over into adjoining streets. There are also vendors selling kitchen and other useful items, such as brooms made of palm fronds, clay pots, and straw craft, often made by the person selling them.

Government House On the south side of town is an ornate Victorian mansion perched on the side of Morne Fortune (which means "hill of good fortune" and is often referred to locally simply as the Morne). It is the official residence of the governor-general. You will consider it your good fortune, too, if you are there to see a St. Lucia sunset.

Fort Charlotte Due to its strategic importance, the hills surrounding Castries harbor were rung with batteries and forts built by the French and British. The best preserved is Fort Charlotte, which crowns the summit of Morne Fortune at 853 feet. Fort Charlotte was begun by the French in 1764 as part of a plan to build Citadelle du Morne Fortune, but was completed by the British in 1794. Many of the original fortifications are still in place. The view from Morne Fortune takes in Castries and stretches from Pigeon Island on the north to the Pitons on the south.

A Drive around the Island

South to Soufrière

South of Morne Fortune the road winds around hairpin turns, up and over steep hills to the lower reaches of the beautiful Cul-de-Sac Valley, intensively green with vast banana plantations.

Marigot Bay At Marigot a corkscrew road drops down precipitously to Marigot Bay, a teardrop lagoon with one of the most beautiful settings in the Caribbean. At sunset the scene is exquisite. The bay, almost completely hidden by steep, heavily wooded hills, is a natural harbor that used to make a dandy hideout for pirate ships and warships in the olden days. In the past, the bay's tropical splendor was used frequently as a movie location. Today it is a popular anchorage for yachts and serves as an Eastern Caribbean base of the Moorings, one of the leading yachting companies in the Caribbean (its home base is Clearwater,

Florida. 888-952-8420; www.moorings.com). Recently, the bay has seen a great deal of development, much of which has taken away from its once gorgeous tropical setting.

Discovery at Marigot Bay (758-458-5300; www.discoveryatmarigotbay.com), a new large resort and villa development is operated by GLA Hotels. In addition to fifty-seven suites and sixty-seven luxury rooms, there are several restaurants, a spa, a sixty-berth marina, and a marina village with shops and water sports. The resort, we are sorry to say, is an intrusion on this once idyllic setting. It's called "progress" and it's enough to make you weep. Across from the resort on the north side of the bay is **The Rainforest Hideaway** (758-286-0511), a rustic, moderately priced restaurant at the water's edge serving very good Caribbean and Pacific Rim fusion cuisine.

After the Marigot turnoff, the main road crosses the Roseau River Valley and passes the fishing villages of Anse la Raye and Canaries, skirting deserted beaches framed by high rocky cliffs, some accessible only by boat. A small side road leads to the old fishing village of Anse la Raye, where you can tour **La Sikwi Sugar Museum** (758-452-6323), a cultural theater, a restored 40-foot water wheel, and botanical gardens by advance arrangements. There is a small admission fee. The serpentine route makes its way along the magnificently lush Duval Ravine and over the hills to the ridge overlooking Soufrière—one of the most fabulous views in the Caribbean. There, on the south side of Soufrière, the majestic peaks of the Pitons jut out of the sea.

The Pitons Petit Piton (2,438 feet), the northern peak, and Gros or Grand Piton (2,619 feet), on the south, are ancient volcanic spikes or extrusions. They rise from either side of a steep, wooded hillside that shelters a deep bay.

The view of the Pitons is magnificent from several hilltops above Soufrière. One of the best, particularly for photographs, is at Ladera, a hotel perched on a cliff south of Soufrière.

Of all the views, nothing beats the approach from the sea, an experience offered by several cruise ships and available on day sails from Castries. To sail into Soufrière Bay, watching the Pitons grow in their dimensions as the ship nears, and to anchor directly in front of them where their peaks tower a half-mile overhead is to enjoy one of the most extraordinary experiences in the world of travel—on par with seeing the pyramids of Egypt and the Taj Mahal. Here the sight is all the more fabulous because it is a natural phenomenon. If your arrival is timed for the late afternoon before sunset, the scene is more magical still as the peaks, bathed in the light of the setting sun, have an almost ethereal quality.

By the beach and on the hillsides between the Pitons is **Jalousie,** a resort that took its name from a former plantation on the site. The hotel was controversial from the day it opened because the resort marred one of the Caribbean's most magnificent natural sites. Nor is the controversy helped by **Bang Between the Pitons,** a beach bar/restaurant whose owner, Colin Tenant, was the original developer of Mustique, as well as Jalousie. Bang is a collection of quaint gingerbread houses that serve as bar, boutique, and restaurant offering local dishes. For hiking the Pitons, see the Sports section later in this chapter.

Soufrière The quaint little port of Soufrière has a spectacular setting at the foot of the Pitons with the mountains of the St. Lucia Rain Forest rising behind it. The town is the oldest settlement on St. Lucia and was an important center of trade and commerce under the French. At its prime in the late eighteenth century, there were as many as one hundred sugar and coffee plantations in the vicinity. During the French Revolution, which took as bloody a turn here as it did in France, members of the aristocracy were put to the guillotine erected in Soufrière's town square. Even after almost two centuries of British rule, the French legacy is still very apparent in the names of people and places, their speech, and to some extent, the architecture of the old town.

Although a great deal of the town's historic houses have been lost to fires and hurricanes over the centuries, there are enough Victorian and French colonial buildings around the main square to give the town character. Restoration of the historic center has been under way since 1989 and will take many years to complete.

Soufrière and southern St. Lucia are known for their wood craftsmen. The furnishings of the Tourist Bureau's visitor's center at the pier were created entirely by local craftsmen using cedar, mahogany, teak, and other local woods. In addition to its fabulous setting, Soufrière is surrounded by scenic wonders and is the gateway to some of St. Lucia's most interesting natural attractions.

Drive-In Volcano Southeast of Soufrière is the remnant of a volcanic crater, which St. Lucians have dubbed "the world's only drive-in volcano." Actually, a road does lead into an area of barren, grayish earth and gravel, with pools of boiling mud. At regular intervals clouds of steam, accompanied by hissing sounds, shoot 50 feet in the air, as sulfuric gases are released from the earth's inner core. Where water flows the rocks have been streaked with yellow, orange, green, purple, and brown, indicating the presence of sulfur, iron, copper, magnesium, and zinc washed from them by the water. A slight, but not offensive, sulfur odor can be detected. There is a small entrance fee, and a park guide must accompany visitors.

The Eastern Caribbean is replete with the remnants of volcanic craters, solfatara, and sulfur springs, but few are as showy and easy to visit as this spot in St. Lucia, and none are more fascinating.

Diamond Falls and Mineral Baths (758-459-7565; www.diamondstlucia; soufestate@candw .lc). After fresh rain water collects in the boiling crater, where it is saturated with minerals and heated to about 180 degrees Fahrenheit, it runs down the mountainside, dropping about 1,800 feet in six waterfalls. You can actually follow the course of the water on mountain trails, but an easier way to see at least one of the falls—lowest and prettiest of the six—is to visit the Diamond Falls and Mineral Baths, less than a mile east of Soufrière. From the entrance to the privately owned Diamond Waterfalls, a narrow bricked path bordered by hedges of tropical plants and shaded by stately palms and gigantic tree ferns leads to the bathhouse and the falls. The beautiful cascade roars out of dense tropical foliage down a mineral-streaked gorge into a stream that flows through the gardens to underground pipes and a series of pools, each a different temperature.

The baths were built originally in 1784 for the soldiers of Louis XVI. The French governor of St.

Lucia had had the water analyzed and found its curative properties to be similar to that of Aix-les-Bains in France. The baths were almost totally destroyed during the French Revolution, and in 1836 the British governor tried to restore them, but without success. Only in recent times, after restoration by their present owner, have the baths functioned again; a part of the original eighteenth-century baths is still in use. The water reputedly has curative powers for arthritis and rheumatism, but even if you do not take the baths, you will find the peaceful gardens a cool, refreshing respite for sun-weary travelers. There are separate fees for the entrance and use of the baths.

Anse Chastanet (758-459-7000; www.anse chastanet.com). On the north side of Soufrière is one of the most enchanting resorts in the Caribbean, with a setting so idyllic you will forgive, if not forget, the terrible road leading there. The road has the merit, however, of having a splendid view of Soufrière and the Pitons. Anse Chastanet is built along a precipitous hillside overlooking a lovely beach. Sunsets here must be seen to be believed. Some of the hotel's furnishings have been made by local wood craftsmen. Take particular notice of the columns of the dining terrace; they are made of local wood and beautifully carved with wildlife scenes by a local self-taught woodcarver, Lawrence Deligny. Anse Chastanet Beach fronts some of the best reefs in St. Lucia only 20 feet from shore. The hotel's dive facilities are open to nonguests for a fee.

St. Lucia Rain Forest The Central Forest Reserve, part of the 54,252 acres of forest and woodlands that cover St. Lucia, is a nature reserve of the central highlands, commonly called the St. Lucia Rain Forest. The Rain Forest Walk, a 7-mile trail, crosses the island through the reserve, between the villages of Mahaut on the east and Fond St. Jacques on the west. From the high ridge there are panoramic views of the central mountains, the Pitons, and Morne Gimie, the highest peak on the island (3,117 feet). Don't be surprised to see farmers emerge from the valleys and mountainsides carrying sacks of produce. Even the high mountains of St. Lucia have been lumbered and cultivated since plantation days.

The forest, with up to 150 inches of rain per year, has a great variety of ferns, bromeliads, wild orchids, anthuriums, and other rain-forest vegetation. Overhead the canopy is often so dense that little sunlight gets through. On the approach to the trail, the air is perfumed by pretty white flowers called wild orchids that grow profusely by the roadside. Bird life is abundant and includes three species of hummingbirds and the highly endangered St. Lucia green parrot, the national bird. Since 1979 St. Lucia has had a tough conservation program to save the parrot, bringing it back from the edge of extinction.

The Rain Forest Trail can be approached from either the east or west coasts, and many people hike straight from coast to coast. The hike is not difficult and takes 3.5 hours, but there are no facilities on or approaching the trail. Permission from the Forestry Department is needed. Forestry Department hikes with naturalists provide the most practical way to go.

Contact the Tourist Office in Soufrière or Anse Chastanet Hotel, which organizes hikes with one of the best naturalists in St. Lucia. The drive from Soufrière to Fond St. Jacques takes about thirty minutes, but the road to the top of the ridge and the trailhead is rutted and must be taken by jeep or on foot. The ridge road runs for about 2 miles to the signposted entrance of the reserve and the start of the trail. From here the hike to the eastern exit takes about 3.5 hours. If your time is limited, an alternative would be to hike for only an hour or two and return to waiting transportation at the western entrance. Wear comfortable walking shoes; trails are often muddy, and showers are frequent.

Morne Coubaril (758-459-7340; fax: 758-459-5759; coubaril@candw.lc) The 200-acre Morne Coubaril Estate, just outside Soufrière, is a working coconut and cocoa plantation and cultural center with costumed guides. It can be visited on foot or horseback. After many years of neglect the property, said to be the oldest estate in St. Lucia, has been restored and is meant to give a glimpse of daily life on a plantation in olden days. In addition to the restored manor house, there is a stable, **Trekkers,** with twenty horses, offering rides through the plantation and the surrounding countryside and to the Sulfur Springs. The estate also offers a two-hour hiking excursion to a waterfall with explanations of plants and herbs. For information: Contact Morne Coubaril or P.O. Box 308, Soufrière, St. Lucia.

To the South Coast

Choiseul The forty-five-minute drive to the southern end of the island passes through the fishing village of Choiseul, known as the arts-and-crafts center of St. Lucia, where many villagers work in their homes as wood carvers, potters, and straw weavers. Their products can be purchased at the **Choiseul Arts and Craft Centre** (758-459-3226), a teaching center, and **Victoria Arts and Crafts,** a roadside stand.

On the north side of town by the roadside, you will pass a rock with a clearly visible Amerindian petroglyph often pictured in St. Lucia brochures. After the fishing village of Laborie, the landscape is flat and dry, unlike most of the island.

Moule-à-Chique Peninsula Vieux Fort is the main town of the south and the site of the Hewanorra International Airport. Hewanorra, meaning "land of the iguana," was the original Arawak name for St. Lucia. Regrettably, very few iguana remain. On the tip of the island, a narrow finger of land, Moule-à-Chique Peninsula, ends in an 800-foot-high promontory overlooking the sea, where the Atlantic Ocean and the Caribbean Sea collide. The view takes in the dramatic seascape, with St. Vincent in the distance on the south and the Maria Islands on the east.

Coconut Bay Resort and Spa (www.coconut bayresortandspa.com), a 254-room, all-inclusive resort on the beach east of Vieux Fort and the airport, opened in March 2005. Those familiar with the area will remember it as the former site of the Club Med. Among the new resort's facilities are three swimming pools and a water park.

Maria Islands Nature Reserve At the end of the airport runway by Sables Bay is the Maria Islands Nature Centre and a half-mile offshore the two small islands of the Maria Islands Nature Reserve. Created in 1982 and operated by the National Trust, the reserve is home to a variety of wildlife including the Maria Islands ground lizard and the kouwes, a small, harmless, nocturnal snake said to be the rarest snake in the world. The

Maria Islands are also a bird refuge, and the waters around the islands are rich in marine life. A visit to the islands must be arranged with the National Trust, but you do not need permission to snorkel, which is best on the southwest side of Maria Major, the larger of the two islands.

The East Coast

The scenery along the east coast is lovely. In some parts there are dramatic rock formations created by pounding Atlantic waves, and other parts have deep bays with quiet waters. Savannes Bay, north of Vieux Fort, is a protected area, with the island's most extensive mangroves. Along this road, if you are lucky, you might see men making dugout canoes from the gommier tree in the same manner used by the Arawak and Carib Indians five hundred years ago.

Continuing en route to Dennery, the largest town on the east coast, the road passes through some of the island's most beautiful, lush scenery, with huge banana groves swooping down from rain-forested mountain peaks to the edge of the sea, where the Atlantic breaks against rocky fingers and barrier islets near the coast.

Mamiku Gardens (758-455-3729; fax: 758-452-9023; www.mamiku.com) The twenty-two-acre botanic gardens at Micoud (on the east coast, about a forty-five-minute drive from Castries) have been carved out of the woodlands surrounding the ruins of an eighteenth-century estate house that originally belonged to Baron de Micoud, a French governor of St. Lucia. Later, it served as a British military post and was destroyed during a battle between the British and the brigands, as slave freedom fighters were known.

The gardens, created by owner-designer Veronica Shingleton-Smith, whose family has owned the estate since 1906, have four distinct selections: **Mystic Garden,** approached by a pretty archway of hybrid gingers, has orchids and a variety of flowers and trees, as well as a small restaurant and souvenir shop in one of the plantation's old buildings. Another path meanders through stands of bay trees, a typical species throughout the estate, to the **Secret Garden,** reminiscent of an English summer garden with a great variety of sage, oleander, and flowering plants. Benches made by local craftsmen from local wood are placed in shady areas throughout the gardens for visitors to sit and enjoy the tranquil surroundings.

The **Woodland's Path** leads to **Grandpa's House,** an old wooden house, formerly used by the estate owners, with a typical Creole garden of fruit trees and herbs and spices used traditionally as natural remedies, as well as in cooking. **Bougainvillea Walk** connects with another path that zigzags up the mountainside to the high point of the estate. Benches along the way are conveniently placed and the foliage trimmed to enable visitors to enjoy panoramic views of the Atlantic coast and Praslin Island. At the summit there is a small wooded picnic area and the ruins of an eighteenth-century plantation house, which are off-limits to visitors until excavations are complete. The new Banana Walk has signs that explain banana cultivation.

Veronica's Garden and the Casse (a small stream), the fourth area, can be visited on the downhill return. The garden follows a watercourse with anthurium along the banks. A fifteen-year-old galba tree, one of the rare indigenous varieties on St. Lucia, can be seen here, along with a variety of other forest species found on the island. There are an estimated five hundred varieties of plants at Mamiku. Fragments of eighteenth-century pottery have also been excavated and are on exhibit at the Archeolo Ruin de Madamede Micoud. Accommodation for the handicapped has been made.

Praslin Bay Once a quiet fishing village, Praslin is now the site of a major billion-dollar resort and residential development, Le Paradis St. Lucia (www.leparadisstlucia.com), covering 554 acres along 2.5 miles of coastline and reefs facing Fregate Island. Phase One, to be completed by September 2008, includes a 232-room Westin hotel, the chain's first on St. Lucia; a spa with 25 treatment rooms; an 18-hole golf course designed by Greg Norman and managed by Troon Golf; conference facilities for up to 600 people; a casino, a specialty restaurant, lounge and bar, and 100 deluxe condo and residential units. Phase Two, with a projected completion date in 2009, will add a five-star boutique hotel, a marina and marina village, and more homes.

Offshore at Praslin Bay, Fregate Island is a nature preserve for the Magnificent Fregatebird that nests here. Through the St. Lucia National Trust, you can arrange to hike the mile-long nature trail circling the national park. In addition to Fregates, the island is home to some rare species of birds and boa constrictors. On a hillside above Praslin Bay is Fox Grove Inn, which some call the best-kept secret in St. Lucia for its restaurant where patrons enjoy a magnificent view of the coast and Frigate Islands. (See Dining section later in this chapter.)

Canopy Tour One of St. Lucia's newest attractions is an aerial tram providing a spectacular ride over the rain forest. The tour begins at Dennery at the foot of the rain forest–covered mountains. After instructions are given, participants gear up to swing on cable wires atop the forest to seven different platforms, directed by guides at each platform. Tours operate on Thursday at 1:00 p.m. and Saturday at 8:00 a.m. Cost is US$60. Tours on other days can be arranged. The tour company, **Palm Services Ltd.** (758-458-0908; mtnbikeslu@candw .lc; www.adventuretoursstlucia.com) recommends you take the tour with a group or, if on your own, via jeep, as the road to the site is not good.

Beyond Dennery, the east-coast road meets the cross-island highway with the Barre de L'isle on its south. About halfway along the road to Castries is the trailhead to the Barre de L'isle Rain Forest Trail that runs along the edge of the rain forest and climbs to the top of Morne la Combe, which towers 1,446 feet on the Barre de L'isle ridge. Those who have the stamina for the difficult, three-hour hike are rewarded with fabulous panoramic views west to the Roseau and Mabouya valleys; shorter hikes have their rewards, too. For information: 758-450-2231.

North to Pigeon Island

St. Lucia's main resorts and some of its best beaches lie along a stretch of coast between Castries and Rodney Bay. Some of the hotels are all-inclusive resorts whose sports and other facilities are available only to their guests; others accommodate day visitors. Inquire at the Tourist Information Desk at Pointe Séraphine.

Union Nature Trail A few miles inland from Sandals Halcyon Beach Hotel on Choc Beach, a nature center at Union has a forty-five-minute trail for a self-guided walk, an herb garden featuring bush remedies used in St. Lucia, and a small zoo of local wildlife, developed in 1987 by the Forestry Department (www.slumaffe.org) to acquaint children with their natural heritage and provide a convenient place to introduce these attractions to cruise passengers and other visitors. The trail is an easy graveled path through a dry forest where hikers are likely to see hummingbirds, warblers, and finches. There is a small admission fee.

Gros Islet Normally a quiet fishing village on the northwest coast, Gros Islet comes to life on Friday nights. A street fair and outdoor disco has become the island's biggest weekly event, with visitors joining residents in a "jump up," the street dancing of Carnival, which has come to mean a big party.

Rodney Bay As part of a resort development plan for northern St. Lucia, the causeway was built in 1971 to connect Pigeon Island to the mainland by closing the north end of Rodney Bay and creating a long sandy beach. Over the years, the land area has been expanded and the south end of the bay, with its yacht basin, has become a major resort area and nightlife center with bars, restaurants, shops, and hotels. In the last five years, the development has been extensive with many more restaurants and shops and the addition of **Bay Gardens Beach Resort** and **The Landings** directly on Reduit Beach, and **Coco Palm** at the edge of hip Rodney Bay Village, which bills itself as St. Lucia's answer to South Beach.

The Body Holiday at LeSport, an all-inclusive spa-resort and the first of its kind in the Caribbean, is only a short drive from Rodney Bay. It has several day passes: Lunch with a swim in the pool or at the beach from 12:30 to 3:00 p.m. costs US$31; half-day package from 10:00 a.m. to 6:00 p.m. includes lunch, drinks, activities, and afternoon tea for US$60; and full-day from 10:00 a.m. to midnight includes lunch and dinner, all beverages, sports, and exercise facilities (except scuba and water skiing) for US$118 per person. Spa treatments are separate.

Pigeon Island National Park Pigeon Island (www.slunatrust.org) has a long and colorful history going back to the Arawaks. It was used as a hideaway by pirates who preyed on merchant ships

in the sixteenth century and was a strategic British fort in the eighteenth century. It has been a quarantine station, whaling station, U.S. naval station, and even a hideaway of an English actress. After the causeway was constructed, the island was made into a park. It has trails leading to a promontory, now known as Pigeon Point, with the ruins of Fort Rodney and grandstand views of Rodney Bay and the north coast. The Pigeon Island Museum and Interpretive Centre is housed in the former British officer's mess, which was completely remodeled to the original 1808 plans. The history is brought to life in exhibits and an audiovisual reenactment of Rodney's famous victory over the French. The park is open daily from 9:30 a.m. to 4:30 p.m. There is a small admission charge.

Ships that stop at Rodney Bay often arrange a barbecue on the beach with water sports, a visit of the park, or tours of the northern part of St. Lucia.

Shopping

Pointe Séraphine has an attractive shopping complex set around a Spanish-style courtyard with dozens of shops selling duty-free goods. Selections are small, but prices are among the best in the Caribbean. You will find fine china, crystal, perfume, liquor, cigarettes, jewelry, and leather goods, as well as locally made fashions and crafts.

Although Pointe Séraphine is primarily for cruise-ship passengers, it is open to other visitors and to St. Lucia residents. Cruise passengers must show their cabin key, landing card, or passport to claim duty-free privileges; island residents pay duty on their purchases. Liquor and cigarettes are delivered to the ship. Store hours are Monday to Friday 8:30 a.m. to 12:30 p.m. and 1:30 to 4:30 p.m. and Saturday to 1:00 p.m., but the hours are usually extended when cruise ships are in port.

On the south side of the harbor, **La Place Carenage Shopping Plaza** is an attractive shopping complex in West Indian design, located at the foot of town and directly in front of the piers. It has many of the same shops as Pointe Séraphine, along with some unique attractions as well. The walk-in **Desmond Skeete Animation Centre,** said to be the only one of its kind in this area of the Caribbean, reproduces the island's colorful history through animation technology. The **Promenade of Artisans** is a showcase of local artisans, where visitors can browse and buy local art and crafts and watch some of the local artists at work on a range of pieces from self-portraits to pottery. **The Arcade of Indigenous Products** reflects St. Lucia's heritage, with cottage industry items such as jams, jellies, sauces, candy, and more, some to be sampled before buying.

There are other shopping centers: **Sunset Shopping Plaza** and **Rodney Bay Marina Shopping Complex.** Beach and street vendors who are licensed by the government and permitted to operate in certain areas usually sell coral and freshwater pearl jewelry. They can sometimes be overzealous, but normally they are good natured and will move on after a smile and a "no, thank you." Artists, often Rastafarians, sell their woodcarvings on the street or beach, too. And don't overlook the **Castries Market**—it's fun, even if you buy nothing.

Art and Artists Eudovic Art Studio (Goodlands, Castries; 758-452-2747; www.eudovicart .net; info@eudovicart.com). Joseph Eudovic is the dean of St. Lucia's wood sculptors and possibly the best of his style in the Caribbean. His works stand on an international level, with many being museum pieces. He carves from the trunks and limbs of local trees—gliricidia, red cedar, eucalyptus, and mahogany—allowing the natural wood to inspire the shape. Each piece is lyric with tension and energy that seem to be struggling to break out, but, at the same time, lines that flow with a calm and grace only a master craftsman can achieve. They evoke the movements of a ballet dancer, graceful and restrained but full of energy. Prices range from US$300 to $3,000 and up.

Eudovic is also a teacher, and other artists and students work at his studio. Visitors are welcome to view works in progress. The small shop also has beautiful trays, masks, and other gifts made from local woods and coconut. Eudovic's wife makes madras-costumed dolls that are whisk brooms and brushes. The fifteen-minute drive south of Castries is well worthwhile for serious art lovers.

Another well-known artist, Llewellyn Xavier, whose work is in the permanent collection of New York City's Museum of Modern Art, has his studio

at Silver Point, Cap Estate (Gros Islet; phone/fax: 758-450-9155). Call for an appointment. Xavier and his wife operate **Art and Antiques** (Point Seraphine; 451-4150), an art gallery selling fine art and antique maps and prints, silver, jewelry and collectibles. The gallery also holds auctions from time to time. In 2007, a 208-page retrospective of Xavier's work was published by Macmillan Caribbean as part of the latter's series on Caribbean artists. The book, *Llewellyn Xavier: His Life and Work*, covers the artist's forty-year creative journey.

In Castries, **Artsibit Gallery** (Brazil and Mongiraud Streets; 758-452-7865) carries local and Caribbean art, as well as posters and prints. The St. Lucia's Artists Association, organized in 1987 to help local artists and create a permanent national collection, exhibits its members' work here. Among the other galleries are **Modern Art Gallery** (Bois d'Orange Highway; 758-452-9079) and, at Rodney Bay, **Caribbean Art Gallery** (758-452-8071), **The Print Gallery** (758-458-0427), and **Zaka** (758-457-1504; www.zaka.cc), which specializes in masks and totems.

Books and Maps Sunshine Bookshop (Brazil Street; 758-458-0633; sunbooks@candw.lc) has the largest stock in town. **Noah's Arkade** (Pointe Séraphine) and gift shops at hotels usually carry tourist books on St. Lucia.

China and Crystal Harry Edwards Jewelers (Pointe Séraphine and La Place Carenage; 758-451-6799) has duty-free china and crystal.

Clothing and Accessories Several companies design and manufacture clothing in their factories in St. Lucia. **Pickwick & Co.** has the best of Britain in cashmere, china, and other goods. **Timbuktoo** (La Place Carenage) has a large selection of casual tropical wear.

Crafts and Souvenirs Batiks, hand-printed fabrics, and silkscreen designs are among the island's nicest products and are available as shirts, skirts, dresses, and a large variety of gifts. The oldest and most distinctive producer is **Bagshaws** (La Toc Road, La Place Carenage, and Pointe Séraphine), which has been in business more than three decades and still uses the colorful designs created by the late founder. The enterprise is now operated by daughter-in-law Alice Bagshaw, a dynamic American who has lived on the island most of her adult life. Bagshaws makes sportswear, leisure wear, and gift items with two dozen distinctive silkscreen designs on a variety of fabrics, including sea island cotton. The fabrics are designed, printed, and sold only in St. Lucia. Prices are reasonable. The retail shop is next to the art studio, where you can watch artisans at work.

Caribelle Batik (Old Victorian Road) has its workshop in a more-than-one-hundred-year-old house on the Morne, where you can watch artists at work making batik using antique Asian hot-wax methods on cotton. Their batik wall hangings, pareos (beach wraps), shirts, skirts, sundresses, evening wear, and more are sold at Sea Island Cotton (Rodney Bay), and other quality shops. Arts and Crafts Cooperative of St. Lucia (La Place Carenage) has a wide selection of gifts and souvenirs made in St. Lucia by different artisans.

The Noah's Arkade stores (Pointe Séraphine, Castries, and Rodney Bay) carry a large variety of crafts: wooden bowls, trays, and carvings; straw mats, baskets, and hats; ornamental shells and shell jewelry; and hammocks, as well as postcards and books on St. Lucia. Handicraft St. Lucie (Sunset Shopping Plaza) is an art gallery with souvenir items of red clay pottery, straw, and wood carvings.

Herbs and Spices Caribelle Batik (Pointe Plaza) stocks Sunny Caribbee Herbs and Spices. Erma of St. Lucia (Rodney Bay Marina) has local products, perfumes and spices from Grenada, and unusual crafts that owner Erma Compton uncovers in her travels throughout the Caribbean and South America.

Jewelry Colombian Emeralds (Pointe Séraphine and La Place Carenage) with stores throughout the Caribbean, has fully guaranteed sapphires, rubies, diamonds, and emeralds. Y. de Lima (William Peter Boulevard) is one of the top stores for fine jewelry, also selling cameras and film. Touch of Class (Pointe Séraphine) has jewelry and electronics.

Liquor and Wines Rums made in St. Lucia are Denros Bounty, Admiral Rodney, and Five Blondes. The latter is particularly popular with vis-

itors as souvenirs for its label, which pictures . . . yes, five blondes. (Presumably the name originally referred to blond or light rum.) Stores at Pointe Séraphine are well stocked and competitively priced; some are even lower than in St. Thomas.

Perfumes and Cosmetics Images (Pointe Séraphine and La Place Carenage) has the best selection of perfume and cosmetics. Perfumes are made locally by Caribbean Perfumes (Vigie Cove; 758-453-7249; caribperfumes@candw.lc) and come in three floral scents.

Dining and Restaurants

Dining choices in St. Lucia range from elegant restaurants in the hills overlooking Castries to rustic seafood ones in villages by the sea. All have the personal stamp of their owners and reflect the island's diverse makeup. European and American fare is readily available, but it is the island's Creole cuisine that deserves your attention. Be sure to sample such dishes as callaloo soup, stuffed breadfruit, banana bread, fried plantain, pumpkin soup, flying fish, and stuffed crab backs. Prices are not high, except in deluxe restaurants. Generally, lunch per person in an inexpensive restaurant will be less than US$15; moderate, US$15 to $25; and expensive, more than US$25. Most restaurants are open daily; some close on Sunday, others close on Monday or Tuesday. Check in advance.

Castries and Environs

Buzz Seafood and Grill (Rodney Bay; 758-458-0450; www.buzzstlucia.com). From the outset, Buzz got lots of buzz because its owner is Pat Bowden, a former owner of San Antonio, the island's trendsetter for many years. Together with Chef Marie, they have created an eclectic, modern, and internationally inspired menu tested from several of their other ventures. You can try such house specialties as spicy lobster and crab cakes, seared tuna, homemade spinach ravioli, and parmesan crusted chicken, along with steaks, fresh fish, and local selection. But unless your ship remains in port for an evening or calls on Sunday during the winter season in time for brunch, you cannot learn what all the buzz is about because Buzz is only open for dinner. Expensive.

The Coal Pot (Vigie Marina; 758-452-5566; www.coalpotrestaurant.com) is a long-established open-air restaurant at the water's edge. Owners Xavier, the chef, and Michelle Elliot, who is an artist and acts as hostess, specialize in New World cuisine, a fusion of fresh Caribbean ingredients with French cooking. Fresh local fish is on the menu for lunch and dinner. The Coal Pot's Caribbean ambience is enhanced by the colorful Caribbean art by Michelle decorating the wood and stone walls, and on moonlit nights the restaurant's ten tables are set under the stars. Moderately expensive.

The Green Parrot (Morne Fortune; 758-452-3399; www.greenparrothotel.com). A local favorite with a grand view of Castries offers West Indian dishes, along with steaks, watched over by Chef Harry, a St. Lucian who trained at London's prestigious Claridges Hotel. There is also a pool and darts room with an English pub atmosphere. Expensive. (Harry has a beach bar/restaurant for groups of ten or more at Anse Jambette, a popular stop for day-sailing excursions south of Castries. Call ahead.)

The Edge Restaurant Bar and Sushi (Harmony Suites Hotel, Rodney Bay; 758-450-EDGE; www.edge-restaurant.com) is one of the best restaurants in St. Lucia due to award-winning Swedish chef Bobo Bergstrom's unusual Eurobbean fusion cuisine. The gourmet fare is served in a stunning, torch-lit waterfront setting, and is also home to the island's first sushi bar. Open daily from 8:00 a.m. to 11:00 p.m. Reservations are recommended; closed September. Moderately expensive.

Ti Bananne Caribbean Bistro & Bar (Coco Palm Resort, Rodney Bay; 758-456-2800; www .coco-resorts.com) Chef Richardson Skinner combines Trinidadian and French cuisine amid colorful murals in a relaxed and distinctly St. Lucian ambience. Moderate.

Jacques Waterfront Dining (Vigie Cove; 758-458-1900; www.froggiejacques.com). Open-air waterside dining on seafood and local specialties in a pleasant, casual setting. Moderately expensive.

The Lime (Rodney Bay; 758-452-0761). Popular at lunch for rôti and light fare, it is a favorite for "limin'" at happy hour and in the evening for the Rodney Bay crowd. Moderate.

Oceana Seafood Restaurant (Castries; 758-456-0300; fax: 758-453-2102). Great food; a local favorite. Inexpensive.

Spinnakers Beach Bar and Carvery (Rodney Bay; 758-452-8491; fax: 758-458-0301). On the beach and very popular, the food is always fresh. Great atmosphere, particularly at lunchtime. Moderate.

Tao (LeSport; 758-450-8551; www.bodyholiday .com). The gourmet restaurant of the spa-resort is one of the best, if not the best restaurant, in the Caribbean. The Pacific Rim cuisine created by the young Filipino chef is extraordinary and very innovative. Tao is a nonsmoking restaurant and the dress code is resort elegant. Expensive.

Soufrière to the East Coast

Trou au Diable Restaurant (Anse Chastanet Resort; 758-459-7000; ansechastanet@candw.lc). Situated directly on the beach just north of Soufrière, the open-air restaurant of Anse Chastanet resort is popular with swimmers, divers, and snorkelers who enjoy the reefs only 20 yards offshore. The menu has a choice of salads, sandwiches, seafood, and other dishes. A Caribbean Buffet is served on Tuesday evening and a special East Indian/Caribbean menu the rest of the week. Best reached by water taxi from Soufrière. Moderate.

Dasheene Restaurant & Bar (Ladera Resort; 866-290-0978; 758-459-7323; www.ladera.com). Set on a mountainside 1,000 feet above sea level with a spectacular view of the Pitons, the restaurant is Ladera's casual, yet sophisticated, dining room, open seven days a week, and serving light cuisine that combines Caribbean Creole fare with modern American cooking. Moderately expensive.

Hummingbird Beach Resort (758-459-7232). Drinks and lunch with a view of the Pitons and a pool for a cool swim makes this an easy place to linger. The menu has seafood and Creole specialties. Expensive.

Whispering Palms (Fox Grove Inn, Mon Repos; 758-455-3271; www.foxgroveinn@candw.lc) on a hillside above Praslin Bay on the east coast is probably the best-kept secret in St. Lucia for its fine restaurant with a wonderful view. The friendly owner/chef Franz Louis-Fernand, who has thirty-five years experience at restaurants in Europe and is aided by wife Esther, serves fish and lobster bought fresh from local fishermen and vegetables, fruits and herbs from local farms and the market in the village. The menu includes meat and poultry selections, too. Moderate.

Nightlife

St. Lucia is low-key, with nightlife revolving around hotels and a few restaurants with light entertainment. There are romantic cocktail and moonlight cruises, and everyone on the island heads for Gros Islet on Friday night.

Rodney Bay has become the center of night action with bars and restaurants, such as **Indies, Lime, Upper Level,** and **Mojitos,** offering live musical entertainment on different nights of the week. For information, check *Tropical Traveler,* a free tourist newspaper that lists nighttime entertainment daily for the week. **The Derek Walcott Theatre** (at the Great House) offers music, dance, and drama productions in a small, open-air theater located in the ruins of the old Cap Estate House. An annual performance by the Trinidad Theatre Workshop and Sunday brunch productions are among the theater's highlights.

Sports

Beaches/Swimming St. Lucia claims to have more than 120 beaches, many accessible only by boat. The beaches closest to Castries are north of the port and easy to reach by bus or taxi. The prettiest ones are in the secluded coves south of the capital, reached by motorboat in about thirty minutes.

Biking Bike St. Lucia (758-451-2453; www.junglereefadventures; junglereef@candw.lc), developed by Anse Chastanet resort, is St. Lucia's only biking-in-the-forest facility, located adjacent to the resort on Anse Mamin, site of one of St. Lucia's oldest plantations. The prepared trails, designed to accommodate both first-time and experienced riders, weave through the plantation grounds, deep into the tropical jungle. There is also a skills-training area and a number of instructors who provide an introductory class or refresher

course. The trails also offer a window into history as participants pedal by the eighteenth-century French-colonial ruins of a sugar mill, an old church, a freshwater reservoir, and more. There are hundreds of fruit trees such as mango, coconut, banana, guava, cocoa, and citrus, as well as wild orchids, birds, and an old-fashioned river swimming hole. The Jungle Biking Adventure costs US$95 per person and includes equipment rentals, water bottle, and introductory lesson; round-trip transfers by water taxi and lunch served at the plantation. Another company is **Cycle St. Lucia** (Rodney Bay; 758-458-0908; www.cyclestlucia.com).

Boating Sailing is one of St. Lucia's most popular sports, where yachtsmen can enjoy safe harbors on the island's deeply indented coastline. There are three boating centers. Marigot Bay is the base for **The Moorings St. Lucia** (758-451-4357; www.moorings.com), a major Caribbean boat charterer. It offers day-sailing from Marigot Bay and has a dive shop and water-sports center. Rodney Bay Marina (www.rodneybaymarina.com) at Gros Islet has **Sunsail Stevens Yachts** (758-452-8648), one of the oldest yachting specialists in the Eastern Caribbean, and **Destination Saint Lucia Yachting** (758-452-8531; www.dsl-yachting.com). Both offer day sails and longer charters.

Castries is the base for large party boats that sail on picnic and snorkeling excursions, such as the Brig *Unicorn* (758-456-9100), US$100, which departs about 8:30 a.m. and returns at 4:30 p.m. Soufrière is the most popular destination; Anse Jambette is also popular.

Endless Summer Cruises (Castries; 758-450-8651; fax: 758-452-0659; www.stluciaboattours.com) offers full-day catamaran cruises from Rodney Bay to Soufrière with tours, buffet lunch on board, and stops for swimming and snorkeling at secluded beaches as well as at Marigot Bay, US$90. Champagne sunset cruises, US$50.

Deep-Sea Fishing Fully equipped sportfishing boats are available for half-day and full-day charters. Contact **Captain Mike's Sport Fishing & Pleasure Cruises** (Vigie Marina; 758-452-7044; www.captmikes.com), **Mako Water Sports** (Rodney Bay Marina; 758-452-0412; makosportfishing@yahoo.com), or **Hackshaws Boat Charter &**

Sport Fishing (Castries; 758-453-0553; www
.hackshaws.com). The main seasons are December
to June for open-sea species, such as wahoo, sailfish, tuna, and kingfish, and July to December,
when the catch is best closer to shore. Fishing is
an old tradition and a way of life for many St.
Lucians.

Dolphin and Whale Watching St. Lucian
waters are home to resident and migrating dolphins and whales. The sight of these mammals in
their natural habitats is surely an unforgettable
experience. The claim is made that twenty-five
varieties have been spotted in St. Lucia waters.
Most frequent are Sperm, Pilot, and Humpback
whales and on rare occasion the Orca (Killer
Whale). On occasion, large pods of Dolphin, up to
150 at a time are sighted. Contact **Hackshaw's
Boat Charters** (758-453-0553 or 452-3909; www
.hackshaws.com; hackshawc@candw.lc), which
operates four boats—three for sportfishing and a
custom-designed whale-watching boat. Hackshaw's is a member of the St. Lucia Whale Watching Association and follows the international
whale-watching rules for the safety of the mammals. Excursions are *Whale Watch Safari*, departing from Vigie Marina in Castries at 8:00 a.m.,
returning at noon for US$40 per person, and
another one that includes lunch and swimming for
US$50. Private whale watching also can be
arranged. **Sunlink Tours** (758-456-9100) arranges
excursions upon request; US$70 adult, $45 child.

Golf The 9-hole golf course at **Sandals Regency
Golf Resort & Spa at La Toc** (758-452-3081),
about 5 miles from the port, is reserved for its
guests and available to others only by prior
arrangement. **The St. Lucia Golf & Country Club**
(Cap Estates; 758-450-8523; www.stluciagolf.com),
about 1 mile from Rodney Bay, is an 18-hole layout.
Greens fees are US$75 to $90 for 9 holes, US$95
to $125 for 18 holes depending on the season,
US$20 for golf club rentals. The course is fully irri-
gated with an automatic system. The Cap Grill is
open daily for breakfast and lunch and Thursday to
Saturday for dinner. In the next several years, two
more 18-hole championship golf courses should be
completed: Pointe at Cas en Bas, designed by Jack
Nicklaus, is part of a resort development, and Le

Paradis, designed by Greg Norman, will anchor a
major development on the east coast.

Hiking The central mountains, particularly the
short trail of the Barre de l'Isle, St. Lucia Rain Forest Trail, and Union Nature Trail, are the most popular for hiking. (See previous sections in this
chapter for details.) These hikes do not require a
great deal of experience or endurance. Wear comfortable shoes, and keep cameras in waterproof
covers. Experienced hikers are allowed to hike the
Gros Piton, a strenuous 2,619 feet up, but they
should have permission of the Forest and Lands
Department (758-450-2078/2231; deptforest@
slumaffe.org) and a knowledgeable guide, which
can be arranged by contacting the Pitons Tour
Guide Association (758-459-9748); maximum three
hikers per guide.

Horseback Riding St. Lucia can be explored
by horseback on trips organized by **Trim's Riding
Stable** (758-452-8273) at Cap Estate. The stable
offers picnic rides along the Atlantic coast and trail
rides overlooking the Caribbean and horse-and-car-
riage tours of Pigeon Point. **International Riding
Stables** (Gros Islet; 758-452-8139) offers a beach
picnic to Cas en Bas with time for swimming. In
the Soufrière area, **Trekkers** (Morne Coubaril
Estate; 758-459-7340) has similar excursions.

Kayaking A fairly new sport in St. Lucia, kayaking excursions are available from **Jungle Reef
Adventures** (P.O. Box 7000, Soufriere; 758-459-
7755; junglereef@candw.lc). The company also
offers mountain biking and Scuba diving excursions.

Snorkeling/Scuba Diving Although St. Lucia
has lovely, unspoiled reefs with abundant fish
along 24 miles of its Caribbean coast, it is a newcomer to diving: Many sites are yet to be explored.
Some of its best reefs with spectacular coral and
marine life are found at Anse Cochon and in the
few miles between Anse Chastanet Beach and the
Pitons. Here, many dive sites are found in calm and
protected waters near the shore; some in only 20
feet of water are close enough to reach directly
from the beach. Indeed, the proximity to shore of
shallow-water reefs makes St. Lucia a good place
to learn to snorkel and dive.

The Pitons drop as deep into the water as they rise above the ground, and their walls offer an exciting and unusual experience for divers, who see huge sponges, underwater caves, and a great variety of fish.

Scuba St. Lucia (Anse Chastanet; 758-459-7755; www.scubastlucia.com) is the leading dive shop and offers beach and boat dives four times daily. It has resort courses for beginners, certification courses, night dives, underwater photography, and others. Facilities include changing rooms, freshwater showers, beach bar/restaurant, and boutiques. The Moorings St. Lucia (Marigot Bay) and Windjammer Landing, north of Castries, have dive operations as well.

Soufrière Marine Management was founded in 1995 to protect and properly manage 7 miles of St. Lucia's most spectacular underwater coastline in the Soufrière area. Rather than simply impose measures to safeguard the marine environment, the SMMA project over a period of three years consulted every community member—fishermen, taxi drivers, dive operators, community groups, restaurateurs, and church organizations—before legislation was implemented. As a result, the coastline was carefully zoned to fill the needs of all users, establishing fishing priority areas, marine reserves, mooring areas, recreational sites, and multiuse zones. Since the SMMA was established, the reefs have started to regenerate, and fish stocks in certain areas have tripled. The SMMA has been recognized for its work with several awards and is seen as the blueprint for marine management to be set up around Anse la Raye and Canaries, and ultimately to create an umbrella organization to manage the entire St. Lucian coastline.

Windsurfing/Kiteboarding Sables Bay facing the Maria Islands is the most popular location for windsurfing, but the entire south coast, bordering both the Atlantic and the Caribbean, is ideal. Strong Atlantic winds and choppy waves are a challenge to experts, whereas the Caribbean's gentle breezes are suitable if you are learning or improving your skills. Most beachside hotels offer rental equipment and instruction.

The sport of kiteboarding or kitesurfing has come recently to St. Lucia, along with the rest of the Caribbean. For information, contact **Club Mistral St. Lucia** (758-454-3418; www.stluciakite boarding.com; www.slucia.com/windsurf) or **Reef Kite & Surf** (Anse de Sables Beach, Vieux Fort, 758-454-3418; kitesurf@slucia.com).

Festivals and Celebrations

St. Lucia's festivities are a blend of its French, British, and African heritage—to the extent that it is hard to tell where one ends and another begins. Two festivals unique to the island are the **Feast of St. Rose de Lima,** August 30, and **Feast of St. Marguerite Mary Alocoque of France,** October 17. Both were founded by St. Lucian singing societies, La Rosa and La Marguerite, and are held on the feast days of the patron saints for which they are named.

Each festival is preceded by months of nightly singing practices called *séances,* which take place in festive settings. A king and queen, who serve as leaders for the events, are selected for each festival. Strict protocol is observed, with participants and visitors bowing to the chosen leaders upon entering the practice hall. A church service is followed by a costumed procession of members clad as kings and queens, princes and princesses, policemen and soldiers—singing and dancing in the streets. The parades are topped off with sumptuous banquets and dancing, with the king and queen leading the grand waltz at midnight.

St. Vincent and the Grenadines

Kingstown, Bequia, Mustique, Mayreau, Tobago Cays, Palm Island, Union Island

St. Vincent

St. Vincent Passage

Miles 0 3
Kilometers 0 4

N

CARIBBEAN
SEA

Fancy
Owia   Owia Bay
De Volet Point   Falls of
Baleine   Sandy Bay

Larikai Point   Sandy Bay

Soufrière
Mountains
Active Volcano
(last erupted 1979)

Orange Hill

Soufrière Trail   Rabacca Dry River
Wallibou   River
Richmond Beach   Trinity   Hell's Gate
Chateaubelair   Richmond   Falls   Falls   Rabacca
Bay

Chateaubelair
Islet   Richmond   Mount   Georgetown
Chateaubelair   Peak   Brisbane

Troumaka Bay   Black Point

Cumberland River

Barrouallie

Vermont
Nature Trails   South Union
Bay

Montreal
Botanical
Gardens   Biabou

Layou   Mesopotamia

Questelles Point   Botanical
Gardens   Yambou Head

Fort Charlotte   KINGSTOWN
Arnos Vale   Stubbs Bay
Cane Garden Point   Villa
Young Island

CARIBBEAN

SEA

ATLANTIC OCEAN

Rugged Terrain and Gentle Beauty

Majestic emerald mountains rising almost directly from a sapphire sea anchor a chain of three dozen exquisite gems that make up the country of St. Vincent and the Grenadines. Situated in the Windward Islands between St. Lucia and Grenada, they are the idyllic Caribbean hideaways for nature lovers, boating enthusiasts, and true beachcombers.

St. Vincent, the capital and largest of the group, is surprisingly different in composition and appearance from the Grenadines. It is covered almost end to end with intensely green, deeply creviced mountains that peak at 4,500 feet in an active volcano that displayed its awesome power as recently as 1979. Roads twist through the steep mountains, providing spectacular views of the interior, thick with tropical forests and cultivated with banana and arrowroot. On the Caribbean coast sheer cliffs drop to the sea, and white- or black-sand beaches hide in the crevices of an irregular coastline. On the windward side the Atlantic crashes against the rockbound shores.

The Grenadines, by contrast, are low-lying islets trimmed with palm-fringed, pristine beaches facing coral gardens. They stretch south from St. Vincent to Grenada over 65 miles of sparkling seas that yachtsmen often call the most beautiful sailing waters in the world. Now cruise ships are discovering them, too. Out of thirty-two islands and cays, six are ports of call.

Discovered by Columbus on his third voyage in 1498, St. Vincent was probably inhabited first by the Ciboneys and later by the Arawak and Carib Indians. Pre-Columbian artifacts have been found throughout the islands, and Amerindian petroglyphs can be seen on rock faces in many places. The island was still occupied by Caribs in 1672 when it was claimed by Britain.

In 1675 a slave ship sank in the channel between St. Vincent and Bequia. Survivors reached both islands and, in time, were assimilated with the Caribs. Their offspring came to be called the "Black Caribs," a name sometimes still used to refer to the villagers on St. Vincent's northeast coast, where their descendants concentrated.

Britain and France fought over St. Vincent for a century, but the Caribs put up such fierce resistance that neither country was able to colonize it. In 1748 the European combatants declared St. Vincent a neutral island. Under the Treaty of Paris, however, St. Vincent was ceded to England in 1763 and, together with Grenada, the Grenadines, and Dominica, formed the Windward Islands Federation. The Grenadines were divided administratively; Grenada got Petit Martinique and Carriaçou, at the south end of the chain, and St. Vincent was made responsible for all the islands north of Petit Martinique.

Except for a brief period of French occupation from 1779 to 1783, St. Vincent remained in British hands. With French support the Caribs made a final attempt in 1795 to regain their territory, but the rebellion was squashed. Hundreds of Caribs were

At a Glance

Antiquities	★
Architecture	★
Art and artists	★
Beaches	★★★★★
Colonial buildings	★
Crafts	★
Cuisine	★★
Culture	★★
Dining/Restaurants	★★
Entertainment	★
Forts	★★★
History	★★★
Monuments	★
Museums	★
Nightlife	★
Scenery	★★★★★
Shopping	★
Sightseeing	★★★★★
Sports	★★★★
Transportation	★

Fast Facts

Population: 109,022

Size: St. Vincent, 18 miles long and 11 miles wide, 133 square miles; Bequia, 7 square miles; Mustique, 4 square miles.

Main Towns: Kingstown, St. Vincent; Port Elizabeth, Bequia; and Clifton, Union Island.

Government: St. Vincent and the Grenadines, a member of the British Commonwealth, has a parliamentary government headed by a prime minister. The parliament is made up of a House of Assembly, elected every five years. The governor-general is appointed by the queen on the advice of the prime minister.

Currency: East Caribbean (EC) dollar. US$1.00 equals about EC$2.70.

Departure Tax: EC$40 (US$15)

Language: English

Public Holidays: January 1, New Year's Day; March 14, National Heroes Day; Good Friday; Easter Monday; May 1, Labor Day; May 31, Whit Monday; July 5, Caricom Day, Carnival Monday; July 6, Mardi Gras; August 1, Emancipation Day; October 27, Independence Day; December 25, Christmas Day; December 26, Boxing Day.

Telephone Area Code: 784

Airlines: There are no direct flights from the United States to St. Vincent. American Airlines, Air Canada, United Airlines, and Air Jamaica connect in San Juan, Barbados, St. Lucia, and Antigua with American Eagle (to Canouan only), LIAT, Grenadines Air (456-6793), SVG Air (457-5124; www.svgair.com), and Mustique Airways (458-4380; www.mustique.com). St. Vincent has an information desk in the arrivals hall at the airport in Barbados, open daily from 1:00 to 8:00 p.m. to assist passengers traveling to/from St. Vincent and the Grenadines.

Information: ww.svgtourism.com; www.bequiatourism.com

In the United States:

St. Vincent and the Grenadines Tourist Information Office, 801 Second Avenue, New York, NY 10017; (212) 687-4981; (800) 729-1726; fax: (212) 949-5946; svgtony@aol.com.

In Canada:

St. Vincent and the Grenadines Tourist Information Office, 333 Wilson Avenue, Suite 601, Toronto, ON M3H IT2; (416) 457-1502; fax: (416) 633-3123; svgtourismtoronto@rogers.com.

In Port:

Kingstown: St. Vincent and the Grenadines Department of Tourism, Cruise Ship Terminal, P.O. Box 834, Kingstown, St. Vincent and the Grenadines; (784) 457-1502; fax: (784) 451-2425; www.svgtourism.com; tourism@caribsurf.com. Hours: weekdays 8:00 a.m. to 4:15 p.m.

Bequia: Bequia Tourism Association, Port Elizabeth; (784) 458-3286; fax: (784) 458-3964; bequiatourism@caribsurf.com. Hours: Monday to Friday from 8:30 a.m. to 6:00 p.m., Saturday from 8:30 a.m. to 2:00 p.m., and Sunday from 8:30 a.m. to noon.

Union Island: Union Island Tourist Bureau; (784) 458-8350. Hours: daily, including weekends, 8:00 a.m. to noon and 1:00 to 4:00 p.m.

---

shipped off to Balliceaux, an islet east of Bequia, and then deported to the island of Roatán, which was part of British Honduras at the time. St. Vincent and the Grenadines became independent in 1979.

Today, St. Vincent and the Grenadines hit the big time with their starring role in Disney's *Pirates of the Caribbean: The Curse of the Black Pearl*. St. Vincent became the base of operations for the cast and crew, and Walillabou was transformed into the bustling Port Royal. The set is still standing and is a popular tour stop.

Budget Planning

St. Vincent is one of the least expensive destinations in the Caribbean, but the limited tourist development limits your options as well. On the other hand, its unspoiled quality is part of the attraction. Plan to enjoy St. Vincent and the Grenadines for their unrivaled natural beauty, and leave your shopping for other ports. Some of the Grenadines—Bequia and Union—are also inexpensive, but those that have been developed as deluxe, private-island resorts, such as Petit St. Vincent and Young Island, are expensive. The islands frequented by cruise ships—Bequia and Mayreau—are visited for their beaches and water sports; activities are generally prearranged by the cruise line.

Port Profile

Location/Embarkation The port is on the southwestern corner of St. Vincent at Kingstown Bay. It is a vital commercial artery for this predominantly agricultural country as well as being its cruise and ferry port. A new pier exclusively for cruise ships was part of a major reclamation project to improve the appearance, access, and facilities of the port area. A walkway from the pier leads directly into the city center, 2 blocks from the Department of Tourism and main shopping street. The Cruise Ship Pier and Terminal offers a number of shops and also includes the offices of the Ministry of Tourism and Culture and the Department of Tourism's Tourism Information Bureau.

Local Transportation Minibuses to all parts of St. Vincent depart from Market Square, or you can wave at a passing bus to stop for you. Sample fares from Kingstown to the main locations: Arnos Vale, EC$1.00; Mesopotamia, EC$2.50; Georgetown, EC$4.00. Cruise-ship passengers seldom use buses except for short distances near Kingstown.

Taxi rates are fixed by the government. The hourly rate is EC$50 (US$19). Taxis can be hired for sightseeing. Some examples of one-way fares from Kingstown to popular destinations: airport, EC$20; Young Island dock, EC$25; Blue Lagoon, EC$35; Mesopotamia EC$50; Lists of bus and taxi fares are available from the Department of Tourism. Fares are likely to be increased in the near future.

Roads and Rentals On St. Vincent the main road system is confined to the southern, most populated, third of the island between Kingstown and Richmond on the west and Sandy Bay on the east. Most are narrow roads that wind through the mountains and along irregular coastlines. No road circumnavigates the island, and only roads on the south coast cross the island between the east and west coasts. There are very few roads in the central area, and almost none in the northern third. The east-coast road north of Georgetown is best covered by four-wheel drive.

Cars and jeeps are available for rent in Kingstown for US$45 and up per day, but you might enjoy your sightseeing more if you do not have to negotiate the winding roads. Taxis can be hired by the hour or for the day; be sure to agree on the route and price in advance. Guides for hiking can be obtained through the Forestry Division or the Government Tourist Office. Local tour companies organize hikes to Soufrière; you should consult them about trail conditions.

Rental companies include **Ben's Auto Rental** (Arnos Vale, 456-2907; fax: 457-2686), which has all-terrain Suzukis and pickup service available; **Greg's Rental Services** (457-9814; gregg@caribsurf.com); **Avis Rental Car** (456-6861/456-4389); and some independent dealers. A local driving license is required and can be obtained for EC$75 upon presentation of your U.S. or Canadian driver's license at the Licensing Authority, Halifax Street, or at the police station on Bay Street. For bike and scooter rentals, check out **Sailor's Cycle Centre** (457-1712) and **Trotman's Depot** (482-9498). Driving in this former British colony is on the left.

Ports of call in the Grenadines have at least one road from the pier to the main community or resort, as well as tracks and footpaths. Bequia, Mustique, and Union have taxis.

Ferry Service Between Kingstown and Bequia ferries leave at two- and three-hour intervals from 6:00 a.m. to 7:00 p.m. Cost is EC$20 one-way. Schedules are subject to seasonal changes. For schedule information contact **Bequia Express** (458-3472) or **Admiral** (458-3348). Ferries to Canouan, Mayreau, and Union operate several days a week. You will find schedules in the Tourist Department's information booklet.

New ferry (sea) service for the Eastern Caribbean is planned, and the vessel *Caribbean Rose*, with the capacity to carry 300 passengers and 55 vehicles, will serve St. Vincent and the Grenadines from Barbados and Trinidad. For schedule information and ticket cost, contact the local agent, **Perry's Customs & Shipping** (457-2920) or

Inter Island Trading Ltd. (457-1172). Also in preparation is ferry service for the East Caribbean by Antigua-based Palm Ferries (George Pigott Building, Market Street, St. Johns, Antigua; [868] 333-3081; www.palmferries.com). As noted elsewhere in this book, Caribbean ferry service has a long start-and-stop history; always check with any ferry service locally before making plans.

Emergency Numbers

Medical: Milton Cato Memorial Hospital, Kingstown; 456-1185

Police and Coast Guard: 999; 911

Shore Excursions

Shore excursions vary from a three-hour island tour with a visit to the Botanic Gardens, to a drive to Mesopotamia, to hikes on nature trails in the Buccament Valley, to hikes to Trinity Falls, to dive and/or snorkeling trips, to trips to Bequia and other Grenadine islands, to a boat excursion to the Falls of Baleine—a magnificent waterfall accessible only by boat—passing spectacular scenery, with stops for swimming and snorkeling. This trip is offered as a day excursion by tour and water-sports companies in Kingstown. Another option is to hike to the summit of the Soufrière Volcano. The excursion from Kingstown takes six hours. A six-hour tour to the Darvue Waterfall stops in Wallilabou where fans of *Pirates of the Caribbean* will see the film set for the movie's town of Port Royal first-hand. A three-hour motor cruise provides an opportunity to view some of the seven species of whales and eleven species of dolphins that frequent the waters off St. Vincent.

For travelers arriving by yacht or coming to St. Vincent to begin a sailing excursion through the Grenadines, these tours can be arranged through your chartering company.

Some tour companies: **Vincy Aviation Services Ltd.** (Arnos Vale; 456-5600; www.vincy aviation.com) specializes in island tours and charter flights, among other services. Yacht cruises to the Grenadines (with or without crew) are available through **Barefoot Yacht Charters** (456-9526; barebum@caribsurf.com; www.barefootyachts .com).

HazECO Tours (Box 325, St. Vincent; 457-8634; fax: 457-8105; www.hazecotours.com). Eco-tours to volcano and other nature sites; "Flora and Fauna," boat tour to the Falls of Baleine and bird-watching excursions.

Sailor's Wilderness Tours (Middle Street; 457-1712; fax: 456-2821; www.sailortours.com, sailortours@hotmail.com). Variety of tour packages, including Mesopotamia Valley, Falls of Baleine; Rain Forest and Parrot Reserve; biking/picnicking volcano tour; catamaran sailing tours; Bike 'n Cruise the Grenadines. All tours include van and other vehicle support on all rides, drinks, snacks, and fruit.

Baleine Tours (457-4089; baleinetours@ hotmail.com), **Fantasea Tours** (457-4477; www .fantaseatours.com; fantasea@caribsurf.com;), **Sea Breeze Nature Tours** (458-4969; seabreeze tours@vincysurf.com), hiking and horseback riding with the **Richmond Vale Nature and Hiking Center** (492-4058; www.richmondvalehiking.com; jesper@richmondvalehiking.com), and **Treasure Tours** (456-6432; treasuretour@vincysurf.com) can arrange hikes to the volcano, orchid farm, and Montreal Gardens.

St. Vincent on Your Own

Kingstown is the only sizable town on St. Vincent. Founded in the early eighteenth century, the historic town stretches around Kingstown Bay and climbs the surrounding hills. It is laid out in a grid of three streets deep and about 10 blocks long. The historic sites, along with browsing in a few shops, can be covered on foot in an hour or so.

A Kingstown Walkabout

In the Cruise Ship Terminal, after you have browsed the shops selling local and imported items, you can walk out onto Upper Bay Street, turn left, and walk along to old, renovated warehouses that now house the **Cobblestone Inn, Basil's Bar and Restaurant,** and a number of small shops.

One block west of this complex is the Kingstown Market, a large building that is open every day except Sunday. At the north end of the market, on Halifax Street, is the **Courthouse and Parliament** building, a large colonial structure and small square at the town's center.

West of the parliament Halifax Street becomes Grenville Street, which has two landmark churches. **St. George's Anglican Cathedral,** at the corner of North River Road, is the oldest church in St. Vincent (1820) and is noted for its stained-glass windows. But more curious is St. Mary's Catholic Church, an extraordinary mixture of Romanesque, Gothic, Renaissance, and baroque styles with pointed arches, round arches, turrets, and square and wedding towers. It was created from pictures of famous European cathedrals by a bishop-architect in 1823, enlarged in 1877 and 1891, and restored in the early 1940s. The interior is as ornate as the exterior. North of the church is **Victoria Park,** a parade ground.

Botanic Gardens About a mile north of town are the oldest botanic gardens in the Western Hemisphere, established in 1765 on twenty hillside acres north of town. The gardens were begun mainly to grow herbs and spices, which in those days were the source of most drugs; the first curators were medical men as well as horticulturists.

After being allowed to deteriorate in the mid-nineteenth century, the gardens were reactivated by 1890 as part of a larger agricultural and botanical scheme. Today they are beautifully maintained, though not well signposted, and have enormous variety; they rank among the most outstanding in the Caribbean. They have nine varieties of ixora, a flowering bush whose small clustered blossom is the national flower. Along with huge mahogany and teak, you might see African tulip, yellow poui, flamboyant, or others in bloom, depending on the month. In October, for example, the nutmeg are laden with fruit, and the cannonball tree, an ugly wiry tree, shows its magnificent, delicate coral blossom.

The gardens' prized species is a sucker from the breadfruit tree planted in 1793 from the original plant brought to the Caribbean from Tahiti by Captain Bligh of *Mutiny on the Bounty* fame. When he arrived in Kingstown in 1793 on the HMS *Providence* on his second voyage, he off-loaded 530 breadfruit plants, of which 50 were planted in the gardens. The gardens' specimen is said to be a third-generation sucker of an original plant. As a clone of the original root, it can be referred to as an "original." The entrance to the gardens opens onto a manicured grass path bordered by hibiscus hedges and shaded by enormous Honduras mahogany trees. Guides are available. The famous breadfruit tree is nearby.

On the east side of the gardens is an aviary for the St. Vincent parrot, the national bird and one of the most endangered parrot species. Their number has decreased from thousands to an estimated five hundred birds today. Their habitat is being destroyed by clearing of the forest for agriculture, logging, hunting, and by the lucrative international pet market for exotic birds. The bird has magnificent coloring, with a distinctive white head and a brownish mauve body and green, deep lavender, and gold on the tail, neck, and wings.

A major effort to preserve the parrot is under way by the Forestry Division with the aid of Peace Corps volunteers, World Wildlife Fund, and RARE, the Philadelphia-based tropical-bird conservation group. A reserve has been established on about six hundred acres of rain forests in the Upper Buccament Valley. The program has involved the entire population—from schoolchildren, dressed as parrots, dancing to a calypso tune written especially for "Vincy," the parrot's nickname, to businessmen who use the parrot in their promotions.

Fort Charlotte From its 650-foot-high perch about 2 miles west of town, Fort Charlotte commands a magnificent view across Kingstown Bay to some of the Grenadines. Built around 1791 during the reign of King George III and named for his queen, the fort was completed about 1812 and was occupied by British troops until 1873. The gun emplacements, which are intact, point inland. This and the moat location, between the promontory and the main island, indicates that the builders may have been more concerned about attacks from the land—from the Caribs or the French—than from the sea. Today an area of the fort is used as a women's prison.

Fort Duvernette Built about 1800 to protect the entrance to Kingstown, the fort sits atop a volcanic spike, 195 feet above the sea. Fort Duvernette is next to Young Island at the entrance to Young Cut, a narrow channel on the south coast where water sports are centered. A visit can be arranged through Young Island Resort (www.young island.com).

A Drive around the Island

The South Coast to the Mesopotamia Valley

From the capital, Queen Elizabeth Drive, one of the main arteries, runs east over Sion and Dorsetshire Hills, providing fabulous views over Kingstown and Fort Charlotte. At Arnos Vale, by the airport, the road splits. One branch skirts the coast along Calliaqua Bay, where most of the hotels and popular beaches are located; and the other climbs the mountains. The east end of Calliaqua Bay, known as the Careenage or Blue Lagoon, is the center for sailing charters.

Mesopotamia Valley The southern third of St. Vincent has two high mountain ridges bridged at two 3,000-foot peaks—Grand Bonhomme and Petit Bonhomme. They form the heads of two large, intensively cultivated valleys: the Mesopotamia Valley on the east and the Buccament Valley on the west. The high slopes of the Mesopotamia Valley are thick with tree ferns and bamboo and planted with nutmeg, cacao, and coconut. The panoramic views are spectacular. The lower reaches of the valley are the country's breadbasket, planted with West Indian staples that include breadfruit, banana, plantain, and root crops such as eddo and dasheen—all plants with huge leafs that enhance the valley's lush appearance. High on the windward slopes of Grand Bonhomme at Richland Park are the Montreal Gardens, a botanical garden and nursery.

Yambou Gorge You can return from the gardens via the Yambou Gorge, where the streams that drain through the Mesopotamia Valley tumble over volcanic rocks on their way to the sea. On the coast large Atlantic rollers break against the rocks and the black-sand beaches at Argyle. Views along the way across the ridges and through the valley to the sea are magnificent.

The West Coast to the Buccament Valley

West of Kingstown the Leeward Highway snakes along the west coast and after about 5 miles crosses the Buccament Valley. The former Pembroke Estate was once a prosperous 1,000-acre sugar plantation whose aqueduct supplied water to power the mill. A road inland along the Buccament River leads to the head of the valley and a rainforest trail on the slopes of Grand Bonhomme.

Nature Trail A loop trail of 1.5 miles, developed by the Forestry Department with the aid of Peace Corps volunteers in 1988, rises from about 1,000 feet to almost 2,500 feet and passes under towering teak, mahogany, silk cotton, gommier, and other hardwoods that form a dense canopy overhead. The forest floor is carpeted with enormous ferns; tree trunks and their limbs are festooned with epiphytes (leafy air plants) and entangled in a curtain of vines. The buttress roots of the oldest trees are among the largest seen in any Caribbean rain forest. The trail has a lookout for viewing parrots.

Beyond Buccament the Leeward Highway snakes north along steep ridges that drop into the sea, passing fishing villages on the way to Chateaubelair, where the road ends. This region of jagged peaks, high bluffs, and deep ravines is the less-accessible part of the island.

Falls of Baleine St. Vincent's prettiest waterfalls are almost at the edge of the sea on the northwest coast, about 7 miles north of Richmond Beach and 18 miles from Kingstown as the crow flies. At the head of a steep-sided gorge on the northern face of the Soufrière Volcano, the falls cascade more than 70 feet in one stage through thick tropical foliage into a rockbound pool ideal for swimming.

Access to the falls from Kingstown is by boat. The forty-five-minute trip is as fascinating as the falls are enjoyable and provide a view of St. Vincent's spectacular scenery from the sea. The falls are located about 500 yards from a small pebble beach. The boat anchors on the new pier that has been constructed and now provides easy access to the beach. A walkway, including a bridge with handrail, also helps in providing easier access to the falls than in previous years. Trips to the falls are offered daily by most tour companies.

Exploring the East Coast

Soufrière Volcano The northern third of St. Vincent is dominated by the Soufrière Mountains, which have one of the most active volcanoes in the Eastern Caribbean. Five eruptions between 1718 and 1979 are documented, but archaeological evidence indicates the volcano probably erupted as early as A.D. 160. During an 1812 eruption—one of the worst, killing two thousand people—ash fell as far away as Barbados, 90 miles to the east. In 1902, the same year as the devastating eruption of Mount Pelée in Martinique, an eruption of Soufrière created the present width of the crater: 1 mile in diameter. In 1971 another eruption caused an island of lava to form in the center of the crater lake.

The most recent, in April of 1979, sent ash and stone thousands of feet into the air and rivers of molten lava down the mountainsides. More than twenty thousand people were evacuated, but, miraculously, no one was killed.

Once again the volcano is safe to climb and may be approached from either the eastern or western side on a trail running along the southern ridge of the crater. The eastern trail is used most frequently and can be followed by experienced hikers on their own. It starts 1 mile north of Georgetown at Rabacca, where the peak first comes in view. A guide and jeep can be provided by a local safari outfitter.

From Kingstown to the start of the eastern trail is 26 miles and takes 1.5 to 2 hours to drive. It is followed by a 2.5-mile drive on a very rutted plantation road north of the Rabacca Dry River, passing through the extensive banana and coconut groves of Rabacca Farms—formerly the 3,000-acre Orange Hill Estate, once the largest coconut plantation in the Caribbean—to the base of the crater at about a 700-foot altitude. From there a 3-mile trail ascends gradually through a rain forest to the crater rim. Along the way are wonderful vistas, sometimes looking back to the coast. The hike to the rim takes about three hours. You should check with the Forestry or Tourism Offices about trail conditions. Bring water and a picnic lunch, and start early to avoid the heat of the sun (but temperatures at the summit are chilly). There are no facilities of any kind once you leave the coast.

Rabacca Dry River A remarkable phenomenon of the St. Vincent volcanic eruptions are the "dry rivers": riverbeds that were filled and choked with scoriae, or lava cinder, and gravel after the eruptions of 1812 and 1902. Water flowing into the river seeps through the scoriae and disappears, becoming a subterranean river as it nears the coast. At the mouth of the river, the surface is bone-dry.

The best examples of dry rivers are at Wallilabou, on the west coast, and on the east coast at the Rabacca Dry River, which enters the sea at Rabacca, north of Georgetown. Where the main highway crosses the riverbed, the dry river is more than a half-mile wide and covered with several feet of loose ash; no water is visible on the surface. But toward the mountain, where the terrain begins to rise, water can be seen. Depending on the time of the year, it might be a small stream or a raging torrent after a sudden downpour.

Sandy Bay and Fancy On the north coast at the base of La Soufrière are the villages of Sandy Bay, Owia, and Fancy. Traditionally, Sandy Bay had the largest concentration of the descendants of the "Black Caribs," who came from the union of African slaves and indigenous Amerindians. After Sandy Bay the coastal road deteriorates and becomes a dirt track.

Shopping

The town center of Kingstown is small, and the shopping of interest to cruise passengers is modest, involving only a few stores on Bay and Halifax Streets. Stores are open weekdays from 8:00 a.m. to 4:00 p.m. and Saturday to noon.

The best selection of crafts, as well as books on St. Vincent, can be found at the **Cruise Ship Shopping Complex.** The courtyard at the Kingstown Market is another place to find everything from jewelry to wood carvings. **Artisans Art & Craft** (Bonadie Building, Bay Street; 456-2306) specializes in local crafts from more than seventy craftspersons throughout the island.

The **St. Vincent Crafts Centre** on the east side of town is a marketing outlet and craft shop for locally made jewelry, dolls, baskets, and other crafts made from straw, clay, coconut, wood, and bamboo; quality is not consistent.

Fibreworks (Penniston; 456-7118; fibreworks@caribsurf.com), in the Buccament Valley, was founded in 1997 by artist Vonnie Roudette, who uses local materials to create unique hand-crafted items. **Wallilabou Craft Centre** (Walliabou Village; 456-0078) was established in 1986 as a co-operative of local villagers and provides training in various techniques of straw and weaving baskets, handbags, hats and even children's toys using fibers from pandanas and wiss plants. The centre's motto is "In every piece of our craft lies a story of interaction with the environment through creativity and open hearts."

Dining and Restaurants

Kingstown has only a few restaurants outside of hotels. Prices are moderate. Check locally about days and hours for serving lunch and dinner.

Basil's Bar and Restaurant (Cobblestone Inn; 457-2713; www.basilsbar.com). The famous watering hole on Mustique has a twin. Situated in a pretty, historic building within walking distance of the pier in Kingstown, the pub offers classic cuisine and seafood. Basil's also has At Basil's (456-2602), an antiques and furniture store.

The Bounty Restaurant (Kingstown; 456-1776) serves Creole dishes using fresh local produce and catch-of-the day.

The Lagoon & Green Flash Bar (Blue Lagoon; 458-4308; www.lagoonmarina.com). In a romantic setting on a beautiful lagoon, the restaurant is part of the marina specializing in yacht charters. The menu features seafood.

Lime 'N Pub (Villa Beach; 458-4227) has West Indian and international food.

Xcape Restaurant and Bar (Villa Beach; 457-4597) on the waterfront is popular with locals. Inexpensive.

Young Island Resort (458-4826; www.young island.com), St. Vincent's only luxury resort, has long enjoyed a reputation for fine cuisine, enhanced by the private-island resort's romantic setting with dining under thatched gazebos smothered in tropical gardens at the water's edge. Reservations required. Expensive.

Sports

Beaches/Swimming The white-sand beaches on the south and black-sand ones on the west are the safest for swimming. The windward, or east, coast is generally too rough and the shoreline too rocky for swimming. All beaches are public. On the south coast a two-minute dock-to-dock boat ride across the cut takes you to Young Island, a private-island resort. Except for a few thatched-roof pavilions by the beach, most of the villas are hidden under curtains of tropical foliage. The resort does not provide changing facilities for day visitors, but you can swim at the beach and lunch in the restaurant.

Boating A sailing trip through beautiful waters of the Grenadines usually starts from St. Vincent. Yachts for up to eight people can be chartered, with or without crew, from **Sunsail Lagoon Marina & Hotel** (Blue Lagoon; 458-4308; www .lagoonmarina.com.com; sunsailsvg@vincysurf .com), **Barefoot Yacht Charters** (Blue Lagoon; 456-9526; barebum@caribsurf.com; www.barefoot yachts.com), and **TMM Bareboat Vacations** (Blue Lagoon; 456-9608; www.sailtmm.com; tmmsvg@ sailtmm.com).

Deep-Sea Fishing Sportfishing is not a developed sport, although the seas around St. Vincent and the Grenadines have abundant fish. Watersports operators can arrange deep-sea fishing upon request, and in the Grenadines you can often go out to sea with a local fisherman. **Crystal Blue Sportsfishing** (Indian Bay, Box 175, Kingstown;

457-4532; www.wefishin.com; wefishin@yahoo.com).

Hiking and Biking St. Vincent has some of the most spectacular scenery in the Caribbean, and it's best seen by hiking. There are easy trails in lush, mountainous settings and arduous ones over rugged terrain. For local people the lack of roads in many places makes walking and hiking a necessity. Guides for hiking are available through the Forestry Division and the Department of Tourism. Local travel companies organize hiking to Soufrière. Contact **HazECO Tours** (457-8634; fax: 457-8105; www.hazecotours.com) for hiking trips and sightseeing tours. **Sailor's Wilderness Tours** or **Sailor's Cycle Centre** (457-1712; fax: 456-2821; sailorstours@hotmail.com) organizes bike tours to remote areas.

Snorkeling/Scuba Diving The best snorkeling in St. Vincent is found along Young Island Cut and the west coast, but even better snorkeling is in the Grenadines, where shallow-water reefs surround almost every island, and huge schools of fish travel through the archipelago.

Diving in St. Vincent has only been explored in the past decade, and experts have been excited by what they have found. Reef life normally found at 80 feet in other locations grows here at depths of 25 feet, and there is an extraordinary amount and variety of tropical reef fish. **Dive St. Vincent** (457-4928; fax: 457-4948; www.divestvincent.com; bill2@divestvincent.com) is located on St. Vincent's south coast; **Dive Fantasea** (457-5560; www.divefantasea.com; divefantasea@vincysurf.com), **Bequia Dive Adventures** (458-3826; www.bequia diveadventure.com; adventures@caribsurf.com), and **Dive Bequia** (458-3504; fax: 458-3886; www.dive-bequia.com, bobsax@caribsurf.com) are in Bequia. Generally, prices for dive excursions and use of equipment are lower than in other Caribbean locations.

Tennis and Squash Grand View Hotel (458-4811; fax: 457-4174; www.grandviewhotel.com; Grandview@caribsurf.com;) on the south coast has a sports center with tennis and squash courts, gym, and an outside pool. Nonguests may use the facilities upon payment of a fee. Tennis facilities are also located at the National Sports Centre in Villa. Contact the **National Sports Council** (458-4201).

Windsurfing Equipment is available for rent from hotels on the south coast. In the Grenadines, all beachside resorts have windsurfing equipment.

Festivals and Celebrations

St. Vincent's Carnival, or **Vincy Mas**, as the Vincentians call it, is a ten-day festival held from the last Sunday in June to the first Tuesday in July. It is one of the biggest celebrations in the Eastern Caribbean, and people from neighboring islands participate.

The last two weeks in December have Christmas celebrations. Starting on the sixteenth people parade and dance through Kingstown every day (except Sunday) for the following nine mornings.

Other festivals are National Heritage Month (March), Emancipation Month Celebrations (August), and Independence Month Celebrations (October).

The Grenadines

The three dozen enchanted islands and cays that make up the Grenadines are like stepping-stones across the 65 miles between St. Vincent and Grenada. These idyllic islands-in-the-sun, where the news comes with the mail boat, are about as far off the beaten track as you can get in the Caribbean.

Scalloped with porcelain-white beaches protected by coral reefs, the Grenadines float on a deep turquoise sea. Long admired by yachtsmen, in recent years they have drawn the attention of cruise ships. Nine islands have settlements; the others are sanctuaries for birds and hideaways for those who love the sea.

Bequia

Information Bequia Tourism Association (458-3286; fax: 458-3964; www.bequiatourism.com).

Lying 9 miles south of St. Vincent across the Bequia Channel, Bequia (pronounced BECK-wee) is the largest of the Grenadines and a cruise-ship port of call. An island of rolling green hills, Bequia has only a few roads, but walking on unpaved roads and footpaths is easy. The island has many pretty beaches with reefs that are often within swimming distance from shore.

Bequia is known throughout the Eastern Caribbean for its skilled seamen, boat builders, and fishermen—descendants of New England whalers, European traders, pirates, and shipwrecked slaves. A haven for yachtsmen from around the world for its excellent anchorage at Admiralty Bay, Bequia has become a mecca for artists, writers, and assorted city dwellers who have opted for the laid-back island life. Unlike some of the Grenadines, Bequia has not been developed for tourists. Most hotels and guesthouses—some in former plantation houses with flowering gardens—are small and unpretentious.

Port Elizabeth, the main town and port where ships dock, can easily be covered on foot. The tourist information office at the pier has free maps and literature. A short walk north of the harbor takes you to the workshops of the island's best carvers of model boats, a craft for which Bequia is famous.

If you walk south from the pier along the main street, you will find a bookshop, Noah's Ark, and other small stores. By the bay, Frangipani Hotel (www.frangipanibequia.com) belongs to a former prime minister of St. Vincent and the Grenadines, who hails from Bequia. The hotel is one of the oldest on the island, and its bar is something of an institution for residents and visiting salts. Next door the Gingerbread is a tiny hotel with a delightful restaurant open to the breezes, an ice-cream parlor, and Dive Bequia, one of the four local dive shops.

In February 2007, construction began on the 100-room Bequia Beach Resort in Friendship Bay on the site of the former Bequia Beach Club and the Blue Tropic Hotel.

Some of Bequia's best snorkeling is found at Friendship Bay on the south coast where a half-mile beach is protected by reef; Spring Bay on the east coast is another. Windsurfing is available through hotels and guest houses. The breakers at Hope Bay are popular for bodysurfing. Sportfishing is available from *The Achiever II* (Grenadines

Adventure Sailing Co.; 458-3817; fax: 457-3172; quest@bequiasvg.com). Local fishermen hook tuna, marlin, wahoo, kingfish, and other big fish with ease.

Every spring the **Bequia Easter Regatta** attracts sailors and spectators from distant lands who join local fishing boats in four days of competition and celebration. Bequia's fishing vessels are wooden craft still made by hand. There are also competitions for model "gum boats" made by young Bequia craftsmen and gaily rigged miniatures made from coconut husks by children. The festival includes sports competitions, music, food, and exhibition of island products. For day-sailing excursions, contact **Michael Tours** (Paget Farm; 458-3782; www.bequia.net/michael_tours; michael toursbequia@yahoo.com).

Frequent daily ferry service connects Port Elizabeth and Kingstown in about one hour. Bequia has an airstrip; Mustique Airways flies daily from Barbados.

Mustique

Developed in the early 1970s by British and international investors, Mustique was put on the map by the British royal family, Mick Jagger, Raquel Welch, and a host of international celebrities who vacation here. The former home of the late Princess Margaret, a six-acre perch overlooking Galizeau Bay on the south coast, is available for rent. **Basil's Bar and Restaurant,** the parent of Basil's Restaurant in St. Vincent, is the best celebrity-watching spot on the island. It also has water-sports equipment for rent. Mustique welcomes visiting yachts but not cruise ships.

Mustique has a more manicured appearance than its sister islands. From the north end covered with gentle hills, the land rises to a steep range in the center and south. Sandy Bay on the north coast has a mile-long crest of white sand with spectacular water whose colors run the full spectrum of blue and green. Off the western point of the bay lies the wreck of the *Antilles*. Other good beaches are found at Pastor Bay on the east and Landing Cove on the west. There is good snorkeling, particularly at Britannia and Lagoon bays.

In colonial times the island had seven sugar plantations, one of whose estate houses is now

The Grenadines

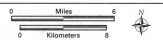

**BEQUIA
ISLAND**

Spring Bay

Admiralty Bay

○ Port Elizabeth

Friendship Bay

Derrick ○

Petit Nevis
Island

Isla Quatre

Bettowia
Island

Baliceaux
Island

C A R I B B E A N

S E A

Dovers ○

**MUSTIQUE
ISLAND**

Petit Mustique
Island

Savan Island

Petit Canouan
Island

Maho Bay

**CANOUAN
ISLAND**

Charleston Bay

North Mayreau Channel

C A R I B B E A N

Mayreau Island

Tobago
Cays

S E A

**UNION
ISLAND**

Clifton ○

Palm Island
(Prune Island)

Martinique Channel

Petit St. Vincent
Island

the Cotton House, the only deluxe hotel in Mustique. There are frequent flights from St. Vincent, which take ten minutes, and direct service from Barbados.

Canouan

Located between Mustique and Mayreau, the island is a popular stop for yachts, with a marina for one hundred boats. **Raffles Resort at Canouan Island** (458-8000; fax: 458-8885; www.rafflescanouan .com; canouan@raffles.com) is the largest hotel in St. Vincent and the Grenadines; another is the **Tamarind Beach Hotel** (458-8044; fax: 458-8851; www.tamarindbeachhotel.com). Both have facilities for water sports, and the Trump International Golf Club at Raffles Resort was designed by Jim Fazio and has been called the "St. Andrews of the Caribbean." There is one main road and a renovated and upgraded airport.

One of the driest islands of the group, Canouan is encircled by beautiful beaches. Charleston Bay on the west is the main port. The mushroom-shaped harbor has a mile-long beach. From the bay a half-mile-long footpath over the hill leads to more beautiful beaches and to some of the best snorkeling in an area called the Pool, where the colors of the water are fabulous.

Moorings Yacht Charters (Raffles Resort; 458-8044, www.moorings.com), one of the major sailing and bare-boat chartering companies in the Caribbean, has a base at the Raffles Resort.

Mayreau

Until Salt Whistle Bay Resort opened in 1987, Mayreau had no facilities. The resort is situated on a palm-fringed crescent of beach; at the north end, a short trail crosses over to the east side and a long stretch of beach. The island's tiny village is on a hill from which there is a lovely view over Tobago Cays and Horseshoe Reef, an area with extraordinary multihued aquamarine waters for which the Grenadines are famous. Mayreau is popular as a cruise-ship stop for its beautiful beaches and reefs. The wreck of a British gunboat, about 300 yards off Grand Col Point on the west coast, is a favorite of divers.

Tobago Cays

East of Mayreau about halfway between Canouan and Union is one of the most beautiful spots in the Caribbean and a highlight of cruising the Grenadines. Tobago Cays are four uninhabited palm-fringed islets etched by pristine white-sand beaches and incredibly clear aquamarine waters. The setting is so serene it seems unreal. From a beach on any islet, you can walk or swim to clusters of reef to view the spectacular marine life. The water flowing between the islands has strong currents, which bring huge schools of fish. On the east the cays are encircled by Horseshoe Reef, the northern half of which has spectacular reefs; parts are shallow enough to wade.

In 1989 at the tenth anniversary of its independence, St. Vincent and the Grenadines' prime minister declared the 1990s as the Decade of the Environment, placing conservation at the top of the priority list. One of its first projects was the Tobago Cays National Park—and not a minute too soon. The islets were declared a marine reserve more than a decade ago, but lack of attention and careless use by fishermen and boaters, coupled with the lack of strong government regulation, put tremendous stress on the coral gardens. Upgrading them to a national park provided the mechanism for the government to acquire the territory and manage it.

Palm Island

A private resort on a 110-acre island, Palm Island was known as Prune Island until the late Texan John Caldwell came along. Known as the Johnny Appleseed of the Caribbean, Caldwell obtained a ninety-nine-year lease (for which he paid US$1 per year) from the St. Vincent government and built a resort, where he replaced the scrub and swamp—not to mention mosquitoes—with two thousand palm trees and hundreds of other flowering trees and plants. He also planted another three thousand palm trees on neighboring islands.

Palm (www.eliteislandresorts.com) is popular with yachtsmen and is an occasional stop for small cruise ships. It is surrounded by pretty beaches protected by reefs that are only a wade or a short swim away. The resort was purchased in 1999 by

Rob Barrett, who owns Galley Bay and other hotels in Antigua and who promptly closed Palm for eight months to make extensive renovations and improvements, before reopening it in 2000.

Petit St. Vincent

Another deluxe, private-island resort, Petit St. Vincent often appears on the Caribbean's "ten best" list. Half of the 113-acre property was left in a natural state, and the other half was turned into a manicured park setting. The island is scalloped with pretty spectacular beaches, and on its north side are two sandbars with gorgeous white sand—Punaise and Mopion—floating in fantastically beautiful water and reefs. In fact, the islands are the western extreme of a 3-mile reef that runs along the north and east sides of Petit St. Vincent to Petit Martinique, one of Grenada's Grenadines. The shallow water offers some of the best snorkeling in the area. Petit St. Vincent welcomes visiting yachts but not cruise ships.

Union Island

Located about halfway between St. Vincent and Grenada, Union Island is 1.5 miles from Palm Island and 4 miles from Tobago Cays. The second-most populated of the Grenadines, Union's 2,500 inhabitants live mostly in Clifton, which is the government and commercial center as well as port. It has a bank, police station, doctor and clinic, and several buildings dating from the early 1800s. A footpath leads to Fort Hills, where there is a gun emplacement with old cannons and a panoramic view.

The T-shaped island has a spine of jagged, slab-faced mountains running north-south along the T-bar with Mount Tabor, at 999 feet, the highest peak in the Grenadines. A road connects Clifton, on the east coast, and Ashton, a fishing village on the south coast. Bloody Bay on the northwest coast and Chatham Bay on the west coast are popular anchorages.

Union has small hotels and an airstrip served by scheduled flights from St. Vincent, Grenada, St. Lucia, and Martinique. Union celebrates Easter with boat races, calypso competitions, and cultural shows. In May the Big Drum Festival is a cultural event to mark the end of the dry season and culminates with the Big Drum Dance, a celebration also seen on Carriacou.

Grenada

St. George's, Grenada; Hillsborough, Carriacou

Grenada and Carriacou

Miles 0 — 4
Kilometers 0 — 6

N

CARRIACOU

CARIBBEAN SEA

Gun Point

PETIT MARTINIQUE

Bay á L'Eau

Dover

Bogles

Belaire

HILLSBOROUGH

Mt. Pleasant

Six Roads

Harvey Vale

Great Bretche Bay

White Island

Saline Island

GRENADA

CARIBBEAN SEA

Sauteurs Bay

Lavera Beach

Caribs Leap ★

Sauteurs

Lavera Nat. Pk. ▲

Duquesne Bay

Morne Fendue

River Sallee

Grenada Bay

St. Mark Bay

Victoria

Gros Point

Lake Antoine

Rum Distillery ★

Gouyave

Palmiste Bay

Mount St. Catherine ▲

Tivoli

Dougaldston Estate (Nutmeg) ★

G R E N A D A

Paradise

Great River Bay

Concord

Halifax Harbour

Concord Falls ★

Mount Qua Qua ▲

Great River

Grenville

Grenville Bay

Seven Sisters Falls

Grand Etang Lake

ℹ

Grand Etang National Park ▲

Great Bacolet Point

Constantine

Gran Mal Bay

Crochu Harbour

ST. GEORGE'S ◉

⚔ **Fort Frederick**

Grand Anse

Morne Jaloux

La Sagesse

Quarantine Point

Woburn

Marquis Point

Point Salines

✈

Lance aux Epines

Hog Island

Westerhall Point

Calivigny Island

Prickly Point

A T L A N T I C

O C E A N

The Spice Island

Mountainous and lush, Grenada is a tapestry of tropical splendor that leaves you breathless with its beauty. Here, where the air is filled with the scent of cinnamon and nutmeg, thick vines climb the telephone poles and trail along overhead wires; the banana trees by the side of the road grow as tall as the palm trees that shade the beaches. Waterfalls cascade through the forested mountains decorated with 450 species of flowering plants and 150 species of birds. Nutmeg, ginger, vanilla, and almost every herb and fruit of the tropics fill the landscape.

The Spice Island, as Grenada is known, is the southernmost island of the Windwards, located 100 miles north of Venezuela. Off the north coast are its dependencies of Carriacou and Petit Martinique—two islands of the Grenadines chain that stretches north to St. Vincent. The trade winds that cool the island—only 12 degrees north of the equator—bring more than 160 inches of rain annually to the interior, creating lush forests and rivers that rush down the mountains to the sea.

From its forested, volcanic peaks, Grenada drops to a varied coastline of steep cliffs with hidden coves of black sand, wide bays with long stretches of white sand, deep harbors sheltering sailing craft, and lagoons and estuaries that host wildlife. Beneath the sea volcanic action continues nearby. Kick 'em Jenny, a volcano, lies submerged only 500 feet under the water off Grenada's north coast.

Sighted by Columbus on his third voyage in 1498, Grenada was probably occupied first by the Ciboneys and later the Arawaks, who were driven north by the fierce Carib Indians around A.D. 1000. English traders attempted to establish a colony on Grenada's west coast in 1609, but they failed due to Carib resistance. In 1650 the French had better luck and established a settlement on the southeast coast at the present site of La Sagesse, which paved the way for it to become a French possession two decades later.

Because of its strategic location, Grenada was coveted by the British, too. Consequently, the island changed hands several times between the French and the British until 1783, when it was ceded to Britain under the Treaty of Versailles. The British expanded sugar production, stepped up the importation of slaves, and established a plantation system. In 1795 Julien Fedon, a mulatto planter of French origin inspired by the ideas of the French Revolution, led a bloody but unsuccessful rebellion against the British. After slavery was abolished in 1834, attempts to continue sugar cultivation by importing indentured laborers from Asia failed. In 1877 Grenada became a British crown colony, and in 1974 it gained full independence.

A few years later in 1979, a bloodless coup led by Maurice Bishop and six of his followers, known as the New Jewel Movement, threw out the government of Sir Eric Gairy, a controversial character with a secret police known as the "Mongoose Gang." Bishop and his group might have been a welcome relief had they not changed the island's name to the People's Revolutionary Government of

At a Glance

Antiquities	★
Architecture	★★
Art and artists	★★
Beaches	★★★★★
Colonial buildings	★★★
Crafts	★
Cuisine	★★★★
Culture	★★
Dining/Restaurants	★★★
Entertainment	★
Forts	★★★
History	★★★
Monuments	★
Museums	★
Nightlife	★
Scenery	★★★★★
Shopping	★★
Sightseeing	★★★
Sports	★★★★
Transportation	★

Population: 102,000

Size: Grenada, including Carriacou and Petit Martinique, covers 133 square miles. Grenada itself is 12 miles wide and 21 miles long.

Main Towns: St. George's and Grenville, Grenada; Hillsborough, Carriacou.

Government: Grenada has a parliamentary form of government and is a member of the British Commonwealth. Parliament consists of two chambers: a Senate of seven appointed members and a House of Representatives of fifteen elected members. The cabinet, headed by the prime minister, is responsible to parliament. The queen is represented by a governor-general.

Currency: Eastern Caribbean (EC) dollar. US$1.00 equals EC$2.70. U.S. dollars and traveler's checks are widely accepted.

Departure Tax: EC$50 (US$20 adults); EC$25 (US$10) ages two to twelve; younger than age five exempted.

Electricity: 220 volts, 50 cycles

Language: English

Public Holidays: January 1, New Year's Day; Good Friday; Easter Monday; May 1, Labor Day; May, Whit Monday; June, Corpus Christi; First Monday and Tuesday in August, Emancipation Holidays; October 25, Thanksgiving Day; December 25, Christmas Day; December 26, Boxing Day.

Telephone Area Code: 473

Airlines: *From the United States:* Air Jamaica, American/American Eagle, and US Airways. *From Canada:* Air Canada; Regional: LIAT from various Caribbean islands. Airlines of Carriacou and SVGAir serve Carriacou from Grenada; the latter connects to Union Island. At Grenada's Point Salines International Airport, services for private aircraft have been added with a VIP lounge with dedicated customs and immigration personnel.

Information: www.grenada grenadines.com

In the United States:

Grenada Board of Tourism: (800) 927-9554 for travel information; cnoel@grenadagrenadines.com; P.O. Box 1668, Lake Worth, FL 33460; (561) 588-8176; fax: (561) 588-7267.

In Canada:

Grenada Board of Tourism, 439 University Avenue, Suite 920, Toronto, M5G 1Y8, Ontario; (416) 595-1339; fax: (416) 595-8278; tourism@ grenadaconsulate.com.

In Port:

Grenada Board of Tourism, Burns Point, P.O. Box 293; St. George's, Grenada, W.I.; (473) 440-2001/2279; fax: (473) 440-6637; gbt@spiceisle .com; www.grenadagrenadines.com.

In Carriacou:

Grenada Board of Tourism, Main Street, Hillsborough; (473) 443-7948; fax: (473) 443-6127; carrgbt@spice isle.com.

Grenada and begun waltzing with Cuba. The Cubans wasted no time in sending experts to train Grenada's security forces and help with its most pressing need: the construction of a new airport. The airport became a bone of contention for the United States, which saw Cuba's involvement as a camouflage to turn Grenada into a military base, enabling Cuba to control the two ends of the Caribbean.

Thus in 1983, when an internal struggle for power resulted in the assassination of Bishop and an attempt by a pro-Cuban faction to seize power, the United States saw an opportunity, and, with the endorsement of the Eastern Caribbean states, it intervened militarily to stop the coup and restore order. The following year a parliamentary government was returned to power. The irony is that the United States completed the construction of the airport, which it had claimed Grenada did not need, and President Ronald Reagan landed there sixteen months after its opening, pointing with pride to its completion.

Despite its turbulent history, Grenada is an easy-living sort of place, with hotels set in flowering gardens alongside beautiful beaches, old fishing villages, and gentle folk whose diverse heritage matches the colorful tapestry of their tropical landscape. British traditions run as deep as African and Asian ones, but the French legacy, too, has endured: in the names of the people and places, the patois that is more French than English, and the cuisine, which is some of the best in the Caribbean.

Budget Planning

Grenada is not an expensive island, with the notable exception of taxis, but since many cruise ships do not stay a full day in port, a taxi with the driver/guide might be your best way to tour—particularly if you have others with whom to share the cost. If you plan to do nothing more than go to the beach, public buses run frequently from town to Grand Anse Beach.

Port Profile

Location/Embarkation St. George's, the capital and port, has one of the most picturesque settings in the Caribbean. The harbor has two sections: one is the docking area for large cruise ships; the other is a well-sheltered inner harbor used as a yacht basin. The new Melville Street—a $24 million cruise-ship port facility that can accommodate at least two mega cruise ships—opened in December 2004. The first phase included the construction of berthing facilities, a welcome center, and parking facilities for taxis and tour operators. Phase two, completed a year later, added the US$11 million Esplanade Mall, with shops selling local crafts, fragrances, electronics, jewelry, gifts, and liquor at duty-free prices. At the Welcome Center you can get information and make phone calls using a major credit card. Simply dial 111 from pay phones.

Local Transportation Grenada does not have a fully developed public transportation system. Instead, private minibuses provide in-town and intraisland services at low rates. They leave frequently from Market Square and Esplanade in St. George's.

Taxis are available at the port and in town, but they tend to be expensive unless you can share the cost with others. Rates are set by the government in cooperation with the taxi union. Sample taxi fares from the pier: to town center, US$3; Grand Anse/Morne Rouge, US$10; golf course, US$10; Point Salines Airport, US$15. It costs US$20 per hour to hire a taxi.

Roads and Rentals One road circumnavigates the island, and another crosses it from coast to

coast over the central highlands. By combining the routes it is easy to make a loop around the northern or southern half of the island. The time most cruise ships remain in port is usually insufficient, however, to cover both circuits in one day. The best roads are those between St. George's and the south coast, and the cross-island highway. Major arteries deteriorate farther north along both the west and east coasts. Secondary roads and dirt tracks reach most villages throughout the island. If you have a good map (on sale at the Grenada National Museum), you can rent a car, but if you are not accustomed to left-side-of-the-road driving, you are probably better advised to hire a taxi, with the driver acting as guide. Often roads are narrow, winding, and in poor condition, and Grenadians drive fast, making for a daunting experience.

Cars and open-sided Mini-Mokes cost about US$60 per day to rent. In winter you should reserve in advance. You need to be twenty-one years of age and have a valid driver's license to obtain a local permit from the traffic department, which the car rental agency will handle for you. Cost is EC$30 or US$12. Driving in this former British colony is on the left. Rental agencies in St. George's include **Avis/Spice Island Rentals** (440-3936; avis grenada@spiceisle.com; **Azar Auto Rentals** (414-2911); **Dollar** (Airport; 444-4786; fax: 444-4788; callisterna@spiceisle.com), and **McIntyre Bros.** (444-3944; fax: 444-2899). Bikes can be rented for about US$15 from **Trailblazers Mountain Bike Tours & Rentals** and jeeps from **Adventure Jeep Tours,** (both at 444-5337; www.adventure grenada.com; adventure@spiceisle.com). Both companies also operate biking and jeep tours.

Ferry Service The *Osprey Express* (440-8126; osprey@spiceisle.com; www.ospreylines.com), a high-speed hovercraft, takes passengers twice daily (only once on Saturday) from St. George's to Hillsborough, Carriacou, and to Petit Martinique in about 1.5 hours. EC$70 or US$27 one-way; EC$140 or US$54 round-trip.

Emergency Numbers

Medical: General Hospital, St. George's; 440-2050
Ambulance: St. George's area, 434
Police: 911

Shore Excursions

The island can be toured in a loop around its northern or southern half—it is not advisable to try to cover both in one day. The following tours are typical of those offered by cruise ships or local tour companies. The places mentioned are described later in this chapter.

Grand Etang and the Central Highlands: 2–3 hours, US$30–$45 for four persons or more. After climbing the lush hillsides with grand views of the harbor, the route crosses the central spine of mountains with the Grand Etang National Park. From the visitor center there are self-guided, signposted trails in the rain forest.

The West Coast: 3 hours, US$45. A drive along the west coast reveals some of the island's most fabulous scenery. Stops are usually made at Dougladston Estate, a nutmeg plantation, and at the processing plant in Gouyave. You can return via the scenic Belvidere Road and the Grand Etang, or turn inland to the Concord Valley and hike the forty-five-minute trail to the Concord Falls.

West Coast and North Coast Loop: 6 hours, US$50–$60. The west coast tour continues to Sauteurs and historic Caribs Leap, stopping for lunch at Morne Fendue, and returning to Grenville via the east coast and the cross-island highway. Some cruise ships charge US$65 per person when passengers travel by car.

City Tour and Bay Gardens: 3.5 hours, US$25. Tour St. George's, Richmond Hill, and Bay Gardens for a walk through the botanical gardens, and visit the Tower, a private estate house.

The Southern Route: 4–5 hours, US$35–$45. The above tour continues to Westerhall Point, a deluxe residential area with a dramatic seascape, and to Grand Anse Beach. Alternatively, you could continue southeast to La Sagesse, a nature reserve and estuary, for a swim or a walk in the woods.

Kayaking: See Sports section later in this chapter.

River Tubing: 1.5 hours, US$45 per person (transfers not included). Balthazar River, fed from sources deep in the interior, flows through tropical rain forest and the historic Balthazar Estate. A forty-five-minute drive from St. George's through the Grand Etang Reserve takes you to the launch site, where participants get a briefing and are provided with a life vest and tube. Guides accompany you down the river, as you gently spin in the currents. At the end, there's an opportunity to swim. It's wet, wild, and wonderful. Age requirement: eight years and older; maximum weight: 250 lbs. Departures: 9:00 a.m., 11:30 a.m., and 2:00 p.m. from launch site. Bring a towel; wear swimsuit, sunblock, and water shoes. Reservations required. **Adventure Jeep Tours** (P.O. Box 857, St. George's; 444-5337; www.grenadajeeptours.com; info@ grenadajeeptours.com).

Whale watching: See Sports section later in this chapter.

Some companies with light adventure and nature tours: In addition to river tubing above, **Adventure Jeep Tours** (444-5337; fax: 444-5681; www.grenadajeeptours.com) specializes in adventure, nature tours by jeep to rain forests for hiking; repast on authentic local cuisine at a restaurant deep in the interior; to scenic west coast to a beach for a swim and snorkel, and sunset return. Available Monday to Friday.

Caribbean Horizons Tours & Services (True Blue Bay Resort; 444-1555; fax: 444-3944; www .caribbeanhorizons.com; macford@spiceisle.com). Day tours to major attractions; rain-forest hikes and ecotours to waterfalls or mountain peaks. Deep-sea fishing, day sails. Admissions and refreshments on all tours; multilingual guides. Car and jeep rentals. Open daily; twenty-four-hour answering service.

Aquanauts Grenada (True Blue Bay Resort, Grand Anse Beach; 444-1126; fax: 444-1127; www .aquanautsgrenada.com) offers guided dive trips to more than thirty dive sites, including wrecks, marine parks, reef diving, shark diving, and Isle de Rhonde. Also snorkel with nurse sharks and stingrays. Free pickup.

Sunsation Tours (Le Marquis Complex, Grand Anse; 444-1594; fax: 444-1103; www.grenada sunsation.com; qkspice@spiceisle.com). Excursions to major attractions, including Concord, Marquis, and Seven Sisters waterfalls and other offbeat sites. Admissions included; lunch and drinks on some tours. Rental jeeps available.

Henry Safari Tours (445-5313; safari@ caribsurf.com) and Telfor Bedeau (440-8163) were among the first to specialize in hiking and nature tours almost two decades ago.

Published prices for a taxi with a driver/guide for up to four persons: **Annandale Falls,** 1 hour, US$25; **Morne Jaloux/Woburn/Grand Anse Beach,** 1.5 hours, US$30; **Bay Gardens,** 1 hour with tour, US$16; **Grand Etang,** 2 hours, US$30; **Grand Etang/Grenville,** 2.5 hours, US$50; **Dougaldston/Gouyave/Spice Factory,** 2.5 hours including tours, US$40. A complete list of car-rental and tour companies is available on the Grenada government's Web site: www.grenada grenadines.com.

Grenada on Your Own

The capital of Grenada is set on a deep bay with a tango of yellow, blue, and pink houses topped with red-tile roofs, clinging to the slopes of the green hills that frame the harbor. One of the Caribbean's most beautiful natural harbors and an important trading center since its founding by the French in the early eighteenth century, St. George's is a popular port of call for cruise ships and yachts sailing the Grenadines.

A St. George's Walkabout

Like its history, St. George's character is part French and part English, yet distinctively West Indian. It is divided into two parts separated by a promontory crowned by Fort George. The lower town hugs the inner harbor, known as the Carenage, and the new town is "over the hill" along the seaside Esplanade. The two are connected by a tunnel under the hill, used by motor vehicles, and by a road and narrow sidewalk over the hill, used by cars and pedestrians. Both parts are best seen on foot, which takes about two hours, but it could take longer if you stop frequently to admire the views or browse in shops and historic sites along the way.

The Carenage (1) A perfect horseshoe in shape, the Carenage is one of the best anchorages in the West Indies and always busy with boats of all sizes and description. It is also the center of life for the town, where schooners loaded with Grenada's bountiful harvest of fruits and vegetables sail for markets in Barbados and Trinidad. Most of the schooners are made in the neighboring Grenadines by local shipwrights.

On the south side of the Carenage, a second harbor known as the **Lagoon (2)** is the yacht basin, marina, and commercial port. The Lagoon is actually the submerged crater of an ancient volcano. On its east are the **Botanical Gardens,** begun in 1887; buildings on the grounds house government offices.

North of the pier **(3),** Lagoon Road/Wharf Road skirts the Carenage past the post office, the **Department of Tourism Bureau (4),** the public library, and small shops on the waterfront. Near the Department of Tourism, overlooking the water, is a shaded pedestrian plaza with seats and pretty flowers around a statue, *Christ of the Deeps.* It was given to Grenada by Costa Cruise Line in appreciation of the island's help to the passengers and crew of the *Bianca C,* which caught fire in the harbor in 1961. For a different view of St. George's, "water taxis" cross the harbor from the pier to the north side of the Carenage for about US 50 cents a ride.

Climbing the hill above the Carenage are old churches that combine West Indian and European architectural elements and government buildings dating from the early 1800s. **York House** holds the supreme court; the neighboring **Registry Building** was built about 1780; and **Government House,** remodeled in 1802, is a fine example of early Georgian architecture. **St. George's Anglican Church (5),** rebuilt in the twentieth century, has wall plaques from the eighteenth and nineteenth centuries; **St. Andrew's Presbyterian** dates from 1830 and **St. George's Methodist Church** from 1820.

Grenada National Museum (6) On the hill up from the Carenage in an eighteenth-century building that was once part of a French army barracks and prison is the National Museum. Here

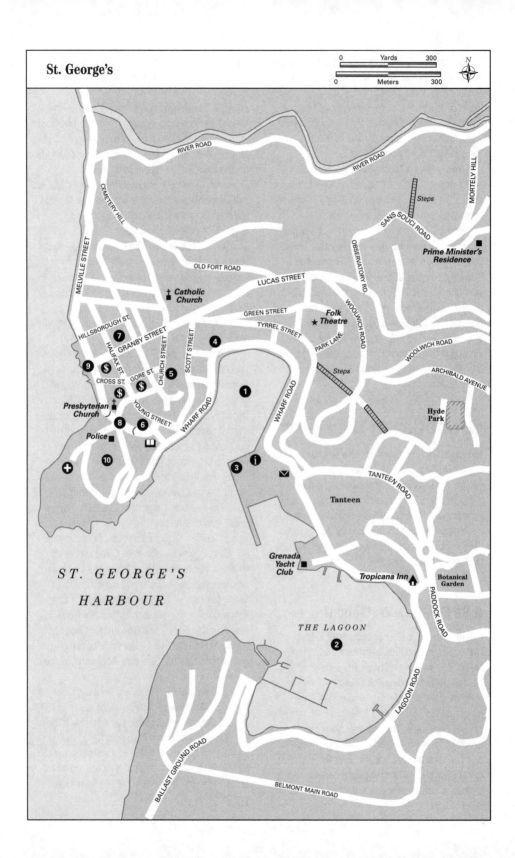

artifacts from archaeological excavation around the island and exhibits trace Grenada's history from the Ciboneys to colonial times. The museum sells books, pamphlets, and maps of Grenada. Hours: weekdays 9:00 a.m. to 4:30 p.m., Saturday 10:30 a.m. to 2:00 p.m., closed Sunday. Admission: US$2.

Market Square (7) A walk from the Carenage up Young Street over the hill or a drive through **Sendall Tunnel (8)** takes you to the other side of St. George's, with Market Square at the center of town. The market is one of the liveliest, most colorful in the Caribbean, particularly on Saturday morning. Vendors, each with their tiny plot and brightly colored umbrella, sell brooms, baskets, and an array of exotic tropical fruits, vegetables, and spices. West of the square the **Esplanade (9),** a strip of coastal road along the outer harbor, has fish and meat markets.

At strategic hilltops around the harbor, the French and the British built a series of fortifications in the eighteenth century to defend the island. Today they stand as testimony to the rivalry that raged between the two powers throughout most of Grenada's colonial history, as well as offering grandstand views.

Fort George (10) The harbor entrance is guarded by an imposing fort built in 1706 by the French as Fort Royal and later seized by the British, who renamed it for their monarch. Built on a promontory with walls more than 4 feet thick, the fort was a master feat of engineering in its day. It has two levels with barracks, ammunition storage rooms, dungeons, and a maze of underground passages. The fort served as police headquarters for many years, and in 1983 it witnessed the coup in which Prime Minister Bishop and many of his supporters were killed.

To visit the other forts, a drive is recommended, as the hillsides are very steep and the sun is hot. Alternatively, you could drive or take a bus from Market Square to the top of a hill and walk down.

Fort Frederick Built in 1779 soon after the French recaptured the island from the British, Fort Frederick is located on the summit of Richmond Hill, between Fort Matthew to the north and Fort Adolphus to the south, occupying the most strategic position of all the fortresses and commanding extensive views. Its thick stone walls, barracks, watchtowers, and underground tunnels are similar to those of Fort George. In the 1983 coup attempt, the fort was the headquarters of the People's Revolutionary Army, the faction that tried to seize power from Bishop. The carcass of a Soviet armored truck, left to rust where it was abandoned, seems a fitting reminder of the grim events.

Bay Gardens East of Fort Frederick in the hillside suburb of St. Paul's on the site of an old sugar mill is a private three-acre spread with an estimated 3,000 different species of flora found in Grenada and the Caribbean. Footpaths covered with nutmeg shells wind through exotic vegetation. In addition to spice and fruit trees—all labeled—Bay Gardens has sections for flowers and various kinds of orchids. The entrance fee includes a walk through the gardens with a guide.

The Tower A private home east of Bay Gardens on St. Paul's Road is the estate house of a working fruit-and-spice plantation, set in gardens of exotic plants. The Tower, built in 1916, is one of the island's few remaining old houses constructed of volcanic rock. It is open to the public by appointment. The owner's private collection of Carib artifacts and antiques is on display.

A Drive around the Island

Along the West Coast

North of St. George's the road hugs the coast, passing through small fishing villages and skirting magnificent scenery of lush, thickly carpeted mountainsides that drop almost straight into the sea and coves, their black-sand beaches almost hidden from view. Offshore at Molinere Bay is the new fabulous *Underwater Sculpture Park* by British artist, Jason Taylor. Located 2 miles north of St. George's, the park has sixty-five sunken figures, positioned in a circle on the sandy bottom, in depths between 6 and 24 feet.

Concord Valley Inland from Halifax Harbour a road along the Black Bay River leads to the head of the Concord Valley, where a triple-stage waterfall in a setting of dense tropical foliage cascades down the central mountains. Above Concord village the road stops directly in front of the falls' lower stage, where concrete steps lead down to a swimming area.

The second stage has a much more beautiful setting, which is accessible thanks to a footpath laid by U.S. Peace Corps volunteers. Large rocks and a few small bridges were placed at strategic points, making it less difficult to cross the river against rushing water. Even so, the hike is not easy unless you are nimble and dressed appropriately in shorts, or bathing suit, and sneakers (the rocks are slippery). Your effort will be richly rewarded: The cascade spills through jungle-thick vegetation into a pool where you can have a delightful swim surrounded by magnificent scenery. The hike takes about forty-five minutes to go and twenty-five minutes to return.

Gouyave Grenada is the world's second-largest producer of nutmeg; the main production center is the area around Gouyave on the west coast north of St. George's. Inland about a half mile immediately before Gouyave is Dougladston Estates, one of the island's oldest and largest nutmeg plantations. Its staff members explain the cultivation of nutmeg and other spices to visitors. In Gouyave you can have a free walk-through tour of a growers' cooperative that is the country's major nutmeg-processing station. You will see workers clean, grade, and prepare nutmeg for shipping.

Gouyave, the main fishing town on the west coast, was the site of the first British attempt to establish a colony in 1609, when they were forced to leave after encountering fierce Carib resistance. Today the town has a reputation for rowdiness.

The North Coast

Caribs Leap North of Gouyave the road passes through Victoria, a quiet town at the foot of 2,757-foot Mount St. Catherine, Grenada's highest peak, and continues to the town of Sauteurs (which in French means "leapers"). There a promontory alongside St. Patrick's Roman Catholic Church and Cemetery, a historic landmark. The steep-faced north side of the promontory, known as Caribs Leap or Leapers Hill, drops more than 100 feet into the sea. The last of the Carib, the inhabitants of the island at the time of Columbus, leaped to their death here rather than surrender to the French, who were intent on exterminating them.

Helvellyn House (Sauteurs, 442-9252; helvellynhouse@spiceisle.com) Located on a hilltop at the northern tip of Grenada, Helvellyn House is surrounded by tropical gardens and commands a great view across the sea to Carriacou. The stone structure was built by the current owner's grandfather, who also made the furniture. A lunch of West Indian specialties is served daily and there are three rooms available for rent. Nearby is the new **Helvellyn Pottery and Learning Centre,** which makes vases, bowls, plates, and other pottery, designed and fired on site.

Morne Fendue On the south side of Sauteurs, the estate house of a former plantation, Morne Fendue, was built at the turn of the twentieth century in the traditional method: with hand-cut local stones and mortar made with lime and molasses. The late owner, Betty Mascoll—the island's best-known hostess of kings, queens, and presidents—opened her house for a Grenadian lunch. You can still enjoy lunch provided you call in advance (442-9330). This is not a restaurant; you dine in the drawing rooms on local dishes, usually fresh vegetables from the garden. Similarly, **Mount Rodney**

Estate (442-9420), a plantation house also near Sauteurs, offers West Indian specialties that owners Lynn and Norris Nelson prepare and serve with style; lunch only. Fixed price, EC$45. Reservations required.

Belmont Estate (442-9524; belmontestate@ caribsurf.com), another plantation in this vicinity, is now open to visitors. The 400-acre estate, dating from the eighteenth century, has been in continuous operation and still produces nutmeg and cocoa. There is a museum and a forty-five-minute tour of the working plantation. Visitors also enjoy demonstrations of traditional cultural activities, such as stick fighting, drumming, and local dances. The estate serves a three-course lunch of local dishes for US$15 for adults; half price for children younger than twelve years of age. It is open Sunday to Friday; reservations are required. Sunsation Tours, among other tour companies, visit the estate on their island tours.

Grenada Chocolate Company (Hermitage, St. Patrick's; 442-0050; http://grenadachocolate .com; info@grenadachocolate.com). Part of Belmont Estate amid the cocoa groves, the chocolate company was founded in 1999 to produce high-quality, organic dark chocolate from local cocoa. The company has its own organic 100-acre cocoa farm, and its little factory can perform all the steps in the production of chocolate, from the planting and growing of cocoa trees to the fermenting of fresh cocoa beans to the processing of fine dark chocolate. Its cocoa is grown without use of chemicals, and solar energy is used to power its machines. Because the making of chocolate in small batches is rare, the company had to create its own processing methods, which involved designing its own machines based on early 1900s designs and refurbishing antique ones. The company's goal is to revolutionize the cocoa-chocolate system that typically keeps cocoa production separate from chocolate-making and thus, takes advantage of cocoa farmers, by enabling farmers to be part of the entire process. The company's products are sold online in the U.S. A colorfully wrapped 4-ounce chocolate bar costs $5.95; 6-pack, $33.20.

Levera National Park East of Sauteurs is a long white-sand beach popular with Grenadians on weekends, but usually deserted during the week. The scenic coast is part of the Levera National Park and nesting grounds for sea turtles, protected from May to September. South of the park the coastline changes to gray sand and weathered rock cliffs.

Lake Antoine and River Antoine Distillery South of Levera Park, the eighteenth-century River Antoine Rum Distillery is a historic landmark on a sugar plantation where cane for rum making is processed in the same way it was two hundred years ago when the plant was built. The distillery has an electrical pump and new boiling machinery, but water from the river is still used to turn the old waterwheel to power the plant. It is the last operational waterwheel in Grenada. Lake Antoine, a crater lake, can be reached on a footpath from the distillery or nearby road.

The Central Highlands

Annandale Falls On the highway from St. George's to the Grand Etang Forest Reserve, on the mountain spine down the center of the island, a short detour can be made to Annandale Falls, the most accessible waterfall in Grenada. Located only a few yards from the road in an area of lush tropical vegetation, the small hillside with steps leading to the falls is planted with an herb and spice garden. A welcome center at the entrance to the falls sells local spices and crafts.

Nearby at La Mode you can visit the St. George's Estate, where a local winery, Grenada Wine Cooler, makes great fruit wines by traditional methods used in Grenada for two hundred years.

Grand Etang Forest Reserve The ridge of mountains that bisect the interior of Grenada are covered by the Grand Etang Forest Reserve, part of a new national parks system established by the government of Grenada with the help of U.S. development agencies, including the Peace Corps and the Organization of American States. The highway that zigzags up the forested mountains crosses the reserve almost at its center at a 1,910-foot altitude and within a few hundred yards of Grand Etang, an extinct volcano that gave the reserve its name; its crater is filled with a lake. (Grand Etang means "large pond" in French.) North of the crater is Mount Qua Qua Peak, one of Grenada's three highest peaks. The flattop cone of Mount St. Catherine can be seen on the north, with Mount Sinai on the south.

Grand Etang Lake is only about 500 yards from the visitor center, where there are displays and information on the self-guided nature trails. The trails range from fifteen minutes to three hours and lead to the lake and surrounding rain forests, which have some of the island's most exotic vegetation and wildlife.

Seven Sisters Trail Southwest of Grand Etang Lake, a trail leads to an area with waterfalls that drop in several stages into a large pool delightful for swimming. The trail takes three hours round-trip for experienced hikers and crosses a cultivated area to reach the virgin forest. Parts of the trail, along steep ridges, are difficult, particularly during the rainy season when the ground is very muddy. An experienced nature guide is essential.

The South Coast

From St. George's, along the Lagoon Road, the highway leads to Grand Anse Beach, one of the most beautiful beaches in the Caribbean, and the southern part of the island. At the southernmost point, Fort Jeudy, the Atlantic crashes against high cliffs, and the scenery is magnificent.

Port Louis Grenada (Lagoon Road, 439-0000; www.portlouisgrenada.com) A comprehensive resort, spa, marina, and residential development, representing an investment of about US$555 million, includes a world-class marina with 350 slips and yachting facilities for yachts up to 100 metres, 36 estate lots for individual homes, 200 residential units varying in size from 900-square-foot village apartments to turnkey 3,000-square-foot houses; a 120-room luxury hotel; a premier spa and lifestyle center; a 120-room mid-priced hotel; revitalization of the southern end of the lagoon area and reclamation and renovation of the seafront; revitalization and augmentation of Pandy Beach to compliment that of Grand Anse, including water sports, beach extension, diving, and other elements; and employment and training of up to 800

staff. Within the Caribbean and West Indies, Port Louis will be a unique mix of charm and character including a vibrant market with a waterfront of exciting activities. Peter de Savary, a well-known British developer of luxury properties, is also developing Mount Cinnamon on Grand Anse, a transformation of the former Cinnamon Hill hotel into 21 luxury villas and the addition of a 200-room hotel and the recently opened restaurant, Savvy, at the base of the complex.

The entire south and southeast coasts from Point Salines on the west, where the international airport is located, to Great Bacolet Bay on the east, is made up of hilly peninsulas, bluffs, islets, and deep bays. Some fingers have hotels and marinas, and others are elegant residential areas with pretty views. The deep bays and islets have recently become popular locations for kayaking. At the water's edge of Lance aux Epines peninsula is **Prickly Bay Waterside,** one of Grenada's newest marina and residential resorts.

La Sagesse Nature Center In the southeast corner, La Sagesse is the site of the first European settlement on Grenada. A nature center here, developed as part of the national parks system, includes palm-fringed beaches and coral reefs, mangrove, a salt pond, woodlands, and an estuary with a large variety of birds. A small guesthouse with a delightful bar and outdoor restaurant has equipment for water sports. A more recent addition is the **La Sagesse Arts & Craft Market,** which showcases the work of Grenada's finest art and artisans.

You can return to St. George's via Marquis, Grenada's capital under the French. The road passes cacao and banana plantations and fields of wild pine whose fiber is widely used in making baskets and other straw handicrafts. In this area of the east coast, the island's French heritage is particularly evident in the names of people and places.

Alternatively, you can continue to the east coast where a lavish resort development at Bacolet Bay was launched in February 2007. Set on forty-three acres of tropical gardens with a white sandy beach, the facilities include a spa, fitness and sports center, restaurants and beachfront bar, water sports, hiking and biking trails, and limited vehicle access.

Shopping

The shopping area of St. George's is compact and easy to cover on foot in an hour or so. Some of the shops are on the waterfront by the Carenage, and others are in the "upper" town, where Young Street becomes Halifax and leads to Market Square. Most stores are open weekdays from 8:00 or 9:00 a.m. to noon and 1:00 to 4:00 or 4:30 p.m.; Saturday 8:00 a.m. to noon. Not all close for lunch. Over the past several years, shopping malls have blossomed in the Grand Anse area, but the most convenient is the new Esplanade Mall at the cruise-ship terminal, which offers a variety of duty-free and other stores as well as an Internet cafe.

Art and Artists Art Grenada Fine Arts Gallery (7 Grand Anse Shopping Center) features a large selection of local artists and holds exhibitions regularly. Look for works by Canute Caliste, Susan Mains, Roger Brathwaite, and Richard Buchanan. Yellow Poui Art Gallery (9 Young Street; 440-3001; yellowpoui@spiceisle.com) features local artists including Grenada's best-known primitive artist, internationally known Canute Caliste, and such well-known Caribbean artists as Boscoe Holder from Trinidad. Also find prints, rare antique maps and engravings, watercolors, and photographs; look for brightly decorated masks on calabash by local artist Ottley Dennis. Closed Monday except by appointment.

Books and Maps Sea Change Book & Gift Shop (Carenage; 440-3402) stocks American and British paperbacks and best-sellers and books on Grenada and the Caribbean.

China and Crystal The Gift Shop (Carenage and Grand Anse Shopping Complex) has famous-name crystal and china, such as Wedgwood and Royal Copenhagen. Caribbean Duty Free (Esplanade Mall; 440-5356) carries a large selection of china and crystal, fine jewelry, and other duty-free items.

Clothing and Accessories Art Fabrik (9 Young Street; 440-0568; info@artfabrikgrenada.com; www.artfabrikgrenada.com) is a batik shop with a selection of handpainted batik art, clothing, and accessories made in its studios. Imagine (Grand Anse Shopping Center; 444-4028) carries Caribbean handcrafts as well as island batiks and casual wear. Gatsby (Spice Island Beach Resort; 444-4258) has new, separate, duty-free boutiques of designer resort wear for men and women.

Crafts and Souvenirs Arawak Islands, Ltd. (Belmont Road; 444-3577; www.arawak-islands.com) has attractively packaged island products that make great gifts to take home. Sold in outlets around the island, the best of the collection are handmade, handpainted ladies' sachets and kits of island specialties packaged in a fabric pouch. Figleaf (Carenage) carries gifts, local handcrafts, resort wear, and Cuban cigars.

Blind Workshop (Carenage) is an outlet for handwork by local blind artisans. Gifts include straw bags, hats, and mats. Closed weekends. Tikal (Young Street; 440-2310; fisher@spiceisle.com), the leading store for handcrafts made in Grenada and other Caribbean islands, has batiks, handpainted T-shirts, and jewelry.

Grand Anse Craft and Spice Market (north end of Grand Anse Beach; 444-3780), managed by the Grenada Tourist Board, was created in response to complaints about persistent vendors roaming the beach. Here, you can find a wide range of local art and crafts, from carvings to homemade sweets and hair braiding. There's a refreshment bar, phones, toilets, and tourist information desk. Hours: daily 8:00 a.m. to 7:00 p.m.

Jewelry Lisa's Island Jewellery/The Jewellery Store (Carenage and Grenville Street; 439-4404) specializes in handmade gold and silver jewelry in West Indian designs as well as international brands. Colombian Emeralds (Carenage; 440-1746), with stores throughout the Caribbean, has a large selection of jewels and jewelry. Spice Island Jewellry Mfg. Co. (Grenville Street, St. George's; 440-3155) features handcrafted gold and silver jewelry.

Liquor and Wines Renwick-Thompson & Co. (Carenage; 440-2625) claims to be "the best little liquor store in town." Tourist Gift Shop (St. George's Pier) stocks duty-free liquor and gifts.

Perfumes and Cosmetics Arawak Islands (Belmont Road) is a store and workshop that produces perfumes, lotions, potpourri, and teas made from native flowers, spices, and herbs. The staff will explain the manufacturing process and let you sample scents such as frangipani, jasmine, and other unusual fragrances. Shampoo, body lotion, and suntan lotion also are available. Products can be purchased at gift stores in town.

Dining and Restaurants

Fresh fish, fresh vegetables and fruit, soups, desserts made from exotic herbs and spices, and tangy cool drinks punched with island rum are some of the taste treats of Grenadian cuisine, one of the most original in the Caribbean. In addition to traditional West Indian dishes, the French, Chinese, Indian, and Middle Eastern influences have added a distinctive variety and nurtured an interest in food not usually found in former British colonies.

Restaurants are small and operated by their owners, who take personal pride in every dish. Many close on Sunday. Major credit cards are accepted unless noted otherwise. For lunch inexpensive means less than US$10; moderate, US$10–$20; expensive, more than US$20. A 10 percent service charge and an 8 percent value added tax are added to the bill. As mentioned earlier in the chapter, several estate homes in the northern part of Grenada serve lunch, usually offering an array of delicious Grenadian dishes. You will want to make it part of your sightseeing, but normally, you will need to make reservations in advance.

Aquarium Beach Club and Restaurant (Magazine Beach, 444-1410; www.aquarium-grenada.com). The fashionable beachside restaurant with its great location in tropical gardens by the sea is one of the island's favorites for lunch or dinner. Fresh fish, local and international specialties. Wednesday night is lobster night; Sunday brunch's beach-side barbecue is the place to be. Moderately expensive.

The Beach House Restaurant and Bar (Point Salines/Ball's Beach; 444-4455). International cuisine with a Grenadian flavor, seafood, and steaks in a relaxed setting by a pretty beach. Just off the airport road or by water taxi from the Carenage. Closed Sunday. Moderate.

Boatyard (Spice Island Marina; 444-4662). As part of the marina, the palm-shaded bar and restaurant is something of a hangout for yachtsmen, where they can catch up on world events via satellite television and enjoy local and international programs. On Friday nights it becomes a disco of sorts. Closed on Monday. Moderate.

Coconut's Beach (Grand Anse Beach; 444-4644). Delightful sand-in-your-feet setting for Creole specialties or refreshing tropical drinks. No credit cards. Moderate.

La Belle Creole (Blue Horizons Hotel; 444-4316; www.grenadabluehorizon.com). Set in pretty tropical gardens, the hotel belongs to a family known throughout the Eastern Caribbean for its inventive, Creole cuisine. Moderate.

The Nutmeg (Carenage; 440-2539). A long-time favorite of townfolk and tourists for its convenient location, this restaurant features a harbor view, sandwiches, and snacks. Moderate.

Rhodes Restaurant (Calabash Hotel, Lance aux Epines; 444-4334; calabash@spiceisle.com; www.calabashhotel.com). One of Grenada's best restaurants serves continental cuisine with a Caribbean touch. Dinner only. Moderate to expensive.

Savvy Restaurant (Mount Cinnamon at Grand Anse; 439-0000; www.mountcinnamongrenada.com). Located at the base of the new Mount Cinnamon resort overlooking Grand Anse Beach, Savvy is Grenada's newest fine-dining experience. Opened in June 2007 by Peter De Savary, a well-known British developer and creator of Port Louis, Savvy serves Mediterranean fusion cuisine laced with Grenadian spices in a casual-chic atmosphere in a beautiful setting with a spectacular view of the beach and sea stretching to St. George's from the bar and every table. Expensive.

Tropicana (Lagoon Road; 440-1586). West Indian and Chinese cuisine and the best Indian rôtis (meat or chicken roll flavored with curry) in town. A local specialty is featured daily. Moderate.

The Victory Bar & Grill II (Port Louis Marina, Lagoon Road) is an unusual bar with casual barbecue grill and the new marina. Open Tuesday to Sunday from 11:00 a.m. until 11:00 p.m.

Water's Edge (Bel Air Plantation Resort; 443-2822; watersedge@belairplantation.com; www.belairplantation.com), the restaurant of the new hotel on Grenada's southeast coast, is headed by a well-known Grenadian chef, Craig Copland, who also operates his own catering company. The menu features Caribbean cuisine with a contemporary flair. Be sure to try the calalou soup. Moderately expensive.

Nightlife

In low-key Grenada nightlife means watching a magnificent sunset while sipping on an exotic sundowner, a leisurely dinner, and maybe a stop at a disco. Larger hotels have a West Indian buffet and live music on different nights of the week. **The Marryshow Folk Theatre** (Tyrrel Street; 440-2385) has concerts, plays, and special events from time to time.

The Rhum Runner (440-4386; runner@spiceisle.com), a large catamaran, sails on Friday and Saturday evenings, departing the Carenage at 7:30 p.m. and returning at midnight. There's music for dancing and free-flowing rum punch. Price is US$12; a dinner cruise on Wednesday evening from 6:00 to 9:00 p.m. for US$40 is also offered. Some cruise ships offer *The Rhum Runner* as a three-hour excursion along the coast to a beach for a swim and rum drinks, US$27.

Sports

Beaches/Swimming Grand Anse Beach is a 2-mile band of beautiful white sand framed by palm trees bowing to a calm Caribbean Sea. It is not only the prettiest beach in Grenada, but one of the loveliest in the Caribbean and the island's resort and water-sports center. The south shore has quiet coves with white-sand beaches hidden between the fingers of its deeply indented coast. The west-coast beaches north of St. George's have steel gray, volcanic sand. Carriacou and its offshore islands are rung by fabulous white-sand beaches that seldom see a footprint.

Boating Grenada is the southern gateway to the Grenadines and has long been known in yachting circles for its sheltered bays, which provide some of the best anchorages in the Caribbean. The **Grenada Yacht Club** (Tanteen, 440-6826; www.grenadayachtclub.com, gyc@caribsurf.com), located just outside of St. George, offers docking and re-fueling facilities and can accommodate boats up to 75 feet long. The south coast offers short excursions for snorkeling and beach picnics and complete charter facilities: **Spice Island Marine Services** (L'Anse aux Epines; 444-4257; www.spiceislandmarine.com; simsco@spiceisle.com). **The Moorings** (True Blue Bay Resort; 444-4439, 888-952-8420; www.moorings.com; secret harbour@caribbeanhighlights.com), one of the region's largest charterers, is based on Grenada's south coast for cruising the Lower Caribbean, particularly the popular stretch between Grenada, the Grenadines, and St. Lucia.

For day cruises, contact **First Impressions** (440-3678; www.catamarancharters.com, starwind sailing@spiceisle.com); or **Rhum Runner** (440-2198; renthom@spiceisle.com). Its party cruises are offered frequently as cruise-ship excursions.

Deep-Sea Fishing Fish are plentiful in Grenadian waters, but sportfishing is not well developed here. The catch includes barracuda, kingfish, red snapper, and grouper offshore; ocean species are sailfish, black-fin tuna, and blue marlin, among others. **Sanvics** (Grenada Grand Beach Resort; 444-4371) arranges half-day charters for about US$350 and US$500 for six hours, or contact **Evans Fishing Charters** (444-4422; fax: 444-4718; bevans@caribsurf.com).

Golf Grenada Golf and Country Club (Woodlands; 444-4128) has a 9-hole course, which is one of the best natural courses in the Caribbean. Visitors may use the facilities for a small fee. Greens fees are EC$40 or US$15 for 9 holes; US$35 for 18 holes; club rental, US$8; caddie, US$10. Club hours: Monday to Saturday 8:00 a.m. to sunset; Sunday to 1:30 p.m.

Hiking With its magnificent scenery and accessible self-guided nature trails in the Grand Etang National Park, hiking is one of Grenada's top attractions for nature lovers. To arrange more difficult hikes requiring a guide, contact **Telfour Hiking Tours** (442-6200) whose owner, Telfour Bedeau, is the most experienced hiking guide in Grenada; **Phinton Ferrier** (444-9241), or Denis Henry of **Henry's Tours** (443-5313; www.henrysafari.com; email: safari@spiceisle.com). The latter's rates range from US$115 for one person to US$55 per person for four or more persons for a hike to Concord or Seven Sisters falls. **Caribbean Horizons Tours** (444-1555; www.caribbeanhorizons.com) is among others that arrange hiking. (See Shore Excursions earlier in this chapter for details.)

Over the last few years, Grenada has developed a new, groundbreaking National Forest Policy involving people from all over the country. One result has been a decision to ban all logging in forest reserves and national parks and establish management priorities such as water production, biodiversity, wildlife conservation, and recreation. Regarding the last, the National Parks and Tourism sector is developing a network of nutmeg-shell-covered nature trails, such as the recently opened Morne Gazo Trail in St. David's Parish, the southeastern district of the island. The trailhead can be reached by bus or car; there is a cafe/shop and restrooms near the car park. The 1-mile trail has steps and handrails where necessary, but you need to be fairly fit to climb the 200 steps to the summit. There, a platform provides views across most of southern Grenada. Entrance: EC$5; information sheet in English is available; open 9:00 a.m. to 4:00 p.m. Monday through Saturday, 10:00 a.m. to 3:00 p.m. Sunday. Other trails being developed are Annandale, starting from the falls; Cross, near where the St. George–Grenville highway crosses Grand Etang; and the more difficult Vendome to Les Advocats Trail in Grand Etang Forest Reserve. For information, contact Rolax Frederick (440-2934).

Kayaking The sport is new to Grenada but it's a natural one with the island multi-indented coastline offering so many shelter bays and off-shore islets. **Spice Kayaking & Eco Tours** (P.O. Box 1518; Allamanda Beach Resort, Grand Anse; 439-4942; cell: 407-1147; info@spicekayaking.com; spicekayaking@caribsurf.com) offer a variety of tours. The half day begins from Clarke's Court Bay to explore Hog Island and untouched bays and coves of Grenada's southeast with a stop for a swim or snorkel in crystal-clear waters. Pedal boats are also available. The four-hour tour cost US$50

per person including drinks and sandwiches; a full-day six-hour adventure takes in Calivigny Island and snorkeling and continues to a secluded beach at Fort Jeudy where a Grenadian lunch awaits. Cost: US$60 per person, including drinks and lunch. All excursions are accompanied by guides.

Snorkeling/Scuba Diving The best reefs are off Carriacou and its surrounding islands, but in the immediate vicinity of Grenada, you can find reefs along the west coast, some within swimming distance of shore. The south end of Grand Anse Beach is well suited for snorkeling. It has some of the largest sea fans in the Caribbean and a great variety of small fish. The north side of Grand Anse Beach at Martin's Bay is a popular dive site and has patch reefs in 30 to 50 feet of water.

About 3 miles from Grand Anse Beach lies Costa Cruise Lines' former ship, *Bianca C,* which caught fire and sank in 1961. The wreck, one of the largest in the Caribbean, is in water more than 100 feet deep and attracts huge turtles, rays, and a variety of other fish. It is a very popular wreck for experienced divers. Unfortunately, recent reports indicate the dive is no longer as thrilling as in the past. Hurricanes have left the wreck broken up and strewn over a larger area, and the lack of protection has enabled souvenir collectors to strip the ship bare of its furnishings.

Molinière Reef, about 3 miles north of St. George's, is the most frequented area for diving. The reef begins at a 30-foot depth and slopes to 60 feet before dropping to 120 feet. Recently, it has become even more popular with the addition of the wonderful new **Underwater Sculpture Park** by British artist Jason Taylor. The site, only a short boat ride from the cruise port, is easily accessible to snorkelers as well as divers.

Aquanauts Grenada (True Blue Bay Resort, Grand Anse Beach; 444-1126; fax: 444-1127; www .aquanautsgrenada.com; aquanauts@spiceisle .com) and **Dive Grenada** (Grand Anse Beach; 444-1092; 444-5875; www.divegrenada.com; info@dive grenada.com) have daily excursions and certified diving courses at all levels. **Spice Island Diving** (Spice Island Beach Resort, Grand Anse Beach; 444-3483; fax: 444-5319; ddresser@caribsurf.com) is a full-service operation with two dive boats and modern dive equipment. It offers daily two-tank dives in the morning, US$70, and single dive in the afternoon, US$40, to popular sites: *Bianca C* wreck, US$50; Molinère Reef, good for beginners and advanced divers as well as snorkelers; Boss Reef, a 5-mile reef; and trips to Isle de Ronde, a volcanic island 4 miles north of Grenada and one of the Caribbean's last virgin dive sites, US$75.

Tennis Public courts are located at the Tanteen Public Court and Grand Anse Public Court. The Richmond Hill Tennis Club allows visitors to use its facilities for a small fee, and most hotels have at least one court. An open lawn tennis tournament is held annually in March.

Whale and Dolphin Watching An estimated fifteen species of whales can be seen in Grenada waters. The best viewing times run from December to April. **First Impressions** (phone/fax: 444-3678; www.catamaranchartering.com) and **Project Ecological Research Station** (phone/fax: 443-7936; kido-ywf@caribsurf.com; www.kido-projects.com) offer whale- and dolphin-watching excursions on catamarans.

Windsurfing Beachside hotels have windsurfing equipment. Board rentals cost about US$15.

Festivals and Celebrations

August is Grenada's month of celebration, with the year's three biggest events—Carriacou Regatta, Rainbow Festival, and Carnival—falling in the first two weeks.

Usually held the first weekend in August, the **Carriacou Regatta,** begun in 1965, has become one of the Grenadines' main sailing events. All types of boats participate—work boats, sloops, five-masted schooners, canoes, and even miniature sailboats propelled by hand. Banana boats exchange their cargo for people, and sailors from throughout the Grenadines converge on the island and camp on its nearby islets to be part of the three days of festivities. The biggest celebration is the Big Drum Dance, a ritual of the islanders' African heritage that has been reborn into the national culture of the Eastern Caribbean.

Either preceding or coinciding with the Carriacou Regatta is the **Rainbow Festival** in Grenville.

The entire parish of St. Andrew, in which the town is located, turns out to paint the town with brilliant colors; music, food, and crafts fill the streets. In mid-August the festivities move into high gear on the "big island" with **Carnival.** The celebrations culminate in the final "jump-up," with the picturesque harbor of St. George's filled with color, music, and dance, and visitors joining the Grenadians in celebration.

Carriacou

Twenty-three miles northeast of Grenada is one of its two Grenadine Islands. Carriacou, a port of call for several small cruise ships, is a 13-square-mile island with an interesting history and a diverse cultural and natural heritage. It is scalloped with white-sand beaches and surrounded by tiny islets and cays with even more beautiful, pristine beaches—all set in turquoise waters with fabulous reefs. A national parks system is being developed to bring the main areas under protection.

About two-thirds of Carriacou is of volcanic origin. The remainder is limestone and contains fossils that have made Carriacou particularly interesting to scientists.

Hillsborough The port and main town is a village where time seems to have stood still. About 4 blocks long and 3 deep, it is worth a quick walkabout, particularly to visit the museum, where there is a collection of Amerindian and other artifacts. It is situated in the island's oldest house, which was recently restored. Sandy Island, facing the harbor, is a popular snorkeling location with a shallow-water reef only a few feet from shore. You can rent a boat at the pier for the five-minute ride to the island, but you'll need to bring your own snorkeling gear or rent it from the dive operator based at **Silver Beach Resort,** north of town.

Most parts of the island have adequate roads; you can make a tour in a leisurely hour's drive. From a hilltop on the north end of the island, known as the Hospital Scenic Overlook, you can get a grandstand view and a quick orientation of the island. High North Peak, the highest point in Carriacou, at 955 feet, is being made into a national park; it is the least-altered area of the island. The forested northwest slope of the peak drops down to L'Anse La Roche, a beautiful reef-protected cove and beach. Here, too, are the stone ruins of an eighteenth-century plantation that once covered about 266 acres of forest and grazing lands.

The northeast coast at Petit Carenage Bay has extensive mangroves that attract a large variety of birds. South of the swamp at Watering Bay is the village of Windward, founded by Scottish seamen and known throughout the Eastern Caribbean for its skilled boat builders. You can often see them by the waterfront making their fishing and sailing boats, which they construct by hand without a blueprint in a traditional manner handed down from generation to generation.

Off the south coast are tiny Saline Island and White Island, surrounded on three sides by sandy white beaches and protected by the best coral reefs in Grenada's waters. Saline is interesting to scientists for its geological formations and to bird-watchers for its shore birds. Red-billed tropic birds, which grow tails up to 20 inches long, breed here from April to May.

Tyrrel Bay, in the southwest corner of Carria-cou, a good anchorage for yachts, has a pretty secluded beach for swimming. North of the bay the village of Harvey Vale is the home of Grenada's leading primitive artist, Canute Caliste, who is in his eighties. He and some of his twenty-three children (yes, twenty-three!) welcome visitors. Cal-iste's inexpensive paintings are collector's items.

Carriacou Silver Diving (Main Street, Hills-borough; phone/fax: 443-7882; www.scubamax .com), the first dive school on Carriacou, opened in 1993. It offers PADI and CMAS-certified interna-tional diving instruction and certification and a vari-ety of dive packages. The thirty sites in the vicinity of Carriacou offer diverse diving grounds, from flat coral reefs to steep, sloped reefs. **Arawak Divers** (Tyrrel Bay; 443-6906; fax: 443–8312; www.arawak divers.com; arawakdivers@caribsurf.com) is another PADI dive operation and offers daily excur-sions.

Carriacou has small, attractive hotels with din-ing: **Caribee Inn,** at Prospect, on the northwest coast; **Cassada Bay,** on the southeast coast; and **Silver Beach Resort** (443-7337; silverbeach@ caribsurf.com), near Hillsborough. You can hire a taxi or rent a car to tour the island, and boats can be rented for day trips to nearby islands. Seafood is the specialty—with dining on the water's edge—at **Scraper's** (Tyrrel Bay; 443-1403). Carriacou, eighteen minutes from Grenada on Air-lines of Carriacou or Region Air Services, is an easy day trip. The taxi fare from Carriacou Airport to Hillsborough is US$4; Windward, US$8. The *Osprey Express* (www.ospreylines.com; 440-8126) hovercraft operates between Grenada and Carria-cou twice daily.

Petit Martinique Located 2.5 miles off the east coast of Carriacou is its sister island of Petit Martinique. The largest and only one of Carriacou's offshore islands that is inhabited, it covers 486 acres and is dominated by a 745-foot volcanic cone. The 900 residents are mainly fishermen and boat builders. The island is also served by the high-speed hovercraft *Osprey Express,* which makes the trip in 1.5 hours and costs US$27 one-way, US$54 round-trip.

Barbados
Bridgetown

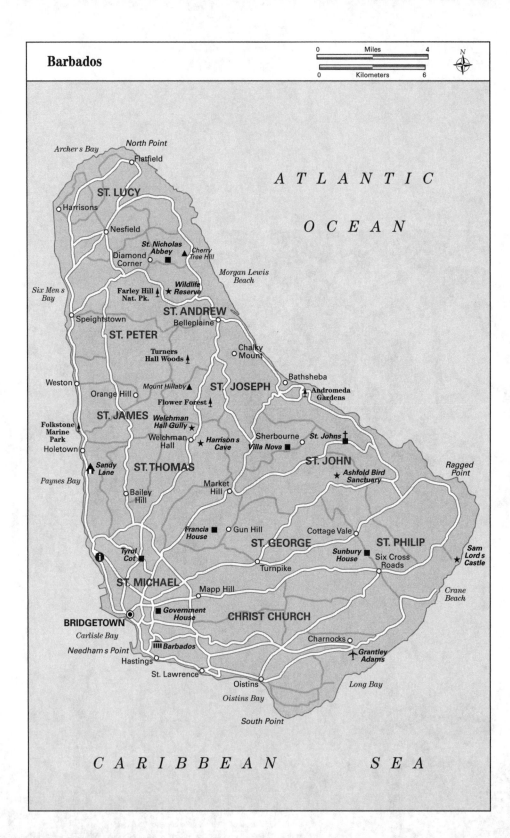

Barbados

Miles 0 — 4

Kilometers 0 — 6

N

Archer's Bay
North Point
Flatfield

ST. LUCY

ATLANTIC

Harrisons

Nesfield

OCEAN

St. Nicholas Abbey ■
Diamond Corner
▲ *Cherry Tree Hill*

Morgan Lewis Beach

Six Men's Bay

Speightstown

Farley Hill Nat. Pk. ▲
★ *Wildlife Reserve*

ST. ANDREW

Belleplaine

ST. PETER

Turners Hall Woods ▲

Chalky Mount

Weston

Mount Hillaby ▲

ST. JOSEPH

Bathsheba
▲ Andromeda Gardens

Orange Hill

Flower Forest ▲

ST. JAMES

Welchman Hall Gully ★

Welchman Hall

★ *Harrison's Cave*

Sherbourne
Villa Nova ■
St. Johns †

St. JOHN

Folkstone Marine Park
Holetown

▲ *Sandy Lane*

ST. THOMAS

★ *Ashfold Bird Sanctuary*

Ragged Point

Paynes Bay

Bailey Hill

Market Hill

Francia House ■
○ Gun Hill

Cottage Vale

ST. PHILIP

Sam Lord's Castle ★

ⓘ
Tyrol Cot ■

ST. GEORGE

Sunbury House ■
Six Cross Roads

ST. MICHAEL

Mapp Hill
Turnpike

Crane Beach

■ *Government House*

CHRIST CHURCH

BRIDGETOWN ◉
Carlisle Bay
Needham's Point
Hastings

▥ *Barbados*

St. Lawrence

Charnocks ○

✈ *Grantley Adams*

Oistins

Long Bay

Oistins Bay

South Point

CARIBBEAN   SEA

Masterpiece Theatre in the Tropics

Barbados is an elegant sort of place in a quiet way. Whether it comes from the three hundred uninterrupted years of British rule, the pride and natural gentility of the Bajans—as its people are called—or from the blue-stocking vacationers who return annually like homing birds to their roost, this Caribbean island is tony. Something like *Masterpiece Theatre* in the tropics.

A limestone and coral island of soft, rolling green hills, Barbados is the easternmost land in the Caribbean, located 100 miles east of the Lesser Antilles. Surrounded by coral reefs that are often within swimming distance from shore, Barbados is fringed with white-sand beaches and calm Caribbean waters on the west and pounded by white-topped Atlantic rollers on the east.

The island's first inhabitants, the Barrancoids, were an Indian tribe from South America who came in the first century A.D. and remained six hundred years. There appears to have been a two-hundred-year gap before the arrival of the peaceful Arawaks, another South American tribe that remained until they were forced north or conquered in about A.D. 1200 by the more warlike Caribs. Early in the sixteenth century, the Caribs met their fate at the hands of the Spaniards who took them as slaves to work in Hispaniola.

Thus when the Portuguese arrived in 1536, they found the island deserted but decided not to settle. A century later, due to a navigational miscalculation by the skipper, Henry Powell, the first English ship arrived in Barbados in 1625, on the west coast at the site Powell called Jamestown for the English monarch. Two years later he returned with eighty settlers to establish the first British colony at the site, known today as Holetown. The settlers raised crops such as yams, cassava, and tobacco, which they had learned from the Indians. But it was sugar, introduced in 1637, that brought Barbados the riches and gave birth to a plantation society that ran the island for almost three hundred years. Unlike most other Caribbean islands, which seesawed between rivaling European powers, Barbados remained British. This continuity helped to make her one of the most stable countries in the Caribbean.

Barbados lays claim to being the third-oldest democracy in the Commonwealth, having established its first parliament in 1639. But, of course, it was hardly a democracy for everyone. As the island developed, the planters imported white indentured servants to fill the need for increased labor. But their treatment of these workers was so inhumane it led to riots in 1634 and 1649, and new arrivals fell to a trickle. To relieve the labor shortage, African slaves were introduced, but from the first slave uprising in 1675 until the abolition of slavery in 1833, rebellion was continuous. In the following century the majority black population matured politically and economically, and a middle class developed.

Although Barbados has been independent of British rule since 1966, in some ways it seems more British than the queen. In Bridgetown, the capital, bewigged judges preside over the country's

At a Glance

Antiquities	★★
Architecture	★★★★
Art and artists	★★★
Beaches	★★★
Colonial buildings	★★★★
Crafts	★★
Cuisine	★★★
Culture	★★★
Dining/Restaurants	★★★★
Entertainment	★★
Forts	★★
History	★★★★
Monuments	★★
Museums	★★★★★
Nightlife	★★
Scenery	★★★
Shopping	★★
Sightseeing	★★★★
Sports	★★★★
Transportation	★★★

Fast Facts

Population: 288,000

Size: 166 square miles

Main Town: Bridgetown

Government: Barbados, a member of the British Commonwealth, has two houses of parliament: the House of Assembly, the lower house, with twenty-eight members elected from each of Barbados's eleven parishes and the City of Bridgetown for five-year terms; the Senate, or upper house, with twenty-one appointed members. The governor-general is appointed by the queen.

Currency: Barbados (BD) dollar. US$1.00 equals BD$1.98. U.S. dollars, traveler's checks, and major credit cards are widely accepted.

Entry Requirements: All visitors must have a valid passport.

Departure Tax: BD$25 (US$13)

Language: English

Public Holidays: January 1, New Year's Day; January 21 (or nearest Monday), Errol Barrow Day; Good Friday; Easter Monday; May 1, Labour Day; May 15, Whit Monday; October 2, United Nations Day; first Monday in August, Kadooment Day; November 30, Independence Day; December 25, Christmas Day; December 26, Boxing Day.

Telephone Area Code: 246

Airlines: Barbados is one of the major transportation hubs of the Eastern Caribbean. *From the United States*, direct service is provided by: Air Jamaica, American Airlines, Caribbean Airlines Continental, Delta and US Airways. *From Canada:* Air Canada flies directly to Barbados. *Interisland:* American Eagle, Air Caraibe, Caribbean Airlines, LIAT, Mustique Airways, and SVG Air.

Information: www.barbados.org

In the United States:

Barbados Tourism Authority

New York: 800 Second Avenue, New York, NY 10017; (800) 221-9831; (212) 986-6516;

fax: (212) 573-9850; btany@barbados.org.

Coral Gables: 150 Alhambra Circle, No. 1000, Coral Gables, FL 33134; (305) 442-7471; fax: (305) 567-2844; btamiami@barbados.org.

Los Angeles: 3440 Wilshire Boulevard, No. 1215, Los Angeles, CA 90010; (800) 221-9831; (213) 380-2198; fax: (213) 384-2763; brala@barbados.org.

In Canada:

Barbados Tourism Authority, 105 Adelaide Street West #1010, Toronto, ON M5H 1P9; (800) 268-9122; (416) 214-9880; fax: (416) 214-9882; Canada@barbados.org.

In Port:

Barbados Tourism Authority, Harbour Road, P.O. Box 242, Bridgetown; (246) 427-2623; (800) 744-6244; fax: (246) 426-4080; btainfo@barbados.org; www.barbados.org.

The Inns and Outs of Barbados, an annual publication, contains a wealth of information useful to visitors. There's also a wealth of information on www.funbarbados.com.

Barbados National Trust, Wildey House, Wildey, St. Michael, Barbados; (246) 426-2421; fax: (246) 429-9055; www.ccanet.net/bnt.; natrust@sunbeach.net. The trust is a private organization concerned with the country's cultural, historic, and natural heritage and responsible for most of its major tourist attractions.

---

law courts, and hotels stop for afternoon tea. Even the rolling countryside bears a striking resemblance to England.

Budget Planning

Barbados has a reputation for being an expensive island, but this may be unfair without some qualification. Certainly, if you travel by private taxi and dine at top restaurants and posh resorts, you will find prices on par with those in New York. But to enjoy Barbados you do not have to go the expensive route. It has good public transportation; taxis for touring, when shared with others, are not unreasonable; and Barbados has many areas where it is easy and pleasant to walk or hike. There are moderately priced restaurants, particularly for Bajan food.

Port Profile

Location/Embarkation Bridgetown, the capital, is situated on the southwest corner of Carlisle Bay. Known as Deep Water Harbour, the port is about 1 mile west of the city center. Cruise ships dock next to the commercial port, which is part of an industrial park; however, it has a separate section of piers with a terminal for cruise passengers. The terminal has a Tourist Information Desk and duty-free shops. Outside the terminal taxis authorized to be in the port area await passengers, most hoping to take you on a tour rather than merely transport you into town.

Local Transportation Barbados has good public transportation serving all corners of the island. Buses operated by the state-owned Transport Board are blue with yellow trim; smaller, privately operated minibuses are yellow with blue trim. To ride the bus you need the exact fare, BD$1.50; you can buy tokens at the bus depot in town. You need have no hesitation about using buses here, but be forewarned: Some bus drivers appear to be in training for the Indy 500. If they are not already deaf from the blast of their bus radios, they—or you—soon will be. Buses operate frequently, from 5:00 a.m. to midnight, but they are crowded from 3:00 to 7:00 p.m.

You can easily identify taxis by the taxi sign on the roof and the letter Z on their license plates. They are not metered, but rates are regulated by law. As always, agree on the price with the driver in advance. Expect to pay about US$100 for a four- to five-hour tour; up to five persons may share the car. Drivers are supposed to be trained to act as guides, but you have to settle for potluck. (The taxi union here is very strong, and some of their members would do well to retire.)

The taxi fare from the port to Bridgetown is BD$10. Some one-way fares from Bridgetown: St. Lawrence Gap, BD$25; airport, BD$38; Harrison's Cave, BD$44; Holetown, BD$37; Speightstown, BD$50; and east to Bathsheba, BD$64.

Roads and Rentals Barbados has more than 800 miles of paved roads. The main arteries are fairly easy to follow, but the maze of small roads and country lanes bordered by tall khuskhus grass and sugarcane tend to look alike to newcomers and can sometimes make even the most accessible place hard to find. The road network starts from Bridgetown, in the southwest, and fans out across

the island like sun rays. The main arteries are numbered 1 to 7 and branch often to connect with other highways, creating a web across the island. A modern 12-mile highway between the airport and west coast skirts the congested Bridgetown/south coast area.

It is easy to take one road on the outbound and return by another route. For example, if you leave the port by Route 1, bordering the west coast where many top resorts are located, and return by Route 2, which is slightly inland from the west coast, you will pass near many of the main attractions.

Good maps are available, but adequate road signs are not. Fortunately, Bajans are friendly and helpful. Their directions, however, are not always clear, because they use the name of the parish—rather than a town or specific locations—as a frame of reference. Bridgetown traffic is heavy; give yourself plenty of time to return to your ship so you won't be inadvertently stranded.

Cars, Mini-Mokes, and vans are available for rent. You can use your valid U.S. or Canadian driver's license, but you must register with the police and pay a fee of BD$10. Your car-rental firm will handle all the formalities for you. Daily rates for cars start at about US$50 for standard shift and US$75 for automatic. *NOTE:* Travelers age seventy and older must present a doctor's letter stating they are fit to drive a vehicle. Some companies will not rent cars for less than two days; it is wise to check in advance. Among those that offer one-day rentals are **Courtesy Car Rentals** (431-4160; courtesyrentacar.com), which has free pickup and delivery; **Voyager Rent-A-Car** (243-0427; www.voyager-rent-a-car.com), **Direct Car Rentals** (420-6372; www.barbadoscars.com), which has Mini-Mokes and jeeps, also with free pickup and delivery; and **Bajan Car Rentals** (429-4327; www.bcrbarbados.com).

Interisland Air Service See Fast Facts.

Emergency Numbers

Medical: Queen Elizabeth Hospital, 436-6450
Ambulance: 511 or 426-0016
Police: 211 or 430-7100
Fire: 311

Shore Excursions

Because of its large number of sightseeing attractions and the extensive road network, there are many routes to be taken for an island tour, and each local tour company has its version. Those described here are typical, but the excursions offered on your ship are likely to differ slightly. The first tour is the one most frequently used. The sites mentioned are described elsewhere in the chapter.

Harrison's Cave/St. Nicholas Abbey/Farley Hill National Park: 4.5 hours, US$70–$90, depending on itinerary. Drive through sugarcane fields of the central highlands to Harrison's Cave, St. Nicholas Abbey, and Farley Hill National Park. Return via Speightstown and the west coast to Bridgetown. Shorter versions available for about US$40–$50.

Gun Hill/Flower Forest/Sunbury Plantation: 3.5 hours, US$35–$45. Drive through Bridgetown via National Square and Government House; to Gun Hill, the Flower Forest, and east to St. John's Church and return via Sunbury Plantation House, a private home open to the public.

Atlantis Submarine Expedition Adventure (www.atlantisadventures.com), US$89.00 adults, US$57.00 teens age 13–17, US$44.50 children; *Above and Below Barbados Tour,* US$152.50 adults, US$84.50 children, combines a scenic catamaran cruise and snorkeling adventure with an underwater tour on *Atlantis III* . Atlantis also offers a *Power Snorkel Adventures* with a handheld power "scooter" for $57 for adults age fifteen and

older, booked for groups of eight or more, Monday to Saturday at 9:00 and 11:00 a.m. and 1:00 and 3:00 p.m. (436-8929; fax: 436-8828; barbados@res .atlantisadventures.com. See Sports section for description.)

Golf/Hiking/Biking Tours. See Sports section.

Rum Factory Tours: Three of Barbados's historic rum factories offer tours, each with a slightly different spin on the tale, which are sometimes included in shore excursions, or you can take your own. *Mount Gay,* on Spring Garden Highway within walking distance of the port, is the oldest factory; it was founded in 1703; *Malibu,* about a mile from the port, is the only working distillery on a beach; and *Heritage Park* in St. Philip district near the east coast, is a modern plant in a history park. (See later in this chapter for descriptions.) For something a bit more spicy, **Island Safari** (432-5337; www.island safari.bb or www.barbadostraveler.com) has a *Rum Shop Safari* for US$42.50, on Saturdays from 10:00 a.m. to 3:00 p.m.

Plantation House Tours: Several of Barbados's many old manor houses are included on island tours, and the one visited usually depends on the route. Those such as Francia, Sunbury (www.barbadosgreathouse.com), and Tyrol Cot can also be visited on your own. From January to mid-April, the National Trust offers special home and garden tours on Wednesday afternoon to specific places, which are open to the public only during this period. Check local newspapers or the National Trust for information.

Island Tours: Among the independent tour companies that offer regular island tours, **Adventureland** (429-3687; fax: 426-3687; www .adventurelandbarbados.com) has an off-road, full-day excursion to less-traveled Barbados for US$77 adult, US$45 children. **J.C. Williams Tour Co.** (427-1043; fax: 427-6007; williamstours@caribsurf .com) has a Historic and Ocean Park Tour to three major sites and Ocean Park Barbados, a marine aquarium, and includes lunch and drinks; another tour circles the entire island. BD$150 (US$75). **Island Safari Barbados** (432-5337; www.island safari.bb) organizes offbeat, caravan-style safari excursions in Land Rovers, among others. **Boyce's**

Tours (425-5366; www.toursbarbados.com) has a variety of heritage, cultural, and nature tours, with departures almost daily, ranging from US$45 to US$57.50 per person. **Bajan Helicopters** (Bridgetown Heliport; 431-0069; fax: 431-0086; www.bajanhelicopters.com) has two flight-seeing tours of Barbados.

Barbados on Your Own

Bridgetown, where approximately one-third of the population lives, has retained enough of its historic character to make a walk interesting. When you come into Bridgetown at **Deep Water Harbour (1)**, you drive (or walk) along Princess Alice Highway, a road built on reclaimed land and paralleling Broad Street, a thoroughfare to the north. You pass **Pelican Village (2)**, a center for local arts and crafts; and, to the north, the eighteenth-century St. Mary's Church. The main road ends by the **Careenage (3)**, the picturesque old harbor where the town began in 1628.

A Bridgetown Walkabout

Still the heart of town, the Careenage lies at the mouth of Constitution River and is spanned by the two small bridges from which Bridgetown takes its name. On the north bank, **National Heroes Square (4)** has a statue of Admiral Nelson by Sir Richard Westmacott, dating from 1815 and predating by twenty-seven years the more famous Nelson Monument in London.

North of National Heroes Square is a group of neo-Gothic buildings, which house the **Barbados Parliament (5)** (www.barbadosparliament.com), originally constructed in 1635. The structures were rebuilt to replace buildings destroyed by fire in 1860. The west wing, dating from 1872, houses the Senate; and the east wing, built in 1874, is the House of Assembly. Note the stained-glass windows with portraits of British monarchs and the speaker's chair, which was a gift from the Indian government when Barbados got its independence.

From the square, Broad Street runs west toward the port, crossing Prince William Henry Street, named for the young naval captain around

whom one of the island's favorite tales was spun. It involves a character named Rachel Pringle, an innkeeper and madam who ran the best little brothel in Barbados, where the prince and his rowdy sailor friends spent a raucous evening. Miss Rachel, history tells us, had no hesitation about sending the prince—who later ascended to the English throne as William IV—a bill for damages. He paid it.

North of Broad Street is Victoria Street, a narrow street with small shops, and Swan Street, a picturesque lane with old balconied buildings, stores selling clothing and jewelry, and pushcarts piled with tropical fruits. Farther north the eighteenth-century **Old Town Hall (6)**, at James and Coleridge Streets, houses the police headquarters. It neighbors the supreme court and the public library, built in 1905 with a grant from the Andrew Carnegie Foundation.

In a triangle east of the library on Magazine Lane (the name comes from a powder storehouse, or magazine, once here) you will see the Montefiore Fountain, donated by a member of the Jewish community in 1864. Across from it stands the recently restored **Nidhe Israel Synagogue (7)**, the second oldest in North America. Originally built in 1656 by Jews from Brazil, the synagogue was rebuilt in the nineteenth century, but the building had long ceased serving as a temple and was in ruins when it was rescued from demolition in the early 1980s. It was restored through the efforts of the local Jewish community, the National Trust, and Jewish groups in the United States, Canada, and the United Kingdom.

Today the building's exterior appears much as it did in the 1830s and has a balustraded roofline, lancet-shaped windows, and thick walls rounded at the corners. Inside, all the additions made in the twentieth century—when it was used alternately as a racing club, warehouse, law library, and business office—were removed, and the walls were stripped to the original coral stone and roof timbers.

To re-create the 1833 temple appearance, the original benches were copied in native mahogany, and eight chandeliers were copied from the originals (now in the Winterthur Museum in Delaware). The main gates, which had been at a private home,

Bridgetown

0 Yards 300
0 Meters 300

N

KENSINGTON ROAD · **HINKSON GAP** · **CHAPMAN STREET** · **GREEN PARK LN.** · **GILLS ROAD** · **BEDFORD LANE** · **LIGHTFOOT LANE** · **COLERIDGE STREET** · **ROEBUCK STREET** · **TUDOR STREET** · **SOBERS LANE** · **WALDRON STREET** · **MAHOGANY LANE** · **MASON HALL STREET** · **REED STREET** · **PINFOLD STREET** · **CRUMPTON STREET** · **EMMERTON CANE** · **ST. MARY'S ROW** · ■ **Police** · ⑥ · ⑦ · **CHEAPSIDE STREET** · **SUTTLE STREET** · **JAMES** · **PALMETTO RICKETT STREET** · ⑨ · **St. Mary's** ✝ · **STREET** · **SPRAY STREET** · **CHURCH STREET** · ② · ✉ · **CHAPEL STREET** · **SWAN STREET** · ⑧ · ① · **REEF ROAD** · **Market** ■ · **LOWER BROAD STREET** · **PRINCE WILLIAM HENRY STREET** · **VICTORIA STREET** · **MARHILL STREET** · **PRINCESS** · **ALICE** · **TEMPLE RD.** · **McGREGOR ST.** · **BROAD STREET** · **HIGH STREET** · **ST. MICHAEL'S ROW** · **HIGHWAY** · **COWELL STREET** · **PRINCE ALFRED ST.** · **NILE ST.** · ⑤ · ④ · **HINKS ST.** · ✦ **Immigration** · **BRIDGE STREET** · **Constitution R.** · ⌂ **Bus Terminal** · **FAIRCHILD STREET** · *Fishing Harbor* · ③ · **NELSON STREET** · **JORDENS** · **LANE** · **BAY STREET** · **WELLINGTON STREET**

C A R I B B E A N   S E A

1. Deep Water Harbour
2. Pelican Village
3. Careenage
4. National Heroes Square
5. Barbados Parliament
6. Old Town Hall
7. Synagogue
8. St. Michael's Cathedral
9. Queen's Park

were returned to their place in the stone wall sur-rounding the property. The cemetery, with 400 old graves, was cleaned and tombstones were repaired. In August 2007 the Nidhe Israel Syna-gogue Museum, adjacent to the synagogue, opened to the public. Exhibits include artifacts dis-covered in the cemetery and are exhibited on a bed of sand, connecting with the religious observance of the sand covered floor in a seventeenth-century synagogue. Hours: Monday to Saturday, 9:00 a.m. to 4:00 p.m. Admission: US$12.50. For information, contact Synagogue Restoration, Box 256, Bridge-town; 432-0840.

East of National Heroes Square, St. Michael's Row leads to **St. Michael's Cathedral (8),** built originally in 1665 and rebuilt in 1789 after being destroyed by a hurricane. It was elevated to a cathedral on the arrival of the first bishop of Barbados in 1825. The Lady Chapel at the eastern end was added in the 1930s. On the south is Queen's College, a prominent girls' school, opened in 1880. At the end of the street is a public park, **Queen's Park (9),** that was once the residence of the commander of the British troops of the West Indies.

From the Careenage, Bay Street (which becomes Route 7) runs south past the Harbour Police Station and St. Patrick's Cathedral, the island's first Roman Catholic church, built in 1849. The road passes the Carlisle Bay Centre, a recreational and water-sports center.

At the corner of Bay Street and Chelsea Road stands Washington House, once identified as the place where George Washington stayed with his brother in 1751 as a lad of nineteen. Recently, however, this historic error was corrected, and Bush Hill House in the Garrison was identified as the home where Washington stayed. Formerly a private house used for offices, **Bush Hill House,** now called George Washington House (228-5461; www.georgewashingtonbarbados.org), has been restored as an eighteenth-century plantation residence and is open to the public weekdays, 9:30 a.m. to 4:30 p.m. Admission: US$12.50 adult, $6.25 children age five to ten, younger than age five admitted free. In any event, Barbados was the only foreign land the first president of the United States ever visited.

At the south end of Carlisle Bay, Needham's Point is a popular resort area with hotels, pretty beaches, and sports and recreational facilities. On the tip are the ruins of Fort Charles and St. Anne's Fort, which were part of a defense system begun in 1694. Behind the forts is the **Garrison Savannah,** a parade ground that is now the racetrack. It is surrounded by more than seventy historic buildings, one of which—a former colonial prison—houses the Barbados Museum.

Barbados Museum (427-0201; www.barbmuse.org.bb; customerservice@barbmuse.org.bb) For history buffs, a visit to the museum is a Barbados highlight where they can enjoy a magnificently displayed, comprehensive collection on the history, culture, and natural history of Barbados and the Caribbean. Among the outstanding exhibits are those tracing the routes of the pre-Columbian people into the Caribbean, along with displays of their artifacts. In 2004, the newest gallery, the "Charles A. Robertson African Gallery: Connections and Continuities" opened to the public. The exhibit introduces the viewer to the geography, history, and heritage of Africa and its legacy in the creation of Caribbean society. The museum has a fine library of old maps and documents on the West Indies and a good bookshop. Hours: Monday to Saturday 9:00 a.m. to 5:00 p.m., Sunday 2:00 to 6:00 p.m. Admission: BD$11.50 adults, BD$5.75 children.

Bordering the residential district of Belleville (too far to walk) on the east is **Government House,** set in lovely gardens. It has been the residence of the governor since 1702. Nearby **Ronald Tree House** (No. 2, Tenth Avenue), formerly the headquarters of the Barbados National Trust (426-2421; fax 429-9055; natrust@sunbeach.net), is a restored Victorian town house named for the trust's founder, Ronald Tree, who also built the original luxury hotel Sandy Lane. Many of the historic homes and sites maintained by the trust rank among the island's main attractions. On Wednesdays from mid-January to early April, the trust sponsors Open Houses, which is a house and garden tour. The houses, often furnished with antiques and rare collections, have beautiful interiors. There is a charge.

Tyrol Cot Heritage Village (St. Michael; 424-2074; www.barbados.org/tyrolcot.htm) High on the lists of Barbados's heritage attractions is the house that belonged to both Sir Grantley Adams, the first premier of Barbados, honored as the "father of democracy," and his son Tom Adams, who followed in his father's footsteps and was the country's second prime minister. Built in 1854, and restored recently by the National Trust, the manor is a good example of mid-nineteenth-century architecture. In the gardens is the **Heritage Village,** an outdoor "living" museum housed in chattel houses, the folk architecture of old Barbados. Each cottage displays the work of a traditional craftsman or artist, who usually can be seen at work. Traditional Bajan food and snacks are served in a "rum shop." Hours: Weekdays, 8:00 a.m. to 4:00 p.m. Admission: BD$14 adults, children sixteen years and younger are admitted free.

A Drive around the Island

Barbados has so many historic homes, gardens, old churches, parks, nature reserves, and scenic sites that you could strike out in almost any direction and find plenty to fill a day. We have divided the excursions into segments to be taken separately as leisurely drives of two to three hours; they can also be combined, depending on your time.

North to Speightstown

(Parishes: St. Michael, St. James, St. Peter)

From Bridgetown, Route 1, skirting the palm-fringed beaches of the Caribbean known as the Platinum Coast, has many of Barbados's most fashionable resorts and fabulous villas.

Mount Gay North of the cruise-ship pier, within walking distance, is Mount Gay Visitor's Center (Spring Garden Highway; 425-8757; www.mountgay.com) at Barbados's oldest rum factory, begun in 1703. On the tour you get a taste of the island's history, culture, rum making, and rum. There is a gift shop and a garden cafe. Hours: Monday to Friday, 9:30 a.m. to 3:30 p.m.; tours every half hour. Admission: BD$14. There is also a luncheon tour on Tuesdays and Thursdays, BD$80 with transportation, BD$68 without transportation; and a cocktail tour on Thursdays, BD$60 with transportation, BD$50 without. Call in advance to reserve for these tours.

Farther along, **Malibu Visitors Centre** (Brighton, Black Rock; 425-9393; www.malibu-rum.com), by West Indies Rum Distillery and the home of Malibu, is Barbados's only working distillery on the beach and offers distillery tours. Hours: Monday to Friday, 9:00 a.m. to 4:00 p.m. The last morning tour is at 10:30 a.m.; last afternoon tour at 3:45 p.m. After a tour you can spend the day on the beautiful beach where chairs, umbrellas, changing rooms, showers, and a small restaurant and bar (where you receive a complimentary drink) are available. Special day pass and lunch tours, including transportation, are also available.

Sandy Lane Once the dowager queen of the group, Sandy Lane Hotel and Golf Club (www.sandylane.com) is set in 380 acres of a former sugar plantation just south of Holetown. Designed by the well-known Caribbean architect Robertson "Happy" Ward, Sandy Lane was built in 1961 by Sir Ronald Tree, M.P., whose famous aristocratic friends helped him establish the resort's reputation as the most exclusive in the Caribbean. The resort was torn down totally and rebuilt from the ground up. It reopened in 2001 as a brand-new hotel, resembling the old one somewhat, but with quite a difference. The rooms are larger and more luxurious, with push-button electronics that even Batman could envy. There's one to open the draperies, another to adjust the lights or the volume on the television or the DVD, and still another to tell the butler on the outside that you are inside your room. The resort, which has a huge spa with eye-popping prices, redesigned and expanded its golf course to 45 holes, including two 18-hole championship courses by famed architect Tom Fazio.

Holetown The site of the island's first settlement, Jamestown, is marked by a memorial and the St. James Parish Church, first built about 1660 and thought to be the oldest on the island. The south porch has an old bell on a pillar, bearing an inscription to King William, 1696—making it older than the Liberty Bell in Philadelphia, which was cast in London in 1750. At the entrance to Holetown is **Chattel House Shopping Village,** which has craft and other shops in colorful cottages patterned after typical local houses. A map of other Chattel House Shopping Village locations around the island can be found at www.barbados.org/maps. With so many of Barbados's best hotels along the west coast, this area has also become a center for many of the island's best restaurants and more sophisticated nightlife.

Folkestone Park/Barbados Marine Reserve North of Holetown, the Folkestone Park is a picnic and swimming spot popular with Bajans and part of the complex that includes the Barbados Marine Reserve, a small marine museum, and the Belair Research Laboratory. Offshore, the marine park is divided into zones according to use for water sports or scientific research.

If you are short on time, you can turn east at Holetown onto Route 1A, for Harrison's Cave, Welchman Hall Gully, and Flower Forest.

Glitter Bay Immediately upon entering the front gate, which opens onto twelve beachfront acres of landscaped gardens, you get the impression that someone important lived here. Glitter Bay (www.glitterbay.com), formerly the seaside retreat of Sir Edward Cunard of British steamship fame, was the gathering place of a glittering array of lords and ladies when Cunard's passengers came to winter in the tropics. Cunard's mansion, or Great House, is the centerpiece of the baronial resort. Stately royal palms lead the way to flower-trimmed walkways, a mile-long beach, and a split-level swimming pool with a waterfall and footbridge. The equally stylish Royal Pavilion is next door.

Cobblers Cove Farther north, Cobblers Cove (www.cobblerscove.com) is a small, romantic resort set snugly in three acres of tropical gardens overlooking a quiet crescent of pearly sand, with just enough history to lend it charm. Cobblers Cove made its American television debut in 1982 when its former neighbor, actress Claudette Colbert, whose house shared the same beach, had old chum Ron Reagan as a guest. The resort's centerpiece is a pale pink villa built as a summer home by a Bajan sugar baron early in this century.

Speightstown Once an important sugar port, Barbados's second-largest town was founded between 1630 and 1635 by a firm called Speight of Bristol (England). So close were the links in trade that the town was known as Little Bristol until the turn of the century. The Manse, the oldest building in the town, dates from the seventeenth century.

Arlington House and Museum This "Single House" on Queen Street was called "Little Bristol" by the early settlers. Now restored, the historic house has an interactive museum on all three floors: "Speightstown Memories" on the ground floor; "Plantation Memories" on the second floor; "Wharf Memories" on the third floor celebrating Speightstown's former glory as a leading port and hub connecting three continents. Hours: Monday to Saturday, 9:00 a.m. to 5:00 p.m. Admission: BD$12.50.

East to Farley Hill

(Parishes: St. Peter, St. Andrew)

At Speightstown, Route 1 leaves the coast and turns east to Farley Hill.

Farley Hill National Park Approached by an avenue of royal palms and casuarina trees, the park is named after a mansion built in 1861 for the visit of Prince Alfred, Duke of Edinburgh. Later it housed George V and other members of the British royal family. After a fire in 1965, the house was taken over by the government, but not rebuilt. The grounds were made into a park of thirty wooded acres and gardens with picnic tables and a children's playground. The views south and east of the Scotland District and the Atlantic coast are spectacular. Several times a year Farley Hill is transformed into a stage for musical and theatrical events, such as the Barbados Jazz Festival (www.barbadosjazzfestival.com). Hours: Daily from 7:00 a.m. to 6:00 p.m.

Barbados Wildlife Reserve Opposite the park entrance a track leads through a sugarcane field to the Barbados Wildlife Reserve (422-8826; www.barbadosmonkey.dhc-ltd.com; info@barbadosmonkey.org), primarily a sanctuary for the green, or vervet, monkey, created in 1985 by primatologist Jean Baulou of the Barbados Primate Research Centre. Monkeys, brought to Barbados from West Africa, were considered agricultural pests as early as 1680. In recent years they had become so numerous and destructive that the government turned to the Primate Research Centre to organize a humane trapping and wildlife management program.

The monkeys, although called green, are brownish gray with yellow and olive green flecks. Naturally shy and difficult to observe in the wild, the monkeys are uncaged here and can be seen in a mahogany grove along with agoutis, caimans, deer, opossums, raccoons, tortoises, and wallabies. The three-acre reserve has tree-shaded paths, a stream with otters, swans, and ducks, and a walk-in aviary of tropical birds. Hours: daily 10:00 a.m. to 5:00 p.m. Admission: BD$23 adults, BD$11.50 children three to twelve years old. Information: 422-8826.

St. Nicholas Abbey East of the park en route to Cherry Tree Hill is St. Nicholas Abbey (www.stnicholasabbey.com), a plantation house built in 1650 and owned a decade later by Sir John Yeamans, the third governor of South Carolina. Still the estate house of a working sugar plantation, the well-preserved structure with curved gables and four chimneys is a fine example of Jacobean architecture. The mansion was recently renovated by the new owner, architect Larry Warren. It is open to the public year-round and is a producer of foundational sugar cane by-products. Hours: Weekdays, 10:00 a.m. to 3:30 p.m.; admission: BD$25 adults; BD$15 children.

To the east, the 850-foot Cherry Tree Hill commands a fabulous view of the Atlantic coast and Scotland District, a large bowl-shaped area that differs geologically from the rest of the island. It is in St. Andrew parish, named for the patron saint of Scotland.

Morgan Lewis Mill About a mile south of Cherry Tree Hill stands the seventeenth-century Morgan Lewis Mill (www.barbados.org/morgan.htm), the only windmill of the three hundred that once operated in Barbados that still has its wheelhouse and arms intact. It was built in Dutch style by Dutch Jews from Brazil who settled in Barbados and pioneered sugar cultivation. The mill was restored by the National Trust. Admission: BD$10 adults, BD$5 children.

South of Morgan Lewis you can continue along the east coast to Bathsheba or join Route 2 to return to Bridgetown through the heart of the island. Mount Hillaby, Barbados's highest point, is in view, and inland, Turners Hall Woods is a forty-six-acre reserve of natural forest popular with hikers and naturalists.

The Central Highlands

(Parishes: St. Michael, St. Thomas)

Three of Barbados's most popular attractions— Harrison's Cave, Flower Forest, and Welchman Hall Gully—are located within a mile of one another about a thirty-minute drive from the port on Route 2. A stop at Earthworks Pottery could be made en route.

Harrison's Cave (www.harrisonscave.com) Among Barbados's many limestone caverns, the most accessible and impressive is Harrison's Cave. First explored in 1781, the cave was developed in the 1970s as an attraction by the government with the aid of Danish speleologists. A battery-powered tram with a driver and guide takes visitors down into the lighted chambers. The spectacular Great Hall, which rises more than 150 feet, has a twin waterfall set among beautiful stalagmites and stalactites glittering under artificial lights. Near the bottom the tram rounds a curve where you see the falls again, plunging into a blue-green pool below. Renovations, including improvements to the ground floors, an interpretive center, reservations section, souvenir shop and snack bar, were completed in May 2007. Tours operate daily every hour from 9:00 a.m. to 4:00 p.m. Admission: US$20, children US$10.

Welchman Hall Gully Across the road from the cave is the south entrance to Welchman Hall Gully, a split in the coral limestone where a nature reserve has been created. The gully, humid and protected from high winds, was converted into a tropical-fruit-and-spice garden in the mid-nineteenth century but was later abandoned. In 1962 the site was acquired and developed as an attraction by the National Trust. A half-mile-long path starts at the south entrance and meanders through the reserve, thick with vegetation that appears to be growing out of the rocks. It ends at the parking lot on the north side, having passed six different sections with trees and plants common to the Caribbean, including huge samples of the bearded fig. Open daily; admission is BD$14. Harrison's Cave and Welchman Hall Gully (438-6671, dbranker@caribsurf.com) can be reached by public bus.

Flower Forest North of Harrison's Cave is a tropical garden developed on fifty acres by a private group of Bajans and foreigners as a "legacy of beauty, peace and quiet . . . to leave our children." Situated on Richmond Plantation, an old sugar estate at 850 feet in altitude, the gardens have a great variety of tropical fruit trees and herbs. Footpaths along the contours of the steep hillside lead past bougainvillea and other tropical flowers. The walk is a bit strenuous, but there are benches and lookouts where you can stop to enjoy views. There is a bar at the entrance serving exotic fruit drinks and also a gift shop. Hours: Daily, 9:00 a.m. to 5:00 p.m. Admission: BD$20 adults, BD$10 children five to thirteen years old (433-8152; www.barbados.org/sightseeing/Flowerforest).

The Central Highlands II

(Parishes: St. George, St. John)

Another excursion from Bridgetown through the central part of the island winds east, past tiny chattel houses and fields of swaying sugarcane, to the windswept Atlantic coast at Bathsheba on Routes 4 and 3B.

The parish Church of St. George, dating from the seventeenth century, was rebuilt after being devastated by a hurricane in 1780. It has an altar-piece painting by the eighteenth-century American painter Benjamin West.

Gun Hill About midway a secondary road leads uphill to Gun Hill at about a 700-foot elevation. Once an important British military camp, it was part of a chain of signal stations. On a hillside stands a huge British lion, 10 feet high and 16 feet long, hewn from a limestone outcrop in 1868. This emblem of Imperial Britain looks a bit incongruous now. Gun Hill, a National Trust property, is open daily. Admission: BD$10 adults, BD$5 children.

Heritage Park The historic site of the Foursquare Sugar Factory in St. Philip has been made into a tourist attraction by the owners in conjunction with the National Trust. Historic buildings (www.windmillworld.com/world/barbados) are alongside the modern distillery of ESAF White Rum. Hours: Monday to Friday, 9:00 a.m. to 5:00 p.m. Admission: free, tours are self-guided. Call 420-9954 for information.

Orchid World On Highway 3B between Gun Hill and St. John's Church, en route to Villa Nova. One of Barbados's newest attractions set in lovely, rolling countryside, Orchid World (433-0306; ffl@ sunbeach.net) is a treasure for orchid lovers, with dozens of exotic species from around the world. Hours: Daily, 9:00 a.m. to 5:00 p.m. Admission: US$7 including VAT, adults, children half-price.

On the southwest, **Drax Hall,** built in 1650, is one of the oldest, finest plantation houses in Barbados and still owned by the Drax family. It is one of the private homes open to the public on the National Trust's homes and garden tours.

Francia Plantation House An elegant manor set on a wooded hillside with lovely terraced gardens, Francia was built in 1913 by a successful Brazilian farmer of French descent who married a Bajan woman. The beautifully maintained mansion is furnished with interesting antiques. Hours: Weekdays, 10:00 a.m. to 4:00 p.m. Admission: BD$9 adults, BD$4.50 children (429-0474; francia@ caribsurf.net).

The East Coast

(Parishes: St. Philip, St. John, St. Joseph)

The lighthouse at Ragged Point marks the eastern-most reach of Barbados; beyond, the next stop is the coast of Africa. North of the point the coast stretches for 16 miles along the Atlantic to Bathsheba and Pico Tenerife. The scenic area is popular for hiking and beachcombing.

Codrington College Founded in the seventeenth century by Christopher Codrington, a wealthy planter who became governor of the Leeward Islands, Codrington College is the oldest British school in the West Indies and one of the earliest institutions of higher education in the Western Hemisphere. Now a theological school, the entrance is marked by a fabulous avenue of stately royal palms—one of Barbados's most frequently pictured settings.

St. John's Church On a hillside above Codrington College is St. John's Church, built in 1836 to replace an earlier one destroyed by a hurricane. The churchyard contains tombstones from 1678; one is the grave of Ferdinando Palaeologus, said to be a descendant of Byzantine emperor Constantine. The hillside offers wonderful views of the Atlantic coast.

Bathsheba Overlooking beautiful Tent Bay and framed by the 1,000-foot-high limestone walls of Hackleton's Cliff, Bathsheba is a fishing village and holiday resort. Often described as Cornwall-in-miniature, it has room-size boulders resting at the water's edge, where large white-topped Atlantic waves break against the shore. Flying fish can be seen here. The Atlantis Hotel, famous for its Sunday brunch of Bajan cuisine, overlooks the dramatic landscape.

Andromeda Gardens (433-9384; www .andromedagardens.com) A cliffside above

Bathsheba is the site of the Andromeda Gardens, a mature tropical spread acquired by the National Trust in 1989. The gardens have a particular interest to botanists and horticulturists, because the late owner's hobby was to transplant species here from different climatic conditions around the world to test their ability to grow in the Caribbean's tropical environment. Laid out along the hillside by a meandering stream, the gardens are known for their orchids. Hours: Daily, 9:00 a.m. to 5:00 p.m. Admission: BD$17.50 adults, BD$9.00 children).

To the South and Southeast
(Parishes: Christ Church, St. Philip)

South of Bridgetown, Route 7 leads 16 miles to Ragged Point. A detour through St. Lawrence Gap or at Maxwell Road takes you through lanes that Bajans call "the Strip." But it's much tonier than the name might suggest, with small resorts and something of a Cape Cod ambience.

Oistins From the fishing village of Oistins, one of the most historic towns on the island, a road leads to South Point, the southernmost tip of Barbados, where there is a lighthouse. The southeastern end of the island has rocky fingers and pretty bays protected by reefs lying just off the coast.

Concorde Experience Museum (www .barbadosconcorde.com) The G-BOAE, the final Concorde to fly supersonically over the Atlantic, is opened for public tours at Grantely Adams Airport. The experience includes a virtual flight school, a departure lounge, an observation deck, a multimedia presentation, and a tour of the aircraft. The project was done in partnership with GAIA Inc., the Barbados Museum and Historical Society, and British Airways. Hours: Daily, 9:00 a.m. to 6:00 p.m. Admission: US$17.50 adults, $12.50 child.

Sam Lord's Castle The elegant Georgian mansion was built on the foundation of an old plantation house in the early 1800s by Samuel Hall Lord, who reputedly made his fortune as a wrecker—a pirate who lured ships onto the rocks to plunder them. Now a National Trust property, the mansion is the restored centerpiece of a hotel and boasts a fine collection of art and antiques. Although it's closed for renovations at press time, when tours are available, admission is BD$15

adults; children younger than age twelve admitted free.

Sunbury Plantation House (www.barbados greathouse.com) An early-eighteenth-century plantation house that was extensively renovated after a fire in 1995, Sunbury House is furnished with antiques and artifacts meant to reflect life on a sugar estate in the colonial era. Hours: Daily, 9:00 a.m. to 5:00 p.m. Admission: BD$12 adults, BD$6 children.

Shopping

Broad Street in Bridgetown is the main shopping center of the island, complete with department stores, shopping malls, and a host of boutiques. The two largest department stores—**Cave Shepherd & Co.** and **Harrison's,** with branches at the port—stock duty-free imports such as perfumes and English bone china. Stores are open weekdays from 8:00 a.m. to 4:00 p.m. and Saturday to 1:00 p.m.

Colorful Swan Street is a place for bargains. Chic boutiques are found on Bay Street. Shopping villages have mushroomed around the island, making it easy to combine a sightseeing and shopping excursion.

Antiques Greenwich House Antiques (Greenwich, St. James; 432-1169), in an old plantation house, is crammed full of wonderful old china, furniture, books, and prints.

Art and Artists The Barbados Arts Council Gallery (Pelican Village; 426-4385) has group and one-person shows year-round in its open-air gallery. It features everything from batik and photography to sculpture and ceramics. **Queen's Park Gallery** (Queens Park; 427-2345), operated by the National Cultural Foundation, stages monthlong exhibitions throughout the year. The spacious gallery is open daily Monday through Saturday 10:00 a.m. to 6:00 p.m.

The Gallery of Caribbean Art (Queen Street, Speightstown; 419-0858; www.artgallerycaribbean .com) specializes in art from around the Caribbean as well as some of Barbados's leading artists. Hours: Monday to Friday 9:30 a.m. to 4:30 p.m., Saturday to 2:00 p.m. **Kirby Gallery** (The Courtyard, Hastings, Christ Church; 430-3032; www.kirby artgallery.com), directed by artist Vanita Comissiong, is one of the island's newest galleries for art by Bajan artists.

Barbados is in the midst of an art explosion, judging from the number of galleries that have opened in recent years. The Web site http://arts happeningsbarbados.blogspot.com has a list and descriptions of galleries. In addition to those named above, there are another dozen or so around the island. *Sunseekers,* a free weekly tourist publication, also has a list. For those with a serious interest, *Art in Barbados, What Kind of Mirror Image?* by Alissandra Cummins, Barbados Museum and Historical Society director; Alison Thompson, an art history teacher; and Nick Whittle, an artist and art teacher, is a book published by the society.

Books and Maps The best is the **Cloister Bookstore** (Hincks Street; 426-2662). Others are **Brydens** (Victoria Street), **Cave Shepherd & Co.** (Broad Street), and **Barbados Museum Bookshop.**

China and Crystal Cave Shepherd & Co. (Broad Street and branches at deluxe hotels; www.shopatcaveshepherd.com) stocks china and crystal such as Wedgwood, Royal Doulton, and Waterford, to name a few. **Little Switzerland** (Broad Street) is another.

Cigars The Caribbean Cigar Co., at the western end of Pelican Village, walking distance from the port, produces four sizes of cigars with tobacco from Cuba, Ecuador, and Cameroon under the brand Royal Barbados. At the workshop you can watch women at work while a guide explains the process done partly by hand, partly by machine.

Clothing and Accessories In addition to department stores, you can find boutiques for beach and leisure wear throughout the island. The most interesting are those of Bajan designers. **Gatsby,** with nine boutiques at Bridgetown Harbour and in west coast hotels, has international designer-label fashions. **Upbeat** (Broad Street and other locations) carries beachwear, including swimwear by local designers, such as Ripples (www.ripples-swimwear.com). **The Monkey Pot** (Pelican Village) sells handpainted dresses and ties.

Crafts and Souvenirs The recent explosion of crafts has resulted in a bewildering variety of decorative and functional products by sophisticated artists, who set the standards and style, and by local craftspeople, who use their intuitive skills and ingenuity to transform clay, beads, seeds, rope, coral, wood, and grass into pottery, sculpture, jewelry, fabrics, and household items. The Barbados Investment and Development Corporation (BIDC), a government agency that provides training, is credited with helping to improve the quality and sophistication of local crafts. BIDC markets the products as Pridecraft. Craft fairs are held throughout the year. The main fairs are Holetown Festival, February; Oistins Festival, Easter; Crop Over, August; and Barbados Museum Annual Craft Fair, December.

Pelican Village (Princess Alice Highway) is a cluster of small shops with curios and crafts. Nearby Temple Yard is the craft center of the Rastafarians, who specialize in leather and paintings with strong African identification.

Earthworks Pottery (Edgehill, St. Thomas; 425-0223; www.earthworks-pottery.com) is the workshop of Goldie Spieler, whose imaginative collection ranges from decorative chattel houses to functional microwave and kitchenware. Hours: weekdays 9:00 a.m. to 5:00 p.m., Saturday 9:00 a.m. to 1:00 p.m.

Articrafts (Broad Street; 427-5767) showcases the work of Roslyn Watson, an artist, designer, and handweaving specialist noted for pretty yet durable basketry and tapestry. Open 8:30 a.m. to 5:00 p.m. Monday to Thursday, until 6:00 p.m. on Friday, and 4:00 p.m. on Saturday. Quality work by other artists is also on display. **Best of Barbados** (outlets at hotels and tourist attractions; www.best-of-barbados.com) is both a group of shops and a marketing label for the distinctive work of Jill Walker, which is widely distributed throughout the Caribbean. She is best known for her watercolors of island folk scenes, which are reproduced in a wide range of gifts and small household items.

The Chattel Village (Holetown). Borrowing from the colorful style of local architecture known as chattel houses, developers have created attractive, colorful shopping villages with each small house devoted to a specialty shop—Barbados's answer to shopping malls, although the island has them, too. Convenient to the port and hotels is the west coast village with **Best of Barbados; Ganzee,** a T-shirt specialist; the **Gourmet Shop,** for island and other food products; and an outdoor cafe, among other shops.

Wild Feathers (Bayshore entrance near Sam Lord's Castle; 423-7758) is the small home studio where Geoffrey and Joanie Skeete carve and re-create indigenous and migratory birds of Barbados. You usually can watch them at work. On display is their collection of more than thirty birds, including some made by their son and daughter-in-law. Larger carvings are made to order, but miniatures are available for sale. Joanie also paints watercolors of Caribbean birdlife. Call for an appointment.

Medford Craft World (Whitehall, Main Road, 425-1919) is the workshop of Reggie Medford, a self-taught woodcarver with an eye for business who has developed an unusual method of carving native mahogany with an electric blade normally used for sanding. His mass-produced products—clocks, dolphins, bowls—range from US$20 to $150, depending on the size and design. His abstract sculptures, which follow the natural contours of the raw wood, are his most interesting work; they start at US$200.

Jewelry You'll find fine jewelry at **Cave Shepherd** and **Harrison's,** among others. Craft stores and trendy boutiques carry handcrafted jewelry of local materials and semiprecious stones.

Liquor and Wines Bajan rum, some of the best in the Caribbean, has been made here since the early seventeenth century. Barbados claims to be the first island in the West Indies from which rum was exported. The best known is **Mount Gay,** whose factory (425-8757) offers one of the best and most comprehensive tours of a rum factory in the Caribbean. A popular brand of aged rum is Cockspur Old Gold. Other rum factory tours are described earlier in this chapter.

Perfumes and Cosmetics Harrison's (Broad Street, hotel outlets, and at the port) stocks most of the well-known French perfumes and at prices competitive with St. Thomas and other Caribbean islands.

Dining and Restaurants

Neither the gourmet capital of the Caribbean nor its Creole center, Barbados nevertheless can hold its own for the range and variety of restaurants, and it's getting better with each passing year. More restaurants are offering West Indian dishes. Local seafood, especially Barbados's famous flying fish, a small fish that can be seen often skipping over the waves on the Atlantic coast, is the star, as are fresh fruits and vegetables.

Other Bajan specialties are pumpkin fritters, curried chicken, pepperpot (a savory stew derived from the Arawak Indians), cou cou (a cornmeal and okra dish), and pickled breadfruit, to name a few. Mauby, a traditional Bajan drink made from tree bark, has a pungent, bittersweet taste meant to stimulate the appetite.

Prices at the best restaurants are high. Inexpensive means less than BD$40; moderate, BD$40–$60; and expensive, BD$60 and up. Reservations are advised. Major credit cards are usually accepted, but inquire in advance. Dress is casual but conservative. Some hotels require a jacket for men at dinner. Some of the best restaurants serve only dinner. Those listed here serve lunch unless stated otherwise, but check locally for times, as these vary.

Bridgetown/Christ Church Area

Chefette (435-6000; www.chefette.com). Barbados's largest fast-food chain with thirteen restaurants, many with playgrounds, offers steaks, chicken, burgers, pizza, salad bar, ice cream. Moderate.

Josef's (St. Lawrence Gap; 420-7638; www.josefsinbarbados.com). Set in a renovated house with an airy touch, the cozy ambience conveys the feeling of dining at a friend's home. A garden has tables at the water's edge. Lunch weekdays; closed Sunday. Expensive.

The Waterfront Cafe (Careenage; 427-0093; www.waterfrontcafe.com.bb). You can enjoy seafood specialties here along with the picturesque setting of the Careenage. Moderate.

West Coast

Aqua Restaurant & Lounge (Hastings; 420-2995; www.aquabarbados.com) An eclectic menu with choices from family style and sushi to a champagne dinner—all in a seaside setting with unobstructed views and ocean breezes.

The Cliff (Derricks, St. James; 432-1922; www.thecliffbarbados.com). In a lovely seaside location and cleverly terraced to guarantee an ocean view for every table, this is the best restaurant in Barbados for sophisticated fare by the creative chef and manager team of Paul "Scally" Owens and "Mannie" Ward. Expensive.

Daphne's (Paynes Bay, St. James; 432-2731; www.daphnesbarbados.com), a sister to the famous London eatery, offers contemporary Italian cuisine at the water's edge at the heart of the island's Caribbean coast. Cocktail hour (5:00 to 7:00 p.m.) offers drinks at half price. Extensive wine list. Expensive.

Fish Pot (Little Good Harbour Hotel, Shermans, St. Peter; 439-3000; www.littlegoodharbour barbados.com), at the water's edge in the fishing village of Shermans, north of Speightstown, is an informal, relaxing, yet smart alternative to Holetown's more snooty establishments. Under the careful eye of chef Trevor Byer, who is considered one of the island's best, the menu and daily specials are mostly seafood, plus local vegetables and fruit. Reservations suggested. Moderately expensive.

Pices (St. Lawrence Gap; 435-6564; www.piscesbarbados.com). Elegant restaurant of chef Larry Rogers and wife, Michelle, (formerly La Terra at the Royal Westmoreland Clubhouse). Imaginative West Indian–inspired menu features an extensive variety of seafood to be enjoyed in relaxed, sophisticated seaside ambience. The twosome also have **Olives Bar & Bistro** (Holetown; 432-2112), situated in an old Bajan house and serving earthy Mediterranean and Caribbean favorites. Dinner only. Expensive.

Ragamuffins (First Street, Holetown, St. James; 432-1295; www.ragamuffinsbarbados.com), set in an authentic small chattel house, is an informal and friendly eatery offering fish, lobster, West Indian curries, vegetarian dishes, and steak. Daily specials are written on a board; dining is outside in the tropical garden setting or inside. The busy bar has specialty drinks and beers until the wee hours. Reservations suggested. Moderate.

Sassafras (Sugar Hill Resort, St. James; 422-6684; www.sassafras246.com). An original and creative menu combines Caribbean and Asian flavors. The wine list is good and prices reasonable. Moderate.

The Tides (Holetown, St. James; 432-8356; www.tidesbarbados.com). Chef Guy Beasley and his wife, Tammie, have teamed up with manager Trevor Parris to create one of the area's most delightful restaurants. Situated at the water's edge in an old coralstone house surrounded by lush gardens, the Tides—as the name indicates—takes its inspiration from the sea in both its decor and cuisine. Fresh local fish is a specialty presented in an innovative, contemporary fashion, with European, Asian, or Caribbean influences. Meat and vegetarian dishes are also on the menu, and there's an extensive wine list. Diners can choose a romantic setting on the seafront terrace with orchids on the table, a more casual bistro style in the courtyard, or a blackboard menu of light fare in the busy bar. The Tides is something of an art gallery, with paintings decorating the walls. Expensive.

Nightlife

Bajan Roots & Rhythms is staged Wednesdays and Fridays from 6:30 to 10:15 p.m. at the **Plantation Garden Theatre** (St. Lawrence Road; 428-5048; www.theplantation.bb). Cost is US$85 adults, $66 teens age thirteen to eighteen, $38.50 children age three to twelve and includes transportation, dinner, and drinks. Or, nondiners: US$49.50 adults, $33.00 teens, $22.50 children. Two hot clubs, both by the beach on Bay Street, are **Harbour Lights** (436-7225; www.harbour lightsbarbados.com) and the **Boatyard** (436-2622; www.theboatyard.com). At the former, you are likely to see more tourists and ex-pats; the latter is more popular with locals than tourists. Both have live music on some nights, free drinks on others, and dancing on the beach and under the stars. For rock and blues, **B4 Blues** (St. Lawrence Gap; 435-6560), a waterfront restaurant, has performers on Monday, Wednesday, Thursday, and Sunday. **The Ship Inn** (420-7447; www.ship innbarbados.com) features live music and DJs nightly with dancing under the stars.

The Waterfront Cafe (Careenage; 427-0093; www.waterfrontcafe.com.bb) has jazz on Friday and Saturday. De Kitchen, next to the Boatyard, is the place to mix with Bajan yuppies on Friday night.

If you want to sample the island's late-night action, head for Baxters Road, a sort of ongoing food fair for Bajan snacks with more rum shops per block than any place on the island or maybe the Caribbean. It's busiest after midnight. The Pink Star is a late-night favorite.

On the cultural scene, Frank Collymore Hall (436-9083; www.fch.org.bb), a modern concert and conference hall in Bridgetown, has a wide range of programs, from poetry reading and jazz to ballet and symphony concerts. The year-round agenda is published in visitor newsletters. Theater has a long history in Barbados, and long-established groups stage plays by West Indian and international playwrights at island theaters regularly. Consult local newspaper or the tourism authority.

Sports

Beaches/Swimming All beaches are public, but access is often restricted by the presence of hotels that crowd the beaches on the west and south coasts. Hotels do not have facilities for day visitors, but you can still use the beach. Much of the north and east coasts is rockbound, with stretches of beaches washed by strong Atlantic waves and too rough for swimming, except in certain places such as Bath, which is protected by a barrier reef. A government-operated picnic site here has showers and toilet facilities. Crane Beach, on the southeast, is one of the prettiest beaches, but it's often rough with Atlantic waves. **Weiser's on the Bay,** on Brandon's Beach about a mile from port, is a beautiful stretch of white sand with calm waters. You'll find beach chairs, lockers, and umbrellas, each US$5, with half credited back for bar drinks. Equipment per hour: snorkeling, US$10; kayaks, US$10; Sunfish, US$20; surf, windsurfing boards, US$10. Flag service on beach 9:00 a.m. to midnight daily.

Biking Highland Adventure Centre (Cane Field, St. Thomas; 431-8928; fax: 438-8070; neilhighland@ hotmail.com) offers a 1.5-hour, 7-mile mountain bike ride from Highland (15 percent uphill), travel-

ing at a leisurely pace on secondary roads through the heart of Barbados, in heavily wooded areas and small remote villages, seeing a side of Barbados that few tourists experience. The guide points out the best photo ops as well as information on the area, and the tour includes a "refueling" stop at a local rum shop. It continues on toward Bathsheba and ends at the Barclays Park Bar in Bathsheba, where you can enjoy a cool drink and get transportation back to Highland.

Boating At water-sports centers on the beach, Hobie-cats can be rented for BD$30 per half hour with skipper. Day sails along the west coast with food, drinks, snorkeling, and swimming are available from several companies. *Jolly Roger,* a replica of a pirate ship, departs Saturdays at 11:00 a.m. and returns about 3:00 p.m. Cost: US$60. The custom-built *Harbor Master* departs on Wednesdays from 11:00 a.m. to 3:00 p.m. Cost: US$65. Both include lunch, drinks, music, and snorkeling lessons, as well as transportation as needed. *Tiami Catamaran Lunch Cruise* departs daily at 10:00 a.m. and returns at 3:00 p.m.; cost: US$80. The *Turtles at Sunset Cocktail Cruise* departs on Sundays at 4:00 p.m. and returns at 7:00 p.m.; cost: US$47.50. Contact **Tall Ship Cruises** (430-0900; www.tall shipcruises). **Cool Runnings** (436-0911; fax: 427-5850; www.coolrunningscruisesbarbados.com) offers a daily *Snorkel Lunch Cruise* from 9:30 a.m. to 2:30 p.m. from the Careenage for US$75; and a *Sunset Snorkel Dinner Cruise* on Wednesdays from 3:00 to 7:00 p.m. for US$60. Boats often change their schedules seasonally; check locally. The **Barbados Yacht Club** (427-1125; www.barbados yachtclub.com) is located east of Bridgetown on the south coast.

Deep-Sea Fishing Sportfishing is good here, with bottom fishing over reefs, trolling along the coast, and deep-sea fishing for big game. Blue marlin is caught year-round but is more plentiful during the winter months. Other fish include wahoo, tuna, kingfish, bonito, mackerel, yellowtail, and amberjack. Anglers who cast from rocks or shallow water can catch small barracuda, jacks, snook, and tarpon. Half- and full-day charters are available from **Dive Shop Ltd.** (426-9947; www.divebds.com), **Blue Jay Charters** (422-2326), **Cannon Charters** (424-

6107), and **Blue Marlin** (435-6669). Most half-day trips run from 8:00 a.m. to noon and 1:00 to 5:00 p.m. and cost US$400 for half-day; full-day trips from 8:00 a.m. to 5:00 p.m., cost $800.

Golf Barbados's golf course most convenient to the port is the spread at **Sandy Lane Hotel** (St. James; 444-2500; golf@sandylane.com); only the 9-hole course is available to nonguests. Farther north the **Royal Westmoreland** golf course is a private club reserved for the owners of the million-dollar homes in this pricey real estate development, their friends, and guests at hotels with whom the club has agreements. Perhaps if you know the "right people," you can get in to play the lovely course designed by Robert Trent Jones Jr. The newest course is the recently redesigned **Barbados Golf Club,** the island's first public championship golf course. Designed by Ron Kirby, the 18-hole, par 72 course is located on the south side of the island and has a clubhouse, bar, and restaurant. The course (Durants, Christ Church; 428-8463; www.barbadosgolfclub.com) was renovated so completely that it's really a new golf course. In 2002 it was sanctioned by the PGA European Tour to host the Seniors Tournament. Green fees are $104 in summer, $135 in winter for 18 holes, $65 and $81 for 9 holes.

Hiking Barbados has many places to hike that combine beautiful scenery and interesting history. On Sundays you can join an early-morning walk organized by the Barbados National Trust. Led by young Bajans, the hikes are designed to highlight the island's history and natural beauty. They are organized into three groups—fast, medium, and slow—start at 6:00 a.m. and last about three hours. Wear comfortable walking shoes or sneakers and a wide-brim hat for protection against the sun. Schedules are available from the National Trust (426-2421) and published in local newspapers.

Horseback Riding Several stables offer beach, trail, and cross-country riding: **Brighton Stables** (425-9381), **Tony's Riding School** (St. Peter; 422-1549), **Ye Old Congo Road Stables** (St. Philip; 423-6180). The **Caribbean International Riding Centre** (422-7433) offers a 1.5-hour mountain and beach tour for $70, $90 with more beach time.

Just Breezing Watersports (Holetown; 262-7960; www.justbreezingwatersports.com) offers a five-hour tour for a minimum of four and maximum of six people that begins with a horseback ride on the dramatic Atlantic side of Barbados. There is a stop for lunch at the stables and riders are then transported to the Caribbean side of the island, where you continue with a ride on the beach. The tour then takes to the water on a glass-bottom boat for snorkeling with green sea turtles and over a shipwreck teeming with fish. Cost: US$166.67 per person. **Boyce's Tours** (425-5366; www.tours barbados.com) pairs a horseback ride on the moors of Waterford and a visit to the Arbib Nature and Heritage Trail with a visit to the Mallalieu Motor Collection that includes a Bentley, a Triumph, and Austins. Cost: US$40 per person.

Kayaking The Kayak and Surf Club (South Coast near Silver Sands Hotel at Kayaker's Point; 428-6750) welcomes visitors; equipment and changing rooms are available. **Weiser's on the Bay** (Brandon Beach), less than a mile from the port, is the nearest location with kayaks for rent, US$10 per hour. **Ocean Adventures** (438-2088; 866-504-1145; www.oceanadventuresbarbados .com) offers coastal kayak tours, some visiting the beaches and coves where participants can swim with sea turtles. A 3.5-hour tour includes a stop for snorkeling and refreshments. The company also has boat excursions on their *Silver Moon* catamaran.

Polo Introduced in Barbados at the turn of the twentieth century by the British Army, polo is played at the **Polo Club** (St. James; 437-5410; www.polonews.com) on Wednesday, Saturday, and Sunday from December to April/May. Admission is BD$5. Polo ponies are bred on Barbados.

Snorkeling/Scuba Diving Barbados is surrounded by coral reefs—an inner one suitable for snorkeling and learning to scuba dive and a barrier reef less than a mile from shore, which has the main dive sites. The best area for snorkeling is the quiet, clear waters of the Caribbean on the west, where reefs in 20 to 30 feet of water are within swimming distance of shore. Equipment is available for rent from the dive shops and water-sport operators.

The main dive locations on the west coast are reached by boat. The formation of the reefs is one of peaks and valleys, with the first dropoff ranging from about 50 to 100 feet. North of Holetown, the Barbados Marine Reserve has an artificial reef and marine park with a marked underwater trail for snorkelers and a segment of the 7-mile outer reef for divers. An artificial reef lies about a half-mile offshore at Prospect and was created by sinking the Greek freighter *Stavronikita,* which had been destroyed by fire in 1976. Most of the ship rests from a 40- to 90-foot depth, but the top of the main mast, marked by a buoy, is only 15 feet below the surface.

Barbados has other shipwrecks nearby. Two in Carlisle Bay, south of Bridgetown, are the closest. The bay, too, is interesting for divers, because the bottom is littered with bottles of different shapes and sizes dating from colonial times, when the Customs House was located here and ships anchored in the bay.

The leading dive operators include **Coral Isle Divers** (Careenage, Bridgetown; 434-8377; www.coralisle.net), **Dive Barbados** (Mount Standfast, St. James; 422-3133; www.divebarbados.net), **Eco Dive Barbados** (243-5816; www.ecodivebarbados.com) and **Dive Shop Ltd.** (426-9947; www.divebds.com). Most have trips daily, departing at 9:30 or 10:30 a.m., 12:30 p.m., and 2:30 p.m. Cost: US$65–$85 for one tank, US$110–$150 for two tanks. Barbados is one of the few places in the Eastern Caribbean with a recompression chamber.

If you are not a scuba diver, there are several alternatives. Snuba is something between snorkeling and diving, with special apparatus, offered by **Snuba/Coastal Kayak Tours** (436-2088; www.oceanadventures.bb). *Atlantis III,* a recreational submarine, takes passengers to depths of 150 feet on the barrier reef. The *Expedition* operates daily with morning and afternoon dive times from the Careenage, where **Atlantis Submarine** (436-8929; www.atlantisadventures) is based, and take about 2.5 hours, with 45 minutes spent on the reef. Cost: US$89.00 adults, US$57.00 children age thirteen to seventeen, US$44.50 children age four to twelve.

And if you don't want to go in the water at all, visit **Ocean Park** (Balls, Christ Church; 420-7405;

www.oceanparkbarbados.com), a marine aquarium that showcases exotic underwater life in twenty-six displays throughout the park. Exhibits include the Freshwater Falls, home to the Red Belly Piranha; the Ray Pool; and the Living Reef, where you can "walk underwater without getting wet." Hours: Tuesday to Sunday, 10:00 a.m. to 6:00 p.m. in summer and daily 10:00 a.m. to 5:00 p.m. in winter. Admission: US$17.50 adults, $10.00 children four to twelve years old, $50.00 family ticket (two adults, three children). There is also **Pirate Adventure Mini Golf,** with two, 9-hole mini putt courses where guests play through cannons, treasure chests, and a sinking ship. Hours: Summer, Monday to Thursday, 10:00 a.m. to 6:00 p.m.; winter, 10:00 a.m. to 5:00 p.m.; and Friday, Saturday, and Sunday throughout the year, 10:00 a.m. to 10:00 p.m. Admission US$7.00 adults, $5.00 children, $20.00 family ticket; or $2.50 with each paid entry to Ocean Park.

Surfing The Atlantic coast in the vicinity of Bathsheba has been the venue for several surfing championships. **Barbados Surf Trips** (262-1099; www.surfbarbados.com), **Zed's Surfing Adventure** (Inch Marlow; 428-SURF; www.barbadossurf.com), and **Surf Barbados** (256-3906; www.surfing-barbados.com) rent boards of all types. Daily rates: US$25–$50. Lessons start at US$50 per person for two hours. Zed Layson, a fifth-generation Bajan and a pioneer of the sport, has been a competitive surfer for more than twenty-four years and is ranked in the top twenty amateurs in the world.

Tennis and Squash Tennis is available at two dozen hotels and at other sites operated by the government. Of the six squash facilities, the one with air-conditioned courts nearest the port is Barbados Squash Club (The Marine, Christ Church; 427-7913).

Windsurfing/Kiteboarding A combination of assets has made Barbados one of the prime windsurfing locations in the world, with conditions particularly well suited for competition. The World Windsurfing Championships have been held here. The main location is the south coast, where there is a reef almost 5 miles long. It protects the inner waters near the shore and provides a calm sea for beginners. Outside the reef, strong Atlantic waves break against and over the reef, providing a real challenge for competitors. Particularly exciting for advanced windsurfers is the sport of wave jumping. In addition, on the south coast the trade winds blow from the east for nine months of the year and enable windsurfers to reach for long distances. Barbados is a popular training base for competitors. For lessons and board rentals contact the **Silver Sands Resort** (428-6001; www.silversand barbados.com).

The same assets that made Barbados so popular for windsurfing are also the features that have made it a center for the fast-growing sport of kitesurfing or kiteboarding. Wind conditions and ocean temperature are said to be best for someone wanting to learn the sport. **Redeye Kiteboarding** (Inch Marlow; 262-KITE; www.kitesurfbarbados.com) rents a range of equipment and boards from $35–$65 per day. Kitesurf lessons range from US$180 for four hours to US$360 for ten hours; private lessons, US$75 per hour.

Festivals and Celebrations

Crop Over, mid-July to early August, is an annual arts festival that is similar to Carnival in fanfare, but different in origin. Based on a seventeenth-century plantation tradition of celebrating the annual sugarcane harvest, the event was revived in the late 1970s as a local festival. It was so popular it evolved into the island's major annual event. In the old tradition the festival began on the last day of harvesting the cane, when the workers decorated themselves and drove to the mill singing that the "crop was over." The next day plantation owners feted the workers with Crop Over parties. Today's version re-creates some of these events with fun and frolic, beginning with the Ceremonial Delivery of Sugarcane and a Decorated Cart Parade. There are concerts, plays, regattas, fancy dress balls, contests, and parades, but the most important event is the Calypso Contest.

PART FIVE

The Southern Caribbean

Trinidad and Tobago

Port of Spain, Trinidad; Scarborough, Tobago; Pigeon Point, Tobago

Trinidad

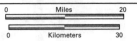

0   Miles   20

0   Kilometers   30

N

CARIBBEAN   SEA

Blanchisseuse

Galera Point

Toco

Medine Point

Northern   Range

Salibea

Monos Island

Chacachacar Island

Chaguaramas

Gaspar Island

Asa Wright Nature Center ★

Aripo Caves ★

San Juan

Tunapuna

Valencia

PORT OF SPAIN ⊙

Caroni River

Arima

Matura Bay

Caroni Bird Sanctuary

Cunupia

Sangre Grande

Chaguanas

Caroni Dam

Talparo

Lower Manzanilla

Manzanilla Point

GULF OF

Barracones Bay

OCEAN

PARIA

Couva

Navet Dam

Biche

Nariva Swamp

Cocos Bay

Point Lisas

Navet River

Guatuaro Point

Pointe--Pierre

Rio Claro

ATLANTIC

San Fernando

Princes Town

River

Mayaro

Point Galba

La Brea

Ortoire

Mayaro Bay

Pitch Lake

Guapo Bay

Irois Bay

Galeota Point

Granville

Rushville

Isolate Bay

San Francique

Moruga

Icacos Point

Erin Point

COLUMBUS   CHANNEL

The Odd Couple

A dual-island nation with some of the most spectacular scenery, wildlife, and unusual attractions in the Caribbean, Trinidad and Tobago are as different in lifestyle and tempo as any two islands in the region.

Trinidad, the birthplace of calypso and steel drums, is the ultimate Caribbean kaleidoscope, with more than four dozen nationalities and ethnic groups making up this richly textured society. Hindu temples stand beside mosques, cathedrals, and Anglican steeples, and rôti and rijsttafel count as local cuisine as much as pepperpot, fish cakes, and shish kebab. A veteran of oil boom and bust, Trinidad is the center of the country's commerce and trade, where visitors are usually more interested in business than beaches. But once a year all business stops and Trinidad explodes in C-A-R-N-I-V-A-L.

Twenty-two miles to the northeast lies tiny Tobago, a quiet and tranquil island so extravagantly beautiful it makes even the worst Caribbean cynic smile. Tobago is the ultimate tropical paradise, scalloped with palm-fringed alabaster beaches bathed by aquamarine waters and framed by lush green mountains that host hundreds of exotic birds.

Even the origin of the two islands differs. Trinidad, only 7 miles off the coast of Venezuela near the delta of the Orinoco River, was originally part of the South American mainland, although scientists are not sure exactly how or when the separation occurred. Tobago, however, was not part of South America; it was volcanic in origin and more closely associated with the islands of the Eastern Caribbean.

Trinidad is only 10 degrees north of the equator. It has three parallel mountain ranges, separated by wide plains that run east-west across the island. The mountainous Northern Range, covering the northern third of the island, is considered to be an extension of the Andes of Venezuela. It has the country's highest peaks, reaching more than 3,000 feet, which separate the Caribbean coast on the north from the rest of the country. The south side of the Northern Range gives way to the wide Caroni Plain, where nine rivers flow from the mountains into the Oropouche River, which runs east to the Atlantic; and the Caroni River, which meanders west through marshland to the Gulf of Paria.

Due to its proximity to and association with South America, Trinidad has flora and fauna found nowhere else in the Caribbean. In contrast to its bustling capital of Port of Spain, Trinidad's forest-clad countryside is home to 700 orchids, 600 varieties of butterflies, and more than 425 species of birds. It also has such strange natural phenomena as mud volcanoes and the world's largest asphalt lake.

Trinidad was first settled by the Arawaks from Venezuela and Guyana more than two thousand years ago. They called the island Iere, meaning "land of the hummingbirds," and remained for many centuries before moving north to the Eastern Caribbean. The Arawaks were followed by the Caribs, also from South America, but apparently the Caribs did not stay long and moved north, too.

At a Glance

Antiquities .... ★
Architecture.................. ★★★
Art and artists .... ★★★★
Beaches .... ★★★★
Colonial buildings .... ★★★
Crafts .... ★★
Cuisine .... ★★★
Culture .... ★★★★★
Dining/Restaurants .... ★★★
Entertainment .... ★★★★★
Forts .... ★★
History .... ★★★
Monuments .... ★★
Museums .... ★★
Nightlife .... ★★★★
Scenery .... ★★★★★
Shopping .... ★★
Sightseeing .... ★★★
Sports .... ★★★★
Transportation .... ★★

Fast Facts

Population: 1.3 million

Size: Trinidad, 50 miles long, 37 miles wide; 1,900 square miles. Tobago, 27 miles long, 7.5 miles wide; approximately 200 square miles.

Main Towns: Port of Spain and San Fernando, Trinidad; Scarborough and Plymouth, Tobago.

Government: Trinidad and Tobago is a parliamentary democracy based on the British Westminster system. The president, elected by parliament, is chief of state and appoints the prime minister.

Currency: Trinidad and Tobago (TT) dollar. US$1.00 equals about TT$6.27. Since both currencies are rendered as dollars, be sure you understand which currency is being quoted. U.S. and Canadian money can be exchanged at banks, where you receive an official receipt. It entitles you to reconvert your unused TT dollars back to your original currency on departure. Without this receipt you will not be able to reconvert TT dollars legally. Major U.S. credit cards and traveler's checks are accepted in most hotels, stores catering to tourists, restaurants, and car-rental firms, but at small operations and out-of-the-way places, be prepared to pay in the local currency.

Departure Tax: TT$100 (US$17)

Entry Requirements: Passports are required for U.S. and Canadian citizens.

Language: English is the national language, but in this polyglot nation Chinese, Arabic, Urdu, Hindi, and other exotic languages are spoken, too.

Public Holidays: January 1, New Year's Day; Good Friday; Easter Monday; May or June, Whit Monday; June, Corpus Christi; June 19, Labor Day; first Monday in August, Emancipation/Discovery Day; August 31, Independence Day; September 24, Republic Day; December 25, Christmas Day; December 26, Boxing Day. Eid-il-Fitr, a Muslim feast, changes from year to year, as does Divali, a Hindu festival. Carnival is not a national holiday, but Carnival Week, and particularly the final two days, might as well be, since little business is transacted.

Telephone Area Code: 868

Airlines: *From the United States:* American Airlines flies twice daily from Miami; Caribbean Airlines (replaced BWIA) flies daily from Miami, New York, and twice weekly from Washington D.C.; Continental flies from Newark and Houston four times weekly from each city; Delta flies four times weekly from Atlanta, and twice weekly from New York; and LIAT flies from various Caribbean islands to Piarco International Airport, 20 miles southeast of Port of Spain. Caribbean Airlines also has service to Trinidad from several Caribbean locations. Traveling to Tobago, American Eagle flies from San Juan and Delta offers once weekly service from Atlanta. *From Canada:* Caribbean Airlines and Air Canada fly from Toronto. *Intraisland:* Caribbean Airlines operates former Tobago Express' shuttles between Trinidad and Tobago throughout the day, beginning at 6:30 a.m.

Information: www.visitTNT.com; www.tntisland.com has a wealth of information, and its directories are better than the phone book.

In the United States:

(888) 585-4TNT; tourism-info@tidco.co.tt

In Canada:

RMR Group Inc., Taurus House, 512 Duplex Avenue, Toronto, ON M4R 2E3; (888) 585-4TNT; (416) 485-8724; fax: (416) 485-8256; assoc@rmrgroup.ca.

In Port:

Tourism Development Company of Trinidad & Tobago Ltd. (TDC), Tragarete Road #63, Port of Spain, Trinidad; (868) 622-0541; fax: (868) 622-9415.

Tobago Tourist Bureau, Crown Point Airport, Unit 12, TIDCO Mall, Sangster's Hill, Scarborough; (868) 639-4333; fax: (868) 639-4514. tour tobago@ihml.com

---

Columbus came upon Trinidad on his third voyage and went ashore at Moruga, on the south coast (some authorities say it was farther east at Erin). He named the island La Trinidad for the three peaks of the southeast mountains, which symbolized to him the Holy Trinity and are known today as the Trinity Hills. Trinidad seemed to have been a low priority for the rivaling European powers, thus enabling the Spaniards to hold it until 1797, when they were dislodged by the British.

In contrast, Tobago was so highly prized for its rich agricultural potential and its strategic location that it changed hands more than a dozen times between Spain, England, France, and other European powers battling for control of the New World. Finally, in 1889, Tobago asked to become a part of Trinidad. The two islands received their independence from Britain in 1962 and became a republic in 1976.

Budget Planning

For many years, the government of Trinidad and Tobago has had a love-hate relationship with tourists and an on-again, off-again desire to attract them. Until the oil bust in the mid-1980s, Trinidad had little need for tourism and indeed, its first prime minister, who ruled the country for thirty years, was openly hostile to it. This attitude manifests itself, I think, in the costs for visitors. You can get the impression that for Trinidadians, costs are reasonable, but if you are a tourist, costs are high. This assessment may be unfair, and, rather, may simply reflect the absence of a well-developed tourist industry with competitive services. Another factor of cost is the 15 percent VAT (value-added tax), which is added to the price of most services.

Generally, food and public transportation are cheap. Taxis are expensive, and tours are overpriced. If you know how to bargain or if a local person negotiates the price for you, the price of a taxi for the day can be reduced by as much as 30 to 50 percent.

Port Profile: Port of Spain

Location/Embarkation Port of Spain, the capital and main port, is situated on the west coast of Trinidad, overlooking the Gulf of Paria. Its cruiseship terminal is part of a complex covering four acres located at the foot of Port of Spain. The complex has a reception area, exchange bureau, post office, communications center from which AT&T calls can be made collect, and a shopping mall with duty-free shops. The Trinidad and Tobago Tourist Development Authority offices are on the second floor. Outside the terminal building are a craft market, a rustic outdoor pub, and the Breakfast Shed, one of the town's best inexpensive restaurants for local food.

Local Transportation Taxis are available at the port to take you sightseeing or to other parts of the city. Fares are posted on a board by the terminal door and in Port Authority literature. In the heart of Port of Spain (walking distance from the port), walking is the most practical way to get around, as traffic moves at a snail's pace. Private taxis are expensive, but there are inexpensive collective taxis and minibuses (Port of Spain, yellow stripe; Tobago, blue stripe) called maxi-taxis. They follow specific routes, stopping to pick up and discharge passengers along the way. Fares are standard; occasionally drivers will take a passenger a short distance off the regular course for an extra fare. Maxi-taxis can be hailed by a hand signal. Port of Spain also has inexpensive bus service on main routes and between major towns.

Taxi rates increase by 50 percent after 9:00 p.m. All taxis have an H as the first letter on their license plates. Sample rates from the port in Trinidad: to the Trinidad Hilton, TT$60; airport, TT$170; Asa Wright Nature Center, TT$500. Taxi for the day costs about US $25 per hour. In Tobago from Pigeon Point: to Plymouth, TT$70; Scarborough, TT$60; Buccoo Point, TT$60; Arnos Vale Hotel, TT$80; Speyside, TT$265.

Roads and Rentals Trinidad has a fairly wide network of roads, including some super highways, reaching most areas of the country within one to two hours from the capital. Roads in and around towns are generally well signposted, but they have very heavy traffic. Small towns have secondary roads, but remote mountain and rural regions are reached by track or walking.

Two north-south roads connect Port of Spain with the northwest Caribbean coast. Directly north, Saddle Road winds up the mountains to the North Coast Road and continues to Las Cuevas and Blanchisseuse. East of the capital the only road across the Northern Range is a steep corkscrew route between Arima on the south and Blanchisseuse on the north coast.

East from Port of Spain, two parallel highways run along the south side of the Northern Range. Eastern Main Road, the older of the two, passes through densely populated suburbs to towns at the base of mountains, from which secondary roads

Author's Favorite Attractions

★ Caroni Bird Sanctuary

★ Asa Wright Nature Centre

★ Diving in Tobago

★ Tobago Nature Trail

climb the southern face of the mountains. Just before Valencia, Eastern Main Road branches north to Toco, on the northeast tip, where it rounds the corner to the Caribbean coast. The other branch of the Eastern Main Road turns southeast via Sangre Grande, the largest town of the eastern region, to Manzanilla, on the Atlantic coast. The Beetham Churchill-Roosevelt Highway, the alternate express-way east from Port of Spain, terminates at Fort Reed (Wallerfield), a former U.S. Army base. It crosses several north-south roads, the main one being Uriah Butler (Princess Margaret) Highway, an expressway between Port of Spain and San Fernando, Trinidad's second-largest city and the heart of the oil industry.

Car rentals are available. Rates start at about US$50 for a well-used car, plus 15 percent VAT. Some firms require deposits. Check out your car carefully, and make notes of all the dents and other signs of wear to avoid being charged for them when you return. U.S. and Canadian visitors with a valid driver's license may drive here for up to three months. At all times, drivers must have with them their driver's license and any travel document that certifies their date of arrival in Trinidad and Tobago. Driving in this former British colony is on the left.

The Tourist Board has a list of car-rental companies and rates. In Port of Spain these include Autocenter (6 Ariapita Avenue; 628-4400; fax: 622-2959; autocenter@wow.net), Bacchus Taxi and Car Rentals (622-5588), Thrifty (800-367-2277), Econo-Car Rentals (622-8072; fax: 622-8074; econocar@trinidad.net), and Singh's Auto Rentals (623-0150; fax: 627-8476; singhs@trinidad.net).

In Tobago, Autocenter (phone/fax: 639-4400; autocenter@wow.net) and Baird's Car Rentals

(Scarborough, 639-2528) also rent motorbikes and bicycles, as does Modern Bikes (639-3275). Econo-Car Rentals Ltd. (Local Road, Crown Point, opposite airport; 660-8728; www.econocarrentalsltd.com) and Sheppy's Car Rentals (639-1543; www.tobagocarrental.com) also have motorcycles, jeeps, and minivans; Sherman's Auto Rentals (639-2292; www.shermansrental.com), Singh's Auto Rentals (Grafton Beach Resort; 639-0191), Thrifty Car Rental (Rex Turtle Beach; 639-8507), and Tobago United Auto Rentals (639-9973; www.tobagoautorentals.com) have jeeps and small buses, as well as cars.

Interisland Air Service See Fast Facts.

Emergency Numbers

Medical: Port of Spain General Hospital, 623-2951
Ambulance: 990
Tobago County Hospital: 639-2551
Police: 999

Shore Excursions

For Trinidad

Local tour companies offer excursions as varied as a visit to a wildlife sanctuary or a working plantation to a day at the beach, golf, or fishing. Tours are expensive unless you are part of a group, and even some group tours are expensive. Prices vary considerably from one vendor to another; those below are average. Prices are subject to a 15 percent VAT.

The first two tours described are likely to be offered as shore excursions by your ship. If you have a keen interest in natural attractions, an excursion led by an experienced nature guide will be more rewarding than traveling on your own. Trinidad has good nature guides who cater to bird-watchers and naturalists. One of the most outstanding is Jogie Ramlal (Milepost 33/4, Blanchisseuse Road, Arima, Trinidad); write to him in advance to make arrangements. Sites mentioned here are described elsewhere in this chapter.

Caroni Bird Sanctuary: 4 hours, US$50 per person for two; US$34 for three persons or more. The 450-acre sanctuary for the scarlet ibis is visited at sunset to watch thousands of birds swoop in to roost for the night.

Port of Spain/Maracas/Saddle Drive: 3.5 hours, US$40 per person for two people; US$30 for three or more. City tour is followed by a drive over the Northern Range to the Maracas Valley and north coast. Or it may include less city sightseeing and more time at the beach.

Asa Wright Nature Centre: 5 hours, US$65 per person. In the rain forest, about 1.5 hours' drive from Port of Spain, is an inn and study center for tropical wildlife with nature trails for self-guided hikes. Excursions are organized by the center (P.O. Bag 10, Port of Spain; 914-273-6333; 800-426-7810) and by travel companies in the capital.

A list of tour companies is available from the Tourist Office and from Trinidad and Tobago Incoming Tour Operators Association (c/o Travel Centre, Uptown Mall, Edward Street, Port of Spain; 623-5096; khackshaw@trinidad.net). In Port of Spain these include Travel Centre, Ltd. (622-0112; fax: 622-0894; www.the-travel-centre.com; info@the-travel-centre.com), which features nature tours, bird-watching, and sightseeing, and Trinidad & Tobago Sightseeing Tours (628-1051; fax: 622-9205; www.trintours.com), with nature tours, sightseeing, and sailing excursions. Caribbean Discovery Tours (624-7281; fax: 622-7062; www.caribbeandiscoverytours.com) offers ecological, cultural, and historical tours. Also check out Sensational Tours (#67 Ariapita Avenue, St. Ann's; 623-3511; www.sensational tours.net).

For Tobago

Buccoo Coral Reef: 1.5 hours, US$25 with transfers. Glass-bottom boat trip over the reef or a longer trip with snorkeling. US$15 for boat excursion directly from Pigeon Point.

Island Tour: 2.5 hours, US$50 per person for two; or five hours, US$120 per person for two; US$30 for three or more. Visit Scarborough, Plymouth, and Caribbean coast. A longer version continues along the windward coast to Speyside and Charlotteville and returns via part of the leeward coast.

Island Tour with Hiking: 4–5 hours, US$55 per person. Nature-guide specialists combine an island tour with stops at places for birding and Main Ridge Nature Trail for hiking. For Tobago

nature tours, contact David Rooks (phone/fax: 639-4276; www.rookstobago.com).

More Tobago nature specialists are listed in the Hiking/Birding section later in the chapter. Other tour companies in Tobago include Good Time Tours of Tobago (7–8 Cruise Ship Complex, Scarborough; 639-6816; fax: 639-6841; www.good timetourstt.com), a full-service tour operator at the cruise-ship terminal that offers island tours in both Tobago and Trinidad.

Fresh Tours Tobago (P.O. Box 520, Scarborough; (748-1220; www.tobagotoday.com/fresh tours) is a small tour company specializing in tailor-made tours for two or more persons to off-the-track nature and beach locations. Prices range from US$35 to $75 per person. On full-day tours, local lunch and cool beverages are included.

Frankie Tours and Rentals, Tobago (Mt. Irvine Beach Facilities Car Park, Tobago; 631-0369; www.frankietourstobago.com) arranges personalized, flexible itineraries and has a wide selection of prearranged activities—taxi service, auto rentals, airport shuttle, and tours to Trinidad—and offers a 10 percent discount for online bookings.

Trinidad on Your Own

If Trinidad and Tobago are the odd couple, Trinidad is a study in contradiction, beginning with the name of its capital. Facing south on the Gulf of Paria with the foothills of the Northern Range rising behind it, Port of Spain is turned inward to its city squares, savanna, and interior streets where the city pulsates. Hot, crowded, and congested, Port of Spain is a defiant city that almost dares you to like it. It is a vibrant, lived-in city with strong, competing images reflecting the multiracial, multi-faceted society that makes up the twin-island nation. And, almost in spite of itself, it even has a plan. The quickest way to get a sense of Port of Spain is to walk through its heart, where the architecture, music, museums, and restaurants mirror Trinidad's cultural mosaic.

A Port of Spain Walkabout

For 250 years under the Spanish, Port of Spain was little more than a tiny village amid swamps and mangroves. The actual Spanish capital, San José de Oruna, was 12 miles inland at St. Joseph, today a suburb. The early 1780s were a turning point, when French and other settlers who had been given land grants in Trinidad arrived and an agricultural and social transformation of the country began. To market their products and supply their needs, the port was improved and expanded. Then, in 1784, José Maria Chacon, the last of the Spanish governors, made Port of Spain the official capital. Merchants built town houses, sugar barons added mansions, and the new prosperity attracted a great variety of people who further contributed to the town's growth. The British arrived in 1797 and added the streets that they named for their kings, queens, and admirals, and which are the heart of the city today.

A fire in 1808 destroyed much of the earlier town, but in 1813 a young and able British governor, Ralph Woodford, set about rebuilding it—a task he apparently relished. He was responsible for many of today's landmarks—two cathedrals, Woodford Square, Queen's Park Savannah, the Botanic Gardens—and his layout remains basically the same.

Now teeming with people, Port of Spain has grown far beyond its nineteenth-century heart into a complex of communities, each with a distinct identity. On the west are the old middle-class suburbs such as Newtown and Woodbrook. St. James, with streets named Bombay and Bengal, has a large Indian community whose ancestors came as indentured laborers to work the plantations after slavery was abolished. On the north you will see the newer affluent suburbs of St. Clair, Maraval, St. Ann's, and Cascade climbing the hills; and on the east in the foothills are Belmont and Laventille,

Afro-Trinidadian communities where the steel band was born and the air is filled with the pulsating rhythms of calypso.

As your ship sails into **port (1)**, the twin towers of the Financial Complex, pictured on Trinidad and Tobago currency and housing the Central Bank and Ministry of Finance, and the Holiday Inn, stand out in the foreground against the city, which is still mostly low rise. Some of the old buildings, which have been well restored, lend the city grace; those that have fallen into disrepair give it a tawdry touch; and here and there, a new high-rise lifts your eyes up from the shacks and rum shops that often greet your view at eye level.

The center of Port of Spain, from the harbor on the south to the Queen's Park Savannah on the north, is laid out in a modified grid of 10 blocks. From the port you cross Wrightson Road, the highway that separates the city from the port at the foot of Independence Square. Once lined with bars and brothels and dubbed the Gaza Strip during World War II when Trinidad was home to an American army and navy base, Wrightson Road was built on part of the four hundred acres of landfill when the bay was dredged in 1935 to create a deep-water harbor.

Independence Square (2), a tree-lined plaza by the sea when it was laid out in 1816, is not a square but two parallel east-west streets. Normally it has the atmosphere and noise of a Middle Eastern bazaar and the confusion of an African market, with honking taxis and cars jostling people and pushcarts while calypso blares from sidewalk stands and storefronts.

(Although I have walked along these streets alone without fear or incident, many Trinis, as

1. Cruise-Ship Dock	9. National Museum and Art Gallery
2. Independence Square	10. Queen's Park Savannah
3. Cathedral	11. Queen's Royal College
4. Columbus Square	12. Emperor Valley Zoo
5. Woodford Square	13. Botanic Gardens
6. Cathedral of the Holy Trinity	14. President's House
7. Red House (Parliament)	15. Trinidad Hilton Hotel
8. Town Hall	

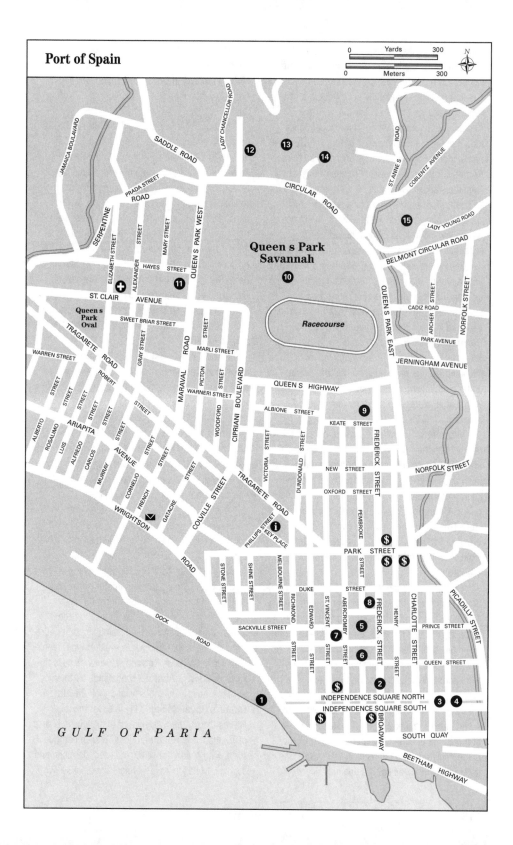

Trinidadians call themselves, do not consider the area safe, particularly from petty theft, and warn visitors to be careful with their purses and wallets.)

In the center of Independence Square at the base of Frederick Street is a statue of Arthur Andrew Cipriani, a pioneer of the independence movement and a former mayor of the city. The east end of Independence Square is anchored by the **Roman Catholic Cathedral (3),** one of the two cathedrals added by Woodford, but completed in 1832 after his death. Built of blue stone from the Laventille hills in the shape of a cross, the structure was renovated in 1984. When the cathedral was constructed, its eastern wall was on the seafront.

Behind the cathedral is **Columbus Square (4),** with a statue of a young Christopher Columbus—an area that is badly in need of renovation.

Frederick Street is the most direct connection between Independence Square and **Queen's Park Savannah.** Traditionally, it has been the main shopping street, but in recent years, as modern shopping centers have been built in the suburbs and the downtown streets have become congested with traffic, better-quality stores have moved away.

Woodford Square (5) The main square, laid out by Woodford, is one of the town's prettiest areas, with enormous flowering trees shading its lawn and walkways. Down through history the square has been a favorite location for political rallies. On the south side is the **Cathedral of the Holy Trinity (6),** the Anglican cathedral built by Woodford to replace one destroyed by the fire of 1808. The church has a memorial statue of Woodford.

On the west is the **Red House (7),** the home of Parliament and other government departments. The sprawling neo-Renaissance structure got its name in 1897 when it was painted red for the diamond jubilee of Queen Victoria. Originally built in 1844, the enormous building was burned down in 1903 during demonstrations that started over hikes in water rates and ended in protests against the colonial government. Defiantly, the British rebuilt it. Again in the summer of 1990, the Red House was at the center of conflict when militants took the prime minister and parliament members hostage, and the building was badly damaged.

The north side of the square, once lined with town houses, has **Town or City Hall (8),** built in 1961 to replace an earlier structure destroyed by fire; the public library; and the modern Hall of Justice.

National Museum and Art Gallery (9) (117 Frederick Street; 623-5911) Founded in 1872 and housed in the Royal Victoria Institute (Keate and Frederick Streets), the National Museum and Art Gallery has an art collection ranging from primitive to abstract to folklore, as well as prints by Cazabon, a Trinidadian landscape artist whose paintings have provided a valuable historical record of Trinidad from about 1850 to his death in 1888. Periodic exhibitions of modern Trinidadian art are held here. The museum has a natural history section and exhibitions on the country's oil industry, transportation, and its history from the Arawaks to the colonial period. Hours: Tuesday to Saturday 10:00 a.m. to 6:00 p.m.

Queen's Park Savannah (10) Once an area of two hundred acres, the Savannah now covers eighty acres of open land with enormous shade and flowering trees. Stretching between the city and the hills, it is both the city's lungs and playground. In the northwest corner a depression known as the Hollows, with enormous shade trees along walkways with flower beds, lily ponds, and rock gardens, is a popular picnic spot. In recent years the park has become a huge traffic circle, with cars circling it in a clockwise direction—not entirely a new role, as the route was a toll road in colonial times. Annually it is the center of Carnival activity.

A group of historic houses of imposing architecture frame the western perimeter of the park. Built at the turn of the twentieth century and known as the Magnificent Seven, each of the ornate structures has distinguishing characteristics. From Frederick Street, walking west along Queen's Park West, you pass **Knowsley,** which houses the Foreign Ministry. After the road bends north, you pass the American Embassy, and then the stately **Queen's Royal College (11),** a boys' school; **Hayes Court,** the residence of the Anglican bishop of Trinidad; and **Roomor,** built in French baroque style, with soaring towers, pinnacles, dormers, and cupolas. Mille Fleurs is a typical town house, with lacy iron fretwork; it is followed by the **Arch-bishop's House,** the home of the Roman Catholic archbishop of Trinidad and Tobago.

Whitehall, which is in Moorish style, was built in 1904 as a private residence and served until recently as the office of the prime minister. The last in line is **Stollmeyer's Castle,** also known as **Killarney,** also built in 1904. It is a copy of a German Rhine castle. Although not one of the Seven, **Boissiere House** (26 Queen's Park West), an eccentric structure known as the Gingerbread House, is the photographer's favorite.

On the north side of the park is the home of the president of the republic.

Emperor Valley Zoo (12) (www.trinizoo.com) Begun in 1952, the zoo has animals from around the world, but emphasizes tropical fauna. Among the natives are the tree porcupine, ocelot, and two species of monkeys, weeping capuchin and red howler. There are agouti; lappe (or paca), an enormous rodent hunted in South America for its meat; and deer. The large number of reptiles includes iguana; spectacled caiman, a small crocodile called an alligator locally; and some samples of Trinidad's forty-seven types of snake. The most colorful birds are the toucan and macaw, but, in fact, the grounds of the zoo, gardens, and park are like an aviary. The zoo gets its name from the once abundant emperor butterfly, one of Trinidad's six hundred varieties.

Botanic Gardens (13) (http://www2.trinidad .net/fobogtt) Laid out in 1820, the seventy-acre Botanic Gardens has manicured lawns with pretty walkways along an avenue of palms and hedges of hibiscus and bougainvillea shaded by large tamarind and saman. Among the flowering trees is the wild poinsettia known as chaconia, named for the Spanish governor who made Port of Spain the capital. The tree's brilliant red blossom is the national flower. Hours: daily 6:00 a.m. to 6:00 p.m.

President's House (14) Built in 1857 in Italian Renaissance style, the home of the president of the republic has Victorian cast-iron columns and railings. Its flowering gardens adjoin the Botanic Gardens and zoo.

Overlooking the park from the east is the **Trinidad Hilton (15),** known as the upside-down hotel because of the manner in which it was built into the hillside. You enter the lobby at the upper level, where there is a magnificent view, and from there descend to the restaurants and guest rooms.

To the west of the capital, Fort George, built in 1804, has been restored as a historic monument. It crowns a promontory at 1,100 feet with a fabulous view; the grounds are a popular spot for picnics. Next to the harbor Fort San Andres, built in 1785, is said to be the place Don Cosmo Damien de Churruca, a Spanish naval officer and astronomer to the king, fixed the first meridian of longitude in the New World in 1792.

On the east edge of town is the most obvious architectural reflection of Trinidad's multifaceted society. The **Jinnah Memorial Mosque,** built in 1947 in South Asian–Islamic style, is named for the founder of Pakistan.

A Drive around Trinidad

Port of Spain makes a good base from which to see the countryside—as different from Port of Spain as Trinidad is from Tobago. Three of Trinidad's national parks—Chaguaramas on the west, Maracas on the north, and Caroni on the south—are less than 10 miles from the capital. Each park is completely different in nature from the others.

Chaguaramas The Chaguaramas Peninsula, the northwestern reach of Trinidad, and its offshore islands, are part of the Chaguaramas National Park, whose highest peak is 1,768-foot Mount Catherine. About a mile off the south shore is Gaspar Grand, a local beach resort connected by daily boat service. The island has caves with stalactites and stalagmites that can be viewed along lighted walkways. There are picnic facilities near the cave entrance. Other islands are popular for sailing and water sports.

Maracas On the north side of Port of Spain, Saddle Road winds up the mountains through the suburbs and descends along forested mountains to Maracas Bay on the Caribbean coast. Long strands of golden sands framed by the lush mountains of the Northern Range stretch from Maracas Bay to Las Cuevas Bay—all part of the Maracas National Park and the most popular beaches in the Port of Spain vicinity.

Caroni Bird Sanctuary National Park After meandering through the Caroni plains and mangroves, the Caroni River empties into the Gulf of Paria 7 miles south of Port of Spain. Within the mangroves, which cover 40 square miles, is the 450-acre Caroni Bird Sanctuary, the home of the scarlet ibis, Trinidad's national bird. Daily at sunset the brilliant scarlet birds stage one of nature's most spectacular shows. As the sun begins to drop, a few of the bright red adults and their smoky pink juveniles appear in the sky. Then they arrive by the dozens, and finally by the hundreds, loudly flapping their 3-foot span of wings as they swoop down to perch on mangrove trees to roost for the night. They are joined by large numbers of snowy egrets and herons, and, by dusk the birds cover the green trees in such numbers that the sanctuary looks like a lake of Christmas trees.

Naturalist Frank Graham Jr., writing in *Audubon, the Magazine of the National Audubon Society* (May 1987), says, "The arrival of the scarlet ibises at their roosting place in the mangroves is the most spectacular exhibition in the avian world. . . ." The ibis gets its fire engine red plumage from the carotene in the crabs, shrimp, and snails on which it feeds. The birds need about three years to achieve their intense sheen.

Boat trips are available from near the sign-posted entrance to the park, west of the Uriah Butler Highway. The boats wind through lagoons and mangrove swamps to the sanctuary. Along the way a guide describes the vegetation and wildlife of the swamp, which includes more than 150 species of birds, 80 kinds of fish, and a variety of reptiles and other animals. Tours also leave daily from Port of Spain. Birders and those with a keen interest in nature should arrange to visit with a naturalist guide, however; otherwise you will get a standard tour—little more than a boat ride to the sanctuary at sunset.

Pointe-à-Pierre Wild Fowl Trust Less than an hour's drive south from Port of Spain is an unlikely combination of conservation and industry, which has resulted in one of the most beautiful spots in Trinidad. Within the compound of the TRINTOC (Trinidad and Tobago Petroleum Company) refineries and petrochemical complex are two lakes surrounded by fifteen acres of coastal wilderness turned into a bird refuge for endangered species and migrants. Established in 1966 with the help of

Texaco (former owner of TRINTOC), the trust is a private, nonprofit effort to protect Trinidad's endangered species and help to rejuvenate their numbers to return them to the wild. It also serves as an environmental educational center, particularly for children.

On nature walks in a beautiful park setting, you can watch a great variety of waterfowl and forest species at close range. If you wish to make a day of it, bring a picnic lunch. The sanctuary is operated by volunteers, and visits must be arranged in advance by contacting the trust (42 Sandown Road, Goodwood Park, Point Cumana, Trinidad; 637-5145; http://users.carib-link.net).

Devil's Woodyard At Princes Town, east of San Fernando, is a mud volcano known as the Devil's Woodyard that is regarded as a holy site by some Hindus. Mud volcanoes are formations in the earth's surface created by methyl gases sweeping through the subsurface mud. As the mud dries, it builds up platforms that form cones sometimes as high as 20 feet. In 1852, when the mud volcano at Princes Town was formed, it was thought to be the only such phenomenon in the country. Twenty mud volcanoes have now been registered in southern Trinidad and are thought to be associated with oil production.

Pitch Lake Trinidad's largest oil fields lie south of San Fernando. To the west, near the coast at La Brea, is Pitch Lake, the largest deposit of asphalt in the world, discovered in 1595 by Sir Walter Raleigh, who used the pitch to caulk his ships. Often described as resembling a gigantic parking lot, the lake covers approximately eighty-nine acres.

The Northern Range

Mount St. Benedict The ridges and river valleys on the southern side of the Northern Range resemble the folds of an accordion. Almost any part of the mountains has great hiking and birding, but the areas most frequented are those near picnic, camping, or lodging sites. A popular one near the capital is Mount Tabor, where the Mount St. Benedict Guest House caters to bird-watchers and naturalists. A road there leads past the Abbey of St. Benedict to the peak of Mount Tabor at 1,800 feet. Lookouts along the way provide fabulous views of

Port of Spain and the Caroni Plains. The trees around the guesthouse and the abbey, particularly in the early morning and late afternoon, are alive with so many birds you can see three dozen or more species on a two-hour walk. For guided tours, contact **Pax Nature Tours** (Mount St. Benedict, Tunapana; 662-4084; fax: 645-4234; www.paxguesthouse.com).

Over the next ridge in the Caura Valley, the Forestry Division has a recreation center with picnic facilities, and over the next ridge, a road along the Arouca River leads to Lopinot, the valley's first coffee and cocoa plantation restored as a tourist attraction.

At Arima a 10-mile road crosses from the south side of the Northern Range to Blanchisseuse on the Caribbean coast. The spectacularly scenic route climbs from sea level to about 2,000 feet in 387 turns, passing through forests laced with gigantic bamboos and carpeted with ferns. Logging tracks and old plantation roads branch from the main road and make good trails on which to explore the rain forest. Arima has about three hundred descendants of the Arawaks, the Amerindians who inhabited Trinidad when the Spaniards arrived. They have a social organization that is trying to keep their heritage alive. The most easily recognized tradition is their distinctive straw craft, similar in design and fabric to that of the Caribs in Dominica and Guyana.

Asa Wright Nature Centre Deep in a rain forest on the slopes of the Northern Range overlooking the Arima Valley is the Asa Wright Nature Centre (667-4655; fax: 667-0493; www.asawright .org; dayvisit@asawright.org), a private institution unique in the Caribbean. Established in 1967 on the Spring Hill Estate, it is a former coffee, citrus, and cocoa plantation at 1,200 feet, located 7.5 miles north of Arima. The center includes a bird sanctuary and wildlife reserve with an inn (in the former estate house) and hiking trails that day visitors may use upon payment of a small fee. Guided hikes are available at 10:30 a.m. and 1:30 p.m. Hours: 9:00 a.m. to 5:00 p.m. The William Beebe Tropical Research Station, begun by Dr. William Beebe of the New York Zoological Society in 1950, is part of the Nature Centre.

The inn's veranda, surrounded by dense tropical vegetation, is like an aviary, except that the birds come and go freely from the surrounding rain forest. The most celebrated species here is a nesting colony of oilbirds, which make their home in a cave located on the property. The oilbirds are found only here and in the northern parts of South America.

The center's five trails, ranging from half-hour strolls to three-hour hikes, are designed to maximize viewing of particular species. The main trail runs downhill from the inn through orchards to the rain forest and is a good route to see tanagers, thrushes, and trogons. From it the Bellbird Trail branches west to where you can hear, if not see, the bearded bellbird, one of the most curious birds of the forest. It has two completely different calls: One is a loud clank like the pounding of metal; the other, from which its name derives, is soft like ringing bells. There is a fee for day visitors: US$10 adults, $6 children. Lunch is served from noon to 1:00 p.m. for TT$100, Sunday TT$140. Reservations necessary.

After crossing the ridge, the Arima-Blanchisseuse Road descends through a pass into the valley with magnificent views of the Northern Range and the Caribbean. In recent years, the once-secluded Blanchisseuse area has become a popular weekend getaway, with holiday homes and guesthouses. The coast is scalloped with small bays and beaches set dramatically at the foot of rain-forest-clad mountains. Small beachside bars offer lunch and shark-and-bake, a specialty of the north coast. Marianne Bay, where the road ends, is the largest and most popular beach, with a freshwater lagoon at its eastern end.

In Blanchisseuse, **Surf's Country Inn** (669-2475), a daytime facility designed as a replica of a seventeenth-century ranch cottage, has a bar, restaurant, and tea terrace overlooking the Caribbean Sea. You will find nature trails and boats available for a cruise along the north coast. Las Cuevas is about 5 miles to the west. The northeast region is wild; even local naturalists do not go hiking without guides.

Matura Beach Matura, on the Atlantic coast, is the nesting beach of the leatherback turtle. The species is protected, and local environmentalists maintain a turtle watch during the nesting season, from March to September, when hunting is prohibited. Black with pink and white spots on its neck and flippers, the leatherback is the largest of the sea turtles and grows up to 7 feet in length and more than 1,000 pounds in weight.

Brigand Hill The best location in eastern Trinidad to enjoy magnificent views and see lots of birds is Brigand Hill, a little-known hilltop near the town of Plum. Once a cocoa plantation overtaken by rain forest, it is now a reserve with a forestry station and lighthouse. The diverse concentration of colorful fruit and flowering trees and forest vegetation attracts an enormous variety of birds. From the summit you have a sweeping view of the east coast from Manzanilla Point on the north to Point Radix on the south, one of the longest stretches of golden sands in the Caribbean.

On the coast the Tourist Board maintains bathing and picnicking facilities. An undertow makes parts of the coast dangerous; ask locally before going into the water to swim, and always stay close to shore. This narrow strip of land, shaded for 17 miles by an estimated one million coconut palm trees, separates the waves of the Atlantic from the great expanse of the Nariva plains and swamp. There is no organized boat trip here such as those at Caroni Swamp, but there is a great variety of birds, easily spotted by the road and along the rice paddies that are characteristic of the area. A controversy is raging locally over proposed development of the region, pitting farmers and environmentalists against commercial and industrial interests.

Shopping

Local crafts, good art, and an array of fashions by local designers are the attractions of shopping in Trinidad. Among the best crafts are wood carvings, hand-beaten copper, dolls, straw products, steel drums, paintings, fabrics, and jewelry. Don't overlook the locally made rum and world-famous Angostura bitters, which can be purchased at the Angostura shop in the port.

Port of Spain's main downtown shopping area is Frederick Street and nearby streets. The stores more likely to be of interest to visitors, however, are in the port terminal and at the Trinidad Hilton (Lady Young Road) and, particularly, the Hotel Nor-

mandie (10 Nook Avenue, St. Ann's), which has quality shops with jewelry and fashions by some of Trinidad's best designers. Shopping malls, popular with Trinis, are found on Frederick and Edward Streets in town and Long Circular Road and Western Main Road in the suburbs and elsewhere.

The port terminal shopping plaza and the Trinidad Hilton are the most convenient places for cruise passengers to shop for china, crystal, perfume, and similar duty-free items.

Art and Artists Art Creators (Aldegonda Park, Apartment 402, 7 St. Ann's Road, St. Ann's, Port of Spain; phone/fax: 624-4369) is one of the town's most serious galleries, with year-round exhibits of aspiring artists and established Trinidadian ones such as Boscoe Holders. Other galleries include **Aquarela Galleries** (Suite 4, 1A Dere Street, Port of Spain; 625-5982; fax: 624-5217; gml@wow.net); **101 Art Gallery** (101 Tragarete Road, Woodbrook, Port of Spain; 628-4081; http://101artgallery.com); and **Gallery 1.2.3.4** (Hotel Normandie, 10 Nook Avenue, St. Ann's, Port of Spain; 625-5502; fax: 624-0856; res@opus.co.tt). **West Mall** has art exhibits and craft markets throughout the year. The **Art Society of Trinidad and Tobago** (623-5461,ext. 228; http://artsocietytt.org) has information about exhibitions and has sample photos of artists work.

Books and Maps RIK Services/Trinidad Book World (87 Queen Street) and **Ishmael M. Khan & Sons** (20 Henry Street) are leading bookshops. Popular travel guides on Trinidad and Tobago are available in shops at the Trinidad Hilton and **Paria Publishing Co.,** which has a branch at the port terminal.

Clothing and Accessories The most attractive fashions by local designers are found at the boutiques that make up the Village Market, the shopping gallery of the Hotel Normandie. These include **Greer's Textile Designs,** the boutique of Greer Jones-Woodham and Verena Mostyn-Numez, who make batiks of exotic designs on cotton, sold as fabrics and attractive fashions. Cool, breezy linen casuals are the trademark of one of Trinidad's best-known designers at **Meiling** (Satchel's House, 6 Carlos Street; 627-6975; meilcltd@tstt.net.tt).

Meiling's fashions are sold at the Coco Reef boutique on Tobago, too. **Radical** (West Mall, Western Main Road; 632-5800), with several locations around Port of Spain, is something of the Gap of the Caribbean and carries men's and women's clothing.

Crafts and Souvenirs Athea Bastien (The Batique; 43 Sydenham Avenue, St. Ann's; 624-3274) is Trinidad's best-known batik artist. Others are **Bambu Ltd.** (Kapok Hotel Shopping Arcade, 16–18 Cotton Hill, St. Clair; 628-4003; fax: 637-6324) and **Pamela Marshall** (Poui Design) (Ellerslie Plaza, Boissiere Village, Maraval; 622-5597; pouides@tstt.net.tt). The **Trinidad and Tobago Blind Welfare Association** (118 Duke Street; 623-0940) has gifts, accessories, and household products of rattan, grass, and banana leaves made by the blind. **Trinidad and Tobago Handicraft Cooperative** (King's Wharf) sells hammocks, salad bowls, and small steel drums. **Kacal** (Trinidad Hilton) has wood carvings and art crafts. **Art Potters Ltd.** (port terminal) specializes in pottery. **Craft Mart** (Long Circular Mall and port) stocks crafts and souvenirs.

Jewelry Baksh Bros (66 Prince Street) has fine silver work. **Kanhai Ragubir** (13 Eastern Main Road, Curepe) is a jeweler in the port terminal.

Music Calypso and steel-band records and tapes can be found at **Rhyner's Record Shop,** which has branches at the Trinidad Hilton and at the port.

Dining and Restaurants

Perhaps nothing reflects the multinational heritage of this dual-island nation better than its cuisine, which includes ingredients and dishes from its Spanish, French, Dutch, African, Indian, Chinese, Syrian, Portuguese, and English ancestry. Add to this melting pot an abundance of exotic fruits, herbs, and vegetables—and an imaginative people whose urge to create is as lively in the kitchen as it is in the costumes of Carnival. Moderate means less than US$20. Check locally for days restaurants are open.

Battimamzelle (Coblentz Inn, 44 Coblentz Ave., Cascade, 621-0541). Chef/owner Khalid

Mohammed garnered rave reviews from the day he opened for innovative, eclectic cuisine such as pomegranate-glazed duck as enticing to look at as to eat. Open daily except Sunday for lunch and dinner. Moderately expensive. Incidentally, the restaurant's name is a local name for the dragonfly.

Melange (Ariapita Avenue, Woodbrook; 628-8687), noted for nouvelle Creole cuisine, is set in a colonial house painted blue. Expensive.

Rafters (6A Warner Street, off the Savannah; 628-9258; rafters@carib-link.net). A popular old rum house with authentic brick walls and hand-hewn ceilings offers sandwiches, chili, and chicken wings in the pub bar; and elegant dining in the room where Pat Bishop's colorful paintings brighten the walls. There's an a la carte menu of house specialties. Moderate.

Solimar (6 Nook Avenue, St. Ann; phone/fax: 624-6267; www.solimarcuisine.com) features local specialties and international cuisine in an open-air garden. Moderate.

Tamnak Thai (Queen's Park East; 625-0647; www.tamnakthai.co.tt), a restaurant in an old renovated mansion facing the Savannah and decorated with Thai artifacts, is the setting for delicious Thai and fusion cuisine. Rooftop bar. Expensive.

Tiki Village (Kapok Hotel, 16 Cotton Hill; 622-5765; kapok@trinidad.net). An excellent Chinese restaurant, it sits on the top floor of a hotel that has been in the Chan family since 1928. Moderate.

Veni Mange (67A Ariapita Avenue, Woodbrook; phone/fax: 624-4597; veni@wow.net). Cordon Bleu–trained Allyson Hennessy and her exuberant sister, Rosemary Hezekiah, prepare some of the best food in town from this small Victorian house. Not to be missed are specialties such as callaloo soup; stewed beef with eggplant fritters; Trinidad hot-pot; and oildown, a classic West Indian dish of breadfruit, pigs' tails, salted beef, and coconut. Lunch only, weekdays 11:30 a.m. to 2:30 p.m. On Fridays people linger in an informal late-afternoon party atmosphere. No credit cards. Moderate.

The Veranda (Rust Street; 622-6287) serves typical Creole cuisine in an elegantly casual style. Open Monday through Friday for lunch; Thursday, Saturday for dinner. Moderate.

Nightlife

Evenings in Port of Spain start when people elsewhere are ready for bed. Clubs pulsate with calypso and soca, and major hotels have everything from piano bars to limbo and steel bands. Check local publications to learn what's happening.

Queen's Hall (St. Ann's Road, off the northeast corner of Queen's Park Savannah) is a venue for popular shows, concerts, and other cultural events.

Trinidad Theatre Workshop (3 Hart Street; 624-4681) produces plays that are staged in Trinidad and other Caribbean islands.

Cricket Wicket (149 Tragarete Road; no phone), a popular pub for after-work drinks, has varied music groups on weekends until 2:00 a.m.

Mas Camp Pub (Ariapita Avenue and French Street; 627-8449) has calypso, pan, and dancing on weekends and live calypso talent night on Wednesdays. When the Mighty Sparrow—one of the world's best-known calypsonians—is in town, his **Hideaway** in Petit Valley is a great place to get into calypso.

62nd & 3rd (62 Tragarete Road, Woodbrook, Port of Spain). Popular with young professionals for dancing and drinks on Friday and Saturday nights. There is an entrance fee. The dress code—no shorts or beach sandals—is enforced.

Sports

Beaches/Swimming The most popular beaches near the capital are on the Caribbean coast from Maracas Bay to Las Cuevas, where there are snack bars and changing facilities. Gaspar, Monos, and other islands off the northwest peninsula are popular for day trips. On the east coast, Salibia is the main resort, and south of Manzanilla a palm-fringed beach stretches for 17 miles, but bathers must be careful about undertow. Don't overlook rivers and pools by waterfalls in the mountains, where there are picnic facilities.

Boating Powerboat racing is a popular sport, with the major race, a 90-mile run between Trinidad and Tobago, in August. Sailing is big but only as a private sport. The **Trinidad & Tobago Yatching Association** (P.O. Box 3140, Carenage Post Office, Carenage; 634-4210; fax: 634-4376) holds races almost weekly and welcomes members of other yacht clubs with prior arrangements. Several tour companies offer cruises from Port of Spain to islands off the northwest peninsula, usually stopping at Gaspar Grande or one of the islands for a buffet lunch and swim. Contact **Travel Trinidad and Tobago** (625-2201).

Deep-Sea Fishing The Bocas Islands off Trinidad are the prime location for deep-sea fishing. Among the companies that arrange sportfishing trips are **Classic Tours** (628-5714) and **Island Yacht Charters** (637-7389; fax: 628-0437; pdella@ trinidad.net). For information, contact **Trinidad & Tobago Game Fishing Association** (91 Cascade Road, Cascade; 624-5304; www.ttgfa.com).

Golf The 18-hole Moka Golf Course (6,705 yards; par 72), also known as **St. Andrews Golf Club** (in the suburb of Maraval; 629-2314; www.golftrinidad .com), is the oldest on the island, having been established in the late nineteenth century. Visitor greens fee: 9 hole, TT$250. For information, contact **Trinidad & Tobago Golf Association** (P.O. Box 3403, St. Andrews Golf Club, Moka Maraval; 629-7127; fax: 629-0411; http://trinidadandtobagogolf association.com; ttga@tstt.tt).

Hiking Trinidad's Northern Range is honeycombed with trails. Monthly field trips are arranged by the **Trinidad and Tobago Field Naturalists' Club** (c/o The Secretary, P.O. Box 642, Port of Spain; 624-8017; www.wow.net/ttfnc). Visitors can be accommodated with prior arrangements. Its members are also the best source of information on trails. Recently, some tour companies offering hiking, birding, and nature excursions have blossomed. Among them are **Wildways Caribbean Adventure Travel, Caribbean Discovery Tours** (see Shore Excursions earlier in this chapter), and **David Rooks Nature Tours** (Maraval; 622-8826; fax: 628-1525; www.rookstobago.com). Other useful sources on guided nature tours and hiking: Hikers 20 (c/o Gia Gaspard-Taylor, Apartment 3, 10 Hunter Street, Woodbrook, Port of Spain; 622-7731) and the **Forestry Division** (Long Circular Road,

Port of Spain; 622-4521/7476). For the Chaguaramas area west of Port of Spain: **Chaguaramas Development Authority Guided Tours** (634-4227/4364).

Kayaking The Kayak Center (Gulf of Paria; 633-7871; kayak@wow.net) and **Kayak Adventures** (7 St. Vincent, Port of Spain; 625-5472) offer rentals and a variety of excursions.

Surfing The north and northeast coasts are the main areas for surfing, a popular sport here. At Maracas Bay wave heights up to 10 feet are best for bodysurfing. The northwestern end of Las Cuevas, known as "the Bowl," has strong wave action for experienced surfers. Damiens Bay, at Blanchisseuse, has the most consistent surf, with waves from 4 to 13 feet. For information, contact Surfing Association of Trinidad & Tobago (P.O. Box 1020, Port of Spain; 625-6463; www.surfingtt.com; info@surfingtt.org).

Tennis The courts closest to the port are at the Trinidad Hilton, where there are two. Public courts are poor quality. Contact the **Trinidad & Tobago Tennis Association** (21 Taylor Street, Port of Spain; tel/fax: 628-0783).

Windsurfing The main areas for windsurfing are Chaguaramas Bay, on the west side of the capital, and the north coast. Contact the **Windsurfing Association of Trinidad and Tobago** (32 Dundonald Street, Port of Spain; 628-8908; www.tntisland .com/sportsassn.html).

Tobago on Your Own

Cloaked almost from end to end in deep green foliage brightened by flowering trees and colorful tropical flowers, tiny Tobago (www.exploretobago .com; www.mytobago.com; www.tobagotoday.com) is an enchanted island scalloped with some of the Caribbean's most idyllic beaches and encircled by incredibly beautiful aqua waters. This quiet, tranquil Eden of tropical splendor rises almost directly from the sea to about 2,000 feet in the Main Ridge, a mountain spine down the center of the island. From the steep slopes covered with magnificent rain forests, hundreds of tiny streams carve their way through the mountains and cascade over rocky cliffs to the sea. The foothills are covered with cocoa and banana plantations and orchards.

Tobago has long been ambiguous toward tourists—most of whom come from Trinidad. An array of stop-and-go development projects by the government in Trinidad has left this out-of-the-way Nirvana with an assortment of rustic inns, funky guesthouses, and overpriced tourist-class hotels. In 1990 the island welcomed its first deluxe hotel, Grafton Beach Resort, in two decades. Yet, in this day of overdevelopment in Paradise, Trinidad's benign neglect may have been a blessing in disguise.

A cruise-ship dock in Scarborough, the island's main town, opened in 1990; some ships also dock off the western tip and tender passengers to Pigeon Point, a spit of land with a picture-perfect, palm-fringed, white-sand beach overlooking the Caribbean, within walking distance of many hotels. It has bathing facilities for day visitors (for a fee).

Tobago has a limited network of roads, which wind along the coast and twist through the mountains. The newest roads are excellent, the old ones are terrible, and others have simply been abandoned for lack of maintenance. One crosses the Main Ridge between the leeward and windward coasts, but no road completely circles the island.

You can rent a car or hire a taxi for the day. In planning an excursion, be aware that distances are deceiving, due to the nature of the terrain and the roads. For example, the 25-mile drive from Pigeon Point along the windward coast to Speyside takes more than 1.5 hours. For information on car and bike rental companies in Tobago, see the Roads and Rentals section earlier in this chapter.

A Driving Tour of Tobago

Scarborough, about 8 miles northeast of Pigeon Point, is a quiet West Indian village with a small botanic garden and a Handicraft Center (Bacolet Street). Fort King George, a well-restored fortification built by the British in 1777, overlooks the town and provides a fabulous view of the Atlantic, or windward, coast. The **Tobago Museum**, housed in

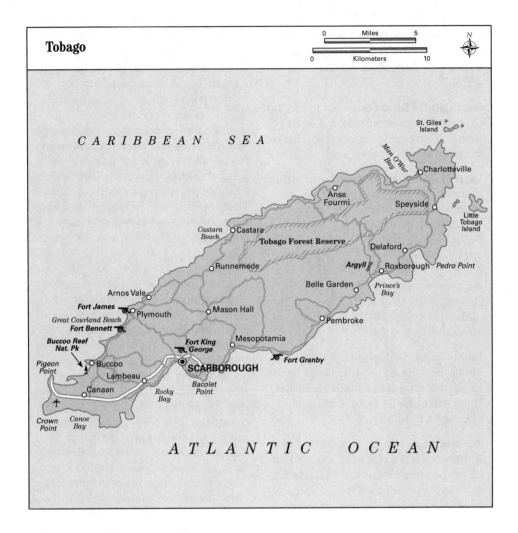

the Barrack Guard House, has Amerindian artifacts, military relics, and documents from the colonial period. The former officer's mess houses a craft shop and the military hospital has the National Fine Arts Centre which displays Tobago art and sculpture. Hours: Monday to Friday, 9:00 a.m. to 5:00 p.m. Admission: TT$5. Its other historic buildings are St. Andrew's Church, constructed in 1819, and the Courthouse, which dates from 1825.

Directly north of Pigeon Point on the Caribbean, or leeward, coast and across the island from Scarborough is Plymouth, Tobago's second town. It, too, has a historic fort, Fort James, built in 1768. One of the island's prettiest strands is just south of the town: Great Courland Bay, better known as Turtle Beach for the turtles who come to nest here in April and May.

Buccoo Reef National Park/Buccoo Reef Trust In the quiet waters between Pigeon Point and Buccoo Bay is the Buccoo Reef National Park, a sea-and-land reserve with shallow-water reefs in the form of a wide horseshoe that shelters the inner reef and a lagoon at the center, where the water is less than 30 feet deep. An area of exceptionally clear water on the east is known as Nylon Pool. The gardens have a great variety of coral—staghorn, starlet, brain, sea fans, and others—that attracts an enormous array of fish.

At low tide the water in parts of the reef is only about 3 feet deep, a feature that has made it popular with snorkelers and nonswimmers who, unfortunately, walk around the reef in sneakers. Although there have been laws on the books for almost three decades to protect the reef, the government has never seriously enforced them, and the reef is in great danger of being destroyed by misuse. The Crusoe Reef Society, a marine research and conservation group in Trinidad, has tried hard to pressure the government for greater conservation measures but has had only limited results. The **Buccoo Reef Trust** (Cowie's Building, Auchenskeoch Road, Carnbee, Tobago, 635-2000, fax: 639-7333; www.buccooreef.org; office@ buccooreeftrust.org), established in 2004, was awarded the Environmental Management Authority's Green Leaf Award in 2007 for its contribution to environmental conservation and protection in Trinidad and Tobago. Perhaps that's a reflection that some progress is being made.

Bon Accord, another lagoon on the south side of the park, is edged by mangroves, which host a great number of birds, including the rufous-vented chachalaca, Tobago's national bird. A trail east of Pigeon Point borders the mangroves. Glass-bottom boat and snorkeling trips to Buccoo Reef leave daily from Pigeon Point.

East of Plymouth is **Adventure Farm and Nature Reserve** (Arnes Vale Road, 639-2839; cell: 797-2940; www.adventure-ecovillas.com; adventure@tstt.net.tt), a twelve-acre estate and organic farm with birds, butterflies, iguanas, mango and citrus orchards, and nature trails. The reserve, which claims to have the largest number of hummingbirds on the island, has a new bird observation area. Admission: US$5, per person, half-price for children. Guided tours are available for groups only on request. Monday to Saturday 7:00 a.m. to 5:00 p.m., Sundays by arrangement. Visitors can also purchase homemade drinks from fresh organic fruits in season on the estate.

Grafton Estate/Caledonia Bird Sanctuary Grafton Estate was a working plantation until it was hit by a hurricane in 1963. The damage was so extensive that the owner, Eleanor Alefounder, decided not to restore it. Another consequence of the hurricane was that the island's birds were desperately short of food. Recognizing this, Alefounder started a feeding program and turned part of her estate into a wildlife sanctuary. After her death in 1983, the estate was placed in trust to preserve the reserve and maintain the feeding program. Birds are fed by the caretaker, James Sampson, daily at 8:00 a.m. and 4:00 p.m., when visitors can see the beautiful mot-mot, cocrico, blue-gray tanagers, bananaquit, doves, and more. On request, Sampson, who is a mine of information on the birdlife of Tobago and the estate, takes visitors on property trails to spot more wildlife. Located north of Plymouth, the entrance is marked by a THE SANCTUARY sign across from the Grand Courlan Hotel. There is no charge, but contributions are welcome.

Kimme Museum (639-0257; www.luisekimme .com; hoppingstick@tstt.net.tt) Located near Bethel village overlooking the Mt. Irvine Golf Course, the museum houses a collection of one hundred incredible, unique works of German sculptor Luise Kimme, who has lived in Tobago since 1979. Her unique, colorful, larger-than-life size sculptures—some 14 feet high—of Caribbean dancers, folklore and religious characters, dancing couples, Nijinsky ballet dancers, and mythological figures, are carved out of oak, lime, cypress, and cedar wood; some are created in bronze. The fascinating sculptures capture the essence of the Tobago people and their culture. The museum, locally called "The Castle" for its fancy, bazaar architecture, is very much worth a visit. The studio and workshop are only open on Sundays, from 10.00 a.m. to 2:00 p.m.; visits at other times can be arranged. Entrance: TT$20.00 (US$3.50) per person.

The Leeward Coast

Tobago's entire Caribbean coast is made up of one beautiful beach after another—some with resorts, others untouched. North of Plymouth, Arnos Vale, a tiny cove with a hillside hotel, is one of the most romantic spots in the Caribbean. Once part of a sugar plantation, the hotel's oldest building is completely encased in tropical foliage like a tree house, with a choir of birds to serenade it. Sunsets here are incredible. The idyllic cove has a fine coral reef suitable for snorkelers and novice divers. North of Arnos Vale an abandoned road of about 2 miles is now a hiking trail to Golden Lane and Culloden Bay.

Arnos Vale West of Arnos Vale on the road between Scarborough and Golden Lane, the ruins of the Arnos Vale plantation (with a waterwheel and other machinery bearing 1857 markings) are the centerpiece of a lovely culture park and museum created by the owners of the Arnos Vale hotel. There is a guided nature trail through the surrounding woods to a waterfall. Hours: daily 8:30 a.m. to 10:30 p.m.; 660-0815. Admission: TT$10. The open-air **Arnos Vale Waterwheel Restaurant** (Franklyn Road, 868-660-0815; www .arnosvalehotel.com; reservations@arnosvalehotel .com) has an eclectic menu of local specialties and light fare.

Tobago has begun to develop specialized eco-resorts that you can visit. **Footprints Eco-Resort** (660-0118; 800-814-1396; www.footprintseco-resort .com), at the end of a long, steep road from Golden Lane to Culloden Bay, opened in 1997 on a magnificent sixty-one acres surrounded by hills and overlooking the sea. The inn uses solar panels, local timber, and recycled piping; produces much of its food; and offers great birding and snorkeling. The resort has two nature trails on the property for guests to use; there is no cost, nor are there guides on the property. Nonresident guests may wander the trails on their own.

Inland, at the end of a rough road from the village of Runnemede is **Cuffie River Nature Retreat** (P.O. Box 461, Scarborough, Tobago; phone/fax: 678-9020; www.cuffieriver.com) on a twenty-one-acre site perched above the gently flowing Cuffie River, a tributary of the Courland River. The center, on the edge of the Forest Reserve amidst lush bamboo groves, wild heliconia, and cocoa trees, has locally made furnishings and fixtures and is an ideal center for birding and hiking. It serves local dishes based on fresh produce. It also has close ties with the villages nearby, drawing on their traditions for entertainment. The retreat offers walks through their nature trails for a TT$50 fee, and lunch is available to nonresident guests for TT$80.

North of Golden Lane along the Caribbean coast, the road snakes through forested mountains along steep cliffs that fall almost directly to the sea. From **Mount Dillon**, a windswept promontory rising 800 feet above the sea, you can have a spectacular view of the leeward coast with Pigeon Point in the southwest and Trinidad on the horizon.

Behind the white-sand beaches rise the green slopes of the Main Ridge.

Castara, a tiny village with a popular swimming beach, has bathing facilities. There are a few local restaurants and rustic inns, but one suspects development is not far behind. Stay tuned. Farther north, Englishman's Bay, Parlatuvier Bay, and Bloody Bay—lovely enclaves of white-sand beaches shaded by giant ferns, bamboo, and palms—can be reached by short trails from the main road. Other trails inland lead to pretty waterfalls.

Main Ridge Rain Forest Trail North of the island's midgirth a good road crosses the Main Ridge between Parlatuvier Bay, on the leeward coast, and Roxborough, on the windward side. At the crest of the ridge is the entrance to the Main Ridge Rain Forest Trail, the most accessible and best-maintained trail in the Tobago Forest Reserve, the oldest forest preserve in the Western Hemisphere (established in 1765). The entrance is marked by Bloody Bay Lookout Site, where the Forestry Department has a small cabin with a map of the trail. The lookout sits high above Bloody Bay and offers magnificent views.

From here a looped footpath of three hours winds down the steep slopes through the rain forest along a stream that empties into Bloody Bay. After the trail crosses the stream, it levels out and returns on an easy walking path to the eastern entrance on the main highway, about 2 miles west of the lookout.

The Windward Coast

Between Scarborough and Speyside, a fishing village near the north end of the island, the Windward Road hugs the serpentine coast, overhung with trees laden with mango, lime, and papaya as it weaves through fishing villages and bayside hamlets. Almost any road into the mountains leads to waterfalls, wooded slopes, and beautiful vistas. Roxborough, the largest town on this stretch, is the access point to the 175 foot **Argle Waterfalls,** the island's highest falls, which drops in stages and at the bottom forms a pool where you can swim. The walk to the falls from the car park area takes about twenty minutes. Admission: TT$30 including guide. Further along at the 110-foot Kings Bay Waterfall, the Tourist Board has trails and facilities, but unfortunately very little water falls except during the rainy season.

Speyside Set against the thick forests of the Main Ridge, the little fishing town of Speyside overlooks Goat Island, one of the most unusual dive sites in the Caribbean, which the Tobago government bought recently and plans to make into a nature reserve. A mile offshore is **Little Tobago,** a 280-acre bird sanctuary, also known as Bird of Paradise Island. There in 1909 an Englishman introduced four dozen birds of paradise, hoping to establish a safe haven for the species, which was being decimated by poachers supplying feathers to the European fashion market. The birds lived until 1963, when a hurricane devastated the island. Seven birds survived, but none have been sighted since 1983. The island has many other birds and wildlife and has been a sanctuary since 1934. Nature trails lead to the eastern side of the island, where the beautiful tropic bird nests in the cliffs. Often birds on their nest can be observed and photographed at very close range.

A boat from Speyside to Little Tobago takes about twenty minutes and is often a rough crossing over white-capped seas. Be prepared for wet landings, as there are no docks, and take water because there is no supply on Little Tobago. Arrangements are best made through a local guide or the Blue Waters Inn in Speyside.

Charlotteville At the north end of Tobago on the leeward coast is Charlotteville, a fishing village on Man o' War Bay. Directly behind the wide horseshoe bay rises heavily forested 1,890-foot Pigeon Peak, the tallest mountain. Due to its isolation, Charlotteville has kept the island's folkways more than any location on Tobago. The Man o' War Bay Cottages on the north side of the bay is a small naturalists' retreat on a 1,000-acre cocoa plantation, open to visitors to wander at will. Recently, the road from Charlotteville to L'Anse Fourmi farther south on the leeward coast was completed, giving access to a part of Tobago that is truly untouched and making possible a longer route to circle the island.

Dining and Restaurants

The following restaurants are moderately priced, ranging from about US$10 to $30.

Blue Crab (Main and Robinson Streets, Scarborough; 639-2737). In a hillside house near the harbor, you will find home cooking offered for lunch. Flying fish, curried or rolled around sweet peppers and eggplant, is a specialty, along with homemade ice cream and locally made fruit wines.

Ciao Cafe' Italian Gelato & Bar (Burnett Street, Scarborough, 639-3001; www.ciaocafe tobago.com) makes two dozen flavors of Italian gelato on site and serves espresso, cappuccino, and pastries as well as being a wine bar and offering light snacks. Open Monday to Saturday 10:00 a.m. to 10:00 p.m. and Sunday 5:00 to 10:00 p.m.

Gemma's Treehouse Kitchen (south of Speyside; 660-4066). The day's catch is cooked to order at this rustic beach tavern, where it's enjoyed on a little "tree-house" veranda by the sea. Only a one-room shack a few years ago, Gemma's has grown into the best-known restaurant on the island and something of an institution. If Gemma's is crowded and there's a wait, we are told by some locals that at two nearby restaurants, **Bird Watchers,** and **Redman Simple,** the food is as good and prices better.

Grafton Beach Resort (Black Rock; 639-0191). One of Tobago's main hotels has a delightful terrace restaurant open to the breezes. Its buffet and a la carte menu have local specialties and international dishes, and they are all good.

La Belle Creole Restaurant and Bar (Bacolet Street, north of Scarborough; 639-3551; www.halfmoonblue.com). Formerly known as Old Donkey Cart House, this island institution is situated on Crown Landsonce owned by King George V in a restored mid-1850s French colonial house that was Tobago's first guesthouse. In 1980, Gloria Jones-Knapp, a former fashion model in Europe, opened the Old Donkey Cart House as a wine bistro. Today, it is home to the Half Moon Blue Hotel and Le Belle Creole restaurant, specializing in Creole recipes from around the Caribbean and the daily fishermen's catch at Bacolet Bay, along with callaloo soup and homemade bread and pastas.

Miss Esmee's stand at Store Bay Beach has great tamarind and sesame balls, coconut muffins, and rôtis (Indian burritos stuffed with meat or chicken and flavored with curry). Miss Esmee is no longer with us but her daughter runs the stand. If you are heading in a different direction, ask your driver to stop at his favorite rôti maker. It's sure to be fresh, hot, and mighty good.

Sports

Beaches/Swimming Almost any place on the island has powder-fine beaches, many that seldom see a footprint. Pigeon Point and Store Bay are the most convenient for ships anchoring off Pigeon Point. Parlatuvier and Bloody Bays, on the Caribbean coast, where bathers arrive by boat or hike in from the main road, are tranquil and secluded.

Biking Mountain bikes are available for rent from **First Class Bike Rentals** (Store Bay; 662-3377), near Crown Point Airport, and **Modern Bike Rentals and Adventure Tours** (Box 122, Scarborough; phone/fax: 639-3275; www.oceanpoint.com/mountainbiking; islandboy@hotmail.com). Rates: Bike rentals, US$15 per day; 1–2 hour tour, US$30 per person, 3–4 hour, US$40 and include bikes, helmet, water bottle, light snacks, refreshments, and an experienced guide. **Mountain Biking Tobago** (P.O. Box 1065, Bon Accord, 639-9709, cell: 681-5695; mtbtobago@tstt.net.tt or icehouse@tstt.net.tt) and **Tobago Mountain Bike/Slow Leak Tours** (635-0641; www.tobagomountainbike.com) offer fun and challenging mountain bike tours around Tobago. The latter's Web site has tour descriptions, including level of difficulty, prices, and tour guide profiles.

Boating Natural Mystic (639-7245, www.sailtobago.com) offers day-sail tours on the *Natural Mystic* trimaran. Tours depart from Mt. Irvine Bay and sail up the Caribbean coast to secluded Cotton Bay. An onboard barbeque is included. The boat takes a maximum of ten passengers.

Angostura Tobago Sail Week (637-6785; www.sailweek.com) usually mid-May, racing in the waters off Tobago is the biggest sailing event of the year and attracts yachties from around the world.

Birdwatching See Hiking section.

Deep-Sea Fishing The north shore of Tobago and the waters around nearby St. Giles Island are the main locations for game fishing. Arrangements must be made in advance through a local travel company. Fishing charters are available from **Dream Catcher** (680-7457, Bon Accord, Tobago; tobagodreamcatcher@hotmail.com). **Dillon's Fishing Charter** (Crown Point, 639-8765; 678-3195; www.tobagogamefishing.com) offers year-round sportfishing on a fully-fitted 38-foot Bertram Sportfisherman with Captain Stanley, who counts thirty years experience in these waters, for full day/nine hours, US$700 including food, drinks, all tackle and bait. It also does fishing/cruising combos with four hours of fishing followed by a stop at a secluded beach for swimming while the fish is prepared for you for lunch. Dillon's also has a restaurant where seafood is the specialty. **Frankie Tours and Rentals** (Mt. Irvine Beach, Tobago; 631-0369; www.frankietourstobago.com) offers several daily excursions: Deep Sea Fishing, all equipment provided, four persons maximum, US$300 half day, US$500 full day; Shark Fishing, four persons, five hours, US$300; Fly Fishing, two persons maximum, five hours, US$150.

Golf The 18-hole championship **Mount Irvine Golf Course** (6,800 yards; par 72) at the Mount Irvine Hotel (639-8737; www.mtirvine.com, mtirvine@tstt.net.tt) is about 5 miles from Pigeon Point. One of the Caribbean's most scenic golf courses, it is situated on 125 landscaped acres of gentle rolling hills overlooking the sea. The clubhouse, which is the headquarters of the Tobago Golf Club, is on a promontory with superb views. It has changing rooms, pro shop, and restaurant. Greens fees are US$35.00 for 9 holes; US$55.00 for 18 holes; cart, US$23.00 and $41.50; caddy, US$8.00 and $18.00. Prices include taxes.

Tobago Plantations Golf and Country Club (7,000 yards, par 72), is the island's only PGA-designed course and was created by architects Bob Hunt and Narcus Blackburn of PGA Management Ltd. Its Golf Academy is staffed by PGA-qualified pros and offers all levels of instruction; there's also a pro shop, with rentals. Greens Fees: 18 holes US$95; 9 holes US$65. Set on the island's windward side, it is adjacent to the Tobago Hilton (639-8000; www.tobagoplantations.com; tpl@tobagoplantations.com.

Hiking/Birding and Nature Tours Tobago offers endless opportunities for hiking. The most accessible is the Main Ridge Rain Forest Trail, a loop off the main highway between Bloody Bay and Roxborough. You can take it as a short walk of an hour from its eastern entrance or try a three-hour hike from the western one. **Environment Tobago** (www.sos-tobago.org; www.scsoft.de/et/et2; envirotobAtstt.tt), a local environment organization, arranges hikes to interesting locations monthly on Sunday mornings, The hikes are free and meant to be fun and an opportunity to meet new people and join Environment Tobago. Call or e-mail for information a week before the hike for details on the current month's hike. Other nature tour specialists on Tobago are **Newton George** (660-5463, cell: 754-7881; www.tka.co.uk/birds); **Wayne Gray** (www.waynesworld-tours.com), who specializes in bird watching and Tobago's natural history; **Jeb McEachnie**, (660-6228, cell: 757-4281; www.angelfire.com/nt2/naturestouch2), who specializes in bird watching, turtle watching, and nature tours and has more than fifteen years of experience; and **David Rooks Nature Tours** (P.O. Box 348, Scarborough; 639-8594; fax: 660-4328; www.rooks tobago.com), headed by David Rooks, Tobago's best-known ornithologist and nature tour guide. His Web site has bird lists, tour descriptions, and prices.

Nature Lovers of Tobago (cell 767-9298; 639-4559 with voice messaging; www.tobagobirding .com) is headed by Darren Henry, a dendrologist (one who studies trees) and birding tour guide. His Web site has bird lists and photos, plus information on his tours, which range from two hours to full day, and prices. Henry, a trained forester and certified tour guide with a vast knowledge of Tobago's flora and fauna, is a group leader for the Audubon Society's annual Christmas bird count in Tobago.

Peter Cox Tobago Nature Tours (Milford Road, Canaan; 385-3909, cell: 751-5822; www .tobagonaturetours.com) provides a wide variety of individualized (no buses except by request) nature and sightseeing tours to the main attractions on Tobago and to Little Tobago, including leatherback turtle–watching tours during the nesting season (March to August). Tour descriptions and prices can be found on the company's Web site. The bird-watching section of the Web site www.simply tobago.com has the most complete information on birding in Tobago, as well as Trinidad, I have found. It also includes an extensive daily diary and bird list written by a contributor.

Kayaking Tobago Sea Kayak Experience (Charlotteville; 660-6186, info@seakayak tobago.com) has kayaking excursions that leave from either Man O War Bay in Charlotteville or from Conrado Hotel on the road to Pigeon Point. The excursions range from an instructional program covering strokes, sweeps, draws, braces, and rescues and some kayaking for US$40 to a half day for novices to a full day geared to experienced paddlers and including kayaking and hiking into the rain forest and lunch for US $60.

Snorkeling/Scuba Diving Tobago is almost completely surrounded by shallow-water reefs, most within swimming distance from shore and easily accessible to snorkelers and novice divers. Marine life is rich in color and the water exceptionally clear. Tobago was one of the earliest locations to be discovered by pioneer divers four decades ago, but the advanced skill needed for diving the best sites has left it as something of a last frontier. It offers great diversity, but the most interesting feature for advanced divers is drift diving.

The main area for snorkelers and novice divers is Buccoo Reef and the reefs along the Caribbean coast. Grouper Ground, on the western tip of the island opposite Pigeon Point, has gentle drift diving for experienced divers. Here basket sponges are the size of bathtubs. The clarity of the waters makes it a delight for underwater photographers.

The northeast coast around Goat Island offers some of the finest diving in the West Indies. Due to the strong surf and surge, the reefs have been dubbed "Flying Reefs" and are only for advanced divers with experience in drift diving. The most celebrated, **Japanese Garden**, begins in about 20 feet of water and drops to 110 feet. The shallow area has huge sea whips, sea fans, and sponges with a great variety of colors. Tobago has dive operators at Pigeon Point, Crown Reef, Turtle Beach, and Speyside. A recompression chamber is in operation at Roxborough. The **Association of Tobago Dive Operators** (660-5445; fax: 639-4416; www.tobagoscubadiving.com) sets standards for membership and operations. Among the members are **Adventure Eco-Divers** (Grafton Beach Resort, Black Rock; 639-8729; fax: 639-0030; ecodiver@ tstt.net.tt), **Man Friday Diving** (Charlotteville; Bjarne Olesen), **Aquamarine Dive** (Blue Waters Inn, Speyside; 660-5445; fax: 639-4416; amd tobago@trinidad.net; mail: P.O. Box 402, Scarborough), **Tobago Dive Experience** (P.O. Box 115, Scarborough, Tobago; 660-4888; fax: 639-7034; 800-544-7631; www.tobagodiveexperience.com), and **World of Watersports** (Ricky Knowles, Tobago Hilton Hotel, Lowlands; P.O. Box 299, Scarborough; 660-7234; fax: 660-8326; info@worldofwater sports.com).

Windsurfing/Kitesurfing Pigeon Point beach, protected by Buccoo Reef, is an ideal tropical lagoon for windsurfing and kitesurfing. The main season is mid-December to June with winds averaging 12 to 20 knots from east to northeast. Kitesurfing is fairly new to Tobago. The lagoon is good for beginners, but more adventurous conditions for experienced kitesurfers are found on windward side of the island at Rockley Bay where the Tobago Hilton is located. **Radical Sports Ltd.** (Pigeon Point, PO Box 299, Scarborough, 631-5150, cell 688-2628; www.radicalsportstobago.com; info@radicalsportstobago.com), at the northern end of Pigeon Point Heritage Park, has kitesurfing and windsurfing equipment for rent. Board and rig rental, TT$250 for one hour or $350 for three hours. It also offers kitesurfing lessons, kayaking, and other water sports.

Festivals and Celebrations

Carnival in Trinidad

Trinidadians say they have two seasons: Carnival and the rest of the year. Carnival in Trinidad is the biggest, most colorful and creative of all Caribbean Carnivals and the one after which the others are patterned.

Carnival is not simply another event, but a celebration of life—a folk festival, sports competition, art exhibit, and dance and music concert rolled into one, involving every age at every level of society. It's street theater where, after months of work, all the island's talent and energy are released in a few delirious days of mirth and madness. It's CAAR-NA-VAAL!

Although Carnival culminates in the last two days before Ash Wednesday and the start of Lent in the Catholic tradition, Carnival in Trinidad actually begins the day after the new year is born.

Trinidad's Carnival tradition began in 1783, when French settlers and others who were given land grants in Trinidad arrived in large numbers, and a festive season from Christmas to Ash Wednesday was initiated. Masked bands of people, often accompanied by musicians, paraded through the streets, stopping to visit friends at homes where elaborate balls were given. But this was sport for the privileged. "Free persons of color," as free blacks and mixed races were known, were not forbidden to mask, but they did not participate in the affairs of high society. Black slaves were prohibited by law from joining the festivities.

The most radical change came with the emancipation of the slaves in 1833, when the celebrations became the people's festival and the scene shifted from fancy dress balls for a few to the masses in the street. With it also came a confluence of national traditions that, over the century, became as mixed as a pot of callaloo, often totally reversing their original meanings. The music of the old bamboo bands was replaced by rudimentary pan bands whose metallic tones were beat out on dustpans, paint cans, and any other metal objects on which innately talented musicians could improvise rhythm and tone.

During World War II Carnival was suspended, but in the backyards of Trinidad the pan technique continued to develop (leading to the term panyard), and the number of instruments and their complexity grew. Not everyone embraced them; many people branded the players as hooligans and tried to prohibit them from playing in the streets.

In 1948 the commercial 55-gallon oil drum appeared in Trinidad for the first time. Soon the discarded drums were being used by pan players who found that tempered steel enabled them to extend their musical range. Rapidly the drums replaced all other pans in use, and a steel band association was formed. The first pan recital, with selections ranging from calypso to the classics, received such acclaim that the respectability of steel band music was assured. The steel band, which has been an essential element of Carnival, has recently become an endangered species during Carnival parade. Gigantic boom boxes mounted on flatbed trunks now accompany the paraders. The canned music is so loud that steel pans wouldn't stand a chance to be heard, even if they tried. Unfortunately, it's having a serious impact on Carnival, too; many revelers often seem as mechanical and uninspired as the canned music.

Today Mas Bands, as the masqueraders are known, are divided into three sizes—small, medium, and large—with the largest having four thousand people. Large groups are broken down into three dozen or more sections, each costumed differently to portray an element in an overall theme created by the band leader, who must excel as an artist, showman, director, and producer with the genius to choreograph theater on a grand scale. The winner of the Mas Band competition is crowned King of Carnival. What greater honor is there? The best are household names throughout the Caribbean.

Calypso is the very essence of Carnival. Always witty, rich in innuendo and satire, calypso contains a variety of verses followed by a set refrain. The lyrics often satirize island politics, society, and other local matters, so you are likely to miss the biting humor of the calypsonian, but this will not lessen your enjoyment. The music is infectious.

From December through the end of Carnival, top calypsonians and two or three dozen hopefuls perform their newest songs nightly at calypso tents. (Years ago the artists performed in outdoor tents and makeshift structures; today's calypsonians hold their shows in theaters with stages, but the term tent remains.) Each calypsonian has his or her own style and fans. The top ones are as well known in the Caribbean as Michael Jackson is in the United States.

Although the Road March, or Carnival Parade, is the greatest spectacle, the competitions for calypsonians, steel bands, and costumed bands are the heart of Carnival activity for Trinis. About three weeks before Carnival, the Steelband Panorama

preliminaries are held over two days and bring together as many as one hundred steel orchestras from around the country, each with as many as fifty or one hundred players. The finals are held on the Saturday before Carnival, when a dozen or so orchestras compete for the championship.

Kiddies' Carnival, also held on the Saturday morning, is when children dressed in full regalia "play mas."

Dimanche Gras: On the Sunday before the two last days of Carnival, the finals of three major competitions take place: Calypso Monarch, the best calypsonian of the year; and the King and Queen of Carnival, chosen for the most beautiful, creative, and magnificently costumed male and female masqueraders. The Dimanche Gras show is staged at the Queen's Park Savannah.

Carnival Monday: Dawn, or *J'ouvert* (French for "the day begins"), is the official start of Carnival Monday and symbolizes the opening of the doors to let King Carnival in. At the end of the Dimanche Gras show, people join the crowds at *fêtes*—public parties that anyone can attend by buying a ticket. (Dozens of *fêtes* are advertised in daily newspapers, many being held at hotels.) On Carnival Monday the *fêtes* end at 4:00 a.m., when the dawn breaks and people spill into the streets to jump to the music of the steel bands. Everyone—young and old, visitors and Trinis—joins "Joovay" and lets the music move them along.

Carnival Tuesday: Early in the morning bands of brilliantly costumed masqueraders line up for the spectacular parade through the streets of Port of Spain to the Savannah, dancing to the music. Carnival ends at midnight with the "Las Lap," an expression for the wind down of the festivities—the last chance to jump in the streets before King Carnival disappears for another year.

Other Festivals in Trinidad

Steelband Music Festival in September/October is almost as important as Carnival. Trinidadians are justly proud of inventing the steel drum, the only new instrument to be added in the twentieth century.

Festival of Hosay, a Muslim observance, is held in Muharram (first month of the Islamic calendar) and commemorates the martyrdom of Hassan and Hussein, the sons of Ali, at the battle of Kerbala in early Islam. The form it takes here is unique to Trinidad and stems from East Indian traditions. The most elaborate events are in the St. James section of Port of Spain, where East Indians are concentrated.

The Muslims prepare goat-skinned tassa drums and secretly build *tadjahs,* which are colorful, elaborate floats of intricate detail, made of paper, tinsel, reeds, and bamboo in the shape of mosques in Asian style. Three mini-celebrations precede Hosay: *Flagnight* on the seventh day of Muharram, when pilgrims parade in the streets bearing flags honoring the battle of Kerbala; *Small Hosay,* the following night when miniature *tadjahs* (representing the tomb of the younger brother, Hussein) are carried through the streets; and *Big Hosay* (the following night), when the large *tadjahs* (symbolizing the tomb of the older brother, Hassan) are paraded. Hosay Day follows with a final parade of the *tadjahs,* which, three days later, are ceremoniously cast into the sea.

Phagwa or **Holi,** the Hindu Festival of Color, has been celebrated in Trinidad and Tobago since 1845. The festival takes place on the full moon of Phagun (February to March), the most beautiful time of the year in North India at the dawn of spring.

Tobago Heritage Festival, held for two weeks beginning in mid-July, is a celebration of Tobago's history and culture, keeping alive the island's traditions of storytelling, dance, drama, and music, and culminating in street carnivals in Plymouth and Scarborough at the end of the month. Villages around the island host festival events and games, band, song, and dance competitions are held throughout the festival.

Bonaire

Kralendijk

Bonaire

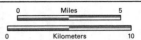

ATLANTIC

OCEAN

Playa Funchi

Chikitu
Beach

▲ Brandaris
Washington
Slagbaai
National Park

Boca Onima

Goto Meer

Playa
Frans

Rinc n

Boca Olivia

Flamingo
Sanctuary

Karpata

Seru Largu

Boca Chikitu

Lagoon

Hato

Noor i Salina

KLEIN
BONAIRE

Antriol

Nikiboko

KRALENDIJK

Tera Kora

CARIBBEAN

Hoop

Bachelor s Beach
Punt Vierkant

Lac
Bay

Sorobon

SEA

Pink Beach

Solar
Salt
Works

Flamingo Sanctuary

Pekel
Meer

Lacre Punt

Nature's Child

Bonaire is an unspoiled island with small-town charm. Although it has seen considerable development in the past decade, the island is devoid of slick commercialism. It has only low-rise hotels along white-sand beaches fronting crystal-clear Caribbean waters within a five- to ten-minute ride from town, the port, and the airport.

Shaped like a boomerang, the island is blessed with a bounty of natural beauty preserved in three nature parks—one for flora and wildlife, another for flamingos, and a third for its coastal waters and marine life. Bonaire has been a mecca for scuba divers from around the world since they discovered its fabulous underwater life three decades ago. But even for those who do not dive or have no higher aspirations than snorkeling, there is more than enough to see here to make a visit worthwhile.

The second-largest island of the Netherlands Antilles, Bonaire is located 86 miles east of Aruba and 38 miles east of Curaçao, its sister Dutch island; Venezuela is 50 miles to the south. The island's landscape is almost as diverse as its seascape and has three distinct areas: The north end, mostly covered by the national park, is hilly and greener than the rest of the island and has freshwater and saltwater lakes.

The central region is semiarid, somewhat flatter, and has a landscape similar to the American Southwest. The south end is the flattest part and is covered with salt pans, sand dunes, and mangroves. Less than a mile off Bonaire's south coast is Klein (meaning little) Bonaire, a flat, uninhabited island of about 3 square miles, which acts like a barrier reef protecting the main island's leeward waters.

In contrast to the calm south coast, Bonaire's north side is battered by strong waves that break against black volcanic and coral rocks, as well as unusual coastal formations with grottoes and caves with Indian petroglyphs. Throughout the island the landscape is dominated by enormous candle and other cacti and the ever-present divi-divi tree, whose asymmetrical shape is sculpted by the strong winds that help keep Bonaire cool.

Bonaire, one of the Caribbean's youngest tourist destinations, was discovered five centuries ago in 1499 by Amerigo Vespucci, the Italian navigator for whom the Americas were named. The tranquil island was inhabited by Arawak Indians at the time, and Vespucci named it Bo-nah, from the Arawak word meaning "low land." For the next century the Spaniards attempted to colonize it but failed. Instead they took the Arawak population to Hispaniola as slaves. In the years that followed, the island was colonized by the Dutch, fought over by the French and British, and leased to a New York merchant.

From 1639, and for the next 160 years, the island was managed by the Dutch West India Company, which developed salt production, and the Dutch imported African slaves to work the salt pans. In 1816 the Dutch government took over Bonaire, after an interlude of British control, and it has remained Dutch to the present.

At a Glance

Antiquities . . . . ★
Architecture . . . . ★★
Art and artists . . . . ★
Beaches . . . . ★★★★
Colonial buildings . . . . ★★★
Crafts . . . . ★
Cuisine . . . . ★★
Culture . . . . ★
Dining/Restaurants . . . . ★★
Entertainment . . . . ★
Forts . . . . ★
History . . . . ★
Monuments . . . . ★
Museums . . . . ★
Nightlife . . . . ★
Scenery . . . . ★★★★
Shopping . . . . ★★
Sightseeing . . . . ★★★
Sports . . . . ★★★★★
Transportation . . . . ★

Population: 12,000

Size: 24 miles long, 3 to 7 miles wide; 112 square miles.

Main Town: Kralendijk

Government: Bonaire is part of the Netherlands Antilles, an autonomous region of the Kingdom of the Netherlands. The governor is appointed by the queen of the Netherlands. The locally elected legislative council has three elected Central Government senators and three elected island commissioners.

Entry Requirements: U.S. and Canadian citizens must have a valid passport and a return or ongoing ticket.

Currency: Netherland Antilles florin (NAf) or guilder. US$1.00 equals NAf1.77. U.S. dollars are readily accepted.

Departure Tax: US$32.00 on international flights; US$5.75 (NAf10) to Curaçao and other islands.

Electricity: 127 volts, 50 cycles

Language: Dutch is the official language, but Papiamento is the island language. English and Spanish are widely spoken.

Public Holidays: January 1, New Year's Day; February, Carnival, Carnival Monday; Good Friday; Easter Monday; April 30, Coronation Day; May 1, Labor Day; Ascension Day; June 24, St. John's Day; June 29, St. Peter's Day; September 6, Bonaire Day; October, Sailing Regatta; December 25, Christmas Day; December 26, Boxing Day.

Telephone Area Code: For international direct dialing from the United States, dial 011-599-717 plus the four-digit local number.

Airlines: *From the United States:* Flamingo International Airport is served by Continental with two non-stops from Newark and from Houston; Air Jamaica from Montego Bay; and American Eagle from Puerto Rico daily. American Airlines serves Bonaire via Curaçao, connecting with Dutch Antilles Express (599-717-0808; reservations@flydae.com), Divi Divi Air (599-9-839-1515), Insel Air (599-9-733-1521), or Tiara Air via Aruba.

Information: www.infobonaire.com

In the United States:

Tourism Corporation Bonaire, 10 Rockefeller Plaza, Suite 900, New York, NY 10020; 800-BONAIRE; (212) 956-5912; fax: (212) 956-5913; usa@tourismbonaire.com.

In Port:

Bonaire Government Tourist Office, 2 Kaya Grandi, Kralendijk, Bonaire, N.A.; 599-717-8322 or 599-717-8649/8322; fax: 599-717-8408; www.infobonaire.com.

Budget Planning

Bonaire is relatively inexpensive as Caribbean destinations go. Diving, deep-sea fishing, windsurfing, and most water sports are about the least expensive in the region. Tours are reasonably priced. Certain elements, such as good restaurants, however, can be expensive.

Port Profile

www.tourismbonaire.com
www.infobonaire.com

Location/Embarkation The pier is located on the south side of town, only a short walk from the town center and a few steps from the **Divi Flamingo Beach Resort and Casino.**

Local Transportation There is no public bus system, but there are taxis and rental cars. To see the most interesting sights, you need a car or a tour, which can be arranged through a local tour company or the Tourist Office. Sample taxi rates: Kralendijk to Harbor Village or to Captain Don's Habitat, US$7; to Lac Bay, US$20. Island tour: US$25 per hour.

Roads and Rentals Bonaire has a limited number of surfaced roads; the rest are dirt roads and tracks. A car or, in some places, a jeep or four-wheel-drive vehicle is necessary for exploring the island and can be arranged upon arrival. A valid driver's license is required. The minimum age is generally twenty-one, but it can be twenty-six for certain car models. Driving is on the right. The tourist office and local tour companies distribute a free booklet, *Bonaire Holiday,* which has a road map.

From Kralendijk a surfaced road of 9 miles runs along the west coast, where most of the island's resorts are located, to the national park boundary. Here it forks with the left road, which continues along the west shore to Nukove, a snorkeling area; the right fork runs east along Goto Meer, a lake, to Rincon, where a road leads northeast to the national park entrance.

South of Kralendijk a surfaced road makes a loop around the southern tip of the island along the Pekelmeer Lagoon and returns north along the east coast.

Daily rates for cars, jeeps, and minivans range from US$40 to $65 with air-conditioning. Rental companies in Kralendijk include **Avis Car Rental** (717-5795) and **Budget** (599-717-4700, fax: 599-717-3325; www.bonaire-budgetcar.com), among others. **Cycle Bonaire** (599-717-2229; www.bonairediveandadventure.com; info@bonairediveandadventure.com) rents bikes for $15 per day. Half-day excursions cost $55–$65 depending on course and include refreshments, escort vehicle, and nature interpretation. **Bonaire Wellness Connexions** (599-717-3637, ext. 608; www.bonairewellness.com; info@bonairewellness.com) also rents bikes for $15 per day; call for guided tour prices. **Outdoor Bonaire** (599-791-6272; www.outdoorbonaire.com; hans@outdoorbonaire.com) offers tours from $40 per person.

Emergency Numbers

Medical: Hospital, (599) 717-8900/8445
Police: 114

Shore Excursions

Bonaire Tours (Box 115, Kralendijk; 599-717-8778; fax: 599-717-4890; www.bonairetours.com, email: info@bonairetours.com), the island's main tour company, especially for cruise-ship passengers, and **Discover Bonaire/Bonaire Dive and Adventure** have similar programs. Transportation is by minivan or jeep, depending on the number of people. Prices are per person for adults plus tax; reduced children's prices are available. All locations are described further in this chapter.

Flamingo View Tour: 2 hours, US$18–$25. Drive along the north coast and through the hills inland to Rincon. Highlights are the Thousand Steps, Goto Meer to observe flamingos, the north coast to see Indian petroglyphs, and to Seroe Largo for a fabulous view.

Southern Island Tour: 2 hours, US$23–$25. The low-lying south is a marked contrast to the hilly north. Highlights are 150-year-old salt pans with sparkling white hills; flamingo sanctuary; stone slave huts; and Lac Bay, a lagoon and wildlife area.

Biking Excursions: half day, US$55–$65. **Cycle Bonaire** (Kaya Gerharts 11d; 599-717-2229; fax: 599-717-7690) offers guiding biking excursions with stops for snorkeling and a seaside picnic. **Discover Bonaire/Bonaire Dive and Adventure** (599-717-2229; fax: 599-717-2227; www.bonairediveandadventure.com), the dive shop at Sand Dollar Condominium Resort, offers bike tours, too.

Kayaking, Snorkeling, Diving, Fishing Excursions: See Sports section later in this chapter.

Bonaire on Your Own

Hard by the sea on the west coast at about midisland is the capital, Kralendijk, which means "coral dyke" in Dutch. It is a pretty little town of pastel buildings of Dutch colonial architecture, reflecting the island's commitment to preserve its cultural heritage as much as the parks preserve its natural one.

A Kralendijk Walkabout

Kralendijk (pronounced KRAH-len-dike) can be covered on foot in less than an hour. It comprises two parallel north-south streets, Kaya Hellmund/Kaya Craane (along the waterfront) and Kaya Grandi (the shopping street), and two east-west streets, Kaya Gerharts and Kaya Brion. A principal artery, Simon Bolivarstraat, begins at Kaya Grandi and cuts diagonally across Gerharts and Brion Streets.

Kralendijk's historic and shopping areas are the same, making it easy to combine a walking and shopping excursion. Many of the shops, bars, and restaurants are housed in colorful old structures that give the town its special character. Some of the most historic buildings are located around Wilhelminaplein (Queen Wilhelmina Park), by the sea on the east side of town. The park has pretty shade trees and benches and three historical monuments:

One commemorating Dutchman Van Welbeek's landing on Bonaire in 1634 is in the center of the park; another honoring Bonairean soldiers killed during World War II is by the sea; and the third remembers Eleanor Roosevelt's visit to Bonaire in 1944, when American troops were stationed here.

Directly behind the park on its east side is an eighteenth-century church; in front by the pier is the customs office; and on the south, Government House. South of Government House is the old fort, which is to be renovated for the Instituto Folklore Bonaire (Folklore Museum), a collection of musical instruments, old utensils, and pre-Columbian and other artifacts.

A Drive around the Island

To the North

As you drive from town toward the island's north coast, the terrain changes from flat and desertlike with short, pale-colored bushes and hundreds of cactus plants to green rolling hills. The road winds along the west coast hugging the coastline of jagged, black coral rock. About 4 miles north of the capital at Barcadera (across from the Radio Antilles tower), there are seaside steps, known as the **Thousand Steps,** a popular dive site.

Another mile north are rock formations whose appearance is so grotesque they have been dubbed the **Devil's Mouth.** After another mile the road becomes one-way in a northbound direction. At Karpata the first of two roads goes inland to Bonaire's oldest village, Rincon. Karpata is the home of STINAPA, the Bonaire National Parks Foundation, which is responsible for the management of the land and marine parks, and of the Karpata Ecological Center, a marine research facility. After another mile the road reaches the gate of Bonaire Petroleum's oil terminal, where the road forks. A left turn continues north to Nukove and Playa Frans, where you will find beaches for swimming, hidden caves, and some of the island's most popular picnicking and snorkeling locations; the right fork takes you along a lake on the southern border of the park to Dos Pos and south again to Rincon. There is no access to the park from the southwest.

Goto Meer Lying outside the southwest border of the park is a beautiful lake, Goto Meer, once open to the sea and still fed by underground springs. The drive along the lake shore is the prettiest in Bonaire and should be a priority. The vegetation is typical of the park with candle cactus, acacia, mesquite, and other trees usually found in dry lowland tropical forests; it becomes leafy green during the rainy season. The southern end of the lagoon attracts large numbers of flamingos, particularly in November and December. Early in the morning you are also likely to see parrots and parakeets in the trees around the lake. The island's highest point, 784-foot Brandaris Hill, is in view on the northeast.

Washington/Slagbaai National Park The northern end of Bonaire is covered by the 13,500-acre Washington/Slagbaai National Park, a wildlife sanctuary and the first of its kind in the Netherlands Antilles when it was established in 1969. Situated on the hilliest, greenest part of the island on a former plantation producing divi-divi trees, aloe, charcoal, and goats, the park showcases the island's flora and fauna and includes Brandaris Hill, which can be seen from most locations in the park.

In 1967 the heir of the Washington estate sold the land to the government on the condition that it would never be developed commercially. The land was designated for a national park, and the Netherlands Antilles National Parks Foundation was made the custodian. Three years later, in 1972, the family of the Slagbaai plantation sold the land to the Parks Foundation, and the two areas were reunited into the Washington/Slagbaai National Park.

The park has a wide variety of birds and landscape that ranges from dry lowland forest and salt licks to freshwater lakes, secluded white-sand beaches, unusual rock formations, and dramatic seascapes along rocky coasts. Candle cactus, which grows as tall as trees; prickly pear cactus; mesquite, a favorite perch of the Bonaire parrot; acacia; and divi-divi trees are abundant.

Bonaire, a flyover for migratory birds between North and South America, has as many as 150 species—some unique to the island. Among the most interesting are the beautiful black, yellow, and white trupial and the colorful parakeets and parrots. The endemic, yellow-winged Bonaire parrot, also called the lora, is protected. The park can be seen by car or on foot.

There are two signposted routes over mostly dirt roads: a short one of 15 miles marked by green arrows and a longer one of 22 miles marked by yellow arrows. The routes can also be used for hiking, and there are additional footpaths to places not accessible by motor vehicles.

At the entrance, located on the southeastern side of the park, you can get a free pamphlet with map or purchase more complete guidebooks that detail the routes and the flora and fauna to be seen along the way. There is also a book on the birds of Bonaire. Hours: daily 8:00 a.m. to 5:00 p.m. Entrance: US$10 adults, US$2 children; cash only. Must enter before 2:45 p.m. Other resources: www.bonairenature.com/washingtonpark and www.washingtonparkbonaire.org.

Both park roads begin at the entrance gate. The yellow one goes first to **Salina Mathijs,** a salt pond populated by flamingos during the rainy season (October to January). After another mile a side road to the right leads to **Playa Chiquito,** a rock-bound cove with a beautiful beach, where the surf is too strong and the water too rough for safe swimming. A short walk north along the rocky coral coast at **Boca Chiquito,** huge waves crash against the shore with such force they send clouds of spray shooting 30 feet and more into the air.

The yellow route continues to the north end of the park at **Boca Cocolishi,** a small secluded cove divided into two parts—a deep, rough seaward side and a calm, shallow basin with a black-sand beach—separated by a coral ridge. The basin and beach were formed by small pieces of coral, mollusks, and their shells (*cocolishi* means "shell" in

Papiamento). Hermit crabs can be seen on the beach and in the shallow water.

Inland along **Salina Bartol,** another salt pond, lies Poos di Mangel, a watering hole for a great variety of birds and a good bird-watching location. Boca Bartol, on the coast, is made up of coral rubble and flat, eroded rock. This bay has abundant elkhorn coral and sea fans and many colorful reef fish.

On the green route about three-quarters of the way from the east to the west coast, the road passes the trailhead for the 1.5-mile hike to the top of Brandaris Hill. Farther on, a side road leads to **Put Bronswinkel,** a watering hole for parakeets and other birds that is one of the park's best birding locations.

Playa Funchi, on the west coast, is the former harbor of the Washington Plantation. Here you can see dozens of multicolored geckos and iguana, particularly bright green baby ones. If you are quiet on the approach, the iguana often remain statue-still and can be photographed.

At Playa Funchi the green route turns south to **Boca Slagbaai,** a large bay with a white-sand beach popular for swimming, snorkeling, and diving. Used as a harbor for exporting salt and meat in the 1800s, the former storage buildings and customs office have been restored. Local scouts and other groups often rent the main house for overnight camping. The buildings sit on a strip of land that once dammed and separated the sea from **Salina Slagbaai,** the saline lake behind the bay. The lake has flamingos, particularly from about January to July.

Bonaire Tours and Vacations (599-717-8778; fax: 599-717-4890; www.bonairetours.com) offers a guided excursion to Washington/Slagbaai National Park for US$55, which includes transportation and stops for swimming and snorkeling. **Discover Bonaire** (599-717-5252; fax: 599-717-7690; www.bonairediveandadventure.com) also has park tours with a naturalist guide.

Across the Central Region and North Coast

The low-lying terrain and scattered hills of the central region stretch from Kralendijk to the north coast through green farm fields with old Dutch colonial farmhouses. The coast is as desolate as the moon, with large fields of coral terraces and deeply eroded rocks, some with petroglyphs. A good road from Kralendijk to Rincon and the entrance to the national park runs through the cunucu (or kunuku), as the countryside is known in Papiamento.

Immediately north of Kralendijk at Noord di Salina, a side road of about 1 mile leads up **Seroe Largo,** a hill of about 500 feet in altitude. There you will be rewarded with a fabulous view of Bonaire stretching from the national park on the north along the resorts of the west coast and Kralendijk to the salt mounds on the south.

Another 4 miles north on the main road brings you to a small sign marking the turnoff onto a dirt road for **Onima,** where there are Arawak petroglyphs on rock faces near the road. Here, too, strong waves break against the rocky shore.

On the main road, about 2 miles north of the Onima turnoff, you will reach Rincon, the first settlement on the island, dating from the sixteenth century. Set in a pretty green valley, the town is anchored by a brightly colored village church and surrounded by old red tile–roofed houses of typical Dutch architecture. From Rincon to the national park entrance is less than 3 miles.

To the South

In contrast to the hilly north, the southern part of the island is flat, dry, and covered with white mountains of salt that shimmer in the bright sun. The salt pans, which are more than 150 years old, have been reactivated after many years of disuse. It takes seven months for the evaporation process to be completed to make salt. The modern plant can load salt by conveyor belt onto ships at the rate of 2,000 tons an hour. It is shipped to the eastern United States, throughout the Caribbean, and as far away as New Zealand for chemical, industrial, water softening, and ice-control applications. On the coast south of the loading pier is **Witte Pan,** or Pink Beach, one of the longest stretches of beach on Bonaire. It parallels the south side of the **Pekelmeer Lagoon,** the large canal that channels sea water to the salt pans.

Flamingo Sanctuary Between the salt pans and the Pekelmeer Lagoon is a 135-acre flamingo sanctuary, a nesting ground for about five thousand birds. You can tour the perimeter of the pans, but access to the sanctuary is prohibited because of the flamingos' extreme sensitivity. Viewers usually leave their vehicles by the road and walk quietly along the edge of the lagoon, where they can get close enough to see the birds with binoculars and photograph them with telephoto lens.

On the south side of the saltworks, you can see tiny stone huts by the side of the road. Built around 1850—about a decade before slavery was abolished here—the huts were used to house slaves when they worked the salt pans.

On the southern tip of the island stands the **Willemstoren Lighthouse,** the oldest lighthouse in Bonaire, built in 1837.

Lac Bay Here the road turns north for about 4 miles to Lac Bay (Lake Bay), which has extensive mangroves and is the most popular place in Bonaire for kayaking. You'll also find the **Kontiki Beach Club,** a small restaurant serving fish and snacks, and open Tuesday to Sunday (closed Monday). On the south side of the bay at Sorobon, there is a pretty beach with a small naturalist hotel; its clothes-optional beach may be used by nonguests upon payment of a fee.

Bonaire Marine Park The growth of Bonaire as a diver's mecca and the development of tourism in the 1970s led to the need for a long-term program to protect the island's extraordinary coral reefs and marine life. With the help of the International Union for the Conservation of Nature and Natural Resources, as well as the World Wildlife Fund, the Netherlands Antilles National Parks Foundation (STINAPA) received a grant in 1979 to create the Bonaire Marine Park (www.bmp.org). It monitors the impact of coastal development, resource exploitation, visitor use, and other variables and manages services and facilities for visitors, including park brochures, lectures, slide presentations, films, and permanent dive-site moorings.

The park incorporates the entire coastline of Bonaire and neighboring Klein Bonaire and is defined as the "seabottom and the overlying waters from the highwater tidemark down to 200 feet." It has more than eighty marked dive sites, often within wading distance from shore. All marine life is completely protected; fishing, spearfishing, and collecting of fish, shells, or corals—dead or alive—are prohibited. All boats must use permanent moorings and cannot anchor except in emergencies.

Bonaire's reefs contain some of the most beautiful coral formations in the Caribbean. They are famous for their variety—the park's guidebook describes eighty-four species—and include an abundance of sponges, particularly purple tube sponges, elkhorn and sheet coral, and four kinds of brain coral. More than 200 species of fish have been identified. *Guide to the Bonaire Marine Park,* available in local dive shops and gift stores, was written by the marine biologists who developed the Bonaire Marine Park, Tom van't Hof and Dee Scarr.

Divers and snorkelers derive the greatest pleasure from the park, but nondivers can see a great deal on glass-bottom boat excursions, because visibility in Bonaire's waters is excellent and major coral formations are close to shore. The park fee, valid for one year, is US$25 for scuba divers; US$10 for snorkelers, windsurfers, kayakers, sport fishermen, and kiteboarders. The fee goes to maintaining the marine park.

Klein Bonaire Less than a mile west of Kralendijk is the small, dry, and rocky islet of Klein Bonaire. Covered with desert vegetation, it has several white-sand beaches, which are popular destinations for day-trippers. Its spectacular reefs are part of the marine park and range from shallow-water gardens thick with elkhorn coral to coral slopes with great varieties of sponges, gorgonians, and large star and brain corals.

After being in private hands for 131 years, Klein Bonaire officially became part of Bonaire in 1999, when it was turned over to the Klein Bonaire Preservation Foundation and the Bonaire government. The island was purchased for US$4.6 million from the Development Company of Klein Bonaire; the firm had intended to turn the island into a resort community. The purchase deed specifies that the island is to remain undeveloped and natural forever. It is known to be a nesting place for sea turtles and birds. The only structure there is a beach shack built from driftwood to give shelter from the sun.

The island will become one of the Antilles National Parks; meanwhile, it is being managed by the Bonaire Marine Park. The island's well-known No Name Beach has been renamed Playa Neme. Water taxis are available from Kralendijk for US$14 round-trip, and private boats usually offer excursions daily.

Shopping

Kralendijk has an assortment of small shops selling jewelry, crystal, leather, perfume, and sportswear at prices competitive with Curaçao and Aruba, but Bonaire is a place for casual, not serious, shoppers. Most shops on Kaya Grandi are housed in brightly painted colonial buildings. Harborside is a small mall in a renovated building with a Dutch colonial facade. Located between Kaya Grandi and seaside, it has nine shops, an ice cream parlor, bar, and restaurant. Hotels also have small gift shops, and these are likely to be your best place to find books on Bonaire, particularly its marine life.

Store hours generally are Monday to Saturday from 8:00 a.m. to noon and 2:00 to 6:00 p.m., although some stores remain open through the lunch hours. When cruise ships are in port on Sundays or holidays, tourist shops usually open for a few hours. U.S. dollars, credit cards, and traveler's checks are accepted; stores often quote prices in dollars.

Art and Artists The Cinnamon Art Gallery / Bonaire Artists Foundation (Kaya A.P.L. Brion #1, Kralendijk, 786-9563; www.avybart.com; africavy@avybart.com) in downtown, is a project of the Bonaire Artists Foundation, a nonprofit entity created to promote the work of Bonaire-based local artists in a permanent gallery setting and has rotating exhibition of their art. The Gallery does not keep any payment for the artists' work purchased there; rather, 100 percent of the monies flow directly to the artist. Private donations provide the funding for exhibits and cost of maintaining the gallery. Its Web site provides a schedule of upcoming events where local artists will be presenting their work, usually during an evening reception with music and refreshment. Hours: Monday to Friday, 10:00 a.m. to noon and 2:00 to 5:00 p.m. or by appointment.

China/Crystal/Jewelry Littman's Jewelers (Harborside; www.bonairelittmanstores.com) is the agent for several well-known brands of European crystal and also carries delft china; it is best known for fine jewelry and quality dive watches. **Atlantis** (Kaya Grandi 32B) is a similar addition

Cameras/Photo Supplies Paradise Photo (599-717-8741) has cameras and photographic equipment, develops film, and takes passport pictures.

Clothing and Accessories Benetton (19 Kaya Grandi) claims its prices are 30 percent less than those in the United States. **Bahia** (Harborside) has pretty sportswear. **Botica Bonaire** (599-717-8905) is like a general store and has a local clientele for clothing, as well as perfume, toiletries, and pharmaceuticals.

Crafts and Souvenirs Littman's Gifts boutique stocks hand-painted T-shirts, Dutch china and island souvenirs, and casual jewelry. A small deli section has Dutch chocolates, cheeses, and other specialties. **Bonaire Gift Shop** (Kaya Grandi 13) has souvenirs, handicrafts, toys, film, wine, liquor, accessories, custom jewelry, and clothing. **Fundashon Arte Boneriano** (Bonaire Art Foundation), located by the post office has local handicrafts, souvenirs, and art.

Dive and Sporting Goods Some stores in town have masks and fins, but you will find the best stocks of quality dive equipment in the dive shops at hotels. **Buddy Dive Shop** (Kaya Grandi) sells water-sports equipment, T-shirts, postcards, and souvenirs.

Perfumes and Cosmetics D'Orsy's (Harborside), a member of a chain found in Aruba and throughout the Netherlands Antilles, has a good selection of French perfumes.

Dining and Restaurants

Bonaire has a surprising selection of restaurants offering fresh seafood and continental specialties, but some of the best are open for dinner only. Those listed here are generally open daily, but some may close Sunday or Monday and serve lunch and dinner. Check locally. These restaurants and more can be found at www.bonairediningguide.com, which is updated annually. Entries range from inexpensive (less than US$9) and moderate (US$10 to $20) to expensive (more than US$20).

Bistro de Paris (Kaya Gobernor 46; 599-717-7070), a new French-owned and -operated restaurant situated in a small white house with a terrace, serves French cuisine. Moderate.

Cactus Blue Bar & Restaurant (JA Abraham Blvd 12, 599-717-4564), a colorful downtown eatery, offers contemporary Caribbean cuisine and some familiar American fare to be enjoyed in air-conditioned comfort or outdoors on the terrace. Some specialties are Cajun tuna sashimi, fresh lobster, lime & ginger shrimp, Argentinean filet mignon and kabritu stoba—Bonairean goat stew. Moderate.

Papaya Moon Cantina (48 Kaya Grandi; 599-717-5025; www.papayamooncantina.com), Bonaire's first and only Tex-Mex restaurant. Serves lunch and dinner in an indoor/outdoor setting. Moderate.

Kontiki Beach Club (65 Kaminda Sorobon; 599-717-5369; www.kontikibonaire.com) features sandwiches, salads, and snacks in the laid-back atmosphere of an outdoor cactus garden. Exhibits art by local artists for sale. Jazz occasionally. Moderate.

Vespucci's Restaurant (Harbour Village Marina; 599-717-2596) offers seafood and Mediterranean-style fare. Moderately expensive.

Zeezicht Bar and Restaurant (10 Curaçao straat, near the pier; 599-717-8434). Established in 1929, its specialties are fresh fish and nasi goring, an Indonesian dish. Happy hour at 4:15 p.m. features live musical entertainment. Moderate.

Nightlife

The nightlife on Bonaire is low-key, in keeping with the ambience of the island. **Karel's Beach Bar** on the water and **City Cafe** in Kralendijk are popular nightspots. Both are open air and usually have live music on weekends.

Bonaire has a casino at **Divi Flamingo Beach Resort and Casino**, Minimum age is eighteen.

Sports

Beaches/Swimming On Bonaire you have the choice of powdery white, pretty pink, or black sand beaches. Most are small reef-protected coves with exceptionally clear water. The best swimming is on the leeward, or western, side where the waters are calm. Swimming on the windward side is generally not recommended due to the strong waves and currents.

Sorobon Beach Resort is a clothes-optional resort with a private beach on Lac Bay. Nonguests are welcome to use the resort's facilities for a small fee.

Pink Beach on the southwest coast takes its name from the pinkish tint of the sand, enhanced by the light of the late-afternoon sun. Popular with Bonaireans on the weekends, it is delightfully empty during the week.

Biking Bonaire has more than 100 miles of trails ranging from goat paths to unpaved roads. Local bike shops offer bike rentals and guided tours. Bonaire's Web site, www.infobonaire.com, has a cycling map and descriptions of six routes. **Cycle Bonaire** (Kaya Gerharts 11d; 599-717-7558; fax: 599-717-7690; www.bonairediveandadventure .com) offers mountain-bike rentals, mapped routes, and guided biking excursions with stops for snorkeling and a seaside picnic, and has permission for mountain-biking tours in Washington/Slagbaai National Park (US$55–$65). Similar tours and rentals are available from **Outdoor Bonaire** (599-785-6272; www.outdoorbonaire.com); and Buddy Dive Resort.

Bird-watching Bonaire boasts over 190 species including the protected Lora (Amazon parrot). The island has no endemic bird species, but does have subspecies or ones restricted to the Aruba, Bonaire and Curaçao area. Bonaire's most famous bird is the pink flamingo, which can be seen in the Washington Slagbaai National Park in the north and a reserve in the salt pans on the south. For bird-watching tours contact **Bonaire Dive & Adventure/Jerry Ligon** (599-717-2098). Ligon, a resident naturalist, leads field trips to the park and bird sanctuaries.

Boating Sailing yachts offer half-day and full-day excursions; most serve beverages and snacks. The *Oscarina* (599-790-7674; www.bonairesailing.com/ oscarina) has trips to Klein Bonaire for swimming and snorkeling, at US$55 per person, half day; US$75 full day with lunch. Other day sails are offered by **AquaSpace** (599-717-2568; info@aqua spacebonaire.com); **Pirate Cruise of Bonaire** (599-790-8330; www.remarkable.com/bonaire/ pirates.html), and **Woodwind** (599-786-7055; www.woodwindbonaire.com).

Deep-Sea Fishing Half- and full-day charters with all provisions are available through watersports operators. Bonaire's offshore fishing grounds beyond the marine park are abundant with mackerel, tuna, wahoo, barracuda, and swordfish, to name a few. **Big Game Sportfishing** (599-717-6500; www.bonairefishing.com/biggame); **Fishing Bonaire** (599-790-1228; www.bonairefishing.com/ siri); **Multifish Charters** (599-717-3648; www .multifish.com); and **Piscatur Charters** (Captain Chris Morkos; 599-717-8774; fax: 599-717-4784; www.bonairefishing.com/piscatur) offer deep-sea fishing trips. Piscatur's charters include gear, bait, beer, soda, and sandwiches: half day, four persons, US$350; and full day, US$500–$600. They also arrange reef fishing, as well as bonefishing and tarpon fishing in the shallows.

Hiking The best hiking is on the trails and footpaths of the national park. (See section on the Washington/Slagbaai National Park.) You can arrange for a naturalist guide at the park entrance for US$10. The companies listed under Biking above can also arrange hiking guides. **Bonaire Tours and Vacations** (www.bonairetours.com) has a Kunuku Trip with walk-on trails in the Rooi Lamoenchi plantation; three hours, US$21.

Horseback Riding The Riding Academy Club at Kunuku Warahama (599-560-7949; www.horsebackridingbonaire.com), is something of an American dude ranch in the Caribbean and is located in the southern wilderness of the island. It offers riding, horse shows, and carriage rides, as well as two playgrounds and a petting zoo for children.

Kayaking Kayaks can be rented from most dive shops. Bonaire's calm waters are ideal for kayaking. Kayaks are available to explore Lac Bay, a lagoon with mangroves, which are a nursery for fish life; to view the coast; or to visit Klein Bonaire. **Bonaire Tours and Vacations** (599-717-8778; fax: 599-717-4890; www.bonairetours.com) has a guided kayaking excursion to Lac Bay for US$45, including transportation and equipment. **Discover Bonaire/ Bonaire Dive and Adventure** (599-717-2229; www.bonairediveandadventure.com) has kayak rentals and mangrove excursions. Others offering guided kayak trips include Outdoor Bonaire (599-785-6272; www.outdoorbonaire.com and **Mangrove Info Center Bonaire** (599-790-5353; fax: 599-717-5622; www.infobonaire.com/kayaking), a research and excursion center, established in 2002 by Gerard van Erp. It has an aquarium for basic research and a research partnership with the Rotterdam Zoo in the Netherlands, which is planning to build a educational mangrove forest. Lac Bay mangroves excursions: 8:30 a.m. two-hour guided kayak tour, including mangrove snorkeling, $42.50; 9:30 a.m. one-hour solar boat tour, $25; 11:00 a.m. one-hour guided kayak tour, $25. Call for reservations.

Snorkeling/Scuba Diving Bonaire is one of the world's leading scuba-diving locations, with more than eighty beautiful dive spots along its magnificent reefs. Rave reviews come from experienced divers because of the great variety and quality of marine life; beginners like it because of the ease and accessibility of the reefs. Indeed, there is no better place in the Caribbean to learn to scuba or snorkel. In many places, you can wade from the shore to the reefs to enjoy unlimited viewing and diving from the beach any time of the day or night.

Snorkel Tour: Bonaire is also the first Caribbean island to have a full-fledged snorkeling program. It teaches participants about the reefs and provides trained guides to take them on reef tours. Tours are available at twelve locations, and each provides a different experience. They are offered one to three times a day, depending on demand; cost is US$55, including rental equipment, map, video presentation, and guide. Tours can be booked through any dive shop in Bonaire.

The best reefs are within the protected lee of the island, where most of the diving and other recreational activity takes place. Here the reefs have a narrow, sloping terrace extending seaward to a dropoff at 33 feet. This is followed by a slope varying from 30 feet to a vertical wall, extending to a depth of 100 to 200 feet. Among the places for walk-in snorkeling and scuba are the Thousand Steps, on the north coast at Barcadera, and farther north at Nukove, where you can picnic and watch birds.

Bonaire is one of the Caribbean's best-equipped dive centers; all hotels cater to divers and have excellent dive shops on their premises. They offer lessons at every level of training, as well as in underwater photography. Divers can hire an underwater camera person to videotape their diving experiences. Deluxe live-aboard boats that carry their own dive equipment are based here. Among the dive operators closest to the port are **Divi Dive Bonaire** (Divi Flamingo Beach Resort; 599-717-8285; 800-367-3484; fax: 599-717-8238) and **Captain Don's Habitat Dive Center** (Box 88; 599-717-8290; 800-327-6709; fax: 599-717-7346; www.habitatdiveresorts.com). A list of the island's dozen or so dive operators and their services is available from the Bonaire Tourist Office and at www.infobonaire.com.

Windsurfing The constant trade winds that keep the island cool make Bonaire an ideal location for windsurfing. All beachfront resorts have windsurfing equipment. **Bonaire Windsurf Place** (Sorobon; 599-717-2288; www.bonairewindsurfplace.com) has rentals and offers lessons. **Jibe City** (Lac Bay, 599-717-5233; www.jibecity.com) rents boards for US$20 an hour or US$60 per day. It also has kayaks.

Festivals and Celebrations

Carnival is celebrated in the traditional pre-Lenten period, and there is the **Bonaire Dive Festival** in June, but the biggest event of the year is the **Bonaire Sailing Regatta** in mid-October. Started as a wager among friends three decades ago, it has evolved into an official event. Fishermen and yachtsmen from all over the Caribbean compete in different categories.

Curaçao
Willemstad

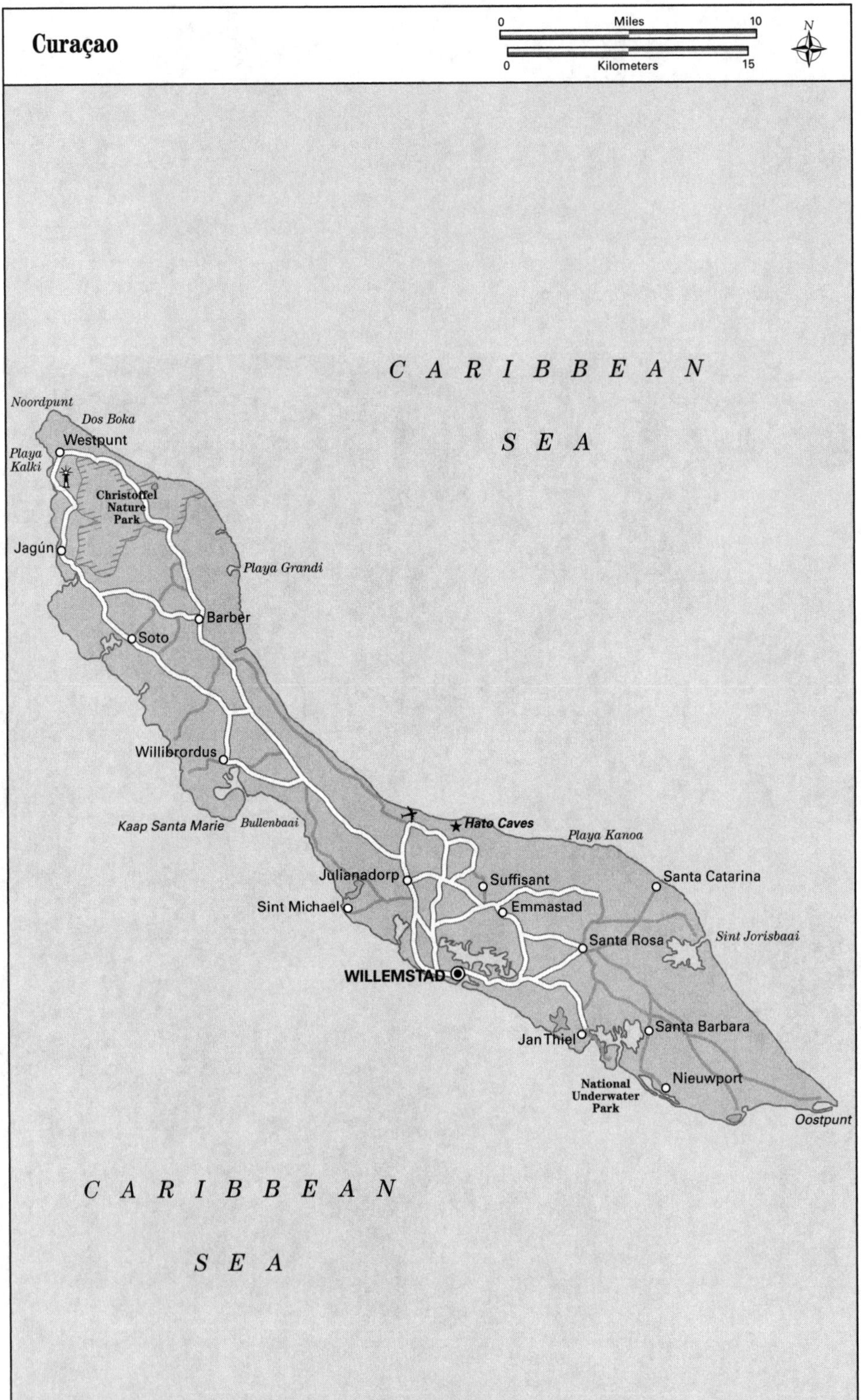

Curaçao

Miles
0   10

Kilometers
0   15

N

C A R I B B E A N

S E A

Noordpunt

Dos Boka

Westpunt

Playa Kalki

Christoffel Nature Park

Jagún

Playa Grandi

Barber

Soto

Willibrordus

Kaap Santa Marie   *Bullenbaai*

Playa Kanoa

Hato Caves

Julianadorp

Suffisant

Santa Catarina

Sint Michael

Emmastad

Santa Rosa

Sint Jorisbaai

WILLEMSTAD

Jan Thiel

Santa Barbara

National Underwater Park

Nieuwport

Oostpunt

C A R I B B E A N

S E A

A Dutch Masterpiece in the Tropics

Known throughout its history as a center for international commerce with one of the world's busiest ports, Curaçao, the cosmopolitan capital of the Netherlands Antilles, has stepped into the role of a sun-drenched Caribbean resort rather recently. But over the past several years, in concert with private interests, the government has made up for lost time by renovating, upgrading, and expanding its many attractions. It has added sporting facilities, shopping plazas, new cruise facilities, and a harborside park, as well as restored and beautified an extensive area around the port.

Lying 39 miles off the coast of Venezuela between Aruba and Bonaire, Curaçao is a surprising combination of worldliness and sophistication, resulting from its long trading tradition and polyglot culture, juxtaposed with a rugged landscape reminiscent of the American Southwest, with dry, cactus-covered reddish soil, undulating rocky hills, chalky mountains, and windswept shores. The land is greener toward the north and along the coast, where narrow waterways lead to large lagoons with fingers and islands used for commerce and sport. These waterways are Curaçao's most distinctive features and one of several elements that make it seem like a mini-Holland with palm trees.

Surrounded by beautiful reefs that divers are now discovering, Curaçao's rocky north coast is pounded by waves, while on the south a placid turquoise sea laps at small sandy coves. Uninhabited Klein Curaçao lies to the southeast.

Cruise-ship passengers have the best vantage point for an introduction to this unusual island when they sail into Willemstad, the capital. There they are greeted by a colorful harborside of brightly painted and gabled Dutch colonial buildings dating from the eighteenth century. So distinctive is the setting that it has become Curaçao's signature and led others to call it a "Dutch masterpiece in the tropics."

The island's early inhabitants were the Caiquetios, an Arawak tribe that migrated north to the Caribbean from South America. Discovered in 1499 by the Spanish navigator Alonso de Ojeda, a lieutenant of Christopher Columbus, the Spanish made their first settlement here in 1527. But a century later the Dutch captured the island and founded their own settlement in 1634. It was made a colony of the Dutch West India Company, starting Curaçao's long trading tradition.

Over the next two centuries, the French and British, eager to have Curaçao for its natural harbors and strategic location, battled the Dutch for possession and dislodged them several times for a year or two. In 1642 a young Peter Stuyvesant was made governor, three years before being named director-general of the Dutch colony of New Amsterdam, which today we call New York.

Under the Dutch Curaçao was divided into plantations, some of which prospered on salt mining rather than agriculture. Slave trading was another important source of revenue. But after slavery was abolished here in 1863, Curaçao

At a Glance

Antiquities	★★
Architecture	★★★★★
Art and artists	★★★
Beaches	★★
Colonial buildings	★★★★★
Crafts	★★
Cuisine	★★★★
Culture	★★★
Dining/Restaurants	★★★★
Entertainment	★★★
Forts	★★★
History	★★★★
Monuments	★★
Museums	★★★★
Nightlife	★★★
Scenery	★★★
Shopping	★★★
Sightseeing	★★★★
Sports	★★★
Transportation	★★

Population: 130,000

Size: 38 miles long and 2 to 7 miles wide; 180 square miles.

Main Town: Willemstad

Government: Curaçao is the largest, most populous of the Netherlands Antilles, which (with Aruba's departure in 1986) consists of Curaçao, Bonaire, St. Maarten, Saba, and St. Eustatius. They form an autonomous region of the Kingdom of the Netherlands, with the seat of government in Willemstad. Their government is a parliamentary democracy with a governor appointed by the Dutch queen. There are three councils: legislative, executive, and advisory; each island territory has its own legislative and executive body, called an Island Council, whose members are elected for four years.

Entry Requirements: Visitors must have a valid passport.

Currency: Netherlands Antilles guilder (NAf) divided into 100 florin or cents. US$1.00 equals NAf1.77. U.S. dollars are widely accepted, and prices are often quoted in dollars.

Departure Tax: US$33 on international flights; US$20 for interisland ones.

Electricity: 127/120 volts; 50 cycles

Language: Dutch is the official language; English and Spanish are widely spoken. Papiamento is the local language and blends Dutch, Portuguese, English, French, Indian, and African words.

Public Holidays: January 1, New Year's Day; Carnival Monday; Good Friday; Easter Monday; April 30, Queen's Birthday; May 1, Labor Day; Ascension Day; July 2, Flag Day; December 25 to 26, Christmas.

Telephone Area Code: From the United States, dial the prefix 011-599-9 followed by the local number.

Cell-phone rentals: RentAFone (Salinja Galleries 599-9-465-8844; rentafone@indel.net).

Internet Cafe: Wireless Internet Café (Handelskade 3, Punda)

Time Zone: Atlantic Standard Time (one hour later than EST)

Airlines: *From the United States:* Air Jamaica, American Airlines, and American Eagle. *Interisland:* Dutch Antilles Express (DAE) and Bonaire

Express (www.bonaireexpress.com) serves the interisland routes between Curaçao, Aruba, Bonaire, and St. Maarten.

Information: www.curacao-tourism.com; www.curacao.com; www.curacao-travelguide.com; www.gaycuracao.com; www.tourism-curacao.com; www.curacaomonument.org

In the United States:

Curaçao Tourist Office, 7951 Southwest Sixth Street, Suite 216, Plantation, FL 33324; (800) 3-CURACAO; (954) 370-5887; fax: (954) 723-7949; jbgrossman@aol.com.

In Port:

Curaçao Department of Tourism, Main Office, Pietermaai 19, Curaçao, N.A.; (599) 9-434-8200; fax: 461-2305; info@ctdb.net.

STINAPA, Netherlands Antilles National Parks Foundation, P.O. Box 2090, Curaçao, N.A.; (599) 462-4242; fax: (599) 462-7780; www.curacao.com.

became a sleepy little island until 1914, when oil was discovered in nearby Venezuela.

Royal Dutch Shell Company, taking advantage of Curaçao's fine harbors, built one of the world's largest oil refineries here. It attracted trade, banks, and other commercial enterprises and created a prosperity that continued throughout the century. Curaçao's trading history had already made it an ethnic melting pot and the oil prosperity that brought workers from many nations enhanced the blend. Today Curaçao claims to be made up of more than fifty nationalities.

Budget Planning

Prices in Curaçao for restaurants and tourist services compare favorably with the rest of the Caribbean. Tourist attractions and facilities are rather spread out; hence touring by taxi tends to be expensive unless you can share costs. Car rentals are moderately priced and public buses inexpensive. You need have no hesitation about using buses since most people speak English and are helpful and friendly. If you like to walk and discover on your own, you'll find Curaçao one of the most delightful ports in the Caribbean.

Port Profile

www.curacao-tourism.com
www.curacao-travelguide.com

Location/Embarkation Your ship's arrival in Curaçao will be one of the most interesting experiences of your cruise—don't miss it! Willemstad is built around Santa Anna Bay, a large deepwater lagoon, which is entered from the sea through a long, narrow finger whose waterfront is lined on both sides with colorful Dutch colonial buildings. The channel, which is 4,200 feet long and only 270 feet wide, opens onto the Schottegat, the inner harbor, spanning 150 acres—the seventh-largest harbor in the world.

On the east side of the picturesque channel is the Punda, with Fort Amsterdam, the oldest part of town. The west side, where your ship docks, is known as Otrobanda (meaning "the other side"). The two sides are connected by the Queen Emma Pontoon Bridge, a century-old bridge that is a pedestrian walkway, near the dock.

Another bridge, the Queen Juliana—whose slender, arched profile is in full view from the time your ship enters the harbor—is used for motor traffic. It spans Santa Anna Bay and connects the two sides of town to the roads that circumnavigate the bay. The bridge, 1,600 feet across, stands at a height of 185 feet; your ship is likely to pass directly under the bridge en route to its dock, and if the ship has a tall stack, watching the tricky maneuver can be a heart-stopping moment.

The port's passenger terminal has local and international telephones and a tourist information desk, and is in walking distance to downtown shopping areas and attractions. Up to five vessels can dock at the inner harbor.

On the west, before entering the harbor, is the megapier, completed in 1999 and used by the ships for which it was built, namely, the new super-megaliners and those ships too tall to pass under the Queen Juliana Bridge. Passengers step off in the Rif area, next to the seventeenth-century Rif Fort, which overlooks the harbor entrance. Here, too, is the main bus stop for the Otrobanda area and a short walk via a landscaped walkway to the Queen Emma Pontoon Bridge and downtown.

Riffort Village has small boutiques, a new Renaissance Hotel, several good restaurants—including Bistro Le Clochard, one of the city's best—and several outstanding art galleries. There is always some sort of live music, usually a local band in the courtyard. One of the biggest advantages of the location of the new megapier is that it has ample space for taxis and tour buses.

Local Transportation Taxis are available at the port and taxi stands at hotels. Fares are set by the government but should be agreed upon with the driver in advance. They are for up to four passengers; for a fifth passenger 25 percent is added; there is an additional 25 percent surcharge after 11:00 p.m. Curaçao taxis can be identified by the sign on their roof and the letters TX after the license number. In 2005 meters were installed in taxis. Sample fares from the port: to airport, about US$20; from Punda to Breezes Beach, about US$24. Sightseeing by taxi costs US$30 an hour for one to four passengers, for a one-hour minimum. To phone for a taxi, call 869-0747; to lodge a complaint, call 461-6577.

When you leave your ship (in Otrobanda) to go no farther than the downtown shopping area (Punda), it is better to walk across the pontoon bridge or take the free ferry; otherwise, a taxi must circle the long distance around the bay.

Public buses operate on regular schedules in Willemstad and to populated areas of the island. The central departure points are Waaigat (next to the post office) in Punda and Riffort in Otrobanda, a three-minute walk from the docks. Between the two bridges in Otrabanda are the renovated buildings of Porto Paseo, now housing hotels, a casino, art gallery, museum, bars, restaurants, parks, and a large crafts center. Also in the immediate vicinity of the port are international phone and e-mail facilities, car rentals, taxis, and "Ask Me" personnel provided by the Curaçao Port Authority.

Roads and Rentals In its urban areas Curaçao has a good road network that fans out from Willemstad and the port on the south for a radius of about 6 miles; there are also major east-west arteries crossing the island. But beyond these principal routes, rural roads are often dirt ones, which

www.curacao.com, may have better rates. Road Assistance: 599-9-9-24-7.

Ferry Service A free ferry crosses the harbor between Otrobanda and Punda regularly through-out the day; when the pontoon bridge is closed for traffic, pedestrians use the ferry.

Interisland Air Service See Fast Facts.

Emergency Numbers

Medical: St. Elisabeth Hospital
Emergency: 599-9-462-4900
Ambulance: 599-9-462-5822
Police: 114
Curaçao Dialysis Center: 599-9-869-5055

Shore Excursions

Cruise ships have tours to the island's best-known attractions, such as the Curaçao Seaquarium and Curaçao Liqueur Distillery, but Curaçao is not a cookie-cutter, beach-lined Caribbean island. It is different, and its differences are what make it interesting, particularly to those with curiosity, a fondness for history, and a sense of adventure. Several local companies offer tours for small groups that will give you a much better picture of this unusual island than standard tours can do. They also tailor tours to off-the-beaten-track places.

Walking Tours: The best walking tours of Willemstad are offered by Old City Tours (Julianaplein 26; 599-9-461-3554), whose archi-tect/owner, Anko van der Woude, is the island's leading expert on historic architecture and some-times leads the tour himself. The company has sev-eral programs of two to three hours, but with advance arrangements, a program can be fitted to your interest. Some other walking tours include those of the Punda with an architect or art histo-rian, starting from the pontoon bridge on the Punda side; for reservations, call 599-9-461-3554; and by appointment with Uniek Curacao (599-9-462-8989; 599-9-462-6632; www.uniek-curacao.an). Another is offered by Jopie Hart (599-9-767-3798), a historian and teacher who grew up in Otrobanda. Historical Otrobanda Tours (599-9-767-3798; lagun@attglobal.net) also has walking tours of Otrobanda. Angelina's Walking Tour is a culinary

can become muddy after a heavy rain; inquire locally before leaving main highways. East and south of Willemstad, good roads run as far as Spaanse Water (or Spanish Water), a large lagoon on the south coast; beyond there are only a few dirt roads and tracks. On the west a major artery from Willemstad crosses the center of the island to the Christoffel Nature Park and Westpunt (West Point). En route it branches to the west coast in three places: Santa Marta Bay, San Juan, and Santa Cruz, where it continues via the coast to Westpunt. Road maps are available.

Bikes, scooters, and motorcycles are available for rent, but if this is your first trip to Curaçao, none are a good mode of travel, unless with a tour guide. For bike rentals, **Dutch Dream** (Landhuis Papaya, 599-9-864-7377; dutchdream@carib-online.net); for motorcycles, the **Bike Shop** (Sta. Rosaweg 599-9-560-3882; bikeshop@curacao-travelguide.com), which handles Harley-Davidson motorcycles, and **Christoffel Park Rental Bike** (Christoffel Park; 599-9-566-6303); for scooters, **Scooby's Rental Scooters** (Breezes Hotel, 599-9-523-8618; www.scooterscuracao.com; info@scooterscuracao.com).

Car rentals are essential for touring on your own. You need a valid driver's license. Traffic moves on the right; road signs are in kilometers. Expect to pay about US$50 and up for a small car. Among the rental firms are **Avis** (599-9-461-1255; www.aviscuracao.com), **Budget** (599-9-868-3466; www.curacao-budgetcar.com) and **Hertz** (599-9-888-0088; www.hertzcaribbean.com), which have jeeps and Mini-Mokes and offer free pickup and delivery. Another dozen local companies, listed on

walking tour (see Angelina's Kitchen in Restaurant section later in this chapter).

Banda Ariba (East Side) or Banda Abao (West): 3.5 hours, US$35–45. The half-day tour to the east usually visits Landhuis Chobolobo, which houses the Curaçao Liqueur Distillery, and **Landhuis Rooi Catootje Museum,** a beautifully restored landhouse owned by the Mongui Maduro Foundation (599-9-737-5119) with a collection of books, documents, and photos of Curaçao's history and its Jewish community, or Hato Caves.

A full-day tour to the west gives you a picture of country life in the eighteenth and nineteenth centuries and visits Landhuis Ascension, restored and furnished in its original style.

Trolley Train: 1.5 hours, US$20. Guided city tour starting from Fort Amsterdam in a caboose-pulled open-sided trolley. Excellent guides. Operated by Miami-based **Atlantis Adventure** (800-SHOREX-1). Cost: US$30–$35 when bought as a ship's shore excursion.

Combination Tours: Half day, US$40–$50 per person. Some island sightseeing, such as visiting the Seaquarium, is combined with swimming or the Botanical Garden and Zoo, a drive west through the countryside, or a visit to a cunucu house or Landhuis Jan Kok. **Taber Tours** (599-9-737-6637; fax: 599-9-737-9539; tabertrs@cura.net) city tour departs daily at 2:00 p.m. Other companies with similar tours are **Touraçao Tourist Services/Explore Curaçao** (Pietermaai 133/135; 599-9-517-7714; touracao@curlink.com; info@explorecuracao.com) and **Island Style Tours** (599-9-747-7777; www.tourism-curacao.com).

Seaworld Explorer: 2 hours, US$35. The semisubmarine departs from a dock at the **Hilton Curaçao Hotel and Casino.** Tours are conducted in several languages; check locally for the English ones (599-9-461-0011; 599-9-461-0012).

Ostrich Farm and Herb Garden: 3 hours, US$49. A visit to the Caribbean's only ostrich farm, located in the northeast corner of the island, can be combined with the Caribbean Herb Garden. You will not save money doing it on your own, unless you rent a car, as the drive to the farm takes more than thirty minutes one-way. (www.ostrichfarm.com)

Adventure Excursions: For biking, hiking, and other such trips, see the Sports section later in this chapter. Among the companies offering them are **Wild Curaçao** (6 Scherpenheuvel; 599-9-561-0027; fax: 599-9-747-0382) and **Cura Curaçao** (599-9-864-4255), which offer hikes to the summit of Mount Christoffel as well as historic hikes. **Dutch Dream Adventures** (599-9-864-7377) has jeep safaris, canoeing, mountain biking, and hiking excursions.

The Beach Express: US$49 adults, US$25 children. The western end of the island has beaches in secluded coves with crystal-clear water for swimming and snorkeling, but without a car, the trip here can be pricey. An alternative is the Beach Express, a colorful, handpainted open-air bus. En route it makes a short stop at the Christoffel Park and Boka Tabla Cave, then to two of the remote tropical beaches of Banda'bou to swim, snorkel, or relax. Prices include all entrance fees, guide, soft drinks, lunch on the beach, and snorkel gear. For reservations, call the Curaçao's Tour Info Center at 599-9-462-6262 or e-mail info@tourism-curacao.com. For more sightseeing options, go to www.tourism-curacao.com.

Curaçao on Your Own

Willemstad is an architectural gem and was given the recognition it deserves when it was named as a World Heritage Site by UNESCO in 1997. The heart of Willemstad, with its colorful historic buildings, straddles Santa Anna Bay. Punda, the east side, has a 5-square-block historic zone, including Fort Amsterdam and the main shopping streets—all easily covered on foot. Otrobanda, the west side, is more residential and has clusters of old buildings, newly renovated as shopping and restaurant complexes. Both historic districts with their narrow lanes—some closed to traffic—are best explored on foot. (For guided walking tours, see previous Shore Excursions section.)

A Willemstad Walkabout

Since 1987 Curaçao has put an extraordinary effort into the renovation of the city center, adding many new facilities. YOU ARE HERE signs with maps of the downtown shopping area are posted at the cruise terminal and other key locations.

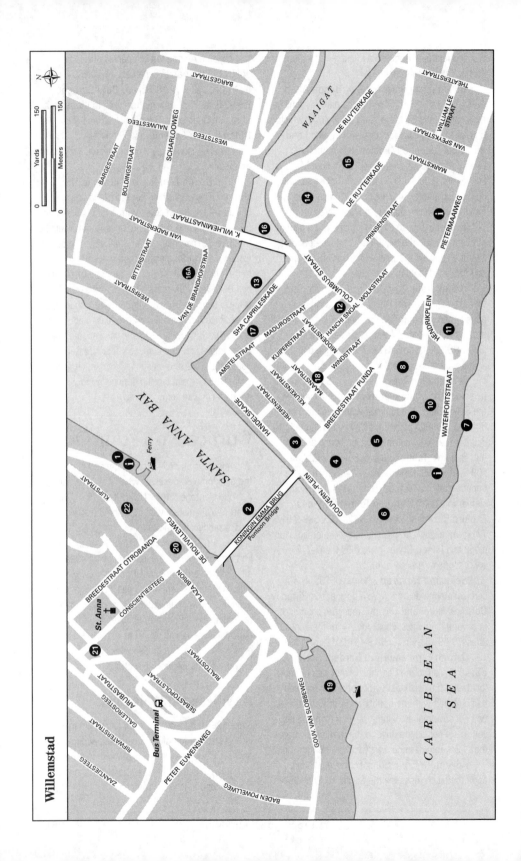

Willemstad

WAAIGAT

SANTA ANNA BAY

CARIBBEAN SEA

Yards
Meters

BARGESTRAAT
THEATERSTRAAT
WILLIAM LEE STRAAT
VAN SPEYKSTRAAT
DE RUYTERSTRAAT
MARKSTRAAT
DE RUYTERKADE
SCHARLOOWEG
NAUWESTEEG
WESTSTEEG
BOLDINGSTRAAT
BARGESTRAAT
VAN RADERSTRAAT
VAN DE BRANDHOFSTRAA
BITTERSTRAAT
WERFSTRAAT
K. WILHELMINASTRAAT
SHA CAPRILESKADE
AMSTELSTRAAT
MADUROSTRAAT
HANDELSKADE
HEERENSTRAAT
KEUKENSTRAAT
KUIPERSTRAAT
MAANSTRAAT
WINDSTRAAT
MIDDENSTRAAT
HANCHI SNOAL WOLKSTRAAT
COLUMBUS STRAAT
PRINSENSTRAAT
PIETERMAAIWEG
HENDRIKPLEIN
BREEDESTRAAT PUNDA
WATERFORTSTRAAT
GOUVERN. PLEIN
KONINGIN EMMA BRUG
Pontoon Bridge
Ferry
KLIPSTRAAT
DE ROUVILLEWEG
BREEDESTRAAT OTROBANDA
PLAZA BRION
CONSCIENTIESTEEG
RIALTOSTRAAT
SEBASTOPOLSTRAAT
GOUV. VAN SLOBBEWEG
BADEN POWELLWEG
PETER EUWENSWEG
ARUBASTRAAT
GALLEROSTEEG
RIFWATERSTRAAT
ZAANTJESTEEG
St. Anna
Bus Terminal

1 2 3 4 5 6 7 8 9 10 11 12 13 14 15 16 16A 17 18 19 20 21 22

1.	Dock	13.	Floating Market
2.	Queen Emma Pontoon Bridge	14.	Central Market
3.	Penha Building	15.	Post Office
4.	Fort Amsterdam	16.	Wilhelmina Bridge
5.	Fort Church	16a.	Maritime Museum
6.	Plaza Piar	17.	Plaza Jojo Correa
7.	Waterfort Arches	18.	Gomezplein
8.	Wilhelmina Park	19.	Riffort
9.	Police Office	20.	Koral Agostini
10.	Courthouse, Council, Bank of Boston	21.	Sebastopol House
11.	Temple Theatre	22.	Museum Kura Hulanda
12.	Mikve Israel-Emanuel Synagogue and Museum		

Queen Emma Pontoon Bridge (2) It is only a short walk from the **dock (1)** to the Queen Emma Pontoon Bridge, which connects the Otrobanda and Punda. The bridge swings open regularly to allow ships to pass. The first pontoon bridge was built in 1888 by L. B. Smith, an American entrepreneur from Maine whose ships brought the first ice (packed in sawdust) to Curaçao; he was also involved in building Curaçao's first power and water plant. A series of postage stamps commemorates his achievements.

Handelskade When you cross the pontoon bridge to the east bank, you arrive on Handelskade, the harborfront street lined with brightly painted eighteenth-century buildings complete with gables and red-tiled roofs. They were once offices of trading companies and warehouses, and were it not for their vivid colors under the bright Caribbean sun, you might imagine yourself in Amsterdam. The red tiles of the roofs came from Europe as ballast in ships. For their return voyages the ships were filled with salt, a major commodity in world trade in colonial days that was used in curing fish and preserving foodstuffs.

Directly in front is the **Penha building (3),** the town's oldest (corner of Handelskade and Breedestraat). Molded on the top is the date 1708, the year of its construction. As you walk along the narrow streets, you will see many old buildings similarly marked. The Penha building was once a social club with a gallery from which members could watch the passing harbor traffic; today it houses one of the town's leading department stores.

Breedestraat, historically, has been a major thoroughfare of Punda and Otrobanda and can be used as a focal point for your walk. (Incidentally, straat is Dutch for street; we have rendered street names as they appear locally in the conviction that they are easier to follow, if not always to pronounce.) On the south is Fort Amsterdam; on the north the shopping streets and several important historic buildings. Look down Breedestraat and you will see typical Dutch colonial–style galleries with their unusual short, round columns.

Fort Amsterdam (4) Originally constructed in 1634 to protect the harbor entrance, Fort Amsterdam was the largest and most important of the eight forts protecting Curaçao from 1648 to 1861, when the capital was a walled city. Now restored, the fort serves as the seat of government. Within its mustard-colored walls are the governor's residence, several government offices, and the eighteenth-century Dutch Reformed Church.

The governor's mansion is a classic colonial structure whose entrance opens onto a courtyard with buildings that house the offices of the central government. Some buildings have retained their old elements, such as heavy oak beams, wide-pegged floorboards, and handblown glass windows. (599-9-461-1139; fax: 599-9-465-7481.) Hours: Monday to Friday, 9:00 a.m. to noon and 2:00 to 5:00 p.m. Admission: NAf3.00 adults, NAf1.50 children.

Fort Church (5) Across the courtyard, the church dating from 1766 occupies the site where a church has stood since the Protestants first came to Curaçao in 1635. Owned by the United Protestant Community of Curaçao since 1824, the first church was probably a wooden shed that served the military garrison at the fort. According to old town maps, by 1707 it had been replaced by a stone building. The church was rebuilt and expanded many times. 599-9-461-1139. Entrance: NAf3.

By the southwest corner of the fort is a small plaza (6) with a statue of Manuel Piar, a gift from Venezuela to Curaçao in memory of one of Curaçao's native sons. Piar, a freedom fighter under the South American liberator Simón Bolívar, was the first foreigner to become a Venezuelan general.

Waterfort Arches (7) On the south side of the fort, by the sea, the turreted and vaulted ramparts were added in 1826 and 1830 to strengthen the fortifications and house provisions. In 1988 the vaults adjacent to the Van der Valk Plaza Hotel were restored and converted into the Waterfort Arches, a plaza with shops, restaurants, and a seaside promenade where you can stroll along the ramparts. If you were on hand to watch your ship sail into port, you can see why the hotel, built directly on the foundations of fortress walls, is one of the few in the world with marine collision insurance.

Attached to the sea wall below the hotel are links of a heavy iron chain used in olden days for protection against invaders. The chain was placed across the mouth of the harbor, attaching it at the Riffort (19), the counterpart fortification on the west side. Built in 1828, the now restored Riffort houses a police station and Bistro Le Clochard, a restaurant with great harbor views. West of Riffort is the new megapier where the largest cruise ships dock.

Wilhelmina Park (8) East of Fort Amsterdam beyond the police office (9) is the Wilhelminaplein, a small park with a statue of Queen Wilhelmina. On its south are several imposing buildings (10). The first, with an impressive balustrade, houses the Council, or parliament, and Courthouse; another, in Georgian style, was built as a Masonic Temple in 1869.

If you were to continue east for a mile or two, beyond the Avila Beach Hotel—too far to walk— you would come to the Octagon House, a museum dedicated to Simón Bolívar. On two occasions Curaçao gave asylum to Bolívar during his struggle to free South America of Spanish rule. The house was visited by Bolívar when his sisters lived there. Hours: weekdays 8:00 a.m. to noon and 2:00 to 6:00 p.m. Admission is free. (599-9-461-4377)

Crossing to the north side of Wilhelmina Park, you reach Columbusstraat, which marked the outer city walls until 1861.

Mikve Israel-Emanuel Synagogue and Museum (12) At the corner of Hanchi Snoa is the oldest synagogue in continuous use in the Western Hemisphere. Built in 1732, some of its artistic treasures are even older than the synagogue itself, dating from the founding of the congregation in 1651 by twelve families from Amsterdam. At services a prayer for the Dutch royal family is chanted in old Portuguese, which was once the common language of the Curaçao Jewish community.

The courtyard museum has artifacts, memorabilia, and replicas of the oldest, most elaborate gravestones in Beth Haim Cemetery, dating from 1659 and said to be the oldest Jewish cemetery in the Western Hemisphere. It is located on the north side of the bay. The architecture of the synagogue, with its curved gables and short columns, is interesting inside and out. As an example, the half columns on the facade do not support the building—they are hollow and function as drains for rainwater. The interior is rich with brassware and woodwork. The symbolism of the white sand on the floor has several interpretations: the wandering of the Jews in the desert, the muffling of the sounds of secret services during the Spanish Inquisition, or God's promise to Abraham that his descendants would be "countless as the sand." Hours: weekdays 9:00 to 11:45 a.m. and 2:30 to 4:45 p.m. There is an entrance fee. Visitors are welcome to attend Sabbath services; tie and jacket are required for men. (599-9-461-1633; fax: 599-9-461-1214; www.snoa.com.)

Floating Market (13) Continuing on Columbusstraat to Madurostraat (another demarcation of the old city walls), you can turn left (west) to see some outstanding examples of rococo gables. The first lane on your right (north) leads to a canal with a picturesque floating market. Each week schooners from Venezuela come here to sell their fruits and vegetables in this open-air market shaded by the sails of the boats. There are also fishermen selling snapper, grouper, conch, and other fish from local waters. Up the street to the east, the large, round building is the **Central Market (14),** a modern town market—but with as much bustle as any Caribbean marketplace. It has a bar and native market-style buffet restaurant serving local food.

Behind the Central Market is the **post office (15),** which has a philatelic window. In front of the market, the **Wilhelmina Bridge (16)** connects Punda with Scharloo, formerly a wealthy residential quarter of early Jewish merchants. The architecture of this area ranges from eighteenth-century Dutch colonial to Victorian gingerbread. Over the past decade most of these mansions have been restored as private homes or offices; the drive along here is one of the main attractions of a city tour.

Maritime Museum (16A) (Van der Brandhofstraat 7, Scharloo; 599-9-465-2327; fax: 599-9-461-9512), opened in 1999 to commemorate Curaçao's 500th anniversary, celebrates the island's seafaring heritage. The museum has guides and a guided tour by boat. Hours: daily except Monday, 10:00 a.m. to 4:00 p.m. Admission: US$8.50 adults, US$4.50 children; with harbor tour, US$15.00 and US$7.00. The combination is sold as a shore excursion on some cruise ships.

Walk west to **Plaza Jojo Correa (17).** You will probably see your ship docked across the bay. Stop and look back (northeast) across the channel to the Wilhelmina Bridge and Waaigat for a nice view. At the plaza turn south onto Heerenstraat, one of the main shopping streets, which has several buildings with elaborate gables. At the end of the street is the Penha building, where you began. If you want to take a break, **Gomezplein (18)** is a pretty pedestrian mall with park benches, or you could continue to Handelskade along the waterfront, where you will find some sidewalk cafes.

Otrobanda

A walk around Otrobanda, except for the immediate vicinity of the port and Breedestraat, is better with a guide through its narrow winding lanes lined with colorful old buildings and private houses, to point out the historic and architectural features that have made them landmarks. A pamphlet, "Discover the Spirit of Historic Curaçao," has a walking tour with a useful map, prepared by the Chamber of Commerce and Curaçao Tourist Bureau. It is outdated, but if you have a good sense of direction and an adventurous spirit, you could use it for a self-guided walk. If you are truly interested in history, arrange to visit with Old City Tours, whose architect-owner has been one of the driving forces behind the area's preservation.

Museum Kura Hulanda (22) The museum (Klipstraat 9, Otrobanda; 599-9-462-1400; fax: 599-9-462-1401; www.kurahulanda.com) is part of one of the most ambitious restoration projects in the Caribbean. It has included the private restoration of sixty-five historic buildings, mostly former private homes, in an 8-block complex, which has become the Hotel Kura Hulanda and conference center, as well as the museum. Opened in 1999, as one of many projects commemorating Curaçao's 500th anniversary, the $6 million Museum Kura Hulanda is dedicated to the island's African heritage. A cultural center and cultural studies center with an auditorium, it is situated only a few blocks from the cruise-ship dock on the site of a former slave yard and prison overlooking the harbor. Guides are available. Admission: US$6 adults, US$3 children. Hours: Monday to Sunday 10:00 a.m. to 5:00 p.m.

South of the port terminal on the waterfront is a group of restored buildings known as **Koral Agostini (20),** which date from 1737. It has small shops, a sidewalk cafe, and the West Indies, a popular balcony restaurant and bar with live Latin and Caribbean music on weekends.

At Breedestraat, Otrobanda's main shopping street, turn west for 2 blocks to St. Anna Church. One block south is Conscientiesteeg, the oldest lane of the quarter; and directly south of it on Sebastopolstraat, the **Sebastopol House (21)** is a good example of an eighteenth-century style that combined elements of a colonial town house with those of a plantation house.

West on Conscientiesteeg past **La Moda de Paris,** once the leading clothing shop in town, to the end of the street, a turn south for 1 block takes you to one of the most attractive areas, with a block of renovated town houses called "the Four Alley." Farther south at Zaantjessteeg and Graven-straat, there is a group of fine houses with their original entrances and pretty gardens facing Pater Eeuwensweg. The houses once overlooked a lagoon that had bridges leading to the Rif area, a sort of lovers' lane in olden days.

You can return to the port via the Riffort area (and to the mega-pier and new Renaissance Hotel) or via Breedestraat for a stop at the **Netto Bar,** a famous neighborhood rendezvous, where you can buy Cuban cigars (but smoke them before you go back through U.S. Customs, because agents are likely to confiscate them). On your return you will pass any number of wonderful houses that have been renovated and the entrance to Kura Hulanda Hotel. The hotel, a collection of renovated old town houses, is like a tiny village and very much worth a visit. (See the Restaurant section for more information.)

Curaçao Museum (Van Leeuwenhoekstraat; Otrobanda; 599-9-462-3873; fax: 599-9-462-3777; curmuseum@yahoo.com). A mile or more from Rif-fort is the Curaçao Museum, housed in a building dating from 1853. Originally it was used as a mili-tary hospital—and not a former plantation house, or landhuis, as is sometimes said, although the style is similar. The museum covers the island's his-tory from pre-Columbian times to the Dutch colo-nial period and has some artifacts of this century.

Permanent exhibits include a replica of a typi-cal kitchen of the colonial era, antique furniture, old industrial tools, and household utensils. You will find old maps of Curaçao and the Caribbean, a natural-history section, and a garden with island plants and trees. In addition to a permanent collec-tion of contemporary art, the museum organizes exhibitions of works by local artists. In 1987 the **Children's Science Museum,** financed by the Rotary Club, was added. It has hands-on models of local industries. Hours: Monday to Friday 9:00 a.m. to noon; 2:00 to 5:00 p.m.; Sunday 10:00 a.m. to

4:00 p.m. Entrance is NAf5.50 for adults, NAf2.75 for children. On the first Sunday of each month, a concert is given in the gardens from 4:30 to 6:30 p.m.

On the south side of Otrobanda by the sea is the Rif Recreation Center, and on the western edge, Piscadera Bay, a popular resort area with several hotels and the modern Convention and Trade Center. **Koredor,** a seafront recreational area on Piscadera Bay, has a jogging track, playground, and picnic area, and the **Sundance Health & Fit-ness Center.**

The **Curaçao Marriott Hotel,** which opened in 1992 (originally as a Sonesta Hotel), was the island's first international chain hotel in two decades. The deluxe resort, set in tropical gardens, has three restaurants, a casino, a pool with swim-up bar, a health club with four tennis courts, and water sports. A welcome addition, the outstanding hotel, designed in Curaçao's classic architecture, is credited with rejuvenating Curaçao's tourism (and hence its economy) and setting new standards for all the island's hotels and restaurants.

Farther west at Blaubaai (Blue Bay) is one of Curaçao's major attractions—**Blue Bay Curaçao Golf and Beach Resort** (Landhuis Blaauw; 599-9-868-1755; fax: 599-9-869-0212; www.bluebaygolf .com). The beautiful layout, designed by Rocky Roquemore, is the island's first 18-hole champion-ship course. It is part of a resort and residential community with a deluxe hotel and executive con-ference center.

A Drive around the Island

Willemstad Environs

You can circle Santa Anna Bay from Piscadera Bay on the west by taking the highway around the bay to the east, or cross over on Queen Juliana Bridge. East of the bridge on the right (south) on a hill is **Roosevelt House,** the U.S. Consul General's resi-dence, a gift from Curaçao to the United States for its assistance in World War II.

After another mile along the highway, a large modern monument depicting six birds leaving the mother's nest commemorates the Netherlands Antilles becoming autonomous in 1954. North of the monument is the Amstel Brewery, said to be the only factory in the world that brews beer from distilled seawater. Tours are offered by appointment.

Landhuis Chobolobo On the eastern edge of Willemstad in a seventeenth-century *landhuis* is the **Curaçao Liqueur Distillery** (P.O. Box 3353; 599-9-461-3526; fax: 599-9-461-3503; www.curacao liqueur.com), where the orange-flavored liqueur Curaçao is made. (The distillery celebrated its 100th anniversary in 1996.) The early Spaniards planted Valencia oranges in Curaçao, and after adapting to the aridity and red-clay soil, the trees bore a fruit too bitter to eat—but an oil extracted from its skin proved to be suitable for making liqueur. The colorful bottles make distinctive gifts to take home. Tours are available weekdays 8:00 a.m. to noon and 1:00 to 5:00 p.m.

Landhuis Rooi Cattotje Since 1853 another plantation house, on a hillside beyond the Curaçao Liqueur Distillery, has been in the Maduro family, one of Curaçao's oldest and best-known families. After the owner died in 1974, his heirs converted the home into a library to house his unusual collection of books, documents, and photos relating to Curaçao's history, particularly its Jewish community. Visits are by appointment (599-9-737-5119).

If you detour in a northerly direction along Schottegatweg, you pass Peter Stuyvesant High School, which has a statue of Peter Stuyvesant in a schoolyard—a reminder of Curaçao's early New York connection.

Landhuis Brievengat About 9 miles on the northeast, you will see an early-eighteenth-century plantation house that was a 12,000-acre cattle ranch until the mid-nineteenth century. It was saved from demolition by the Preservation of Monuments Foundation, which restored it in 1954 as a cultural center. By day it functions as a museum showcasing eighteenth- and nineteenth-century furniture and household artifacts. In the evening it becomes a restaurant and one of the island's most popular night spots, with ear-shattering music and dancing several nights a week. Hours: Monday to Friday 9:15 a.m. to noon and 3:00 to 6:00 p.m. Admission: NAf3.50 adults, NAf1.75 children. (Brievengat; 599-9-565-2156; fax: 599-9-736-8120; paul&mieke@hoetjes.net)

West of Willemstad

Too often cruise passengers confine their visit to Willemstad and miss some of Curaçao's best attractions: rugged windswept terrain, pretty inland lagoons, adobe houses, and patchwork fields with fences of neatly crisscrossed candle cactus where sheep and goats graze, plus two of the best nature parks in the Caribbean. These are all the more fascinating for their obvious contrast to Curaçao's cosmopolitan capital.

The road crosses the tranquil countryside, or *cunucu (kunuku)*, an Arawak word originally used to mean a piece of land given by a landowner to a slave to grow crops for his personal needs. The dry landscape is covered with cactus that grows as tall as trees and the ever-present divi-divi tree, whose wind-sculpted branches grow in one direction at a right angle from the trunk.

Dotting the countryside are former plantation houses, or *landhuizen*, some dating from 1650. Most were surrounded by walls and fortified against marauding pirates and rebelling slaves. About sixty houses remain, and several are maintained as museums.

Landhuis Daniel Just beyond the Santa Maria turnoff at Daniel is one of the island's oldest plantation houses, dating from 1634. Landhuis Daniel was never a farmhouse, but a rest stop for travelers and their horses traversing the island. The house has been restored and once again is a rustic rest stop, with ten modest rooms, a pool, a vegetable garden, and facilities for diving nearby (599-9-864-8222).

Landhuis Jan Kock At Daniel the road forks west to Sint Willibrordus, a village, and the seventeenth-century Landhuis Jan Kock, where once salt from nearby ponds was produced for the herring industry in Holland. The manor house is now a private home that serves as an art gallery. Today, the salt pans are home to Curaçao's only permanent flamingo colony.

Hato Caves Set on a bluff on the north coast near the airport, the ancient caves were recently renovated, lighted, and made more accessible. The caverns have stalagmites, stalactites, and bats. Beautiful orange-and-black orioles, known here as troupial, flit about in nearby trees, and iguanas scamper in the undergrowth near the snack bar and souvenir shop at the caves' entrance (F. D. Rooseveltweg; 599-9-868-0379; 599-9-868-8114; hotel holland@cura.net). Hours: daily except Monday 10:00 a.m. to 5:00 p.m.; guided tours on the hour until 4:00 p.m. Admission: US$6.50 adults, US$5.00 children younger than age thirteen.

Landhuis Papaya Originally built as a "house in the country" since the area was never fertile enough for agriculture, the three-part structure is characteristic of nineteenth-century architecture in western Curaçao. Typically, the building began as a single unit with more rooms added as the family expanded. Restored and reopened in 1993 as a restaurant and tourist center, it is located ten minutes west of the airport. The house has some samples of artistic woodwork of the period; only local materials were used in the restoration. It has an information center, bar and outdoor terrace, a children's playground made from wood scraps and old tires, and a small art gallery with local works. The restaurant offers international and local dishes. The plantation's former warehouse was converted into three rental apartments. Hours: Tuesday to Friday 9:00 a.m. to 6:00 p.m.; Saturday and Sunday noon to 11:00 p.m. Sunday, live music (599-9-869-5950).

Christoffel Nature Park On the hilly north end of the island is a 3,500-acre nature park whose most prominent feature is Curaçao's highest peak: 1,238-foot Mount Christoffel. The park begins north of Mount Hyronimus, a tabletop mountain, and comprises three contingent plantations—Savonet, Zorgvlied, and Zevenbergen—acquired by the government and managed by STINAPA. The **Savonet Museum of Natural and Cultural History** near the park entrance is housed in Landhuis Savonet, the former estate house. Hours: Monday to Saturday 8:00 a.m. to 4:00 p.m., Sunday 6:00 a.m. to 3:00 p.m. Admission: US$9 adults, $5 children, including entrance to the park. The park is a forty-minute drive from Willemstad (599-9-864-0363).

The park, opened to the public in 1978, has more than 500 varieties of plants and trees, an estimated 150 resident and migrant bird species, iguana, feral donkeys, and the Curaçao deer. You can see unusual rock formations, caves with bats, and Indian petroglyphs. The vegetation is dry with abundant mesquite, century plants, divi-divi, and gigantic cacti.

Twenty miles of road, divided into four color-coded signposted routes, wind through the park. Three are driving routes of about an hour, each highlighting different points of interest. The fourth route is a footpath to the top of Mount Christoffel. A nature guide for hiking, birding, and deer watching can be arranged through the park or the tourist office. Guided nature walks are offered by the park for US$15; check with the park for days and times as they vary by season (599-9-864-0363; reservations should be made in advance).

The park also arranges jeep tours for $85 (including entrance fee) for up to five persons; horseback riding, day and moonlight rides, for $40 for two hours; and deer watching 4:00 to 6:30 p.m. year-round (599-9-864-0363; fax: 599-9-864-0170). Guides lead small groups (maximum of eight people) on a ten-minute walk to the observation tower. Cost: $9 for adults and $5 for children younger than age fifteen; reservations are required. For more information about hiking in Curacao, www.hiking curacao.com has a wealth of information and links to local companies that offer hiking and other outdoor excursions.

Savonet Route is a good introduction to the park's vegetation and to the most common trees and plants of Curaçao. It starts at the visitor center and winds through the eastern part to the north coast. You might see one of the two hummingbird species—ruby topaz and blue-tailed emerald—that breed here. Near the center of the area is a watchtower from which hikers can spot Curaçao deer come to a nearby watering trough.

Zorgvlied Route is a ninety-minute circuit through the central and north areas; it returns along the eastern flank of Mount Christoffel, crossing the footpath to the summit. Two abundant trees and plants are the calabash, whose large fruit has a hard shell used throughout the Caribbean since the time of the Arawaks as a bowl and cooking utensil; and the enormous kadushi, a type of candle cactus, used to make cactus soup.

Zevenbergen Route winds over the undulating hills of the southwest. The trail to the top of Mount Christoffel offers grand vistas extending the length of the island and, on a clear day, as far east as

Bonaire and south to Venezuela. The hike from the visitor center is a three-hour round-trip, but by driving to the base of the mountain, you can cut off an hour.

Westpunt An old fishing town, Westpunt (or West Point)—on the rocky cliffs at the north end of the island—sits above a quiet, turquoise sea. Below is a small beach of coarse sand, surrounded by walls of rock. The area has undergone extensive development in recent years with private homes and weekend cottages. The most significant addition is the **Lodge Kura Hulanda & Beach Club,** which was opened in 2005 by the same group that created the historic Kura Hulanda Hotel and museum in Willemstad. The attractive lodge replaced the old **Kadushi Cliffs.** From Westpunt you can return south through the undulating hills of the west coast, where there are rocky coves with pretty little beaches, some reached by dirt roads.

Landhuis Knip (Kenepa) This restored plantation house is a good example of the island's seventeenth-century-style landhuis. It was one of Curaçao's most prosperous plantations and the site of the island's largest slave rebellion in 1795. There is a small museum and portrait gallery, and it occasionally hosts folklore shows with displays of local handicrafts. Hours: Sunday to Friday 9:00 a.m. to 4:00 p.m. Admission: NAf3.50 (599-9-864-0244). The landhuis is located in Bandabou, the local name for western Curaçao, near Playa Grandi and Klein Knip, two of the island's best beaches. By the sea, the dive resort **Habitat Curaçao,** a sister to Bonaire's famous **Capt. Don's Habitat,** opened in 1996, underscoring Curaçao's appeal as a dive destination.

On the south side of Santa Cruz, Santa Marta Bay is a large serpentine lagoon with beaches and rocky shores surrounded by green hillsides. The cultivation of the orange tree, from which the liqueur Curaçao is made, is a specialty of the area.

East of Willemstad

Curaçao Underwater Park The biggest boost to the development of Curaçao as a dive center has been the creation of the 1,500-acre Curaçao Underwater Park, stretching for more than 12 miles from the Princess Beach Hotel, just west of Jan Thiel Lagoon, to the eastern tip of the island. Developed by STINAPA, the Netherlands Antilles National Parks Foundation, with a grant from the World Wildlife Fund of the Netherlands, it protects some of Curaçao's finest reefs, which can be enjoyed by snorkelers as well as divers. Jan Thiel Beach and Santa Barbara Beach provide access to the park, where visibility is up to 150 feet. An excellent guidebook by the marine biologist Jeff Symbesma has an explanatory profile of the reef.

There are sixteen permanent mooring buoys for boats. The first mooring in front of the Princess Beach Hotel has diverse and colorful formations typical of Curaçao's reef structure. It starts in shallow water, suitable for snorkelers, where elkhorn and staghorn corals and gorgorians are abundant, dropping to 30 to 40 feet, from which the reef slopes at a 45-degree angle. The upper slope has mountain star coral, leaf coral, flower coral, and yellow pencil coral, as well as a variety of sponges. On the lower slope are brain corals, sheet coral, and star corals. The fish seen here are typical of Curaçao reefs, too, and include chromis, wrasses, four-eyed butterfly fish, and sergeant majors, among others.

Seaquarium On the west end of the marine park is the Curaçao Seaquarium, a private facility with more than four hundred species of marine life native to Curaçao waters. The Seaquarium uses no chemicals, pumps, or filters in the tanks, helping to promote the natural reproduction of sea life. Hours: daily 10:00 a.m. to 10:00 p.m. Admission is US$15.00 adults, $7.50 child younger than age twelve. Cruise-ship shore excursions usually visit the Seaquarium (Bapor Kibra, P.O. Box 3102; 599-9-461-6666; fax: 599-9-461-3671; www.curacao-sea-aquarium.com).

Animal Encounters Here's your chance to face down a shark or pet a stingray. Next to the Seaquarium divers can enter a 15-foot-deep open-water enclosure, which is a natural tidal pool, to play with the ray, angelfish, grouper, and other fish. At one end of the enclosure, divers are separated by a mesh fence from large sea turtles; on the other side, they can watch reef, lemon, and nurse sharks through a thick Plexiglas wall while they pass food to the sharks through small openings.

Admission is US$54, which includes a full dive tank, wet suit, weights, a bucket of fish, and an hour of basic instruction on the use of dive gear from a professional diver who will accompany you. Photographs or a video of you can be taken for an additional charge. It's probably as close to a shark as most people ever want to be, but it's still thrilling. About half of those who participate are donning dive gear for the first time. (I recommend, however, that you have at least taken a scuba diving resort course.) Nonswimmers can watch from a semisubmersible submarine at the site. Hours: 8:30 a.m. to 5:30 p.m. As a shore excursion, the cost will probably be $30 more, but they will include round-trip transportation from the pier in town.

Dolphin Academy A new attraction at the Seaquarium offers a variety of programs to interact with dolphins, starting with a free daily educational presentation. Participants are given instructions and accompanied in the water by a trainer. Children younger than age eight must be accompanied by a paying adult. Prices are per person.

Dolphin Encounter: Interaction with dolphins in shallow water; minimum age of participants, three years, US$79. *Dolphin Swim:* For experienced swimmers at least 4'3" (1.30 meters) tall, who swim with the dolphins, US$159. *Dolphin Snorkel:* Learn about the bottlenose dolphin while snorkeling with them in a saltwater lagoon, $169. *Dolphin Dive:* For certified divers only, US$200. Hours: Daily 8:30 a.m. to 4:30 p.m. Entrance (tax included): US$15.00 adults, US$7.50 children younger than age twelve. Reservations: 599-9-465-8900; www .dolphin-academy.com.

Another new Seaquarium program, similar to the dolphin one, enables participants to interact with sea lions. There are four levels: *Sea Lion Encounter:* A thirty-minute session in basic behaviors with the animals while training techniques are explained, US$39. *Sea Lion Swim/Snorkel:* Learning about sea lion behavior and aquatic ecosystem and conservation, and interacting with the animals, US$69. *Sea Lion Dive:* Certified divers swim/interact with sea lions at an open-water dive site, US$99. *Sea Lion Training:* Behind the scenes with trainers and work with the animals, US$149; *Sea Lion Wedding:* Couples can get married underwater with sea lions as their ring bearers and witnesses (available only by advance request).

Most of the attractions can be booked on the Seaquarium's Web site. However, there are a bewildering range of prices, so you might want to contact the facility with questions before making a booking.

Spanish Water Near the eastern end of the island, Spaanse Water, or Spanish Water, one of the island's largest and most beautiful lagoons, is a sheltered natural harbor with many hilly green fingers and coves, islands and beaches, and a long, very narrow opening to the sea. It is the island's boating and fishing center, with marinas and other water-sports facilities. The Curaçao Yacht Club is based here, and many Willemstad residents have weekend houses here. A new Hyatt Hotel is going up here and due to open in 2008.

East of Spanish Water you can see a chalky table mountain, 637-foot Tafelberg, from almost any height on the island. At one time as much as 100,000 tons of phosphate were mined here yearly; mining continues on a small scale. Beyond to the east is an arid, desolate area of rocky, rugged terrain.

Curaçao Den Paradera: Also known as Dinah Veeris's Botanical Garden, the owner is on a one-woman crusade to preserve the traditional medicinal flora of Curacao. At Den Paradera, began in the 1980s, Dinah Veeris grows more than 300 species of wild plants to help save them as well as the knowledge of how to use them—information that was being lost due to urbanization and industrialization that has changed much of the wild landscape of Curaçao. The name "Den Paradera" comes from the Paraguiri Indians who once had a large garden on the island. Some of the plants come from neighboring Bonaire and Aruba. Veeris, known locally as a healer, blends herbs for medicinal purposes to sell and has published books that are often used by local botanists.

Curaçao Ostrich Farm Across the island from the Seaquarium on the north coast at St. Joris Bay is a farm, unique to Curaçao and the Caribbean; it's one of the biggest ostrich ranching operations outside Africa. Here you can see the majestic creatures, which are the world's fastest animals on two legs, and learn about all aspects of ostrich ranching in an Africa-like environment.

Hours: 8:00 a.m. to 5:00 p.m. Reservations: 599-9-560-1276. Guided tour every hour. Closed Monday. Admission: US$10 adults, US$6 children age two to twelve years (West Goot Sint Joris; 599-9-747-2777; 599-9-747-2766; www.ostrichfarm.net; info@ostrichfarm.net).

The farm has a gift shop with African crafts and a restaurant, **Zambezi** (599-9-747-2566), serving ostrich meat specialties and South African wines. It is housed in a large thatched-roof hut similar to dwellings that might be seen in Africa. Open from noon to 7:00 p.m. daily except Sunday evening and Monday.

Aloe/Curaçao Ecocity Projects (Aloe Vera Plantation, Weg Naar Groot Sint Joris z/n; 599-9-767-5507/5577; fax: 599-9-767-5577; www.aloe curacao.com; ecocity@cura.net) is located near the Ostrich Farm on the same dirt road beyond the farm. It is open 8:00 a.m. to 2:00 p.m. weekdays and to noon on Saturday. Lotions, gels, sun cream, and other products are available for purchase.

Shopping

Willemstad's cosmopolitan ambience is reflected in its shops filled with goods from around the world, including an abundance of European items: from fine jewelry to designer fashions, perfumes, and Japanese electronics. Cruise passengers are usually most interested, however, in Dutch goods, such as chocolate, rounds of Edam and Gouda cheese, delftware, and even wooden clogs. Breedestraat and Heerenstraat are the main streets of Punda, where quality stores are housed in colorful eighteenth-century colonial buildings.

Curaçao is not a duty-free port, but in 1988 the government removed tariffs on most luxury items, so prices represent a savings of 20 to 30 percent off those in the United States. A knowledge of stateside prices is the best way to recognize a good bargain. "Curaçao Holiday," a free tourist pamphlet, has a keyed map of store locations that is a convenient reference guide.

Punda stores are open Monday to Saturday from 8:00 a.m. to noon and 2:30 to 6:00 p.m. Some remain open during lunch, particularly when cruise ships are in port. They also open for cruise passengers on Sundays and holidays, except Christmas and Good Friday.

Art and Artists Curaçao has an active artist community, and in the last few years an amazing number of galleries have opened to showcase the work of local artists. Most galleries are open Monday to Saturday from 9:00 or 10:00 a.m. to 6:00 p.m. and on Sunday by appointment. Call to confirm hours. **Kas di Alma Blauw** (67 De Rouville-weg, by the cruise terminal; 599-9-462-8896; www.galleryalmablau.com) sells art and gifts by local artists. Also near the cruise docks are **Carib Fine Art** (Hotel Kura Hulanda, Langestraat 8, Otrobanda; (599-9-465-5759; www.caribfineart.com), featuring paintings, sculptures, ceramics, glassware, and gift items created by local and Caribbean artists plus a collection of unusual nineteenth-century engraved sea charts of the New World; and **Gallery Mon Art** (Riffort, Unit 103, Otrobanda; (599-9-462-2977; monartgallery_riffort_curacao@hotmail.com), showing the paintings, ceramics, and mixed media by members of Artevisho, a local artists association. It also sells calendars, diaries, and books.

Slightly farther away is **D'art Gallery** (Bitterstraat 11/Werfstraat 6; (599-9-462-8680), situated in the Schaloo district behind Villa Maria, which carries contemporary works by local and international artists, including some South American ones. **Open Atelier** (F.D. Rooseveltweg 443; Mahuma, Willemstad; (599-9-868-6027; artliesdek@hotmail .com) promotes Curaçaoan artists and sells paintings created by youngsters from various children's organizations.

Studio-galleries of several leading artists include **Jean Girigory Gallery** (Riffort, Unit 205, Otrobanda; 599-9-461-8205), with paintings, sculptures in bronze and ceramic, masks, and glassworks; **Nena Sanchez Gallery** (Bloempot Shopping Center; 599-9-738-2377; www.nena sanchez.com), whose Web site shows why this self-taught women is one of Curaçao's most popular artists with a colorful, distinctive style; and **Yubi Kirindongo** (Kaya Reis 390, Souax Ariba, Ser'I Kandela; 599-9-869-3268), one of Curaçao's top artists with international standing, who works with materials and metals that when put together give a rough texture and special energy to his work. By appointment only.

Books and Maps Van Dorp (Breedestraat) is one of the main bookstores.

Cameras and Electronics Boolchand's (Heerenstraat) and Palais Hindu (Heerenstraat) have large selections of photographic equipment and electronic gadgetry. Come with prices from home.

Clothing and Accessories The most easily recognized store in Curaçao is the yellow-and-white rococo front of Penha & Sons, a department store in the town's oldest building. It has a wide variety of goods from perfumes and designer clothes to delft china and cashmere sweaters. Bamali Boutique (Waterfort Arches) carries stylish fashions in Indonesian batik, plus art and wood carvings. Gifi (Trompstraat 20) specializes in Italian designers such as Valentino, Krizia, and Armani. Emilia (Gomezplein), another trendy boutique, specializes in chic French and Belgian apparel for men, women, and children, including Naf Naf and European footwear.

Crafts and Souvenirs Obra di Man (Bargestraat in Scharloo) is both a shop and workshop for handmade folkloric dolls, wall hangings, ceramics, and other local crafts, with an outlet on Gomezplein. Kas di Arte (Breedestraat 126) stocks local crafts. Curaçao Creations (Schrijnwerkerstraat off Breedestraat, in Otrobanda; 599-9-462-4516) has handicrafts fashioned by Curaçaoans, including pottery, leather goods, glasswork, jewelry, woven baskets, and art. The Public Market in Punda (near the Wilhelmina Bridge) is another place to find local crafts. (Market closes at 2:00 p.m.)

Dutch Antilles Ceramics (Tera Cora, Kaya Diabaas 120, Band Abou; 599-9-864-9105) makes by hand a large selection of original items that are sold in most souvenir shops. Check the bottom of an item for the trademark. The workshop can be visited weekdays. Keramos (Rio Canario, Kaya Col. Kay Winkel 2; 599-9-737-4676), a twenty-five-year-old pottery store run by local artists, sells handmade ceramic souvenirs, plates, mugs and dishes with local motifs, and miniature landhouses and kunuku cottages.

Gourmet Food Products Rounds of Gouda or Edam can be purchased at supermarkets at about a 30 percent savings over U.S. prices. And don't forget Curaçao liqueur. Zuikertuintje (meaning "the sugar garden") is a supermarket in a seventeenth-century landhuis on the east side of town, just beyond the Curaçao Liqueur factory. It has selections of Dutch cheese and chocolates and a large assortment of European gourmet products—plus a cafe where you can sample some of the products.

Jewelry Among the best-known names is Gandelman Jewelers (Breedestraat 35), which creates its own designs and also sells Piaget and Movado watches and Gucci accessories.

Linens New Amsterdam (Breedestraat) is a variety store, with goods ranging from sports gear and Gottex swimsuits to Chinese cloisonné and Lladro figurines, but it is best known for fine linens. Little Holland (Breedestraat) has lovely linens, too.

Perfumes and Cosmetics Yellow House (Breedestraat), the leading perfume shop, is as pretty as it is complete in its stock of French and other perfumes and cosmetics. It also carries Hummel figurines and other gifts.

Dining and Restaurants

Curaçao's long trading history and diverse population made up of Dutch, Portuguese Jews, Africans, Chinese, Indians, Indonesians, and a host of Europeans is reflected in its food and wide selection of restaurants. They range from pizza parlors and Dutch taverns to French bistros and elegant continental restaurants. Some offer harbor views; others are set in historic forts and charming old plantation houses. Entries range from moderate (less than US$10) and moderately expensive (US$10 to $25) to expensive (more than US$26).

For *criollo*, or local fare, try *empana*, a pastry inherited from the Spaniards; *sopito*, a fish-and-coconut soup served with *funchi*, a cornbread taken from the Africans; *keshi yena*, a cheese shell filled with meat, learned from the Dutch; and *rijsttafel*, a multidish treat the Dutch learned in Indonesia.

Angelica's Kitchen (Hoogstraat 49; 599-9-562-3699; www.angelicas-kitchen.com) is a Curaçao culinary option that enables guests to play chef and gourmand when a minimum of ten participants, beginning at 6:00 p.m., dress up as chefs and read over the recipes that will serve as dinner. The dishes are based mostly on French or Italian cuisine with local influences, but they can be Caribbean fare. Dinner is ready by 8:30 p.m., and the evening ends at 10:30 p.m. Owner Angelique Schoop, a Curaçao native, studied in Amsterdam, the Peter Kemp Cooking School in New York, and La Varenne near Paris. She has created her kitchen in her century-old landmark childhood home, which she restored. Reservations are necessary. Moderately expensive.

Recently, Angelica introduced two culinary walking tours by request. One tour includes lunch of local food at the Old Market and on the other, participants make their lunch at Angelica's Kitchen. Tours start at 9:30 a.m. at the Otrobanda side of the Pontoon bridge and visit parts of Otrobanda and Punda, including the historic synagogue and the Floating Market, where participants buy ingredients for their hands-on lunch. The tour ends about 2:00 p.m. Cost per person: US$45 with lunch at the Old Market or $70 with hands-on lunch at Angelica's Kitchen. Reservations for a minimum of four participants: e-mail info@angelicas-kitchen.com.

Astrolab Observatory Restaurant (Langestraat 8, Willemstad; 599-9-434-7700; www.kurahulanda.com), situated next to the garden of the Hotel Kurá Hulanda, is named for a world-class collection of scientific instruments on display nearby. It serves contemporary gourmet cuisine indoors and alfresco. Specialties include fresh fish, lobster, and beef dishes. Good wine cellar. Moderately expensive.

Avalon (Caracasbaaiweg 8 Salina; 599-9-465-6375; www.avaloncuracao.com). Edgy, art deco design reminiscent of South Beach, Avalon is cool. The relaxed, lounge-like atmosphere draws locals and tourists with its imaginative menu and specialty drinks that combine flavors from around the world with a Caribbean twist. Executive Chef David McHugh, a graduate of Atlanta's School of Culinary Arts, has among his signature dishes Crispy Red Devil Snapper, Adobo Crusted Hanger Steak, and vegetarian dishes, including Thai Red Curry Bowl. Avalon also offers sushi by Venezuelan sushi chef Carlo Marcano. There's a martini menu, extensive wine list, and Cuban cigars. Expensive.

Bistro Le Clochard (Riffort, Otrobanda; 599-9-462-5666; clochard@attglobal.com). In this restaurant, set in an old fortification and former prison by the harbor, you can sit almost close enough to touch the passing ships. The menu is French and continental with fresh seafood, veal, cheese fondue, and sinful desserts. Expensive.

Dokterstuin Plantation House (Dokterstuin in northwest Curaçao; 599-9-864-2701). If you find yourself on the main road to West Punt, Band Abou, or Christoffel Park at lunchtime, this restaurant is worth your stop for authentic Curaçao, or criollo, cuisine. Here, in an outdoor picnic setting of a seventeenth-century plantation house (also known as Klein Ascencion), you can feast on Creole chicken for only US$6; cactus or okra soup or stewed papaya or cucumber (squash) for US$8; and goat meat, conch, or snapper for US$10. The manor, restored in 1996, houses a small museum. Closed Monday. Inexpensive.

Fort Nassau (599-9-461-3086; fortnassau@curacao.com). Known for its view, it offers a pretty hilltop setting overlooking Willemstad, as well as an ideal perch for an aperitif on its terrace bar. Moderately expensive.

The Grill King (Waterfort Arches 2–3, Punda; 599-9-461-6870) is a good place for steaks and lobster in a convenient town location by the sea when you are really hungry and appreciate good service. Moderate.

Golden Star Bar (Socratesstraat 2; 599-9-465-4795). The informal Curaçaoan bar/restaurant is not much to look at, but it's everyone's favorite for criollo cuisine. You can try a zesty *carco stoba* (conch stew), *bestia chiki* (goat-meat stew), *bakijou* (salted cod), *locrio* (a chicken-mixed rice), *concomber stoba* (stewed meat and cucumber), fish, and *funchi*. Moderate.

Portofino Restaurant (Marriott Beach Hotel; 599-9-736-8800). Situated in an air-conditioned dining room and an outdoor garden terrace, the delightful restaurant features a variety of Northern Italian dishes. The atmosphere is casual, but elegant. Moderately expensive.

Rijsttafel Indonesia (Mercuriusstraat 13; 599-9-461-2606). In Salinja, just east of Princess Beach, it has as good a rijsttafel as you will find east of Indonesia. In May 2006, the management changed to Sawasdee Thai restaurant. So now, it offers two cuisines: Thai and Indonesian. Moderate.

Tu Tu Tango (Plasa Mundo Merced; 599-9-465-4633; fax: 599-9-465-1399; info@tutu-tango .com) is a fun place that consistently gets rave reviews for its tapas, music, ambience, and waiters. Tu Tu's are the appetizers that you select from a chalkboard, and Tango is the main meal selected from an eclectic assortment. Moderate.

Zambezi International (Ostrich Farm, Groot Sint Foris West; 599-9-747-2777; fax: 599-9-747-2766; www.ostrichfarm.com) If you have ever wondered what ostrich meat tastes like, here's your chance to sample it straight from the farm and enjoy it with South African wine in surroundings meant to resemble a typical African restaurant. Moderately expensive.

Nightlife

Most of Curaçao's nightlife centers around hotels, restaurants that have music for listening or dancing, and discos. Ten hotels have casinos; the closest to the port is **Kura Hulanda** hotel. There are popular bars for happy hour, piano bars for a quiet rendezvous, and seaside cafes where you can watch the parade of people and ships.

Banana's (Schottegatweg Oost 193) serves food early, then a young, hip crowd arrives and hangs out til late—bring your dancing shoes. Wet & Wild Beach Club (Seaquarium Beach, Bapor Kibra; 599-9-561-2477) is a popular local hangout where the dance floor meets the sand along with pumping loud beats and cold drinks. Zen (Salinja 124), a laid-back lounge/bar that fits its name, is another option, and when you want a change of scenery, K-Oz (Salinja 124, above Zen) has an outdoor patio leading into a hip club with a retro feel and DJ music bouncing off the red walls and large dance floor.

Blues Cafe (Avila Beach Hotel; 599-9-461-4377) offers jazz by leading local musicians on the east side of town. The Latin in the Curaçaoans comes out most in their popular music and dance. Tumba music is Curaçao's answer to salsa.

Sports

Most of the island's hotels and water-sports centers are located along the south coast immediately east and west of Willemstad. They welcome day visitors.

Beaches/Swimming Several beaches on the leeward coast within a mile or so of Willemstad have been developed. They have changing facilities and water sports; there is an admission fee. There are pretty bays and coves with beaches, which swimmers are likely to have to themselves, except perhaps on weekends. You will find free public beaches at Westpunt, Knip, Klein Knip, and Daaibooi. Private beaches, charging a fee per car, are Blauw Bay and Jan Thiel, which have changing facilities. On the southeast, Santa Barbara, at the entrance to Spanish Water, is a popular beach with Curaçaoans. The windward coast generally is too turbulent for safe swimming.

Caracas Bay Island, on the southeast corner of Curaçao, is a beach club with water sports and a variety of other attractions: mountain biking, kayaking, horseback riding, hiking, as well as swimming, snorkeling, and boating. Entrance: US$3, includes beverage. All activities are priced separately, and are moderate. For example, forty-five minutes of horseback riding, US$35 per person; one-hour mountain-bike tour, US$15.

Biking Mountain bikes are available for rent at **Christoffel Park** (599-9-864-0363; fax: 599-9-864-0170), which is the best place for biking excursions. Several companies offer bike rentals as well as biking excursions: the **Bike Shop** (Sta. Rosaweg 23; 599-9-560-3882; fax: 599-9-738-0027; bikeshop@curacao-travelguide.com), **Dutch Dream** (Landhuis Papaya; 599-9-864-7377; dutch dream@attglobal.net), and **Rancho Alfin** (599-9-864-0535). **Curaçao Actief** (East Commerce Park Unit, C10 Heelsumstraat; 599-9-433-8858; www .curacao-actief.com) organizes mountain biking excursions as well as kayaking, sailing, windsurfing, diving, snorkeling, and ecosafari tours. Log on to www.hikingcuracao.com for links to those providing biking and hiking in Curaçao and around the Caribbean.

Boating A cruise along the coast to Klein Curaçao off Curaçao's eastern end, to enjoy its sandy beaches and snorkeling, is a favorite sailing excursion offered by water-sports operators. A full-day sail on the *Insulinde*, a 120-foot traditionally rigged sailing vessel, is US$55 (599-9-560-1340). *Kristel-Ann II* (599-9-737-5416) and **Water World Curaçao** (599-9-747-0656) offer day trips to Klein Curaçao or Porto Maria Bay and sunset trips to the Spanish Water. **Mermaid Boat Trips** (599-9-560-1530; www.mermaidboattrips.com) sails three times weekly with up to sixty people to Klein Curaçao for the day. The schooner *Bounty* (599-9-560-1887; www.bountyadventures.com) has party cruises. Check with operator for days and time as they vary considerably. For private sailing, contact **Curaçao Yacht Club** (Brakkeput Ariba; 599-9-767-4627; www.curacaoyachtclub.com).

Deep-Sea Fishing Half-day charters for about US$300 and full-day ones for about US$600 leave from major hotels and the marinas at Spanish Water almost daily, offering great deep-sea fishing for four to six persons, with tackle and bait provided. Arrangement can be made through water-sports operators. Anglers go for marlin, tuna, wahoo, sailfish, and other large fish. Only hook and line fishing is permitted in the Curaçao Underwater Park. Fishing charters can be arranged by **Curaçao Seascape** (599-9-462-5000; 599-9-462-5905) and **Second Chance** (599-9-560-1367). **Let's Fish** (Caracasbayweg 407N; 599-9-561-1812; www.letsfish.net) offers half-day outings (six people maximum) for US$350; full day, US$525. It also runs day trips to Klein Curaçao (up to eleven people). **Miss Ann Boat** (Jan Sofat 232-A; 599-9-767-1579; www.missannboattrips.com) has fishing trips for wahoo, tuna, marlin, sailfish, dorado, and barracuda. Six people, half day: US$400, full day, US$600. **Pro Marine Yacht** (jarojaro@cura.net) has seven boats. The **Curaçao Yacht Club** (see Boating) organizes an annual Blue Marlin Tournament in early March.

Golf and Squash Blue Bay Curaçao Golf and Beach Resort (Blaubaai, or Blue Bay; 599-9-868-1755; fax: 599-9-869-0212; www.bluebaygolf.com), one of Curaçao's main attractions, is the island's first 18-hole championship course. Located on the south coast west of Willemstad, the 6,815-yard, par 72 course is laid out over the natural undulating terrain between the hills, rocks, and beach, and enjoys views of the sea from many locations. Designer Rocky Roquemore says players should bring their cameras as well as their skills. The clubhouse has a pro shop and restaurant. Greens fees: January to April and November to December, US$100 per person or US$85 after 2:00 p.m.; April 15 to December 15, US$85 or $65 after 2:00 p.m. Use of driving range and putting green, US$10. Clubs ($35) and shoes ($10) are available for rent. The golf club is part of a resort and residential community and an executive conference center.

The **Curaçao Golf and Squash Club** (Wilhelminalaan, Emmastad; 599-9-737-3590) welcomes visitors. The strong winds and sand greens of the 10-hole course are the challenge. Clubs and pullcarts are available for rent. Greens fee: US$15. There is a clubhouse with bar, open daily in the morning. The club also has two squash courts open daily from 8:00 a.m. to 6:00 p.m. There are special hours for visitors.

Hiking The best hiking is in the Christoffel Nature Park, where marked routes highlight special features and show the variety of Curaçao's natural features and attractions. Many parts of the north coast have only dirt tracks, where hikers can enjoy the wild desolate scenery of strong waves breaking against rock shores.

In addition to the guides at Christoffel Park, **Uniek Curaçao** (599-9-462-6632) has jeep safaris, and **Wild Curaçao** (599-9-561-0027) offers hiking excursions. Log on to www.hikingcuracao.com for links to other companies providing hiking in Curaçao and around the Caribbean. **Curaçao Actief** (East Commerce Park Unit, C10 Heelsumstraat; 599-9-433-8858; www.curacao-actief.com) organizes hiking excursions as well as kayaking, sailing, windsurfing, diving, snorkeling, and ecosafari tours.

Horseback Riding Rancho Alegre (Landhuis Groot St. Michiels; 599-9-868-1181) offers riding in the countryside Tuesday to Friday, US$50. So too, does **Ashari's Ranch** (599-9-869-0315). Arrangements should be made in advance. Riding tours of Christoffel Park are offered by **Rancho Alfin** (599-9-864-0535) and the park by appointment through **Landhuis Savonet** (599-9-864-0363).

Kayaking/Canoeing Curaçao's fingered coastline with many bays is ideal for kayaking. Among the companies that offer excursions are **Atlantis Adventure** (599-9-461-0011) and **Nacawok** (599-9-666-0193). **Dutch Dream** (Kleermakerstraat 48c; 599-9-461-9393) offers canoe trips on Thursdays from 8:00 a.m. to 5:00 p.m., about US$46. **Curaçao Actief** (see Hiking above) offers kayaking excursions.

Snorkeling/Scuba Diving Long overshadowed by its sister island of Bonaire for diving, Curaçao is only now beginning to get the attention it deserves. The island is surrounded by fringing reef, much of which is virgin territory. The structure comprises gently sloping terraces, shallow walls, and sheer dropoffs. The marine park protects some of Curaçao's finest reefs and can be enjoyed by snorkelers as well as divers. (See the Curaçao Underwater Park section earlier in this chapter.)

In addition, Curaçao has more than three dozen coves and beaches with reefs within swimming distance from shore at places that can be reached by car. One of the most convenient is Blauw Bay, 5 miles from Willemstad, just west of Piscadera Bay.

Curaçao Watersports Operator Association (599-9-868-8044; fax: 599-9-868-8114) is made up of the island's main water-sports operators, dive shops, and tourism interests. Most operators are located at hotels and can make arrangements for fishing, waterskiing, day sailing, and glass-bottom boat excursions, as well as diving and snorkeling.

Among the major dive shops are **Atlantis Diving** (599-9-465-8288; www.atlantisdiving.com), **Caribbean Sea Sports** (Marriott Beach Resort; 599-9-462-2620; www.caribseasports.com), **Habitat Divers Curaçao** (Rif Santa Marie; 599-9-864-8800), **Ocean Encounters** (Bapor Kibra z/n; 599-9-461-8131; www.oceanencounters.com), and

Seascape Curaçao/Dive & Watersports (Hilton Resort, Piscadera Bay; 599-9-642-5905; www.seascapecuracao.com). All offer excursions for beginners to experienced divers as well as resort courses. Rates range from US$45–$55 for a single dive and $70–$80 for two dives, including tanks, weights, and belt. *Ocean Encounters* at the Seaquarium has a new dive-with-dolphins for US$200.

Tennis Courts are available at the Curaçao Caribbean, Marriott, Holiday Beach, and Princess Beach hotels. The dive shop at the Curaçao Renaissance will be the closest to the cruise docks when it opens in 2008.

Windsurfing/Kiteboarding The strong trade winds that cool the island and shape the divi-divi trees have also made windsurfing and kiteboarding two of Curaçao's most popular sports, with international recognition and an Olympic windsurf champion. Annually in June, the **Curaçao Open International Pro-Am Windsurf Championship** attracts the masters from around the world. The meet is an official stop on the Caribbean World Tour and is sanctioned by the Professional Windsurfers Association as a part of the World Cup title. The most popular windsurfing area is on the southeast coast between Princess and Jan Thiel beaches, which is also the venue for the annual championships. The protected waters of Spanish Water are best for novices. **Top Watersports Curaçao** (by the Seaquarium; Box 3102; 599-9-461-6666; fax: 599-9-461-3671) specializes in windsurfing. It rents boards and other water-sports equipment and offers lessons. **Windsurfing Curaçao** (Caracas Bay Island, 599-9-738-4555; cell 599-9-524-5249; www.windsurfingcuracao.com) has boards for rent at the Marriott, Spanish Waters, and other locations: one hour US$14, half-day $35, full-day $50; lessons $46 for one hour.

Curaçao Kiteboarding (599-9-511-1094; www.curacaokiteboarding.com; curacaokiteboarding@gmail.com) provides lessons from beginner to independent kiteboarder. Kiteboarding is an extreme sport and can be dangerous. Lessons, given at your own risk, start at 9:00 a.m. at St. Joris Bay. Students must be fifteen years of age or older, be able to swim, and not be afraid of water; they need to have watershoes, T-shirt/rash guard, sunscreen, and insurance. The first lesson covers equipment, safety, the wind window, kite setup, kite control, and more. Three-hour lesson for one: US$115, for two people: $165. Pickup service: $15. Equipment is available for rent.

Festivals and Celebrations

Curaçao gets the year off to a good start with Carnival and closes it with a big **Christmas**—after all, jolly old St. Nick was Dutch. In between there is a full calendar of sports and cultural events. In addition to the international windsurfing competitions, Curaçao hosts a big fishing tournament in spring, the **Troubadours Song Festival** usually in July, and the **Curaçao Jazz Foundation Festival** in November.

For the most complete list of events, tours, attractions, and day- and nighttime activities taking place during your visit, check out the free weekly publication *K-Pasa Curaçao This Week* (599-9-463-6393) or its Web site: www.k-pasa.com.

Aruba
Oranjestad

Aruba

Miles
0 — 4

Kilometers
0 — 6

N

CARIBBEAN

SEA

Cudarebo Point ☀

Malmok ○

○ Westpunt

○ Bakaval

✝ *Alto Vista*

Palm Beach

○ Noord

Calabas ○

■ *Bushiribana Gold Mine*

○ Bubai

Eagle Beach

Druif Beach

○ Paradera

○ Ayo

Boca Andicuri

ORANJESTAD ◉

Hooiberg ▲

Catashi ○

↑ *Arikok National Park*

✝

Simeon Antonio ○

Santa Cruz ○

Boca Prins

Fontein Cave ★

Spanish Lagoon ➤

Jamanota ▲

Guadirikiri Cave ★

Sabana Besora ○

Tunnel of Love ★

Savaneta ○

○ Brasil

San Nicolas ○

Boca Grandi

Rodgers Beach

Sereo Colorado ○

☀ *Colorado Point*

Baby Lagoon

CARIBBEAN

SEA

Island of Surprises

By any measure Aruba is an unusual island. It combines city polish, frontier ruggedness, and a people who are as warm and gracious as they are ingenious. Dutch orderly and clean, this modern miracle was little more than sand and brush four decades ago. Now the island is one of the most popular, sophisticated destinations in the Caribbean, with tourist facilities catering to visitors from three continents. And it never stops. New hotels, restaurants, shops, and other attractions continue to pop up, adding to Aruba's already impressive range and variety.

In contrast to the glitter and glamour of its resorts, Aruba's arid, rocky terrain is similar to the American Southwest. The land is flat, except for the 541-foot Hooiberg—a conical-shaped hill rising in the center of the island—and small, undulating hills on the north side.

Yet for a small, low-lying island, Aruba has surprisingly diverse landscape and natural attractions.

Located only 15 miles off the coast of Venezuela, Aruba is ringed by coral reefs. Its leeward coast, where tourist development has been concentrated, has miles of calm, palm-fringed white-sand beaches, which are among the most beautiful in the Caribbean. In contrast, strong winds and big waves crash against the northeast coast, where the landscape is as desolate as the surface of the moon. Along the rockbound shores are coves with white-sand or black-pebble beaches, caves with prehistoric drawings, and sand dunes. The countryside is dotted with tiny, colorful Dutch colonial villages and farms against a landscape of gigantic rock formations sculpted by the strong winds, and shrub and cactus fields that overnight can turn from a lifeless brown to flowering green after a good rain.

Inhabited by the Arawak Indians of the Caiquetio tribe as early as 500 B.C., more is known about their civilization since first excavation took place in 1882 by Mr. Van Koolwijk. The island was claimed for Spain in 1499 by Alonso de Ojeda and became a Dutch possession in 1636. Except for a short period of British control in the nineteenth century, it has remained Dutch.

No Europeans settled on Aruba until 1754, but it was another forty years before colonization began. Aruba was largely ignored until 1824, when gold was discovered. Its production lasted almost a century and was followed by an oil prosperity that began in 1924, when the Lago Oil and Transport Co. built an oil refinery here. Eight years later the company became a subsidiary of Exxon and prospered until 1985, when Exxon closed its refinery due to the drop in world demand. It was a move that might have devastated most islands, but not Aruba. Almost without skipping a beat, the Arubans quickly got their affairs in order—including leaving the Netherlands Antilles in 1986 to become a separate entity under the Dutch crown—and redirected their energies into developing other sectors of their economy.

Arubans say their population is made up of forty-three nationalities. One look at the astonishing

At a Glance

Antiquities . . . . ★
Architecture . . . . ★
Art and artists . . . . ★
Beaches . . . . ★★★★★
Colonial buildings . . . . ★★
Crafts . . . . ★
Cuisine . . . . ★★★
Culture . . . . ★
Dining/Restaurants . . . . ★★★★
Entertainment . . . . ★★★
Forts . . . . ★
History . . . . ★
Monuments . . . . ★
Museums . . . . ★
Nightlife . . . . ★★★★
Scenery . . . . ★★★
Shopping . . . . ★★
Sightseeing . . . . ★★★
Sports . . . . ★★★★
Transportation . . . . ★★★

Population: 97,931

Size: 20 miles in length and 6 miles in width; 70 square miles.

Main Town: Oranjestad

Government: Aruba was a member of the Netherlands Antilles until 1986, when it became a separate entity within the Kingdom of the Netherlands with political autonomy, which allows Aruba to conduct its affairs without ratification by the central government as required of the other five Dutch Islands. The Netherlands government is responsible for defense and foreign affairs. Aruba has a governor appointed by the queen for a six-year term of office. The parliament is made up of twenty-one members elected for four-year terms. The Council of Ministers forms the executive power, headed by a prime minister.

Currency: Aruba's currency is the florin (Afl), divided into 100 cents. US$1.00 equals Afl1.77. Dollars and traveler's checks are widely accepted.

Departure Tax: Afl65.5 (US$37). U.S. passengers returning home from Aruba pass through U.S. immigration in Aruba before their departure. Others on international flights, $33.50.

Language: Dutch is the official language, but Papiamento is the local language, used increasingly in the schools. It evolved from Spanish, Dutch, and Portuguese and is sprinkled with African, English, and French words. Most Arubans have an amazing aptitude for languages and often speak Dutch, English, and Spanish.

Public Holidays: January 1, New Year's Day; Carnival Monday; Flag Day; Good Friday; Easter Monday; April 30, Coronation Day; May 1, Labor Day; Ascension Day; December 25 and 26, Christmas and Boxing Day.

Telephone Area Code: In February 2003 Aruba expanded the telephone numbers from six to seven by adding a 5 in front of the former six-digit number. For example, if the old number was 881-111, the new number is 588-1111. To call a cell phone, add a 9 in front of the old number. For example, 981-111 becomes 998-1111. To call Aruba from the United States, dial 011-297 plus the seven-digit local number, which now should always start with 5.

Airlines: *From the United States:* There are daily flights from New York, Newark, Baltimore, and Miami. Regularly scheduled carriers servicing Aruba include American Airlines, Continental, Delta, JetBlue, United Airlines, and US Airways. *From Canada:* Air Canada. *Interisland:* American Airlines/American Eagle, Martin Air, and BonaireExpress (www.bonaireexpress.com). In July 2007, Tiara Air began six weekly, non-stop flights between Aruba and Bonaire. Aruba opened a brand-new facility for private jets in January 2007.

Information: www.aruba.com

In the United States:

Aruba Tourism Authority:

New Jersey: 1000 Harbor Boulevard, Main Floor, Weehawken, NJ 07087; 800-TO-ARUBA; (201) 330-0800; fax: (201) 330-8757; ata.newjersey@aruba.com.

Chicago: 5901 North Cicero, Suite 301, 60646; (847) 517-1243; fax: (847) 517-1245; ata.chicago@toaruba.com.

Fort Lauderdale: One Financial Plaza, Suite 2508, Fort Lauderdale, FL 33394; (954) 767-6477; (954) 767-0432; ata.florida@aruba.com.

Houston: 12707 North Freeway, No. 138, Houston, TX 77060; (281) 362-1616; fax: (281) 362-1644; ata.houston@aruba.com.

Atlanta: 1001 Garden View Drive, No. 418, Atlanta, GA 30319; (404) 892-7822; fax: (404) 873-2193; ata.atlanta@aruba.com.

In Canada:

5875 Highway No. 7, Suite 201, Woodbridge, ON L4L 1T9; (905) 264-3434; fax: (905) 264-3437; ata.canada@aruba.com.

In Port:

Aruba Tourism Authority, 172 Lloyd G. Smith Boulevard, Aruba (P.O. Box 1019); 297-582-3777; fax: (297) 583-4702; ata.aruba@aruba.com.

range of physical and facial characteristics of the people will convince you the claim is not far-fetched. But the most pronounced feature the Arubans have retained is the legendary Arawak traits of a gentle, smiling nature. For most visitors this is Aruba's biggest attraction.

Budget Planning

Aruba can be expensive if you travel by taxi and dine at the top restaurants. Bus transportation is reliable and cheap, however; car rentals are reasonable and the best mode of travel; sightseeing tours are moderately priced and well executed; and there is a wide range of restaurants. If you want to tour off-the-beaten-track, you will probably need a guide on rural roads, because there are very few signs and no gasoline stations. On the other hand, if you are adventurous and have a good sense of direction, you can probably manage on your own. Arubans are so friendly and helpful, you are not likely to be lost for long. There are also savings to be had if you pick up a copy of *Aruba Nights* or *Aruba Experience,* tourist booklets that are chock full of discount coupons on car rentals, tours, and water sports, at restaurants, and in shops.

Port Profile

Location/Embarkation Ships pull dockside at the port, which is located on the west side of Oranjestad, the capital, less than a quarter mile from the town center and within walking distance of the main shopping area.

Staff from the Cruise Tourism Authority (CTA) booth on the pier welcome passengers with a booklet called *Aruba for You,* containing sightseeing, shops, and dining information as well as discount coupons for services and shops. Passengers with prearranged rental cars or tours are met inside the terminal lounge. Activities desks are set up outside on the dock for immediate bookings.

The cruise terminal has four information kiosks with cruise greeters positioned there to offer services to cruise passengers. The kiosks are equipped with touch-screen access to information, a DVD and video about the island, and surveys in various languages.

Major changes and renovations are under way at the port. The cargo and loading docks are being moved from Oranjestad south to Barcadera, enabling these areas to begin being transformed into a multimillion-dollar waterfront redevelopment project scheduled to begin in late 2007. It will include a waterfront marina with residential, retail, and commercial components, in addition to new cruise-ship facilities.

Local Transportation Taxis are at the port to meet ships, and can be requested by phone from a dispatch office (582-2116). Taxis are expensive,

unless you share the cost with others. They do not have meters, but rates are fixed and should be agreed upon in advance. The one-way fare from the port to a Palm Beach hotel is US$12; from Palm Beach hotels to the airport, US$20–$25; and from the port or town to the airport, US$13. All taxi drivers participate in the government's Tourism Awareness Program and receive a Guide Certificate.

Local buses are inexpensive and can be recommended. Drivers speak English and are very helpful. The buses run at about fifteen-minute intervals along Smith Boulevard, the main seaside thoroughfare paralleling the port. The main bus terminal is directly across from the cruise dock exit on Smith Boulevard. Buses heading east from the port take you to the downtown area and beyond. Buses going west take you to the resorts along Eagle and Palm Beaches. Bus stops are marked *bushalte.* One-way fare is US$1.50 and can be paid in U.S. currency. **Arubus** (582-7089) and the Tourist Bureau have information on buses and schedules.

Roads and Rentals Aruba has a network of paved and rural roads that make it possible to drive to any part of the island. *Aruba Holiday,* a free tourist guide with a road map, is available from the Aruba Tourism Authority, hotels, and shops. Most roads radiate from Oranjestad, from which the main arteries run west to the resort center of Palm Beach, east to the airport, and southeast to San Nicolas. No road completely encircles the island, but by using a series of connecting roads, you can make a loop from Palm Beach around the northwest end and return via Noord to the Natural Bridge.

Toward the south beyond the airport, the highway continues to Spanish Lagoon, Savaneta, and San Nicolas. You can loop through San Nicolas to the southeast coast and return via Santa Cruz, a crossroad town almost in the center of the island, with roads branching north to the Natural Bridge; west along the Hooiberg, Casibari, and to Palm Beach; and south through Frenchmans Pass (Franse Pas) to Barcadera.

Car rentals are abundant and the best mode of transportation around the island. Cars range from US$35 and up per day. An open-air jeep, the most popular choice, costs about US$60 to $70 per day. A valid foreign driver's license is needed to rent and drive a car. The minimum driving age for rental cars is twenty-one to twenty-five and the maximum age is sixty-five to seventy-five, depending on the rental company. Major U.S. car-rental companies have licensees in Aruba, and there are reliable local companies. Driving is on the right side of the road.

George's ATVs, Scooters & Cycles (993-2202) rents jeeps, scooters, and motorcycles and has pickup service. Bikes cost about US$15; scooters, US$20. Open 9:00 a.m. to 5:00 p.m. **Pablito's Bike Rental** (587-8655) is open 9:00 a.m. to 6:00 p.m.

Heli-tours Aruba (965-5906; www.aruba helitours.com) offers island tours, using a new R44 helicopter for a minimum of two passengers.

Emergency Numbers

Medical: Dr. Horacio Oduber Hospital, Smith Boulevard; 587-4300

Police: 582-4000/582-4100; 911

Fire Alarm Center: 115; 911

Shore Excursions

An island tour can be taken several ways: a standard motorcoach or jeep excursion, on horseback, or by ATV, helicopter, or hiking with a nature guide or other specialist, visiting the less accessible parts of the island and focusing on its more unusual aspects. More information is available on sightseeing and sports later in the chapter. Prices are per person.

Island Tour: 3 hours, US$25–$35. A drive around the island from the port passes the Hooiberg en route to the Atlantic coast. The return

probably will be via Ayo and the resorts along Palm Beach.

Cunucu Safari: 4–5 hours, US$50–70 with lunch. An excursion with more emphasis on the natural environment accompanied by a naturalist guide takes you to the interior of Aruba. You travel by a jeep-type buggy, breakfast at an Aruban cunucu home, tour the "outback" sites, and end with lunch in town.

Learn to windsurf: 2 hours, lesson package US$40–$55. Aruba is one of the Caribbean's major windsurfing locations. Lessons are available at beachside hotels and Windsurf Village.

Atlantis **submarine:** 2 hours, US$89 adults, $79 teen, $49 children. For those who do not swim or dive, the recreational submarine that dives down 150 feet is an opportunity to see the beautiful reefs and marine life along Aruba's shores.

Seaworld **Explorer:** 2 hours, US$37 adult; $22 child (two to twelve years). The semisubmersible submarine offers an experience similar to the *Atlantis* sub but can go only along the surface of the water.

Golf at Tierra del Sol: 5 hours, US$160 in season. The interesting Robert Trent Jones II course is on the northwestern end of Aruba. (See Sports section for details.) As a cruise-ship excursion, it will include transportation.

Scuba diving: 3 hours, US$70. Dive operators offer learn-to-dive courses as well as dive excursions for certified divers: one-tank dive, US$50; two-tank dive, US$55–$65. Snorkeling excursion, US$30–$35. Another version combines hiking and snorkeling, US$51.

Sea Trek: Exclusively on De Palm Island. Walk at leisure among the fish and marine life on the ocean floor. A large helmet keeps your face out of the water, and you breathe through a tube attached to a floating tank. Half-day US$89, including round-trip transportation.

Kayak Adventure: 3 hours, US$99, as ship-to-shore excursion. Kayaking from Spanish Lagoon and mangroves on the south coast to Bacadera Channel to a beach for swimming and snorkeling. Participants must be ten years or older to participate.

Heli-tours Aruba (965-5906; www.arubaheli tours.com), located behind the Seaport Casino in Oranjestad, offers several tours. The northwestern half of Aruba for fifteen minutes, $75 per person; or combined with the island interior, thirty minutes, $115 per person, for minimum of two passengers.

Aruba on Your Own

The capital of Aruba, Oranjestad, is a neat, clean town of Dutch colonial and modern architecture. It is easy to cover in an hour's stroll or to combine with a shopping excursion. From the port you can walk along Smith Boulevard to the Renaissance Village Complex, a mall with moderate-priced boutiques and outdoor cafes overlooking the harbor. Farther along is Wilhelmina Park, a small tropical garden named for the Dutch queen.

An Oranjestad Walkabout

From Schuttestraat, turn right on Oranjestraat for 1 block to reach Fort Zoutman, the oldest-standing structure on Aruba. It was built in 1796 to protect Aruba's harbor; the Willem III Tower was added in 1868 to serve as a lighthouse. The fort houses the **Aruba Historical Museum** (582-6099), which focuses on the last one hundred years of Aruba's history. Hours: 9:00 a.m. to noon and 1:30 to 4:30 p.m. Entrance: US$3.

The **Bonbini Festival,** a folkloric fair, takes place in the courtyard of the fort every Tuesday evening from 6:30 to 8:30 p.m. year-round. Admission is Afl5.31 (US$3.00). It features a folkloric show, native food, and crafts by local artisans. The fair proceeds go to local charities whose members man the stalls. (Bonbini in Papiamento means "welcome.")

As an alternative route from Smith Boulevard, just before the small bridge over the Renaissance Aruba Beach Resort lagoon, you can detour through the Renaissance Village, a shopping complex of the Renaissance Aruba, to the town center. Guests board a boat, directly from the lower lobby, to go to the resort's private beach. An escalator in the atrium takes you from the street level by the lagoon to the main floor, where the casino and disco are located. On the north side of the hotel are sidewalk cafes overlooking the town square.

Aruba Archaeological Museum (Irasquin-plein 2A; 582-8979; archeo@setarnet.aw). The

museum, inaugurated by Princess Margriet of the Netherlands in 1986, was created to preserve the artifacts of Aruba from precolonial times to the present. Aruba is placing increased emphasis on its cultural and historic heritage for the benefit of its citizens as well as visitors. Hours: weekdays 8:00 a.m. to noon and 1:00 to 4:30 p.m. Entrance is free. A booklet, *The Indians of Aruba,* published by the museum, is helpful in understanding the island's ancient history.

On Wilhelminastraat is the Protestant Church, dating from 1846 and rebuilt in the 1950s in Dutch-Aruban architecture. It faces a small square, which was redesigned in the late 1980s as the town plaza and pedestrian mall, surrounded on all sides by shopping complexes behind colorful facades of Dutch colonial architecture. The north side of the square is Nassaustraat, the traditional commercial street. West of the square is Havenstraat, with several of Aruba's best restaurants.

The **Numismatic Museum** (Weststraat just beyond the cruise dock; 582-8831) displays more than thirty thousand different coins and paper money, some dating from ancient Greek and Roman times. Hours: weekdays 7:30 a.m. to noon and 1:00 to 4:00 p.m. There is a small entrance fee.

Ricki Shells (Salina Serca 35A; 586-2119; www.museumaruba.org) displays excavation findings and many rare and unusual shells that make wonderful souvenirs. By appointment only, so phone in advance.

Aruba Antiquity Museum (Timbalstraat 11,Tarabana; 583-2039) displays a private collection of island antiques, housed in a private home. It is open to the general public by appointment.

West of Oranjestad

At Druif Bay, where the coastline bends north, a talcum powder–fine white sand stretches for almost 7 miles. It is the most developed part of Aruba, containing the majority of its luxury hotels, casinos, restaurants, and water-sports facilities. The first mile or so, known as **Eagle Beach,** has a jogging track at the western end, and on its north side are wetlands known as **Bubali Pond,** a small bird sanctuary.

Aruba Aloe Museum and Factory (115 Pitastraat, Hato; 588-3222; www.arubaaloe.com).

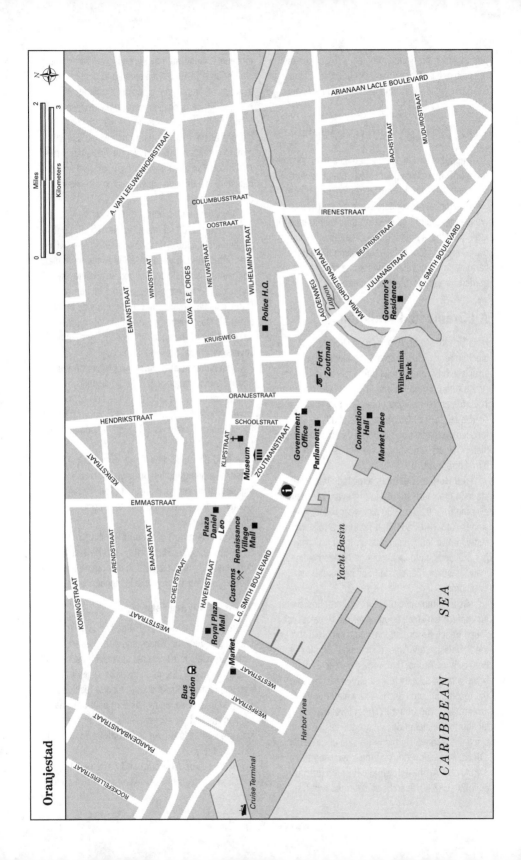

Long a local tradition that aloe brings good luck and can cure many ailments, the plant is often found hanging from home ceilings and planted by the front door. In the past the plant brought prosperity to Aruba and is still cultivated commercially for use in lotions, suntan creams, hair-care products, and fragrances. Tours: Monday to Friday, 9:00 a.m. to 4:00 p.m., Saturday, 9:00 a.m. to 2:00 p.m. US$6 adults, $3 child. The shop sells aloe products nicely packaged for gifts. They can also be purchased in supermarkets and gift and souvenir shops.

Palm Beach The next stretch of 5 miles is gorgeous Palm Beach. Each of its seaside hotels is surrounded by flowering gardens that provide privacy and relieve an otherwise-barren landscape with color. Each hotel has its own swimming pool, beach bar, and water sports. The prettiest of the group is the deluxe **Hyatt Aruba,** designed in Spanish architecture with tropical gardens and terraced pools and lagoons interconnected by waterfalls overlooking a beautiful palm-graced beach. It is the headquarters of **Red Sail Sports** (586-1603 or in the United States 800-255-6425; www.redsail aruba.com), which also handles sports arrangements for day visitors.

Butterfly Farm Aruba (586-3656; www.the butterflyfarm.com). Located near the south end of Palm Beach, Aruba's Butterfly Farm is home to thirty-two species of butterflies from around the world, accounting for the 600 to 700 large and small butterflies visitors can see here. The farm raises them from egg to caterpillar to butterfly. Visitors are given a guided tour and explanation of the process; afterward, they are free to walk on their own through the different, mesh-enclosed gardens, each intended to attract and sustain various species. The butterflies are from the Caribbean, Central America, the Middle East, and Pacific, as well as Aruba, which has eleven native species. Admission: US$12 adults, $6 children, which allows for return visits. Hours: daily 9:00 a.m. to 4:30 p.m. Both the Aruba farm and the Butterfly Farm in St. Maarten have the same owners.

California Point The scenic northern end of Aruba is marked by the California Lighthouse, a historic landmark. It takes its name from the ship *Californian,* wrecked in 1891 and lying in 15 to 30 feet of water off the northwest tip.

En route to the point after Palm Beach is a stretch of beach known as Fisherman's Huts; it is the island's prime windsurfing area and home of **Windsurf Village.** At the foot of the lighthouse is **Tierre del Sol,** Aruba's golf course (see Sports).

The main road from California Point returns southeast along a stretch of dry, desolate terrain characterized by towering rocks and scattered hills. The highest is Alto Vista, 236 feet, from which there are lovely views. Here, too, is the chapel of Alto Vista, consecrated in 1750. In the village of Noord, St. Anna Church, with a seventeenth-century Dutch hand-carved altar, is one of the island's oldest churches and a fine example of Dutch colonial architecture.

A Drive around the Island

Aruba's surprising diversity can be revealed only on a tour of the island—a total change from the beaches and glittering casinos of the south coast. After leaving the placid turquoise waters and white sands on the leeward shores, the road north passes an area of gigantic rock formations and the ever-present Aruban landmark, the divi-divi tree, whose curious shape is sculpted by strong prevailing winds.

Hooiberg East from Oranjestad toward the airport is the conical-shaped 541-foot Hooiberg, known as "the Haystack," in view on the eastern horizon. Located almost in the center of the island, the curious volcanic formation is visible from most any location. It is covered with dry woodlands of kibrahacha, or yellow poui, a common tree of the Caribbean that usually blossoms after a rain. A flight of several hundred steps leads to the summit, where you can see the coast of Venezuela in the distance on a clear day. Among the birds populating the hill is the spectacular orange-and-black trupial (or troupial).

On the south side of the Hooiberg, the Canashito area has caves with Arawak petroglyphs—one of several places where they are found. The area between the Hooiberg and Casibari, on the north, is littered with huge boulders that have been carved and weathered into bizarre shapes by the strong winds that blow across the island.

Ayo Directly east of Hooiberg, an area strewn with enormous rocks has been dubbed "the Stonehenge of Aruba." Footpaths make it easy to walk through the area and examine the formations at close range. If you are very quiet, you will probably see a variety of birds, particularly colorful parakeets that populate these parts.

Donkey Sanctuary (584-1063; www.aruba donkey.org) In Santa Lucia, near the Ayo Rock formations, the Save Our Donkeys Foundation has rescued some forty animals in a few short years. Visitors are welcome to spend time with the donkeys, feed them, and participate in the adopt-a-donkey program. The guides enjoy explaining the history of the donkeys in Aruba while escorting you around. Open daily from 8:00 a.m. to 12:30 p.m.

The Atlantic Coast Across the island from Oranjestad on the northeast coast between Boca Mahos and Andicuri Bay, the land drops sharply into a turbulent sea where waves crash endlessly against the rocky shores. At a natural bridge—once a prime tourist attraction until it collapsed in September 2005—the force of the water was so great it gave rise to the popular notion that the bridge was carved out of the coral by the sea. Scientists say, however, that the bridge and other similar formations along the coast were formed when weak spots in the coral terraces, which make up the north coast, were dissolved and washed away by abrasive action of fresh rainwater. They explain that the sea could have polished, enlarged, and even smashed the bridge by its force, but only fresh water could have dissolved the rock on the land side. Another bridge, known as Boca Druif, or Dragon Mouth, can be seen at Boca Prins on the windward coast.

The road between Santa Cruz and Boca Prins runs through the Miralamar Pass between Aruba's highest hills and the countryside of rolling hills, farms, and colorful cunucu houses. Originally, *cunucu* in the Arawak language meant a plot of land for agriculture; now it is widely used to mean rural areas. Arubans also use the Spanish word *campo* for countryside.

Aruba Ostrich Farm (585-9630; www.aruba .com/whattodo/ostrichfarm; greatoutdoors@ setarnet.aw) Located by Bushiribana Goldmine ruins on the road to the former Natural Bridge, the Aruba Ostrich Farm is a sister to the bigger farm on Curaçao. Guided tours by truck are offered daily 9:00 a.m. to 4:00 p.m. among the pens and to the incubation station. Cost is US$12 adults, US$6 children. There is no charge to visit the restaurant, bar, or gift shop, which is stocked with interesting African carvings and clothing.

Arikok National Park Mount Arikok, 577 feet, is the island's second-highest peak and the center of the Arikok National Park, which lies between Boca Prins, San Fuego, and Boca Keto. It was created by FANAPA, Aruba Foundation for Nature and Parks, the principal group working to preserve Aruba's natural heritage. At the foot of the hill is a restored country house with a small garden that has samples of trees and bushes found on Aruba.

Aloe vera grows wild throughout Aruba. Widely cultivated for medical purposes in the past, its production declined due to competition from lower-priced synthetics, and most plantations were abandoned. Small-scale cultivation continues, and a few of the outdoor ovens where the juice of the leaves is boiled and hardened are still in use on the island. The juice is used in making sunscreen lotions and cosmetics at a local plant. You can treat a cut or sunburn simply by breaking off a leaf and rubbing the sap on your skin.

Mount Yamanota The south side of the San Fuego/Boca Prins Road is known as Yamanota (or Jamanota), an area that has been earmarked as a national park and includes the island's highest hill, 617-foot Mount Yamanota. You can take a paved road to the summit, where you will find grand views of the island. The Yamanota area is the home of the Aruban parakeet, a bright green-and-yellow bird that is almost as large as a parrot.

Guadirikiri and Fontein Caves The most accessible of Aruba's many caves are two on the east coast: the Fontein Cave, with fine Arawak petroglyphs, and the large Guadirikiri Cave, with two high ceiling chambers, one with an opening at the top that allows in some light. A third chamber, entered by a small low opening, is home to a large number of bats. Be forewarned: The room is hot and humid.

South of Oranjestad

Spanish Lagoon The road south from the airport returns to the coast at Barcadera, where there is a long island waterway, Spanish Lagoon, with mangroves and a bird refuge at its northeastern end.

Linear Park In late 2007, work was scheduled to start on Aruba's Linear Park. Covering 10 miles from the airport to Eagle Beach, the park is expected to be the longest linear park in the Caribbean. The $10 million project will include green zones and walking/jogging paths.

About 600 yards from shore in front of Barcadera Harbor is a reef that starts at the surface and drops to about an 80-foot depth. It is part of a 2-mile reef along the south coast and is popular for snorkeling and diving. The *Atlantis* submarine is based here, and there are also two beach developments: The north one belongs to the Renaissance Hotel; the south one is De Palm Island, a privately developed recreation and sports center. The area is also a favorite for sportfishing.

Savaneta, on the south side of Spanish Lagoon, was the first European settlement and the former capital of Aruba.

Frenchmans Pass A road inland around the north end of Spanish Lagoon goes through Frenchmans Pass (Franse Pas), a tree-lined drive and site of a historic battle between French and Spanish buccaneers in 1700. Tracks from the main road go to the ruins of the Balashi gold mill, a relic of Aruba's gold rush, built in 1898.

San Nicolas (Sint Nicolaas), Aruba's second-largest settlement, grew up around the oil refinery, owned by Standard Oil of New Jersey until it closed in 1985. Now, the town will have a new lease on life when an ambitious urban renewal project—to make it a cultural and tourism center—is completed. **Charlie's Bar,** in the heart of the town, is an island mainstay not to be missed. Charlie came to Aruba several decades ago to work in the oil refinery, but after a time decided a bar was more fun. So too is the bar's decor—everyone who visits is supposed to leave something, and they have! South of the oil installation, there are two secluded beaches, popularly known as Rodgers Beach and Baby Lagoon, where you can snorkel from shore. Both beaches lie at the foot of Seroe Colorado, a residential community originally built for Exxon Oil executives.

Enroute to Baby Beach, you might treat your kids to a stop at the **Aruba Model Trains Museum** (Koolbaaibergstraat 12, Lago Heights, San Nicolas; 584-7321), housed in a private home, where they can see a variety of trains, the oldest dating back to 1895. Hours: Tuesday to Saturday 10:00 a.m. to 5:00 p.m., Sunday by appointment. No entry fee.

The southeastern end of the island, marked by the Colorado Lighthouse, overlooks some of Aruba's main dive locations. Along the east coast Boca Grandi, a wide bay, is a popular picnic spot. The area is popular for windsurfing and sportfishing.

North of San Nicolas is an arid, windswept region with little vegetation, even during the rainy season, where the divi-divi tree is abundant. Its asymmetrical shape is caused by the passaat, the Papiamento name for the strong winds that blow mainly from the east.

Although all wind-sheared trees with this shape are commonly called divi-divi, several species grow in this manner. Divi-divi means "ear" in the Arawak language and is derived from the watapana tree, which has thick, curled pods resembling a human ear.

Shopping

Aruba is not officially a duty-free port, but in 1989 duties on luxury items were lowered from 40 to 7.5 percent, turning it into a shopping mecca. Of greatest interest to most visitors are the Dutch products, such as delft blue pottery and Dutch pewter; Gouda, Edam, and a variety of other Dutch cheeses and chocolates; and Indonesian crafts.

Traditionally, Nassaustraat (Caya Croes) has been the shoppers' street, but a downtown renewal project, begun in 1988, changed the face of the town center. Several complexes set behind pastel-colored facades of traditional Dutch Caribbean architecture, complete with gables, added many stores.

The town square is anchored on the east by the Strada, a long-established department store, which has been rebuilt as a complex with eleven boutiques. On the west is the Holland Aruba Mall, another shop-and-restaurant complex. On the south is Renaissance Village Mall, the shopping and restaurant complex of the **Renaissance Aruba Resort and Casino** (583-6000). By the waterfront on the east is the Renaissance Marketplace; to the west, directly in front of the port, is the Royal Plaza Mall, with its fancy "Taj Mahal" architecture. Aruba's newest shopping mall is the beautiful **Paseo Herencia**, located directly in front of the Holiday Inn. Together these malls have several hundred stores with sports and casual wear, leather, shoes, swimwear, designer fashions, jewelry, Dutch cheeses, and crafts—all within walking distance or a short ride from the docks.

Malls are open Monday to Saturday, 10:00 a.m. to 6:00 p.m. Downtown store hours are Monday to Saturday from 9:00 a.m. to 1:00 p.m. and from 2:00 to 6:30 p.m.; however, many stores remain open during the lunch hour. When cruise ships are in port on Sundays and holidays, some shops in the Renaissance Marketplace, Port O Call, and Royal Plaza malls are occasionally open.

Art and Artists Creative Hands (5 Socotorolaan) carries ceramic cunucu houses and divi-divi trees, and other folklore objects. **Gaspirito,** on a country road near Palm Beach, and **Que Pasa?** (Wilhelminastraat 2) are both restaurants and art galleries with local and Caribbean art. **Mopa Mopa** (Renaissance Village Mall) sells unusual gifts that appear to be handpainted but are not. The specialized craft is made from the buds of the mopa mopa tree, which are boiled to form a resin. Vegetable colors are added to the resin, which the artist then stretches by hand. The material is cut into small pieces and layered to form intricate designs on wood.

Access Art Gallery (Caya Betico Croes 16-18, Oranjestad; 588-7837) displays local and international artists, with a focus on design as functional art. A cultural evening with lectures and arts presentations is held Thursday evenings. **Art Studio Insight** (Paradera Park 215; 568-9168) emphasizes visual and theater arts. **Captain's Art Gallery** (Palm Beach 6-D Noord; 586-1991), a small, noncommercial gallery, shows up-and-coming artists. **Eterno Gallery** (Emanstraat 92,Oranjestad; 583-

9607) carries local and international artwork. **Osaira Muyale Contemporary Art Studio** (Stadionweg 3,Oranjestad; 582-1350) is the studio of contemporary conceptual artist Osaira Muyale. Rotating exhibits can also be seen at the Cas di Cultura, National Library of Aruba, Numismatic Museum Aruba, and the Aruba Investment Bank in Oranjestad.

In San Nicolas, the **San Nicolas Foundation for the Arts** (SiNFA) (Van Zeppenveldtstraat 10; 584-2969) covers the visual arts, theater, music, literature, photography, and dance. **South End Art Foundation** (584-6976) exhibits a large selection of paintings, crafts, and sculptures by local artists.

China and Crystal Aruba Trading Company (Caya G. F. Betico Croes 12; www.arubatrading .com) is a large department store, established in 1930, with a section for china and crystal. **Little Switzerland** (Nassaustraat; 800-524-2010; www .littleswitzerland.com) is one of the Caribbean's mainstays for fine china and crystal.

Clothing and Accessories There are many boutiques of women's fashions in the various shopping malls, but if you are looking for high fashion, **Agatha at Les Accessoires** (lower level, Renaissance Aruba Resort; 583-7965) is run by transplanted New York fashion designer Agatha Brown, known for her unique styles. **Benetton** (Holland Plaza) is here, too, but a check of prices did not reflect a savings over New York stores; the same can be said of **Fendi,** whose store is located on the town square. There's also **Tommy Hilfiger** (Royal Plaza Mall) and **Polo Ralph Lauren** (Renaissance Mall). For funky upscale fashions, **Tropical Motion** (Renaissance Village Mall) has Indonesian batiks and French-designer outfits. **Gimmick** (Renaissance Village Mall; 583-9244; fax: 587-4195; gimmick@setanet.aw) is operated by a mother and daughter team who import top European lines, from sexy to business attire. **Azul** (Caya G. F. Betico Croes 10; 583-0131) is a two-story boutique for men's and women's clothing by Nautica, Lacoste, Ralph Lauren, Kenneth Cole, and others. The new Paseo Herencia has Diesel, Lacoste, and many other popular brands. The Web site www.arubahouse.com has a good list of clothing and souvenir shops with addresses and phone numbers.

Food Specialties Le Gourmet, in the Aruba Trading Company, stocks pâté, caviar, fine Dutch chocolates and cheeses, liqueurs, wines, spices, and more. Supermarkets, such as **Pueblo** and **Ling & Sons,** are good places to buy Dutch cheese, chocolates, and other edibles, as well as liquor.

Jewelry The best-known jewelers are **Gandelman** (www.boolchand.com), a long-established quality store that has a large selection of fine gold jewelry and watches and a customer-service office in the United States, and **Colombian Emeralds.** Both are located in the Renaissance Village Mall and certain hotels.

Leather Gucci (Renaissance Village Mall) has its own store facing the town square, where the savings are about 20 percent over U.S. locations. There are many stores in Oranjestad selling Louis Vuitton–type handbags and luggage at prices considerably lower than in the United States. You would need to be familiar with the manufacturer's goods to know if those here are the genuine item or merely good replicas. But if you don't care, they are very good buys. **Ferragamo** (Emmastraat 1, Plaza Daniel Leo) is one of the newest high-fashion stores to open in town, and **Hugo Boss** (Caya Betico Croes 15) recently moved into a new shop with women's as well as men's fashions.

Perfume and Cosmetics Every shopping complex in town and at resort hotels has perfume shops. **Aruba Trading Company** (Caya G. F. Betico Croes 12) has a well-stocked perfume-and-cosmetics section. **Sadini's** (Holland Plaza) has a large selection and exceptionally pleasant staff. The **Aruba Aloe Factory and Museum** (588-3222; www.arubaaloe.com) makes a variety of perfumed lotions, sun, skin-, and hair-care products from the gel found in aloe plants grown at the site. Locals have used this wonder plant for generations to treat all types of ailments: cuts, burns, sunburn, and more. Products are sold in the gift shop, along with aloe candles in unusual shapes. Aruba Aloe also has shops downtown and at the airport.

Dining and Restaurants

Oranjestad has a surprising range and variety of restaurants—Chinese, American, Italian, French, Indonesian, and more—reflecting the multifaceted nature of the country. In recent years, too, Aruban specialties have come out of home kitchens onto restaurant menus at places specializing in local cuisine. Some of the best restaurants—Chez Matilda, LeDome, Gasparito, Papiamento, Que Pasa?—are open for dinner only; some may open for lunch during the winter season. Most restaurants close Sunday or Monday. Inquire in advance. Through a Dine-Around program, monitored by the Aruba Gastronomic Association (AGA), visitors can try more than twenty fine restaurants at special rates with purchase of a coupon booklet priced from US$110. Contact De Palm Tours (582-4400) or AGA (588-5700; www.arubadining.com).

Aqua Grill (J.E. Irausquin Boulevard 374, Palm Beach, 586-5900; aqua-grill@setarnet.aw) serves a wide range of fresh seafood in a setting of contemporary decor that combines New England fish house traditions with Caribbean ones. Moderately expensive.

Brisas del Mar (by the sea near San Nicolas; 584-7718). This open-air restaurant with fishnets hanging from the ceiling and a direct view of the Caribbean is a thirty-minute drive from Oranjestad to Savaneta—but well worth it for seafood and local cuisine. Phone in advance to know if lunch is being served. Expensive.

Cuba's Cookin' (Wilhelminastraat 27 588-0627; cubascookin@visitaruba.com) Conveniently located in town, it has a great reputation for authentic Cuban cuisine. Expensive but portions are enough for two meals.

Driftwood Restaurant (Klipstraat 12, Oranjestad, 583-2515) Popular for seafood with an Aruban flavor. Expensive.

Dutch Pancake House (Renaissance Marketplace; 583-7180) serves handmade bakes from an old family recipe of the Dutch owners; seventy-five varieties in this seaside setting. Open 9:00 a.m. to 9:00 p.m. except Monday. Moderate.

Flying Fishbone (Savaneta 344; 584-2506), a charming beach restaurant specializing in fresh seafood, is set in Aruba's oldest fishing village. You can dine by soft candlelight with your feet in the sand and starlight overhead. Reservations required. Moderately expensive.

Laguna Fish Market (Radisson Aruba Resort and Casino, Irausquin Boulevard 81; 586-6555) likes to say that the only thing fresher than the fish is its setting along freshwater lagoons and tropical foliage. On Monday and Friday, dining starts at a seafood tasting bar and an appetizer bar and continues with a menu of fresh fish and Caribbean specialties. Other nights have Italian, Mexican, barbecue, and other themes. Moderate.

Le Petit Cafe (Royal Plaza Mall; 583-8471; lepetitecafe1@visitaruba.com) is a fresh and lively cafe on the town square where your chicken or meat is cooked on a hot-stone platter in front of you. They also serve salads, sandwiches, hamburgers, and light meals. Moderate to expensive.

For some budget-easy alternatives, try the delicious local cuisine and seafood at **Cafe Bahia** (588-9982); the **Grill House** (31 Zoutmanstraat; 583-1611), which has Aruban-style fish and Dutch steak in a cozy setting; and **Mambo Jambo** (Royal Plaza Mall; 583-3632), which offers light lunch and is open for cocktails during the day and becomes a nightclub in the evening. There's also a **Carlos 'n Charlie's** of the famous Mexican chain (582-0355), Hooters, and pizza parlors galore.

Nightlife

Aruba has a very lively nightlife. Each major hotel has a nightclub with international entertainment or disco with a distinct ambience. If you would like some help in sampling the nightlife, **De Palm Tours** (582-4400) offers a "Bar Hopper" tour. Or, bar hop in the gaily painted **Kukoo Kunuku Party Bus** (586-2010; www.kukookunuku.com) or the **Banana Bus** (993-9757; www.bananabusaruba .com) with a big yellow banana on its roof. The Banana Bus also runs an island tour with a swim and snorkeling at Baby Beach, Tuesday to Saturday from 9:00 a.m. to 1:30 p.m. for US$30 per person.

The island's eleven casinos are found mostly in hotels. The **Alhambra** (www.alhambracasino.com), a large independent gaming house, is part of an entertainment-and-shopping complex near Eagle Beach. The complex also has a theater, shops,

restaurants (including Dunkin Donuts and Subway), and a big-screen sports bar.

The Lounge (overlooking the casino in Renaissance Aruba Beach Resort; 583-6000) is a new, sophisticated late-night spot for drinks, light fare, and people-watching until 6:00 a.m.! **Black Hog Saloon** (Bubali, across from LaCabana Resort; 587-6625) jumps to the wee hours. This is biker's bar serving mode: huge drinks, bar-stool races, and trick rides on Harley Hogs.

If you would prefer something on the more cultural side, the 220-seat theater **Cas de Cultura** (Culture Center, Vondellaan 2; 582-1010) stages concerts, ballet, folkloric shows, and art exhibits. Check with the Aruba Tourism Authority to learn what's happening during your visit.

Sports

All hotels here have a swimming pool and water sports, and they can arrange scuba, fishing, and windsurfing. De Palm Island, south of Oranjestad, is a water-sports center of **De Palm Tours** (582-4400; in United States, 800-533-7265; www .depalm.com).

Beaches/Swimming The most beautiful waters for swimming are along the soft sands of Palm Beach, but you can find other white-sand beaches with calm waters along the leeward coast. At Baby Beach on the southern coast, the water is only 4 to 5 feet deep. Its calm waters are especially suited for children.

Biking and Motorcycling Because most of Aruba is flat, biking can be an easy way to get around, and the trade winds help keep you cool. **Bike & Locker Rental** (L. G. Smith Boulevard 234, Oranjestad; 587-8655) and **Pablito's Bike Rental** (L. G. Smith Boulevard 234; 587-8655) rent bikes for $15 a day. Or, you can go big time with a Harley Davidson from **Big Twin Aruba** (L. G. Smith Boulevard 124-A; 582-8660, www.harleydavidson-aruba.com; hours: Monday to Saturday, 9:00 a.m. to 6:00 p.m.) for $99 for a half day; $149 full day, including insurance and helmets, and a $1,000 deposit. The shop also sells Harley clothing and accessories. **Donata Car and Cycle** (L. G. Smith Boulevard 136-D; 583-4343) rents mopeds and motorcycles; **George's Cycle Center** (L. G. Smith Boulevard 136; 592-5875) has scooters and all-terrain vehicles; and **Semver Cycle Rental** (Noord 22, Noord; 586-6851) has scooters and motorcycles. Guided tours on all-terrain vehicles are available from **De Palm Tours** (L. G. Smith Boulevard 142; 582-4400; 800-766-6016, www.depalm.com) for $75 to $100.

Boating Water-sports operators offer sail and snorkel cruises on catamarans and other sailboats and glass-bottom ones for viewing the coral.

Deep-Sea Fishing Sportfishing is a big sport in Aruba. Less than a mile or so from shore, the sea is rich with kingfish, tuna, bonito, wahoo, blue and white marlin, and more. About a dozen boat operators offer half- and full-day, fully equipped charters, some for a maximum of four persons; others for up to six persons. The price ranges from US$220 to $320 for half-day and $400 to $600 full day. You can obtain a list from the Tourist Office. **De Palm Tours** has daily departures at 8:00 a.m. and 1:00 p.m.

Golf Tierre del Sol (866-978-5158; www.tierre delsol.com), Aruba's first 18-hole championship golf course (6,811 yards; par 71) was designed by the Robert Trent Jones II Group and can accommodate golfers of all ages and abilities. There is a driving range, putting green, and practice chipping area complete with a bunker. Located near the California Lighthouse, it is part of a planned community with apartments and villas, an excellent spa and health club, a handsome clubhouse with a popular restaurant, swimming pools, and tennis complex. The development has its own irrigation system and water supply (a major consideration of this arid island). During construction of the course, which is landscaped with Aruba's indigenous plants, environmentalists were consulted to protect local wildlife, particularly the birds at a nearby sanctuary. Reservations: (586-0978; fax: 586-0671). Greens fees with cart range from US$92 to $159, depending on time of day and season of the year. Club rentals, US$45 to $55.

The **Links at Divi Aruba** (adjacent to Divi Village Golf and Beach Resort; 583-2300; www .divigolf.com) is a new 9-hole course that also plays as 18 holes. There is a golf school, pro shop,

and restaurant. Play is open to the public, but guests at Divi's four hotels get preferred tee times. Non-hotel guests, US$70 to $80 for nine holes in season; club rentals, $30 to $35 per round.

Joe Mendez Adventure Miniature Golf (Bubali; 587-6625) features an 18-hole elevated course surrounded by water and a full complement of entertainment venues: paddleboats, go-kart racing, and batting cages.

Hiking Aruba's only marked hiking trails are in Arikok National Park (Piedra Plat 42, 582-8001; pna@setarnet.aw), but there are many tracks branching from main arteries to almost any place of interest. Nature hikes, birding, archaeological excursions, and jeep safaris lasting three to six hours are led by naturalists from **De Palm Tours** (582-4400; 800-766-6016). For an interesting early-morning climb—and a more accessible one—try the Hooiberg (known locally as the Haystack), the mound rising conspicuously in the center of the island about 6 miles east of Oranjestad. The climb to the top via several hundred carved steps affords great exercise, and you're rewarded with a spectacular view of the island. Information on hiking, jeep, horseback, and bicycle tours through the park are available at the National Park offices.

Horseback Riding Rancho Daimari (Tanki Leendert 249, San Nicholas; 587-5674; www.visit aruba.com/ranchodaimari) offers a two-hour guided tour including a swim for $64 per person. Others include **Rancho del Campo** (22 East Sombre; 585-0290; www.ranchodelcampo.com) and **Rancho Notorious** (Boroncana 8–E; 586-0508; www .ranchonotorious.com), which offer trail rides daily except Sunday. The mounts, imported from South America, are the famous paso fino horses noted for their smooth gait. Trips can be arranged for all levels of skill. Rancho Notorious also offers guided bike tours.

Kayaking Aruba Kayak Adventures (Ponton 90, Oranjestad; 582-5520; www.arubawavedancer .com/arubakayak) offers excursions Monday through Saturday starting at 8:30 a.m. and 2:30 p.m. Contact them in advance to make arrangements. A kayaking and snorkeling excursion costs $99 per person. **De Palm Tours** (L. G. Smith

Boulevard 142, Oranjestad; 582-4400; 800-766-6016, www.depalm.com) has a four-hour guided kayaking/snorkeling tour for $80 including lunch.

Landsailing The sport of gliding over sand and land using a kart with a sail propelled by wind is called landsailing. The small, light kart is mounted on three wheels with the front wheel attached to a system that enables riders to steer the kart with their legs and control the kart with the sail, using techniques similar to sailing. **Aruba Active Vacations** (Salina Cerca 25-K, cell 297-741-2991) offers landsailing as well as other active sports such as windsurfing, kite surfing, and mountain bike rentals and tours.

Rock Climbing Near Grapefield, a small town at the southeastern end of the island, is a series of 50-foot-high limestone cliffs, known as the Fontein Cliffs. In 1996 some local and Dutch climbers mapped the cliff faces and put in place the material necessary for climbing. Now, the cliffs have become a popular climbing site for locals and visitors. If you don't have the gear necessary to climb, the **Club Active Aruba** (585-3433) rents the equipment and provides instruction for novices. Due to Aruba's intense sun and heat, climbers are advised to plan their climb before 10:00 a.m. or after 3:00 p.m.

Snorkeling/Scuba Diving Aruba is surrounded by coral reefs, and there are interesting shipwrecks. The reefs in the calm leeward waters range from shallow-water corals within swimming distance of shore—suitable for snorkelers and novice divers—to deepwater reefs and walls that drop 100 feet and more. Snorkeling and diving can be arranged directly with dive operators, most of whom are located at the hotels on Eagle and Palm Beaches. A beginner's dive lesson costs about US$70. **Pelican Tours and Watersports** (P.O. Box 1194, Oranjestad, Aruba; 587-2302; fax: 587-2315; www.pelican-aruba.com), one of the island's oldest dive operators, offers a full range of packages: one-tank dive, US$35; two-tank dive, US$55; night dive, US$39. The dive center is located on Palm Beach next to the Holiday Inn.

There are another dozen dive operators, all PADI certified and with their own boats. A list is available from the Tourism Authority. If you don't

dive, you don't have to miss the fun. SNUBA (582-4400) is an apparatus that enables you to see more than a snorkel, but it does not require the skills to scuba dive. Cost: US$15–$55, depending on package inclusions.

Arashi Beach, north of Palm Beach, is ideal for snorkeling and shallow-water dives directly from the beach. The reef of elkhorn coral lies on a sandy bottom in 20 to 40 feet of water. There are two shipwrecks that can be viewed by snorkelers as well as divers. The *Pedernales,* an oil tanker from World War II, lies in 20 to 40 feet of water near the Holiday Inn; the *Antilla,* a German cargo ship scuttled by the Germans at the start of the Second World War, lies at 60 feet in two parts.

At Barcadera, a 2-mile reef runs along the south coast and has abundant gorgonians and elkhorn and staghorn corals, which attract a great variety of fish common to the Caribbean. Farther south Baby Lagoon offers the greatest visibility for snorkeling.

If you are in Aruba the first week in July, you can get a free dive by participating in the Aruba Perrier Reef Care Project (582-3777), an annual reef cleanup program.

Atlantis Submarine Expeditions (866-546-7820; www.atlantisadventures.com) departs from the Atlantis downtown office (opposite Aruba Renaissance) where you board a boat that transfers you to the submarine off the southeast coast. The guided excursion takes you over the Barcadera reefs and two sunken wrecks. Price: US$89 adult, $79 teen (twelve to sixteen years old), $49 child.

Sea World Explorer, a semi submarine with viewing windows onto the underwater sea life, 5 feet below the surface, provides viewing of the Arashi reef and the *Antilla* wreck. The guided excursion departs from the Pelican Pier (Holiday Inn) where you board a transfer boat. Tours daily: 11:30 a.m. and 1:30 p.m. US$37 adult, $22 child (two to twelve years old). Contact Atlantis or De Palm Tours (582-4400).

Several water-based thrill rides are also available from De Palm Tours: *Rhino Rider,* a two-person, self-drive, 10-foot inflatable motorboat; *Screamer,* with high-speed runs and 180-degree spins in a 1000-horsepower turbocharged jet boat; and *Thriller Aruba,* which zips across, around, and into the high seas.

Tennis Most hotels have tennis courts, but Aruba's strong winds are not conducive to play, except at well-protected courts. The **Aruba Racquet Club** (Rooi Santo 21, Palm Beach; 586-0215; www.arc.aw) is a world-class tennis center. It has eight lighted courts, an exhibition center court, pro shop, swimming pool, fitness center, bar, and restaurant. Hours: 8:00 a.m. to 11:00 p.m. Rental fee: US$10 per hour per court.

Windsurfing/Kiteboarding The same strong winds that shape the divi-divi tree and keep the island cool have made Aruba one of the leading windsurfing locations in the Caribbean. Most of the year the winds blow at 15 knots and, at times, up to 25 knots. Windsurfers from around the world meet here annually in June for the **Aruba Hi-Winds Pro-Am World Cup,** where the winds get up to 25 knots or more. The most popular windsurfing areas are north of Palm Beach at Fisherman's Huts, the beach fronting **Windsurf Village** (www.aruba house.com). All beachside hotels have windsurfing equipment. If you want to learn or polish your skills, the **Sailboard Vacations Flight School** at the Windsurf Village is best. Lessons from a skilled full-time instructor cost US$40 per hour or US$150 for five hours and are given in the warm shallow waters of Fisherman's Huts, where winds are consistent.

Kiteboarding has literally taken off in Aruba, motivated by the same strong winds that made windsurfing so popular. If you know what you're doing, the best spot to "fly" is Arashi Beach near California Lighthouse. At Boca Grande on the south shore, you can watch local experts show off their radical moves. Those eager to learn can take lessons and rent equipment at **Vela Windsurf Resorts** (Fisherman's Huts Windsurf Center (101 L. G.Smith Boulevard, Palm Beach, 586-9000; 800-223-5443, www.velawindsurf.com). Prices range from beginner group lessons for one-hour instruction and one-hour equipment rental afterwards for $50 to one hour of private instruction with equipment not included for $125. Or, try **Aruba Boardsailing Productions** (486 L. G.Smith Boulevard, 586-3940 or 993-1111, www.visitaruba.com/aruba boardsailing), where kiteboarding rental costs are about $55 per day.

Festivals and Celebrations

Carnival, celebrated during the pre-Lenten period, has long been the main celebration in Aruba, and it has all the costumes, color, calypso, parades, and floats of any Caribbean Carnival. Aruba usually has a major music festival in the summer season.

For the most complete listing of events, tours, attractions, and day- and nighttime activities taking place during your visit, check out the free weekly publication *K-Pasa Aruba This Week* (588-7928) or its Web site: www.k-pasa.com.

PART SIX

South America's Caribbean and the Panama Canal

Venezuela

Venezuela is a country of dazzling variety. On its west are the snowcapped Andes Mountains soaring to more than 16,000 feet; on the north lie more than 1,000 miles of Caribbean coast; and to the south and east, the Amazon jungle. Deep in the southland of strange tabletop mesas is Angel Falls, the tallest waterfall in the world; through the central plains flows the Orinoco River, the second longest in South America.

The people come from backgrounds as varied as the Venezuelan landscape. In addition to the Amerindians, whose Arawak ancestors populated the Caribbean at the time of Columbus, and the Spaniards who conquered South America, Venezuela has had large influxes of Europeans, Mediterraneans, and Asians, and after the discovery of oil, a steady stream of Texas oilmen and New York bankers. The hodgepodge is what Venezuelans call their own brand of crillos.

Clearly, one day—or even one month—is not enough time to see this diverse country. And even with the little time you have during a day in port, what you see of the country depends on which of Venezuela's ports your ship visits.

La Guaira

Located about midpoint on Venezuela's Caribbean coast, La Guaira is the port for Caracas, the capital, situated on the south side of the Avila Mountains, which rise almost directly from the coast. All cruise ships which call at La Guaira offer a day's motorcoach excursion to Caracas; most also have one to Angel Falls, which departs from the international airport, about a ten-minute drive from the port.

La Guaira is a scruffy port town with very little to recommend it, except for some good seafood restaurants and the old section of pastel colonial buildings and cobblestone streets centered on Plaza Vargas. **Guipuzcoana House,** on the shore road, is the former trading and customs house built in the early eighteenth century and restored as the town hall. It houses the local tourist office. Behind it is the **Boulton Museum,** which displays antiques and memorabilia of John Boulton, a wealthy nineteenth-century English trader whose descendants lived in the house until the 1960s.

East of La Guaira are the main beach resorts of the north coast. Be careful about where you swim, as some places have strong undertow; *balnearios,* or public beaches, with changing facilities and lifeguards, and hotel beaches are best. Macuto has several deluxe hotels with good sports facilities.

Caracas

Stretching 12 miles east-west along the Cuaire River Valley, Caracas sits at 3,000 feet above sea level, enjoying spring weather year-round, even though it is only 10 degrees north of the equator. Free-spending and fun-loving, the oil-rich capital has grown from a small town of 400,000 to a sophisticated metropolis of almost 4 million in less than four decades.

One of South America's most modern and dynamic cities, with a skyscraper skyline to rival New York or São Paolo, it is also one of the oldest, founded by the Spaniards in 1567. Its historic heart is **Plaza Bolívar,** a tree-shaded square with an equestrian statue of Simón Bolívar, the native son who led the revolution that liberated Venezuela—and, ultimately, most of South America—from Spanish rule. His birthplace, **Casa Natal,** a lovely restored colonial home, the **Bolívar Museum,** and the **National Pantheon,** where the Great Liberator's ashes are enshrined, are nearby. Also on the plaza is the **Cathedral of Caracas,** first built in 1595, containing works by Rubens and Murillo and other art treasures; to the southwest is the **Capitol** building.

Modern Caracas is best reflected in the monolithic Parque Central, a complex of ultramodern towers housing offices and apartments, with the striking **Museum of Modern Art** at the center. Two other museums, the **Museum of Fine Arts,** where Venezuela's many fine artists are displayed, and the **Museum of Natural Science** *(Ciencias Naturales),* with pre-Columbian artifacts and a fauna collection, are at the entrance to **Los Caobos Park.** Other attractions include the **Botanical Gardens, University City** (started in 1725), and **La Rinconada Racetrack,** one of the most beautiful in the world.

Caracas has super restaurants and shopping, particularly for stylish but inexpensive fashions, in high-rise malls. It is famous for its nightlife, which, unfortunately, cruise passengers will need another visit to enjoy—most ships stay in port only long enough for a day tour. This short time points to a potential problem in visiting Caracas on anything but your ship's organized tour. Traffic is horrendous, despite a network of superhighways stretching forever. Some have suggested that instead of being called the city of eternal spring, Caracas might more appropriately be named the city of eternal traffic jams. A subway, which is fairly easy to use and costs about 10 cents, has made getting around the city easier for people who want to be on their own.

That's the good news. The bad news is that the 12 miles between Caracas and your ship in La Guaira—normally a thirty-minute drive—has been known to take two hours. If your tour bus of your cruise ship's tour gets stuck in traffic, the ship will not leave without you. So if you do decide to go off on your own—and many do—be sure to allow ample time for the return to port.

Excursion to Angel Falls Angel Falls and nearby Canaima, a remote base camp and airstrip, are hidden deep in the Gran Sabana, a 14,000-square-mile region of towering, tabletop mesas with truncated peaks known as *tepuis,* likened to the Grand Canyon in the jungle. The only way to get there is by air on Avensa, the domestic airline, which has regular service. En route the plane flies into the canyon of Auyantepuy, or Devil Mountain, whose top covers an area of 180 square miles at 5,000 feet in height. It is said to be the setting of Arthur Conan Doyle's classic *The Lost World.*

At the head of the canyon, through the clouds and mist, passengers see slender Angel Falls sprouting from the top of the mountain and dropping for 3,212 feet—twice the height of the Empire State Building and fifteen times that of Niagara Falls. The falls were named for American pilot Jimmie Angel, who discovered them in 1933. As the plane flies through the narrow canyon, the walls seem so close you wonder how the pilot can avoid scraping the plane's wingtips. This is not a trip for the fainthearted!

Canaima has a lodge, also operated by Avensa, set on a beach by an amber-hued lagoon whose color comes from the water's high tannic acid content. In the distance La Hacha Falls, made up of seven cascades on the Carrao River, roars into the lake. You can take a canoe trip on the lake for a closer look at the cascades, swim, and have lunch before flying back to your ship.

Los Roques Archipelago Directly north of La Guaira is an atoll of coral islands and reef surrounding a transparent lagoon protected as a national park. It is an occasional stop for small cruise ships where passengers can enjoy snorkeling and scuba diving to see the rich marine life. Los Roques are only some of the seventy-two islands that dot Venezuela's Caribbean coast.

Puerto La Cruz

Set on a wide bay in an amphitheater of green hills, Puerto La Cruz is one of Venezuela's fastest-growing resort towns but a rare cruise port. The port in town is near hotels, which offer water sports, tennis, racquetball, a health spa, and a golf course. The principal sightseeing attraction is **Barcelona,** the capital of the state of Anzoátegui, 8 miles from Puerto La Cruz. Founded by the Spaniards in 1693, Barcelona is a typical Spanish colonial town with neat, narrow cobblestone streets lined with whitewashed houses and a plaza with the Church of San Cristobal, the municipal building, and a museum. Next to the plaza are the ruins of **Casa Fuertes,** called the Venezuelan Alamo. It was formerly a monastery where Simón Bolívar established his headquarters during the War of Independence.

Cumaná Forty-five miles east of Puerto La Cruz, Cumaná is the oldest city in South America, an occasional port of call, and a ferry departure point for Margarita Island. It is rich in history, churches, and other colonial buildings and boasts the **Museum of the Sea.** It can be visited on a day trip from Puerto La Cruz. From either Puerto La Cruz or Cumaná, a day's excursion can be made to the **Guacharo World Sanctuary,** a 1,000-acre national park with wildlife and caves with rare oilbirds, known in Spanish as guacharo.

Margarita Island

Famous for pearls, pirates, and earthly pleasures, Margarita Island is one of Venezuela's leading resorts, popular for its pretty beaches and duty-free shopping. Located 23 miles off the coast, northeast of Puerto La Cruz, Margarita and its satellites of Cubagua and Coche make up Venezuela's three-island state of Nueva Esparta.

On Cubagua in A.D. 1500, the Spaniards founded **Nueva Cadiz,** their first settlement in South America, which thrived on pearling until the Spaniards depleted the oyster beds and Mother Nature finished the Spaniards with a tidal wave. The Spaniards then took up residence on Margarita, fending off pirates who preyed on ships carrying treasures from the Spanish Main.

Mountainous and green, Margarita—about 40 miles long and 20 miles wide—comprises two islands joined by the narrow, 10-mile-long Isthmus of La Arestinga bordered by a large mangrove, which is protected as a national park. Porlamar, the port and tourist center, is booming with new shops, restaurants, cafes, and resorts. Elegant shops with duty-free European fashions are found along Cuatro de Mayo and Santiago Marino Avenues; the **Museum of Contemporary Art** and more shops are located between Calles Iguaidad and Zamora.

In town and elsewhere are a great variety of restaurants—seafood, Creole, Spanish, Italian, Chinese—but the highlight of any menu is the prices. Margarita is one of the Caribbean's least-expensive islands. The main beaches are east of the town, from Bella Vista to El Morro; others edge the north shores.

Porlamar has more than a dozen car-rental agencies, including Avis, Budget, Hertz, and National. Most are located at the airport, but some have offices in town and at leading hotels. Porlamar is connected to other parts of the island by good roads, which lead to another world of colonial towns, mountain vistas, quiet fishing villages, and deserted beaches.

La Asunción, 6 miles north of Porlamar, is the state capital, founded in 1565. Nestled in the Santa Lucia Valley, surrounded by green hills, its location was selected for its relative inaccessibility to pirates in olden days. Among its historic sites are the **Cathedral of Nuestra Señora de La Asunción,** built in 1568 and considered the model for churches built in Venezuela up to the nineteenth century; **Museum of Nueva Cadiz,** housed in the former government headquarters; and the seventeenth-century **Fort of Santa Rosa,** which guarded the eastern approach to the capital. It is one of three forts, underscoring the island's strategic location to the Spanish fighting off the English and others in colonial times.

Pampatar, a pretty whitewashed colonial town on the east coast, has the **Fort of San Carlos Borromeo,** dating from 1662 and restored as a museum in 1968. **Casa Amarilla,** the seat of the short-lived Republic Government during the War of Independence against Spain, has been restored as the customs house.

About 2 miles northwest of Porlamar, **El Valle del Espiritu Santo,** dating from 1529, was the first capital of Margarita. Here the **Sanctuary of the Virgin of the Valley,** long venerated by fishermen and boatmen, was consecrated by Pope John Paul II as the patron saint of the Venezuelan Navy. The Virgin's feast day, September 8, is cause for a weeklong celebration.

The 26,000-acre **La Restinga National Park,** 22 miles west of Porlamar, is one of the island's main attractions. Boats take you through the beautiful bayous, rich in plant and wildlife. You are likely to see cormorants, heron, white ibis, and an occasional scarlet ibis. Farther west, the Macanao Peninsula—the other island of Margarita beyond the isthmus—is mostly wilderness with beaches that seldom see a footprint.

Orinoco River

Some nature-oriented cruises combine visits to the Roques Archipelago with a voyage on the Orinoco, the eighth-largest river in the world. Its serpentine course flows over 12,500 miles from its Andean sources to the huge delta where thirty-seven "mouths" empty into the Atlantic. When your ship enters the delta, you see the color of the water change immediately from deep blue to muddy brown.

The most interesting cruises take passengers by Zodiacs or other small inflatable boats into the tributaries to see birds and other wildlife and to visit remote villages. About 60 miles up the river, Curaipo, a village of about 1,000 Warao Indians, has houses on stilts to protect them when the river rises 60 feet during the rainy season of July and September. The step back in time here is quite a contrast to the industrial area around Ciudad Guayana, from which passengers can take an excursion to Angel Falls.

Information

Consulate of Venezuela, 7 East 51st Street, New York, NY 10022; (212) 826-1660; fax: (212) 644-7471; www.consulate-ny-gov.ve

Venezuela Tourist Office, c/o Embassy of Venezuela, 2445 Massachusetts Avenue NW, Washington, DC 20007; (202) 797-3800; www.embavenez-us.org

The language of Venezuela is Spanish and the currency, the bolivar. US$1.00 equals about 2,145 bolivars. You need a valid driver's license to rent a car; driving is on the right side of the road. A note of caution: When you go ashore, do not take valuables with you, and at the beach, even on the most secluded beaches of Margarita, never leave your personal belongings unattended.

Colombia

Cartagena

Cartagena, about midpoint on Colombia's Caribbean coast, is both a historic monument and a modern beach resort. Founded in 1533, the city became the main port of Spain's New World empire, serving as the staging ground for conquest and plunder of the continent. It was the departure port for treasure ships laden with the gold, emeralds, and other riches that sailed with their loot to the mother country.

The Old City was protected by 7 miles of walls, 40 feet high and wide enough for cars to drive along the ramparts. Inside the walls you will discover narrow lanes with whitewashed houses and flower-filled balconies. In one place the dungeons and storerooms have been converted into an arcade of craft shops, where you can find excellent regional crafts. Among the architectural gems to visit are the **Palace of the Inquisition,** housing the **Colonial Museum,** facing Plaza Bolívar and its statue of Simón Bolívar; several churches; and the restored mansion of the Marques de Valdehoyos, where the **National Tourist Office** is located.

The sixteenth-century **Fort San Felipe,** standing guard above the Old City, is considered the best-preserved example of Spanish military architecture in the Western Hemisphere. Outside the city atop a hill called **La Popa** is the Monastery of Santa Cruz, from which you will find a grand view of Cartagena and the Caribbean.

Today Cartagena is Colombia's main Caribbean resort, with deluxe hotels in the modern beachfront stretch of Bocagrande, offering a wide range of sports and fashionable shops with resort wear, leather goods, and emeralds, for which Colombia is famous. Shore excursions usually end here. Be prepared for your tour guides to hustle you into certain shops—the ones where they get the highest commissions—and where you will stay much too long, if you are not a shopper.

Cartagena has a golf course, tennis courts, and charter boats for deep-sea fishing. Boat excursions are available to nearby Bocachica, offering beautiful beaches, snorkeling, and diving; and to Pirate's Island, one of fifty Rosairo Islands, which are protected as a nature preserve.

A note of caution: When you go ashore, do not take valuables with you, and when at the beach, never leave your personal belongings unattended.

Information

Embassy of Colombia, 2118 Leroy Place NW, Washington, DC 20008; (202) 387-8338; fax: (202) 232-8643; emwas@colombia emb.org

Colombian Consulate, 10 East 46th Street, New York, NY 10022; (212) 949-9898

Fondo de Promocion Turistica Colombia, Carrera 16a No. 78 Of. 604, Bogota, Colombia; (571) 611-4330; fax: (571) 236-3640

Panama

Panama Canal: The Vital Link

www.pancanal.com

History is replete with great endeavors but few were as bold, difficult, dangerous, and controversial—yet successful and beneficial—as the Panama Canal. An engineering triumph by any measure, the Big Ditch, as it is often called, is a 50-mile-long channel traversing Panama at the narrowest point between the Atlantic and Pacific Oceans. A vital link in international trade for 100 years, it has had a profound effect on world economic and commercial development. Annually, as many as 20,000 ships pass through it, carrying more than 200 million tons of cargo bound for destinations in the four corners of the globe.

From the time the Spanish explorer Vasco Nuñez de Balboa crossed from the Atlantic to glimpse the Pacific in 1513, the dream of a waterway through the Isthmus of Panama was born. Under Charles I of Spain, the first survey for a proposed canal was made in 1534. During the California gold rush of 1849, when the lack of a safe way across the United States by land hampered those in the eastern United States from participating in the bonanza, the search for a shortcut across Panama found new motivation. With the permission of Colombia, which controlled the isthmus area, a group of New York businessmen financed the building of a railroad, completed in 1855. It provided travel from the eastern United States to Panama by sea, crossing the Isthmus of Panama by rail and sailing up the Pacific coast to California.

Yet the idea of a waterway persisted. In 1876, Colombia gave a French financial syndicate, headed by Lt. Lucien Napoleon Bonaparte Wyse, a French army officer, permission to construct a canal. The syndicate engaged Ferdinand de Lesseps, who built the Suez Canal, for the project. De Lesseps, with little evidence to support it, said that a canal at sea level was feasible.

Despite tremendous support, enthusiasm, and feverish activity, the project was doomed from the start. For reasons of geography and topography,

engineers say, digging a canal at sea level would not have worked regardless of how much money, men, and machines de Lesseps had used. And if technical miscalculations had not been enough to defeat the French, tropical diseases were. Approximately 20,000 men died from yellow fever, malaria, and other illnesses in the two decades the French toiled. To these trials were added mismanagement and financial chicanery by no less than de Lesseps's son Charles and Gustave Eiffel, builder of the Paris tower. After US$300 million in payout, the syndicate went bankrupt in 1889.

Meanwhile, Theodore Roosevelt, a visionary who personified the American spirit of the times, wanted the United States to build a canal, which he saw as strategic for an expanding America and the link between the eastern United States and its new Pacific possessions—Hawaii and the Philippines—gained from the Spanish-American War in 1898.

After engineers studied sites in Nicaragua and Panama and a long, public debate was held, Congress approved Panama in 1902. But the battle was not over. Colombia said no and demanded more money for granting the United States permission. The Panamanians, wanting the canal and eager for independence from Colombia, had their own ideas. With French aid and U.S. encouragement, they revolted; U.S. troops prevented Colombia from moving forces to stop them.

In 1903, the United States and Panama signed a treaty allowing the United States to build the canal. The following year, the United States bought the rights, property, and equipment of the French Canal Company for $40 million. Ironically, the equipment had deteriorated so much by then that most of it was worthless.

Faced with the difficulties of removing the rock necessary to create a sea-level canal, U.S. engineers, headed by Col. George W. Goethals, an Army Corps of Engineers career officer, concluded that a lock system would be less costly and provide better control. But the first order of business was to improve health conditions and particularly to control the mosquitoes that carried yellow fever and malaria. The job was given to Col. William C.

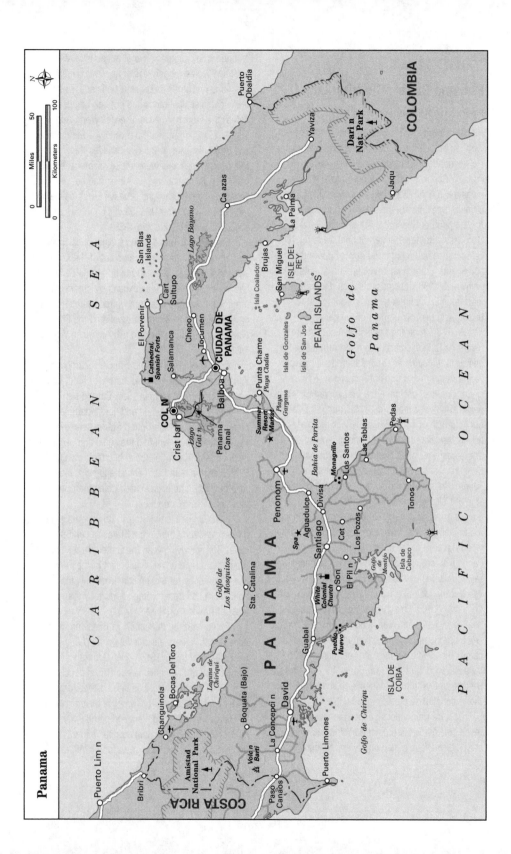

Gorgas, who set about draining swamps and installing sewer systems. By 1906 yellow fever had been brought under control and malaria reduced dramatically.

Building the canal entailed three major projects on a grand scale: cutting a channel through the Continental Divide; digging an earthen dam—the largest ever built up to that time—across the Chagres River to create Gatun Lake, which became the largest artificial lake of its time; and designing and building three sets of enormous parallel locks and gates.

Cutting the 9-mile channel through Panama's mountain spine at the Culebra Cut—later named Gaillard Cut for Col. David DuBose Gaillard, the engineer in charge—was the most difficult part and took ten years. Enormous amounts of rock and shale were removed and hauled by rail to the Pacific to fill in marshes and build a causeway. Like the French, the U.S. team was plagued by rock and mudslides caused by the area's heavy rains.

The canal opened to traffic on August 15, 1914, six months ahead of schedule and at a cost of $387 million—$23 million below estimates. In the intervening years, the United States invested more than $3 billion in the canal, 70 percent of which was recovered, but basically, the original structure is intact. Even though ships have gotten larger, the canal can still handle 90 percent of the world's oceangoing liners. By the time the canal had marked its 75th anniversary in 1989, more than 5 billion tons of goods and 700,000 ships had transited it. More current numbers reflect that more than 922,000 vessels have used the waterway since its opening.

In his *The Path Between the Seas,* the leading book on the history and construction of the Panama Canal, author David McCullough says that of its many achievements, perhaps the most remarkable is that "so vast and costly an undertaking . . . [was] done without graft, kickbacks, payroll padding [or] any of the hundred and one forms of corruption endemic to such works. . . . nor has there been even a hint of scandal . . . [or] charge of corruption in all the years that it has been in operation."

The canal's value is impossible to calculate. Just one example provides a dramatic illustration: From San Francisco, the voyage around South America is 13,000 miles and takes three weeks; via the canal, it's 4,600 miles and can be made in a week.

For Panama, it has meant jobs—more than 9,000 employees—and income, and tolls and other revenues of about $921 million a year, which, in the past, were heavily invested in maintenance and modernization.

A New Day

At the stroke of midnight on December 31, 1999, while the world ushered in the new millennium, Panama celebrated its own once-in-a-lifetime event: the transfer of the Panama Canal, along with about $4 billion worth of property, from the United States to Panama. It included the 569 square miles of real estate that came with it, transforming the barracks, hospitals, schools, airstrips, churches, houses, offices, and manicured lawns into private housing, hotels and other tourist facilities, a university, sports centers, and industrial parks.

Long before the big day, Panamanians had laid plans and committed resources—an estimated $1 billion from Panamanian and foreign investors—to develop the Canal Zone for tourism, primarily in two directions: **Colon 2000,** an umbrella project to develop the city of Colon at the western mouth of the canal into a major Caribbean deepwater port for cruise tourism, trade, and as a convention center with the makeover of the city's historical waterfront; and a similar, smaller development at the Pacific entry point. In between, they are creating a tourism infrastructure with an eye to ecotourism particularly, with preservation of the Panama Canal watershed a top priority.

Panama claims to be giving more than lip service to ecotourism. Almost one-third of Panama is under protection through its national park system, which shelters more than 10,000 species of plants, including 1,200 orchid species, and 940 types of birds. Since the canal is surrounded by pristine rain forest, alive with wildlife, such projects as the **Gamboa Rainforest Resort at the Panama Canal** (877-800-1690; 314-900; www.gamboaresort .com) seem to be ideal.

Located about midway across the Isthmus of Panama, about 25 miles from the Atlantic and

Pacific Oceans, the resort sits at the fork of the Chagres River and the Gatun Lake, in the Soberania National Park, which is part of the watershed. In addition to its facilities—145 deluxe rooms, three restaurants, pool, spa, marine, and meeting facilities—the resort has an education and research program, partly in cooperation with the Smithsonian Tropical Research Institute, which has trained the resort's guides. It has hiking trails, an observation deck over the canopy for bird-watching, fishing, and other nature-oriented activities, and offers river excursions and visits to nearby Indian villages.

Among Panama's other ambitious projects, the $60 million restoration of the Panama Railroad has enabled passengers to travel by rail from ocean to ocean. The eighty-two-acre site of the former school of the Americas, 5 miles from the Canal Free Zone, was transformed into the Melia Panama Canal (470-1100; www.solmelia.com), managed by the Spanish hotel chain, Sol Melia. The 285-room hotel has a large pool, three restaurants, and a marina.

To expand the benefits of the cruise traffic, Panamanian authorities have encouraged cruise lines to design new itineraries that begin and end in Panama as well as having some ships turn around in the Gatun Lake at midpoint. The effort has paid off, as now many cruise ships have added Panama and the Canal Zone as shore excursion destinations in their own right.

Recently, a $5.25 billion expansion project was approved to build a new lane of traffic along the Panama Canal through the construction of a third set of locks to accommodate supertankers and larger cargo ships carrying 12,000 containers each, as opposed to the 5,000 containers carried now by Panamax ships, the largest that can currently run the canal. The project will double the canal's capacity, allowing more traffic and longer, wider ships, including mega-cruise ships that are too large to transit the present canal. Some 14,000 ships use the canal annually.

On Friday, July 13, 2007, the first bid to widen the Canal was issued to a Panamanian company, Constructora Urbana SA (CUSA). The $41 million bid is to dig a 4.1-mile channel to accommodate larger ships, moving an estimated 46 million cubic feet of sediment and earth on the Pacific side of the canal. Work is to begin in 2008 and end in 2010. The entire project, controversial for its environmental impact, calls for a construction timetable for the work to be completed in 2014, with the new locks open for transit in 2015.

Shore Excursions

Samples of the excursions available to cruise passengers in the canal area follow. Your ship is also likely to have the more traditional city tours of Colón at the canal's eastern end and Panama City on the west.

Rainforest Aerial Tram: 4.5 hours, US$99 adults, $79 children. The **Gamboa Rainforest Resort at the Panama Canal** and five-star hotel is located on the Chagres River in the 55,000-acre Soberania National Park. Here in this spectacular setting an aerial tram enables you to see the forest canopy and get a bird's-eye view of the countryside. The tram rises from the forest floor and understory into the sunlit canopy to an observation tower. The Serpentarium, a butterfly house, botanical and orchid gardens, reptile exhibit, and model Embera Indian village are also visited. Were you to visit on your own, the resort charges US$43 for the aerial tram tour. The cruise-ship excursion includes transportation and perhaps another stop.

An Ecological Adventure on Gatun Lake: 5.5 hours, US$49 adults, $39 children. At Gamboa Pier, you board a 25-foot boat and travel to the cargo ships waiting to cross the canal to Cerro Balboa on Gatun Lake, where the ecological tour begins. Your guide explains the flora and fauna and its surprising importance to the canal operation. The visit continues to Monkey Island, where it is common to see monkeys and other wildlife. The last stop is the Miraflores Locks to watch the operation of the Panama Canal and see a model of the canal, with a narrated video on its building and operation. Here, too, is the visitor center with excellent exhibits.

Discover the Emberá Indian Culture: 5.5 hours, US$99 adults, $73 children. Panama's rich and diverse indigenous population accounts for about 8 percent of the total population and is composed of seven tribes. Although threatened by environmental degradation of their lands and incursions by outsiders, these tribal people have managed to preserve much of their culture. Upstream along the Chagres River, you will come into contact with the Emberá Indians.

Also called Choco Indians, the Emberá live in houses built on stilts with cone-shaped roofs made of palm leaves. They sit on the floor, sleep on straw mats, and use a stepladder to climb up to their houses. Both men and women create crafts: basket weaving and ceramics for the women; woodcraft—cooking utensils, walking sticks, ritual sculptures, and altars—for the men. Perhaps their best skill is making piraguas, or dugout canoes, from cedar or yellow pine.

El Valle Ecological Paradise: 8 hours, US$69, adult, US$54 child. The 1.5-hour drive from Panama City to El Valle on the Pan-American Highway crosses the Bridge of the Americas and passes through beautiful, lush countryside. El Valle, at the edge of an extinct volcano, is famous for its ecological environment, resplendent with flora and fauna; the town is a popular weekend escape for Panamanians. Visits are made to El Chorro Waterfall and Nispero Zoo.

Portobelo: The Pirate's Trail: 4.5 hours, US$43 adults, $31 children. Portobelo, one of the most important Spanish settlements in the New World, is an hour's scenic ride from Colón on a road bordering the Caribbean coast much of the way. An excellent harbor (visited by Christopher Columbus), Portobelo was connected by a stone highway to Panama City—both transshipment ports for riches destined for Spain—and the end of two trails that crossed the jungles of the isthmus. When enough treasure had been accumulated here, caravans of sailing ships began their voyage back to Spain, trying to avoid pirates lying in wait.

Sir Francis Drake died of fever before he could capture the port, and was buried in the bay. But other English buccaneers sacked the settlement several times, including Sir Henry Morgan in 1688. In those days, Portobelo was said to be the most heavily fortified Spanish coastal control point in the Americas. After viewing the early Spanish fortifications and customs house, you visit the Church of the Black Christ and hear its legend.

Atlantic to Pacific Railway Journey: 4.5 hours, US$149 adults, $119 children. The dome railway car, a 1938 Vintage Deluxe Observation Car recently refurbished, has full-length observation windows and booth-style seating. There are no preassigned seats, and capacity is limited. The air-conditioned car has restrooms and a bar. It shares an outside observation area with an executive train car.

Transiting the Panama Canal

Some two dozen cruise ships offer transcanal cruises regularly in the winter season, and another three dozen offer them seasonally in spring and fall when they make their way between the Caribbean and Alaska, or the West Coast and the East Coast, or en route to and from South America in winter and Europe for the summer. See the chart at the end of the book for specific ships.

The Isthmus of Panama, the neck of land connecting North and South America and traversed by the canal, lies northeast/southwest across mountainous, tropical jungle terrain. Due to the lay of the land, ships sail mostly on a north/south course, rather than east/west as might be assumed.

Ships approaching from the Caribbean enter the waterway at the Port of Cristóbal in Limón Bay; Colón, Panama's second-largest town, is to the east. Port Cristóbal is also the northern terminus of the railroad that runs alongside the canal. There may be as many as fifty ships waiting to transit, but cruise ships are given priority over cargo vessels. Normally, cruise ships complete the crossing in about eight hours, but it can take longer, depending on the number and speed of the ships ahead. Pilots from the Panama Canal Commission board all ships to guide them through the canal. The commission also provides every cruise ship with a commentator who gives a running account over the ship's public address system of the vessel's passage through the canal and of the history and operation of the canal.

From Cristóbal, your ship follows a 6.5-mile course at sea level along a 500-foot-wide channel south to the Gatun Locks, the first of three locks where your ship is lifted 85 feet in three stages to the level of Gatun Lake. As your ship inches forward on its own steam into the first and lowest of the three chambers, a tow line is tossed to a Panamanian seaman, who connects it to a messenger line from an electric 55-ton towing locomotive known as a mule, which runs on rails at the top of the lock on each side, pulling the ship into place in the chamber. Each mule can pull 70,000 pounds; the number attached to a ship is determined by the ship's size.

Above the first chamber is the control tower, where the operator controls the flow of water through huge 18-foot culverts, or tunnels, located in the center and side walls of the locks. When the pilot gives the signal, the mules begin to roll forward to position your ship into the first chamber; slowly the great doors at the stern close.

With your ship inside the huge chamber, the tower operator opens the valves and water spills out through the culverts at the rate of three million gallons a minute. It is like being on the bottom of a gigantic swimming pool, watching your ship rise as water fills the enclosure. No pumps are used to fill or empty the chambers; the system works by gravity, with water flowing from one level to another through the large culverts to smaller culverts that open to the floor of the chambers.

The huge chambers—1,000 feet long by 110 feet wide—have concrete walls from 8 to 50 feet thick and floors from 13 to 20 feet deep. Each set of locks has parallel chambers of the same size to allow passage in both directions at the same time. Each lock holds 65.8 million gallons of water; every time a ship makes a complete transit, 52 million gallons of water flow into the sea. The colossal steel doors or gates—still the originals—at the end of each chamber are 65 feet wide and 7 feet thick, and vary from 47 to 82 feet in height; the largest weighs more than 700 tons. Yet they can be opened and closed with only a 40-horsepower motor.

When the water in the first chamber reaches the level of the water in the next lock, the gates between the two open, the mules pull your ship forward, and the doors behind your ship close. Again, water fills the chamber, and your ship rises to the water level of the third and final stage. When that step is completed, your ship sails onto Gatun Lake.

Covering an area of 163.38 square miles, Gatun Lake was created by carving out an enor-

mous earthen dam across the Chagres Valley at the north end of the canal. The Chagres River flows into Gatun and Madden Lakes on the north side of Continental Divide, and together with Miraflores Lake on the south side, supplies the water to operate the locks. The lakes' water levels are controlled by dams, ensuring a constant supply.

Your ship sails under its own power for 24 miles across Gatun Lake to the Gaillard Cut through a pretty landscape of forested hills and islets (the tops of submerged hills), where you can observe some of the region's wildlife. The most frequent visitors around your ship are brown pelicans; the treetops are often heavy with vultures; and high in the sky, magnificent frigate birds glide overhead. If you are good at spotting birds, off in the forest you might see toucan and macaw; and as the ship moves closer to the Pacific, you might begin to see boobies.

You will also be able to watch ships transiting the canal from the other direction; most will be cargo vessels, but occasionally, a small private yacht or another cruise ship will pass, too. Expect a shower or two; depending on the time of year, the air can be balmy and pleasant or steamy. This is, after all, the middle of the jungle, even if it appears mechanized and manicured.

Some cruise ships on one-week Caribbean cruises go only as far as Gatun Lake, where they turn around and depart through the Gatun Locks back to the Atlantic side.

At about the midpoint of the canal, your ship leaves Gatun Lake and sails into the Gaillard Cut. This V-shaped channel, cut from granite and volcanic rock, is the narrowest stretch of the canal and was the most difficult to build. More than 230 million cubic yards of earth and rock were excavated from the 9-mile stretch to make it navigable. Originally, the channel was 300 feet wide; later, it was widened to 500 feet, and there is discussion about widening it farther. It has a depth of 42 feet. The sides have been stabilized, they are monitored constantly, and dredging never stops. About halfway along the cut on the west side, a bronze plaque honors the builders of the canal and the workers who died.

The cut ends at the entrance to the first of two sets of locks: Pedro Miguel Locks with only one step of 31 feet, followed by the Miraflores Lake and the Miraflores Locks, which drop 54 feet in two steps. Here, the process is reversed. Your ship will enter a chamber full of water, and as the water is drained out, your ship is lowered to the next level, and finally to the level of the Pacific. At the exit of the final lock is the Port of Balboa and, off in the distance to the south, Panama City. Directly in front is the lofty Bridge of the Americas, the bridge connecting the two sides of the waterway and part of the Interamerican Highway between North and South America.

Trivia buffs may like to know that for years the largest cruise ship to pass through the canal was Cunard's *QE2,* which is 963 feet long with a beam of 105 feet—just 5 feet short of the locks' 110-foot width. However, most of the new large ships, which have been built to the specifications that allow them to transit the canal and are referred to as Panamax ships, are a fraction longer and/or wider than the *QE2.* For example, Norwegian Cruise Line's *Norwegian Star* is 971 feet in length with a 107-foot beam; and Celebrity Cruise's Millennium Class ships are 965 feet long and have a 105.6-foot beam. The amount these ships pay has increased as well, normally up to $300,000 and more, but the least is still the 36 cents paid by Richard Halliburton to swim the canal in 1928.

The Panama Canal Operation

The Panama Canal operation is the model of efficiency. It operates 24 hours a day, 365 days a year, with as many as forty ships passing through daily. For most ships, the average Canal Waters Time—the total time spent at the Panama Canal, including waiting time and in-transit time—is just less than twenty-four hours. A reservation system is available to provide a guaranteed priority transit upon request.

Its ability to work at peak efficiency is attributed to its skilled technicians and year-round maintenance, which accounts for about one-quarter of the canal's annual operating budget, or about $221 million. These include annual major overhauls of the lock gates, culverts, and valves; towing locomotives, which are reconditioned at a repair facility designed especially for them, and tow track; and continuous dredging of the 50-mile channel and anchorages.

Miraflores Visitors Center Located on the east side of the Miraflores Locks, the center enables visitors to watch vessels transiting the canal from a very short distance and learn about the canal's operation, history of its construction, and the watershed and its vital role in world trade. The center has a theater, observation terraces, snack bar, restaurant, gift shop, and four exhibition halls. The exhibitions include historic pieces, interactive modules, video presentations, models of the canal, and objects used in its operations.

The *History Hall* provides the background, explains the technical innovations integral to the canal's construction, and honors the hundreds of men and women who made it possible.

The *Hall of Water* emphasizes the importance of water; the protection of the canal watershed, the environment, and biodiversity; and Canal Authority's commitment to managing this resource and the surrounding region.

The *Canal in Action* is an amusing depiction of the canal operation. Viewers go inside a simulator and one of the lock culverts to view a virtual ocean-to-ocean transit. It also features the canal's ongoing improvements, modernization, and maintenance projects.

The *Canal in the World* focuses on the canal's importance to world trade; the routes it serves; its users, the types of vessels that transit, and the commodities they carry. It also gives an overview of studies conducted to guarantee the canal's future competitiveness and benefits to Panama.

Center hours: 9:00 a.m. to 5:00 p.m. daily; restaurant open noon to 11:00 p.m. Admission for nonresidents: $8 adults, $5 children age five to seventeen, younger than age five admitted free. Information: (507) 276-8325; fax: (507) 276-8469; cvm@pancanal.com.

The San Blas Islands

Of all the exotic destinations cruise ships visit in the Western Caribbean, none is more unusual than the San Blas Islands off the northeast Caribbean coast of Panama. An archipelago of low-lying islands, upon approach their thatched-roof dwellings shaded by crowds of palm trees look more like the islands of the South Seas than the Caribbean.

These islands are the home of the Kuna Indians, the only tribe of island dwellers in the Caribbean who have both survived and been able to maintain their ancient folkways more or less intact despite 500 years of contact with Europeans and other alien cultures.

The San Blas Islands comprise about 400 islets plus a strip of land on the Panamanian coast, over which the Kuna claim sovereignty and maintain self-rule. There are forty-eight Kuna villages with a total population of about 40,000, represented in a tribal council. The people move between the islands in dugout canoes, little changed from those of their ancestors. Their main crop is coconut, which they use as currency. Despite their isolation on these islands, they are unusually worldly and have accepted certain innovations, such as communications and education, while retaining their traditional way of life.

Normally, your first glimpse of the Kuna will be from your cruise ship, where as many as ten boats, full of Kuna women, will be doing a brisk business selling their colorful, unique molas for which they are famous. Do not think these are the last of their stock.

When you go ashore to visit a Kuna village, you will see the molas displayed on clotheslines strung the entire length of the village. Some are squares that can be made into pillow covers or framed; others appear on shirts and dresses. All are remarkably inexpensive, ranging from US$10 to $40 or more depending on the intricacy of the design. There is no need to try bargaining; these women may not be able to speak your language, but they understand money.

Molas represent a Kuna woman's wealth, like a dowry. They are elaborate reverse-applique in bold, bright colors, incorporating stylized flowers, animals, birds, and supernatural motifs, and were made originally for the front and back panels of the blouse that the petite Kuna women wear. Occasionally you will see a mola that incorporates current events, such as the U.S. landing of troops in Panama, which crept into designs in 1990. To a newcomer, molas may all seem alike, but upon closer examination, the fineness of the stitches and sophistication of the motifs are the telling signs of a master craftswoman.

Kuna women also wear beaded bracelets drawn tightly on their arms and legs, gold nose rings, and layers of gold around their necks. They are a colorful bunch, irresistible to photographers. Most are happy for you to take their picture, often posing with a bright green parakeet, monkey, or iguana, but you must pay them—25 cents per click.

The villagers are friendly, although rather stone-faced unless you take the time to admire someone's beautiful child—a gesture that usually draws a broad smile from the young mother. Their straight hair is jet black and their facial features are similar to those of other Indian tribes of South America's Caribbean coast, whose common ancestors were the Arawaks once populating all the islands of the Caribbean.

More and more, the San Blas Islands are being included on transcanal itineraries, particularly the westbound ones sailing from the Caribbean to the Panama Canal. See the chart at the end of the book for specific ships.

Information

www.visitpanama.com
www.ipat.gob.pa
Instituto Panameno de Turismo, Apartado No. 4421, Panama City 5, Republic de Panama; (800) 231-0568; (011) 507-226-7000; fax: (011) 507-226-5043.

Chart of Cruise Ships Sailing the Caribbean

Chart of Cruise Ships Sailing the Caribbean

Every effort has been made to ensure the accuracy of the information regarding the ships' ports of call and prices, but keep in mind that cruise lines often change itineraries for a variety of reasons. Before you make plans, you should obtain the most current information from your cruise line, its Web site, or your travel agent.

Prices are for "cruise only" unless indicated otherwise and are based on per-person, double-occupancy rates, ranging from the least expensive cabin in low season to the best cabin in high season. Prices include port charges unless noted otherwise, and they are full-rate brochure prices. However, almost all cruise brochures now include early-bird saving prices, which are often discounted 50 percent and more. Holiday, special, or positioning cruises are not included.

Cruise Line/Ships	Ports of Call	Price Range	Duration/Season
American Canadian Caribbean Line			
Grande Mariner	Bahamas/Turks & Caicos from Providenciales to Nassau via Mayaguana Island, Long Island, Acklins Island, Exuma Cays, Staniel Cay, Norman's Cay.	$2,970–$3,795	11 days/winter
	Caribbean from St. Thomas to St. John, Tortola, Salt Island. Or St. Maarten to Antigua via Marigot, Saba. St. Kitts, Nevis.		
	Bahamas round trip from Nassau to Spanish Wells, Eleuthera, Harbour Island, Governor's Harbour, Exuma Cays, Staniel Cay, Warderick Wells Cay.		
Carnival Cruise Lines			
Carnival Conquest	Western Caribbean round trip from Galveston to Montego Bay, Grand Cayman, Cozumel.	$1,669–$2,619	7 days/year-round
Carnival Destiny	Southern Caribbean round trip from San Juan to St. Thomas, Dominica, Barbados, St. Kitts, La Romana (overnight).	$1,669–$2,619	7 days/to April
	Round trip from San Juan to St. Kitts, Antigua, St. Lucia, Barbados, Dominica, St. Thomas.		From March 2, 2008

Cruise Line/Ships	Ports of Call	Price Range	Duration/Season
Carnival Cruise Lines *(continued)*			
Carnival Dream (debuts 2009)	tba		
Carnival Freedom	Alternating Eastern/Western Caribbean round trip from Miami to San Juan, St. Thomas, St. Maarten; or Cozumel, Grand Cayman, Ocho Rios, 3 days at sea; or Half Moon Cay, St. Thomas, San Juan, Grand Turk.	$1,419–$2,869	7 nights/to April 2008
	Western Caribbean round trip from Fort Lauderdale to Key West, Grand Cayman, Ocho Rios. Alternating Western/ Eastern Caribbean round trip from Fort Lauderdale; or to Costa Maya, Limón, Colón or San Juan, St. Thomas, Antigua, Tortola, Nassau.		6 days/November 2008– April 2009; or 8 days
Carnival Glory	Port Canaveral to Nassau, St. Thomas/St. John, St. Maarten; or Cozumel, Belize City, Costa Maya, Nassau.	$1,669–$2,619	7 days/year-round
Carnival Legend	Western Caribbean round trip from Tampa to Grand Cayman, Cozumel, Belize; Costa Maya with 2 days at sea.	$1,669–$2,619	7 days/year-round
Carnival Liberty	Alternating Western/Eastern Caribbean round trip from Fort Lauderdale to Costa Maya, Puerto Limón, Colón, or San Juan, St. Thomas/ St. John, Antigua, Tortola/Virgin Gorda, Nassau; or Freeport, Grand Cayman, and Cozumel; or Freeport, Key West or Nassau, Grand Cayman and Costa Maya or Ocho Rios.	$1,419–$2,869	6, 8 days/winter to May 2008
	Eastern Caribbean round trip from Miami to Half Moon Cay, St. Thomas, San Juan, Grand Turk.		7 days/May–October
	Alternating Eastern/Western Caribbean round trip from Miami to San Juan, St. Thomas, St. Maarten; or Cozumel, Grand Cayman, Ocho Rios.		7 days/June 2008– May 2009
Carnival Miracle	Alternating Southern/Western Caribbean round trip from Fort Lauderdale to St. Maarten, St. Lucia, St. Kitts or Colón, Limón, Belize.	$1,819–$2,869	8 days/to Feb 2009
	Eastern Caribbean round trip from New York to San Juan, St. Thomas, Tortola with 4 days at sea.		8 days/June, August– October 2008
Carnival Splendor (debuts 2008)	Eastern Caribbean from Fort Lauderdale to San Juan, St. Thomas, Casa de Campo/ La Romana.	$1,819–$2,819	7-day/November 22, 2008–February 2009
Carnival Triumph	Alternating Eastern/Western Caribbean round trip from Miami to Half Moon Cay, St. Thomas, San Juan, Nassau or Grand Turk; or Cozumel, Grand Cayman, Ocho Rios.	$1,669–$2,619	7 days/to April 2008
Carnival Valor	Alternating Eastern/Western Caribbean round trip from Miami to Nassau, St. Thomas, St. Maarten; or Grand Cayman, Belize City, Roatan, Costa Maya.	$1,669–$2,619	7 days/year-round

Cruise Line/Ships	Ports of Call	Price Range	Duration/Season
Carnival Cruise Lines *(continued)*			
Carnival Victory	Alternating Eastern and Western Caribbean round trip from Miami to San Juan, St. Maarten and St. Thomas, or Costa Maya, Grand Cayman, Ocho Rios.	$1,669–$2,619	7 days/winter
	Bahamas round trip from Charleston to Nassau and Freeport or round-trip from Norfolk.		5 days/May, June, October
	Southern Caribbean from San Juan to La Romana/Casa de Campo, St. Kitts, Barbados, Dominica, St. Thomas.		7-day year-round from November 2, 2008
Celebration (leaves Carnival fleet April 2008)	Jacksonville (FL) to Freeport, Nassau (4 days); or Key West, Nassau (5 days).	$849–$1,749	4, 5 days/year-round
Carnival Ecstasy	Galveston (TX) to Cozumel (4 days); or Cozumel, Calica/Playa del Carmen (5 days).	$849–$1,549	4, 5 days/year-round
Carnival Fantasy	Western Caribbean round trip from New Orleans, 4 days, alternate Thursdays to Cozumel; 5 days, alternate Mondays and Saturdays to Costa Maya and Cozumel.	$849–$1,549	4, 5 days/year-round
Fascination	Miami to Nassau (3 days); or to Key West, Calica/Playa del Carmen or Cozumel (4 days).	$699–$1,279	3, 4 days/year-round
Holiday	Western Caribbean round trip from Mobile alternate Thursdays to Cozumel (4 days); or alternate Mondays to Cozumel, Calica/Playa del Carmen or alternate Saturdays to Cozumel, Costa Maya (5 days).	$849–$1,749	4, 5 days/year-round
Carnival Imagination	Miami to Key West, Calica/Playa del Carmen (4 days); or Grand Cayman and Ocho Rios (5 days).	$849–$1,549	4, 5 days/year-round
Carnival Inspiration	Tampa to Cozumel (4 days); or to Grand Cayman, Cozumel or Calica (5 days).	$849–$1,549	4, 5 days/year-round
Carnival Sensation	Bahamas round trip from Port Canaveral, Thursdays to Nassau (3 days); Sundays to Freeport and Nassau (4 days).	$699–$1,279	3, 4 days/year-round
Celebrity Cruises			
Azamara Quest	Eastern Caribbean round trip from Miami to Virgin Gorda, Dominica, St. Vincent, Tobago, St. Barts, St. John, USVI, Ponce, Samaná, Dominican Republic; Grand Turk, Turks and Caicos. Or Mayaguez and Ponce, Puerto Rico; St. John, Antigua, Dominica, Guadeloupe, St. Barts, Samaná, Grand Turk.	$2,129–$6,049	14 days/winter
Celebrity Century	Western Caribbean round trip from Miami to Key West, Cozumel or Cozumel, Grand Cayman; or Grand Cayman; Key West.	$389–$2,849	4, 5 days/winter
	Bahamas round trip from Miami to Nassau.		2 days/January 2008

Cruise Line/Ships	Ports of Call	Price Range	Duration/Season
Celebrity Cruises	*(continued)*		
Celebrity Constellation	Eastern/Western Caribbean round trip from Fort Lauderdale to St. Thomas; St. Kitts; Barbados; St. Lucia; St. Maarten; or Grand Cayman, Aruba; Cristobál/Panama; Cartagena, Cozumel.	$1,149–$5,149	10, 11 days/winter
Celebrity Galaxy	Southern Caribbean round trip from San Juan, to Tortola, St. Maarten, St. Lucia, Barbados, Margarita Island, Curaçao, Aruba (10 days) or Dominica, St. Kitts instead of St. Maarten (11 days); or Aruba, Curacao, Grenada, Barbados, Dominica, St. Kitts, Tortola.	$769–$3,199	10, 11 days/winter
Celebrity Infinity	Between Fort Lauderdale and San Francisco via Montego Bay, Cartagena, Panama Canal, Puntarenas, Costa Rica; Huatulco, Mexico; Acapulco, Cabo San Lucas.	$1,549–$4,299	15 days/spring/fall
Celebrity Millennium	Eastern Caribbean round trip from Fort Lauderdale to San Juan, St. Thomas, Casa de Campo, Dominican Republic; Labadee, Haiti.	$699–$3,949	7 days/winter
Celebrity Summit	Southern Caribbean round trip from San Juan to St. Maarten, Dominica, Grenada, Bonaire, Aruba.	$669–$3,299	7 days/winter
Costa Cruises			
Costa Fortuna	Alternating Western/Eastern Caribbean round trip from Fort Lauderdale to Cozumel, Grand Cayman, Ocho Rios (or Montego Bay), Grand Turk. Or to San Juan, St. Maarten, Tortola, Nassau or San Juan, St. Thomas, Catalina Island/La Romana, Nassau.	$999–$2,799	7 days/winter
Costa Mediterranea	Alternating Eastern/Western Caribbean round trip from Fort Lauderdale to San Juan, St. Thomas, La Romana, Grand Turk, or Key West, Grand Cayman, Roatan, Cozumel.	$1,049–$2,999	7 days/winter
Crystal Cruises			
Crystal Serenity	Caribbean/Panama Canal from Miami to Costa Rica via Grand Turk, Tortola, St. Barts, Aruba, Panama Canal; reverse. Or round trip from Miami to Tortola, St. Maarten, St. Barts, Antigua, St. Lucia, Barbados, Curaçao, Aruba.	$7,090–$51,915	11, 14 days/December
Crystal Symphony	Caribbean/Panama Canal from Miami to Costa Rica via St. Thomas, St. Maarten, Antigua, Aruba, Panama Canal; reverse.	$5,195–$28,585	11, 13, 16 days/ December–January
	From Miami to Los Angeles via Cozumel, Panama Canal, Acapulco, Cabo San Lucas; or from Los Angeles to Miami via Cabo San Lucas, Costa Rica, Panama Canal, Aruba, St. Kitts, San Juan.		

Cruise Line/Ships	Ports of Call	Price Range	Duration/Season
Cunard			
QM2	Panama & Caribbean round trip from New York to Limón, Cristobál, Curaçao, Bonaire, St. Lucia, St. Thomas.	$1,289–$30,119	4 days/February–March
	Caribbean between New York and Fort Lauderdale via St. Kitts, Grenada, Bonaire. Or round trip from Fort Lauderdale to Curaçao, Grenada, Barbados, St. Lucia, St. Kitts, St. Thomas. Or to Panama, Bonaire, Grenada, Barbados, St. Lucia, Dominica, St. Kitts, Tortola.		8, 10, 14 nights/ November–December 2008–2009
Disney Cruise Line			
Disney Magic	Alternating Eastern/Western Caribbean round trip from Port Canaveral to St. Thomas, Castaway Cay or Key West, Grand Cayman, Cozumel, Castaway Cay.	$849–$6,199	7 days/year-round
	Bahamas round trip from Port Canaveral to Nassau with 2 days at Castaway Cay.		5 days/September
	Round trip from Port Canaveral to Costa Maya with 2 days at Castaway Cay.		7 days/September– December
Disney Wonder	Port Canaveral to Nassau, Castaway Cay (3 days) plus a day at sea (4 days).	$429–$3,999	3, 4 days/year-round
	Cruise can be combined with Disney World packages for a 7-night vacation.		
Holland America Line			
Eurodam	Eastern/Southern Caribbean round trip from Fort Lauderdale to Nassau, Half Moon Cay; or Grand Turk, Tortola; or Puerto Rico, St. Thomas, Half Moon Cay; or Half Moon Cay, Aruba, Curacao.	$499–$4,799	3, 7 days, winter
Maasdam	Eastern/Southern Caribbean round trip from Fort Lauderdale to St. Maarten, St. Lucia, Barbados, Martinique, Tortola or Half Moon Cay, St. Thomas, Dominica, Curacao, Aruba.	$1,789–$14,764	10, 15 days/winter & fall
	Or Fort Lauderdale to San Diego via Half Moon Cay, Cartagena, Panama Canal, Golfo Dulce, Puntarenas, Puerto Chiapas, Santa Cruz Huatulco, Acapulco, Cabo San Lucas. Reverse via Cabo San Lucas, Mazatlan, Puerto Vallarta, Puerto Quetzal, San Juan del Sur, Panama Canal, Cartagena, Nassau.		
Noordam	New York to Grand Turk, Tortola, St. Maarten, St. Thomas, San Juan.	$999–$5,999	10, 11 days/winter & fall through March 2008

| --- | --- | --- | --- |

Holland America Line *(continued)*

Cruise Line/Ships	Ports of Call	Price Range	Duration/Season
Prinsendam	Caribbean/Amazon round trip from Fort Lauderdale to Grand Turk, Aruba, Bonaire, Grenada, Devil's Island, Amazon River, Santarem, Boca de Valeria, Manaus, Parintins, Alter do Chao, Barbados, Dominica, St. Thomas, Half Moon Cay.	$4,199–$31,999	26 days/November
Statendam	Southern Caribbean round trip from Fort Lauderdale to Half Moon Cay, St. Thomas, St. John's. St. Lucia, Barbados, Trinidad, El Guamache, Curacao, Aruba, Grand Turk. Or round trip from Tampa to Key West, Belize City, Santo Tomas de Castilla, Costa Maya.	$1,879–$11,199	14 days/December
Veendam	Caribbean round trip from Tampa to Half Moon Cay, St. Thomas, Dominica, Barbados, Grenada, El Guamache, Bonaire, Aruba. Or to Costa Maya, Montego Bay, Grand Cayman.	$649–$31,396	14, 7 days/winter & fall
	From Tampa to San Diego, or Vancouver via Grand Cayman, Cartagena, Panama Canal, Golfo Dulce, San Juan del Sur, Puerto Chiapas, Santa Cruz Huatulco, Acapulco, Cabo San Lucas.		15–19 days/April
	Panama/Amazon/Caribbean from Vancouver or San Diego to Tampa via Victoria, San Diego, Cabo San Lucas, Acapulco, Santa Cruz Huatulco, Puerto Chiapas, Puerto Caldera, Panama Canal, Aruba, Grenada, Santarem, Boca de Valeria, Amazon River, Barbados, Grand Turk, Half Moon Cay.		32, 36 days/ September–October
Volendam	Caribbean/Panama round trip from Fort Lauderdale to Half Moon Cay, Aruba, Curaçao, Panama Canal, Limón Bay, Manzanillo Bay, Puerto Limón; or reverse.	$1,199–$13,349	10 days/winter to April 2008
Westerdam	Eastern Caribbean round trip from Fort Lauderdale to Grand Turk, San Juan, St. Thomas, Half Moon Cay.	$499–$4,959	7 days/winter & fall
	Or alternating Eastern/Western Caribbean round trip from Fort Lauderdale to Half Moon Cay, Grand Turk, Grand Cayman, Costa Maya or Grand Turk, St. Maarten, Tortola, Half Moon Cay.		
	Eastern Caribbean from Fort Lauderdale to Nassau and Half Moon Cay.		3 days/April & October
Zuiderdam	Eastern Caribbean round trip from Fort Lauderdale to Grand Turk, Tortola, Half Moon Cay, or San Juan, St. Thomas, Half Moon Cay.	$649–$4,959	7 days/winter & fall
	Caribbean/Panama round trip from Fort Lauderdale to Half Moon Cay, Aruba, Curaçao, Panama Canal, Limón Bay, Manzanillo Bay, Puerto Limón; or reverse.		From November 2008

Cruise Line/Ships	Ports of Call	Price Range	Duration/Season
MSC Cruises			
MSC Lirica	Fort Lauderdale to San Juan, St. Maarten, St. Lucia, Antigua, Tortola, and Cayo Levantado (Dominican Republic); or to Cozumel, Puerto Limón, Cristobál, Cartagena, Cayo Levantado.	$699–$3,500	10 days/winter
MSC Orchestra	Alternating Eastern and Western Caribbean round trip from Fort Lauderdale. Itineraries tba.	From $499	7 days/winter 2009
Norwegian Cruise Line			
Norwegian Dawn	Eastern Caribbean round trip from Miami to Samaná (Dominica Republic), Tortola, St. Thomas, Great Stirrup Cay.	$449–$2,099	7 days/winter
Norwegian Gem	Southern Caribbean round trip from New York via St. Thomas, Antigua, Barbados, St. Maarten and Tortola; 11 nights add Grenada and Dominica, instead of St. Maarten.	$1,099–$2,999	10, 11 days/ January–February
	Bahamas round trip from New York via Grand Bahama, Nassau, Great Stirrup Cay, Port Canaveral.		7 days/February–April and December; January-April 2009
Norwegian Jade	Miami to the Bahamas via Grand Bahama Island.	t.b.a.	December
Norwegian Jewel	Alternating Southern Caribbean round trip from Miami to Samaná, Tortola, Antigua, Barbados and St. Lucia.	$299–$3,999	9 days/winter
	Western Caribbean round trip from Miami to Cozumel and Grand Cayman.		5 days/winter 9 and 5 day itineraries can be combined into 14 day cruise
Norwegian Majesty	Charleston (SC) to Grand Cayman, Cozumel, and Key West.	$429–$2,849	7 days/winter
Norwegian Pearl	Alternating Southern/Western Caribbean round trip from Miami via Samaná, Tortola, Antigua, Barbados, and St. Lucia. Or 5 nights, via Cozumel and Grand Cayman.	$329–$2,779	9, 5, 14 days/winter
	Or 9-day and 5-day can be combined into 14-night round trip from Miami.		
Norwegian Spirit	Western Caribbean round trip from New Orleans to Roatan (January to March sailings) or, to Costa Maya (November to December sailings), Santo Tomás de Castilla (Guatemala), Belize, Cozumel.	$499–$4,399	7 days/winter
Norwegian Sun	Western Caribbean round trip from Miami to Roatan, Belize City, Cozumel, Great Stirrup Cay.	$399–$1,899	7 days/winter

Cruise Line/Ships	Ports of Call	Price Range	Duration/Season
Oceania Cruises			
Regatta	Eastern Caribbean round trip from Miami to Virgin Gorda, St. Barts, Dominica, St. Lucia, Antigua, Tortola, Samaná, Grand Turk and reverse.	$2,998–$16,598	10–12 days/winter
	Or Western Caribbean/Panama from Miami to Los Angeles via Playa del Carmen, Cozumel, San Andres, Panama Canal, Puntarenas, Puerto Quetzal, Acapulco, Cabo San Lucas.		
	Or Western Caribbean/Central America round trip from Miami to Playa del Carmen, Cozumel, Belize, Santo Tomas, Roatan, Puerto Limón, Colón, Cartagena, Grand Cayman.		16, 14 days/winter
Princess Cruises			
Caribbean Princess	Fort Lauderdale to St. Thomas, St. Maarten, Princess Cays.	$799–$4,349	7 days/winter
	Eastern Caribbean round trip from New York to Grand Turk, San Juan, St. Thomas, Bermuda (West End) and reverse.		
	Bermuda/Eastern Caribbean between New York and San Juan to St. Kitts, Antigua, St. Thomas.		May–August
	Southern Caribbean between Barbados, St. Lucia, Antigua, Tortola and St. Thomas; or Aruba, Bonaire, Grenada, Dominica and St Thomas.		7 days/October November 2008– May 2009
Coral Princess	Panama Canal round trip from Fort Lauderdale to Aruba, Cartagena, Panama Canal to Gatun Lake, Cristobál, Costa Rica, Ocho Rios or Montego Bay.	$1,199–$3,624	10 days/winter
	Eastern Caribbean round-trip from Fort Lauderdale to Princess Cays, St. Maarten, St. Thomas, Grand Turk.	$599–$4,349	7 days, October 2008– May 2009
Crown Princess	Southern Caribbean round trip from San Juan to Barbados, St. Lucia, Antigua, Tortola, St. Thomas. Or to St. Kitts, Grenada, Bonaire, Aruba; or San Juan, Tortola, St. Thomas, Antigua, St. Lucia, Barbados.	$599–$3,249	7 days/summer
Emerald Princess	Alternating Southern/Eastern Caribbean round trip from Fort Lauderdale to Aruba, Bonaire, Grenada, Dominica, St. Thomas, Princess Cays.	$899–$4,149	10 days/winter
	Or round trip from Fort Lauderdale to Princess Cays, St. Thomas, St. Kitts, Barbados, St. Lucia, Antigua, or reverse.		
	Or, Princess Cays, St. Thomas, Dominica, Grenada, Bonaire, and Aruba; or Antigua, St. Lucia, Barbados, St. Kitts, St. Thomas, and Princess Cays.		October 2008– May 2009

Cruise Line/Ships	Ports of Call	Price Range	Duration/Season
Princess Cruises	*(continued)*		
Grand Princess	Western Caribbean round trip from Fort Lauderdale to Ocho Rios, Grand Cayman, Cozumel, and Princess Cays.	$599–$4,349	7 days/winter
	Aruba, Curaçao, Trinidad, Barbados, St. Vincent, St. Kitts, St. Thomas, La Romana, and Grand Turk.		14 days, December 2008–April 2009
Island Princess	Panama Canal between Los Angeles and Fort Lauderdale via Huatulco, Puerto Quetzal, Puerto Corinto, Costa Rica, Panama Canal, Cartagena, Aruba, Ocho Rios. Or Fort Lauderdale and Acapulco to Ocho Rios, Panama Canal, Fuerte Amador, Costa Rica, San Juan del Sur, Puerto Quetzal, Huatulco; reverse adds Puerto Corinto, Cartagena, Aruba.	$1,199–$4,824	15 days/winter
	Panama Canal between Acapulco and San Juan to Huatulco, Puerto Quetzal, Puerto Corinto, Costa Rica, Panama Canal, Cartagena, Aruba; reverse adds Curaçao, San Juan del Sur.		10–11 days/winter
Royal Princess	Caribbean/Amazon River between Fort Lauderdale and Manaus to St. Barts, St. Lucia, Tobago, Devil's Island, Amazon River ports of Santarem, Boca da Valeria, Parintins, and Manaus; and reverse.	$2,049–$6,449	14 days/winter
Ruby Princess	Western Caribbean round-trip from Fort Lauderdale to Ocho Rios, Grand Cayman, Cozumel, Princess Cays.	$599–$4,349	7 days, November 2008–May 2009
Sea Princess	Alternating Eastern Caribbean round trip from Barbados to St. Lucia, Antigua, St. Maarten, St. Thomas, Grand Turk, Montego Bay, Grand Cayman, Aruba, Bonaire, Caracas, Grenada.	$1,399–$4,999	14 days/winter
	Or from Montego Bay to Curaçao, Bonaire, Isla Margarita, Trinidad, Barbados, Antigua, St. Maarten, St. Thomas, Grand Turk.		
	Transatlantic between Montego Bay or Barbados and Southampton via Grand Cayman, Bonaire, Caracas, Grenada, Barbados, St. Vincent, St. Lucia, St. Maarten, St. Thomas, Antigua, Azores.		7–14 days/April
	Or from Barbados to Dominica, Antigua, St. Maarten, Tortola, Samana, Montego Bay, Curaçao, Bonaire, Isla Margarita, Grenada, Trinidad, or, St. Lucia, Antigua, St. Kitts, Tortola, Samana, Montego Bay, Grand Cayman, Aruba, Bonaire, Caracas (La Guaira), and Grenada.		14 days, October 2008– April 2009

Cruise Line/Ships	Ports of Call	Price Range	Duration/Season

Regent Seven Seas Cruises

Port and handling charges are additional. Cruise-only fares include gratuities, wine with lunch and dinner, soft drinks and juice throughout the cruise, in-cabin bar setup.

Seven Seas Mariner	Caribbean round trip from Fort Lauderdale.	$5,795–$27,295 + port charges	7–12 days/May
Seven Seas Navigator	Caribbean/Mexico round trip from Fort Lauderdale on varying itineraries.	$4,995–$28,295 + port charge	7–14 days/winter
Seven Seas Voyager	Caribbean round trip from Fort Lauderdale to Aruba, Curaçao, St. Kitts, and St. Lucia.	$4,995–$23,295 + port charges	7–11 days/ December 2008–January 2009

Royal Caribbean Cruise Line

Adventure of the Seas	San Juan to Aruba, Curaçao, St. Maarten, and St. Thomas. April–October alternate to St. Maarten, Antigua, St. Lucia, Barbados.	$599–$3,699	7 days/year-round
Brilliance of the Seas	Western Caribbean round trip from Miami to Curacáo, Aruba, Ocho Rios, Labadee.		
	Southern Caribbean/Panama Canal round trip from Miami to Aruba, Panama Canal, Cristobál, Puerto Limón, Grand Cayman (10 nights); or Labadee, Aruba, Curaçao, Panama Canal, Cristobál, Puerto Limón (11 nights); or add Grand Cayman.	$1,099–$3,299	10, 11 days/winter
Empress of the Seas (leaves fleet after March 7 sailing)	San Juan to St. Maarten, St. Barts, St. Kitts, Antigua. St. Lucia, Barbados, Isla Margarita, Curaçao, Aruba (11 nights); to St. Maarten, St. Lucia, Barbados, Isla Margarita, Curacáo, Aruba (9 nights); or St. Thomas, St. Maarten (3 nights); or St. Kitts, St. Maarten (3 nights).	$368–$1,799	3, 11 days/winter to March 2008
Enchantment of the Seas	Western Caribbean round trip from Fort Lauderdale alternating Thursdays to Key West, Cozumel; Mondays to Belize City, Cozumel, Key West; Saturdays to Grand Cayman, Costa Maya. Or Thursdays to Coco Cay, Key West.	$249–$1,309	4–5 days/year-round
	To Grand Cayman, Costa Maya, Cozumel, Coco Cay.		7 days/April
Explorer of the Seas	Southern Caribbean round trip from Cape Liberty to St. Maarten, Antigua, Dominica, Barbados, St. Kitts, St. Thomas, San Juan.	$799–$2,799	7 days/winter
	Bermuda round trip from Cape Liberty to Kings Wharf, Bermuda.		
	Or Eastern Caribbean to Labadee, Casa De Campo, St. Thomas; San Juan.		
	Or Bermuda/Caribbean round trip from Cape Liberty to Kings Wharf, St. Maarten; St. Thomas; San Juan.		9 days

Cruise Line/Ships	Ports of Call	Price Range	Duration/Season
Royal Caribbean Cruise Line *(continued)*			
Freedom of the Seas	Western/Eastern Caribbean round trip from Miami to Labadee, Ocho Rios, Grand Cayman, Cozumel. Or to San Juan, St. Thomas, St. Maarten.	$699–$3,599	7 days/year-round
Grandeur of the Seas	Western Caribbean round trip from Tampa to Grand Cayman, Progresso, Belize, Cozumel.	$599–$2,049	7 days/winter
	Bermuda, Caribbean, and Canada/New England from Norfolk, Virginia and Baltimore, MD.		5, 7, 9 days/summer
Independence of the Seas	Eastern/Western Caribbean round trip from Fort Lauderdale to San Juan, St. Thomas, St. Maarten, Labadee, or Belize, Costa Maya, Cozumel.	$549–$2,299	Winter 2008–2009
Jewel of the Seas	Eastern/Western Caribbean from Fort Lauderdale to San Juan, St. Maarten, St. Thomas, Tortola, Nassau or Key West, Cozumel, Playa del Carmen, Belize.	$549–$2,299	8, 6, days/winter
Legend of the Seas	Southern Caribbean round trip from Santo Domingo to St. Kitts, Guadeloupe, Martinique, Barbados, St. Lucia. Or St. Maarten, Dominica, Grenada, Margarita Island, Aruba.	$649–$5,299	7 days/winter
Liberty of the Seas	Western/Eastern Caribbean round trip from Miami to Labadee, Montego Bay, Grand Cayman, Cozumel. Or to San Juan, St. Maarten, Labadee.	$649–$3,699	7 days/winter
Majesty of the Seas	Miami to Nassau, Coco Cay (3 days) plus Key West (4 days).	Starting at $279	3, 4 days/year-round
Mariner of the Seas	Eastern/Western Caribbean round trip from Port Canaveral to Coco Cay, St. Thomas, St. Maarten; or to Labadee, Ocho Rios, Grand Cayman, Cozumel.	$599–$2,249	7 days/year-round
Navigator of the Seas	Western Caribbean round trip from Fort Lauderdale to Cozumel, Belize, Key West; or to Cozumel, Key West; or to Cozumel, Belize; or to Ocho Rios, Grand Cayman, or Cozumel.	$349–$2,059	6, 5, 4 days/year-round
Radiance of the Seas	Eastern Caribbean/Western Caribbean round trip from Fort Lauderdale to San Juan, St. Thomas, Antigua, St. Maarten, Nassau; or Key West, Cozumel, Grand Cayman, Montego Bay.	$509–$1,349	8 days/winter
Serenade of the Seas	Eastern/Southern Caribbean round trip from San Juan to St. Thomas, St. Maarten, Antigua, St. Lucia, Barbados.	$549–$2,599	7 days/winter
Sovereign of the Seas	Port Canaveral to Nassau, Coco Cay (3 days) plus a day at sea (4 days).	Starting at $279	3, 4 days/year-round
Voyager of the Seas	Western Caribbean round trip from Galveston to Montego Bay, Grand Cayman, Cozumel; or to Cozumel, Roatan, Costa Maya, Progreso.	$699–$2,849	7 days/winter

Seabourn Cruise Line

Cruise-only fares include gratuities, wine and spirits, and a complimentary shore experience when itineraries allow.

Seabourn Legend	Panama, Belize & Costa Rica, from Fort Lauderdale to Puerto Caldera, Belize, Roatan, Costa Rica, Panama Canal transit, Puerto Quepos, San Juan del Sur.	$8,325–$61,031	14–28 days/winter
	Panama Canal & Caribbean, from Fort Lauderdale to St. Thomas via Panama Canal, Puerto Moin, Roatan, Belize, San Juan, St. John, Guadeloupe, Antigua, St. Martin, Virgin Gorda.		7–25 day/winter

SeaDream Yacht Club

SeaDream I	Eastern Caribbean round trip from San Juan to Culebrita, Esperanza, St. John, St. Martin, St. Barts, Virgin Gorda, Jost Van Dyke.	$4,900–$14,750	7 days/winter
	Round trip from St. Thomas to San Juan via St. John, St. Barts, Guadeloupe, Nevis, Jost Van Dyke.		
SeaDream II	Southern/Eastern Caribbean round trip from Barbados to St. Thomas, San Juan, Antigua or from St. Thomas to San Juan; San Juan to St. Thomas; St. Thomas to Barbados; Barbados to Antigua.	$3,900–$29,500	4–14 days/winter

Silversea Cruises

Cruise-only fares include all gratuities and beverages aboard ship, including select wines, champagnes, and spirits.

Silver Wind	Barbados to San Juan round trip; or reverse on varying itineraries.	$3,895–$14,695 + port charges	7–8 days/March

Star Clippers

Royal Clipper	Barbados to St. Lucia, Iles des Saintes, Antigua, St. Kitts, Dominica, Martinique; or Grenadines, Grenada, Tobago Cays, St. Vincent, St. Lucia, Martinique.	$1,745–$4,865 + port charges	7 days/winter

Windstar Cruises

Wind Spirit	St. Thomas to St. Martin, St. Barts, Tortola, Jost Van Dyke, and overnight on board in St. John and Virgin Gorda.	$1,849–$3,449	7 days/winter
Wind Surf	Caribbean round trip from Barbados to either Tobago, Bequia, Dominica, St. Lucia, Mayreau, Grenada, Tobago; or Nevis, St. Martin, St. Barts, Isles des Saintes, St. Lucia.	$1,749–$3,649	7 days/winter

Index